COLONIALITY AT LARGE
LATIN AMERICA AND
THE POSTCOLONIAL DEBATE

A book in the series
LATIN AMERICA OTHERWISE:
LANGUAGES, EMPIRES, NATIONS

SERIES EDITORS:
Walter D. Mignolo, *Duke University*
Irene Silverblatt, *Duke University*
Sonia Saldívar-Hull, *University of Texas,
San Antonio*

COLONIALITY AT LARGE

Latin America and the Postcolonial Debate

EDITED BY
Mabel Moraña,
Enrique Dussel, and
Carlos A. Jáuregui

DUKE UNIVERSITY PRESS   Durham & London 2008

Designed by Jennifer Hill
Typeset in Quadraat by
Keystone Typesetting, Inc.

Library of Congress
Cataloging-in-Publication
information and republication
acknowledgments appear on the
last printed pages of this book.

CONTENTS

ABOUT THE SERIES

Latin America Otherwise: Languages, Empires, Nations is a critical series. It aims to explore the emergence and consequences of concepts used to define "Latin America" while at the same time exploring the broad interplay of political, economic, and cultural practices that have shaped Latin American worlds. Latin America, at the crossroads of competing imperial designs and local responses, has been construed as a geocultural and geopolitical entity since the nineteenth century. This series provides a starting point to redefine Latin America as a configuration of political, linguistic, cultural, and economic intersections that demands a continuous reappraisal of the role of the Americas in history, and of the ongoing process of globalization and the relocation of people and cultures that have characterized Latin America's experience. *Latin America Otherwise: Languages, Empires, Nations* is a forum that confronts established geocultural constructions, rethinks area studies and disciplinary boundaries, assesses convictions of the academy and of public policy, and correspondingly demands that the practices through which we produce knowledge and understanding about and from Latin America be subject to rigorous and critical scrutiny.

Featuring a variety of disciplinary and ideological perspectives from internationally recognized scholars working in Anglo-American, Latin American, and European universities, *Coloniality at Large* connects a state-of-the-art view of the postcolonial debate to issues in the field of Latin American studies. It offers a thorough examination of the contributions and inadequacies of the concept of postcoloniality for Latin American studies, and its contributors differ on many occasions about the merits of the term in the Latin American context. By focusing on the dissemination of colonial and neocolonial practices that interweave with emancipatory and nationalist projects during the periods of nation formation and modernization in the Spanish and Portuguese ex-colonies, *Coloniality at Large* documents and analyzes the impact that colonialism has had on the construction of power relations, collective subjectivities, and cultural/political projects in Latin America.

The editors have gathered seminal studies, many in English for the first time, and new works produced for this project. The essays address ways in which colonialism in Latin America, the oldest colonial system in the West, differed from its later expressions in the nineteenth and twentieth centuries by reinscribing a notion of holy war (e.g., the Crusades) and the vision of the colonized as a tabula rasa on which the principles of Western morality should be written. Similarly, this volume examines the special conditions governing the distribution of power between metropolitan and vernacular elites—a creolization of power—that distinguish the Latin American case. Other studies discuss the critique of Occidentalism and modernity that is inseparable from the colonial project, and analyze the political, social, and cultural practices that resist imperialism, with special attention to the topics of violence, identity, otherness, memory, heterogeneity, and language. In analyzing resistance this collection discusses the marginalized imaginaries, the alternative epistemologies, and the surviving and emerging subjectivities that have resulted from colonialism. It also focuses on the roles intellectuals have played, from the construction of the Creole cultural and historical archive, to the writings and practices associated with the process of independence and the foundation of national states, to the modernization and imposition of neoliberalism in the global era. *Coloniality at Large* gives particular attention to the contributions of Marxist thought, dependency theory, and liberation theology.

ACKNOWLEDGMENTS

The editors of this book would like to thank all of the scholars who have participated in this project for their insightful contributions to the study of coloniality in Latin America and for their patient and generous cooperation in the preparation of the general manuscript. We are particularly grateful for the Ford–Latin American Studies Association (LASA) Special Projects Award we received in 2003, which allowed us to advance the project as planned. Finally, this book would not have been possible without the warm encouragement of Reynolds Smith and the assistance of Sharon Torian at Duke University Press. To them, to the colleagues and students who enriched us with their critical input during the preparation of this work, to the journals and publishing houses that authorized the reproduction of materials, and to those who helped with translations, editing of articles, and bibliographical research, our special recognition.

[Year 2019]: A new life awaits you in the off-world colonies: the chance to begin again in a golden land of opportunity and adventure.—*Blade Runner* (1982)

COLONIALISM AND ITS REPLICANTS

Mabel Moraña, Enrique Dussel, and Carlos A. Jáuregui

The invitation made in a familiar rhetoric by the advertising machine at the beginning of Ridley Scott's film suggests, among other things, that at least in some forms of political imagination it would be impossible today to depict a future in which some notion of colonialism and enslavement is not present. The quote also suggests that the world itself might be becoming too small a place to satisfy, within its traditional parameters, the ambition of colonial domination; it expresses a vision of another New World, for which yet another colonial beginning is imagined. Postcolonialism, *transcolonialism*, or *coloniality* at large, finally on the loose, unconfined, universal?[1]

The purpose of this book is to explore and to interrogate, from the cultural perspective of the Latin American *difference*, current theories dealing with both the historical phenomenon of colonialism and the plurality of discourses it has generated from the beginning of colonial times. In coordinating a collective reflection on these topics, our critical and theoretical project has been twofold: we have been particularly attentive to the strategies utilized by imperial powers in American territories, since the initiation of the "Hispanic" era. This interpretive level implies not only a critical analysis of historical sources, humanistic archives, and classical traditions, but also a *located* critique of the political and philosophical paradigms that underlie the concept and the implementation of imperial expansion. In the particular case of Latin America, a discussion of *post-* or *neo-* colonialism—or that of *coloniality*, a term that encompasses the transhistoric expansion of colonial domination and the perpetuation of its effects in contemporary times—is necessarily intertwined with the critique of Occidentalism and modernity, a critique that requires a profound but detached understanding of imperial rationality.[2] Concurrently, our goal has also been to register, analyze, and interpret the political, social, and cultural practices that reveal the resistance against imperial powers exercised by individuals and communities in a variety of contexts, throughout the *longue durée* of Latin America's colonial and neocolonial history.[3] In analyzing practices and discourses of resistance, topics such as violence, identity, otherness, memory, heterogeneity, and language have been particularly recurrent. These topics, reformulated during the last decades from the theoretical perspective of poststructuralist theories, focus on the cultural mediations that connect historical events, political philosophies, and institutional protocols with the much more elusive domains of social subjectivity and symbolic representation.

The critique of Occidentalism—that is, of the philosophical, political, and cultural paradigms that emerge from and are imbedded in the historical phenomenon of European colonization—is essential to the understanding of the aggressive strategies used in imposing material and symbolic domination on vast territories in the name of *universal reason*, as well as of the opposition this domination generated over the centuries in "New World" societies.

Modernity and violence have intertwined throughout the whole course of Latin American history. The Latin American modern subject is the product of a traumatic origin.[4] From the beginning of the conquest, the encounter of indigenous peoples with the European other was defined by violence. Territorial devastation, slavery, genocide, plundering, and exploitation name just some of the most immediate and notorious consequences of colonial expansion. Social and class relations were shaped by what Sergio Bagú called the "omnipresent violence" of the colonial reality (1952, 129). Given these foundational conditions, the elaboration of loss (of entire populations, cultures, territories, and natural resources) and, later on, the utopian myths that accompanied the ideology of modernity (the construction of a teleology of history which would include the conquest of social order, technological progress, and industrial growth, as well as the promised admission of Latin America as the belated guest in the feast of Western civilization) constituted the underlying forces that guided the construction of cultural identities in transatlantic societies. As Frantz Fanon indicated, the trauma of colonialism permeates all levels of social subjectivity. Taking into account some of these issues, this editorial project has assumed both the complexity of Latin American history and its social and cultural heterogeneity as a vantage point from which a new perception of early and late processes of colonial expansion and globalization could be elaborated.

Many of the pieces included in this volume make reference to a series of essays which initiated, in 1991, a reflection in U.S. academe on the pertinence of postcolonial theory for the study of Latin American history and culture. These essays were intended as a response to Patricia Seed's review essay titled "Colonial and Postcolonial Discourse," which appeared in the *Latin American Research Review* in 1991.[5] Two features were identified by Seed as the common denominator in the studies she reviewed: first, the relations of authority in colonial and postcolonial states; second, the connections between this new interdisciplinary scholarship and contemporary trends such as poststructuralism, new historicism, subaltern studies, and the like. Seed recognized that a distinct field of study was being configured around the process of colonial representation and that the critique of the supposed transparency of language was at the core of critical inquiries.[6]

In his response to Seed's article, particularly in reference to the discursive edge of colonial criticism, Walter Mignolo emphasized a topic that soon became commonplace in the field of critical theory: the *locus of enunciation* as the disciplinary, geocultural, and ideological space from which discourses of power and resistance are elaborated. In order to overcome the hegemony of the *alphabet-oriented notions of text and discourse* Mignolo proposed the term *colonial semiosis* as the overarching concept that, in addition to materials of the lettered tradition, could include cultural artifacts such as quipus, maps, myths, calendars, oral narratives, and discourses produced in indigenous languages, thus allowing for a wider exploration of dominated cultures (Mignolo 1992b, 1993). Mignolo's idea of "descentering" and "multiplying" the centers of power and production of knowledge has also been at the core of the critique of colonialism in recent decades. In this direction, perhaps the most fruitful strategy has been the recovery of both a Latin American tradition that starts in the colonial period and continues in the following centuries, and the production of pre-Hispanic and contemporary indigenous cultures that intersect and challenge Creole culture from the margins and interstices of national cultures. The studies gathered in this book make frequent references to what could be called the Latin American archive. This plural and conflictive repertoire, which includes a wide range of representative genres, cultural orientations, and ideological positions, has been mostly ignored in central debates, despite the fact that in many cases that repertoire's production has anticipated theories and critical positions that intellectuals working mainly in American and European institutions popularized many years later.

This initial debate also included other topics. Hernán Vidal saw the emergence of the postcolonial field in the context of a double crisis which according to him involves both the academic and professional status of literature and literary criticism, and the political vacuum that followed the collapse of socialism. By discussing the formation and function of the Latin American literary canon since the nineteenth century, Vidal offered a panoramic view of the changes registered in the field of literary criticism, divided at the time, according to Vidal, between a technocratic and a culturally oriented approach. The emergence of postcolonial studies as a distinctive field, and one with a particular orientation toward discursive analysis, was seen by Vidal as an effort to find a common ground that could allow for the articulation of both sides of the issue. But his main contention was for the need to restore a political dimension in the study of symbolic representation and social subjectivity, a claim that echoed what has been a constant issue in Latin American cultural criticism.[7]

As for Rolena Adorno's contribution to the debate, it focused, first of all, on the narratives that depicted interactions between dominating and dominated cultures through antagonistic and oversimplified categories (villains/heroes, aggressors/victims, etc.). Secondly, Adorno returned to the concept of "colonial discourse," following in part the arguments developed by J. Jorge Klor de Alva, who challenged the application of the term *colonial* to the early period of Spanish domination in America.[8] These articles, elaborated from very diverse analytical perspectives, contained most of the topics that would become part of the theoretical agenda in this field of study.

As an ample and representative collection of theoretical and ideological approaches, this volume constitutes an attempt to contribute, in the first place, to the Latin American field, particularly to the areas of scholarship in which the social sciences intersect with humanistic studies and cultural critique. Problems related to the scenarios of neoliberalism, globalization, migration, social movements, cultural hybridity, and the like cannot be appropriately analyzed without an understanding of Latin America's coloniality. At the same time, given their transdisciplinary nature and the often comparative perspectives at work in the analysis of the peripheral Latin American region, the studies gathered in this volume could also be read as a critical and challenging contribution to the vigorous postcolonial debate that has been developing in the United States since the 1980s. It should be stated, however, that this collection of studies represents neither an attempt to force an entrance for Latin America in central debates, nor a deliberate effort to analyze the systematic exclusion of the region from the vast repertoire of historical experiences and philosophical and political discourses often examined in connection with the topic of colonialism.[9] Nevertheless, in both their intellectual scope and their critical perspectives, these studies draw attention to some of the philosophical and ideological blind spots of postcolonial theories, which have been elaborated mainly in American academe in reference to decolonization processes that took place, for the most part, after World Wars I and II.

While scholarly opinion regarding postcolonial theory's contributions to the specific field of Latin American studies varies, for many intellectuals in that field the analysis of Latin America's *postcoloniality* seems far more problematic than analysis of the scenarios of decolonization that have resulted from contemporary experiences of imperial expansion. Many critics would argue that, at different levels, due to the specificity of Latin American colonial history, no matter what interpretation may ultimately be adopted for the polemic prefix attached to the term, the application of postcolonial theories to the study of this region would require a great deal of ideological and theoretical refinement. Perhaps the field of Latin American studies has been affected, not as much by the influence of postcolonial *theories*—some of which have been crucial for the understanding of historical processes and the deconstruction of colonial rhetoric—but by the *critique of colonialism and coloniality* in their diverse temporal and spatial manifestations. This critique has not only challenged the limits and agendas of traditional disciplines but has also destabilized reductive ideological and cultural dualisms, mobilizing instead an ample array of new topics and approaches distinctively connected to the experience of colonialism. The work around the notions of colonial semiosis and collective subjectivity; the intersections between metropolitan power and colonial discourse; the studies on language, institutions, and cultural textualities; the analysis of orality, cartography, iconography; the revision and critique of the literary canon; the critique of the concepts of nation, identity, ideology, and hegemony—all have been instrumental for the understanding of political and cultural structures related to Latin America's coloniality. At the same time, scrutiny of the methodology of anthropology, of historiography, and, more generally, of the social sciences, along with analyses of popular resistance in its many forms and critiques of the role intellectuals play in appropriating and resignifying hegemonic models of thought and in exploring alternative forms of knowledge and belief have put into question the adequacy of traditional paradigms for studying a world that is undergoing rapid political and social transformations. But even more important, in spite of its sometimes obvious discursive proclivity, this line of questioning has prompted a productive reinscription of political analysis in the examination of culture and society, an approach that had been diffused, to some extent, by cultural studies and by the postmodern debate, which favored a more fragmented and volatile perspective of political and episte-mological issues.

Within this framework of problems and possibilities, the recognition of the particulars that constitute Latin America's history from the beginning of colonial times should not be read as a claim of *exceptionalism* (a position explored in this volume by Peter Hulme, Amaryll Chanady, and others), but rather as an attempt to elaborate on what Walter Mignolo and other scholars have called *colonial difference*, understanding by that the differential time-space where a particular region becomes connected to the world-system of colonial domination.[10]

To begin with, it should be taken into consideration that Latin American coloniality originates in the transoceanic adventures from which European modernity itself was born, following the arrival of Columbus to the Carib-bean islands. The conquest of overseas territories by peninsular powers—that is, the foundation of the oldest colonial system in the West—is not the expression of the logistics of an imperialist search for transnational markets implemented from the centers of advanced capitalism—as it would be the case with English and French territorial appropriations during the nine-teenth and twentieth centuries—but, instead, an unforeseeable outcome of adventurous commercial explorations, as well as a function of political abso-lutism and religious expansionism. The prolonged crusades against Islam provided the model of the Holy War that would be implemented, with many variations, in the New World, creating a trade-off in which Indians would occupy the place of Moors within the Christian project of religious dissemination. In spite of the prolonged effect of classical and medieval ideas in the modern era, with the "discovery" of America during the first decades of the sixteenth century many epistemological and geopolitical paradigms of the Renaissance from which the enterprise of territorial conquest and colonization had originally emerged came to an end. A *new world*, one that encompassed both metropolitan and colonial territories, appeared on the horizon of European imaginaries. The "peoples without history" who, according to G. W. F. Hegel, would constitute the new frontier of European civilization were conceptualized as the tabula rasa on which the principles and accomplishments of Western rationality (religious beliefs, scientific advances, and humanistic paradigms) could and should be inscribed. The European expansion over transoceanic territories and the domination of subjugated cultures not only resulted from the willingness to pursue economic profit and prove military superiority, but also constituted the historic outcome of political and religious transcendentalism. With the colonization of America, Europe became, at least within the limits of Occidental consciousness, the center of the universe. From then on, the Spirit of Civilization would not only mobilize the Angel of History, but also incarnate in the Specter of Capitalism.

Another defining characteristic of Spanish colonialism not present in more contemporary practices of European expansion was the particular distribution of power implemented among metropolitan and vernacular elites in America. For some scholars, the division of colonial societies into two parallel "republics" (the República de españoles and the República de indios) instituted a unique social and political organization which, by incorporating Creoles (those born in America from Spanish descent) into the dominating Spanish system (the República de españoles), co-opted, at least to a certain degree, a very important sector of viceregal society. Although Creoles occupied a position of relative subalternity with respect to peninsular authorities, their active participation in the Spanish administrative and ecclesiastic apparatus during the period of "viceregal stabilization," as well as their ongoing control over indigenous and African American populations after the so-called emancipation, make it difficult to apply the terms *colonial* and *independence* to the New World without a careful consideration of the power structure and social organization of the colonies. Multiplicity and heterogeneity (of projects, of social strata among dominant and dominated subjects, of political articulations within the vast space of colonial societies, of languages and cultural traditions), as well as perpetuation of social and political structures after the termination of Spanish rule, characterize colonial domination in America. As for Brazil, its colonial history has obvious similarities to that of the Spanish possessions. Nevertheless, it is also true that the region has a unique and ambivalent condition as the only colony that became the official site of its correspondent metropolitan monarchy, when in 1808 the Royal family transferred its residence to America in order to flee Napoleon's threat. Brazil's colonial and postcolonial condition, as well as Portugal's rather peripheral position in the world-system with respect to the British Empire, creates, as Boaventura de Souza Santos has also suggested, "an excess of alterity" that divides Brazilians in two groups: "those that are crushed by the excess of past and those that are crushed by the excess of future" (2003, 9–43).

The differential quality of Latin American colonial history suggests that the phenomenon of imperial expansion has, in the Western world, a genealogy that is much longer and more complex than the one generally considered by postcolonial studies. Spanish and Portuguese colonialism triggered, during the sixteenth and seventeenth centuries, a long series of political, economic, and cultural processes which—with the support of an intricate and diversified web of projects and discourses—instituted modernity as the space of intelligibility where colonial domination could be implemented and legitimized as the strategy that would allow the installation and consolidation of Western civilization as defined by metropolitan standards. With the emergence of Spanish colonialism at the end of the fifteenth century—and not just with the Enlightenment, as is usually assumed by postcolonial studies—Eurocentrism became a conceptual and a political reality, and the periphery emerged as the repository of material and symbolic commodities that would nurture, from then on, the economies and cultures of the Old World. As Enrique Dussel has indicated, the ethnographic conception of the *temporal deficit* of the Other (someone without property, law, writing, etc.) and the practices to which this Other was consequently subjected to (exploitation, evangelization, etc.) constituted, at the time, both conceptually and historically, *modern* colonial experiences in the New World. Ethnography, as well as cartography, history, law, theology, and the like, contributed to define both American otherness and modern (colonial) rationality (1995a). The "peoples without history" were relegated to a pre-modern condition, while barbarism and primitivism were proposed as the defining features of cultural alterity. As Aníbal Quijano has shown in his studies, the political and philosophical thought emerging from colonialism "invented" *race* as the pivotal notion that supported the process of world classification. Situated as one of the axes of modernity, the issue of race became the "rationale" used to support, justify, and perpetuate the practice of imperial domination. As Quijano noted, *race* emerges as a key category to define and justify colonial arrangements and to "legitimize" the system of forced labor in the New World. The concept of *coloniality*, a term coined by Quijano, facilitates an understanding of how race and labor were articulated in the colonial period —a subject often neglected in postcolonial studies—and of its perpetuation in modern times.[11]

After the wars of independence, and in addition to the dominating practices inherited from the colonizers and perpetuated by Creole oligarchies, the subalternization and marginalization of vast social sectors within the framework of national scenarios constituted a constant reminder of the limits of hegemonic episteme as well as of the perversions that accompanied, in different stages, the "civilizing," "emancipatory," and "developing" missions in Latin America. Following the foundation of nation-states, with the secularization of society, the liberalization of commercial trade, and the adoption of Enlightened thought, the "coloniality of power" described by Quijano manifested itself in multiple ways: social hierarchies; economic, racial, and sexual inequality; economic and cultural dependency.

As modernization processes intensified and new forms of colonialism were implanted in Latin America, internal dissidences and resistances increased, thus jeopardizing the advancement of national projects. Often, national bourgeoisies were involved in "neocolonial pacts" with international powers (mostly England, France, and the United States), which strengthened economic and political dependency and deepened inequality in Latin American societies.[12]

In addition to internal problems derived from the continuation of colonial structures, Latin America also endured, since the beginning of its independent life, the effects of both economic interventions and political aggressions. With the Spanish-American War of 1898 and more clearly after World War I, the international hegemony of the United States reformulated Latin America's neocolonial condition, thus providing new evidence of the multiple faces adopted by colonial expansion, its always renewed dominating strategies, and its devastating repercussions.[13]

If the nineteenth century had been the setting for Great Britain's *neocolonial* control over Latin America's economy—as well as of France's cultural influence on newly emancipated societies—the twentieth century saw the consolidation of U.S. international preeminence, which materialized in numerous military and political interventions. The increasing control and conquest of international markets and the development of an imperial foreign policy consolidated U.S. power at a global level, leading this country's expansion into the Pacific and the Caribbean. When in 1898 Spain lost to the United States the territories that remained from the old empire—the Philippine Islands, Cuba, and Puerto Rico—U.S. supremacy was inaugurated. In Latin America, still within the spirit of the Monroe Doctrine of 1823 and as direct application of the "Dollar Diplomacy" approach to foreign policy, the United States intervened—sometimes repeatedly—in Cuba, Mexico, Guatemala, Honduras, Nicaragua, Panama, Colombia, Haiti, and the Dominican Republic, in some cases occupying national territories for many years. Later, the United States engaged in sometimes-disguised political involvements in the internal affairs of numerous other countries (Pinochet's coup d'etat in Chile, Plan Colombia, etc.), as well as in direct military operations in El Salvador and Grenada, to name just some of the most conspicuous U.S. interventions in recent history.

The uninterrupted practice of colonialism has marked Latin American history from its beginning. Even today, at the beginning of the twenty-first century, it would be difficult to analyze Latin America's position, both at the national and at the international levels, without an understanding of its colonial and neocolonial history. But this history should not be written only as a mere enumeration of grievances—a "memorial de agravios"—that renders testimony of the enduring effects of colonial domination and its importance as a determining factor in Latin American historical development. This heterogeneous history must be written, also, as an account that registers the multiple voices, actions, and dreams that have contributed to shaping the collective expression of political rebellion against external aggressions, discrimination, marginality, and social inequality, as well as the search for social transformation and cultural integration. Continuous mobilizations—such as defensive wars, uprisings, subversions, riots, insurgencies, popular demonstrations, and revolutions intended to repel, undermine, or overthrow the dominating powers since the "discovery," in addition to the more institutionalized resistance channeled through the work of political parties, unions, student organizations, and the like—constitute persistent testimonies of an ongoing liberating struggle that traverses the limits of historical and geocultural demarcations.

In other words, from Canudos to the Mexican Revolution to the guerilla wars of the 1960–1980s, Latin American history is also the history of its many replicants and its multiple forms of systemic and nonsystemic resistance against colonialism and the rule of capital. Likewise, the social movements that appeared in the Latin American scenario during the last decades of the twentieth century (the Madres de la Plaza de Mayo in Argentina, the Movimento dos Trabalhadores Rurais Sem Terra in Brazil, the Zapatista movement in Mexico, indigenous mobilizations in the Andean and Central American regions, to name just some of the most notorious expressions of popular struggles) are evidence of the peoples' determination to resist economic inequality, political repression, and social injustice, which are functions of the surviving apparatus of neocolonial domination—what the Peruvian thinker José Carlos Mariátegui called "colonialismo supérstite" (surviving colonialism)—in contemporary times.

But such resilient practices, as well as the numerous manifestations of collective sentiments of discontent and rebellion often expressed through the symbolic practices of everyday life and popular culture, are only possible because they are rooted in solid cultural and epistemological foundations. In fact, the history of Latin America's resistance to colonialism is constituted by the interweaving of multiple narratives that include testimonies of dominated cultures which have survived the devastating impacts of homogenization, repression, and censorship, managing to maintain their alternative and challenging quality through the different stages of Latin American history. For this reason, any study of social and political resistance in the contexts we focus on in this book necessarily implies an analysis of marginalized imaginaries and alternative epistemologies, surviving and emerging subjectivities, and modes of representation which exist in colonial and neocolonial societies under—and in spite of—specific conditions of production, reception, and dissemination of knowledge.

It could be said, that by exposing the perpetuation and metamorphic strategies utilized over the centuries by colonial and neocolonial domination, Latin American history challenges the concept of postcoloniality from within. This is particularly true when the prefix is used to connote the cancellation or overcoming of political, cultural, and ideological conditions imposed by foreign powers in societies that existed under colonial rule.[14] Although a periodization of Latin American coloniality is not only possible but necessary in studying regional developments, the idea of a stage in which colonial domination had been economically, politically, and culturally erased and/or transcended (as suggested, in some interpretations, by the prefix post) seems more the product of a depoliticized evaluation of contemporary history—or even an expression of hope and desire—than the result of a thorough examination of Latin America's past and present. This book offers a thorough examination of the contributions and the downsides of the concept of postcoloniality in the region, and the contributors differ, on many occasions, about the merits and applicability of the term for our field of study. It is precisely this plurality of critical approaches and ideological positions that makes this book a challenging contribution to the debate.

In any case, it is obvious that for Latin America both globalization and neoliberalism stand as new incarnations of neocolonialism, and capitalism continues to be the structuring principle which, by ruling all aspects of national and international relations, not only allows for but requires the perpetuation of coloniality. The consolidation of a *new world order* in which the concentration of power and the redefinition and strengthening of hegemony is taking place at a formidable pace also calls for a thorough examination of peripheral societies where most of the struggles for economic, political, and epistemological liberation are being fought, with variable results. It is within this framework of theoretical problems and political realities that this book has been structured.

But the scenarios of coloniality cannot be thoroughly analyzed without a study of the role intellectuals have played, over the centuries, in conjunction with political and religious institutions, in the definition of social and political agendas, as part of the educational apparatus, in the fields of art, communications, and the like. All processes related to the production, appropriation, and/or dissemination of knowledge in peripheral societies are crucial for the advancement of emancipatory projects. In Latin America, the intertwining of intellectual work and coloniality has been a defining characteristic since the beginning of colonial times, from the construction of a Creole cultural and historical archive in viceregal societies, to the writings and practices associated with the process of independence and the foundation of national states, to the modernization and imposition of neoliberalism in the global era.

Creole *letrados* as hermeneutists and cultural translators, indigenous thinkers as the memory and voice of dominated cultures, national intellectuals as the Messiahs of Enlightened rationality, academics, artists, writers, technocrats, "organic" and public intellectuals as cultural advisors, disseminators, and/or facilitators of national and transnational exchanges of symbolic commodities—none of these categories capture per se the social and ideological paradoxes and ambiguities of intellectual agency in colonial and neocolonial scenarios, and the negotiations imbedded in the production and manipulation of epistemic and cultural paradigms.[15] It could be said that, at all levels, from colonial times to the present, intellectual action has been developed in an attempt to confront the traumatic effects of colonialism. From diverse ideological positions, the narratives that elaborate on the concepts of history, emancipation, collective subjectivity, political and cultural agency, and the like are all permeated in one way or another by the remainders of colonial domination, whether the geocultural site of enunciation is located inside or outside Latin America.

Beginning with the early discourse of Creole letrados who reacted against Spanish authority, many critiques of colonialism have been elaborated by Latin American intellectuals. In modern times, during the periods of independence and modernization, critiques of colonialism proliferated, emerging from different political and ideological perspectives. Very few, however, have been acknowledged in postcolonial studies and debates. The general resistance to postcolonial theory in Latin America is due, in part, to the perception that the concept of neocolonialism should replace that of postcolonialism, which seems to imply—at least in some interpretations of the prefix post—that colonial times have passed. The locus of enunciation has also been challenged. Postcolonial theory has been elaborated from "inside the belly of the monster," as José Martí said in reference to his own struggles against imperialism. At the same time, critical discourses elaborated from peripheral societies have often been ignored, considered in themselves objects of study but never been valued as theoretical contributions worthy of debate. Nevertheless, the long and rich Latin American debate on colonialism includes schools of thought which, incorporating Marxist analysis of imperialism and combining it with other sociological and political approaches (such as those represented by dependency theory and liberation theology), provide incisive deconstructions of colonialism.

From the Latin American Marxist tradition, the critique of imperialism has included, among other things, a long reflection on colonial and neocolonial exploitation. José Carlos Mariátegui's analysis of race, class, land ownership, and national culture in Peru constitutes a good example of an original re-elaboration of materialist thought applied to the specific Latin American reality. Topics related to colonization, Indian exploitation, slavery, and the emergence of nation-states and peripheral capitalism, as well as the long history of popular insurgencies and different forms of cultural resistance, have been thoroughly studied. José Carlos Mariátegui, Julio Antonio Mella, Juan Marinello, Luis Carlos Prestes, C. L. R. James, Sergio Bagú, Nelson Werneck Sodré, Ernesto González Casanova, and Agustín Cueva are just some of the most representative intellectuals concerned with problems related to Latin America's neocolonial history and dependent development. Latin America's coloniality was understood—as early as the 1930s and 1940s—not as a derivation of feudalism but as the result of early capitalism's expansion and of the correlative emergence of peripheral modernity in the region. C. L. R. James, for instance, analyzes the *modernity* of colonial exploitation of labor in slave plantations in Atlantic territories, applying his arguments to the study of the Haitian revolution (1938). The Argentine Sergio Bagú focused on the capitalist characteristics and historical determinations of Latin America's colonial economy and racial relations. His analysis contested traditional assumptions of a Latin American *late feudalism* with the theory about the region's introduction into a system of peripheral but quite modern *colonial capitalism* (1949).

Another seminal theorization on Latin America's peripheral capitalism and its colonial relations with hegemonic centers was undertaken by dependency theory, which emerged in the late 1950s and was developed throughout the 1970s by liberal and Marxist economists such as Raul Prebisch, Andre Gunder Frank, Fernando Henrique Cardoso, Osvaldo Sunkel, Pedro Paz, and Theotonio Dos Santos.[16] From different but convergent perspectives, dependency theory was mainly concerned with the continuity of colonial structures still imbedded in modern capitalism and with the critique of developmentalism. From the perspective of this theory, the projects of development in and for Latin America were interpreted as a "neocolonial pact" between international capital and national elites that perpetuated relations of international dependency and social inequality in the region. Development and underdevelopment, powerful international centers and struggling peripheries, internal and international division of labor, exploitation of national wealth and widespread internal poverty, copious exports of raw materials and ominous hunger—all were aspects of the "colonial capitalism" already analyzed by Sergio Bagú. *Dependentistas* examined this asymmetrical configuration as a contemporary form of the colonial system applied in America and Africa by European empires. To a certain extent, dependency theory constituted a clear acknowledgment of Latin America's "coloniality at large" and a serious attempt to undertake a materialist analysis of the region's economic relations both at a national and an international level.[17]

Divergent and at the same time related to dependency theory, Theology of Liberation provided an alternative reflection on problems related to capitalist oppression in the so-called Third World.[18] In the aftermath of the Cuban Revolution and during the crisis of populism in the 1960s, progressive religious thinkers such as Camilo Torres, Gustavo Gutiérrez, and Juan Luis Segundo, in direct contact with grassroots groups, articulated a theological reading of social reality and a programmatic answer to social problems in Latin America. Liberation theology not only theorized alienation, capitalism, and colonialism, but also inspired a large and influential social mobilization nurtured by a solid religious and political agenda which developed intricate relations with popular insurgency and liberation movements. As an episte-mological and theoretical critique of colonialism, liberation theology tran-scended traditional Marxist notions of alienation, resignified religious nar-ratives as discourses of liberation and popular resistance, and created a new rhetoric and a new concept of social change which connected with popular beliefs and emancipatory political agendas. Finally, liberation theology of-fered a new framework to rethink the articulation of religion and politics, culture and community.

One of the challenges of this volume is to incorporate into current post-colonial debates the fundamental inputs made by Marxist thought, depen-dency theory, and liberation theology to the study and understanding of Latin America's coloniality; furthermore, to engage the reader into a serious reassessment of these contributions vis-à-vis new critical and theoretical approaches. In other words, this volume proposes the integration of "ver-nacular" academic traditions into the reflections and discourses that are rethinking colonialism today from the scenarios impacted by the transfor-mation of hegemony at a planetary level, taking into account the challenges of late capitalism, multiculturalism, and globalization. At the same time, it is important to acknowledge the fact that, in creating new grounds for trans-disciplinary and transnational debates, it is essential to contemplate the specificities of the actors involved in intellectual dialogue, and to ponder the circumstances surrounding the processes of discourse production in various and sometimes conflicting loci of enunciation. Paradoxically, it is in these foundational, though peripheral, analyses that we can find some of the economic and materialistic approaches that we miss today in postcolo-nial theory.

In the specific case of the debate on (post)colonialism, Latin American intellectuals, who are justly wary of the well-known risks of cultural penetra-tion, often resent the adoption of First World paradigms in the analysis of peripheral societies. This is true in the case of "Creole" thinkers and schol-ars as well as among indigenous intellectuals who inhabit the domains of cultures dominated by means of internal colonialism and who think and write in nonhegemonic languages and from nonhegemonic places. Some-times, a fruitful dialogue can still be established, particularly due to the fact that cultural frontiers are today more permeable than ever, and Latin Amer-ica not only exists in its original territories but is also disseminated in adoptive countries, a fact that tends to facilitate the exchange of ideas and collaborative work. But this dialogue can be not only challenging but also difficult to establish. Latin American scholars often seek refuge in different forms of cultural fundamentalism, thus precluding the possibility of taking advantage of theoretical, critical, and political positions that could illuminate regional developments. On other occasions, "central" intellectuals approach Latin American cultural history with variable degrees of theoretical arrogance, paternalism, or "colonial guilt." Time and again, local histories and alternative epistemologies are treated as if they were experimental constructs which have come to existence in order to confirm the place of the Other in the realm of Universal History and to legitimize its inquisitive gaze. Likewise, neocolonial societies as a whole, or specific sectors in particular, are the object of new forms of social classifications that homogenize historical, political, and cultural differences and inequalities by subsuming them in rigid and compartmentalized conceptual systems which reveal more about the nature of the observer than about the quality of the object of study.

In any case, and regardless of the chosen definition of intellectual agency, it is obvious that in spite of the enduring effects of colonial and neocolonial domination, Latin America should not be conceptualized as the residue of colonialism but rather as a space where coloniality has been perpetrated and perpetuated as a function of capitalism, and where cultural, social, and political transformations have been taking place for centuries, in search of emancipation and sovereignty—an arena where multiple and conflictive struggles are being fought and where knowledge is not just appropriated and recycled but *produced* both in dominant and dominated languages and cultures. Consequently, the region as a whole can and should be seen as a much more complex scenario than the one usually approached through concepts such as postnational, posthistoric, posthegemonic, post-ideological, and the like. These fashionable notions, which in certain contexts could mobilize theoretical reflections, capture very specific aspects of a much broader political, cultural, and epistemological reality, and when taken as totalizing critical paradigms, provide limited and limiting knowledge of Latin America's cultural and political problems. This editorial project is precisely an attempt to bridge the different cultural, ideological, and institutional spaces where Latin Americanism is being developed as a transnational intellectual endeavor.

Many scholarly strategies, disciplinary protocols, and ideological positions are combined in this book. Hopefully, the reader will be able to travel these avenues forging his or her own path in approaching the fascinatingly complex Latin American history, and the narratives it has inspired. If, as

Stuart Hall has stated, postcolonial theory entails the task of "thinking at the limits," the study of *coloniality* implies, in turn, the challenge of thinking *across* (frontiers, disciplines, territories, classes, ethnicities, epistemes, temporalities) in order to visualize the overarching structure of power that has impacted all aspects of social and political experience in Latin America since the beginning of the colonial era. Without a doubt, the struggle for emancipation and equality is fought in the region with varying degrees of intensity and success on different fronts. It includes the battles for the recuperation of interstitial spaces of intercultural communication and for the creation of new epistemological platforms from which new forms of political imagination could emerge and proliferate. Divergent forces and impulses traverse the vast territories of coloniality: desire and rejection, mourning and oblivion, passion and melancholia, the harms of spoliation and the need for restitution. But none of them exist outside of the political realm, be it in Latin America itself or in the multiple, transnational domains in which Latin America is studied, imagined, or remembered. It is our hope that this book will be read as not only a contribution to but also as an intervention in the study of Latin America, where coloniality and its replicants exist, at times— still—undetected.

NOTES

1   *Blade Runner* could also be said to represent the political limits of colonialism. From those off-world colonies something returns to challenge the colonial order: the insurgence of the exploited, the insurrection of reified labor, the violent defiance of races condemned to submission. It seems that unlimited colonialism might have limits after all.

2   The concept of "coloniality" coined by Aníbal Quijano has been pivotal to the understanding and critique of early and late stages of colonialism in Latin America, as well as of its long-lasting social and cultural effects.

3   We are aware of the wide application of the term *colonialism* throughout the book, as well as of the use of *postcolonialism* and *neocolonialism* by different authors. Since each contributor makes a specific case for the interpretation of the concept and the term of preference, we have respected this terminological plurality and welcome the different critical and theoretical avenues they open to the reader.

4   The term *colonial subjects* is being used here in its ample semantic spectrum, referring to both hegemonic and oppressed subjectivities within the context of Latin American coloniality.

5   Seed's essay, which initiated a series of responses around the politics and discourses of colonialism, focused on five books on Latin America and the Philippines published between 1979 and 1991: *Colonial Encounters: Europe and the Native*

Caribbean by Peter Hulme (1986), *Discursos narrativos de la conquista: Mitificación y emergencia* by Beatriz Pastor (1988), *Unfinished Conversations: Mayas and Foreigners between Two Wars* by Paul Sullivan (1989), *Contracting Colonialism: Translation and Christian Conversion in Tagalog Society under Early Spanish Rule* by Vicente Rafael (1988), and *Pasyon and Revolution: Popular Movements in the Philippines, 1840–1910* by Reynaldo Ileto (1979).

6   This initial debate is extensively discussed by Fernando Coronil in his essay in this volume.

7   Interestingly enough, in his discussion of the initial debate on postcolonialism, Bill Ashcroft (1998) reduces Vidal's argument to a "stubbornly ethnocentric" and characteristically fearful rejection of outside critical movements. He misses, in our opinion, the point made by the Chilean critic regarding the need to go beyond the limits of textual deconstruction in order to reach "the political dimension in cultural analysis." Ashcroft focuses, rather, on Vidal's concern about the technocratic turn of literary criticism, a preoccupation shared, in the text offered to the same debate, by Rolena Adorno.

8   Klor de Alva's argument appears in his polemic and often quoted article "Colonialism and Postcolonialism as (Latin) American Mirages," which is commonly associated with the postcolonial debate.

9   Anouar Majid has referred to the solidly Anglo-Eurocentric limits of the postcolonial: "As established and practiced in the Anglo-American academy, postcolonial theory has been largely oblivious to non-western articulations of self and identity, and has thus tended to interpellate the non-western cultures it seeks to foreground and defend into a solidly Eurocentric frame of consciousness. Postcolonial theory thus operates with the paradoxical tension of relying on the secular, European vocabulary of its academic origins to translate non-secular, non-European experiences. Despite brilliant attempts to elucidate (or perhaps theorize away) this dilemma, the question of the non-western Other's agency remains suspended and unresolved, while the material conditions that generate a culture of dubious virtues (such as 'hybridity' and 'identity politics') acquire more theoretical legitimacy. The question finally is: Will the subaltern be allowed to speak?" (2001).

10   Walter Mignolo defines *colonial difference*: "The colonial difference is the space where coloniality of power is enacted. It is also the space where the restitution of subaltern knowledge is taking place and where border thinking is emerging. The colonial difference is the space where *local* histories inventing and implementing global designs meet local histories, the space in which global designs have to be adapted, adopted, rejected, integrated, or ignored. The colonial difference is, finally, the physical as well as imaginary location where the coloniality of power is at work in the confrontation of two kinds of *local* histories displayed in different spaces and times across the planet" (2000d, ix). We use the term *colonial difference* with a slightly modified, more punctual meaning, in order to emphasize the *specificity* of Latin America's colonial history, that is, its particular historical, political, social, and cultural modes of articulation within the world-system of colonial domination throughout the centuries.

11 Quijano defines coloniality as a global hegemonic model of power in place since the Conquest that articulates race and labor, thus combining the epistemological *dispositifs* for colonial dominance and the structures of social relations and exploitation which emerged with the Conquest and continued in the following stages of Latin America's history.

12 Fanon makes reference to colonialism as one of the ineluctable "pitfalls of national consciousness" (1991, 148–205).

13 *Coloniality* and *imperialism* name, respectively, the condition resulting from colonial domination and the modern phenomenon of territorial expansion. Colonialism is considered a form of imperial domination. The term *imperialism* is usually restricted to the type of empire building that accompanies the emergence of the modern nation-state in the West, and usually refers to European territorial expansion during the nineteenth and twentieth centuries. Although there is evidence of the use of the term *empire* as early as the sixteenth century, *imperialism* became popular in the mid-nineteenth century, particularly after 1858, the period of the Pax Britannica.

14 Negotiating the concept of postcoloniality as one that makes primary reference to the "political and discursive strategies of colonized societies" (Ashcroft 2001, 24) is not enough. In an attempt to respond to the "perceived threat to Latin American intellectual integrity posed by outside critical movements" and salvage the validity of the term *postcolonialism* Bill Ashcroft proposes some interpretive alternatives, particularly the one that defines "postcolonialism [as] the discourse of the colonized" (2001, 24). This possibility, proposed as a well-intentioned but rather condescending way of dealing with the "fear" of Latin American intellectuals, overlooks the decisive influence that the discourses of power have in constituting the discourses of resistance—that is, the impact of dominating narratives, hegemonic epistemologies, political "rationales," and the like, which inevitably intertwine with the elaboration of emancipatory agendas in colonial or neocolonial domains. If this is the chosen use for the term *postcolonial*, it would provide a truncated account of the cultural, political, and ideological scenarios emerging from colonialism. In my opinion, any analysis of postcolonial discourses should take into account both sides of the coin, as well as the difficult negotiations imbedded in the process of cultural appropriation and intellectual production.

15 The topics of Creole subjectivity and the Januslike identity developed by this group in the colonial period and even in the formation and consolidation of national estates have been studied by many critics. For a critique of the Manichean interpretations of subjects confronted in colonial encounters, see, in this volume, Seed, Adorno (particularly their discussions of what Seed calls "tales of resistance and accommodation"), and Mazzotti. Santiago Colás has also contributed to the study of subject positions and colonial *desire* (1995).

16 For a succinct historic presentation and analysis of dependency theory, its proposals, and its debates, see Theotonio dos Santos's *La teoría de la dependencia: Balances y perspectivas* (2003).

17 "Latin America is today, and has been since the sixteenth century, part of an

international system dominated by the now-developed nations. . . . [Its] under-development is the outcome of a particular series of relationships to the international system" (Bodenheimer 1971, 157).

18   As is well known, in the 1980s the concept of postcolonial(ism) displaced that of the Third World. The term *Third World* was coined in 1952 by the French economist, historian, and anthropologist Alfred Sauvy, and it soon came to be used worldwide in reference to a cluster of nations that, due to the impact of colonialism, had not reached the standards of development that characterized North American and European societies. The term *Third World*, derived from the expression *Tiers Etat* (used during the French Revolution in reference to politically marginalized sectors of society), gained popularity in reference to countries aligned neither with the U.S.S.R. nor with NATO during the Cold War. Since then, *Third World* has been used as a homogenizing and sometimes derogatory denomination applied to underdeveloped nations in Africa, Asia, and Latin America (a group also known as the Global South) regardless of their economic, social, and cultural differences.

PART ONE

COLONIAL ENCOUNTERS, DECOLONIZATION, AND CULTURAL AGENCY

The three essays in this section discuss issues related to the production of knowledge and the confrontation of culturally diverse imaginaries in Latin America. Although the studies focus on different periods and aspects of the process of cultural production under colonial rule, they share a series of critical and theoretical concerns. Gordon Brotherston's piece challenges the term *postcolonial*, noting that the prefix places colonization in the past. In his opinion, concepts such as transculturation, *antropofagia*, *nepantlismo*, contact zone, and in-betweenness are more effective than the historically marked concept of postcolonialism in capturing the complexity of intercultural relations and the overlapping of different codifications in cultural exchanges. His main concern is to illuminate knowledge systems that are alternative to the cultural models imposed by colonial domination. His examinations of both the *Codex Mexicanus* and the Aztec Sun Stone constitute paradigmatic approaches to the interpretation of cultural artifacts which have resisted intellectual colonization. In a similar manner, José Rabasa confronts the problem of intercultural communication in his analysis of the Nahuatl version of the conquest of Mexico, as contained in the *Historia general de las cosas de la Nueva España*, by Bernardino de Sahagún. Rabasa is concerned with the problem of "cross-cultural subjectivity," that is, with the conflictive intersection of cultural categories and the emotional reaction it enlists in the subjects involved in this experience. But Rabasa's study is also an insightful exploration of the limits of representation, as well as of the loci of enunciation and structure of feelings we recognize in *ourselves* and attribute to *others*. As part of a deliberate attempt not to privilege theory over primary sources, Rabasa firmly roots epistemological questions in the analysis of literary and cultural textualities. The problems of *translation*—not only between languages but also between cultural and epistemological categories—as well as the interrelations between symbolic production, power systems, and cultural survival are at the core of Rabasa's and Brotherston's inquires. Looking at colonial scenarios from another perspective, José Antonio Mazzotti's reflections on Creole *agency* focus on the pivotal Peninsular-Creole relationship, particularly under Habsburg rule (1516–1700), but also examine aspects of the postcolonial debate in the context of the transformations that have been taking place at a disciplinary level since the 1980s. From the vast repertoire of postcolonial theory, Mazzotti—as well as other critics— salvages above all Homi Bhabha's concept of *ambivalence* as a defining characteristic of colonial subjectivity.

AMERICA AND THE COLONIZER QUESTION:
TWO FORMATIVE STATEMENTS FROM EARLY MEXICO

Gordon Brotherston

Postcolonial defines itself first of all in time, putting the colonizer into the past.[1] In discourse after
World War II, the term was readily identified with the
formal expulsion of Europe from much of Asia and
Africa and the explicit rehabilitation of prior settlers'
rights. From this perspective, however, the term could
never be as comfortably applied to America, where independence from Europe, a century or more earlier,
had led to more ambiguous repudiation of imported
languages, legal systems, religions, economies, and
races. This was so even though, on the map, states
declaring themselves "independent" most often effectively occupied only part of projected national territories, much of those territories never having been fully
subject to Europe in the first place. Witness, for example, the subsequent plundering of Algonkin towns in
the Ohio Valley, the machine-gun "pacification" (dispossession) of the Mapuche in the Southern Cone and

of the Sioux and many others in northern plains, or for that matter the "caste war" assault on the federated Maya of Yucatán. Furthermore, certain of these former American colonies soon developed into predatory and colonizing powers in their own right, within and beyond their projected borders, the United States being the supreme example.

If the concept of postcolonial in America is fraught in these terms, it is no less so with respect to our capacity from the western point of view to assess the original colonial imposition. So much of what was imposed lives on, unquestioned, in our discourse as literary scholars and academics, in our choice of sources, modes of reading, and historical perspectives. With this, in the projection of a scarcely articulate "other," there has been a general reluctance to admit or recall Europe's own severe intellectual limitation (in its own terms) at the time of the first invasions.

It is for just these reasons that received notions of the postcolonial have been questioned with respect to the Americas, as they were, for example, in 1997 at the Associação Brasileira de Literatura Comparada (ABRALIC) conference in Rio, which was addressed by Homi Bhabha. As a result, wider attention is perhaps now being paid to the transculturation early identified by Fernando Ortiz and promoted by Rama, to anthropophagy in the style of Oswald de Andrade, to notions of periphery attributed to writers as diverse as Borges and José María Arguedas, and to the space-between encoded in both León-Portilla's *nepantlismo* (also fundamental for Anzaldúa and Mignolo) and Mary Louise Pratt's contact zone. Far from exhausted, these approaches direct us historically to the colonial as a huge complexity that everywhere underlies and bedevils European triumphalism. And they encourage the geocultural exploration typified by Rama when, guided by Darcy Ribeiro and Arguedas, he discovered the commonwealth of Amazon and Andes and gestured toward its counterpart in what anthropology and archaeology recognize as Mesoamerica.

Along just these lines, I offer here a reading of two texts that have common roots in ancient America: the *Mexicanus Codex* of the late sixteenth century and the Aztec Sun Stone, which dates from a century or so earlier. The former offers a critique of the Christian calendar and the philosophy articulated in it; the latter, an embodiment of American cosmogony, has resisted repeated attempts at intellectual colonization. Together, they may help us assess—from the other side, as it were—factors involved in both the colonial imposition and modes of emancipation from it. They are especially relevant to questions of knowledge systems, hybridity, and the resistance of mind and culture to European and Western control.

Written in the Mesoamerican script known as *tlacuilolli*, both texts disallow the erasure desired by invading Europeans when they heaped up and burned books in New Spain and quipus in Peru (whole "libraries" of both, to use the Spaniards' own term). As such, tlacuilolli script, like the hiero-glyphic writing of the Olmec or the Maya, is inseparable from the calendrical system of Mesoamerica, which, in articulating time/space, privileges series of conceptually rich numbers and signs (Nowotny 1961; Brotherston 1995; Boone 2000). To this degree, the use of tlacuilolli and comparable recording systems in America may of itself establish epistemological premises no less valid than those attributed to the Greeks in the interests of Europe's idea of itself. Consider, for example, the line of Maya works in phonetic script, which extends, unbroken, for over one-and-a-half millennia, from the early classic inscriptions to the *Books of Chilam Balam*, which went on organizing life according to the Katun calendar well after "independence" (Brotherston 1992, 131–55); the tlacuilolli annals that, formally covering millennia, antici-pated the Corn Riot of 1692 (keenly reconsidered in its colonial context by Moraña 2000) and that furnished Vico's disciple Boturini with his "new idea" of America in 1746 (*Idea nueva de una historia de la América septentrional*); or, again, the import of quipu taxonomy and literary genre in Guaman Poma's *Coronica* into an order of transcription examined in Catherine Julien's superb *Reading Inca History* (2000; see also Urton 2003).

At the moment of contact, the knowledge represented in tlacuilolli texts was by no means readily containable by, or translatable into, the thought-systems authorized by invading Christendom (Rabasa 1993, and in this vol-ume). In this sense, Ricard's classic notion of a spiritual conquest that followed seamlessly on the military one was no less flawed from the start than is the current assumption by certain philosophers that their discipline began to exist in America only with the arrival of Columbus (León-Portilla 1963; Maffie 2001). Considered in this light, the corpus of tlacuilolli texts to which the *Codex Mexicanus* and the Sun Stone belong may tune our notions of "colonization imaginaire" and help balance more finely dualistic character-izations of the colonial as hybrid, or "pensée métisse" (both terms are Gruzinski's). Mapping resident memory, the *Codex Mexicanus* and the Sun Stone show clearly continuities from before to after the invasion, which in certain modes survive the formal fact of coloniality itself.

THE CODEX MEXICANUS

Now housed in Paris (Mengin 1952), the *Codex Mexicanus* (hereafter *Mexicanus*) may be understood as a wry reflection on the course that Aztec history had taken before and after 1519. On the evidence of its own annals, it was completed in the decade immediately after the Gregorian reform of the Julian calendar took effect in New Spain in 1583. Its authors state an interest in the College of San Pablo, founded in 1575 in Teipan by the Augustinian friar Alonso de la Veracruz, on a property in the southeast quarter of Tenochtitlan that had been endowed by Moctezuma's grandson Inés de Tapia (Toussaint et al. 1990, 139). The resources and high intellectual standing of this college, which eclipsed anything the Franciscans or other orders had previously accomplished, became proverbial in native annals of the time. For their part, chroniclers of the Augustinian Order note how the library of books freshly imported from Europe was adorned with maps, celestial and terrestrial globes, astrolabes, planispheres, chronometers, and other state-of-the-art instruments (Grijalva 1985, 327).[2] Used by the Vatican in its attempt to redefine the time of Western Christendom in the Gregorian Reform (Parisot and Suagher 1996), instruments such as these were observed by native eyes in Mexico that had nothing of Europe's innocent other, but rather were informed by many centuries of precise local knowledge, as *Mexicanus* makes plain.

In a Nahuatl gloss in the annals section of *Mexicanus* (36), the last of this text's several authorial hands, a certain Juan, states that the book had been given to him by a descendant of the royal Aztec house of Acampachtli (Inés de Tapia?) and that, loyal to the calendrical and philosophical tradition of that house, he will do his best to expose the intellectual limitations and oppressive ideology of his country's new rulers.

Mexicanus is hybrid in at least three senses, deliberately occupying a space between (*nepantla*) Aztec and European. It is made materially of native paper, yet is paginated in European style rather than as a screenfold book, being bound at the spine. It is written in tlacuilolli yet also makes use of European alphabetic script (for words in Nahuatl, Latin, Spanish, and other languages) and numerical notation; moreover, it treats these latter with an ingenuity characteristic of the former (Galarza 1966): according to need, numerals may be arabic or upper or lower roman, and letters may be upper or lower case, more roman or more gothic, even uncial (a fourth-century amalgam of Latin and Greek). Thoroughly imbued with Mesoamerican calendrics, it works easily with the rules and structure of the Christian liturgy and chronology, and it construes the time-depths and eras of both its own and the Christian calendars, implicitly asking who entered whose history in 1519 (Aveni and Brotherston 1983).

Mexicanus was written at a time when, as the Gregorian Reform indicates, Europe was endeavouring to bring its chronology and astronomy up to

American levels (Prem 1978). Unlikely as it may seem, before Charles V's protégé Mercator (Gerhard Kremer) published his *Chronologia, hoc est temporum demonstratio . . . ab initio mundi usque ad annum domini 1568, ex eclipsibus et observationibus astronomicis,* Europe had no formal means of projecting dates accurately far into the past (years "B.C." were simply not conceived of) and therefore was ill-equipped to match the Mesoamerican Era, let alone the larger cycles that era was set in. And the corrections eventually made by Gregory had unfortunate side effects: the liturgically (and socially) disruptive loss of ten days, and the elimination of the night sky as a chronological reference.

Within its own tradition, *Mexicanus* furthers the achievements of millennia, synonymous with the unbroken history of Mesoamerican calendrics and script, which begins with the Olmec inscriptions of the first millennium B.C. and projects back to a Mesoamerican Era date of 3113. As a book, the text represents each of the two literary genres known in the surviving corpus of the classic screenfolds of paper and skin. For part of *Mexicanus* belongs both to the ritual or dream-book genre (*temicamatl*), which consists of thematic chapters (1–17, 89–end), and part belongs to the annals genre (*xiuhtlapoualli*), which narrates events through time (18–88). In other words, each component of *Mexicanus,* outer and inner, has its own genre and hence mode of exposition, means, and principles of reading.

For its part, the annals component begins its count of years with the Aztecs' departure from Aztlan in 1 Flint 1168 and ends, after Gregory's Reform, in 7 Rabbit 1590, covering 423 years in all. The narrative records a particular version of Aztec history, standing somewhere between the earlier plebeianism of the *Boturini Codex,* which concentrates on the migration from Aztlan (Boone 2000, 210–20), and the direct imperialism of the *Mendoza Codex,* in which surviving members of the Aztec ruling class argue that their involvement is indispensable to Spanish attempts at running the colony.

An indication of how the annals interweave the stories of the invaders and the invaded can be found in the account of the year 1559, 2 Reed in the Aztec calendar, a year of major moment for both. In November New Spain was ordered to commemorate Charles V, who had died the year before, in a grand funeral, and this was duly done in an elaborate night-time ceremony which involved the construction of a large wooden edifice, the Túmulo imperial, described in great detail at the time (Cervantes de Salazar 1972). This "tomb" is depicted in several other native annals besides *Mexicanus,* saliently *Aubin* (Vollmer 1981). In that source, there is another image above the tomb, the year-bundle (*xiuhmolpilli*) that represents the kindling of New Fire and the beginning of a new fifty-two-year cycle in native chronology, of "our years" (toxiuh), as the Nahuatl gloss puts it. Overall this evidence suggests that the chance was seized to heighten the link between the two events— funeral and New Fire ceremony—since by then the Spanish colonial authorities would not tolerate overt celebration of the latter. Native prompting led to the funeral being held at night, in darkness dramatically broken by the lighting of a candle in the four-sided edifice, whose flame and fire was then spread outward. As a result, in many key respects emperor Charles's funeral became a covert kindling of New Fire, and it was done on a night in November well placed in the Aztec calendar for this purpose. It is a good example of how ceremony and performance could be infused with meaning invisible and incomprehensible to the invaders (cf. Alberro 2000).

While wholly historical in this sense, the annals convey further messages through their sheer disposition of year-dates on the page. This highlights the slippage between the solar year and the sidereal year of the night sky, a slippage known as the precession of the equinoxes, which over the four-fire kindlings during the migration from Aztlan amounts to the loss of three nights (Mexicanus's fine measurement of precession is noted by Prem 1978, 278). The layout of years further contrives to ransom the native night-sky cipher 11 from the duodecimal system imposed by the colonizers. In his Nahuatl commentary on the imported zodiac, Juan demands the "annihilation" of the sign Libra, or "peso," which epitomizes unwelcome foreign weight and coinage ("niman nimitz micquitiz peso") (24–36). Libra is in fact the only one of the twelve that is not a life-form (zoodion), having been later inserted in the interests of Old World imperialism and the duodecimal standard. The elimination of Libra was to be done out of loyalty to Acamapachtli, and in Mesoamerican terms the effect, clearly, is again to defend local understandings of the night sky in which eleven is privileged as a cipher.

The "ritual" outer frame of Mexicanus that encloses the annals consists of eight chapters, which dwell on the relationship between the two calendars as this is exemplified historically in the annals and as was foregrounded by the Gregorian Reform. The chapters are defined according to categories proper to the genre of dream books, and therefore necessarily have as their constant premise one or other of the two main cycles of the Mesoamerican calendar: the year of 18 feasts of 20 days; and the gestation period (tonalpoualli) of nine moons, or 13 x 20 days.

In opening up the concept of the year, the first chapter focuses on the cycles of Aztec and Christian liturgy. Running from May to December (in the text as it now stands), a narrow marginal column to the left on each page furnishes such details as zodiac sign, month name in alphabetic script and tlacuilolli, and length of the month in days. On each page, the lower register is dedicated to glyphs of the corresponding twenty-day Aztec Feasts, mementos of the great metamorphoses and catastrophes deep in the time of creation. In images and phonetic glyphs, the upper register offers a selection of Christian Saints' and Holy Days: which are chosen and how they are depicted make a complex argument in its own right.

Page by page, the lower and upper registers are separated by a double band of letters, consisting of the seven-letter count a–g that begins on New Year's Day in any given year, and the twenty-seven-letter count of the sidereal moon, that is, its passage through the zodiac (the "lunar letters"). Rooted, as it were, in popular custom below, four chosen feast days grow upward, stemlike, through this double band of letters, indicating that they may continue to flourish within the new colonial order. The lordly Feast Tecuilhuitl rises to become the solstitial St. John's Day in June, and similar though less confident links are made between the hunting Feast Quecholli and St. Martin's Day in November, and between the "falling water" Feast Atemoztli and St. Thomas's day in December. The depiction of Feast Toxcatl in mid-May is the most striking, since the emblem of that Feast, Tezcatlipoca's triple-ring scepter, thrusts into the upper Christian register, higher on the page than the Holy Cross that just before and beside it denotes 2 May. Glossed in Latin as the living tree (arbor), this pagan scepter would recall for every native reader Tezcatlipoca's role in creation no less than in the Aztec expulsion of Cortes and his army from Tenochtitlan in that feast in May 1520. The principle of such stem feasts remains alive in the timing of ritual today (Broda and Baez Jorge 2001).

The days of two saints, Francis and Martin, are noted as those of the arrival in Mexico-Tenochtitlan of Cortes and viceroy Suarez de Mendoza, in 1519 and 1580 respectively. The fashionable black hats and bearded faces of these Spaniards can also be seen in the annals at these dates, and as conquistador and viceroy they complement the church as the three arms of power extended by Europe into sixteenth-century Mexico. Cortes's intrusion on St. Martin's Day, 11 November, links him with the Feast Quecholli (f. 2.3), when migrant birds arrived from the north and the hunting season started on the lakes around the capital, a coincidence relished in many an Aztec narrative. On that day Cortes is reported to have kidnapped Moctezuma, having failed to convince him that the Bible was any kind of match for American accounts of genesis. Noting Suarez and Cortes in this way here means formally integrating historically specific events into the year cycles of both Christian and Aztec ritual.

The second chapter deals with the main question addressed by Gregory's Reform, that is, the need to measure the solar year more accurately than the Julian calendar had done in simply adding a leap day every fourth year. Julian practice is represented by the wheel of 4 x 7 Dominical Letters, a cycle of twenty-eight years derived from the seven-letter count. Thanks to a reference to the final year of Mendoza's reign as first viceroy (1540), the cycle is located here in the Christian Era as the years *anno Domini* 1551–1578. Matching it to the right is the comparable Aztec cycle, the fifty-two-year xiuhmolpilli, of 4 x 13 rather than 4 x 7 years. The two wheels touch and mesh at the xiuhmolpilli ending in 1 Rabbit 1558 and the subsequent New Fire year 2 Reed 1559. Technically, the wheels are engineered so as to reproduce a leap-day formula not of 28 x 52 years but of 29 x 52 (their lowest common denominator), flexibly used in the many regional variants of the Mesoamerican calendar and found at early dates in its far longer era (Edmonson 1988). Visually, the Christian wheel defines its year units by means of rigid lines radiating from a centrally authoritative St. Peter, papal master of locks and clocks and the printing press. The turquoise years of the Mesoamerican wheel are more like the segments or vertebrae of a coiled snake, which carry the attentive reader back to the start of the Mesoamerican Era.

The opening set of chapters concerned with the year culminates in the night sky, in the form of the Old World zodiac, the twelve stations the sun passes through annually, into which are inset the twenty-eight stations of the moon (derived from the twenty-seven lunar letters). The zodiac appears twice, first in Aries, traditionally the spring equinox in March (*Codex Mexicanus*, 10), and then in Aquarius, traditionally January (11), reflecting Christian indecision about when the year should begin.

The Aries zodiac concentrates on the further concomitant problem tackled by Christianity in the centuries-long Paschal Controversies and again in the Gregorian Reform: how best to determine the date of Easter, as the first Sunday after the first full moon after the spring equinox. The *Mexicanus* contribution to this problem, on pages 10 and 15, reveals how, as far as its liturgy went, in 1582 Rome as it were gave up, if not on the phases of the moon, then on the lunar letters of the zodiac and the night sky in general (a fact of some historical and philosophical consequence). To begin with, it obscured the rationale by which the very advent of Christianity was thought to have coincided with the equinoctial sun's precession from Aries toward the constellation Pisces.

In this, *Mexicanus* develops its ideological as well as practical critique of the imported system, affirming local norms under the new colonial rule. Such is the argument of the page dedicated to Christ's body (12), which contrasts exemplarily with the bodies of Tezcatlipoca and Tlaloc in the classic texts, and of the page on Lent (15), which celebrates the Mercury-cycle span between Septuagesima and Ember Day, misunderstood and then forgotten by the Christians themselves. The Aquarius zodiac (11), which complements the Aries zodiac (10), goes in a similar direction.

This page-table arranges, one above the other, the two halves of the zodiac which begin with Aquarius and Leo, including the stations of the sidereal moon (two or three per zodiac sign), along with Aristotle's "four elements"—the *aer*, *aqua*, *ignis*, and *terra* of medieval science—to each of which belong three zodiac signs: Aquarius, Gemini, and Libra belong with air; Pisces, Cancer, and Scorpio belong with water; and so on. In presenting this second zodiac, *Mexicanus* subtly modifies the received design, in the detail of both the zodiac signs and the four so-called elements. Following the correlative principle which so mechanically informs the Old World table, the Aztec scribes take it further in order to turn it on itself and make their own case.

In the first set of three signs—Aquarius, Gemini, and Libra, or those identified with air—play is made with the idea of being double, which as such is plain enough in the case of the Gemini twins and the two weighing pans of Libra's scale. Here, however, Aquarius, too, becomes double, through the fact that the water-bearer holds not one but two jars. Moreover, the streams of water pouring from them are shown to swirl one above the other, in an aquatic pattern altogether reminiscent of tlacuilolli water glyphs (a-tl). At one level, all this recalls the strange coincidence, explicitly noted in Tovar and other companion codices of the sixteenth century, whereby in the sixteenth century the January water jar of the Old World Aquarius found a counterpart in that of the Aztec "falling water" Feast Atemoztli, which fell at a similar time of year (Kubler and Gibson 1951).

In turn, this detail further suggests that the Twins of Gemini also "intermingle," indeed that they are not normal twins at all but a fornicating couple, sitting face to face in a sexual posture likewise found in the classic codices, the legs of the female overlaying those of the male. Finally, this causes us to notice that the doubleness of the third Air sign, Libra, carries through the same idea of superimposition, at the expense of balance, one pan being higher than the other. Hence, as a sequence, the three modified Air signs reinforce each other visually, proposing an overall statement. That

is, they may be read as a complex but altogether coherent response to colonization, a protest against a calendar that validates Aquarius at the expense of
the Feast Atemoztli, against the conquistador-like promiscuity of the "false
twin" Gemini, and against the injustice patent in Libra's tilted weighing
scales—the execrable "peso" Juan sought to annihilate.

The next set of signs—Pisces, Cancer, and Scorpio, assigned to Water—
appears here as two fish (the standard representation), another fish (instead
of a crab), and a crablike scorpion. The fish of Pisces have incipient legs,
which the single fish of Cancer no longer has, implying decline down deeper
in time and, in the context of Mesoamerican cosmogony, suggesting regres-
sion down the evolutionary scale from higher to lower vertebrate, then to
crustacean. These are concepts elaborated in the account of origins and
world ages recorded on the Sun Stone and narrated at length in the *Popol vuh*
(Edmonson 1971; Tedlock 1985).

The third and fourth sets of signs, which belong to Fire and Earth,
concentrate on the true animals of the zodiac, as well as anthropomorphic
Virgo. Play is made with the link that all these creatures ultimately have with
the ideas of being domestically protected (Virgo), domesticated (the herd
animals Aries the ram, Taurus the bull, Sagittarius the half horse, and Capri-
corn the goat), or tameable (Leo the lion). In native America, herd animals,
along with the economy and ideology of pastoralism, were unknown outside
the Andes, and their introduction into Mexico was profoundly resented at
practical and philosophical levels. The damage they did to crops became the
subject of endless legal disputes presented to the Real Audiencia. *Mexicanus*
draws attention to their "tails" and thereby to the process of sexual selection
basic to pastoralism. The bull's pizzle (Taurus) is enormous and contrasts
exemplarily with the tiny or absent members of the Fire creatures Aries, Leo,
and Sagittarius. All nonetheless have long proper tails (even Virgo holds up
a tail-like frond), except for Aries. Indeed, with his tiny, docked tail, Aries
proves to be not a ram at all, but a shorn yearling, and recalling the Paschal
lamb of Easter, looks as ineffectual as Christ's agents most often proved to
be as defenders of their newly acquired Indian flock. As the other side of the
same coin, the bull continues to symbolize the worst of European aggres-
sion in native-paper codex-style books still produced in Mexico today (Sandstrom and Effrein 1986).

Overall, the twelve zodiac signs in this second *Mexicanus* zodiac (11) remain quite recognizable as the Old World configuration they are. Yet they are
persistently modified, a fact easily confirmed by comparison with the un-
modified Paschal zodiac on the previous page (10). Thanks to this, and to the

appeal to the kind of visual logic found in the classic codices, the adapted zodiac comes to undermine the culture from which it stemmed. This process is yet more obvious in the case of the four elements with which the zodiac signs are correlated, where, moreover, a positive counterstatement is also made. Each of the four is deliberately traduced, not just satirically, but in the name of quite another philosophy, and this process is incremental, with each successive representation of the same element, and from one element to the next.

Air, usually clear or transparent, is instead puffed out as black breath onto the white page, from a mouth set in a face with European features and framed by curly (as opposed to straight, Indian) hair. As the year turns, the head moves from side to side, the mouth opens wider, and the blackness cumulatively spreads. The act of exhaling darkness in this way, shamanic in origin, is clearly registered in the classic codices (e.g., Brotherston 1995, 134). Hence, within an image that is wholly European in style, there is again a native message, one which sums up the negative commentary on Spanish colonization made so far.

Yet, more decisive, this black air simultaneously invokes the nighttime, in which the zodiac constellations may actually be seen, a breath which precisely in the attempt to destroy cannot but recall native intelligence. In rejecting Christianity the Aztec priests invoked the powers of the Night and the Wind (*in ioualli in ecatl*). That is, the Air image calls for a zodiac which signifies not by virtue of the existence within it of the night-obliterating sun, as it did for the Christians; and it prefers a zodiac which could effectively be integrated into the measurement of time, as thanks to precession it no longer could be in the Christian calendar, despite the token references, in the lunar letters, to the passage through it of the sidereal moon.

The same order of ideas carries through to the element of water, which, being no more sweet or welcome than European breath, issues from ice crystals far above, arriving as hard hail and cold rain. The image as such, however, is now firmly native, rather than European, and corresponds, quite exactly, to that seen in the account of the altiplano winter given in the *Tepepulco Manuscript* (f. 283), also known as Sahagún's *Primeros memoriales* (Sahagún 1993 [ca. 1547]), where Itztlacoliuhqui the Ice Lord threatens newly planted crops with his hail, in the seasonal cycle parallel to that produced by the three zodiac sets of "four elements." In other words, the idea of destructiveness is transposed from the European face and elements to be incorporated into a wholly native meteorological cycle. At the same time, there is an appeal to the idea of how physical state may be determined by altitude and changes in temperature—solid ice forms as water rises and melts as it falls—and to numeracy—the falling streams of liquid always number eleven.

Now fully integrated into native teaching, the third element, Fire, develops this line of thought. For Fire is not some mysterious essence like phlogiston but a fire (tle-itl), like the one purposefully lit by the metal-workers in the codices, or like that drilled at the New Fire ceremony every fifty-two years. The image again relates temperature change to verticality and to physical state, showing how flames of gas rise from solid coal. And it again invokes numeracy, this time with more complexity. For the coals and flames always present the same overall unit-total of eleven, which repeats that of Water; yet as the fire grows hotter, they visibly shift their inner proportion, as 7:4, 6:5, and 5:6. In Mesoamerican culture the celestial valency of these flames will always be implicit thanks to the ceremony of New Fire, when the exact moment for the fire-drilling was determined by the night sky.

Of the four elements, the last, Earth, is the one most defiantly reclaimed from Old World philosophy. On the *Codex Mexicanus* (11), Earth signifies not as god-given but because it is worked and tended. It is the field (tlalli), imaged as such, as in countless sixteenth-century legal documents, by its regular edge and exactly patterned "plantation" infixes (pairs of dots; laterally inverted and square-sided Cs). In the seasonal planting cycle seen here the field is tended by a definitely native hoe for two-thirds of the year—twelve planting feasts, or eight months—while the hoe is withdrawn from the earth during the six nonplanting feasts, or four months. In the codices, the sophistication of the elements which make up this earth glyph is such that they could mathematically specify field area and form, and type of soil. (They are unfortunately too effaced to be fully decoded). By comparison, European ideas on the subject were so crude as to ruin native practices of land management (Harvey and Williams 1986).

Just as the modified zodiac signs imply a critique, so the set of four correlative elements proposes another thesis, one which points to ideas of production, to the importance not of immutable "elements" but of human effort and intelligence, all within a larger idea of natural origin. If the thought registered in the second *Mexicanus* zodiac is to be termed *astrology* like that of its scholastic prompt, then it is one based on a longer worldview and a more accurate calendrics.

Prompted by the Gregorian Reform, *Mexicanus* responds with immense finesse to the European invasion and its practical and intellectual demands. It does this precisely by remaining loyal to a philosophy of time and space which avoids the easy binaries of the West, and it deploys a much better mathematics and astronomy. Above all, it relies on and furthers the genre expectations of the tlacuilolli literary tradition, tracing subtle interplays between theme and narrative, cyclic pattern and historical moment.

Mexicanus was written at a time when Europe felt threatened intellectually by America on these and several other counts. Try as it undoubtedly did, even in the Old World Rome could no longer hold on to the central authority that it had proclaimed for centuries in such matters. Caught by Ptolemy, as well as by its own dogmas and philosophical priorities, the Roman world lost the night sky to the far more accurate yet heartless, socially abstract, and unreflexive mechanisms of the "science" that Europe was beginning to embrace precisely when the Augustinians arrived in San Pablo Teipan with their astrolabes. And it soon found itself burning the treatises of those scientists with the same enthusiasm with which it had burned tlacuilolli screenfolds in Mexico and quipus in Peru.

Mexicanus survives as the most discreet reminder of all this, just as it serves as a fine and much-needed guide to tlacuilolli literature, to wondrous articulations of time and relivings of genesis, no more than hinted at here, which Europe suppressed, ignored, or simply failed to understand.

THE SUN STONE

While *Mexicanus* remains for most a closed book, replete with knowledge of huge subversive potential, the Sun Stone (also known as Stone of the Suns, Piedra de los soles, and Aztec Calendar Stone) could hardly be more celebrated (Matos Moctezuma and Solís 2002, 19–21). Inscribed in the same script and calendar system a century or so earlier, it incorporates into the Mexican, indeed American, story of genesis exactly the science of sun and night sky, cosmic and calendrical eras found in *Mexicanus* (Monjarás Ruiz 1987; Brotherston 1992).

A visual statement that once dominated Tenochtitlan's main temple, the Sun Stone today ranks second to none as a memento of ancient Mexico, and it serves as a kind of high altar in the Museum of National Anthropology in Mexico City. It is immense and encompasses the world ages, or suns of creation, in a series of concentric circles. Laid out around the center as the four that inhere in the present fifth, these suns are identified by *tonalpoualli* names (number plus sign) which recall the catastrophes they respectively culminate in. Forming a quincunx, they may be and have been read in more than one narrative sequence, depending on the theme or argument at stake.

To the left stand the Water (IX) of the flood and the Jaguar (XIV) representative of the sky monsters that descend to devour and excoriate during the prolonged eclipse. To the right stand the Rain (XIX) of fire produced by volcanic eruption and the hurricane Wind (II) that sweeps away all before it. The four signs, one per each of four limbs, then come to configure the quincunx sign of the present age, Ollin (XVII), the movement or earthquake in which it will end. From any point of view, it is a monumental text, unquestionably pre-Cortesian, that draws fully on the resouces of tlacuilolli in configuring the origins of the world and time.

With the destruction of Tenochtitlan's temple in 1521, the Sun Stone was buried under the rubble as yet another example of idolatry and belief that fitted ill with the biblical Genesis; and it was lost to the view of the colony before its recovery in 1790. The worldview it represented, however, was by no means obliterated; other carvings on the same theme, even if smaller and far less comprehensive, were known. Then, in order the better to counter native belief, the church solicited accounts of genesis, of the kind found in the *Codex Vaticanus*, or *Ríos Codex* (Brotherston 1992, 298–302); this text deals with the same world ages and makes explicit the chronology which culminates in the 5,200 years of our present era, Four Ollin. Beyond that, for a variety of political reasons, Nahuatl scribes produced alphabetical narratives wherein first beginnings coincide with the world-age paradigm. Gathered in the *Codex Chimalpopoca* (Bierhorst 1992), two of these Nahuatl texts to some degree actually transcribe the tlacuilolli statement on the Sun Stone; they are the *Cuauhtitlan Annals* and the *Manuscrito de 1558*, or *Legend of the Suns*.

The *Cuauhtitlan Annals* run unbroken from Chichimec beginnings in the seventh century to Cortés's arrival: every year is counted from before the Chichimec calendar base in 1 Flint 648 to the fateful encounter with Europe in 1 Reed 1519. In describing how the survivors of the ancient Toltecs came to found highland Tula at the turn of the eighth century A.D., the text casts back, via tonalpoualli signs and year names, to the start of the Mesoamerican Era itself and the world ages that inhere in it.

> The first Sun to be founded has the sign Four Water, it is called Water Sun. Then it happened that water carried everything away, everything vanished and the people were changed into fish.
>
> The second Sun to be founded has the sign Four Jaguar, it is called Jaguar Sun. Then it happened that the sky collapsed, the sun did not follow its course at midday, immediately it was night and when it grew dark the people were torn to pieces. In this Sun giants lived. The old ones said the giants greeted each other thus: "Don't fall over," for whoever fell, fell for good.

The third Sun to be founded has the sign Four Rain, it is called Rain Sun. It happened then that fire rained down, those who lived there were burned. And they say that then tiny stones rained down and spread, the fine stones that we can see; the *tezontli* boiled into stone and the reddish rocks were twisted up.

The fourth Sun, sign Four Wind, is called Wind Sun. Then the wind carried everything away. The people all turned into monkeys and went to live in the forests.

The fifth Sun, sign Four Ollin, is called Earthquake Sun because it started into motion [*ollin*]. The old ones said in this Sun there will be earthquakes and general hunger from which we shall perish. (f. 2; adapted from Bierhorst 1992, 26)

Adhering perfectly to the Sun Stone quincunx of tonalpoualli-named world ages, this text as a narrative follows the sequence we began with. In so doing, it specifies registers of meaning that the West later came to identify as geology and zoology. Below the earthquake of Four Ollin lie the sedimentary rock of the flood and the igneous rock produced by volcanic action. In sixteenth-century European thought, the only way rocks could have been formed was by sedimentation, as a result of the biblical flood. In this American context not only was the sedimentary model insufficient from the start, so were the doctrines of fixity, stability, and insurance built on it. For the word-sign for earthquake in Nahuatl, *ollin*, also means movement, elasticity, the material rubber (*hule*, unknown outside the American tropics before Columbus), and hence chance, as in the game *ulama* first played by the "rubber people," the Olmec.

If Water (bottom right) is characterized by metamorphosis into fish, that is, fossil evidence of the first vertebrate life-forms, then at the other diagonal extreme the Wind Sun (top left) marks the most recent metamorphosis in that same vertebrate story, in the form of the monkeys that immediately precede humans and our time. This frankly evolutionary understanding of our origins is what underlies *Mexicanus*'s satirical treatment of the Old World zodiac and the four elements. It is an account developed at great narrative length in other Mesoamerican texts, notably the *Popol vuh* of the highland Maya, which has more to say about the "giants" who perished during the eclipse, about intermediary bird-reptiles who include saurians strong enough to make the earth shudder and erupt, and about our kinship with "elder brother" monkeys.

Overall, this world-age paradigm is amply confirmed in the *Ríos Codex* and the *Legend of the Suns*, which add further details (albeit in other narrative arrangements), confirming, for example, the world age common to bird metamorphosis and the Rain of fire. The legend also establishes a precise chronology for this era, within the multimillennia ascribed to the world-age paradigm in the *Ríos Codex* (in the *Codice Madrid*, 57, 69, rocks twist into shape over millions of years) (Brotherston 1992, 303). From the xiuhmolpilli end-year 1 Rabbit 1558 after which it is named, the legend counts back 2,513 years plus another two millennia (41.5 xiuhmolpilli), to reach the Mesoamerican Era start date of 3113 B.C. used already in Olmec and Maya inscriptions.

Daunting as it clearly was for Western minds of the time, this astounding account of genesis caught the attention of few of Mexico's early colonizers. From the little it learned, the church on the whole actively shied away from it, even more after the Counter-Reformation began to impose its strict limits on what was admissible knowledge. In his capacious *Historia de las cosas de la Nueva España* (ca. 1575–80) Bernardino de Sahagún significantly had nothing at all to say about it, fearing as much as he failed to understand the knowledge of sky and earth that it implied. Yet, in what might be thought of as a small pre-Tridentine window, certain secular chroniclers—among them Francisco López de Gómara—urged the case for America as a world new also in this kind of ideas. In *Historia general de las Indias* (1552), dedicated to emperor Charles V, López de Gómara includes a chapter entitled "Cinco soles, que son edades," which reports,

> Afirman que han pasado después acá de la creación del mundo, cuatro soles, sin éste que ahora los alumbra. Dicen pues cómo el primer sol se perdió por agua, con que se ahogaron todos los hombres y perecieron todas las cosas criadas; el segundo sol pereció cayendo el cielo sobre la tierra, cuya caída mató la gente y toda cosa viva; y dicen que había entonces gigantes, y que son de ellos los huesos que nuestros españoles han hallado cavando minas, de cuya medida y proporción parece como eran aquellos hombres de veinte palmos en alto; estatura es grandísima, pero certísima; el sol tercero faltó y se consumió por fuego; porque ardió muchos días todo el mundo, y murió abrasada toda la gente y animales; el cuarto sol feneció con aire; fue tanto y tan recio el viento que hizo entonces, que derrocó todos los edificios y árboles, y aun deshizo las peñas; mas no perecieron los hombres, sino convirtiéronse en monas.

> [They affirm that since the creation of the world four suns have passed, not including the one that shines on them now. They say then that the first sun was lost because of water, in which all mankind was drowned and all created things perished. The second sun perished when the sky fell to earth, the fall killing the people and every living thing; and they say that at that time there were giants, and that theirs are the bones that our Spaniards have found excavating mines; from their measurement and proportion it seems they were men twenty-palms tall, a

huge stature, but most certain. The third sun failed and was consumed by fire, for the whole world burned for many days and all people and animals died in it. The fourth sun ended because of air; at that time, the wind was such and so strong that it demolished buildings and trees, even rock faces; yet humans did not perish but turned into monkeys.] (López de Gómara 1979 [1552], chap. 206, my translation)

The chapter goes on to detail the transition to the present era, or quinto sol, giving precise details of year names and dates, and adding that the Christian task of conversion was made easier by the fact that the old creator gods were thought to have died. López de Gómara also recognizes the importance of calendar and script for this record ("ha muchos años que usan escritura pintada"), and he refers to the Nahuatl year name ce tochtli (1 Rabbit) in a way consistent with the count back over "858 años" from 1552 to 694. These and other details make it certain that he was drawing closely on the corpus typified by the Codex Chimalpopoca texts; differences from those texts seen in his translation may therefore be considered significant.

Above all, the changes reflect the need to make the Sun Stone paradigm at all recognizable to Old World minds of the day. Failing to find any trace of the monotheist authority indispensable to the biblical Genesis, López de Gómara resorts to the same old Aristotelian model of the four elements that medieval Christianity had loosely incorporated. From water on, each world age is systematically reduced in these terms: eclipse becomes just a fall to earth; volcanic rain becomes simple fire; and wind is first stated as air. Unhappily, even today certain European commentators on the Sun Stone paradigm are afflicted by the same elementary compulsion, which Mexicanus understandably found so anodyne. With this reduction, we lose the specific references to types of rock (tezontli) and the evidence of metamorphosis found in them (fish). The giant bones remain and indeed are more thoroughly measured, though now, curiously, they function less as evidence of other worlds, their discovery being made subject to practical mining enterprise on the part of the colonizers, "nuestros españoles."

As for the present world, López de Gómara says that while he was told about the transition to it, he was not told how it would end, about its name and characteristic in this sense. In practice, this meant he could make his four-element scheme work better; and it relieved him of the need to contemplate the multivalent concept of ollin. López de Gómara's omission of Four Ollin further has the effect of separating the past off as a block from the unnamed present, enhancing linearity in that past. All of this goes radically against the common time/space articulated on the Sun Stone as a quincunx of world ages, each with its own potential time depth, rhythm, and life-form, and named by tonalpoualli signs and numbers which calendrically allow them to be endlessly relived and experienced.

Tying López de Gómara's Spanish prose back to the Sun Stone illuminates both texts. The same is true of a possible comparison forward in time, with the French version of it that was adapted by Montaigne in his "On Coaches." In this piece, Montaigne ponders the achievements of the ancients, not just the Greeks and Romans of Europe but the Inca and Aztecs of America. He finds grandeur manifest in the architecture, roads, gardens, institutions, and philosophy of the New World, ever careful to recall that the capacity to think is as much the privilege of "savage" as of urban human beings. In this case, for his American example of philosophy, Montaigne turns to the world-age paradigm he found in López de Gómara, in a passage here reproduced in the celebrated 1603 English translation by John Florio.

> They believed the state of the world to be divided into five ages, as in the life of five succeeding Suns, whereof four had already ended their course or time; and the same which now shined upon them was the fifth and last. The first perished together with all other creatures by an universal inundation of waters. The second by the fall of the heavens upon us which stifled and overwhelmed every living thing: in which age they affirm the Giants to have been, and showed the Spaniards certain bones of them, according to whose proportion the stature of men came to be the height of twenty handfuls. The third was consumed by a violent fire which burned and destroyed all. The fourth by a whirling emotion of the air and winds, which with the violent fury of itself removed and overthrew divers high mountains: saying that men died not of it but were transformed into monkeys. (Oh what impressions does not the weakness of man's belief admit?) . . . In what manner this last Sun shall perish my author could not learn of them. But their number of this fourth change does jump and meet with that great conjunction of the stars which eight hundred and odd years since, according to the astrologians supposition, produced diverse great alterations and strange novelties in the world. (Montaigne 1893, bk. 3, chap. 6)

In viewing the Sun Stone through López de Gómara's eyes, Montaigne stays close to this last while making a few eloquent changes. Even if the old gods died for López de Gómara, for him new ones have "day by day been born since." Then, rather than talk of "us" and "them" he includes himself in "us," effectively (and heretically) integrating the "universal flood" of the Bible into his larger American genesis. In so doing he mitigates the rigidity of the four-element scheme imposed by López de Gómara (earth becomes "us," air starts as whirling emotion), and he restores to the Indians full credit for finding and construing the giants' bones. To the one metamorphosis (into monkeys) that López de Gómara transmits he adds a heavily loaded parenthesis, both satirical of Christian dogma and strangely prophetic of Darwin, of the kind that earned his work its place on the papal Index.

Caught as he is by this account, Montaigne is no less intrigued by the European "astrologians" who at that very moment were establishing the bases of what would become Western science, and perhaps for that reason he omits all reference to the native calendar, removing native year names (*ce tochtli*) and rounding down to "800 and odd years" the precise 858 of the Spanish and the Nahuatl. At all events, he treats the world-age story with an openness characteristic of certain other agnostic contemporaries (notably Christopher Marlowe and the School of Night) (Kocher 1962; cf. Arciniegas 1975), which, however, quickly evaporated as science replaced Christian faith as dogma and became a powerful validator of colonialism in its own right.

The worldview represented on the Sun Stone was suddenly reinvigorated when colonial rule in New Spain was nearing its end. Possessing latent power even as an archeological ruin, the huge disk was excavated in 1790, along with the awe-inspiring earth-goddess Coatlicue, in circumstances detailed in León y Gama's *Descripción histórica y cronológica de las dos piedras que con ocasión del nuevo empedrado que se está formando en la plaza principal de México, se hallaron en ella . . .* (1792; quoted in Matos and Solís 2002). The unearthing of its sheer physical weight was matched in spirit by the message it bore as a text, one in every way destructive of the creeds of fixity promoted by Christianity and the Enlightenment alike. The very foundations of the viceroyalty were felt to be threatened, in a rethinking of the colonial order that drew in the Creoles. This much is clear from the reading of the Sun Stone made by Ignacio Borunda (in his *Clave de los jeroglíficos americanos*), and from the account that Fray Servando Teresa de Mier, the future hero of Mexican independence, gave both of his association with Borunda and of tlacuilolli as a political and intellectual resource (a story satirically retold by Reinaldo Arenas in *El mundo alucinante*).

In the larger view, these first postcolonial rumblings seem the more telling since on the Sun Stone was written an understanding of genesis, of world ages and cataclysms, that the West was at last catching up with in just those decades, thanks to its fledgling sciences of geology and zoology. Thereafter comes the whole literature and performance of the quinto sol.

IN SUM

Given the technical complexity of Mesoamerican calendrics and hence cosmogony and philosophy, these readings of *Mexicanus* and the Sun Stone can
no more than gesture toward the question of how colonizing Europe was
challenged intellectually in America. The matter at stake of course includes
the discourses preferred by the colonizers and the modes of indigenous
resistance to them. Yet beyond or behind all that lies the larger and rarely
broached notion of knowledge systems as such: of continuities in native
thought that still await acknowledgment; and of a certain limitation the
West has assumed it somehow never suffered from and would in any case
soon displace with its "universal" science.

Finally, having this order of text as a yardstick helps define postcoloniality
in Spanish American writing more generally, these sixteenth-century Mexican cases being an often neglected precedent for comparable declarations of
selfhood that would later come with independence. Among these, we may
mention the passages in "Nuestra América" where José Martí extols native
literacy and the schools of Teotitlan, also invoking the *Popol vuh* and the
classics published in Brinton's Library of Aboriginal American Literature;
Montalvo's acid application of Quechua logic to Creole prejudice ("Urcu
sacha" [2000]); or Francisco Bilbao's impassioned equation of independence with both the philosophy and the still-free territory of the Mapuche (El
evangelio americano [1864]). The paradigm may be extended in turn to include
the other main language traditions imported to America, sharpening awareness of (Latin) American "difference." Just as he mediated Nahuatl thought
in one of his *Essays*, so, in another, Montaigne quoted examples of Tupi-
Guaraní poetry, which would have a strong impact on the Americanistas of
nineteenth-century Brazil. As for English-speaking America, Leslie Marmon
Silko's *Almanac of the Dead* (1992) initiates a similar program of restitution
against what has long been endured as a particularly insidious intellectual
colonization.

NOTES

1   Similar concerns about the temporality of colonialism has been expressed by
    critics like Peter Hulme, in this volume. Aníbal Quijano's concept of coloniality
    also points to the continuity of colonial structures and practices in modern
    times.
2   I am extremely grateful to Elly Wake for this reference.

THINKING EUROPE IN INDIAN CATEGORIES, OR, "TELL ME THE STORY OF HOW I CONQUERED YOU"

José Rabasa

In the prefatory remarks to Book 12: *De la conquista mexicana* (ca. 1569) of the *Historia general de las cosas de la Nueva España*, which provides a Nahuatl version of the conquest of Mexico, the Franciscan friar Bernardino de Sahagún gives two reasons for writing this history: first, "quanto por poner el lenguaje de las cosas de la guerra, y de las armas que en ella vsan los naturales: para que de alli se puedan sacar vocablos y maneras de dezir propias, para hablar en lengua mexicana cerca desta materia" [to record the language of warfare and the weapons which the natives use in it, in order that the terms and proper modes of expression for speaking on this subject in the Mexican language can be derived therefrom]; second, "allegase tambien a esto que los que fueron conquistados, supieron y dieron relacion de muchas cosas, que passaron entre ellos durante la guerra: las cuales ignorarõ, los que los conquistarõ" [to this may be added that those who were conquered knew and gave an account of many things that transpired among them during the war of which those who conquered them were unaware]. Sahagún closes his remarks by stating that the history was written "en tiempo que eran vivos, los que se hallaron en la mjsma conquista: y ellos dieron esta relacion personas principales, y de buen juizio y que se tiene por cierto, que dixeron toda verdad" [when those who took part in the very conquest were alive: and those who gave this account [were] principal people of good judgment, and it is believed that they told all the truth] (Sahagún 1950–82 [ca. 1579], pt. 1, 101).[1] This extraordinary text, which solicits a version of the conquest from the conquered, is actually one of a series of texts that were produced in the sixteenth century to document how Indians perceived the conquest and the colonial order.

To think Europe in Indian categories or to respond to the demand to tell the story of how one was conquered occasions cross-cultural intersubjectivity.[2] The demand seeks to understand the Indian mind, but the response inevitably conveys the destruction of a world as well as the anguish, if not resentment and grief, for a lost worldview. Anguish, resentment, grief, and loss expose the violence of the conquest, but the query also seeks to provoke an internalization of the defeat in terms of an epistemological and moral debacle. The request to tell the story of how one was conquered had the unexpected effect of soliciting the gaze of the indigenous subjects—a brilliant instance of the observer observed.

To appeal to Freud's classic essay "Mourning and Melancholia" has become commonplace in studies of trauma and oppression. Freud's view of the healing process involved in mourning and the pathological clinging to the past in melancholy has been the subject of debate. Already in Freud, there is an opening to an understanding of melancholia as leading to self-knowledge, but even more interesting for colonial and postcolonial studies is his statement that "melancholic . . . reaction . . . proceeds from a mental constellation of revolt, which has then, by a certain process, passed over into the crushed state of melancholia" (1953–74, vol. 14, 258). Both Homi Bhabha and Judith Butler have noted this passage. In Bhabha's view of postcolonial melancholy, the concept of ambivalence suggests a hybrid "in-betweenness," a third space beyond the colonizer-colonized binary. Bhabha underscores the "crushed state of revolt" when he writes, "All this bits and pieces in which my history is fragmented, my culture piecemeal, my identification fantasmatic and displaced; these splittings of wounds of my body are also a form of revolt. And they speak a terrible truth. In their ellipses and silences they dismantle your authority" (1992a, 66). This third space, where

grief and ambivalence dismantle authority, involves going beyond the colonizer and the colonized, but insofar as Bhabha reinscribes the revolt in
terms of one more version of Western discourse, in which Bhabha's *self*
stands for *his* oppressed peoples, he ends up erasing the possibility of conceiving a space that is altogether different from the Freudian-derived discourse that Bhabha elaborates in English. There is no room for an elsewhere
to Greco-Abrahamic tradition from which the colonial order is observed.
Butler (1997) underscores that the "crushed state of melancholia" can lead
to mania, rage, and ambivalence as psychic states that enable an active form
of melancholia, an affirmation of life that demands the restitution of sovereignty, reparations for damages, and social transformation.[3] Indians thinking Europe in indigenous categories and the responses to the demand to tell
the story of how one was conquered run through this gamut of possibilities.
As in Bhabha, these tales of conquest speak a terrible story, and there is
certainly a dismantling of authority, but as in Butler, the passage to rage
conveys a state in which rebellion follows the crushed state of melancholia.
Melancholia in its interplay with mourning would convey the refusal to
recognize that something has been lost, a refusal to internalize a law that
demands self-deprecation and conceives of melancholia as a form of sin.
Because of the nature of the demand to tell the story of conquest, the passage
from mourning to melancholia is never completed, and the possibility of
mania haunts the observers' (i.e., Spanish lay and religious authorities)
certainty about the expected story of victory and defeat.

In reading the Nahua versions of the conquest, the Freudian concepts of
melancholy, mourning, rage, and ambivalence serve as heuristic categories
that at some point we must abandon and whose limitations we must expose.
If appealing to these Freudian categories certainly makes sense from our
present Western interpretative modes, we should also keep in mind that in
projecting psychoanalytical categories on Nahuatl expressions of grief and
mania we may be universalizing our own provincial schemas and modes of
understanding affect. This projection has less to do with the dangers of
anachronism, since I would argue with Willard Van Orman Quine that there
is no outside to these provincial schemas, only a wide range of acceptable
possible translations: "Wanton translation can make natives sound as queer
as one pleases. Better translation imposes our logic upon them, and would
beg the question of prelogicality if there were a question to beg" (Quine
1960, 58). Even if I were to concur with Quine that the development of better dictionaries and other linguistic tools might soften the indeterminacy
of radical translation (one with no previous linguistic contact with native

speakers), though I am not certain that we have advanced much from what Sahagún, Molina, and Carochi knew of what we term Classical Nahuatl, our modern production of commentary using letters remains blind to the visual communication of iconic script, in spite of our disparagement of the early colonial written glosses to the codices. The preference for better translations and the imposition of our logic over wanton translation—frolicsome, gay, playful, and so on—is not self-evident. In fact, the queer may turn out to be queer.[4] Quine does not entertain a world in which his *Word and Object* or, for that matter, Butler's and Bhabha's psychoanalytical discourse would be translated into Nahuatl categories.[5] If today a Nahua understanding of Quine, of Western discourse in general, seem unlikely (and I wonder if this isn't so because of ethnocentrism), Sahagún and other missionaries actually asked sixteenth-century Nahuas to make sense of the Spanish world in their own provincial modes of thought. If it is pointless to speculate what terms sixteenth-century Nahuas might use to speak of psychoanalytical under-standings of melancholia, mourning, and mania in Nahuatl, we may legiti-mately trace early modern understandings of melancholy in these Nahua texts. We must insist that there was a time when melancholy was not yet melancholia. Even if Freud (by this proper name I include Bhabha, Fanon, Lacan, and Butler, just to mention the most prominent) informs our dis-course on melancholy, we may trace phrases, expression, and forms of mourning and grieving that cannot, *must not* be subjected to "better" transla-tions, but allowed to retain their queerness. We may also find the incorpora-tion of typical figures of melancholy, such as the melancholic Renaissance prince, in particular when afflicted with acedia, that Walter Benjamin has written about in *The Origin of German Tragic Drama*.

I will first discuss the semblance of a pathological Moctezuma, the most commonly cited example of melancholia in Indian accounts of the conquest, and then move on to visual and verbal texts in which we find instances of mourning, melancholy, and mania that cannot be reduced to Freud's or to Benjamin's understanding of these terms. The best-known melancholic Moctezuma appears in chapter 9 of Book 12. Even if the heading speaks of the whole population of Tenochtitlan as awestruck—"Ninth Chapter, in which it is told how Moctezuma wept, and how the Mexicans wept, when they knew that the Spaniards were very powerful" (Sahagún 1950–82 [ca. 1579], bk. 12, pt. 13, 25, 26)—the chapter emphasizes the fear, melancholy, and paralysis of Moctezuma: "And when Moctezuma had thus heard that he was much inquired about, that he was much sought, that the gods wished to look upon his face, it was as if his heart was afflicted; he was afflicted. He would hide himself; he wished to flee" (ibid., 26). A few lines farther down, the translation reads, "No longer had he strength; no longer was there any use; no longer had he energy" (ibid.).[6] This semblance of an afflicted Moctezuma cannot but echo the Renaissance commonplace of the melancholic prince suffering from acedia. It should not surprise us that the Tlatelolcas— better, that the collegians who had been trained in Latin, Nahuatl, and Spanish by Sahagún—knew this figure and deployed it. It forms part of a whole set of European forms—that is, perspective, omens, horses, guns, chairs, terms—that the collegians use to imprint symbolic meaning in their verbal and pictorial versions of the conquest. The story of Moctezuma's melancholy does not exhaust the Tlatelolca account, since it can be read as an expression of mania that derives pleasure in its perverse rendition of the Tenochca ruler's infamous character in terms that would have been readily recognized as Spanish.[7] This melancholic Moctezuma is a commonplace in Spanish accounts of the conquest, but Nahuatl verbal and visual texts do not depict a paralyzed, indecisive Moctezuma. This melancholic Moctezuma suffering from acedia differs from other instances in Book 12 in which the informants mourn and grieve for a lost Nahua world. In the melancholic telling of the story of loss and destruction resides the survival of the Nahua life-forms. The story of the loss constitutes an act of rebellion that displaces the military victory to a spiritual and epistemological terrain in which Spanish and Indian forms coexist yet do not suppose a third space of in-betweenness, instead there is a retention and reinscription of differences in which Western forms are quoted and fulfill a symbolic function within a Nahua semantic space. This last point is crucial for understanding the phenomenon of the observer-observed in Indian texts, since they conduct the observation in Indian categories.

In examining Latin American colonial texts we need to reconsider a whole array of binaries that, following the contributions of postcolonial studies and subaltern studies (mainly those of Edward Said and Ranajit Guha), we have attributed to Spanish missionaries and lay officials with no hard evidence. I am thinking, in particular, of the opposition between "people with history, writing, or state vs. people without any of these forms."[8] The power of these binaries, which were prevalent in nineteenth-century French and British imperial texts, is nowhere more evident than in today's generalization to all colonial pasts. In the sixteenth-century and seventeenth-century Americas under colonial rule, the binary we must consider is one between Christian and not-Christian peoples (which for Spaniards would include Protestant heretics). Christianity is not simply a question of accepting a dogma: that is, believing stories in the scriptures, the existence of one God, the effectiveness of the sacraments, and perhaps the mysteries of grace. (I say "perhaps" because grace cannot be reduced to accepting a dogma.) Christianization in the sixteenth century also entailed an epistemology that sought to prove the demonic nature of Mesoamerican gods, to expose false beliefs in magic, and even to reveal superstitions in everyday life-practices that followed the *tonalamatl*, the book of the days or calendar of destiny. Indigenous peoples were subjected to verbal and physical abuse which was intended to instill in them self-deprecating attitudes and the consciousness of sin, but there is no evidence that Indians internalized as a stigma the fact that they lacked letters or history. Indians might have corrected their accounts with knowledge derived from the Bible, but there is no indication that in writing in Nahuatl they sought to imitate European historiography, nor is there any evidence in their colonial pictorial texts that they tried to imitate Western forms out of a desire to gain recognition from Spaniards that they were capable of writing and painting like Westerners. Nor is there any indication that they felt pressed to prove that Nahuatl was a language capable of doing history, literature, and philosophy, as if these clear-cut distinctions were current in the European sixteenth century. The places where Spanish historians question the existence of writing or of history in Mesoamerica are so few that we seem to quote the same places repeatedly. A desire to prove that one and one's language could reproduce European life-forms would be evidence that the negation of writing or history was a prevalent form of abuse and that it had been internalized. But there is no indication that such a desire existed. There was, to be sure, a great amount of anxiety over Christianity, but it was expressed in Indian categories and styles of writing and painting. There was in fact widespread mastery of and experimentation with both verbal and pictorial European forms.

Questions pertaining to the applicability of postcolonial theory and subaltern studies to Latin America have defined current debates in Latin American literary and cultural studies. Personally, I don't believe that theories, in general, should be applied or privileged as texts over those we tend to call primary sources—rather, theories and primary sources should be juxtaposed in the manner of a montage, with literary and cultural artifacts being accorded as much authority as theory. We must theorize and construct theories, but this imperative has nothing to do with application. In reading the wonderful writings of the South Asian Subaltern Studies collective or of postcolonial theoreticians, I have found that it is precisely, paradoxically, to the extent that they do not apply theory that we learn from them about the specificity of Latin American texts. The inapplicability of the binary "peoples with history vs. peoples without history" became particularly clear to me in reading Guha's essay "An Indian Historiography of India." There, Guha traces the origins of the nineteenth-century project to facilitate an Indian history written by Indians in terms of the Hegelian master-slave dialectic. Guha defines history as a late-eighteenth-century European invention that turned to look at India when the British faced the necessity to understand land tenure and tribute systems in their capacity of tribute collectors, or Diwans. Guha poses as unquestionable, as a matter of fact, the distinction between memory and history. For Guha, history is a Western practice that Indians learned in the course of the nineteenth century—there is no Indian history outside the models imported from English liberalism. The apprenticeship entailed imitating European models and the development—Guha speaks in terms of a maturing—of Bangla as an appropriate language for history. The dynamics is, then, one in which Indian historians seek the recognition of their capacity to write history in Bangla. The evolution is also one in which historians move from an acceptance of the inevitability of colonial tutelage to a questioning of the colonial system—a questioning which is bound to the limits of liberalism. This is a brilliant piece by Guha, but it is one that has nothing to do with sixteenth-century New Spain, or with nineteenth-century Latin America for that matter. As Guha underscores it, history as a disciplinary practice is a Western invention of the late eighteenth century. Within this schema, neither the Nahuas nor the Spaniards practiced history.

In his recently published lectures on world history, which he delivered at the Italian Academy for Advanced Studies at Columbia University, Guha (2002) draws an analogy between the use of history to define the inferiority of Indian culture in English imperial literature to the use of writing in Spanish colonial texts; his source is Walter Mignolo's *The Darker Side of the Renaissance* (1995). I would argue that there are no indications that Nahuas took to heart the sporadic references concerning their lack of letters or history. Guha's essay teaches us about the Spanish colonial project inasmuch as what he says about colonization in India enables us to grasp the radical difference of colonization in Mexico. Guha merely repeats Mignolo with no further reflection. He assumes that the same kind of opposition with different terms, operated in the subjection of Amerindians, without further reflecting on how this binary was an invention of the Enlightenment. As much as I think Latin American colonial studies can learn from postcolonial and subaltern studies, I am always struck by how uninformed and ready to generalize are such figures as Edward Said and Ranajit Guha, who with a stroke of the pen reduce the Spanish enterprise to robbing and abandoning the land with no civilizing mission. Take the following passage from Guha's essay: "For purposes of comparison, one could turn to that well-known instance of European expansion chronicled by Bernal Díaz in his classic account, *The Conquest of New Spain*. There, the author writes of the relation between language and conquest in all its lucidity and brutality. The Spaniards, we are told, taught some of the natives taken prisoners and used them as interpreters in their attempt to communicate with the indigenous peoples. The object of such communication was to acquire gold. The pattern was significantly different in the case of the British conquest of Bengal" (1997b, 176).

Postcolonial studies and subaltern studies presume an exteriority to the colonial; whether this exteriority is expressed as a temporal moment that comes after the colonial or as an identity or differential positioning that entertains the possibility of constituting anticolonial discourses, it assumes epistemic and ethical claims to an exception to colonialism and Eurocentrism. From a countercolonial position, one would undermine the colonial from within with no illusion of dwelling outside the Greco-Abrahamic traditions that have defined the languages and the disciplines from which we make sense of the world. Countercolonial moves, as such, would be specific to the spaces of intervention and resistance; resistance would no longer be conceived as responding to power but as generating new space of freedom which power then seeks to dominate. By Greco-Abrahamic languages I have in mind not only the languages we speak and write but also the conceptual apparatuses we deploy in our discourses. We may write philosophy in Nahuatl, for instance, but the disciplines and concepts of philosophy are inevitably bound by a Greco-Abrahamic tradition.[9] The mere fact of speaking of a Nahuatl philosophy entails a process of translating statements not conceived as philosophical into the languages of aesthetics, ethics, epistemology, ontology, and so on. This gesture posits the universality of the disciplines and categories that Western philosophy has developed over the centuries. As such, translation would erase the specificity of the worlds articulated in not-Western terms. Indeed, of worlds from which Western forms of life are reflected on and translated into—in a nutshell, a two-way street of inscription and circumscription. This will enable us to read countercolonial moves in indigenous texts that may very well be read as acts of resistance while seeking an accommodation in the colonial world.

Codex Telleriano-Remensis (ca. 1562) and Book 12: *De la conquista mexicana* (ca. 1569) provide answers to the request to "tell me the story of how I conquered you." They provide a narrative of moral and epistemological disintegration; we can also trace a return of the gaze. In addition to texts that respond to Spanish demand, there are others that were written—in both iconic script and alphabetical writing—outside the supervision of secular and religious authorities, such as the alphabetized *Historia de Tlatelolco desde los tiempos más remotos* (in *Anales de Tlatelolco*), the pictorial and alphabetical *Codex Aubin*, and the pictorial *Codex Mexicanus* and *Codex of Tlatelolco*.

The resistant, subversive, or collaborative nature of texts produced outside the supervision of missionaries or lay authorities cannot be simply an issue of European alphabet versus Indian painting. Paraphrasing Jack Goody's *The Domestication of the Savage Mind* (1977), a study on the consequences of literacy, we can make a distinction between "savage literacies" (alphabetic texts produced using Latin script with no supervision of the missionaries) and "domesticated glyphs" (pictorial texts produced to document collaboration in the imposition and perpetuation of a colonial order). Goody's parody intends to undermine the absolute separation between literacy, orality, and painting. As instances of indigenous textualities, these savage literacies and domesticated glyphs undo any appeal to a writing-versus-orality binary whether it is produced to undermine indigenous cultures or to recuperate a suppressed oral text. Contrary to the commonplace that presumes that the opposition between orality and writing is transhistorical, I would not only argue that it assumes different values in different historical moments and cultures but also insist that this binary was hardly central to sixteenth-century Spaniards.[10] There are, of course, instances of Spaniards claiming superiority on the basis of possessing a phonetic alphabet, such as in Joseph de Acosta's *Historia natural y moral de las Indias*, Juan Ginés de Sepúlveda's *Democrates alter*, and in Juan de Torquemada's *Monarquía Indiana*, the texts that are most commonly cited to buttress arguments that generalize the opposition of oral and writing cultures. Paradoxically, critics and historians bent on recuperating the orality of indigenous peoples in the Americas— the assumption being that these are oral cultures!—contribute to the same prejudice against nonalphabetical writing forms.[11] The proliferation of texts using iconic script from the colonial period to the present suggests not only that Spanish colonial authorities viewed pictorial texts as holding documentary evidence but also that Indians valued and retained their forms of writing often in juxtaposition to alphabetized records of verbal performances.

The concept of indigenous textualities enables us to conceptualize a fluidity between a broad array of writing forms—textile, glyph, landscape,

| Codex of Tlatelolco. Courtesy of the Biblioteca Nacional de Antropología e Historia, Mexico City.

inscription on gourds and other durable materials, tattoos, and alphabetical writing—and speech forms that might underlay the production of written texts or might elaborate further the recorded stories. This fluidity entails an understanding of reading as performance, rather than as the silent, private activity we tend to associate with the bourgeois reader in the solitude of the sunrooms of the nineteenth century. Recent studies in the ethnography of reading enable us to modify the terms of the debate.[12] Not only Goody but also other scholars who follow him, like the early Serge Gruzinski and Walter Mignolo, ignore the fact that people read in historically and culturally defined ways. In sixteenth- and seventeenth-century Mesoamerica texts were primarily read and performed in public rather than read in private. This is still a practice in Native American communities where *lienzos*, *títulos*, and

cartographic histories provide scripts for ritual. Indeed, there is plenty of internal evidence that texts were written collectively and hence reveal a multiple sense of authorship. The use of the alphabet did not exclude the practice of performing and producing texts in collective settings.

Whereas the *Historia de Tlatelolco*, which is part of the *Anales de Tlatelolco* (Berlin 1948), actualizes savage literacy in that it records a Nahuatl oral performance of a pictorial history that condemns the conquest in absolute terms, the *Codex of Tlatelolco* (Berlin 1948) exemplifies domesticated glyph in that it represents Tlatelolca leaders negotiating a privileged position from within the colonial order (figure 1). To all appearances, the pictorial *Codex of Tlatelolco* was produced with a Spanish audience in mind, while the *Historia de Tlatelolco* was produced for a performance within the community of

Tlatelolco. The apparent subordination to the Spanish authorities in *Codex of Tlatelolco* demands the recognition (as in knowing again) of an iconic artic-ulation of the role Tlatelolco played in the Mixton War. As for the *Historia de Tlatelolco*, take as exemplary of the denunciation of the conquest the follow-ing descriptions of the massacre of the Templo Mayor and the devastation of Tlatelolco: "While dancing they went bare [of weapons], with only their net cloaks, their turquoise [ornaments], their lip plugs, their necklaces, their forked heron-feather ornaments, their deer's hooves. The old men who had their tobacco pots and their rattles. It was them they first attacked; they struck off their hands and lips. Then all who were dancing, and all who were looking on, died there" (Lockhart 1993, 259). A view of Tlatelolco in ruins offers a most terrifying description of war: "And on the roads lay the shat-tered bones and scattered bones and scattered hair, the houses were un-roofed, red [with blood]; worms crawled in and out of the noses of cadavers; and the walls of the houses were slippery with brains" (ibid., 313). Note that this graphic—indeed, photographic—image could only be conveyed verbally and by the mimetic faculty of alphabetic writing that, allow me to insist again, does not stand in place of the pictorial version, but rather reproduces speech, a verbal performance of a pictorial history that in using pre-colonial conventions excluded the depiction of such gruesome particulars. Writing like photography inscribes the dead for their invocation as ghosts, as reve-nants that reading and performance bring about.[13] This is savage literacy in its most resistant countercolonial mode. It is also clearly an instance of resistance preceding power in that the Spanish religious and lay authorities could never anticipate Indian understandings of writing and reading for invoking the dead; moreover, their attempt to suppress the calling forth of ghosts would entail the destruction of writing itself.[14]

The condemnation of the conquest in the *Historia de Tlatelolco* leaves no room for a narrative of collaboration or an apology for the colonial order. The internal date of the *Historia de Tlatelolco* is 1528: "This book, as it is written, was done here in Tlatelolco in the ancient times, in the year of 1528" (Berlin 1948, 31). Lockhart holds that this text could not have been written before the 1550s. This latter date would suggest disparate views between those who wrote and painted history in Tlatelolco when we compare the unequivocal denunciation of conquest in the alphabetical *Historia de Tlatelolco* to the narrative of collaboration and accommodation within the colonial order in the pictorial *Codex of Tlatelolco*, which bears as its last date 1565. The melancholic remembrance of the destruction of Tlatelolco and Tenochtitlan, still alive during the years of the Mixton War, would seem to have not affected the decision of the Nahuas from central Mexico to participate in the war against the Cazcanes, another Nahuatl speaking group in the so-called Chichimeca, in what is today the State of Zacatecas. Even if this disparity were to suggest that the internal date of 1528 is correct, we would still have to account for the place the performances of the *Historia de Tlatelolco* and *Codex of Tlatelolco* occupied in the imagined community of Tlatelolco. Can we assume that whereas *Historia de Tlatelolco* was a text to be performed within the community, *Codex of Tlatelolco* was to be performed for the colonial authorities? Then why use alphabetical writing in a text for internal performance and a pictorial writing in a text for external performance? Perhaps the pictorial texts carried a rhetorical force that authenticated their representation of the community in front of Spanish authorities, and perhaps the practice of alphabetical writing to record a verbal performance entailed a magical understanding of writing as the space that certified the death of words as it embalmed them but also their continuance as ghosts as they emerged in reading. One may also speculate on the possibility that the verbal performance of *Codex of Tlatelolco* might have been recorded with the alphabet. Even if it seeks accommodation within the colonial order, the *Codex of Tlatelolco* exceeds a mere subordination. In its surrender lies a countercolonial gesture that enables Tlatelolco to retain its own memory.

Note in this section of the *Codex of Tlatelolco* (see figure 1) the miniature rendition of the Spanish soldiers underneath the gigantic representations of a Tlatelolca cacique and two warriors (one Tenochca and one Tlatelolca) who went to Nochistlan (glyph: flowery cactus) in the 1542 Mixton War to suppress the rebellion of the Cazcanes.[15] The severed head under the glyph indicates that this was a war of conquest. We are missing the first part of the *tira*, in which most likely there was a Texcocan or a Tlacopan warrior behind the last Spanish horseman on the far left. The Tenochca and the Tlatelolca wear a mixture of Spanish and Indian dress. The Tlatelolca's dress is the more elaborate: note the sword, the socks, the short pants, and the *jubón* (doublet) made out of jaguar skin. In front of these figures, we see the cacique of Tlatelolco, don Diego de Mendoza Huitznahuatlailotlac, sitting on a Spanish chair, the new symbol of authority that has replaced the indigenous mat. Below him, we find the glyph of Tlatelolco, and he appears recounting to the eight Spaniards the exploit of the Tlatelolcas during the Mixton War in the year 10 tochtli (Rabbit) 1554. The box adorned with quetzal feathers contains a chalice and host, symbols of the Eucharist. The hanged man stands for the two Tlatelolcas who refused to pay tribute when the system of alcaldes, or Spanish mayors, was instituted in 1549. We read in

Codex Aubin that "it was in the year of 1549 when it was imposed and ordered to elect *alcaldes* and it was then that tribute was first charged, and because two caciques resisted that Natives paid tribute, they were hanged" (cited by R. H. Barlow in Berlin 1948, 114). The minor place the hanged man occupies in the pictorial narrative suggests that a reading would mention the event but only to further buttress the loyalty and subordination of the current Tlatelolca leadership to the Spanish. This detached citation of a hanging in the *Codex of Tlatelolco* contrasts with melancholic reminiscences of atrocities committed against Tlatelolcas and other Nahua peoples from the Valley of Mexico in the *Historia de Tlatelolco*: "There they hanged the ruler of Huitzilopochco, Macuilxochitzin, as well as the ruler of Culhuacan, Pitzotzin. They also hanged the Tlacateccatl of Quauhtitlan, and they had the Tlillancalqui eaten by dogs. And they had some Tezcoca, one of whom was Ecamaxtlatzin, eaten by dogs. They just came to stay. No one accompanied them, they just brought their painted books [*ymamatlacuilollo*]" (Lockhart 1993, 273). Observe that the statement "they just brought their painted books" lacks any doubt as to the status of writing; we ignore the reasons why they brought the books and why the writers felt the need to mention them, but we do know that this is one of many mentions of painted books in the *Historia de Tlatelolco*, which suggests their centrality in native life. It is also worth mentioning that the *Historia de Tlatelolco* closes with a statement on events that followed the fall of Tenochtitlan: "Then the Captain proclaimed war against Oaxaca. They went to Acolhuacan. Then to Mextitlan. Then to Michuacan. Then to Ueymollan y Quauhtemallan and Tehuantepec" (Lockhart 1993, 273; Mengin 1945, 162; cf. Berlin 1948, 76). Does this passage express solidarity with the peoples of Oaxaca, Guatemala, and Michuacan? It certainly places them as foes of a common enemy. The *Historia de Tlatelolco* closes with the enigmatic, reflexive statement "With this this book ends in which it was told how it was made" [Ca zan oncan tlami ynic omopouh ynin amatla yn iuhqui omochiuh] (Mengin 1945, 162; cf. Berlin 1948, 76). Spaniards could not but appreciate the importance of writing and its documentary value in native culture. For the Spaniards, both the form and content held authority. The *Codex of Tlatelolco* continues this pictorial tradition and testifies to its adaptability within the colonial power struggles.

Although these texts were not produced to respond to the request to "tell me the story of how I conquered you," they certainly are instances of "thinking Europe in Indian categories." There is no suggestion of an attempt to reproduce a European historical model to gain recognition. In the *Codex of Tlatelolco* recognition is sought for the deeds not for the mastery of European historiography and painting. These are Tlatelolca deeds told in a Tlatelolca style.

Let us now turn to texts that respond to the request to "tell me the story of how I conquered you" with a page from *Codex Telleriano-Remensis* (Quiñoñes-Keber 1995) (figure 2). The *tlacuilo* (scribe) manages to depict a plurality of worlds on this page. On the left side of the page, we find a Dominican identified by a clean white habit, shoes, and ceremonial dress, imparting baptism to an Indian, who appears to be jumping into the baptismal fount. On the other side of the page, we see a Franciscan—identified by a worn-out brown habit, the knotted cincture, and bare feet—holding what seems to be a bilingual confessional; the *tlacuilo* links the Franciscan to a European representation of the sun and to maize plants that symbolize the planting of the doctrine. The *tlacuilo* codifies Dominican and Franciscan missionaries in terms of their differences on key evangelical practices and preferences for the sacraments of baptism and penitence. These differences ultimately manifest different ways of worldmaking, to borrow Nelson Goodman's phrase.[16] In a nutshell, the Dominican emphasis on baptism conveys an understanding of the development of a habitus that prepares the neophyte for baptism and the ability to recognize grace and avoid sin; on the other hand, the Franciscans' holding a confessional evokes the practice of multitudinal baptisms and the expectation that once baptized the neophytes would be indoctrinated thoroughly and subjected to a confessional discipline in which the acceptance of the dogma would measure the disposition of the will. These preferences go back to the philosophical traditions of the individual orders: St. Thomas Aquinas for the Dominicans; Bonaventure, Duns Scotus, and Ockham for the Franciscans.[17]

We can further document and verify the depth of this characterization of the two orders in other Indian and Spanish sources. Take, for instance, the following passage from Chimalpahin, the historian from Chalco, wherein he cites the testimony of don Feliciano de la Asunción Calmazacatzin, the *principal* from Tzacualtitlan Tenanco, who died in 1611: "My uncle don Juan de Sandoval Tecuanxayaca was a new Christian, and that is why he did not know what he was saying when he spoke of the Franciscans, he talked nonsense when he spoke thus: 'What kind of religious people are those of my brother don Tomás Quetzalmazatl, with their dirty rags and cracked feet? See, in contrast, my Dominicans, how distinguished they are, with their clean and not torn habits, and with their feet wearing shoes'" (Chimalpahin 1998, 195). Elsewhere in the *Séptima relación* (as it is known), Chimalpahin mentions that the people of Amaquemecan paid no attention to the Franciscans,

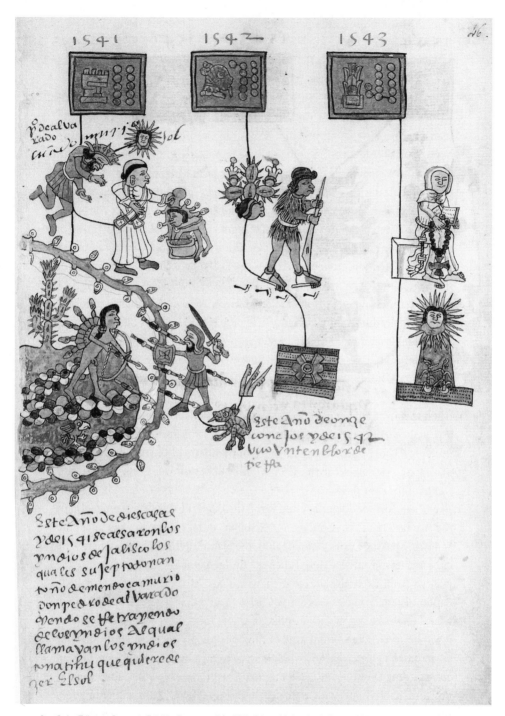

2   *Codex Telleriano-Remensis.* Fol. 46r. Courtesy of the Bibliothèque Nationale de France, Paris.

who eventually left Amaquemecan and were substituted by the Dominican order. Chimalpahin seems to take a certain delight in telling anecdotes, especially the one about don Tomás Quetzalmazatl's description of the shredded habits of the Franciscan and the cleanliness of the Dominicans.

If we were to take as an indication of Chimalpahin's spirituality an *exercicio quotidiano* which was found among his papers, we can adduce his spiritual affinity with the Dominicans. At the end of the exercicio, we find a note by Sahagún stating: "I found this exercise among the Indians. I do not know who produced it, nor who gave it to them" (Chimalpahin 1997 [ca. 1620], 183). Sahagún goes on to say that it was redone rather than just emended. This suggests that it was not a Franciscan who wrote it, but also that there were religious texts circulating in a savage form. I would argue that one can unequivocally trace in the exercicio a Dominican insistence on developing habits for the reception of grace, rather than a mere insistence on accepting the articles of the faith, as was the case in Franciscan confessionals and doctrines. The subject of the exercicio has been baptized and is reminded that he or she has made certain vows, which would hardly be the case for a subject who had been part of a multitudinal baptism. As a baptized subject, he or she is responsible for the doctrine, but the text goes beyond mere repetition by rote, which is the tendency among Franciscan documents, and presupposes a subject who will meditate on the meaning of Christianity and keep vigilance over his or her spiritual health: "These meditations, the acts of spiritually doing things with prudence, which are called an Exercise, which I set before you, and show you, are to be thought about each and every week, and each thought is to be thought about each and every day. . . . For if you accustom yourself to them your soul will consider them a great satisfaction, great good fortune. A Great light, a torch, a great brilliance will proceed with it; it will guide you; it will go before you; it will show you the way that goes direct to Heaven" (Chimalpahin 1997 [ca. 1620], 133). This spirituality is very far from the objective expressed in *Doctrina cristiana: Mas cierta y verdadera para gente sin erudicion y letras: En que se contiene el catecismo o informacion pa indios con todo lo principal y necessario que el cristiano beue saber y obrar. Impressa en Mexico por mandado del reverendissimo señor don fray Juan de Zumárraga: Primer Obispo de Mexico*, which Fray Juan de Zumárraga published in 1546. As the lengthy title indicates, *Doctrina cristiana* has less to do with the specifics of the doctrine than with a theoretical justification of its minimalist tenets. This treatise is mainly concerned with less-educated Indians and Blacks—"los indios menos entendidos y mas rudos y negros" (Zumárraga 1546, 100)—but the reasoning that compares Indians and Blacks to children entails a

counter-argument to the Dominicans' insistence on a thorough catechization before baptisms. Whereas spirituality in the *exercicio* would entail in-
culcating a *habitus*, for the *Doctrina cristiana* cathechization would involve
learning the doctrina by heart and stuttering the articles of faith: "y los
indios . . . comienzen a tartamudear en ella" (Zumárraga 1546, 2v). The
tlacuilo of *Codex Telleriano-Remensis* appears to capture these differences in his
representation of the two orders: on the one hand, the Dominican would
favor thorough catechization before baptism, hence the expectation of a
subject able to understand and practice the introspective self-discipline of
the exercicio; on the other hand, the Franciscan's inquisitive look suspects a
lying subject behind every neophyte. These two positions express irreconcilable understandings of the subject and conversion.

We find the tlacuilo representing two other ways of worldmaking in the
confrontation between Viceroy Antonio de Mendoza and Francisco Tenamaztle, the Cazcan leader of the indigenous uprising that led to the Mixton
War. The tlacuilo juxtaposes the nativistic revival that motivated the rebellion to the *requerimiento* that demanded the subjection to Spanish rule. *Codex
Telleriano-Remensis* records events from the colonial period in a native style
that invents a vocabulary for depicting European objects and subjects; it also
includes pre-Hispanic materials such as the calendar, the monthly feasts,
and the history of Mexico-Tenochtitlan up to the conquest. In seeking information, in asking the tlacuilo to represent the colonial order, the ethnographic gaze found itself inscribed with the eerie spectral sensation that the
tlacuilo resided behind the look of the Franciscan staring at us. The practice
of the confessional and the inquisition are superbly symbolized in this Franciscan facing us, one of the two instances in which the tlacuilo used perspective to depict a frontal image. (The other corresponds to Fray Juan de
Zumárraga, the first bishop of Mexico, who held inquisitorial powers.) This
brilliant instance of the observer observed must have annoyed the missionaries, in particular the Dominican Fray Pedro de los Ríos, who took over the
production of the codex a few pages later (figure 3). His replacement of
indigenous codes, color, and style with shoddy writing was soon abandoned
as he must have realized the futility of continuing a project that, in the first
place, had the finality of recording native ways of writing—not scribbling
mere facts.

Codex Telleriano-Remensis, however, lacks the alphabetical version of an oral
text telling the stories of the depicted colonial events. The oral texts that tell
the story of Tenamaztle's nativistic rebellion, even if told from the tlacuilo's
central-Mexican perspective, can only be extracted from Spanish sources or

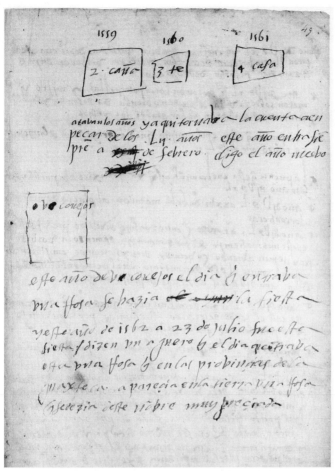

3   *Codex Telleriano-Remensis.* Fol. 49r. Courtesy of the Bibliothèque Nationale de France, Paris.

the Nahuatl accounts of central Mexicans who participated in the conquest. The glosses added to the pictorial text identify the represented objects or events and correct the information written by others, but they do not elaborate a narrative, nor can we find an indigenous account. Nevertheless, we know that missionaries and indigenous historians wrote alphabetical histories in which we can trace not only the kinds of oral stories elders told based on codices like *Codex Telleriano-Remensis* but also the pictorial style of thinking historically.

The *Florentine Codex*, or *Historia general de las cosas de la Nueva España*, takes a radically different approach in that it reproduces the oral accounts given by elders subjected to ethnographic inquiries. Paradoxically, the response to the

teca, cempoalteca, injc qujmo
ichteca tlatlanjque: conjtoque
ca amoie iehoatl totecuioane.
Inm kioac popocatzin, qujnj
xiptlatica in. Motecuçomatzin:
qujlhujque. Cujx ieie inti Mo
tecuçoma? Conjtv. Ca nehoatl
in namo techiuh cauh in nj Mo
tecuçoma. Auh njmã qujlhuj
que. Nopa xiauh, tleica in ti
techiztlacavia, acti techmati
amo vel ti techiztlacavis, amo
vel tica timocaiaoaz, amo vel
titech quamanaz, amo vel ti
techix mamatiloz, amo vel ti
techich chioaz, amo vel ti techix
cuepaz, amo vel ti techix pa
tiliz, amo vel ti techtlacuepi
liz, amo vel ti techixpopoloz,
amo vel titechix mjmjctiz, a
mo vel titechix çoqujviz, amo
vel ti techix çoqujmatocaz, a
motehoatl cavnca in Mote
cuçoma, amo vel tachnetla
tiliz, amo vel mjnaiaz, cam
paiaz, cujx totvtl, cujx pa
tlanjz, cujnoço tlallan quj
quetzaz yiovi, cujx canaca
tepetl coionquj yitic calaqujz

125

Ni Motecuçoma se nos podra ascondor
por mucho que haga, aunque sea ave
y aunque se meta debaxo de tierra
no se nos podra ascondor de verle
a vemos y de oyr avemos lo que
nos dira. Y luego con afrenta em
biaron aquel principal y a todos

4   *Florentine Codex.* Biblioteca Medicea Laurenziana, ms. Laur.Med.palat. 220, c. 425r. Courtesy of the
Biblioteca Medicea Laurenziana, Florence, and of the Italian Ministry of Cultural Affairs. See also
Bernardino de Sahagún, *Florentine Codex: General History of the Things of New Spain,* trans. and ed.
Arthur J. O. Anderson and Charles Dibble (1950–82).

demand to tell the story of conquest in Book 12 must communicate the destruction of a world and its corresponding anguish using the same terms of the banishing worldview. Thus, the telling of destruction preserves the object that is supposed to have been destroyed. Sahagún wrote a revision in 1585. He explains his motivation in a parenthetical remark: "(En el Libro nono, donde se trata esta conquista, se hicieron ciertos defectos: y, fué, que algunas cosas se pusieron en la Narracion de esta Conquista, que fueron mal puestas: y otras se callaron, que fueron mal calladas. Por esta causa, este año de mil quinientos ochenta y cinco, enmende este libro)" [(In this book nine, in which the conquest is treated, some mistakes were made: and it was that some things were put in the narration of the Conquest that were badly put: and other that were silenced, that were badly silenced. For this reason, in this year of fifteen eighty five, I corrected this book)] (Sahagún 1989 [1585], 147) (figure 4). The earlier text consisted of a Nahuatl version derived from Nahua elders who witnessed the conquest, a Spanish version whose language and syntax bore no resemblance to the original Nahuatl and often paraphrased or elided whole passages, and a visual version that should be read as a text of its own and not merely as an illustration. If the visual component in the other books in Sahagún's *Historia general* functions as illustration, this is mainly due to the lack of antecedents in pre-Columbian texts for painting daily life or natural history. And even in the illustrations of daily life or nature, we would have to evaluate each individual case. Images in these other books also function as albums of illustrations to which the alphabetical text provides a commentary. Sahagún's earlier text, the *Primeros memoriales* (ca. 1558–60), best exemplifies this approach.

The visual text of Book 12, however, can be read on its own terms. Indeed, one can read the Nahuatl narrative as an oral rendition of the pictorial version. Because Sahagún apparently did not include a pictorial version in 1585, scholars have limited their speculations to Sahagún's need to revise the Nahuatl verbal text and the paraphrased translation to Spanish. I say "speculated" because the Nahuatl version is lost. It seems that Sahagún was concerned with both the contents of the narrative and with the style, the "cosas mal puestas" [badly put] pertaining to the Nahuatl diction. The 1585 version included three columns: "La primera es, en lenguaje indiano, así tosco como ellos lo pronunciaron, y se escribió en los otros libros: la segunda columna, es enmienda de la primera, así en vocablos como en sentencias: La tercera columna esta en romance sacado según las enmiendas de la segunda columna" [The first is in Indian language, thus coarse as they pronounce it, and was written in the other books: the second is an emendation of the first, in the words and sentences: the third column is in romance drawn according to the emendations of the second column] (Howard Cline, in Sahagún 1989 [1585], 147–48). The "mal puestas" refers to a specifically Nahuatl conceptualization of the events that Sahagún might have considered subversive, but underscores that he is including the original Nahuatl version so that it be known that the faults emended in the second column were not done on purpose ("para que todos entienden que no se erró adrede" [ibid., 148]). To my mind, it remains a mystery how the inclusion of the original Nahuatl would lay to rest the suspicion that the faults were not committed "adrede," on purpose. Sahagún clearly does not censor the original Nahuatl, but leaves it there for comparison with the emended version. These revisions suggest at least two different readers: on the one hand, bilingual Nahuatl-Spanish readers, most likely but not exclusively missionaries, would benefit from the emendations in their use of the Nahuatl language of war in their sermons; on the other, Spanish readers would get a less offensive version. The absence of a visual text could be read as a suppression of the story told by the elders; a story that depicts the atrocities committed provides visual information regarding warrior's insignia and other symbols infused with magical powers, and juxtaposes, hence confronts, European and native systems of representation. But since Sahagún says nothing about the visual text in the preface to the 1585 revisions, this amounts to pure speculation.

Whatever the changes of the Nahuatl version might have been, the "enmiendas" we read in the 1585 Spanish version are for the most part additions, corrections, and suppressions that could not have been part of a revised Nahuatl account, whose main purpose was linguistic. Clearly, extrapolations by Sahagún could not have been part of a new Nahuatl text. Other changes in the Spanish column merely further the softening of language already in place in the Spanish translations in the *Florentine Codex*. Take, for instance, the encounter of the Spaniards near Popocatepetl. The Nahuatl text reads, "When they had given [the Spaniards] [golden banners, precious feather streamers, and golden necklaces], they appeared to smile; they were greatly contented, gladdened. As if they were monkeys they seized upon the gold. It was as if their hearts were satisfied, brightened, calmed, they stuffed themselves with it; they starved for it; they lusted for it like pigs" (Sahagún 1950–82 [ca. 1579], pt. 13, 31). The Spanish version of the Florentine translates: "Alli los recibieron y presentaron el presente de oro que llevaban, y según que a los indios les parecio por la señales exteriores que vieron en los españoles, holgaronse y regocijaronse con el oro, mostrando que lo tenian en mucho" [There they received them and gave them the present of gold that they brought, and according to the external signs that the Indians saw in the Spaniards, it seemed to them that they were pleased and greatly rejoiced over the gold, for they held it in great esteem] (Sahagún 1946 [1829–30], 3, 36; Lockhart 1993, 99). The 1585 Spanish emendation reduces the passage to "presentaron su presente al capitan ordenandolo a sus pies: lo cual y todos recibieron con gran gozo" [they gave the Captain their gifts, placing them on the ground: all received them with great joy] (Sahagún 1989 [1585], 176). These Spanish stories of the encounter in Popocatepetl censors the Nahuatl in different degrees, but we need to ask ourselves what Sahagún meant when he characterized the language of the first column as a "lenguaje Indiano, asi tosco como ellos lo pronuncian" [Indian language, coarse as they speak it], and adds that the second column "es enmienda de la primera, asi en vocablos, como en sentencias" [is an emendation of the first, both in the words and in the opinions] (ibid., 147). Is the speech *tosco* (coarse) because it lacks the civilizing effect of the style and rhetoric of proper historiography as exemplified in the Spanish version, or is it coarse because it denounces the Spaniards in unequivocal terms? I would go for the second instance, given Sahagún's praise of the rhetorical complexity and beauty of Nahuatl in the *Historia general* and other writings. It seems that Sahagún is treating the deficiencies of the Nahuatl version and the Spanish translation as independent cases. We may thus speak of the Nahuatl version in the *Florentine Codex* (unfortunately we do not have the 1585 version) as an instance of savage literacy. As Sahagún points out, the errors were not "adrede." Even if the Nahuatl version was produced at the request and under the supervision of Sahagún and his *colegiales*, who arguably produced just an alphabetical transcription of the oral text, we cannot trace their influence, much less the imposition of a grammatical ideal of logical and narrative refinement ("tosco como ellos lo pronuncian"). The Nahuatl version (and there are plenty of others we can draw from in the *Florentine Codex* and other Nahuatl texts) suggests that the alphabet could remain neutral, that is, function merely as a mimetic technology that records speech. The presence of savage literacy in a text that was solicited and supervised by Sahagún corroborates the fact that the Spaniards never held a monopoly over the uses of alphabetical writing, and that reading and writing was a two-way street in New Spain.

Two corollaries: first, the concept of "tyranny of the alphabet" would miss its target by assigning power to the technology rather than to a certain definition of grammaticality. As a mimetic devise, the alphabet has the purpose of recording speech, not taking the place of, painting; the writing, and not only the reading, of alphabetical texts entails a performative act that cannot be appropriated by the historiography of missionaries and lay Spanish or even mestizo historians. Grammars such as Horacio Carochi's, one of the finest examples of seventeenth-century linguistic studies, speak of Nahuatl as lacking syntax. Syntax is thus presumed to pertain to Latin and, by derivation, to Spanish, but in *Grammar of the Mexican Language* (1645) Carochi suggests that Nahuatl morphology fulfills an analogous function: "En el quarto, en lugar de sintaxi (que esta lengua no la tiene) se pone el modo con que vnos vocablos se componen con otros" [In the fourth, in place of syntax, which this language lacks, I give the manner in which some words are compounded with others] (Carochi 2001 [1645], 15). Shouldn't we be scandalized and underscore that this denial of syntax betrays an ethnocentric prejudice that assumes that all languages should have a syntax? No. The last thing Carochi or Sahagún had in mind was to produce an *arte de la lengua* that would impose syntax or any other linguistic form purportedly lacking in Nahuatl. Perhaps in time, under the influence of Spanish, Nahuatl would develop similar patterns, but that is mere speculation with little use for someone learning to speak and to write Nahuatl in the sixteenth and seventeenth centuries. And there is no indication that Carochi would have entertained such an objective. If anything, Sahagún and Carochi deplore the hispanization of Nahuatl. The end is to understand Nahuatl in order to speak it and write it correctly—that is, make sense in it. A form of classical Nahuatl was certainly embalmed in the grammars. But there is no reason to assume that a Nahuatl grammar would be more or less effective in controlling change and innovation in speech and writing than a Spanish counterpart. Grammars, ultimately, are instruments of power insofar as they seek to control and regulate the language of the elite, of those charged with governing. The governability reinforced by Spanish and Nahuatl grammars perpetuates the structures of power through the education of criollos and the native elite, much in the same way that Antonio de Nebrija spoke of grammar and empire as going hand-in-hand not because of the need to regulate the language of the *populus* or because he sought to impose Spanish over all the territories (the multiple languages spoken in the peninsula and the endurance of indigenous languages in the Americas would indicate a monumental failure), but because Spanish would become the language of empire, of the bureaucratic machinery. And this would be true even within the Morisco community, where on the eve of the second Alpujarras rebellion in 1568 very few spoke, as J. H. Elliot has pointed out, "any language but Arabic" (1963, 233).

Second, sixteenth-century Spaniards were not particularly given to privilege data derived from alphabetical writing over data taken from iconic script, as witnessed by the pictorial documents that circulated in the courts. Authorities were prone to trust the expertise of a tlacuilo, a letrado in his own tradition, over an alphabetical text produced by a suspect Spanish or Indian source. Often iconic script carried more force than an alphabetically recorded oral testimony. Writing conveys the weight of tradition, which in both Spanish and Nahuatl contexts was defined by the status and trustworthiness of the source. We must not assume a priori that pictorial texts would be more resistant to colonial power than an alphabetical rendition of a verbal performance. Numerous pictorial texts seek the recognition of compliance to the evangelization and of participation in the military conquest. But the same heterogeneity that should keep us from inventing a homogeneous Indian culture furthered the exercise of power by fostering conflict among the different ethnic groups. As such, pictorial texts reinforced the identity of the ethnic groups that claimed a right to privileges. Thus, we find in the *Codex of Tlatelolco* a record of the Mixton War (1541) in which the Tlatelolca leaders figure prominently in comparison with the miniaturized Spanish soldiers riding their horses. Certainly, this text preserves a pictorial tradition and worldview in its representation of the colonial order. On the one hand, a verbal performance telling the accomplishments of the Tlatelolcas would articulate a magic-religious understanding of time and space; on the other, the performance of the codex in front of the Spanish authorities would then require switching codes and articulating a discourse clad in Spanish legal terms. Spanish authorities invited versatility in languages and worldviews by recognizing pictorial texts throughout the colonial period.

Telling the story of how one was conquered is not unlike telling the story of one's personal conversion to Christianity, given that it involves telling the story of resistances to the missionaries' revelations of the idolatrous nature of their beliefs. If the Nahuas continued to paint histories *that sought the recognition of their rights and desires as ethnic groups or individual litigants* (pictorial texts whose categories and narrative styles retain their authority in Spanish courts as well as for Spanish historians), then the solicited story of how one was conquered would *seek to implant in the Nahua the recognition of a lost world by prompting an account of how the gods, the magic of warriors and sorcerers, and the system of mores had failed them.* The story of how one was conquered is one in which the gods anticipate the end of their life-forms, the Spaniards ridicule the magic of the sorcerers and the magical force of the warrior's ensigns, and accoutrement proves ineffectual. And yet the melancholic rendition refuses to recognize the Spanish conquest as liberation from magic, superstition, and Satan. It is much like a confession where one fails to recognize conversion as a turning point in one's life, instead indulging in a sweet melancholy that postpones indefinitely the realization of living in a state of sin, of that loss symbolized by original sin. It is also a story of resistance inasmuch as the Tlatelolcas denigrate and mock the Spaniard's desire for gold, denounce the terror of the massacres, and in telling the story in their own categories retain an indigenous memory of the end of their world, which in fact testifies to its survival. Telling the story of how magic and the warrior's insignia failed to impart fear among the Spaniards retains a memory of magic and, paradoxically, enables Indian warriors to continue to wear their accoutrement. Magic may thus continue to exist within the new order. As we saw in the *Codex of Tlatelolco*, the Tlatelolcas wore their traditional dress, even if hybrid, when they fought at the Mixton, and the representation of the *tlatohuani* (in Nahuatl, "he who speaks well") who solicited from Spanish officials recognition of the Tlatelolcas' role in the Mixton War follows pre-Columbian conventions. As such, the Spanish order assumes a particular value in the pictorial text. The specific meaning of the Spaniards within this textual mesh would demand knowledge of Nahuatl and, of course, of the stories told regarding the event.

One cannot but wonder what would have happened if the Tlatelolcas had identified themselves with the Cazcan uprising and joined forces to expel the Spaniards from their lands. It is in these instances where the heterogeneity of Indians works in tandem with the perpetuation of the colonial order. One explanation for failing to support and participate in the rebellion could be the lack of a common culture with the peoples from the north, but heterogeneity also worked against peoples who shared language and culture in the immediate vicinity. Witness the splintering of opposing forces and alliances with the Spaniards that enabled the conquest of Tenochtitlan. Joining forces with the Cazcan, the Zacatecos, the Huichol, and other groups in the Chichimeca would not necessarily have implied abandoning one's ethnic identity in the pursuit of some sort of common ideology, but rather joining forces in the constitution of a multitude fighting a common enemy. We may also wonder why the pages pertaining to the early years of the conquest were removed from *Codex Telleriano-Remensis*. And why the Dominican Pedro de los Ríos felt pressed to take over the production of the text rather than incorporate a tlacuilo more of his liking. The depiction of the Dominican friar baptizing an Indian, the Franciscan holding the confessional, Mendoza enforcing the language of history, love, and war of the requerimiento, and the figure of Tenamaztle imbued with magic-religious symbolism capture four independent worlds. The inclusion and relativization of these worlds reminded the friar of the fragility of the colonial order. Perhaps it was not Ríos, but another Dominican who resented the fragmentation of the world. Perhaps Ríos as a Dominican was in full agreement with Las Casas's condemnation of the conquest and justification of the rebellion in terms of the right the Indians had to erase the Spaniards from the face of the earth. Perhaps Ríos truly believed that he was continuing the project with his scribbling of dates. The question would then be, why destroy the physical integrity of the codex with scratches, blobs, crude writings, if Ríos supported the Indian world in the Lascasian mode of an unconditional acceptance that would have justified sacrifice and anthropophagy as instances of the religiosity of the Nahuas? There is also the possibility that there was a rush to finish the codex, something we find in the case of the hurried translation of Book 12 and the incomplete paintings of *Florentine Codex*, and in the famous note at the end of *Codex Mendoza* wherein the commentator complains of the short notice to write the glosses: "Diez dias antes de la partida de la flota se dio al ynterpretador esta ystoria el cual descuido fue de los yndios que se acordaron tarde y como cosa de corrida no se tuvo punto en el estilo que convenia interpretarse" [The Interpreter was given this history ten days prior to the departure of the fleet, and he interpreted carelessly because the Indians came to an agreement late; and so was done in haste and he did not improve the style suitable for an interpretation, nor did he take time to polish the words and grammar or make a clean copy"] (Berdan and Anawalt 1992, 4, 148). This observation conveys the perplexity of a specialist in native things ("como es el ynterpretador dellas buena lengua mexicana") who fails to furnish an adequate alphabetical interpretation of a native pictorial history. It is as if the letter could not match the complexity of iconic script, even when the intepreter blames his poor interpretation on the Indians who came to agree too late. This comment also provides further evidence of the collective authorship in native historical writing. No internal evidence in *Codex Telleriano-Remensis* points to a time pressure, and we can only speculate on the reason for the shoddy writing and the interruption of its production.

We also lack any clues regarding the removal of pages corresponding to the early years of the conquest. There is a similar text in the Vatican, *Codex Vaticanus A*, also known as *Codex Ríos*, which includes some of the pages pertaining to the early years of the conquest. *Codex Ríos* was produced in Rome by an Italian hand who used a native text as a prototype. There has been speculation about a third text that might have served as a model for

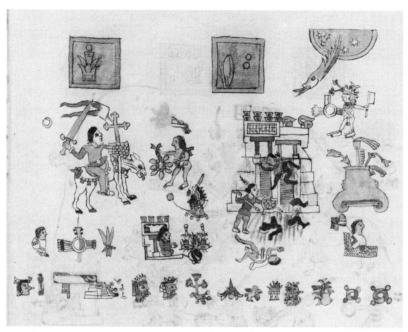

5   *Codex Vaticanus A.* Fol. 89r. Courtesy of the Biblioteca Apostolica Vaticana, the Vatican.

both *Codex Telleriano-Remensis* and *Codex Ríos.* Others speculate that it was *Codex Telleriano-Remensis* itself that served as a model for *Codex Ríos* and that the painter chose not to include the dates scribbled by Ríos at the end of *Codex Telleriano-Remensis.* But then what was the source for the early years in *Codex Ríos?* These early years are bloody and apparently were not offensive to those in Rome (figure 5). *Codex Ríos* and *Codex Telleriano-Remensis* must have functioned as a defense of Native American cultures at the Vatican by Dominicans seeking an indictment of the conquest. One thing that differentiates *Codex Telleriano-Remensis* from the *Florentine Codex* is that the latter provides both a pictorial and a verbal rendition. Does this have to do with the importance Sahagún gave to language as a key to the mentality of the Nahuas? Why would the Dominicans, if this is an apologetic text, cut the tongue of the tlacuilo, reducing all speech in the codex to the glosses written by Indian and Mestizo scribes, which for the most part merely name and describe the painted objects, and the lengthier, interventionist glosses by Ríos and other missionaries? Or is it that we have failed to identify some of the glosses, obviously not the ones that destroy the beauty of the text with scratches and scribbles, as a product of the tlacuilo, as if she could not have learned to use Latin script?

Whatever answers we provide to these questions, they will inevitably further complicate the apparent opposition between "people with writing, history, and so on versus people without these forms." The texts we have examined suggests that the request "tell me the story of how I conquered" and the more generalized instance of texts in which we can observe how Europe was thought and represented in Indian categories entails cross-cultural communication in which alphabetical script coexists with iconic script. We find Indians partaking of the modernity of the colonial order, in fact as active participants in its creation, while also dwelling in an enchanted world. Magic and pre-Columbian life-forms in general were targets for destruction by the missionaries. The story of conquest sought the internalization of how magic failed, but paradoxically the missionaries solicited stories that would only make sense in terms of a world infused by a sense of magic. In soliciting a representation of the colonial order, they encountered a gaze that relativized their world, that showed the multiple ways of world-making that operated in Spanish institutions, texts, and practices. The return of the gaze, the actual looking back of the tlacuilo, made evident the fragility and tenuousness of colonial power. Beyond an understanding of melancholy as crushed rebellion, we find a sweet melancholy that gives place to mania, to the exhilaration, if not happiness, of crossing languages and forms of life.

The continuity and endurance of native cultures up to our present is bound to the refusal to seek the recognition of their capacity to reproduce European forms. In the sixteenth century there was no such expectation from secular and religious authorities, and in the late colonial period it was the criollos and mestizos who manifested such desires. Even today, when indigenous peoples in Mexico demand the recognition of their right to autonomy and to govern themselves according to their juridical institutions, the recognition they seek is not of how they approximate European systems of law.

One of the ironies of pursuing the recognition that one can write history like Europeans and that one's language is capable of doing so is that the attainment of mastery—in the unfolding of the Hegelian master-slave dialectic—constitutes an elite that takes the place of the old master vis-à-vis subalterns that cannot speak, as the subaltern studies narrative wants us to believe.[18] In the case of Mexico, it was an elite comprised of criollos and mestizos which came to assume a position of mastery, and the texts we have examined in this essay should remind us that the gulf separating subalterns and native elites never was nor is as absolute as in the case of India.[19] The lesson we can learn from postcolonial scholars resides precisely in the radical difference and the awareness of a long history of internal colonialism by mestizos and criollos who have sought to speak, if not to stand for Indians. Whereas the solicitation of the story of how one was conquered entailed a belief in cross-cultural intersubjectivity, the cultural artifacts that it provoked manifest the indeterminacy of translation. We should cultivate this indeterminacy since it will keep us from assuming the position of the new masters, of the cry for a "let me do it instead!" Only then will we be able to recognize the force of and position ourselves within countercolonial spaces of resistance.

NOTES

Unless otherwise indicated, all English translations are my own.

1   Sahagún's *Historia general de las cosas de la Nueva España*, which was produced in collaboration with trilingual collegians who spoke Nahuatl, Spanish, and Latin and interviewed elders in different locations in the Valley of Mexico, consists of twelve books in which he collected samples of proper Nahuatl speech about social and natural phenomena: the gods, the feasts, the calendar, fauna, flora, the human body, rhetoric, and so on. Sahagún solicited both literal and figurative meanings. These records of speech where intended to serve as models for sermons and to aid priests in confession. Book 12 is a sampler of the language of war, collected by asking informants to tell the story of the conquest from the perspective of the Tlatelolcas, who next to their cousins, the Tenochcas, resisted the Spaniards to the end. Tlatelolco and Tenochtitlan, the two Mexica cities, shared the central island on Lake Texcoco—today the Avenida Reforma in downtown Mexico City separates the two neighborhoods. I purposely avoid the term *Aztecs* because it erases the specificity of the ethnic groups that inhabited the Valley of Mexico at the time of the Spanish invasion; in fact, its use in sixteenth- and seventeenth-century texts is very sporadic and alternates with the variation *Aztlanecas*, from Aztlan, the mythical region in the north from which both the Mexica-Tlatelolcas and the Mexica-Tenochcas migrated. I prefer to speak of the Nahua and Nahuatl language when generalizing and to provide the specific names of the *altepetl* (atl [water] + *tepetl* [hill]), the term commonly used for the political and territorial units in central Mexico. Tlatelolco was subjected as a tributary of Tenochtitlan in 1475, and, as collected by Sahagún, the Tlatelolcan version of Tenochtitlan-Tlatelolco's fall to the forces of Cortés reflects this bitter past. One cannot underscore enough that this is a particular version that should not be taken as representative of all the altepetl of central Mexico.

2   This epistemological shift, to think Europe in Indian categories, constitutes both a theoretical and hermeneutical point of departure also in Brotherston's essay in this volume.

3   Freud's essay appears in volume 14 of the *Standard Edition*. Freud further refined

his understanding of mourning, melancholia, and mania in *The Ego and the Id* (vol. 19, 3–66) and in *Group Psychology and the Analysis of the Ego* (vol. 18, 65–143). Judith Butler's "Psychic Inceptions: Melancholy, Ambivalence, Rage" in *The Psychic Life of Power* (1997) provides a thorough close-reading of Freud's thoughts on mourning and melancholia; the comments that follow have benefited from Butler's essay. For the commissions for reconciliation in South Africa and Guatemala, consult the websites http://www.doj.gov.za/trc/ and http://shr.aaas.org/guatemala/ceh/report/english/toc.html.

4   To my mind, the best study of queer tropes in native colonial culture is Michael J. Horswell's.

5   Bhabha draws his concept of "minimal rationality" from Charles Taylor and Satya Mohanty. Quine generalizes the provincialism of all cultures, which enables us to conceptualize a form of radical relativism grounded in the necessity to retain a linguistic and cultural "elsewhere" to which all translation must return for the verification of accuracy—a movement between languages that necessarily involves a process of infinite regress. Quine (1960) allows for the possibility of more or less precise translations on the basis of our dictionaries and linguistic knowledge; however, his concept of "radical translation" would ultimately constitute the background of translations of languages and cultures outside the semantic fields of Greco-Abrahamic traditions. Just because we make those languages and cultures sound Greek does not mean that we have captured their own provincial modes of naming and understanding the world. Minimal rationality merely proves that elsewheres are much like us. For a full discussion of radical relativism, see my "Elsewheres: Radical Relativism and the Frontiers of Empire" (Rabasa 2006).

6   A full analysis of the terms I am here subsuming under *melancholy* would demand a paper of its own; here I mention only that Alonso de Molina does not include an entry for *melancolía* in his authoritative dictionary (1971). The early-twentieth-century French scholar of Nahuatl Remi Simeon (1988) provides *el que es melancólico* as an option for translating the verb *tequipachiui*, which is composed of *tequitl* (tribute) and *pachiui* ("destruirse, hundirse en algo, asi como la sepultura").

7   In his *Historia de las Indias de Nueva España e islas de Tierra Firme* Fray Diego de Durán describes Moctezuma sobbing when he addressed the rulers of Texcoco and Tlacopan, the other two altepetl that constituted the triple alliance (misnamed as the Aztec empire), before Cortés's entrance to Tenochtitlan with thousands of Tlaxcalteca allies, but the scene is far from suggesting the pathological melancholy of Book 12 (Durán 1984 [ca. 1581], vol. 2, 535).

8   Said's work, in particular *Orientalism* (1994a), marks a break between the post-Enlightenment imperialism, which he finds to have been imbued by a civilizing mission defined by scientific and technological advances and the earlier forms of colonialism, which he characterizes as having been devoid of a civilizing mission and instead characterized by a raping and subsequent abandonment of the land. The post-Enlightenment civilizing mission also divided the world between peoples with history and peoples without history. See also Said's introduction to *Culture and Imperialism* (1993).

Guha (1997b) traces the development of history written in Bangla in the nineteenth century: Guha's trajectory replicates the Hegelian master-slave dialectic, his study spanning from the English historians writing history in order to retrieve information concerning landed property and land management to the production of pamphlets by revolutionary organizations at the beginning of the twentieth century. In the process, Bengalis under the supervision and direction of English colonial administrators aspired to make Bangla an appropriate vehicle for history, which Guha defines in purely Western terms: "The English who commissioned [the first prose narrative] defined its epistemic character as history and its function as an administrative teaching manual. . . . As such, [Ramram Basu] set out consciously to produce a history rather than yet another puranic tale" (182). History is seen as lacking in India; hence, the project of making Bangla an appropriate vehicle for the new life-forms: "The maturation of historiography coincided with that of the Bangla language as well. A belief had begun to gain ground that if the latter could lend itself to creative use for something so complex and so radical in its break with tradition as a rationalist representation of the Indian past, it could be trusted to do anything" (187). The Bengali elite who—according to Guha's reading of the evolution of Bangla and historiography in terms of the Hegelian dialectic—constitute themselves as the new masters conducted this elaboration of a "modern" Bangla. In this regard the Bengali elite are not unlike the constitution of criollo and mestizo elites in Latin America. Guha (2002) further elaborates the binary between "peoples with and without history."

9   For an elaboration of the inevitability of dwelling and articulating worlds from within the Greco-Abrahamic, see Rabasa 2006.

10   David Rojinski (1998) has written a most elaborate dissertation that dismantles the universality of this binary by reminding us of how writing operates as a fetish that magically erases oral culture, in what cannot be but an equally fetishistic construction of orality.

11   For a brilliant exposition of this prejudice, see Brotherston 1992.

12   See Boyarin 1993, in particular Johannes Fabian's essay (80–98).

13   In his commentary on Walter Benjamin and photography, Eduardo Cadava (1998) draws parallels between the mimetic faculty of writing and of photography, suggesting that the written descriptions of graphic visual details are in fact possible because of the concept of photography that pre-exists the development of the technology. Writing and, even before that, language and the interpretation of the stars anticipate photography: "To say that the history of photography begins in the interpretation of the stars is to say that it begins with death" (Cadava 1998, 30). The connection between writing and death and the return of ghosts through the performance of the recorded voice could not have escaped the Tlatelolcan tlacuilo's adoption of the new mimetic technology; I say "tlacuilo" since the new form of inscription would not have posed a challenge once the principle was understood, and there would have been none more readily inclined to learn the use of letters than those who specialized in iconic script. In passing, given that I am involved in translating the Nahuatl, we should

also meditate on translation as a naming of the death's continuance: "If the task of translation belongs to that of photography, it is because both begin in the death of their subject, both take place in the realm of ghosts and phantoms" (ibid., 18). For a most elaborated thesis on the invocation of ghosts in Native colonial songs, see Bierhorst's introduction to his edition and translation of the *Cantares Mexicanos* (1992). The Dominican Fray Diego de Durán was well aware of native songs that called forth the warriors of old, and in response to these practices he conceived his version of the rise of Tenochtitlan in his *Nueva España* as a resurrection of the ancient grandeur: "Ha sido mi deseo de darle vida y resucitarle de la muerte y olvido en que estaba, a cabo de tanto tiempo" [My desire has been to give it life and resurrect it from the death and oblivion in which it has rested for such a long time] (1984 [ca. 1581], 2, 27–28). However, we should read this passage in terms of a Western historiographical tradition that seeks to produce inscriptural tombs to prevent the return of the dead (see de Certeau 1988, 2).

14 On resistance as preceding power, see Hardt and Negri's comments on Deleuze and Foucault (Hardt and Negri 2000, 25).

15 For a detailed reading of the *Codex of Tlatelolco*, see R. H. Barlow's interpretation in Berlin 1948.

16 With Nelson Goodman (1978), we could argue that Western philosophical styles comprise a plurality of irreconcilable worlds. Each of these worlds would claim universality but their coexistence would entail a de facto relativism. Our Nahua tlacuilo could not have failed to see these radical differences in the missionaries' doctrines. For the Nahuas felt no compelling reason that this coexistence of a plurality of horizons of universality should not be extended to include native life-forms. A record from the Inquisition explains that the cacique of Tezcoco, Don Carlos Ometochtzin, was burned in 1539 precisely for expressing this view: "Consider that the friars and the secular clergy each has its own form of penance; consider that the Franciscan friars have one manner of doctrine and one way of life and one dress and one way of prayer; and the Augustinians another; and the Dominicans another; and the secular clergy another . . . and it was also like this among those who kept our gods, so that the ones from Mexico had one way of dress and prayer . . . and other towns had another; each town had its own way of sacrificing" (Rabasa 1998). For a discussion of this passage and the debates on baptism in the 1530s and 1540s in Mexico, see Rabasa 1998, wherein I argue that philosophical backgrounds inform not only doctrinal practices but also the ethnographic styles the different missionaries practice.

17 For a detailed discussion of the philosophical tradition in which Dominicans and Franciscans were trained, see Rabasa 1998.

18 The by now classic text on the impossibility of subalterns speaking is Spivak's "Can the Subaltern Speak?" But this position underlies the perception, held by other members of the Indian Subaltern Studies Group, of a gulf separating the intellectual middle classes and the tribal societies. This separation is pertinent to both the colonial and the postcolonial worlds. The adoption of European science and history, as among the demands of the colonial authorities, only

exacerbated the differences between the castes (see, for instance, Guha 1997b, 2002; Spivak 1985, 1999, 2000; Chatterjee 1986, 1993; Chakrabarty 1997, 2000). The divide between the worlds of the Nahua elite and the commoners assumed different forms after the Spanish invasion, but the native intellectual elite did not forsake their intellectual traditions as they continued to write/paint history using Nahua life-forms. Another great difference was the impoverishment of the native worlds and the rise of a criollo and mestizo elite, but then, I would argue, this emergent elite had more in common with the Bengali middle classes than with the marginalized Nahuas of the colonial period, the republican period, and today.

19 Mazzotti's essay in this volume analyzes the specificity of Creole agency in Spanish America and the ambivalence of mestizo and criollo subjectivities in colonial times.

CREOLE AGENCIES AND THE (POST)COLONIAL DEBATE IN SPANISH AMERICA

José Antonio Mazzotti

The postcolonial debate in Spanish America has tended to focus on the relationship between dominant and dominated colonial subjects, that is, between Europeans and their descendants on the one hand, and the populations of indigenous and African origin on the other. In contrast, I focus in this essay on the relationship between peninsular Spaniards (those born in Spain) and Creoles (people of Spanish descent born in the New World). By exploring some of the legislation, social practices, and discursive manifestations of what has generally become known as "colonial" Spanish America, I show how pivotal the peninsular-Creole relationship is to an understanding of the complexities and uniqueness of the New World societies under Habsburg rule (1516–1700). In the second part of this essay, I argue that postcolonial theory and criticism, while instrumental in helping to frame some of the contours and conflicts of this period in Spanish American history, have so far been unable to fully explain the specific social, cultural, and literary formations of Creoles within the Spanish New World empire, especially those from the core areas of Mexico and Peru. I hope thereby both to contribute to current scholarship on colonial Latin America and to suggest ways to broaden our approach to postcolonial studies so as to include this region-specific perspective.

Any analysis of Creole discursive production and its role within New World societies must first situate Creole literary and historiographical writings within contemporary debates in Spanish American colonial studies. As those familiar with the colonial literary field are aware, a large body of work dealing with at least one sector of Creole discourse has emerged in recent years. I refer, of course, to those studies which revisit texts by Sor Juana Inés de la Cruz, Carlos de Sigüenza y Góngora, Pedro de Peralta Barnuevo, and other canonical authors. Such contributions have enriched and expanded the colonial field in important ways, renovating questions about the location of these Creole authors within a totality of colonial writings, and examining in greater detail the internal contradictions and ambiguities that such canonical texts present.[1] For their part, studies from outside the traditional boundaries of literary analysis have led to a productive inquiry into the relationship between Creoles and non-elite colonial subjects. The research suggests that Creoles' postures toward the indigenous population varied in accordance with the need to ally, defy, or negotiate with Spanish metropolitan power. Creoles often maintained a complicit silence with official colonial discourse, but at other times they produced their own characterizations—some paternalistically favorable, others scornful—of the poor and dominated colonial subjects.[2]

Overall, Creole discourses have proven to be more ambiguous than is generally recognized in the traditional stereotypes about Creoles' supposedly unconditional allegiance to the Spanish Crown or their alleged proto-nationalism during the Habsburg era. In fact, the very term *colonial* becomes problematic when applied to these Creoles and to the complex societies that existed in Spanish America prior to the advent of the Bourbon era in the eighteenth century.[3] To avoid such generalizations, I begin by acknowledging once again this essay's historical specificity (within the Habsburg era and the first decades of the eighteenth century) and its particular regional dimensions (within the "cores" of Mexico and Peru). Furthermore, although elements of postcolonial theory will sometimes be useful to this analysis of pre-Enlightenment Spanish America, theoretical advances from within Latin American scholarship are often just as useful, if not more so, in determining the profile and specific characteristics of Creole discourses.

SOME INITIAL CLARIFICATIONS

The modern polemic about whether or not the term *colonies* should be applied to pre-Enlightenment Spanish America dates back to at least 1951, with the publication of the Argentine historian Ricardo Levene's *Las Indias no eran colonias* (The Indies were not colonies). Levene wrote in response to the widespread use of this term within the traditional, anti-imperialist rhetoric of Spanish American nationalism. However, much of the subsequent historiography, with its emphasis on the socioeconomic aspects of Spanish domination, only reaffirmed the traditional use of *colonial* to refer to the entire period of Spanish rule in the New World.[4] Given this traditional usage, and the cognate between the Spanish term *colonia* and the English term *colony*, it is understandable that when postcolonial theory first emerged in the 1980s, it, too, began to be applied to post-independence Spanish America. No doubt this application was also a function of the predominance of North Atlantic theoretical frameworks in the study of Latin American literatures; a predominance that has too often eclipsed the important theoretical contributions of such regional authorities as Ángel Rama and Antonio Cornejo Polar. In any case, several Latin American specialists have come to criticize the inaccuracy of the term *colonial* in reference to the sixteenth- and seventeenth-century juridical structure of the Indies, and to question the use of *postcolonial* to describe nineteenth-century and twentieth-century Spanish American societies that are so continuous with their pre-independence pasts.[5] Other critics have bemoaned the "colonial" gesture of those Latin Americanists who simply apply First World paradigms to the region without asking questions or introducing any refinements.[6]

The truth is that the term *colony* was used very infrequently in Spanish America before the second half of the eighteenth century. The sporadic mentions of *colony* in earlier writings, from the sixteenth and seventeenth centuries, relate to its original meaning in Latin, spelled out by Sebastián de Covarrubias in his 1611 *Tesoro de la lengua castellana*: "puebla o término de tierra que se ha poblado de gente extranjera, sacada de la ciudad, que es señora de aquel territorio o llevada de otra parte" [town or piece of land that has been populated by foreigners who were removed from the city, or from some other place, and who exercise dominion over that territory] (f. 224v). In early modern Spain, this ancient Roman form of domination implied the transplanting of soldiers and citizens into distant territories, but did not necessarily include the transplantation of institutions or the transformation of the identities of the dominated people. This is the sense in which Peter Mártir of Anghiera used the word *colony* in 1530 to refer to the Villa Rica de la

Veracruz, the first urban settlement founded by Hernán Cortés in Mexico. "De Colonia deducenda, Progubernatore Cubæ Dieco Velaſquez incõſulto, conſilium ineunt" [They discussed the founding of a colony, although they did not include the Vice-Governor of Cuba, Diego Velázquez], wrote Mártir, who went on to state that "ad leucas inde duodecim in gleba fortunatiſſima fundãdæ Coloniæ locum deſignant" [twelve leagues from there, in a very fertile section of land, they marked the spot to found a colony] (1966, Decade Four, chap. 7, f. 6ov, 154). It would appear that Mártir envisioned a type of "colony" that was synonymous with "town" or "settlement," and that constituted a necessary first step in a grander project to eventually evangelize and assimilate the indigenous peoples. Clearly, such a project exceeded the military and strategic functions originally envisioned by the term *colony*.[7]

That the concept of a colony was initially detached from the idea of evangelization and tied instead to the agricultural, economic, and/or military uses of settlement is apparent even in the writings of El Inca Garcilaso. In "Preface to the Reader," from his *La Florida del Inca* (1605), Garcilaso recommends that the Spanish royal authorities "ganar y poblar [la Florida], aunque ſin lo principal q˜ es el aumento de nuesſtra ſancta fè Catholica, no ſea mas de para hazer colonias, donde embie a habitar ſus hijos, como hazian los antiguos Romanos, quando no cabian en ſu patria" [conquer and populate La Florida, even without the most important thing, which is the spread of our holy Catholic faith; and even if it is only to start colonies where [Spain] can send her children to live, just as the ancient Romans used to do when there was no longer room for them in their fatherland] (Vega 1605, unnumbered folio).[8] This important text communicates an understanding of "colony" as a strictly political endeavor with no relation to an evangelizing mission.

The word could, however, have a different meaning. Covarrubias's *Teasaurus* makes this clear by adding a second, equally important, definition: "También se llamaba colonias las que pobladas de sus antiguos moradores les avia el pueblo romano dado los privilegios de tales" [The name colonies also referred to those places populated by their ancient inhabitants, to whom the Romans had granted the privileges corresponding to such peoples] (1611, f. 224v). In short, a colony was understood in seventeenth-century Spain to be either an enclave with no necessary transformation of native religious and social practices, or a subjected population that was actually granted the privilege of retaining some of its ancient customs (such as its institutions and methods of social organization).

Both meanings seem to have circulated during the sixteenth and seven-

teenth centuries, and neither one was linked to Spain's ultimate goal, presumably, in the Americas. Certainly there was scandalous economic extraction of both labor and precious metals, not to mention the decimation of the
indigenous population. However, Spain's overall design was rather more
ambitious. In addition to the coerced labor and tribute, Spanish domination
ultimately sought the elimination of native "idolatrous" practices, forms of
social organization, and patterns of settlement. To this end, groups of indigenous people were transplanted into *reducciones*, or urban Indian settlements,
under the control of Spanish officials. The overarching narrative which justified such a radical reorganization of native peoples was, of course, the
triumphant implantation of Catholicism and the transformation of indigenous peoples from *rústicos* (uncivilized) or *menores* (minors) into mature political subjects; a transformation which required their proximity to, and
surveillance by, "civilized" or Christian people. At no time during the Habsburg era was the word *colony* identified with this ambitious project.[9]

Two pieces of evidence in this regard come from Fray Luis Jerónimo de
Oré and Juan de Solórzano. The former was a Peruvian Creole who sug-
gested in his 1598 *Símbolo Católico Indiano* that the name "*Colonia*" should
supplant all other names given to the Indies, as a tribute to Cristóbal Colón
(Christopher Columbus). Similarly, the Spanish jurist Juan de Solórzano
argued in *Política Indiana* that "el Nuevo Orbe ſe debio llamar Colonia, o
Columbania, del nombre de don Christobal Colon, o Columbo" [the New
World should have been called Colonia, or Columbania, after the name of
Don Christopher Colon, or Columbus] (1648, f. 79). Both arguments reveal
that the term *colony* was not immediately charged with a universal meaning and could have had more immediate historical connotations. In fact,
their suggested use of the term would have brought the seventeenth-century
meanings of *colony* more into line with the actual relationship of Spain to the
societies of the New World.

Both officially and popularly, the conquered territories of the New World
were generally referred to as either the "reinos de la Corona de Castilla"
[kingdoms of the Crown of Castile] or simply as the "Virreinatos" [vice-
royalties]. In terms of their peculiar political and social organization, the
first, the Viceroyalty of New Spain (including Mexico and Meso-America),
was created in 1535, and a second, the Viceroyalty of Peru (including all of
South America excluding Portuguese Brazil), was created in 1544. Up until
the eighteenth century, these were the only two viceroyalties in Spanish
America.[10] They were conceptualized and designed like other outlying Spanish provinces, with much of the same legislation as the central kingdom but

with their own specific laws as well. To call these viceroyalties "colonies," in the seventeenth-century sense of the word as mere extractive settlements, was somewhat inaccurate and anachronistic.[11]

At the same time, however, the Spanish American viceroyalties were not carbon copies of fifteenth-century Mediterranean viceroyalties and Aragonese possessions (such as Naples, Milan, Sicily, Sardinia, Piombino, and Mallorca). Although there were some points of comparison between the two provincial models, the Spanish American viceroyalties had their own peculiar features which became increasingly unique over time. As the historian Sigfrido Radaelli points out,

> (1) En las Indias españolas el virrey no somete ni desconoce a la población que se halla en sus dominios, sino que por el contrario esta población es incorporada al Imperio, y sus integrantes son equiparados a los integrantes del país descubridor; (2) en los virreinatos aludidos [del Mediterráneo] se establece un vínculo con un país que ya tenía instituciones propias y que las conservaba. Sicilia, por ejemplo, se mantuvo como un reino por completo aparte de los demás reinos de la Corona de Aragón y Castilla, y su autonomía nacional y política no fue jamás tocada.

> [(1) In the Spanish Indies the viceroy does not subject or ignore the population of his domains, but instead this population is incorporated into the Empire, and its members are put on a par with those of the discovering country; (2) in the aforementioned viceroyalties [of the Mediterranean], a linkage is established with a country that already had its own institutions and that preserved them. Sicily, for example, remained as a kingdom completely apart from the other kingdoms of the Crown of Aragon and Castile, and its national and political autonomy was never touched.] (1957, 18)

Unfortunately for the Amerindians, most of their native institutions were simply wiped out, especially those governing religion, economics, and sexual exchange. In terms of the first point in Radaelli's description, the incorporation of the indigenous population was undoubtedly attempted, although not always with great success (as evidenced by the meager accomplishments of the campaigns to extirpate idolatry). In general, however, his point is well taken about the Spanish American institution of the viceroyalty being unique in terms of its characteristics and internal legislation. Of course, the idea of a viceroyalty or something similar was also common in British imperialism, albeit with different characteristics (Radaelli 1957, 17). However, the peculiar internal division of the Spanish viceroyalties into a república de españoles (including the Creoles) and a separate república de indios with its own laws and obligations (regarding issues of tribute and forced labor, for example) is one of the defining features of the Spanish system and an important element to keep in mind in terms of the contradictory processes of nation formation in nineteenth-century Latin America (see Thurner 1997 for the Peruvian case and Guardino 1996 for the Mexican, although both analyses are regional, rather than national, in scope).

In terms of Radaelli's second point, regarding autonomy, there was certainly a specific character to the interplay between peninsulars and Creoles within the Spanish American viceroyalties, but the allegiance to the broader concept of the identity and authority of the Spanish Crown was also very real. Solórzano, for example, even as he developed descriptions of Mexico and Peru as provinces with their own unique features, nonetheless insisted that the Spanish American possessions formed part of the larger political body of the empire. He noted that political integration into this larger body owed much to the explicit comparisons with the Roman Empire, for "en términos de derecho común lo enſeñan con el exemplo de las colonias de los romanos varios textos y autores de cada paso" [in terms of common law, various texts and authors teach it through repeated reference to the example of the Roman colonies] (Solórzano 1648, bk. 2, chap. 30, f. 245). Little wonder, then, that one of Charles V's titles was "Sacra Cesárea Real Majestad." Ideas about empire were informed by the old concepts about the Roman empire, although logical differences did present themselves in the case of a Christian confederation of kingdoms, such as the one over which the Spanish king presided (Pagden 1990, 3).

Moving beyond a comparison to other Mediterranean viceroyalties, it is important to acknowledge that the Spanish American possessions were characterized by the same kind of foreign domination and exploitation that we identify today with the term *colony*, informed as it is by the model of the "Second British Empire" (1776–1914).[12] In this sense, there were many "colonial" aspects to the experiences of indigenous peoples living under Spanish rule. To begin with, the internal differences between indigenous groups began to be blurred by the common denominators of being "Indian" (born in the Indies) and being exploited by the same entity, that is, Spanish authorities. Despite eloquent efforts by the Crown to implement protective laws and the brave testimonies of clergymen denouncing atrocities and abuses by Crown officials (all influenced by the *arbitrista* genre), the realities of tributary control and forced labor in the mines continued.[13] King Philip IV himself was quite conscious of this fact. In an edict of 3 July 1627 (reproduced in part by Solórzano in his *Política Indiana*), the king reiterated the official intention of imperial policy toward the Indians: "Encarezco el cuidado, i vigilancia en procurar la salud, amparo, i defenſa temporal de los Indios, i en deſpachar, i promulgar caſi todos los dias, leyes y penas graviſſimas contra los tranſgreſſores" [What matters to me is to be careful and vigilant in procuring the health, protection and moral defense of the Indians, and to swiftly promulgate laws and hand down the harshest punishments to transgressors] (Solórzano 1648, unnumbered folio). He further acknowledged the existence of such transgressions in dictating that "del todo ſe quitaſſen, i caſtigaſſen las injurias, i opreſſiones de los Indios, i los ſervicios perſonales, q̃ ſe endereçaban à particulares aprovechamientos, i grãgerias" [any offenses against, oppression of, or exaction of personal service from the Indians shall be completely eliminated and punished, for this only benefits private interests and profits] (ibid.). Ultimately, the king emphasized,

> Quiero que me deis ſatiſfaccion a Mi, i al Mundo, del modo de tratar eſſos mis vaſſallos, i de no hazerlo, con que en reſpueſta de eſta carta vea Yo executados exemplares caſtigos en los que huuieren excedido en eſta parte, me darè por deſervido . . . por ſer contra Dios, contra Mi, i en total deſtruiciõ de eſſos Reinos, cuyos Naturales eſtimo, i quiero ſean tratados, como lo merecen vaſſallos, que tanto sirven à la Monarchia, y tãto la han engrãdecido, e ilustrado

> [I want you [the viceregal authorities] to assure Me, and the World, of the way my vassals [the Indians] are being treated, and if you do not respond to this letter I shall make sure that exemplary punishments are applied to those who have committed excesses, for I will consider Myself poorly served . . . because [harsh treatment] goes against God, against Myself, and leads to the total destruction of those Kingdoms, whose Natives I esteem, and I want them to be treated as deserving vassals who have served the Monarchy so well and have so much enhanced and enriched it.] (Ibid.)

King Philip's position on the Indians was hardly original; Crown intervention protecting Indians from Spanish overlords was common in the sixteenth century. Even before the promulgation of the New Laws in 1542, largely inspired by Bartolomé de las Casas's passionate defense of the Indians, there had been protests by other heroic members of the clergy, including a well-known denouncement by Fray Anton de Montesinos in 1511. These protests generated in Spain a wave of support favoring the severe limitation of the power and hegemony that conquerors and their direct descendants were consolidating in the kingdoms of the Indies. The 1542 New Laws were aimed at dismantling the system of *encomienda*, wherein a Spanish official (generally a conqueror) was given charge over a particular part of the indigenous population, collecting the royal tribute in return for protecting and evangelizing these new vassals of the king. This economic system, in conjunction with the system of *repartos*, or land grants handed out to the conquerors, created a group of New World aristocrats with so much wealth and power that they even dared to challenge the Crown itself (in the 1544–48 rebellion of Gonzalo Pizarro in Peru) and to propose perpetual ownership of the lands for themselves (in a 1555 proposal by Peruvian encomienda holders, or *encomenderos*, to the Crown).

Another inspiration for the New Laws came from Spanish neoscholasticism and its views on the relationship between Natural and Divine Law. By the mid-sixteenth century, a constant stream of writings began to appear by critics and philosophers who challenged the right of Spain to dominate the New World and debated the primary moral responsibility that Spain shouldered as an imperial force. The many prominent members of the so-called School of Salamanca produced an extensive corpus of treatises and other writings exposing different points of view on these issues. Scholars such as Francisco de Vitoria, Melchor Cano, Domingo de Soto, and (decades later) Luis de Molina, Juan de Mariana, Francisco Suárez, and others meticulously theorized about the ethical and theological limits of the Spanish Crown's possession and exploitation of the New World (see Pérez-Luño 1992, chaps. 5 and 6; Pagden 1990, 13–36). With the promulgation of the New Laws and the continued harsh criticism by Bartolomé de las Casas and the neoscholastics, the encomenderos came to feel that their efforts and sacrifices were being poorly compensated. Certainly the new legislation was damning to their self-assumed rights and *señorío* (lordship).[14] Furthermore, because the implementation of the New Laws was such a slow-moving and piecemeal process, the Crown also proceeded to establish the more centralized system of *corregimientos*, or publicly administered districts of land and people, as well as the unified and generalized series of legal exemptions, or *fueros*, for indigenous natives known as the república de indios.

Despite whatever good intentions might have inspired this triumphant metropolitan hegemony, the new legislation did not result in population growth or better living conditions for indigenous communities. In the Andean case, the excessive tribute charged by the encomenderos and *corregidores*, together with the epidemics of 1525, 1546, 1558–59 and 1585, decimated the indigenous population, which fell from an estimated 4 to 15 million under Incan rule to only 1.3 million by 1570, and again to only 700,000 by 1620 (Klarén 2000, 49–50). In the face of this population decline Viceroy Francisco de Toledo in the 1570s further expanded the system of

reducciones and corregimientos. Such a radical reorganization of the indigenous population, built on the widespread use of forced, unpaid labor,
distorted the essence of the Andean labor system of mit'a, which the Incas
had formerly utilized for agricultural and military purposes and the Spaniards had appropriated for mining. As a result of the Toledan reforms,
agricultural production fell off dramatically, which caused even more de-
population (Millones 1995, chap. 2) and further crippled the economic development of an American conquistador and Creole nobility.[15] At the same
time, the wealth of the Royal Treasury increased significantly, invigorated by
the new system of mining extraction and land redistribution. By the final
decades of the sixteenth century, then, many Creoles felt that their situation
was simply desperate.[16] In a letter dated 12 December 1588 the "Procurador
de los Pobres de la Ciudad de los Reyes" [overseer of the poor people of
Lima] wrote to King Philip II that "justamente piden los necessitados de aca
que les alcançe parte, mayormente, siendo muchos dellos, hijos, hermanos y
parientes de los que las conquistaron y ganaron y a V. mag. han seruido y
quedado sin gratifficacion ni premio" [The needy people here justly seek
their share of [the wealth], for many of them are children, brothers and
relatives of those who conquered and won [this land] and they have served
Your Majesty but have been given no compensation or reward] (Archivo
General de Indias, Seville, Spain, Lima 32; emphasis added).

Under such circumstances, the Spanish American possessions began to
acquire their original form, both socially and culturally. Although the república de españoles included all those born in the New World to peninsular parents, it was not unusual to hear about the "dark origin" of some
Creoles and mestizos of the first two generations. This was especially the
case among the mestizos, for their Indian blood was believed to incline them
toward idolatry. Creoles, however, were also suspect, and understandably
so, for somewhere between 20 and 40 percent of all Creoles were biological
mestizos whose assimilation as Creoles was linked to their Spanish fathers'
efforts to retain certain privileges (see Kuznesof 1995; Poot-Herrera 1995;
Schwartz 1995). The phenomenon of miscegenation was common during
the first few decades after the conquest; because very few European women
came to the New World in those years, Spanish soldiers and adventurers
treated the women of the vanquished Indians as their sexual prey. In any
case, whether "pure" Creole or camouflaged mestizo, many members of the
republica de españoles felt abandoned by the Crown on seeing their parents
(and therefore themselves) increasingly dispossessed. To add to the suffering, Creoles were constantly suspected of engaging in rebellious behavior,

and as such were often discriminated against in their efforts to obtain land or positions of prestige.[17]

The use of the term *Creole* to refer to the neo-Europeans dates back to at least 1567 and probably carried with it the insulting connotation of being the same name used for the children of African slaves born outside Africa (see Lavallé 1993, 15–25). The term *Creole*, at least as it was used in the first decades after the conquest, indicated a social and legal category more than a biological one (Mazzotti 1996). To be "Creole," and in particular to be a direct descendant of a conqueror or one of the earliest *pobladores*, or settlers, was to also possess the feelings of belonging to the *patria*, or fatherland, and of being entitled to the privileges of señorío in the new kingdom. As Jacques Lafaye (1976 [1974], 7–8), Solange Alberro (1992), and Bernard Lavallé (1978, 39–41) point out, these were the feelings of many of the conquerors themselves.

The claims made by American-born Spaniards for *prelación*, or preferential treatment, from the Spanish Crown were a constant presence in almost every aspect of viceregal law and social organization. Viceroy Conde del Villar attested to this presence explicitly in a letter to King Philip II dated 12 May 1588: "Pretensores ay gran numero en este Reyno porque como los conquistadores y primeros pobladores han dejado hijos cada uno de ellos pretende la gratificaçion entera de lo que su padre sirvio" [There are a great many claimants in this Kingdom because the conquerors and first settlers have left children, each one of whom expects to be fully compensated for the service of his father] (Archivo General de Indias, Seville, Spain, Lima 32). In some cases, such claims received support from the highest viceregal authorities, and even at times from the viceroy himself.[18] Juan de Solórzano, for example, who was an *oidor*, or judge, on the Lima Audiencia, or High Court, and was himself married to a Creole woman from Lima, was an outspoken supporter of the Creoles.

> No ſe puede dudar que ſean [los Criollos] verdaderos Eſpañoles, y como tales hayan de gozar ſus derechos, honras y privilegios, y ſer juzgados por ellos, ſupueſto que las Provincias de las Indias son como auctuario de las de Eſpaña, y acceſoriamente unidas e incorporadas en ellas, como expresamente lo tienen declarado muchas Cédulas Reales que de esto tratan.
>
> [There can be no doubt that Creoles are true Spaniards, and that they should enjoy the rights, honors and privileges as such, and that they should be judged as Spaniards, because the provinces of the Indies are just like those of Spain, and are linked to and incorporated with them, as many Royal Decrees dealing with this issue have expressly declared.] (Solórzano 1648, chap. 30, f. 245).

Ultimately, Solórzano reasoned that:

> Los Criollos hazen con eſtos [los Eſpañoles] un cuerpo, i un Reino, i ſon vaſſallos
> de un mesmo Rey, [i] no ſe les puede hazer mayor agravio, que intentar excluirles
> de eſtos honores.

> [Together with [the Spaniards], the Creoles form one body, and one Kingdom,
> they are vassals of the same King, [and] nothing could be more offensive to them
> than trying to exclude them from those honors.] (ibid., f. 246)

Given the influence of many Creole claims and the centralizing reforms
which increased the size of New World viceregal administrations, a certain degree of Creole presence in government positions was not altogether
unwelcome. This was especially so because of an increasing shortage in
Spain of able and willing officers to fill the burgeoning New World administrations. The eighteenth-century High Court of Lima, for example, offers
ample evidence of Creole infiltration (see Lohmann Villena 1974). The legal
grounds to legitimate Creole participation was clearly established in Law 13,
Title 2, Book 2, of the *Recopilación de Leyes de Indias* (1681), which reads,

> Porque siendo de una Corona los Reinos de Castilla y de las Indias, las leyes y
> orden de gobierno de los unos y de los otros, deberán ser lo más semejantes y
> conformes que ser pueda; los de nuestro Consejo en las leyes y establecimientos
> que para aquellos estados ordenaren y procuren reducir la forma y manera de
> gobierno de ellos al estilo y orden con que son recogidos y gobernados los Reinos
> de Castilla y de León en cuanto hubiere lugar y permitiere la diversidad y diferen-
> cia de las tierras y naciones.

> [Because the kingdoms of Castile and those of the Indies belong to one Crown,
> the laws and governmental structure of the former and the latter shall be as
> similar and consistent as possible; the laws and judgments that this Council [of
> the Indies] decides for those states [will] be aimed at bringing them into line with
> the style and form of government which reign in the kingdoms of Castile and
> Leon, to the extent permitted by the diversity and difference of those lands and
> nations.]

Notwithstanding such legal and practical rationale, there remained a tendency to systematically exclude Creoles from the highest offices, as the
Crown generally appointed only members of the peninsular aristocracy to
the most critical and lucrative posts.[19]

Many Creoles believed that the disdain implicit in their systematic marginalization in terms of receiving land grants or political posts in the first

decades after conquest stemmed from what Antonello Gerbi would later call the "dispute for the New World." During the sixteenth and seventeenth centuries, the bitter debate between Europeans and Americans over identity on both sides and who could best govern the Indies set the bases whose contours continued to inform conceptualizations of the Americas into the eighteenth century. Undoubtedly a marked disdain for Creoles can be discerned in many Spanish writings from the sixteenth and seventeenth centuries. In one representative case from 1617, Cristóbal Suárez de Figueroa put the following words into the mouth of the "Doctor," one of the characters from his El passagero.

> Las Indias, para mí, no sé qué tienen de malo, que hasta su nombre aborrezco. Todo quanto viene de allá es muy diferente, y aun opuesto, yua a decir, de lo que en España posseemos y gozamos. Pues los hombres (queden siempre reseruados los buenos) iqué redundantes, qué abundosos de palabras, qué estrechos de ánimo, qué inciertos de crédito y fe; cuán rendidos al interés, al ahorro! . . . iNotables sabandijas crían los límites antárticos y occidentales!

> [I don't know what is so wrong with the Indies that I even abhor their name. Everything that comes from that place is very different, or even opposite, I meant to say, from what we have and enjoy in Spain. The men from there (with the exception of the good ones), how redundant they are, how verbose, how weak-spirited, how unreliable in their credit and their word, how given in to their interests and to their savings! . . . How notably nasty are the insects that breed in the outer reaches of the Antarctic and the West!] (1914 [1617], 225–26)

To symbolically compensate for these kinds of disdainful remarks, Creoles would insist that their blood was even purer than that of the Spaniards themselves. In 1681 Juan Meléndez, a Creole Dominican priest from Lima, declared that "hacemos pues mucho aprecio los Criollos de las Yndias de ſer Eſpañoles, y de que nos llamen aſſi, y nos tengan por tales, y en orden à conſeruar eſta ſangre Eſpañola pura, y limpia ſe pone tanto cuydado, que no tiene ponderacion" [we Creoles of the Indies greatly appreciate being Spanish, and being called as such and considered as such; and we go to any length to preserve the cleanliness and purity of this Spanish blood] (1681, vol. 1, ff. 353–54). However, Meléndez also noted that Creoles identified themselves as different from peninsular Spaniards, who in their ignorance toward Creoles, were seen as "safios" or idiots and less than human: "Para diſtinguirnos de los miſmos Eſpañoles que nacieron en Eſpaña, nos llamamos allà Criollos, voz que de cierto en Eſpaña ſe ríen mucho: pero con la razón con que ſe ríen algunos de todo lo que no entienden: propiedad de gente ſafia indigna de tener figura de hombres" [In order to distinguish ourselves from the Spaniards born in Spain, we call ourselves Creoles, a term that Spaniards undoubtedly laugh at very much; but they laugh using the same logic as those who laugh at everything they do not understand. This is typical of stupid people who do not deserve to figure as human beings] (ibid., f. 353).

The early identity of the new Creole subjects was founded on the "glorious" conquest, and eventually the Creole elites came to see themselves as strong enough to compete with the peninsular aristocracy for economic domination in the New World. In Peru this competition became very heated in the seventeenth century, when Creole merchants began to figure prominently in viceregal commerce and trade. Because of the considerable influence of Creole-generated wealth, many Creoles began to declare their capital city of Lima to be the center of human civilization and the highest peak of New World religiosity.[20] An extensive descriptive bibliography attests to the extent of Creole exaltations of their cities and the physical richness of their lands. From Mexico, the examples extend from Bernardo de Balbuena's *Grandeza mexicana* to Carlos de Sigüenza's *Paraíso occidental*; in Peru, from Rodrigo de Valdés's *Fundación y grandezas de Lima* (1681) to Pedro de Peralta's undervalued *Lima fundada*. In all cases, the superlative descriptions of American cities and territories reveal not just the psychological profile of their authors but also the subjective *locus* of their articulations and, consequently, their constitution as discursive and social subjects. These particular features would clearly differentiate the Creoles from the other social subjects within the viceroyalties (see Mazzotti 1996, 173–75).

In short, Creoles found diverse ways to negotiate with and confront Spanish power, whether as writers, merchants, officeholders, or landed elites. Those who did not belong to the powerful Creole merchant elites tried their best to reach an accommodation of sorts within the viceregal bureaucracy and the church, making strategic alliances with the Spaniards while continuing to insist on their own rights as Creoles. Lettered Creoles, especially, responded time and time again to the marginalization implied in the privileged, Eurocentric disdain wielded by Suárez de Figueroa and others, producing numerous pages of their own dedicated to exalting the character and appearance of the distinguished descendants of the conquerors. In doing so, these Creole intellectuals carried out the immense task of creating a discursive corpus to articulate their own conception of Hispanic identity. Although this American perspective surely differed in many respects from a peninsular Spanish one, we should be careful not to assume that it necessarily prefigured the struggle for independence, nor that it in any sense suggested an essentialist kind of biological or spiritual kinship between Creoles and the majority of underprivileged Amerindians, blacks, and "castes," or racially mixed groups.

Another indication of the development of separate Creole cultural and communicational practices was the unique kind of Spanish that came to be spoken in the Americas. Although originally sharing many characteristics with Andalusian Spanish, this multiregional, New World Spanish became increasingly differentiated by morphologic and lexical changes, and by its many possible prosodic variants.[21] Creoles were not at all ashamed of their different manner of speech; in fact, they boasted of it, and even used it to recriminate Spaniards for speaking so poorly. Bernardo de Balbuena, a sort of naturalized Mexican Creole, offers a very clear example of this in his *Grandeza mexicana.*

> Es [México] ciudad de notable policia
> Y donde ſe habla el Eſpañol lenguaje
> Mas puro y con mayor corteſania.
>
> Veſtido de un belliſſimo ropaje
> Que le da propiedad, gracia, agudeza,
> En caſto, limpio, liſo y graue traje
>
> [[Mexico] is a city of notable order
> Where the Spanish language is spoken
> More purely and with greater elegance.
>
> Dressed in very beautiful clothing
> Which gives it propriety, grace, shrewdness,
> In a chaste, clean, smooth, and serious garment.]
>
> (Balbuena 1604, estrofas 30–31, f. 111v)

Turning from the linguistic differentiation to the particular spiritual qualities expressed through American Spanish, we find that Creole self-glorification is even more colorful. Examples abound, but a few will suffice. In describing Mexican Creoles, Juan de Cárdenas, in Book 3 of his *Problemas y secretos maravillosos de las Indias* entitles one chapter "*Los Eſpañoles nacidos en las Indias[, que ſon] por la mayor parte de ingenio biuo, tracendido y delicado*" [Spaniards born in the Indies, [who are] for the major part quick-minded, transcendent, and delicate] (1945 [1591], f. 176v).[22] Of Peruvian Creoles, Buenaventura de Salinas boasts that "son con todo estremo agudos, viuos, sutiles, y profundos en todo genero de ciencias . . . [y] este cielo y clima del

Pirú los leuanta, y ennoblece en animos" [they are extremely intelligent, shrewd, subtle and well-grounded in all kinds of sciences . . . [and] this sky and weather of Peru elevates and ennobles their spirit] (1951 [1630], 246). One of the Salinas's sources (Duviols 1983, 108, 114) was Francisco Fernández de Córdoba, an admired scholar from Huánuco, who had made similar public pronouncements in 1620, describing "the Creoles" as "hijos de la nobleza mejorada con su valor, . . . siendo más aventajados en esta transplantación, [de lo] que fueron en su nativo plantel" [Creoles are children of the nobility, [but] improved by their valor . . . for they are more advantaged in this new setting than they were in their native soil [i.e., Spain]] (1976 [1620], 8). Antonio de la Calancha would put Peruvian Creoles at the top of mankind's entire biological and intellectual pyramid, naturally above the Spaniards.[23] According to Calancha (1638), the Creoles' innate talents and their familiarity with the land and indigenous populations made them more suitable to govern the Indians. Through such glorifications, lettered Creoles sought the symbolic authority necessary to achieve more administrative access and a viceregal government more dedicated to "the common good" (see Mazzotti 1996).

Up to this point, our emphasis has been on the ways that Creoles sought to differentiate themselves from peninsular Spaniards in terms of speech, courtly manners, moral and spiritual qualities, and familiarity with the land and its indigenous population. It is time now to situate these examples within a theoretical framework of Creole subjectivity. Given the many different postures assumed by lettered Creoles, it makes sense to forego the more common notion of "subject," which tends to be static and omnipresent, almost essentialist, in favor of some redefined notion of "agency." John Mowitt has identified agency as "the general preconditions that make the theoretical articulation of the critique of the subject possible" (1988, xii). In the case of the Creoles, it would obviously be impossible to articulate specific traces of Creoleness without first identifying those "general preconditions" in which specific individuals and groups in the pre-Enlightenment Spanish American context interacted. Furthermore, the Spanish term for agency—*agencia*—actually refers to the capacity of a mutable subject to negotiate, adapt, and actively seek the most beneficial position. One of the most important outcomes of shifting the conceptual category from "subject" to "agency," then, is that we can posit a positional identity or subjectivity among lettered Creoles, or as Cornejo Polar would call it, a "relational identity" (1994a, 89). In this sense, it would not only be fruitful but absolutely essential to recognize the ambiguous position that many Creoles adopted vis-à-vis the Spanish authorities (exemplified in the saying "Acato pero no cumplo" [I obey but do not execute] [see Lavallé 2000]). After all, Creoles were Spaniards, but not completely; they were also Americans, but clearly distanced themselves from the indigenous, African, and mixed-raced peoples with whom they shared the territories.[24] It makes no sense to extract some of the Creoles' common features in order to piece together some monolithic Creole identity, for doing so runs the risk of erasing the dialogic and interactive nature of Creoles' engagement with their social environment. Paul Smith was no doubt correct when he pointed out that "[in some way] theoretical discourse limits the definition of the human agent in order to be able to call him/her the 'subject' " (1988, 30). For this reason, I prefer to work with the more flexible category of agency, agreeing as I do with Smith that "the human agent exceeds the 'subject' as it is constructed in and by much poststructuralist theory as well as by those discourses against which poststructuralist theory claims to pose itself " (ibid.).

Creole agencies are defined by their own multilayered and multifaceted profiles in the economic, political, and discursive realms. At the same time, however, Creoles did demonstrate a persistent capacity to establish clear boundaries between their vision and all other forms of ethnic nationhood.[25] That constant practice of self-definition was the result of the peculiar system of Spanish domination in the New World, which not only permitted Spanish institutions and laws to be translated into regional terms, but also allowed for the development of a new, native-born social elite, an elite that would eventually become a force for ideological (and biological) transformation of the indigenous people.

In most modern classifications of colonial systems in Western history, Spanish American peculiarities are evident. Jürgen Osterhammel provides a perfect example. He classifies only three types of colonial systems: colonies of exploitation, maritime enclaves, and colonies of settlement. Although he places the Spanish American variant squarely within the first category, he does add the qualification that "European immigration led to an urban mixed society with a dominating Creole minority" (Osterhammel 1997, 11). Such a phenomenon is apparently uncommon in other cases of the history of Western colonization.[26] It is precisely this long-standing Creole presence in the cultural, social, and economic sectors of nineteenth- and twentieth-century Spanish America that has given rise to questions about whether or not the term *postcolonial* should be applied to this region (see Klor de Alva 1995, 270). Critics have pointed out that the wars of independence were led by interstitial sectors like the Creoles and therefore resulted in early-nineteenth-century nation-states which prolonged the ethnic, this time neo-European, domination over the populations of indigenous and African descent. From this perspective, the prefix *post* seems woefully inadequate to describe the historical and ongoing experience in the region.[27]

In order to further explore this alleged inadequacy, it will be useful to review some basic characteristics of the postcolonial theoretical framework, an approach which has undoubtedly reinvigorated the study of Asian and African cultural production within North Atlantic academia and which has also exercised some influence over the Latin American field.

POSTCOLONIAL THEORY IN THE SPANISH AMERICAN (POST)COLONIAL DEBATE

As scholars of colonial Spanish American literature are aware, the field has undergone significant renovation since the 1980s. This is due in part to the critical influence that poststructuralist theory has exercised throughout the social sciences and the humanities since the 1960s. In fact, it has become nearly impossible to rethink any area of study without some reference to the writings of Michel Foucault, Jacques Lacan, and Jacques Derrida, the major figures of poststructuralism. Foucault's notion of "discursive formations" reconceptualized academic disciplines, critiquing traditional notions of these as fixed compartments of knowledge production with static objects of study (1969, 35). By suggesting the relative nature of epistemological categories within each discipline, Foucault challenged traditional disciplines to modify their understanding of the relationship between knowledge production and political power. As a result, these disciplines began to redefine their objects of study and reevaluate their own social and political roles.[28]

In the case of Latin American literature many scholars began taking a more interdisciplinary approach in their work in order to shed more light over the complex webs of meanings generated by texts both literary and nonliterary. The traditional paradigms of "author" and "text" were replaced by those of "subject" and "discourse." Eventually, the widely accepted notion of discourse was further broadened by the idea of "semiosis" in an effort to recognize nonwritten documents (*códices*, quipus, drawings, etc.) as part of the totality of cultural production which took place after 1492 (Mignolo 1989a, 1992b, 1993). In this sense, colonial Latin American *literary studies*, as the interdisciplinary name itself denotes, partially de-aesthetized its own object of study. Many forms of nontextual representation began to be studied, revealing a rich cultural production which had been invisible to previous generations of critics more narrowly focused on canonical authors. The new, interdisciplinary approach became a vehicle for conceptual liberation and a means of resistance for Latin Americanist literary critics, who, tired of being manipulated by obsolete, Eurocentric frameworks, could now allow the many silenced voices of the past to be heard.[29]

At the same time that European poststructuralism was making its influence felt, there were significant advances within the Spanish American tradition of literary scholarship which helped to conceptualize "colonial" discourse as a vast corpus which could not possibly be reduced to conventional forms. Of fundamental importance in this regard was Angel Rama's pathbreaking La ciudad letrada (1984) and the many works of Antonio Cornejo Polar outlining the paradigm of cultural heterogeneity (see Mazzotti 1996). As early as the 1970s, these authors had argued that the literature produced in the Spanish New World was nurtured by, and in dialogue with, a dense sea of voices and collective memories, and that "colonial" literature was often a direct result of, or manipulation of, the indigenous or other dominated voices. By insisting on the value of those elements of Latin American cultural production which are not directly dependent on European models but which present their own complex, internal array of meanings, these two Latin American critics opened the floodgates to a healthy interrogation of the canon. Rama's concepts of transculturation and the "lettered city" and Cornejo Polar's notion of heterogeneity provide us with two theoretical frameworks capable of explaining the relationship in Latin America between oral sources and professional writing, a relationship born of the enormous social and cultural contrasts inherited from the "colonial" past.[30]

Equipped with these new, Latin American analytical tools, colonialist scholars began to insert previously understudied forms of production into the general corpus of colonial studies, thereby reconfiguring the map of privileged texts and semiotic exchanges. Indigenous orality was central to this process of reconceptualizing the object of study. However, this orality had been subjugated for so long by the general framework of linguistic diglossia that it was foreign to the communicative practices of traditional scholars. The importance of this unknown genre encouraged some among recent generations of "colonialists" to appropriate methodological tools from other disciplines (especially linguistics, anthropology, and history) as well as new theoretical frameworks in order to offer novel readings of both canonical and noncanonical discourses and forms of communication.

One of these frameworks was postcolonial theory. The origins of this growing field are many, but are generally identified with the publication of

Edward Said's *Orientalism* (1978) and with Said's most visible precedents, Frantz Fanon and Aimé Césaire, two relevant figures in the mid-twentieth-century anticolonial struggles for national liberation.[31] Over two decades later, postcolonial theory has a wide array of exponents and almost no fixed form or methodology. In the works of Said, Gayatri Chakravorty Spivak, and Homi Bhabha, although to different degrees, the direct influence of "high" French theory (Foucault, Lacan, and Derrida, respectively) has been crucial, and in many ways parallels the influence that those same French theorists have exercised on the Latin American colonial field. However, some of the most generalized concepts of postcolonial theory (in particular, the special attention paid to cultural phenomena through interdisciplinary approaches) have come under increased scrutiny. For example, some critics claim that postcolonial theory does not adequately explain how the economic elements of colonial domination relate to the formation of subjectivities in both the metropolis and the periphery.

In this sense, it is important to differentiate between postcolonial theory and postcolonial criticism. Critics identified with the latter take up a dual position of accepting, and rejecting, the writings of the postcolonial theorists. Some critics (including Aijaz Ahmad, Benita Parry, Arif Dirlik, Chinweizu, and in some aspects Spivak herself) accuse leading theorists of lacking a serious political commitment to Third World liberation struggles. Another issue for critics is whether some postcolonial theory is simply a translation or variation of French poststructuralism designed for consumption by an English-speaking academia. The creative use of class analysis and modes-of-production models by postcolonial theorists has also been called into question by many critics who privilege traditional Marxist approaches to the colonial problem. At the same time, there are other critics (including Paul Gilroy, Wole Soyinka and Robert Young) who question the value of Marxism at all, recognizing it instead as yet another product of the European Enlightenment whose commitment to a universal Reason homogenizes rationalities which depart from a narrative of progress and modernity, and ignore or reject the particular cultural traces of non-Western societies.

Equipped with this broad map of the development of postcolonial studies, it is now time to turn our attention to the importance of postcolonial theory as it relates to our understanding of the Spanish American "colonial" context. In this particular sense, there are a few features of postcolonial theory that need particular underscoring. To begin with, one needs always to keep in mind that the concept of postcolonial was originally applied to the situation of the former French and British colonies in Africa and Asia which became independent in the post–World War II period (Ahmad 1995, 5–7). Scholarly meditation on cultural production within this specific context became a therapeutic means of coming to grips with the posttraumatic effects of colonialism, and the result was a rigorous examination of the subjective consequences of colonial domination and its racial violence. Scholars claimed that postcolonial amnesia, or the "desire to forget the colonial past" (Gandhi 1998, 4), was symptomatic of the urgent need for self-reinvention, a need that was frustrated, according to scholars, by the persistence of the colonial past in all forms of daily life and many types of artistic expression. Postcolonial studies, then, first emerged as "a disciplinary project devoted to the academic task of revisiting, remembering, and, crucially, interrogating the colonial past" (ibid.).

Another relevant aspect of scholarly interrogations of the recent past in Asia and Africa has been the attempt to reverse the universalizing flow of Enlightened Reason by symbolically provincializing Europe.[32] This attempt includes the positing of an "illness"—"the darker side of the Enlightenment," to paraphrase Mignolo 2000d—that cuts through the center of the logic of colonial domination and its alleged "liberating" episteme. Bhabha, for example, claims that remembering the colonial past is more than just a simple act of introspection; it is also an act of re-membering, of putting back together the pieces of a mutilated body in order to recover the traces of a lost identity (1994a, 63). Bhabha's analysis of colonial discourse clearly relies heavily on Bakhtinian and Lacanian logic, at least during what Moore-Gilbert (1997, 14) has classified as his early period (1980–88). For instance, Bhabha focuses on the phenomena of mimicry and hybridism, this time within the context of the colonial subject under British rule in India. In his famous 1984 essay, "Of Mimicry and Man" (later revised and included as chapter 4 in *The Location of Culture*), Bhabha locates the effects of mimicry in the response the colonizer articulates to the simulacrum performed in his presence by the colonized. According to Bhabha, this simulacrum is a destabilizing imitation of the identity of the colonizer, who cannot recognize himself in this "other" who speaks to him in English and wears English-type clothes. Beginning with Bakhtin's concept of hybridity, Bhabha comes to formulate his own definition: "Hybridity is a problematic of colonial representation . . . that reverses the effects of the colonialist disavowal, so that other 'denied' knowledges enter upon the dominant discourse and estrange the basis of its authority" (1985a, 156). In other words, the colonized produces a series of destabilizing messages which reflect his metonymic use of the dominant discursive and cultural imperatives. At the same time, the performance of the simulacrum does not completely conceal the features of the colonized and therefore causes deep paranoia in the dominating subject. This kind of mimicry, claims Robert Young, "implies an even greater loss of control for the colonizer, of inevitable processes of counter-domination produced by a miming of the very operation of domination, with the result that the identity of colonizer and colonized becomes curiously elided" (1995, 148). In this sense, paranoia seems a logical consequence of colonialism, even more profound than ambivalence, for it implies dual identifications in both the colonizer and the colonized (ibid., 161). For Bhabha, mimicry becomes an agent without any particular subject; an agency that resembles an other without being completely other in the eyes of the colonizer (ibid., 148).

The methods and categories of Lacanian psychoanalysis have been used in postcolonial studies to describe those subjective fissures which emerge from the dominating episteme of universal Reason.[33] When postcolonial theorists have studied the effects of British colonization on the native Indian population, their use of concepts such as mimicry and hybridism has revealed an entire universe of meaning that more traditional, socioeconomic approaches had failed to uncover.[34] Much more could be said, in this regard, about the works of Bhabha on colonial ambivalence, of Albert Memmi (1967 [1957]) on the notion of basic dualism, of Ashis Nandy (1983) on internal enmities, and of the contributions of subaltern studies to the historiography of South Asia.[35]

And yet, despite the implications of such an important conceptual body, a classic postcolonial approach cannot fully render a satisfying analysis of the core regions of pre-Enlightened Spanish America. In the first place, the particular nature of sixteenth- and seventeenth-century relations of power and domination were driven by an official imperative to bring what was believed to be the irrefutable religious Truth to the dominated subjects, in this case, the Amerindians.[36] The discursive and juridical proof of the existence of this imperative by no means negates or overlooks the practical consequences of systematic, imperial, economic domination or the individual actions of many opportunistic Spaniards seeking sudden wealth. However, in order to remain faithful to the context, any analysis of "colonial" Spanish American discourse must incorporate the transcendental motives behind some elements of the dominating culture, including the neoscholastic preoccupation with Natural Law, that is, with such things as the "common good" and the "external glory of God." This concern was widespread among the many religious orders of the period and stemmed not only from sixteenth-century neoscholasticism but also from medieval texts (the Franciscans were avid readers of John Duns Scotus) equating Natural and Divine Law (see Mazzotti 1998). Sixteenth-century Spanish religious beliefs, and in particular the demonization of indigenous beliefs and religious practices, must also be taken seriously in terms of understanding the way the native peoples and cultures were treated in the decades following the conquest. The Spaniards were clearly not cultural relativists and had no understanding of the internal logic of Amerindian rituals and beliefs. The specific characteristics of the conquering Spanish *mentalité* certainly took a heavy toll on the very rich heritage of indigenous cultural production.[37]

A second shortcoming of postcolonial theory in terms of its capacity to understand Spanish American Creoles is that the concepts of mimicry, simulacrum, and hybridity are not entirely appropriate to the object of study. After all, the Creole was not exactly the other who would transform himself in the eyes of metropolitan authorities, nor was his hybridism the same as that of the oscillating mestizo positioned between two cultures. Furthermore, although Creoles did conceive of themselves as natives of the dominated lands, they were certainly not as dominated as the native indigenous peoples; indeed, they were also very much a part of the imperial power structure. How, then, can this complex and paradoxical subjectivity best be defined?

Perhaps the postcolonial concept that makes the most sense from a New World perspective is Bhabha's notion of ambivalence. In the context of sixteenth- and seventeenth-century Spanish America, ambivalence does seem to characterize the simultaneous loyalties and disavowals of an ontologically unstable Creole subject, one who moves between a constant sense of inferiority within the system of political representation and equally present self-proclamations about Creole cultural and biological superiority over the Spaniards.[38] However, the concept of ambivalence is only useful for our purposes if we pay attention to what Mowitt (1988) called the "general preconditions"; otherwise, what results may be an oversimplified translation of postcolonial theory rather than a complex portrayal of colonial Spanish American societies.[39] In this sense, it is important to keep in mind that the dimensions of Creole ambivalence were not always static and predictable, but alternated at different times between loyalty and rejection. If not carefully analyzed within its own specific context, this constant but irregular posturing could result in a Creole subjectivity metaphorically diagnosed as schizophrenic. To refine the general concept of ambivalence, then, it might be useful to link the analysis of Creole discourses with an idea like "differential imitation," as developed by Claude-Gilbert Dubois (1979, 12) in his analysis of Mannerist art. Within a colonial Spanish American context, the concept of differential imitation could encompass both the mimetic features of Creole cultural manifestations and the specific character given to Spanish and European models when resignified in the New World. This multiple positionality gives the protohegemonic Creole groups a dual and paradoxical status of belonging and estrangement. When analyzing Creole cultural production, it is useful to keep Spivak's words in mind: "It is hard to plot the lines by which a people (metonymically that group within it that is self-consciously the custodian of culture) construct the explanations that establish its so-called cultural identity" (1999, 8).

Over the more than twenty years since postcolonial theory first appeared, it has received numerous critiques from scholars both inside and outside the English-speaking world.[40] Despite these critiques, it is still possible to appropriate certain elements of postcolonial theory while subverting others, including the meaning of the prefix *post* which, in its original sense, seems not to correspond to the continued (neo)colonial realities of contemporary Spanish America. Let us recall Lyotard's argument here about the inherent opposition implied by the prefix coming before any context of domination. For Lyotard, the prefix suggests that "it is possible and necessary to break with tradition and institute absolutely new ways of living and thinking" (1992, 90). In a very broad sense, and to echo Gianni Vattimo in *The End of Modernity* (1991), the prefix *post* does not always imply a temporal sequence, but simply an oppositional practice (see also Klor de Alva 1995, 245). With this alternative meaning, the prefix *post* would make sense even for communities that continue to live in foreign-dominated states, or in the case of Spanish America, where, as rigorous historical examination has shown, "colonies" as such really did not exist in the pre-Enlightenment era of the Habsburgs. The alternative interpretation of the prefix *post* would indicate a desire among the dominated subjects to alter or overcome "colonial" domination, and it would also recognize that this desire generates a variety of subjective positions and agencies.

Creole agencies inevitably had to involve negotiations with the Amerindian other, as Creoles positioned themselves to achieve symbolic authority in the New World. This was the case throughout the Habsburg era, but with the coming of Spanish absolutism and the Bourbon Reforms in the eighteenth century, followed by the founding of new nation-states in the nineteenth century, such negotiations would become more frequent and more complex. Creole writings increasingly borrowed from, manipulated, and appropriated the long tradition of indigenous oral and written sources in order to reaffirm their privileged status within Spanish American societies. Bhabha implicitly recognized the nature of such a process when he stated that "the epistemological 'limits' of those ethnocentric ideas [of post-Enlightenment rationalism] are also the enunciative boundaries of a range of other dissonant, even dissident histories and voices" (1994a, 4–5).[41]

It is both telling and unfortunate that the field of colonial Spanish American literary studies is very seldom incorporated into the postcolonial debate and has benefited little from the influential presence that postcolonial theory has established within North Atlantic academia. A quote from Leela Gandhi will help to illustrate my point; the statement by this outspoken critic came as she was chastising certain postcolonial theorists for domesticating Third World systems of knowledge, that is, for altering epistemic categories central to post- or neocolonial cultures in order to accommodate those categories within the more widely accepted and canonical Western episteme. "Rarely does [postcolonial theory]," observed Gandhi, "engage with the theoretical self-sufficiency of African, Indian, Korean, or Chinese knowledge systems" (1998, x). Gandhi was no doubt correct in her observation. However, what is most obvious from her statement is that Spanish American and Latin American knowledge systems and cultural productions are completely absent from such (English-speaking) criticisms of (English-speaking) postcolonial theory.

CONCLUSIONS

It seems important in closing to once again emphasize that the particular historical conditions of Habsburg rule in the New World created forms of social and personal relations that cannot be simply equated with those created under other imperial systems. At the same time, however, creative borrowing from postcolonial theory of such conceptual tools as "camouflage," "hybridism," and "mimicry" can be most fruitful in terms of furthering our analysis of this complex and peculiar period of Spanish American history. This is especially the case in studying Creole subjectivities which oscillate so constantly between the Hispanic and the locally based extremes of identity construction. It is precisely this oscillation which explains why Creole agencies appear so differently in different contexts. There is, for example, a major difference between the way the Mexican Creoles embraced the old Mesoamerican indigenous cultures (as in Sigüenza's 1680 *Teatro de virtudes políticas*) and the adversarial view of the Incas held by seventeenth-century Creoles in Lima (as observed by Phelan 1960; Pagden 1990, 92, and chap. 5; and Brading 1991, 13). There were also significant differences between aristocratic Creoles and lower-class Creoles in terms of their respective relationships to the Spanish Crown. Despite such differences, but also because of them, the "colonial" relationship with the metropolis was almost always dual in nature. And whether we understand Habsburg Spanish America as colonial or as viceregal, the fact remains that Creole subjectivities within that context often adopted expressions and political strategies that reinforced their boundaries with other "nations" (in the ethnic sense of the word), and clearly declared their unquestioned superiority vis-à-vis the Spaniards. An understanding of this process certainly helps to explain the Creoles' reaction to what John Lynch (1973) has called Spain's "second conquest," that is, those Bourbon Reforms which sought to undermine Creole authority in the New World. Richard Konetzke (1950) actually argues that the ultimate Bourbon goal of uniting Spaniards and Creoles into a single "cuerpo de Nación" (national body), was doomed to fail because a collective identity and an ontological difference had already emerged among the Creoles of the New World, an identity and a difference that could not simply be erased by imperial decree.[42]

Given the immense discursive variety, both within and beyond Creole groups, it is certainly difficult to define monolithic subjectivities and divide these into bipolar categories, such as colonized and colonizer. In regard, specifically, to the earliest groups of elite Mexican and Peruvian Creoles, these began to develop their own forms of consciousness about their differences with, and their subjection to, the Spanish Crown on reaching adulthood (around the 1560s) and finding themselves in danger of being completely disinherited by that same Crown. In Creole claims of inheritance, there were constant references to the principle of the *pactum subjectionis* between the king and his vassals, that is, the mutual agreement that popular sovereignty would revert to the king as long as he was the caretaker of the common good. This principle is evident in such pre-independence texts as Juan Pablo Viscardo y Guzmán's "Letter to the American Spaniards" (1799) and the writings by Fray Servando Teresa de Mier, as noted by Góngora and others (see especially Lavallé 2000; Stoetzer 1979, chap. 5; and Pagden 1990, 18).

In addition to exploring Creole positioning vis-à-vis the Spanish Crown, any examination of Creole agencies must necessarily also deal with the dialectics between the white Creoles and the immense majority of the New World populations who more clearly were of indigenous and African descent. Special attention would also need to be paid to certain privileged cases, such as the works of Inca Garcilaso de la Vega (the emblematic mestizo) and Guamán Poma de Ayala (of strictly indigenous descent). Analyses should also reach beyond the core regions of Mexico and Peru in order to examine contrasting terms of identity construction which might emerge from non-nuclear cities and territories where Creole presence was much less significant and therefore posed little or no obstacle to Spanish officials' rule over the indigenous populations. And, of course, the complexities of Brazil and the Caribbean should be carefully studied, so that the particular histories of these areas are not simply wrapped up in the same conceptual package as the rest of Spanish America.

What remains absolutely clear is that Creole discourses and agencies can only be understood within their own, internal, historical coordinates. The (post)colonial debate is pertinent to the study of colonial Spanish America only in so far as it helps to understand the formation of local subjectivities, albeit through the use of interdisciplinary tools and conceptual categories invented to study postcolonial cases from the Old World. At the same time, however, given all the attention garnered by theoretical advances within North Atlantic academia, there is the risk that the rich, internal, tradition of interdisciplinary work by Latin American scholars will go unnoticed and underappreciated. Preventing this from happening is certainly one of the merits of the present volume.

NOTES

Unless otherwise indicated, English translations are my own.

1 A brief survey of innovative readings on canonical authors would include Merrim 1999, Martínez-San Miguel 1999, Ross 2000, Jerry Williams 2001, Falla 1999 (albeit from a polemical perspective which recovers the national in Peralta), and Moraña 1998a (especially chap. 2). Such readings are an indirect consequence of the paradigm shift operating within U.S. academia since the late 1980s, specifically in regard to indigenous and mestizo authors such as Waman Puma, Alvarado Tezozomoc, Titu Cusi Yupanqui, and Joan de Santacruz Pachacuti. For a basic understanding of this paradigm shift, see Adorno 1986, 1988a; Mignolo 1995 (afterword); Lienhard 1989, 1992; Chang-Rodríguez 1988, 1991; and López-Baralt 1988.

2 See the important works by Lavallé on Peruvian Creoles, especially those within religious orders (1978, 1993, 2000); and in regards to Mexican Creoles, see Alberro 2000, Liss 1986 [1975], Lafaye 1976 [1974], Brading 1991, and Pagden 1990 (chap. 4).

3 On the Bourbon era and the years leading up to the wars of independence, see Kinsbruner 1994 (chap. 2), Lynch 1973, Stoetzer 1979, and Konetzke 1950, among others. John Lynch even suggests that it is possible to speak of a "Creole state" between 1650 and 1750, the period when Creoles were able to assume

some important roles in the viceregal economy and administration. The subsequent Bourbon Reforms were actually aimed in large part at dismantling these privileges (Lynch 1996, 40). For their part, Creoles rested their alleged rights to greater participation in viceregal decisions on the Spanish juridical tradition. Richard Konetzke presents several precedents which Creoles invoked from the *legislación Indiana*, or the set of laws governing the Indies, in order to support their claims in the wake of the high tariffs and new state-run monopolies imposed by the Bourbon reforms after 1760. One such frequently invoked precedent was "una pragmática de Enrique III en las Cortes de Madrid del año 1396, en la cual con las más rigurosas cláusulas se prohíbe a los extranjeros que puedan obtener beneficios algunos en Castilla" [a decree by Henry III to the Spanish Parliament in 1396, in which foreigners were strictly prohibited from enjoying the benefits of public office in Castile] (Konetzke 1950, 52).

4   See, for example, the response to Levene in Kossok and Markov 1961 (I thank Teodoro Hampe for the reference). In a later work, Kossok would insist on Levene's categorization of the Spanish American revolutions as a bourgeois reaction to the colonial feudalism of Spanish dominion in the New World (1968, 13).

5   In terms of the nineteenth century, one important argument raised by critics is that the so-called national states were essentially led by Creole elites rather than native, indigenous peoples. As such, they argue, Western (i.e., neocolonial) domination remains. See for example, Klor de Alva 1992a and its expanded version, Klor de Alva 1995. For a conservative view of the entire period of Spanish presence in Peru as a "kingdom," see Altuve-Febres 1996.

6   Critics have argued that such "submissiveness" within U.S. Latin Americanism is common, despite the fact that the leading postcolonial theorists hail from the Middle East and India and have now been consecrated within U.S. and British academia, thereby exercising discursive authority from the core and not from the periphery. Rojo 1997, for example, suggests the limitations implicit within the privileged place of enunciation of this sector of postcolonial theorists and their Latin American followers within U.S. academia.

7   This same meaning is preserved in the 1681 *Recopilación de Leyes de Indias*, which recorded the 6,377 laws of the Indies decreed during the sixteenth and seventeenth centuries. One of the very few laws which explicitly mentions the word *colonia* states that "cuando se sacare colonia de alguna ciudad" [when a colony is removed from a city], the purpose would be "hacer nueva población" [to create a new settlement] for people with no land (law 18, title 7, bk. 4). This important legislative history registers no complete identification between the word *colony* or *colonies* and the overall system of Spanish domination in the New World. Moreover, the etymology of *colony*, from the Latin *colonus* (farmer), implies a specific interest in land, not in the native peoples who inhabit that land.

8   This work by El Inca Garcilaso is an edifying history of Hernando de Soto's expedition (1537–42) to the region then known as La Florida, which included not only present-day Florida, but all of the southeastern and south-central regions of the United States (i.e., Georgia, the Carolinas, Alabama, Tennessee, Mississippi, Louisiana, and Texas).

9   Both Pagden 1995 (6, 128) and Klor de Alva 1995 point out the contrast with the British experience in North America. Although the Spanish and Portuguese conquests of the New World were previous to, and more extensive than, the early British settlements, all three branches of European expansion belonged to the first wave of imperialism. This would be followed in the eighteenth century by a second, much more commercial expansion. Only then did the term *colony* begin to be used with any frequency in Spanish America.

10   In 1719 the northern part of the Viceroyalty of Peru was separated to create the new Viceroyalty of Nueva Granada; in 1776 the southern section was separated to form the Viceroyalty of Río de la Plata.

11   O. Carlos Stoetzer clarified years ago the nature of Spanish dominion in the New World, stating that "the incorporation of the Indies into the Crown of Castile meant that they became provinces, not colonies, and represented integral parts of the monarchy" (1979, 1). Anthony Pagden defines the political status of the Spanish possessions in the New World as follows: "The Spanish-American dominions were not colonies—that term is never used to describe any of the Habsburg possessions—but discrete parts of the crown of Castile. As early as the 1560s they had come to be seen by their inhabitants as quasi-autonomous kingdoms, part of what came to be called 'Greater Spain,' *Magnae Hispaniae*, no different, whatever the realities of their legal status, from Aragon, Naples, or the Netherlands" (1990, 91; see also Pagden 1987, 63, 64).

12   This is especially so for South Africa and India. For a summary of the periods and modalities of British Imperialism, see Simon C. Smith 1998, esp. chaps. 1–3; the British Library of Information 193[9]; and Marshall 1996, 318–37. The compilation by Roger Owen and Bob Sutcliffe (1975 [1972]) also contains a general and useful review of colonialism in relation to imperialism.

13   The arbitristas denounced social problems and offered practical solutions, addressing the king as an authority who should act as the universal physician of his kingdoms in order to "cure" them. For Spanish examples of arbitrista texts during the Spanish seventeenth century, see Maravall 1990, 55–127.

14   As alluded to earlier, 1542 is just a formal date for a phenomenon that had already been prefigured for many years. Esteban Mira-Caballos (1997, 105) has studied the process whereby the governor of La Española, Nicolás de Ovando, began to favor Crown officials over former conquerors in granting new repartimientos and encomiendas. Allegedly, Ovando was following the Crown's instructions to protect Indians, although he was evidently also avoiding paying officials' salaries while securing their loyalty to his own administration. In a 1514 letter from La Española the former conquerors bemoaned their impoverished situation: "Nosotros fuimos los que derramamos nuestra propia sangre e hobimos infinitas enfermedades a los principios desta conquista, e ahora nos estamos allí con nuestras mujeres e hijos, porque nos habéis destruido quitándonos los indios, e dándolos a los que ahora nuevamente vienen a la mesa que nosotros teníamos puesta" [We were the ones who shed our own blood and suffered infinite illnesses at the beginning of this conquest, and now we are in this situation with our wives and children because you have destroyed us by

taking away our Indians and giving them to the newcomers to the table that we had set [for ourselves]] (Pacheco, Cárdenas, and Torres 1864–89, vol. 1, 311; I thank Paul Firbas for this reference). Thus, the desserts of the New World banquet were fought over intensely from early on, causing tensions which resulted in the major (but not the final) episode of the 1542 New Laws.

15   This process, it should be noted, was a gradual one, with both forward and backward movements. In terms of the New Laws specifically, the Law of Malinas in 1545 was an important modification which partially reestablished the encomiendas, extending them for a "second life" (i.e., they could be inherited by the eldest son of an encomendero). However, the Malinas Laws continued to prohibit indigenous personal service and stressed that tribute payments be regularized and paid only in metal (not in kind). In 1629, there were some cases of encomiendas being extended for a "third life," and in 1704, a few were even extended to a "fourth life." The final abolition of the encomienda institution came in 1718, by which time the encomiendas had lost economic importance (Ots Capdequí 1993, 27). For more details about the Crown's concessions to some Creole descendants of the conquerors, see Konetzke 1950.

16   Pagden (1987, 56) notes that by 1604, there were only 733 noble Creoles in Mexico. According to a study by Pilar Latasa (1999), there were at least 500 noble Creoles in Peru in 1609 (see n. 18 below).

17   Generalized discontent among Creoles was manifested in more than just gossip, bad-mouthing, and official complaints, both written and oral. Sometimes it resulted in a conspiracy like the one described by Juan Suárez de Peralta in the second part of his *Tratado del descubrimiento de las Indias* (1589) (see Ross 2000). Other times, discontent turned directly into open, but aborted rebellions, in which alliances between Creoles and mestizos took place (see López Martínez 1971, chap. 1 for cases from Cuzco in the 1560s; see also Lavallé 1984, 1992 [esp. chaps. 6 and 7], in relation to the 1592–93 Quito rebellion against the *alcabalas*, or sales taxes).

18   Latasa Vassallo (1999) has examined documentation from the period and quotes a relevant letter by the Viceroy Marqués de Montesclaros to Philip III, dated 22 February 1609 from Lima. The viceroy complains of the more than 500 files with requests from the *beneméritos*, or Creole "patricians," who were descendants of the conquerors and "first settlers" of Peru. The documentation was so abundant that " 'aun quitando las horas del descanso común' no había conseguido hojear más de 200" [even taking hours away from [my] leisure time, I had only managed to read through some 200] (Latasa Vassallo 1999, 2).

19   Konetzke 1950 cites several examples of royal legislative decrees limiting the participation of Creoles in the clergy, the administration, and the army. Such limitations were apparently deemed excessive by aspiring Creoles.

20   Margarita Suárez (2001) has studied the economic realities of the Peruvian viceroyalty during the 1600s and details many of the political and financial transactions that situated Creole merchants in a privileged position. On the grandeur of Lima, the many writings by Buenaventura de Salinas, Antonio de la Calancha, Bernabé Cobo, Juan Meléndez, and others include exaggerated de-

scriptions of the picturesque qualities of the city. In one noteworthy example Salinas denies that Lima is a mere appendix of European culture and power, insisting instead that the city is the very center of the civilized world: "Reconozca [mi eſtilo] en este nuevo mundo la Roma ſanta en los Templos, Ornamentos, y divino Culto de Lima; la Genoua ſoberuia en el Garvo, y brio de los que en ella nacen; Florencia hermoſa, por la apacibilidad de los Temples; Milan populoſa, por el concurſo de tantas gentes como acuden de todas partes; Venecia rica, por las riquezas que produce para Eſpaña, y prodigamente las reparte a todas, quedandoſe tan rica como ſiempre; Bolonia pingue por la abundancia de ſuſtento; y Salamanca por ſu florida Vniuerſidad, y Colegios; pues quien nace en ella no tiene que embidiar meritos, pues ſus padres, y abuelos ſe los dexaron" [Let [my style] recognize Holy Rome in the Churches, Statues and divine Devotion of Lima; proud Genoa in the elegance and bravery of those who are born to her; beautiful Florence in the tranquility of her valleys; populous Milan in the great numbers of people who arrive here from all over the world; rich Venice in the wealth [Lima] produces for Spain and which she generously shares with all the other provinces without ever losing her own richness; plentiful Bologna in the abundance of her foods; and Salamanca in her flourishing University and colleges. He who is born in Lima has no cause for envy, for his parents and grandparents have left him everything] (1951 [1630], vol. 1, unnumbered folio). Meléndez even compares Lima to Jerusalem, claiming that both were designed by God: "Y pues ſe parecen [Jerusalén y Lima] en la forma, bien puede preſumirſe piadoſamente, que la diſeñò Dios, para que la fundaſſen los Eſpañoles, por caueza de las nueuas tierras, y nueuos Cielos, que ſe deſcubrieron, y conquiſtaron. Es pues la planta de la Ciudad de Lima perfectiſſima" [And since Jerusalem and Lima are similar in character, it can be piously presumed that God designed Lima in such a way so that the Spaniards could make her the ruler of the new lands and new skies that they discovered and conquered. Therefore, the design of the City of Lima is most perfect] (1681, vol. 2, f. 155).

21   Various features of American Spanish were accentuated by the common Caribbean experience of the *baqueanos* (Spaniards of long residence in the New World) and were later spread to the rest of the Spanish and Creole inhabitants of the viceroyalties. Notable among these were the multiple lexical borrowings from native languages, the *seseo* (a preference for the "s" sound, instead of the traditional Spanish "z") and *yeísmo* (a preference for the "y" rather than the "ll")—all features which persist in contemporary Latin American Spanish (see Rivarola 1990, 47–56, and chap. 3 on lexical borrowings; for more information on the linguistic variables in American Spanish, see Lope Blanch 1968, Fontanella de Weinberg 1993, Rosario 1970).

22   In the same chapter Cárdenas simulates an informal conversation between a lower-class Creole and a peninsular Spaniard, but first notes, "Oyremos al Eſpañol nacido en las Indias, hablar tan pulido[,] corteſano y curioso, y con tantos preambulos[,] delicadeza, y eſtilo retorico, no enſeñado ni artificial, ſino natural, que parece ha ſido criado toda ſu vida en Corte, y en compañia muy hablada y diſcreta, al contrario veran al chapeton, como no ſe haya criado entre

gente ciudadana, que no ay palo con corteza que mas bronco y torpe sea" [We will hear the Spaniard born in the Indies talking in a very polished, courteous and distinct manner, with so many preambles and in such precise rhetorical style—in a manner not learned or artificial, but natural—that it seems he must have spent his whole life in the Court, surrounded by very well-spoken and discreet company; while on the contrary you will observe the chapetón [Spaniard], who has not been raised among polite people, so that even a log with much bark is rougher and more awkward [to hear]] (1945 [1591], ff. 176v–177r).

23   "Si el Peru es la tierra en que mas igualdad tienen los dias, mas tenplança los tienpos, mas benignidad los ayres i las aguas, el ſuelo fertil, i el cielo amigable; luego criarà las coſas mas ermoſas, i las gentes mas benignas i afables, que Aſia i Europa" [If Peru is the land where the days are most similar, the weather most temperate, the air and waters most benign, the soil fertile, and the sky friendly; then it will raise the most beautiful things, and its peoples will be more benign and kind than those of Asia and Europe] (Calancha 1638, f. 68). See also Cañizares Esguerra 1999 for an examination of the so-called patriotic astrology in Calancha and other Creole writers.

24   Although archival documentation makes it difficult to establish a clear numerical separation between Spaniards and Creoles (since both groups belonged to the república de españoles), the proportion of whites as opposed to other racial and ethnic groups can be approximated with some accuracy. In the Viceroyalty of Mexico, whites made up about 0.5 percent of the total population in 1570, and 10 percent by the mid-seventeenth century (Alberro 1992, 155). In the Viceroyalty of Peru in the mid-seventeenth century, there were only some 70,000 whites in a total population of 1.6 million, or not even 5 percent (Rosenblat 1954, vol. 1, 59).

25   I am obviously using the concept of nation here in its archaic sense. After all, Pagden (1987, 91) and others have utilized the term "Creole nation" to refer to that community of Creoles formed through recognition of the same regional origin, dynastic aspiration and through common language and interests in order to create boundaries against other groups.

26   Anne McClintock's distinction (1994, 295) between a "deep settler colonization" (Algeria, Kenya, Zimbabwe, Vietnam) and a "break-away settler colonization" (United States, South Africa, Australia, Canada, New Zealand) seems overly schematic for the Spanish American case. Walter D. Mignolo (1997, 54) argues that one must differentiate between cases of "deep settler colonization" occurring before 1945 and those occurring after. Among the former, Mignolo includes the case of Peru, which McClintock did not take into consideration.

27   See McClintock 1994 for another critique of the term postcolonial.

28   Although a full discussion of the complex array of ideas and forms of epistemic renewal that poststructuralist thinkers have introduced is beyond the scope of this essay, it is important to acknowledge the relationship between the leading poststructuralists (Foucault, Lacan, Derrida, Barthes, and Baudrillard) and postmodern thinkers like Kristeva, Lyotard, and Vattimo. The latter group rounds out the European set of intellectuals who have examined the epistemological crisis of the Western world within Western contexts (see Kearney 1991, 172).

Their works have contributed in myriad ways to the development of both Latin American "colonial" studies and African-Asian postcolonial theories.

29 In this volume some essays (such as Brotherston's and Rabasa's) illustrate this effort to make textual and nontextual (*other*) representations—many of them of indigenous origin—visible in academic debates. They point to the significance of alternative epistemologies and to the need to overcome the limitations of Eurocentric critical and theoretical paradigms as well as the risks of cultural translation.

30 For a detailed summary of the concept of transculturation, see Spitta 1995, chap. 1; for a comparison between Rama's and Cornejo Polar's proposals, see Bueno 1996 and Schmidt 1996. A useful comparison between transculturation, heterogeneity, and hybridity in the Spanish American context is in Armas Wilson 2000, 78–82.

31 Although this essay does not detail the origins of postcolonial theory, there are several introductions and edited works which do. Among the inevitable references are the edited works by Ian Adam and Helen Tiffin (1990); Bill Ashcroft, Gareth Griffiths, and Helen Tiffin (1989); Peter Hulme (1994); and Patrick Williams and Laura Chrisman (1994). Also mandatory are the critical introductions by Leela Gandhi (1998) and Bart Moore-Gilbert (1997).

32 For Fernando Coronil, who is concerned about the shift from Eurocentrism to globalcentrism, critical responses to colonialism from "different locations take different but complementary forms. While from an Asian perspective it has become necessary to 'provincialize' European thought . . . , from a Latin American perspective it has become indispensable to globalize the periphery" (see Coronil in this volume).

33 Lacan's distinction (1977b) between a Symbolic Order that configures reality but that cannot necessarily apprehend the Real suggests the possibility of interpreting the colonial relationship as being based on unstable images of the Other.

34 For a recent discussion on hybridism and "its discontents" in colonial Spanish American art, see Dean and Leibsohn 2003.

35 Works by Ranajit Guha, Partha Chatterjee, and other Indian historians have generated important debates in other areas of regional study, as is evident in the entries in the present bibliography, the edited volumes *A Subaltern Studies Reader, 1986–1995* (Guha 1982–89) and *Selected Subaltern Studies* (Guha and Spivak 1988), and Spivak's well-known article "Can the Subaltern Speak?" (1994 [1985]). On the "native informant" in Western philosophy, literature, history and culture, see Spivak 1999. On the role of subaltern studies within Latin Americanist (but not necessarily Latin American) debates, see the "Founding Statement" of the Latin American Subaltern Studies Group (LASEG) (1994), the response by Florencia Mallon (1994), and the counterresponse by José Rabasa and Javier Sanjinés (1994). Unfortunately, the LASEG has disappeared in recent years. A compilation that includes works by members of LASEG and other scholars is *Teorías sin disciplina* (Castro-Gómez and Mendieta 1998).

36 The political and philosophical tendencies within the religious orders in Peru often clashed with the initiatives of the governors and the military, which were

clearly geared more toward increasing the Royal Patronage or *patronato real*. The Crown itself was responsible for the division, since it had stipulated that priests be present during the first stages of conquest in order to enforce the Crown's evangelizing policy. The goal was to maintain a relative equilibrium between the political and ecclesiastical powers (Mazzotti 1998, 79). Antonino Tibesar's work confirms as much, pointing out that this equilibrium would be broken under Viceroy Toledo's administration between 1569 and 1581 (1991 [1953], 76 n. 3). The process of evangelization would continue extensively throughout the entire period of Spanish domination.

37   Most published descriptions of Amerindian religious systems coincided in their satanic characterization of indigenous beliefs. This is recurrent in Pedro de Cieza de León, José de Acosta, and many others, including the earliest descriptions of the Aztecs by Cortés in his *Letters*. More sympathetic approaches, like Bartolomé de las Casas's *Apologética historia sumaria*, Bernardino de Sahagún's *Historia del México antiguo*, and Cristóbal de Molina's *Ritos y fábulas de los incas*, remained unpublished until the nineteenth century because of a 1556 royal prohibition on all writings that detailed "idolatrous" religious practices.

38   Two early manifestations of Creole resentment and indignation can be found in Francisco de Terrazas's *Nuevo Mundo y conquista* (ca. 1580) and Antonio de Saavedra's *El peregrino indiano* (1599). Both of these Mexican Creole poets, in expressing general dismay over the demise of the encomienda system as signaled by the New Laws, articulate positions of anger and frustration vis-à-vis what they perceived as the historical displacement of Creoles by the Spanish Crown (Mazzotti 2000).

39   Bhabha himself recognizes the importance of local contexts when he insists that his own work emerges from a particular rhetoric and context and that the concrete experience of colonial history must serve as the basis for any subsequent reflection, in which "private and public, past and present, the psyche and the social develop an interstitial intimacy" (1994a, 13).

40   In the case of the former, see Ahmad 1992a, Robert Young 1995, and McClintock 1994; for the latter, see the Rojo 1997, esp. 12–17.

41   For further discussion on the importance of the postcolonial critic's self-positioning vis-à-vis the validity of his or her own perspective, see Mignolo 1997.

42   Lynch notes that by 1800, there were some 2.7 million whites in the Spanish New World possessions, making up 20 percent of the total population. However, only 30,000 of these whites were peninsular Spaniards, little more than 1 percent of the entire population of the república de españoles (Lynch 1996, 39–40).

PART II

REWRITING COLONIAL DIFFERENCE

The authors in this section focus on the narratives that elaborate on Latin American colonial history from colonial times to the present. The first essay, by Russell Hamilton, discusses the applicability of postcolonial theory to Brazil vis-à-vis the contributions made by Brazilian scholars such as Darcy Ribeiro, Manuel Querino, Ildásio Tavares, and others to the interpretation of the country's colonial condition. For Hamilton, postcolonialism is a "floating signifier." "Figuratively speaking," he writes, "the postmodernists might be seen as marching face first into the future while carrying modernism on their backs. On the other hand, the postcolonialists can be characterized as moving backwards into the future with their eyes fixed on the pre-colonial, or traditional, and especially colonial past." His reflection questions the applicability of postcolonial theory to the specific case of Brazil and analyzes key moments in the constant rewriting of Brazilian coloniality.

In her contribution, Sara Castro-Klaren deals with the colonial period, but her analysis spans up to the twentieth century, tracing the historic trajectory of Latin America's colonial condition and the critique it has generated over time. Her essay focuses on Andean writing, particularly historiography, beginning with its predisciplinary form, in the works of Guamán Poma de Ayala and Inca Garcilaso de la Vega, to contemporary manifestations, particularly José Carlos Mariátegui. Her intention is to explore both the "points of intersections and of divergence" between postcolonial theory and Andean thought. Following the concept of coloniality defined by Aníbal Quijano and recuperated by Walter Mignolo, Castro-Klaren sees in Mariátegui a precursor of postcolonial critics, particularly in his understanding of Peruvian history as one that "belongs outside the parameters of European historiography."

Elzbieta Sklodowska's essay is an "against the grain" reading of Antonio Benítez Rojo's "Heaven and Earth," which she examines "under the sign of 'undisciplined' Caribbean politics." The story provides an articulation between Cuban political reality and African-based spirituality, particularly through the influence of vodou and other elements of Haitian culture. Otherness, ambiguity, and collective memory are some of the levels Sklodowska connects in order to explore the blurring of antagonistic paradigms (rational/irrational, life/death, order/disorder) and the specificity of a region that requires attention to local differences, as well as to the effects of cultural processes of hybridization. Sklodowska disbelieves in the applicability of master discourses to the Caribbean region. *Caribbeanness* is, for her, the scenario in which society performs the fantasy of an unreachable homogeneity.

EUROPEAN TRANSPLANTS, AMERINDIAN IN-LAWS, AFRICAN SETTLERS, BRAZILIAN CREOLES: A UNIQUE COLONIAL AND POSTCOLONIAL CONDITION IN LATIN AMERICA

Russell G. Hamilton

Much of what applies to Brazil with respect to socioeconomic and political factors also holds true for most, if not all, of the former colonies of the so-called New World. Similarities notwithstanding, for a number of historical reasons Brazil also occupies a unique place in Latin America and the world beyond with respect to both its colonial and postcolonial condition.

THE LUSO-BRAZILIAN COLONIAL EMPIRE

As regards the most salient sociohistorical and cultural factors that have contributed to Brazil's unique colonial and postcolonial condition, I begin with a brief consideration of some recent publications. The first of these relevant works is Douglas L. Wheeler's *The Empire Time Forgot: Writing a History of the Portuguese Overseas Empire, 1808–1975*.[1] In his essay Wheeler elucidates several important events and conditions related to Portugal's early maritime explorations. Wheeler emphasizes, for example, the significance of the transfer, in 1808, of the Portuguese royal family to Brazil. He also focuses on the political and economic dependency inherent in Portugal's long-standing alliance with Great Britain, and he puts into perspective the historical factors that paved the way for the emergence of Creole elites in the Portuguese overseas empire, especially in Goa and the Cape Verde islands. The members of these Creole elites are mixed-race and culturally hybridized members of a relatively privileged community among the colonized.[2]

In calling for an update of Charles Boxer's *Race Relations in the Portuguese Colonial Empire* (1415–1825), which Wheeler characterizes as a "useful yet controversial work" (1998, 37), he elucidates how the ideology known as "luso-tropicalismo" propounded a process of biological, social, and cultural creolization that applies, in both real and imagined ways, to Brazil. As for the historical significance of the Lusitanian imperial experience as it was brought to bear in Africa and Asia, as well as in South America, Wheeler concludes with six explanations as to why the Portuguese Empire differed so markedly from its British equivalent. Of particular significance, with respect to Brazil, is the following explanation: "Far more than was the case with Creole elites in the British Empire, Creole elites in Portugal's empire played a larger political, social, and intellectual role in manning the empire as well as the Metropole" (ibid., 40).

In a similar vein, with respect to that which distinguishes the Portuguese Empire from the British Empire, is "Between Prospero and Caliban: Colonialism, Postcolonialism, and Inter-identity," an article by Boaventura de Sousa Santos (2002). As do Wheeler and other social scientists, Santos sees the historical relationship between Portugal and Great Britain as one based on the former's alliance with and, simultaneously, its political and economic dependency on the latter. As the title of his article indicates, Santos makes allegorical use of Prospero and Caliban, who are, of course, two of the main characters in Shakespeare's tragicomedy *The Tempest*. In Santos's article Prospero, the master and colonizer, is Great Britain, and Caliban, the slave and colonized, is Portugal.[3] Santos also characterizes Great Britain as a hegemonic center and Portugal as occupying a "semiperipheral position in the world system" (2002, 19).[4] He makes a particularly perceptive observation regarding Portugal's historically ambivalent position in the world-system as it relates to Brazil when he states: "This double ambivalence of representation affects both the identity of the colonizer and the identity of the colonized. It may well be that the excess of alterity I identified in the

Portuguese colonizer could also be identified in those he colonized. Particularly in Brazil, one could imagine, hypothetically, that the identity of the colonized was, at least in some periods, constructed on the basis of a double other, the other of the direct Portuguese colonizer and the other of the indirect English colonizer" (ibid., 19). This observation is especially relevant to salient aspects of Brazil's colonial and postcolonial condition as depicted by João Ubaldo Ribeiro in his monumental novel *Viva o povo brasileiro*. Santos goes on to affirm that "this doubleness became later the constitutive element of Brazil's myth of origins and possibilities for development. It inaugurated a rupture that is still topic for debate. It divides Brazilians between those that are crushed by the excess of past and those that are crushed by the excess of future" (ibid.). This brings to mind a popular saying which citizens of that South American nation often utter with self-deprecating humor: "Brazil is and always will be the country of the future."[5]

At this juncture, what must be emphasized with respect to Brazil's unique position in the Western Hemisphere is that it defies simple categorization as a breakaway colony. When in 1808 the then prince regent and soon-to-be monarch João VI fled to Rio de Janeiro because of the Napoleonic threat to the Iberian Peninsula, Brazil in effect became the metropole of the Portuguese colonial empire, or, more appropriately, the Luso-Brazilian Empire. This transference of the royal family set the stage for Brazil to acquire, in 1815, the status of kingdom, to peacefully gain its independence and become an empire in 1822, and finally, in 1889, to proclaim itself a republic.

HOW POSTCOLONIAL THEORY APPLIES TO BRAZIL

In the ongoing culture wars and debates in Euro-American academic circles the term *postcolonialism* has become something of a floating signifier (as confirmed by the plurality of positions represented in this volume). Depending in large measure on critical ideologies, postcolonial theory can be said to apply to the entire chronologically postcolonial world.[6] On the other hand, many proponents of postcolonial theory, whose origins date back to the late 1970s, maintain that this contemporary theory applies most appropriately to those nonbreakaway former colonies of Asia, the Middle East, and Africa, which gained their independence from European powers after World War II. Many would agree, however, that there are new nations that were white breakaway colonies, such as South Africa and Zimbabwe (formerly Southern Rhodesia), to which postcolonial theory does apply. In these nations, as in the other relatively new countries of Africa and Asia, the majority population and those who hold political power are for the most part members of the territories' formerly colonized indigenous groups.

For the last several years it would seem that most scholars who teach and do research on temporally postcolonial societies inevitably accept that post-colonial theory applies not only to most of Africa and parts of Asia and the Middle East, but also to Latin America as well as the Anglophone and Fran-cophone Caribbean. Along with the present volume, another indication of this acceptance on the part of scholars is *Postcolonial Perspectives on the Cultures of Latin America and Lusophone Africa* (2000). The introduction and eight essays, only one of which deals with Lusophone Africa, stand as ample proof of postcolonial theory's relevance to Latin America. These former colonies, whether breakaway or not (and most of them are), qualify with respect to the major criteria as denoted and connoted by the *post* in *postcolonialism*.

In his essay titled "Is the Post- in Postmodernism the Post- in Postcolo-nial?" Kwame Anthony Appiah analyzes convergences and divergences that contribute to an understanding of the prefix's denotative and connotative values. In considering a work of contemporary African sculpture, Appiah states that "if postmodernism is the project of transcending some species of modernism, which is to say some relatively self-conscious, self-privileging project of a privileged modernity, our *neotraditional* sculptor of *Man with a Bicycle* is presumably to be understood, by contrast, that is, traditional. (I am supposing, then, that being neotraditional is a way of being traditional; what work the *neo-* does is a matter for a later moment)" (1991, 343).[7] Upon reading Appiah's essay one concludes that the *post* of *postmodernism* and *postcolonial* can be seen as clearing new spaces. But with regard to postcolo-nialism it is not a matter of turning one's back on the colonial and the pre-colonial. Figuratively speaking, the postmodernists might be seen as march-ing face first into the future while carrying modernism on their backs. On the other hand, the postcolonialists can be characterized as moving back-wards into the future with their eyes fixed on the pre-colonial, or traditional, and especially colonial past.[8]

Semantically, the prefix *post* can denote both "after" and "since." Thus, *post-independence* can mean "after independence was gained" and/or "since independence was established."[9] At this juncture it would seem that at least most of those who employ *postcolonial* and *postcolonialism* in English dis-course agree that in temporal terms the hyphenated *post-colonial* refers to the termination of forced occupation and imposed rule by interlopers or an invading force. In the case of breakaway colonies, whereby the colonizers or their descendants rebelled against the metropole, temporal *postcoloniality* also holds true. It can also be argued that even in white breakaway colonies, such as the United States, Canada, and Australia, some measure of postcolonialism has existed since independence with respect to facing the future with at least occasional glances over the shoulder if not with the eyes fixed on the colonial past. In these white breakaways, racial minorities, whether members of the original Amerindian or aboriginal inhabitants, or the descendants of African slaves, may be more apt to dwell on the colonial past.

In the majority of the breakaway colonies of Latin America and the Antilles, the founders and ruling-class members are generally descendants of European settlers. On the other hand, the large numerical presence of persons of Amerindian and/or African descent makes these countries racially and ethnically more prone to postcolonialist assessments than the United States, Canada, or Australia.

To the extent that contemporary postcolonialism applies more appropriately to developing countries, Latin America certainly qualifies as a region of the so-called Third World. It seems legitimate to accept that there exist, however, degrees of "Third-Worldism." Such being the case, Brazil, along with several other countries of South America, is not what one might characterize, especially in terms of economic development, as "hard core" Third World. On the other hand, as dependency-theory economists have demonstrated, Brazil, along with other Latin American countries, has had to march, as it were, to the beat of First World drummers. And globalization, in its current usage, is in many ways a contemporary manifestation of that which dependency-theory economists and other social scientists put forth during the 1960s and 1970s.[10]

The sizeable gap between "haves" and "have nots" in a developing country has considerable significance with regard to Brazil's evolving national ethos. This ethos, along with the formulation of Brazilian ideologies for export, constitute the manner in which members of Brazil's ruling and middle classes and intelligentsia have constructed the country's unique multiracial and Creole social and cultural history.

NATIVIST IN-LAWISM AND ASSIMILATION

History books commonly identify those who carried out the West's overseas expansion as discoverers, explorers, and adventurers. Of course, those historians and others who depict these excursions as intrusions often see the discoverers, explorers, and adventurers as invaders, conquerors, and imperialists. Although Western overseas expansion was predicated in large measure on economic imperatives—for example, control of the spice trade, the quest for gold and other riches, and crop production—the backers of and participants in these expeditions often characterized them as primarily civilizing and Christianizing missions. For the European powers, such sacred missions served to ameliorate and even justify the forced servitude of indigenous peoples and the Atlantic slave trade.

Their documented nefarious impact notwithstanding, the "discovery" and ensuing foreign settlement of the so-called New World also have to be seen in a broad historical context with respect to colonies eventually becoming nation-states. Darcy Ribeiro is one of several Brazilian historians and anthropologists who have contributed significantly to an interpretation of their country's social, linguistic, and cultural evolvement. *O povo brasileiro: A formação e o sentido do Brasil* (The Brazilian people: The forming and meaning of Brazil), Ribeiro's major work, which since its publication in 1995 has gone through two editions and twenty printings. "Gestação étnica" (Ethnic gestation), the work's second chapter, consists of three sections. "Criatório de gente" (People-breeding farm), the first of these sections, includes a subsection titled "O cunhadismo," which Ribeiro explicates in the following passage: "A instituição social que possibilitou a formação do povo brasileiro foi o cunhadismo, velho uso indígena de incorporar estranhos à sua comunidade. Consistia em lhes dar uma moça índia como esposa. Assim que ele a assumisse, estabelecia, automaticamente, mil laços que o aparentavam com todos os membros do grupo" [The social institution that made possible the forming of the Brazilian people was *cunhadismo*, an old indigenous usage that refers to the custom of incorporating strangers into the community. It consisted of offering the stranger an Indian girl as his wife. Upon accepting this offer, the outsider automatically established a thousand ties that made him a relative of all of the members of the group] (1995, 81). *Cunhadismo* translates literally as "brother-in-lawism." In Brazil's Amazon region *caboclos*, individuals of mixed Indian and white parentage, traditionally have addressed each other as *cunhado*.[11] As a form of address, *cunhado*, along with being the Portuguese word for "brother-in-law," can also mean "friend," "companion," and "member of one's extended family."

Sexual exploitation of indigenous and, eventually, African females by the dominant colonizing males certainly has occurred in Brazil, as it has occurred in all territories where people have been subjugated by a group of intruders. Many Brazilian and not a few foreign social scientists have seized, however, on certain historical realities to explicate an apparent penchant among Portuguese seafarers and explorers for forming relationships with

Amerindian and African women and then recognizing their mixed-race off-spring as their legal heirs. One explanation for the proliferation of these interracial marriages or common-law relationships is that early Portuguese settlement of Brazil, unlike British colonization in the Western Hemisphere, was largely male. In this regard, Darcy Ribeiro identifies the presumably pre-colonial Amerindian institution of cunhadismo as a social practice that was acceptable to both the colonizers and the colonized. According to many present-day nativists and patriots, this purportedly mutually acceptable biological and social assimilation initiated the formation of the Brazilian people.

The chapter titled "O processo civilizatório" (The "civilizatory" process) delineates what Ribeiro sees as essential distinctions between British and Portuguese colonizers. In the subsection "O barroco e o gótico" (The baroque and the gothic), Ribeiro attests to a Lá-Cá (There-Here) dichotomy. "There" refers to the British colonies of North America. Ribeiro asserts, "Lá, o gótico altivo de frias gentes nórdicas, transladado em famílias inteiras" [There, the haughty gothic of cold Nordic peoples, transported as entire families] (1995, 69). According to Ribeiro's generalization of northern Europeans, "Para eles, o índio era um detalhe, sujando a paisagem que, para se europeizar, devia ser livrada deles" [As far as they were concerned, the Indians were a detail that besmirched the landscape, which, in order to be Europeanized, needed to be freed of them] (ibid.). Ribeiro makes an invidious comparison when he next characterizes the Spanish and Portuguese colonizers: "Cá, o barroco das gentes ibéricas, mestiçadas, que se mesclavam com os índios, não lhes reconhecendo direitos que não fosse o de se multiplicarem em mais braços, postos a seu serviço" [Here, the baroque of the Iberians, already an interbred people who then interbred with the Indians, although not acceding them any rights except that of multiplying as a labour force] (ibid.).[12]

Perhaps in keeping with a time-honored set of philosophical beliefs on the part of the Brazilian elite, Darcy Ribeiro's characterizations are imbued with a kind of nineteenth-century positivism, as professed by Auguste Comte. At the same time, Ribeiro's conceptualizations of the colonial past and his postcolonialist discourse are in themselves somewhat baroque. He indulges in sweeping ethnic characterizations and stereotypes. In spite of the occasional overstatements and baroque hyperbole of his discourse, Ribeiro does not overtly refute the subjugation and exploitation of the indigenous peoples and imported Africans that came about with the Iberian peoples' arrival in the New World. He does place considerable emphasis, however, on the assimilatory origins and nature of the Brazilian people.

With regard to the sui generis character of Brazil's colonial and postcolonial condition, any number of Brazilian intellectuals who have written on and/or spoken out about such social and economic issues as class disparities and racial discrimination, see assimilation, based on hybridity and creolization, as an essentially positive historical factor.

BRAZIL'S AFRICAN COLONIZERS

In *O povo brasileiro* Darcy Ribeiro devotes considerable attention to the role of the Amerindian, but he also makes reference to the contributions of Africans and their descendants to the formation of the Brazilian people. It was, however, Manuel Querino, reputedly the first black Brazilian historian, who, before anyone else, focused on the contributions of Africans. In 1918 Querino wrote the essay *O colono preto como fator da civilização brasileira* (The black colonist as a factor of Brazilian civilization).[13] In 1954, some thirty-one years after Querino's death, the piece was republished with the title *O africano como colonisador* (The African as colonizer).

What might immediately catch the reader's attention is Querino's reference to the African as "colonist." Indeed, the slave as "colonist," "colonizer," and even "settler" may seem oxymoronic.[14] On reading the six short chapters that make up Querino's essay, one does perceive, however, the thematic validity of *colono* and even the posthumous usage of *colonisador*. (E. Bradford Burns eschews the use of *colonist, colonizer,* and *settler* in the title of his translation of Querino's essay: *The African Contribution to Brazilian Civilization.*)

The theme and thesis of Querino's essay, as Burns's English title conveys, are indeed the nature and extent of Africans' and their descendants' contribution to the formation of Brazilian civilization. In measured tones and without resorting to the binary opposition of evil master and noble slave, Querino offers a historical interpretation, beginning in the sixteenth century, of the Portuguese and African presence in Brazil. He offers a brief but convincing analysis of those factors that led to the coercive transfer to the New World of large numbers of Africans. In fixing on the Africans' skills and abilities as agriculturalists, miners, and craftsmen, Querino prepares the reader for his use of *colono* to depict the slave. To shore up his thesis, in chapter 2, "Chegada do africano no Brasil: Suas habilitações" (The arrival of the African in Brazil: His qualifications), Querino quotes Manuel de Oliveira Lima, who, in his *Aspectos da literatura colonial brasileira* (Aspects of colonial Brazilian literature), makes the following assertion: "Foi sobre o negro, importado em escala prodigiosa, que o colono especialmente se apoiou para o arrotear dos vastos territórios conquistados no continente sul americano. Robusto, obediente, devotado ao serviço, o africano tornou-se um colaborador precioso do portuguez [sic] nos engenhos do norte, nas fazendas do sul e nas minas do interior" [It was on blacks, so prodigiously imported, that the colonist especially depended in order to cultivate the vast territories that had been conquered on the South American continent. Robust, obedient, devoted to service, the African became a precious collaborator of the Portuguese on the sugar plantations of the north, the ranches of the south, and the mines of the interior] (quoted in Querino 1954, 17). According to Querino's theme and thesis of black people's contribution to Brazilian civilization, because the African "collaborated" with the Portuguese, even as the member of a forced-labor contingent, the slave became, in effect, a colonist.

By portraying the African as collaborator and thus as colonist or settler, Querino by no means depicts the African as generally being submissively accepting of his or her status as a slave. In "Primeiras idéias de liberdade, o suicídio e a eliminação dos senhorios" (Emergences of ideas of freedom, suicide, and the elimination of the landlordships), the essay's third chapter, Querino documents those overt acts of resistance that stand as evidence of many captives' nonacceptance of their condition as chattel. In "Resistência coletiva, Palmares, levantes parciais" (Collective resistance, Palmares, partisan uprisings), the essay's fourth chapter, Querino waxes dramatic, comparing Brazilian slave uprisings with Spartacus's heroic role in leading an army of bondsmen to freedom in ancient Rome.

Querino's account of the Africans' resistance to bondage focuses on the *quilombos*, which were settlements of fugitive slaves in the sparsely inhabited Brazilian backlands.[15] Beginning in the seventeenth century, dozens of runaway-slave communities were established in the interior northeast, in the northern Amazon region and south and southwest in Minas Gerais, Goias, and Mato Grosso. The Quilombo dos Palmares, founded in 1630 in what is today the northeastern state of Alagoas, was undoubtedly the largest of these African settlements. Burns terms Palmares "a pseudo-African state with a population of approximately twenty thousand" (1993, 47). In 1694, after years of sustained resistance led by its legendary chief Zumbi, Palmares finally was conquered by forces of the Portuguese Crown.

Querino was one of the first, if not the first, Brazilian intellectual to focus on Palmares in particular and on the quilombos in general. These settlements and their inhabitants' attempts to regenerate sub-Saharan social and cultural institutions also lend validity to Querino's characterization of the African as colonizer. Because of Querino's and eventually other scholars' documentation and validation of these African colonies, in contemporary Brazil the quilombo has attained symbolic significance. This is the case among adherents of the Black Consciousness Movement and particularly among members of Quilombhoje (Quilomotoday), an Afro-Brazilian literary-cultural association founded in 1980. With regard to quilombo's symbolic force, Claudete Alves, a councilwoman for the city of São Paulo, made the following comment as part of a statement printed on the backcover flap of volume 25 of *Cadernos negros: Poemas afro-brasileiros* (Black notebooks: Afro-Brazilian poems): "Continuemos por aí, ocupando os espaços e fazendo deles os nossos grandes e felizes quilombos" [Let us continue this way, occupying the spaces and making of them our great and felicitous quilombos].

Returning to the matter of Querino's essayistic conceptualizations: despite the chapters devoted to collective resistance, uprising, and the establishment of quilombos, Querino's thesis, as it relates to Africans' contributions to Brazilian civilization, is predicated on social integration and cultural creolization rather than on colonialist separation or anti-Portuguese isolation. Apropos of integration and creolization, the title of the essay's final chapter reads, "O africano na família, seus descendentes notáveis" (The African in the family, his notable descendants). The reference is, of course, to the Brazilian family, and the descendants are those black and mixed-race individuals who prior to and after independence achieved recognition because of their contributions to the broader society. Querino goes on to cite more than twenty Afro-Brazilians who since colonial times had achieved fame and celebrity. Included among these figures is, of course, Machado de Assis, Brazil's premier nineteenth-century novelist. According to Brazilian racial categorizations, Machado de Assis was *mestiço* (mixed race) or, more precisely, a quadroon (i.e., one-quarter black and three-quarters white). For many Brazilians, mestiços have represented racial hybridity and thus the Amerindian and African contribution to the formation of a unique Creole civilization, one that qualifies as a "melding pot" if not Cape Verde's status of quintessential "melting pot."

A contemporary work with a title very similar to that of Querino's essay is Ildásio Tavares's *Nossos colonizadores africanos* (Our African colonizers) (1996). Subtitled *Presença e tradição negra na Bahia* (Black presence and tradition in Bahia), the volume consists of three parts and a total of twenty-three essays. As the subtitle indicates, all of the essays speak to the presence and traditions of Afro-Brazilians in the State of Bahia, and especially the city of Salvador, often referred to as the Black Rome of Brazil.

Because a majority of native Bahians are black and mulatto, Tavares's use of "our African colonizers" has a unique postcolonialist meaning when applied to Salvador. In effect, Tavares, who is himself phenotypically white, applies postcolonialism, both temporally and in theoretical terms, to the Africanization of Bahia. According to a thesis defended either explicitly or implicitly in nearly all of the essays in Tavares's volume, Bahia is more African than Africa. An essay that overtly defends this rather bold contention bears the admonitory title "Vamos baianizar a África" (Let's Bahianize Africa). Recalling the gothic-baroque dichotomy put forth by Darcy Ribeiro in *O povo brasileiro*, Tavares indulges in colorfully expressed, if somewhat "politically incorrect," invidious comparisons based on religious practices: "Quando vejo negros iorubanos da Nigéria, aqui, fanaticamente tentando nos converter como testemunhas de Jeová ou pregando um novo surto maometano na Bahia de Todos os Santos, fico feliz de poder, ao menos aqui, saber que um dia, na África, houve uma religião tão bela, tão encantadora e viva, na qual convivemos com os orixás, os voduns, os niquices, os encantados. Precisamos baianizar a África" [When I see black Nigerians of the Yoruba ethnic group here fanatically trying to convert us like Jehovah Witnesses or preaching a new surge of Mohammedanism in the city of the Bay of All Saints, I'm happy to be able to know that once upon a time in Africa there existed a religion as beautiful, as enchanting and alive, as that which we, at least here, share with the *orishas*, *voduns*, the clever ones, the enraptured ones. We need to Bahianize Africa] (1996, 55–56).

Intellectuals, writers, and artists, many of them white, have long been supportive of and actively involved, as Tavares is, in Candomblé, the name by which the religious sects of African origin are known in Bahia. Visitors, including tourists, to Candomblé ceremonies are attracted by the stirring drumming and captivating dancing. Significant numbers of local intellectuals, writers, and artists, while inspired by the aesthetic, also openly follow Candomblé's religious tenets and practices and actively participate in the cults as lay members.[16] For reasons having to do not only with sociohistorical changes in the countries where *orixá* worship originated but also with how the religion was introduced to the New World, ethnologists and religious scholars generally agree that the Candomblé ceremonies of Bahia have always been more spectacular than those of the African lands from whence they came.[17] One reason is that among the Yoruba people, for example, often only one orixá is revered in a given village or area. Because slaves of Yoruba ethnicity came to Brazil from many villages and areas, the cults that evolved in Bahia have a pantheon of deities. Thus, while in a ceremony in a Yoruba village usually only one god descends to dance among the mortals, as Tavares implies, in Bahia the faithful dance among a number of colorfully attired orixás. One might indeed assert that the Bahian ceremony is more baroque than its African counterpart. Moreover, Brazil's African religions have long been syncretized with elements of folk Catholicism. Although in recent times some Candomblé leaders and followers reject this syncretism, for many cult followers nearly every orixá has a Christian saint as a counterpart. In sum, much of Candomblé's appeal to believers stems from its creolization.[18]

In the essay that bears his volume's title, Tavares elaborates on a theme put forth by Querino, also a native Bahian, in *O africano como colonisador*: slave resistance. In Tavares's essay, "Nossos colonizadores africanos," the contemporary Bahian postcolonialist writes that "aqui, além da resistência física e orgânica, os negros tiveram de usar toda sua astúcia para sobreviver" [here, along with the physical and organic resistance, blacks had to use all of the astuteness they could muster in order to survive] (1996, 86). Tavares attributes to the African colonizers a culturally adaptive ability not only to resist being Europeanized but to "empretecer os brancos" [blacken the whites] (ibid.). The presumed Africanization of European settlers, who adopted much of the black colonists' cultural practices, leads Tavares to make his invidious comparison with respect to the de-Africanization of blacks in colonial and postcolonial Africa. In this regard, Tavares makes the following observations about a visit he made to Portugal: "Frequentei a Associação do Cabo Verde, Lisboa, onde tem dança toda quinta. E lá estavam os neguinhos africanos todos durinhos, dançando. E lá estava um conjunto negro todo durinho tocando. Suingue zero. Aqui é ao contrário. Branco tem suingue. Branco mexe os quadris. Há exceções, é claro, mas a verdade é que na África o negro foi colonizado; na Bahia ele é colonizador. No Rio também" [I frequented the Association of Cape Verde, in Lisbon, where every Thursday there's a dance. And there were those little African black brothers and sisters dancing as stiff as boards. And there was a group of black musicians, as stiff as boards, playing their instruments. Zero rhythm. Here in Brazil it's the other way around. White people have rhythm. Whites know how to swing their hips. There are exceptions, of course, but the truth of the matter is that in Africa blacks were colonized; in Bahia there are colonizers. In Rio de Janeiro too] (ibid., 87).[19]

What Tavares fashions in his essays is a simultaneously mythifying, mystifying, and engaging portrayal of the African contribution to the formation of the Brazilian people and culture. With a touch of humor, he also deplores what he sees as the postcolonial de-Africanization of Africa. On the other hand, despite his avowals of Bahia as a kind of black African diaspora that has preserved much of the cultural authenticity of the motherland. Tavares concomitantly celebrates the biological, social, and cultural hybridity that exist in Bahia, that former African colony in the New World.

As a man of letters, and especially as a poet, Ildásio Tavares contributes to the myths and realities of Brazilians as a people and Brazil as a nation. A volume of especially compelling poems with respect to Brazilianness is Tavares's IX sonetos da inconfidência (Nine sonnets of disloyalty) (1999).[20] In "O novenário artístico de Ildásio Tavares" (Ildásio Tavares's artistic prayer book), the introduction to the collection, Fábio Lucas, a highly regarded Brazilian literary scholar, writes, "O poeta, ao mesmo tempo que se insere no terreno pantanoso da metáfora, deixa-se impregnar pelos eflúvios da memória coletiva, trazendo ao rigor da composição literária o drama da formação da gente brasileira" [The poet, at the same time that he inserts himself in the swampy terrain of metaphor, allows himself to be impregnated by the emanations of collective memory, thus bringing to the rigor of literary composition the drama of the formation of the Brazilian people] (Tavares 1999, 7).

"LONG LIVE THE BRAZILIAN PEOPLE"

Viva o povo brasileiro (1984), a title whose English equivalent is "Long Live the Brazilian People," qualifies as one of Brazil's quintessential postcolonial literary works. This best-selling, award-winning novel by João Ubaldo Ribeiro, was translated into English by the author himself and published in the United States. Interestingly enough, the title of the English translation is An Invincible Memory (1989). Although it apparently has not been verified, some contend that Ubaldo Ribeiro originally did opt for a literal translation of his original title. Rumor has it that the American editor deemed "Long Live the Brazilian People" to be unacceptable because some potential readers might find it trite and mawkish. This was perhaps a valid concern for a U.S.-based publisher. Not surprisingly, the title in Portuguese is also a hortatory slogan, but one that effectively serves the author's intentions to celebrate and at times satirize, with wry humor, the Brazilian people's search for collective identity and national identification. And the author's intentions are not lost on Brazilian readers of the novel. In selecting Viva o povo brasileiro as a title, Ubaldo Ribeiro more than likely had in mind the kind of patriotic pride that led Afonso Celso to label his turn-of-the-century work Porque me ufano do meu país (Why I am proud of my country) (1900). This extremely popular book, as Burns notes in A History of Brazil, "was required reading in most primary schools" (1993, 319). *Ufanismo*, which can be defined as ultra-patriotism, gave rise to a number of optimistic nationalistic slogans in the years immediately following Brazil's independence from Portugal.

Along with the good-natured parody inherent in the title, throughout the novel Ubaldo Ribeiro also employs the slogan and its variations as a populist motif. Two of the novel's characters, for example, paint the following message on the sides of buildings and garden walls: "Viva nós, viva o povo brasilerio, viva nós, viva o povo brasileiro que um dia se achará, viva nós que não somos de ninguém, viva nós que queremos liberdade para nós e não para os nossos donos" [Long live us, long live the Brazilian people, long live us, long live the people who one day will find themselves; long live we who don't belong to anyone; long live we who want freedom for us and not for our owners] (Ubaldo Ribeiro 1984, 425; translation by Ubaldo Ribeiro 1989, 319). Ubaldo Ribeiro obviously selected the English translation's title in keeping with the novel's theme of collective identity and national identification. The collective invincibility is that of those souls who down through the centuries are incarnated as the heroes and heroines of the racially and ethnically hybrid Brazilian family.

The epigraph that introduces Ubaldo Ribeiro's epic work reads "O segredo da Verdade é o seguinte: não existem fatos, só existem histórias" [The secret of Truth is as follows: there are no facts, there are only stories]. Technically speaking, *Viva o povo brasileiro* does fit the category of historical novels. Ubaldo Ribeiro makes no claim to being a historian; he identifies himself as a storyteller. With regard to the words and phrasing of the novel's epigraph, *história* is, of course, a Portuguese homonym denoting "history," the latter being a branch of knowledge dealing with past events, as well as "story," which refers to a narrative, either true or fictional. The Portuguese word and the English words *history* and *story* all derive, both etymologically and semantically, from the Latin *historia*. In the Portuguese and English editions Ubaldo Ribeiro plays very effectively and with aesthetic appeal on the denotative and connotative convergences of history, stories, and past events as the novel's third-person narrator and a plethora of characters weave tales that reveal the truths and myths behind the chronological facts of the formation of the Brazilian people and nation.

In keeping with the historical sequence of events, albeit not always in chronological order, each of the chapters, with the exception of the untitled first chapter, has a heading that consists of a real place name and a date. Chapter sections, including those in the first chapter, also bear such spatial and temporal headings. Much of the novel unfolds on the island of Itaparica, in the State of Bahia's Bay of all Saints, where Ubaldo Ribeiro was born and raised. Other frequent settings are in and around the villages and towns of the *recôncavo*, a fertile coastal region of the Bay of all Saints, as well as in Bahia's capital city of Salvador. Most of the stories unfold in the nineteenth century, especially beginning in the year of Brazil's independence from Portugal. There are, however, chapters and chapter subsections wherein the action takes place in other Brazilian cities, specifically Rio de Janeiro and São Paulo. Brazilian citizens also have encounters in Corrientes, in neighbouring Argentina, and in Lisbon, the capital of the metropole of the former Portuguese Empire. The earliest and most recent years in which the novel is set are, respectively, 1647 and 1977, with the action taking place in the seventeenth, nineteenth, and twentieth centuries.

Within this extensive time frame and multiple geographical settings the large cast of characters acts out and recounts stories that elucidate the many issues and themes that make up the evolution of a people in their secular search for identity and identification. *Viva o povo brasileiro* has a number of outstanding nineteenth- and twentieth-century antecedents with regard to literary works that deal with the formation of the Brazilian people. But this contemporary novel consists of tales that give life to all significant historical factors and many of the historic events that make up life in a nation in the process of determining its identity. The novel evokes Amerindian "in-lawism," Brazilians' historically ambivalent stance as they have related to the Portuguese, the British, the Dutch, and the French. *Viva o povo brasileiro* also consists of stories about slavery, African colonization, and nineteenth-century pseudoscientific theories on race as well as the cults of the noble savage and the enchanted mulatto woman, miscegenation as a heightened component of race as a social construct, and what many have come to refer to as the myth of Brazil as a racial democracy. The often complex relations between and among many of the novel's characters also elucidate social hierarchies, regionalism, class struggle, and populism, with an emphasis on the *povinho* (the common folk or rabble) and the *povão* (the people standing tall and proud).[21]

Viva o povo brasileiro lends proof to the assertion that art formulates life. Moreover, Ubaldo Ribeiro's literary art and the other texts considered in this essay elucidate the degree to which Brazil occupies a unique place among Latin America's and, indeed, the world's postcolonial nation-states. Ubaldo Ribeiro's *Viva o povo brasileiro* also stands as a postcolonialist novel par excellence because it transcends nationalist perceptions and conveys a universality that plays on the intriguing aspects of present-day globalization.

NOTES

Unless otherwise indicated, all English translations are my own.

1   This essay, which was published in booklet form, is based on a presentation by Wheeler at the Pós-Colonialismo e Identidade (Postcolonialism and Identity) conference that took place in 1998 at Fernando Pessoa University in Porto, Portugal.

2   The word *Creole* came into English by way of French, but, along with the Spanish *criollo*, it derives from *crioulo*, one of the Portuguese language's earliest international loan words. The noun is based on the verb *criar*, which means to rear, breed, and raise. Originally, *crioulo* referred to the slave raised in the master's house. Subsequently, it came to mean the African slave born in Brazil, where today it is often used as a synonym for any black person. In the language of ethnology and sociology *Creole* refers to "home-grown" racial, linguistic, cultural, and, in some cases, culinary hybridization. Among Portugal's former colonies, Cape Verde's Creole society qualifies as a quintessential melting pot.

3   The Prospero-Caliban metaphor has been widely applied by writers, scholars, and others to the relationship between the colonizer and the colonized in Africa and other areas of the so-called Third World. It is thus a term that has much to do, figuratively, with anticolonialism and postcolonialism.

4   *The Tempest* has been a central reference in postcolonial debates. See, for instance, in this volume, Peter Hulme's recognition of the dilemma of Caliban as a signifier open to multiple ideological, ethnic, and historical interpretations.

5   Marshall C. Eakin authored a book whose title, *Brazil: The Once and Future Country*, plays on a variation of this popular saying. Eakin's work very effectively delineates Brazilians' historical struggle with their own sense of nationhood.

6   According to some researchers nearly three-quarters of the inhabited world has existed under some form of colonialism.

7   The type of African art that incorporates elements of the nontraditional—in this particular piece of sculpture, a bicycle—is known in certain Western art-history circles as Fourth World art.

8   The *post* of *postcolonialism* is discussed in this volume by Peter Hulme, Román de la Campa, and Santiago Castro-Gómez, among others.

9   In "Keeping Ahead of the Joneses," an op-ed report on the semantic variables of the prefix *pre*, the linguist Geoffrey Nunberg "prefaces" the piece with the following pertinent observation: "You can tell a lot about an age from the way it adapts prefixes to its purposes. Take our enthusiasm for using 'post-' in new ways. Sometimes it means 'late' rather than 'after,' as in postcapitalism, and sometimes, as in postmodernism, it means something like 'once more without feeling' " (2002, 4).

10   On the connections between dependency theory and postcolonialism see Ramón Grosfoguel in this volume.

11   *Caboclos* is a Tupi-Guarani word that came to refer to individuals of mixed Indian and white parentage.

12   With respect to the interbred Iberians, the Portuguese, although basically of

Mediterranean stock, are also an admixture of Semitic (i.e., Moorish, Jewish) and, in the northern regions of the Iberian Peninsula, Celtic and Visigoth ethnicity. There is also some historical documentation in support of the biological assimilation of sub-Saharan Africans, brought to Portugal's southern Algarve province early in the slave trade.

13   E. Bradford Burns's translation of the essay was published in 1978 as *The African Contribution to Brazilian Civilization*.

14   The word *colono* translates as both "settler" and "colonizer." *Colonisador*, which Querino himself does not use in his original work but which appears in the title of his posthumously republished essay, most often translates as "colonizer," although occasionally as "colonist." (As a minor orthographic observation, in the 1950s *colonisador* was written with an *s*; today it is spelled with a z, that is, *colonizador*.)

15   *Quilombo* derives from *kilumbu*, a word found in Kimbundu, Kikongo, and Umbundu. In these three languages, which are spoken in the Congo-Angola region of southwest Africa, *kilumbu* refers to an enclosed encampment. *Quilombo*, the Brazilian derivative, came to mean "village" or "African settlement."

16   Ildásio Tavares is a novelist, short-story writer, playwright, poet, and lyricist, as well as an essayist and has published works on Candomblé. He also holds a post in Ilê Axé Opô Afonjá, one of Bahia's oldest and most prestigious Candomblés.

17   *Orixá*, which derives from the Yoruba word *orisha*, refers to an animistic deity who may represent one or more of the forces of nature.

18   Ironically, while membership in allegedly "more-African-than-Africa" Bahia evangelical Christianity is surging, the mainly black and mulatto members of these churches are usually among those Brazilians most vehemently opposed to the religious sects of African origin.

19   Tavares's account of what he observed in Lisbon brings to mind an incident that I witnessed a few years ago in the Cape Verdean city of Mindelo. One evening, in a hotel restaurant, a young female performer, accompanied by guitarists and fiddlers, was singing a selection of *mornas* and *coladeiras*, the archipelago's traditional music. During the performance I noticed that a customer, clearly a foreigner, was becoming increasingly disturbed by what he was hearing. Finally, unable to contain himself, this individual, who turned out to be a French tourist, jumped to his feet and shouted that the music being sung and played was not African. One of the musicians yelled back, "É nossa!" [It's ours!]. The performer was attesting to the fact that although the morna, Cape Verde's signature music, has an almost Italianate, *fado*-like melodic structure, it is a quintessentially Creole, transcultural mode with a distinctly rhythmic base, even if without the marked syncopation and drumming associated with African musical expression.

20   The volume's title refers, of course, to the Inconfidência Mineira, a nineteenth-century abortive attempt to overthrow Portuguese rule.

21   With the election in 2002 of Luiz Inácio Lula da Silva as Brazil's first working-class president, the novel's characters may seem prophetic in their proclamations of "long live the Brazilian people, long live us."

The universal, ecumenical road we have chosen to travel, and for which
we are reproached, takes us ever closer to ourselves.—José Carlos Mariátegui,
Seven Interpretative Essays on Peruvian Reality

POSTING LETTERS: WRITING IN THE ANDES AND THE
PARADOXES OF THE POSTCOLONIAL DEBATE
Sara Castro-Klaren

The postcolonial debate irrupted in the North
American academy in the 1980s. At this time the
field of Latin American colonial studies was being re-
vamped in light of the questions prompted by the generalized reading of Felipe Guamán Poma de Ayala's *El
primer nueva corónica y buen gobierno* (1616?), Edmundo
O'Gorman's *La invención de América: El universalismo en
la cultura de Occidente* (1958), and the general opening
in interpretation occurring as a result of structuralism
first and postmodern theory later. The reading of Guamán Poma and O'Gorman, who were widely separated
in time but not in their hermeneutical thrust, inaugurated a thoroughgoing inquiry into the modes and
consequences of Western historiography. Both authors
pushed the field beyond its standing empirical and
philological parameters. Read in conjunction with new
developments in semiotics and French theory, both
Guamán Poma and Edmundo O'Gorman posed ques-

tions that went far beyond the untrustworthiness of the Spanish chroniclers and their narratives of conquest in Mexico and the Tahuantinsuyo.[1]

In very different languages and styles both the Andean Indian writing a letter to the king of Spain and the contemporary Mexican historian understood that the problem of writing history rested in the occlusion of the epistemological assumptions underlining and regulating this narrative mode as an imperial modality of thought. Their focus on narrative rhetoric and the politics of writing—how is authority constituted, under what conditions has the information been gathered, from what power-knowledge perspective is the narrative constructed, what is the author's locus of enunciation, who is the ideal reader of the narrative, what modes of persuasion are being deployed in the construction of the truth of the narrative—placed Guamán Poma and O'Gorman at the center of unprecedented scholarly discussions that shook received understandings of the "colonial period."[2] The subsequent revision of the colonial period entailed deep consequences for the whole of the study of Latin America. In the field of "literature" the challenge posed by Jorge Luis Borges's intertextual theory and the undermining of the high-culture literary canon by the emergence of *testimonio* had initiated an "internal" process of repositioning period, genre, and cultural boundaries that implied a thorough and profound movement of all the existing posts and signs that allowed for the constitution of objects of study.

It should thus not be surprising to see that the appearance of *Orientalism* (1978), by Edward Said, received a mixed reading. On the one hand the thesis advanced in *Orientalism* seemed similar to the claims made in O'Gorman's own thesis on the "invention"—the nonreferential disposition of the epistemological object—of America by the historiography of the sixteenth century. Said's sweeping inquiry was a brilliant investigation of Europe's invention of the Orient as its nineteenth-century other, and it rang surprisingly familiar themes for scholars in the Latin American field. Reading *Orientalism* produced in students of Latin America "the shock of recognition," an effect that, postcolonial theory claims, takes place in the consciousness of postcolonial subjects as they assess their experience of coloniality in comparison with other colonial subjects. Said's daring reconnoitering of Europe's construction of its other at once went beyond and also confirmed O'Gorman thesis and insight into the nature of the writing of the history of empire and its hierarchical impulses. Informed by Antonio Gramsci's views on culture and Michel Foucault's discourse theory, Said, not unlike José Carlos Mariátegui in his *Seven Interpretative Essays on Peruvian Reality* (1928), brought under his scope not just historiography but also literature and the human sciences to show the regulatory power of ideology. However, *Orientalism* provided yet another shock to students of colonial Latin America. This time it was a shock of misrecognition, for Said's imagination seemed to equate the history of colonialism exclusively with Europe's penetration of the "Orient." Thus, his inquiry ignored the Spanish conquest, the avatars of colonialism, and the inception of modernity in Ibero-America. Moreover, it seemed wholly unaware of the thinking that Latin American intellectuals—from the Inca Garcilaso de la Vega (1539–1616) to Javier Clavijero (1731–1787) and César Vallejo (1892–1938)—had been doing on the epistemological violence of the conquest and the subsequent subalternization of the knowledge of the other.

The purpose of this essay is to map out the points of intersection and of divergence between the most salient and influential aspects of postcolonial theory, its paradoxes and thinking in the Andes on the questions of empire and coloniality. Since the span of thinking in the Andes is as wide as it is fractured and as deep as it is heterogeneous, my effort herein can thus only be preliminary. However, in going over the different ways in which this mapping could begin to place some posts and markers on the surface in order to sketch some lines and directions, I have found that the inquiry undertaken by Mariátegui on the question of the discourse of colonialism is indeed paradigmatic; I therefore focus on his main theses as points of departure, placing Mariátegui's inquiry into the workings of colonialism and the cultural force that it deploys in dialogue with key topics and themes in postcolonial theory. But first a word on coloniality and another on postmodern theory.

COLONIALITY

Coloniality is a concept put in circulation by Walter Mignolo (see his essay in this volume). In his recent *Local Histories/Global Designs: Coloniality, Subaltern Knowledges and Border Thinking* (2000, 14) Mignolo offers a sustained and ample treatment of coloniality. Based on Aníbal Quijano's conception of the coloniality of power as the innermost chamber of capitalism, as an energy and a machine that transforms differences into values (Quijano 1998a), Mignolo conceives of coloniality as a world-system which constitutes the underside of modernity and whose duration has yet to reach its limits. For Mignolo, the colonial difference is the space where the coloniality of power is enacted, where the confrontation of local histories, displayed in different spaces and times across the planet, takes place (Mignolo 2000d, ix). The coloniality of power implies a fractured locus of enunciation as the subaltern

perspective takes shape in response to the colonial difference and hegemonic discourse (ibid., x). Together with Quijano, Mignolo sees the constitution of the coloniality of power through the following operations:

1   The classification and reclassification of the planet's population, an operation
    in which the concept of culture (primitive, stages of development, Europe as
    the norm) plays a key role.
2   The creation of institutions whose function is to articulate and manage such
    classifications (state institutions, universities, church, courts).
3   The definitions of spaces appropriate to such goals.
4   An epistemological perspective from which to articulate the meaning and the
    profile of the new matrix of power from out of which the new production of
    knowledge could be channeled (ibid., 17).

The idea of coloniality of power as a world-system intersects in many areas
with several of the main postulates of what has been configured as postcolonial theory in the work of scholars who write on the discursive characteristics of the imperial expansion of Europe over Southeast Asia, Australia,
Canada and the Middle East. One of the chief tenets in the concept of the
coloniality of power is that the inception point of the modern/colonial as a
world-system must be set back to the time of the Spanish conquest of
Amerindian societies and that one cannot assume, as postcolonial theory
does, the Enlightenment to be the origin of Janus-like modernity. Consequently "post-colonial" theory, with its orientalist perspective, is reposi-
tioned. It is not the canvas. Rather it is merely an item within the larger
canvas of struggles that 1492 brought about for the entire planet. Coloniality
of power overcomes postcolonial theory in its temporal and spatial reach.
Nevertheless, it is interesting to see that in the entry for "imperialism," the
editors of Key Concepts in Post-Colonial Studies (1998), relying mainly on Said's
Culture and Imperialism (1993), write that "for post-colonial theory there was a
continuous development of imperial rhetoric and imperial representation of
the rest of the globe from at least the fifteenth century" (Ashcroft, Griffiths,
and Tiffin 1998, 126).

Moreover, the idea of "coloniality at large," proposed by the editors of
this book, makes it easier to understand how within the evolving colonial
distribution of tasks across and hierarchies over the world's cultures and
peoples, it was possible for Orientalism to ignore the history of Latin America
in the making of a postcolonial world, if by postcolonial we understand all
developments after contact between Europe and its othered or subalternized
civilizations. One of the effects of the coloniality of power has been the

production of hierarchies and differences among the colonized. The imperial English-speaking world, even at the fringe location of its colonial outposts, has considered itself a notch "above" Latin America in the tree of knowledge. This perspective is itself the result of the imperial struggles between Spain and northern Europe, a story much too complex to even allude to here, but one which is critically entwined with the rise of modernity and the location of Latin America in the mapping and distribution of knowledge. The coloniality of power had classified Amerindian and all subsequent knowledge forged in Latin America as subaltern. They understood knowledge and power to reside at the seat of the colonizer, the subject position occupied, by definition, by the interlocutors of their writing. Much as Guamán Poma addressed his letter to the king of Spain, these English-writing and -speaking postmodern thinkers address their inquiry to the northern Euro-American academy.

Despite the fact that we do not yet have a South-South dialogue between, let us say, Southeast Asian and Latin American scholars, a dialogue which was one of the objectives of the Latin American Subaltern Studies Group, concepts such as the coloniality of power, elaborated by Latin American scholars, and certain claims made by postcolonial theory make it possible to think of a critical, a plurotopic approach to cultural theory. A plurotopic approach would be more fitting with the critique of hegemony imbedded in postcolonial theory than would monolingual, isolating, North-South, two-way dialogues between imperial and "former" subaltern subjects who, because of the accidents of history, share the same colonial language. In other words, a lot could be gained if Latin American scholars established a dialogue with scholars like Said or Homi Bhabha in order to cross the divide established by coloniality itself and to inaugurate the plurotopic space of debate. Of course, a predisposition to listening, on both sides, would be necessary. It is important to remember that such a plurotopic dialogue is not without precedent. We are not inventing the wheel. The postcolonial hermeneutic of the modern/colonial world-system that the Spanish conquest inaugurated was already rendered plurotopic by Garcilaso's maneuvering of the Renaissance.[3] What follows in this essay is thus not a search for unanimity, but rather a mapping of convergences, differences, and paradoxes projected onto an uneven ground that shares a common imperial horizon as this planet is enveloped by the vapors and flows of the power of empire.

COLONIALITY AND THE BATTLEFIELD

There are various ways of approaching a discussion of the terms of coloniality in the Andes and a possible intertextual and intersubjective conversation with postcolonial theory across English, Spanish, Portuguese, and
Amerindian languages such as Quechua and Aymara. Before beginning in
any of the possible ways available to the analysis of the problem it is important to remind the reader that just as coloniality is marked by an intense
heterogeneity, so is the series of claims and topical discussions that "postcolonial theory" entails. Bart Moore-Gilbert in *Postcolonial Theory: Contexts,
Practices, Politics* wrestles with the distinction and hostility between postcolonial theory and postcolonial criticism (1997, 5–17). He notes the emphasis
on resistance in postcolonial criticism. Scholars and intellectuals who see
the sign of postcolonial thinking as resistance to colonial discourse also
express a persistent hostility to postcolonial theory, which they find too
closely associated with postmodern theory, a critique suspected of complicity with the very modernity that it deconstructs. As inaugurated by Edward Said, postcolonial theory entails "an approach to [colonial discourse]
analysis from within methodological paradigms derived . . . from contemporary European cultural theories" (ibid., 16). Moore-Gilbert discusses amply
the various critiques that have been leveled at postcolonial theory as it appears in the work of Said, Bhabha, Gayatri Spivak, and Bill Ashcroft. Any
reader of the work of these influential theorists knows that the differences
between them are enormous, as each is closely associated with different and
competing currents in European philosophy and theory. To read Bhabha is
never to forget Lacan, and to follow Spivak is always to be more than aware
of Derrida, Marx, and the ins and outs of the controversies in philosophy and
literary theory in the U.S. academy. Postcolonial theory is by no means a set
of coherent and integrated approaches, assumptions, or methods in cultural
analysis, but it has been an exceptionally important institutional development in the English-speaking world. Moore-Gilbert emphasizes the "elasticity of the concept 'postcolonial.'" He thinks that its capacity to change
directions and to appropriate situations and concepts has brought it to the
point that it is "in danger of imploding as an analytical concept with any real
cutting edge" (ibid., 11).

Postcolonial theory, in all its heterogeneity and ambition, redeploys key
aspects in postmodern theory—opacity of language, decentering of the subject, suspicion of authority, demolition of epistemological and cultural universal claims, relocation of subjects—in order to show the complicity of

"knowledge" and systems of imperial domination. In this sense I find a great deal in postcolonial theory to run very close to Foucault's own discourse theory and its implications for historiography.[4] That move, it is true, risks invigorating and universalizing even more the epistemological power of the imperial centers, but like many aspects of postmodern theory (and Marxism earlier, and the avant-garde earlier, and romanticism earlier), postcolonial theory has a liberating potential when engaged in *critical dialogue*, as Mariátegui was with Marxism and the Inca Garcilaso de la Vega was with Spanish historiography, for nothing is autochthonous and insular or pristine after contact. Postcolonial theory articulates, as do Latin American critiques of empire, a double and/or multiple set of critical languages, trying often but not always succeeding in mounting a challenge to hegemony, saying always with Ranajit Guha that the state of colonial affairs amounts to "domination without hegemony" (Guha 1997a).

Thus, what behooves the student of colonialism, not unlike Foucault's own enterprise or for matter the sense of discovery that Michel de Certeau practices and theorizes, is to look and act in the cracks and crevices of the system in order to break open the homogeneous surface that power/knowledge is always smoothing over. Postcolonial theory, once inflected as a dialectical and critical investigation of the myriad ways in which the coloniality of power constructs center-periphery relations, does not have to be seen as entirely divorced from the work of Latin American intellectuals. Much of the thinking carried out in the "Latin" South entailed finding forms and ways of material and epistemological challenges, creating spaces and subsequent freedoms from the domination of empire. This struggle has not been brought to an end by any of the "posts" for the colonial outpost everywhere continue to post messages and letters that seem new only to those readers who are unfamiliar with the past and "other" colonial histories. It is important not to forget, as Darcy Ribeiro remarked, that the legacy of empire has been deeply damaging and is still very much with us. Ribeiro reluctantly points out that even high-ranking Latin America intellectuals "[have seen] themselves as occupying a subaltern position" (quoted in Mignolo 2000a, 21). Starting with the Inca Garcilaso de la Vega, the same can probably still be said of many a diasporic intellectual today, even those who seem most successful. It thus follows that occlusion is not the Achilles tendon of the center alone.

To offer a proper account of the avatars of the critique of imperial hegemony in the Andes, one would need a much deeper revision of the historiography of thinking in the Andes, one that is not available to us now. I will therefore take some shortcuts and weave my way back and forth between the seminal essays authored by Mariátegui in the first quarter of the twentieth century, the challenge to the Spanish conquest in the work of the Inca Garcilaso de la Vega, and Guamán Poma.

PARADIGMS ON TRIAL

In his *Seven Interpretative Essays* Mariátegui captures the essence of the gearing of problems that at once constitute coloniality in Peru and stand in the way of understanding their meaning as a space for possible critique and action. Mariátegui, like Garcilaso de la Vega, develops a discourse that allows him to keep track of two or more lines of trends and locations in the evolution of events within coloniality. This move has little to do with Homi Bhabha's concepts of hybridity or mimicry, for the latter stresses the idea of "*mim-ando*" or clowning, of imitation and mockery, of copy that denies the idea of an original (Bhabha 1994b). Mimicry, it is true, produces an ambivalent subject not unlike Garcilaso. But Garcilaso was not so much undecided and *ambi-valent* (as in mimicry) about his values or his terrain as he was trying to occupy both sides in the duality of worlds brought about by the conquest. The ambition of his operation was to deploy an ambidextrous cultural competency that allowed him to roam freely and firmly in both worlds and not to feel, as V.S. Naipaul does, that no matter how English he becomes, he still is not "quite white." Naipaul, the model for Bhabha's concept of colonial mimicry, is therefore always left with a feeling of insufficiency, itself the hallmark of mimicry. This is not to say that mimicry is not a condition given in coloniality. It may even be the general condition of colonial subjects. Such a feeling of fraudulent imitation and inflictive mockery is best captured in the Peruvian word *huachafo*. The novels of Mario Vargas Llosa are filled with *huachafos*. But that is not at all the case to be found in the enterprise of Mariátegui, who follows in the line of Garcilaso's ambition to occupy fully both cultural traditions.

Perhaps anticipating Foucault, Mariátegui sees Peru, and by extension the scope of Andean history, as an uneven space of alternating and transformative ruptures and continuities. The conquest and the rule of coloniality mark and deploy in every possible way—economic system, legal system, domination by direct and epistemological violence, linguistic break—the irreparable break that Garcilaso and Guamán Poma recognized and tried to suture and repair in their own, different ways. But the land itself, the territory made by man, and the "problem of the Indian" lead Mariátegui to understand the presence and force of deep economic and cultural continuities that, although denied, arch over the rupture of the conquest and haunt the idea of the modern (European-like) nation. The opening paragraph of *Seven Interpretative Essays* holds the key to Mariátegui's break with positivist historiography and also with the Hegelian model of history, a move that postcolonial theory offers as its operational ground. Mariátegui's salvo against idealist history declares, "The degree to which the history of Peru was severed by the conquest can be seen better on an economic than on any other level. Here the conquest most clearly appears to be a break in continuity. Until the conquest, an economy developed in Peru that sprang spontaneously and freely from the Peruvian soil and the people. The most interesting aspect of the empire of the Incas was its economy. . . . The Malthusian problem was completely unknown to the empire" (1971, 3).

Mariátegui opens up three major problems for thinking history in the Andes. First, contrary to the established Eurocentric perspective initiated by the Spanish chronicles and later affirmed by the rest of European historiography (coloniality of power), Mariátegui posits a break in Peruvian history because he introduces the radical notion that the temporality of Peruvian history has its origins and indeed achieves its formative structure during the long duration of Andean civilizations. The nation's past therefore belongs outside the parameters of European historiography which at best can make room for the "peoples without history," but cannot account for their devolution in their own time. This elsewhere delineates a time line that is not coincidental with Europe's view of its own single temporal development. Thus, on this point Mariátegui's thinking interrogates, as do postcolonial theory and subaltern studies, the question of historical agency and the homing/homelessness of history. The Peruvian theorist is here proposing that history in the Andes, to be properly understood, must stretch back and perhaps even forward in a temporality of its own. In order to do so it must recognize other peoples and other sectors of the nation's peoples as historical actors. Mariátegui thus follows in the wake of the challenge to European historiography already started by Garcilaso and by Guamán Poma. While his interest in the land and the economic structure shows the importance of Marx for Mariátegui's radical inquiry into time and agency, it is just as important to see that his radical thinking comes from a long line of rerouting and rerooting European thought into the matrix of colonial living and thinking to produce a difference capable of conveying the sense of life in the Andes. This difference, I argue, has little to do with either hybridity or mimicry as understood in postcolonial theory.

The second point made by Mariátegui in the opening paragraph questions the universality and predictive capacity of European models for understanding human action in the world. For if the Malthusian problem did not
develop within the structure of Inca economy, then it follows that one has to
question the explanatory and predictive power of Malthus's demographic
theory. To what extent is Malthus's "discovery" then no longer an economic "law" affecting all human stages of demographic change, but simply
an inspired analysis of a local situation in Europe's capitalist and imperial development? Do these three moves in Mariátegui—multiple historical temporalities, replacement and repositioning of the subject of history,
and refusal of European modes of historical explanation—not "provincialize" Europe in a manner similar to the one developed by Dipesh Chakrabarty's brilliant *Provincializing Europe: Postcolonial Thought and Historical Difference* (2000)? Mariátegui in Peru in the 1920s, with the epistemological tools
available at the time—Gramsci, Marx, Schopenhauer, Nietzsche, Garcilaso
de la Vega, archaeology in Peru, fieldwork in Peru—engages three operations
fundamental to postcolonial theory, the latter writing in the wake of postmodern theory.[5]

CHANGING THE SUBJECT

In the second chapter of *Seven Essays* Mariátegui addresses "the problem of the
Indian." This "problem" is one created by criollo state-building historiography in its attempt to build a national history that "mimics," in Bhabha's
sense of the word, the history of the old European nations, such as France or
England. The problem of the Indian, Mariátegui shows, is colonialism itself.
He turns the problem on its head. He shows that the Indian is not the
problem. Rather the Indian is the bearer of the system of economic and
cultural exploitation that holds colonialism in place. The Peruvian State does
not know how to resolve this problem inasmuch as it is an apparatus that is at
once colonial and "modern." As Quijano later theorizes, Mariátegui argues
that colonialism, in order to exploit and continue suppressing the labor force
that the Indian represents, has put in place a complex set of institutions that
reproduce *coloniality at large*. No amount of schooling and republican "modernization" in general can unglue this complex, for colonialism as the foremost expression of capitalism does indeed constitute the underside of modernity. In order to free the Indian from racist and economic oppression, a
whole new system of land tenure, one that challenges the notion of private
property that thus challenges capitalism itself, would be necessary.

Striking a blow to nineteenth-century pieties that predicate the improvement of the "uncivilized" or subalternized peoples of the globe, Mariátegui writes, "The tendency to consider the Indian problem as a moral one embodies a liberal, humanitarian, enlightened nineteenth-century attitude that in the political sphere of the Western world inspires and motivates the 'leagues of human rights.' The antislavery conferences and societies in Europe are born out of this tendency, which always has trusted too much of its appeals to the conscience of civilization" (1971, 25). Once again, Mariátegui offers a critique of Eurocentric thinking, even when it appears to be sympathetic to those suffering the ill effects of imperialism, for Mariátegui's thinking seems founded on the capacity and the will to think otherwise under any and all circumstances. As many have pointed out, postcolonial theory is part and parcel of the age of suspicion inaugurated by Marx, Nietzsche, and Freud. As such it must be careful not to allow itself to be complicit with the liberalizing forces in theory which in fact mask the continuation of coloniality, as Mariátegui points out.

Mariátegui is obviously aware of such a trap. The trajectory of his thought, as seen in his indictment of literature, describes a constant radicalization and self-vigilance. This merciless critique was inaugurated in Peru by Manuel Gonzalez Prada (1884–1918). This iconoclastic and fearless critic of the embrace of coloniality/modernity is recognized by Mariátegui and other radical thinkers of his generation as the "maestro." Mariátegui's suspicion of the good intentions of liberalism were of course reinscribed in José María Arguedas's own critique of indigenismo, of transculturation theory, and of anthropology itself. Such suspicion is also at play in the reception that postcolonial theory has been accorded in Latin America in general. Invested with the prestige of the new, with the glow of the promise of liberation, situated at the center of the newest imperial power, postcolonial theory nevertheless often seems to be sounding themes and approaches developed in Mariátegui's analysis and thus is well known to Latin Americans.

EDUCATION, (NON)LEARNING, AND IDEOLOGY

In his essay on "Public Education" Mariátegui investigates the forms in which education in Peru has been complicit with the establishment and prolongation of empire despite the fact that independence from Spain and national republican educational reforms were supposed to produce a national subject capable of thinking and solving the problems of the nation. Of course Mariátegui knows, as postmodern theory later posits, that the nation is a construct. He calls it an "illusion," a "myth." But he nevertheless understands it to be a necessary construct for the accomplishment of other important human goals, goals which without a nation could perhaps never be reached. He sees the lettered city inaugurated by Spanish colonial rule, with its universities and colleges in the hands of various clerical orders and its emphasis in the humanities as "factories for the production of writers and lawyers" (1971, 79). These institutions of learning are, in fact, an impediment to learning and to the formation of the nation. *Letrados*, as in Spain before, by virtue of their expertise in baroque linguistic games, have continued to manage and advance the interests of the coloniality of power. Up to the very day when Mariátegui wrote, education remained a privilege, its democratizing potential always reigned in by the very class of letrados whose aim was to reproduce themselves in the institutions controlled by their elders.

Mariátegui himself was not the product of any great university or doctoral program. He was a self-taught man who, while in exile in Italy, continued his education, reading voraciously but selectively. He developed a very keen mapping system that enabled him to quickly determine what could fit into his general project of economic, political, and intellectual liberation. He made extremely careful choices and was quick to drop fads and even classics when he determined that their thought was not liberating in the Latin American context, as he felt to be the case with Marx's thought on religion. He found that Antonio Gramsci, Benedetto Croce, and George James Frazer, for instance, opened widely the avenues for thought that he had already begun clearing as a result of his own empirical observation and the works of many other minor but important local intellectuals. The footnotes in *Seven Essays* offer a singular bibliography that not only lets us see what European and American cultural thinkers and philosophers Mariátegui was reading but also how he was noticing, selecting, and absorbing the work of local intellectuals. Here his approach and method differs considerably from Said's, Bhabha's, and Spivak's, diasporic intellectuals who hardly ever draw on the work of "oriental" or other local intellectuals.

Latin America was at the time awash in cultural magazines, and it seems that Mariátegui, the editor of the epoch-making *Amauta*, received and read them all. Indeed, southern Peru, with its historical ties to Argentina, never missed an issue of *Clarín*, *Martin Fierro*, or *Sur*, much less the cultural pages of the great newspapers from Buenos Aires or Mexico City. Radical thinking and abundant publishing in seemingly remote locations like Cuzco, Puno, and Arequipa was the order of the day. This is probably one of the strongest and key differences between the overall configuration of postcolonial theory and Latin American radical thinking. The first seems to be the work of isolated, highly educated, diasporic intellectuals situated in prestigious academic positions in the United States. Their work is mainly in reference to the discursive dimensions of the colonial encounter, as conceived in the matrix of postmodern theory, while Latin American intellectuals like Mariátegui or Arguedas or even Borges, for that matter, come from long traditions of "their own" that entwine, as a matter of course, the ongoing colonial encounter with a locally established critical discourse. Mariátegui's footnotes freely and unselfconsciously mix citations from the work of Emilio Romero, a Cuzqueño historian, with Gramsci. He considers Benedetto Croce's aesthetic in relation to Abelardo Gamarra's poetics, and Waldo Frank's comparative approach to the cultural formation of the English-speaking American colonies and the legacy of the Iberian conquest is set in dialogue with the cultural theory of the Mexican José de Vasconcelos. Mariátegui's liberated vantage point is, by implication, the result of an education that, like a via negativa, gained its freedom by virtue of having been denied entry into the institutions that perpetuate the coloniality of power. Mariátegui sits comfortably on both sides of the Atlantic and takes it for granted, like Borges did at the same time in Buenos Aires, that he, as a Peruvian intellectual, is free to roam in all libraries and archives. Likewise he is free to debate any of the views extant in the extensive intertext in which he navigates. His critique of the colonial legacy in Peruvian education addresses precisely the educational system's cultivation of closure, omission, and learning by rote, and its penchant for establishing repressive thinking and academic authority.

Drawing on Waldo Frank's *Our America* (1919), Mariátegui indicts the energy-sapping Spanish education and compares it, unfavorably, with the energy and strength available in the culture of the Puritan and the Jew, who, in settling what was to be the United States, "directed their energies to utilitarian and practical ends" (1971, 81). Citing his Peruvian contemporary César A. Urgarte, Mariátegui, a Marxist, offers a psychological interpretation of Peru's marginal position in the world of capital: "The Spaniard of the sixteenth century was not psychologically equipped to undertake the economic development of a hostile, harsh, unexplored land. A warrior . . . he lacked the virtues of diligence and thrift. His noble prejudices and bureaucratic predilections turned him against agriculture and industry, which he considered to be occupations of slaves and commoners. Most of the conquistadores were driven only by greed for easy and fabulous wealth and the possibility of attaining power and glory" (quoted in Mariátegui 1971, 85).

What is more, this psychological interpretation for Mariátegui does not necessarily exclude religion. In fact he credits Puritanism with the economic development of the English colonies. He even asserts that "Spanish colonization did not suffer from an excess of religion" (ibid., 83). This consideration of psychology together with religion and as second only to economy as historical forces, shows that Mariátegui, like Arguedas later, and Guamán Poma and Garcilaso earlier, is not always ready to throw out the baby with the bathwater. Culture for Mariátegui is indeed the matter at hand. The long-held practices of debate, selection, and appropriation of ideas coming from the imperial centers are taken for granted as naturalized modes of operation by Mariátegui, who does not evince anguish and fear, as in the mimicry model, but rather seeks the foundation for a definite break with the coloniality of power in a deeply historicized critique of the power of discourse, institutionalized education, and other sites of ideological deployment. This postcolonial move offers much more than just resistance—the hallmark of postcolonial criticism, according to Moore-Gilbert (1997, 16). It is, and it calls for, creative thinking on a grand scale.

However, appropriation has its limits and holds many dangers. It is a neutral tool that can be put to the service of both progressive, decolonizing forces as well as reactionary recolonializing drives. That is why Mariátegui, a keen reader of French philosophy and literature, condemns the anachronistic educational reform that the Peruvian universities underwent when they adopted the French model. He bases his assessment on two legs: an examination of French education in France at the time, its reactionary tendencies; and the discursive and political places or receptors where such a philosophy of education falls as it is imported into Peru. With his eyes always on the local play, Mariátegui draws from the work of French intellectuals who are critical of the system put in place by Napoleon, a system that gutted the democratizing thrust of the educational model created by the French revolutionaries. The Napoleonic reforms, intent on the training of bureaucrats, prolonged, like the colonial system inhered in Peru, the ignorance of the educated classes "for there was nothing to awake intellectual freedom" (Mariátegui 1971, 84). According to Mariátegui, Edouard Herriot in *Creer* (1919) outlines the major ills of the French educational system. They amount to a failure to have created a primary and secondary school system capable of offering technical training. Moreover, Mariátegui observes that the "Third Republic has been able to break with this [Napoleonic] bondage, but it has not been able to break away completely from the narrow concept that tended to isolate the university from the rest of the nation" (85). For Mariátegui, the

Peruvian reforms, based on the North American system, go a long way toward remedying the distance between learning and the interests of the nation at large. There would have been a great stride forward were it not that the reforms have been thoroughly sabotaged by the reactionary forces stationed in the faculty system of sinecures and other privileges. But the most important failure of the reform rests on the fact that it leaves the study of economics outside the core curriculum and is indifferent to the "indigenous element" (86).

Taking public education as microcosm of coloniality Mariátegui is able to show how coloniality reproduces itself in layers and layers of imperial expansion. His analysis points out how under each attempt to reform there lies, as Foucault would show with his archival and geological metaphors, in deep and truncated air pockets, discourses always ready to reemerge. Thus it is clear that the thrust of Mariátegui's analysis of public education in both the imperial centers and ex-colonial spaces shows that the sense of a "real" postcolonial situation is only a temporary and precarious condition. This sense of overcoming the past can never be definitive. It can only be maintained in constant struggle. It cannot be totally overcome, not even with the wars of independence, for the system tends to its own reproduction. Mariátegui's theory of cultural change and intellectual freedom is not, therefore, that far away from Gayatri Spivak's advocacy of the notion that liberation struggles cannot, now that there is nothing outside the text and now that there is no sovereign subject, construct bounded subjects of resistance or impregnable counterhistories. Instead, what is possible for both cultural theorists is the construction of temporary but strategic critical perspectives, "strategic essentialisms," and provisional resisting subjects.

Mariátegui, of course, wants to go beyond a critique circumscribed by the halls of the academy. The academic nature of French education is precisely his dissatisfaction with the adoption of the French model. "Strategic" and "provisionary" for Mariátegui mean the recognition of the inadequacies of thinking in the world both at the center and at the margins. Above all, Mariátegui thinks of culture as the realm of political struggle where there is nothing more certain than change. As an engaged intellectual, he and his comrades having spent time in jail and suffered exile, Mariátegui always already knew that all epistemological and political positions can only be contingent. Thus his study of public education in Peru evinces many of the key items in the problematic of the subaltern group of historians in Southeast Asia, as well as some of the hallmarks of postcolonial theory.[6]

The universities' links to society concern Mariátegui because of their inextricable connection to the question of formation of the national subject and to the uses and places of knowledge in the political arena. In a sharp difference with postcolonial theory, even with the postulates of the "teaching machine" in Gayatri Spivak's work, Mariátegui looks on the intellectuals as a sector of society called on to provide "intellectual guidance" to the working classes (1971, 95). Today, with the university in ruins, as Bill Readings has shown, we have a clearer perspective on the relationship of the humanities and the formation of the national (bourgeois) subject. We view with suspicion the deployment of the study of literature as a discursive formation integral to shaping national (bourgeois) subjects. But at the time when Mariátegui was writing, the connection between the teaching of the humanities and the formation of national subjects was scarcely ever made. Mariátegui was writing at the margins a full fifty years before Readings takes up the question at the center. The liberation of knowledges and of the knowing subject was paramount for Latin America as its societies entered the heated battles of modernity and the universities seemed then, as they still do today, to offer the best vehicle for breaking the walls of ignorance constructed by coloniality. Mariátegui recognizes that education, malgre lui, is instrumental in the formation and identity of the national or international, bourgeois or revolutionary, reactionary or liberated subject. This cannot be changed, and the question at hand is, once again, not to throw out the baby with the bathwater, but to harness education for the project of national liberation and the construction of national identity that is not oppressive.

Mariátegui's examination of the student-led university reform that started in Cordoba, Argentina, in 1919, and spread throughout Latin America, culminating in the International Congress of Students in Mexico City (1921), is prompted by the urgency to understand this sociopolitical movement at the microlevel. Moreover, Mariátegui feels that this "new generation" of Latin Americans holds the key to a continental union, the cherished Bolivarian dream that Mariátegui also considers indispensable in the struggle against colonialism. Again, Mariátegui's vision is focused on the local, concrete effects of thinking. He takes up topics whose examination yields radical departures from the established understanding of the world. His intent is to compel changes in thinking. The poetics of César Vallejo and José Maria Arguedas later share in Mariátegui's sense of thinking in and for the world, a sensibility and conviction only exacerbated by the urgency of the lived.

But this is not the same as saying that Mariátegui is after short-term results only. Quite to the contrary, his interest in changing the world entails a radical search that destabilizes the certainties that underpinned colonialism itself. For that reason he is also critical of the student movement. He asserts that the failure of the student movement had to do with confusing enthusiasm with carefully studied, long-term plans. A reader of José de Vasconcelos, the Mexican cultural critic, Mariátegui points to the underside of the wide-open appropriation and indiscriminate undertaking of projects whose dimensions are not properly understood. He agrees with Vasconcelos's assessment when he writes that one of the gravest dangers in Latin American culture is the lack of follow-through: "The principle weakness of our race is its instability. We are incapable of sustained effort and, for that same reason, we cannot execute a project. In general we should beware of enthusiasm" (Vasconcelos, quoted in Mariátegui 1971, 109). Mariátegui thinks that the student-reform movement has been erratic and unstable, with vague and imprecise goals, themselves prepared and underscored by a rhetorical and pseudoidealistic education which has not yet understood the value of science and the stimulus that it provides to philosophy (110).

However, the best of the student spirit of reform flourishes not in Lima, still the center of colonialist reaction, but in Cuzco, where the project for a great center of scientific research evidences Mariátegui's conviction that "civilization owes much more to science than to the humanities" (1971, 120). And the Cuzco intellectuals have understood another key step in the intellectual liberation that university education ought to entail: to erase the distinction between "superior" and "inferior" cultures, because such a distinction is false and ephemeral. It stands to reason that "there could not be high culture without popular culture," for the definition of one depends on the other (119). It would take an entire monograph to explain how the Cuzco intellectuals came to this understanding in 1919. Nevertheless one cannot but be tempted to say that due to their daily and concrete contact with the suppressed indigenous culture and the centuries-old struggle between Spanish hegemonization of the cultural space and the local intellectuals' attempt to occupy that space, they came, on their own, to a conclusion very similar to that of cultural studies. That is to say that as a result of merging Marxism and the postmodern critique of the sovereign subject, cultural studies began to dismantle the differences established between high and low culture as constructed in the work of Matthew Arnold at the end of the nineteenth century and which owe their construction to the specificities of English history. Mariátegui recognizes that any distinction between high and low culture is tied in colonial situations to the consequences of conquest and that as such the distinction is inexorably tied to the construction of race. In the Andes this and other differences made their first appearance with the

Spanish chroniclers as they began establishing the difference between Europe and its conquered civilizations.[7]

In his concluding remarks Mariátegui stresses the fact that his intent has been to "outline the ideological and political basis of public education in Peru" (1971, 121). He places little hope in the liberating power of literacy, for literacy is not a neutral value. The letter (writing) carries a heavy ideological burden. Furthermore, in Mariátegui's estimate, it is not possible to liberate the mind of the Indian without liberating his body and the practices of everyday life that enchain them both. Liberating the Indian is not just a pedagogical project, for "the first step to his redemption is to free him from serfdom" (122). Thus, Mariátegui lays the fundamental ground for Quijano's later theory on coloniality. Mariátegui's thesis on the coloniality of power is crystal clear when he writes that "our Spanish and colonial heritage consists not of a pedagogical method, but of an economic and social regime" (121). This statement echoes through the chambers of Foucault's own power/knowledge theory. By implication, academic freedom is thus but an illusion if it does not interact with the struggles in the society at large. Perhaps here we have a true point of divergence with what until now has been called postcolonial theory. This separation of theory and practice is an argument leveled against postcolonial theory by many a contemporary Anglophone critic, as a cursory review of *Colonial Discourse and Post-colonial Theory, A Reader* (1994) would indicate.[8] It is also one of the points of resistance to postcolonial theory in Latin American circles.

RELIGION

Mariátegui's reading of George J. Frazer's *The Golden Bough* (1890) enables him to set up a perspective on religion that allows him, as cultural criticism later would, to turn the gaze fixed on the rituals and beliefs of the West's others onto its own normative religion: Judeo-Christian theology and practices. This is indeed a bold and daring step, for it levels the previously established hierarchy between "true religions" or monotheistic creeds and the rituals and beliefs of polytheistic peoples. Mariátegui thinks that now that the concept of religion has been broadened by anthropology and myth studies, it can be understood as much more or much less than considerations on the institution of the church, theology and sacraments. Mariátegui sees the possibility of investigating religion as one more dimension of the ideological formation of subjects. Cast in this fashion, religion permits him to delve into and compare the formation of the Puritan subject to the Catholic subject, and these two in turn enable him to investigate the formation of the indigenous subject. The examination of religious practices and beliefs Mariátegui thinks could perhaps hold the key for understanding indigenous subjectivity. Mariátegui uses anthropology to lend legitimacy to Indian religion itself. In doing so he operates a complete reversal of the colonial claim to monopoly and hegemony over the sacred and subjectivity. This move is of course not lost on Arguedas, who in his peerless novel *Los ríos profundos* (1957) asks: how can the force of religious belief be turned into political action in the modern world, how do men become both paralyzed and moved to action by the force of belief?[9] This investigation into the constitution and the force of belief in the lives of illiterate, colonized people was also Gandhi's great question and finding in India's struggle for freedom from British colonialism. It remains a fruitful question in subaltern historiography.

Reading Waldo Frank's popular *Our America*, Mariátegui brings to bear a Nietzschean perspective on the American journalist's comparative approach to the cultural differences separating the Americas. Mariátegui concludes that the Puritan protest in England was rooted in the will to power (1971, 125). Desiring power in England and finding it impossible to acquire, the puritan developed a self-discipline by which he turned the "sweets of austerity" into a power over himself and later over others. The frugal and self-denying life released energy far better than any other self-discipline. This energy accounts for all the characteristics of subject formation associated with the agents of U.S. capitalism. The question then is, what forms of self-discipline permit the formation of channels that release positive energy into the body politic? If religion is one of those channels, then one needs to ask: how does the Catholic superimposition of rites over indigenous beliefs constitute the subjective energies of the Indian population, and how can those energies be released to the benefit of the Indian and the nation.

Although, like the Inca Garcilaso with regard to the Spanish chroniclers, Mariátegui also must correct Frazer's idea that the original religion of the Incas was similar in its "collective theocracy and materialism" to the Hindu religion (1971, 126), he nevertheless finds the operations of the study of religions in comparative perspective productive and liberating. The comparative study of religion opens the way for a new thinking on how Inca religion actually worked in the Andes. Mariátegui here disputes the established notion that the priesthood preceded the formation of the state in all cultures. For him, Andean culture has to be accorded its own space and specific modes of continuity. To try to understand it under the guidance of "universal" laws only contributes to and perpetuates ignorance of the particulars. The examination of Andean religion that he configures, based on the many works of the indigenista intellectuals of the Cuzco group, leads him to assert that "state and church formation were absolutely inseparable; religion and politics recognized the same principles and the same authority" (ibid.). Thus, like the Greco-Roman identification of the political with the social, the Inca religion could not outlive the demise of the state. "It was a social and not an individual discipline" (ibid., 127), and as such it was ready to accept another ritual without changing its beliefs.

Citing Emilio Romero's pioneering work on the system of deity substitution in the Andes, Mariátegui moves quickly past the problems in Frazer's misunderstanding of Andean religion and its encounter with the Catholic calendar and ritual. In Romero's "El Cuzco católico" (1927) Mariátegui finds that, as Arguedas would later narrate, "the Indians thrilled with emotion before the majesty of the Catholic ceremony. They saw the image of the sun in the shimmering brocade of the chasuble and cope, they saw the violet tones of the rainbow woven into the fine silk threads of the rochet" (Mariátegui 1971, 134). Examining the cultural process of negotiations, borrowings, transpositions, and transformations that would later be called "transculturation" by the Cuban anthropologist Fernando Ortiz and, indeed, later be built into one of the constitutive points of postcolonial theory (Ashcroft, Griffiths, and Tiffin 1998, 233–34), Mariátegui clarifies that "the missionaries did not instill a faith, they instilled a system of worship and a liturgy, wisely adapted to the Indian costume" (Mariátegui 1971, 135). This point would have shocked Garcilaso who did believe in the possible and complete substitution of Andean religion with Christianity based on the idea that one ethical code was not all that distant from the other and on his own comparison of Roman and Inca religion. Guamán Poma, who always claimed that Andean religion was indeed more consistent and straightforward in the relationship between belief and behavior, would have been gratified to read Mariátegui's analysis, for in many ways it coincides with his own diagnosis of what was going on in the Andes during the campaigns for the extirpation of idolatries circa 1600. Mariátegui inflects Frazer—like Garcilaso bends the entire Renaissance to read Andean matters, like Homi Bhabha inflects Lacan and Renan—to read and reposition the "location of culture."

LITERATURE ON TRIAL

Mariátegui begins the last of his seven essays by clarifying that "trial" is used in a legal sense, for he will make the institution of "literature," as the maximum expression of the coloniality of power, responsible for the work it has performed through the centuries. In this scenario an intellectual like

Mariátegui is a witness for the prosecution. He regards his seventh essay as an open trial on the colonialist mentality that has ruined the past: "My responsibility to the past compels me to vote against the defendant" (1971, 183). Cultural critique is thus a question of conscience, not a mere exercise in analysis or a display of rhetorical games. The indictment of the letrado culture that follows could not be stronger or more to the point, and it is not surprising to see that it contains the seeds for Angel Rama's La ciudad letrada (1984).

At the outset, and as usual, Mariátegui, aware of the impossibility of absolutely objective knowledge in an always political cultural milieu, warns the reader that he does not pretend to be impartial (1971, 183), although such admission of positionality does not necessarily mean the negation of universal human aspiration or solidarity. He regards admitting to positionality as part and parcel of the individual's ethical and political responsibility. His politics, he says, are philosophy and religion, not Marxism or scientific materialism (ibid.). While Mariátegui poses the problem of national literature, he does not see that the aesthetic aspect of literature is divorced from the politics. Quite to the contrary, he regards the one as intrinsically related to the other.

In a definition of nation that surprises us for its similarities with the theses of Benedict Anderson and Homi Bhabha, Mariátegui advances that for him "the nation itself is an abstraction, an allegory, a myth that does not correspond to a reality that can be scientifically defined" (ibid., 188). The similarities might be due to a common reading of Ernest Renan's essay "What Is a Nation? (1882), wherein the French philosopher advances the thesis that the nation is not a territory, not a language, and not a religious tradition, but rather a cultural construct woven in the loom that entwines memory with forgetting. Therefore it follows that, for Mariátegui, the idea of an autochthonous and authentic national literature is an illusion. Only the Chinese, he says, if they had managed to achieve their desired total isolation, could then claim a "national literature." Mariátegui takes cultural contact and transformation as a given. Consequently he has no trouble stating that Quechua grammar and writing are the work of the Spaniards. Quechua literature more properly belongs to bilingual men of letters like "El Lunarejo" (Juan de Espinosa Medrano, 1632–1688) or to the appearance of Inocencio Mamani, the young author of Tucuipac Manashcan (in Mariátegui 1971, 184), a comedy written under the influence of the contemporary bilingual poet Gamaliel Churata. Mariátegui's view of this perennial exchange is not unlike the transculturation theorized by Ortiz, and it does not imply a one-way street with the colonized always assimilating forms and forces emitted by the center. This point appears with greater clarity in his essays on César Vallejo.

Mariátegui goes on to characterize the colonial following of Góngora and other Spanish fashions as servile imitation. When carefully considered today, Mariátegui's assessment of the colonial imitation of Spanish literary fashions has a great deal in common with Homi Bhabha's own sense of mimicry. However, that servile imitation—that is to say, mimicry—has little to do with the double or triple cultural competency to be found in Garcilaso's writing practices.[10] Garcilaso's work along with Mariátegui's or Vallejo's must be considered a creative and capable model of a postcolonial discourse that claims agency, competency, and the power of inflection that the discourse of colonized can have on the knowledges of the center, as any history of the reception of Garcilaso's work in Europe can attest.

The cultural "dualism" that has constituted Peru since the rupture of the conquest has obfuscated the need for a critical perspective on European modes of analysis. According to Mariátegui, a questioning of the methods and assumptions in the exegesis of metropolitan literatures is in order, for when they are uncritically assumed as a hermeneutic, they alter the object of study. Thus they have to be either radically altered or abandoned (Mariátegui 1971, 88). Owing to the shape of their own historical situations, colonial, bicultural literatures prove refractory to methods that assume a unified national subject or language. With the exception of two writers—Inca Garcilaso de la Vega and "El Lunarejo"—literature written during the colonial period was, according to Mariátegui, a "servile and inferior imitation" (ibid., 188) of Spanish practices and models. These bombastic and empty texts had no understanding of or feeling for the Peruvian scene. These bad imitators, even when satirical, sustained only by the force of imitation, lacked the imagination necessary for a reconstruction of the preconquest past and therefore failed to ground their discourse on anything concrete. They were incapable of establishing ties with the common people (ibid., 190–93). For Mariátegui, satire and sarcasm are not necessarily critical or subversive positions. They can in fact be part and parcel of the same servile imitation that blocks the way, dilutes the paths of confrontation, and shrinks the possibilities of imagining a world in which the relationship of master and slave does not predicate all relations. It is not till the appearance of Ricardo Palma (1833–1919) in the late nineteenth century that satire and mockery acquire a sharper edge due to Palma's interest in the colonial past. In disagreement with most of Palma's political critics, Mariátegui's sharp eye detects the fact that Palma's is not a nostalgia for the viceroyalty, as many argued, but rather a distancing from it by the effect of a laughter that ridicules, a snickering that reveals the hypocrisy of the master as well as the consent of the slave and thus levels down the authority that supports claims to power and rule.

In his interpretation of the colonial and republican literature in the Andes, Mariátegui advances several key theoretical positions later developed by Antonio Cornejo Polar, Angel Rama, and postcolonial criticism and theory. Mariátegui posits the heterogeneous discursive practices given in a plurilingual and pluricultural environment as he distinguished between texts written in Spanish or Quechua by bilingual subjects and texts written in either Spanish or Quechua by monolingual subjects. He also establishes a difference between servile imitations and texts written in Spanish which are nevertheless connected to the "Andean scene" and speak of the lived experience in the colonial world. He further distinguishes between complicit and critical satire. Mariátegui thus lays the ground for the debate on transculturation that Angel Rama's thesis (1982), based on Ortiz's own analysis of the formation of culture in Cuba ([1940] 1978), brought about in the consideration of Latin American culture as a whole, a debate that has been a dominant force in cultural and literary theory during the last thirty years.

It is important to note here that while Rama chooses the work of José María Arguedas as one of the prime examples of transculturation, some critics have uncritically deployed the idea to explain myriad aspects of Latin American culture in a celebratory move. Others, like Antonio Cornejo Polar, have warned that this re-dressing of the "mestizaje" metaphor hides within it the same potential for oppressive homogenization that is hidden in mestizaje.[11] Others have even pointed out that transculturation also occludes the hierarchical difference implicit in all colonial situations and that it itself could be considered a deployment of the same letrados who erected the colonial teaching machine. Arguedas himself never embraced transculturation as a proper description of either his work or cultural dynamics in the Andes. As it is well known, in his acceptance speech of the Inca Garcilaso Prize (1968) Arguedas rejected the notion that he was an "aculturado."[12] I think that he would also have rejected the notion of transculturation if by that we mean a one-way flow of cultural goods from the colonizer to the colonized and an appropriation process going on exclusively at the colonized end, where either the remnants or the jewels of the imperial center are recycled. This latter notion of cultural exchange has little to do with "exchange" between two asymmetrical and contending subject positions and much to do with the notion of bricolage. The notion of one-way cultural flow is not what Mariátegui has in mind either when he speaks of cultural exchange or when he analyzes the work of César Vallejo, for Mariátegui argues that Vallejo brings about the definitive rupture with the colonial legacy. Thus his "creative" and original poetics would be beyond processes such as transculturation whether it is read in a celebratory or a suspicious way. Arguedas's vocation as a writer was defined and transformed by his reading of Mariátegui when, as an insecure and impoverished Andean youth, Arguedas first came to reside in Lima. The author of *The Fox Up Above and the Fox from Down Below* (1971) writes fully informed by Vallejo's poetics.

Positing the problematic of duality of Peru's culture as a foundational concept for the understanding of all colonial formations, including literature mostly written in the colonizer's language, Mariátegui's cultural theory is not at all far from the influential discoveries of postcolonial theory. Given the constraints of space, I will simply list the topics in *Key Concepts in Post-Colonial Studies* (1998) and highlight the areas of discussion of mutual concern to Mariátegui, his generation, and postcolonial theory: indigenous people/colonizer, agency, ambivalence, anticolonialism, appropriation or catachresis, binarism, center/periphery, class and postcolonialism, colonial discourse, colonial desire, contrapuntal reading, counterdiscourse, cultural diversity/cultural difference, decolonization, dependency theory, essentialism/strategic essentialism, ethnicity, ethnography, Eurocentrism, hegemony, hybridity, imperialism, mestizaje, mimicry, nation and language, national allegory, orality, testimonio, and transculturation.

Mariátegui's negative assessment of colonial literature acquires greater depth in light of the figure of César Vallejo, the author of the epoch-making *The Black Heralds* (1918) and *Trilce* (1928), and now widely recognized as the greatest poet of the Spanish language in the twentieth century. Vallejo's radical inquiry into language and the world won Mariátegui's immediate admiration. Writing at a time when most of the established critics rejected Vallejo's departure from romanticism and symbolism, Mariátegui praises Vallejo for ushering in "poetic freedom and autonomy" and for bringing in "the vernacular in writing" (Mariátegui 1971, 250). Vallejo, according to Mariátegui, does what the entire colonial period failed to do: "For the first time indigenous sentiment is given pristine expression. . . . [H]e creates a new style, . . . a new message and a new technique" (ibid.). Mariátegui astutely recognizes that the novelty, originality, and force in Vallejo's poetry are truly beyond commentary. In order to convey a sense of the compactness of Vallejo's poems and the arresting effect of the poems on the reader, Mariátegui compares it to music: "Indigenous sentiment has a melody of its own and [Vallejo] has mastered its song" (ibid.). It is interesting to note that Arguedas also uses music as the metaphor for capturing the sense of sublime expression.

For Mariátegui, Vallejo has overcome the dualism of form and substance as well as the dualism that the conquest created. Vallejo has achieved the total integration of language, form, and meaning that allows the poem to speak the world. He has also overcome the problem of description, the rhetoric that underscores the distance between language and the world. Vallejo offers a critique of what we would call today "representation" and uses the word instead to close the gap between the world and the word. Vallejo's poetry is above all genuine. It is at one with itself. "Vallejo does not explore folklore. Quechua words [when they appear in his writing] are a spontaneous and integral part of his writing. . . . [H]e is not deliberately autochthonous. His poetry and language emanate from his flesh and spirit; he embodies his message. Indigenous sentiment operates in his art perhaps without his knowledge or desire" (Mariátegui 1971, 252). Mariátegui is especially interested in pointing out that Vallejo's nostalgia is not a nostalgia of a specific past, but it is rather a "metaphysical protest, a nostalgia of exile, of absence" (ibid.). A homelessness, one might say today, but a nostalgia that "throbs with the pain of three centuries" of affliction and endurance (ibid., 254). Mariátegui is quick to point out, however, that Vallejo, even when he confronts God ("You have always been well") or when he feels God's pain, is neither a satanic nor a neurotic poet (ibid.). I think that in Mariátegui's interpretation of Vallejo, which is amazingly on the mark, we find one of the key divergences and differences with postcolonial theory, for Vallejo is truly a child of the age of suspicion, and neither Mariátegui nor Vallejo, for all their devastating critique of the modes of knowledge/power of the colonial centers, really shared in the nihilist narcissism of some aspects of the West's modernity. Vallejo's sorrow is for the whole of humanity and even for God, and as Mariátegui points out, "Nothing in his poetry is egotistic [or] narcissistic" (ibid., 257). On the contrary "he achieves the most austere, humble and proud simplicity" (ibid.).

The same may be said of Mariátegui's own cutting but always direct writing. It is well known that the style of some postcolonial theorists is rather baroque, that there is nothing austere or simple in their texts. In Vallejo, Mariátegui finds not only beauty and a compelling critique of metaphysics but the much desired break with colonialism: "Today the rupture is complete" (1971, 287). Vallejo's art announces the birth of a new sensibility, of a new world. Indeed, Mariátegui feels satisfied with the yield of the trials he has conducted. He thus closes his book by asserting the productive side of the colonial paradox: "The universal, ecumenical road we have chosen to travel, and for which we are reproached, has taken us ever closer to ourselves" (ibid.). This assertion stands in clear opposition to the fear, suspicion and continuous mutilation of mimicry.

CONCLUSIONS

No doubt Mariátegui's singular and seminal analysis of coloniality in Peru had the theoretical power to reach well beyond the borders of the Andean nation and Latin America. But precisely because of the coloniality of power his work, as well as the work of many other Latin American intellectuals, did not readily circulate beyond the borders of the Spanish language. Until the rise of the Spanish American novelists in the international cultural arena (the boom), Spanish remained a subalternized language. It was, as Walter Mignolo has argued, a European language subalternized in the quarters of the powerful second modernity of the Enlightenment, the time when the rest of the globe came under the aegis of the British Empire and with whose Commonwealth postcolonial theory is most deeply and closely associated.

Mariátegui's radical thinking does in many ways anticipate the preoccupations of postcolonial theory, despite the fact that Mariátegui does not depart from a body of postmodern theory that in a way lays the basis for the postcolonial questioning and decentering of the West's power/knowledge primacy. Mariátegui, like Garcilaso de la Vega and Guamán Poma before him (although Mariátegui did not read Guamán Poma, whose work was lost until basically the 1930s) and José María Arguedas afterward, never ceased to learn and to inform their thinking with and from local knowledges. In fact, these four theorists could say that they think as they do, write as they do, and occupy the intellectual space that they do "porque soy indio" as Garcilaso wrote in his classic *Royal Commentaries* (1609).

In this claim made by indigenous mestizos, rests, I think, the most important difference between one of the most easily embraced and frequently deployed concepts in postcolonial theory and the radical, decolonizing thinking of these four Andean intellectuals. It's the difference between mimicry as originally developed in Homi Bhabha's *The Location of Culture* (1994) and the conception of mestizaje as a doubled-layered, but not split, cultural competence of the colonial subject. When Garcilaso, writing in Spain and hoping to pass the censors in order to publish his commentaries on Inca history and society, writes that he disputes the portrayal of the Inca Empire in the Spanish chronicles and that he does so "porque soy indio," he is not contradicting himself. He is already disputing the colonizing notion that the subject must be culturally univocal and that therefore he chooses to suppress part of his lived experience and his multiple knowledges. Garcilaso is establishing the fact that postcolonial subjects walk on two legs, that they can achieve cultural competence on both registers. Mutilation of one of his several cultural registers is not necessary in order to inhabit the postcolonial world. The bicultural colonial subject is a capable subject precisely because he can move from one side to the other, keep them apart, bring them together, cross over, set them side by side in dialogue, struggle for complementarity and reciprocity, or simply keep them at distance depending on the play of the given moment. Garcilaso, who claimed authority on things Inca by virtue of his knowledge of Quechua, nevertheless mastered Hebrew, Latin, and Italian in order to write in Spanish the preconquest past. He posits the postcolonial subject as a subject who must learn to occupy multiple strategic positions. This multiplicity does not imply a schizophrenic subjectivity. Likewise, Guamán Poma, who wanted the Spanish to leave the Andes entirely, decided nevertheless that keeping scissors and writing would be beneficial to the reconstitution of the Andean world.

The Andean concept of doubling and multiplying cultural competencies is indeed divorced from the concepts of mimicry and hybridity in Bhabha. Coming from Lacan, as they do, mimicry and hybridity imply a sense of lack, fear, suspicion, and perennial disencounter and joylessness. The camouflage that takes place in mimicry, the dissembling that breeds suspicion and pain in the colonial encounter that Bhabha so ably portrays does indeed take place in Andean coloniality, and it has no better representation than in the empty imitators of Góngora that Mariátegui describes as part and parcel of a servile literary production which does little to elucidate and much to obfuscate the workings of coloniality. But such mimicry is not universal and determining of all colonial situations, and indeed the four intellectuals singled out in this essay define the colonial struggle precisely as the capacity to achieve competence in all power/knowledge situations and thus stem the tide of mimicry, the paralyzing suspicion of inauthenticity, and the practices of thoughtless imitation.

NOTES

1   In my essay "Writing with His Thumb in the Air" I develop at greater length the process of change in the field of colonial studies. As in this essay, I show therein the reconfiguration of the field due to changes brought about by Latin American scholars working in Latin America and by high French theory at large (Castro-Klaren 2002).

2   Many of these issues, some of which were initially raised in the so-called initial

debate on postcolonialism in Latin America (Seed, Vidal, Adorno, Mignolo, et al.), were later on developed by Mignolo, Castro-Gómez, Achugar, and so on (see Mignolo and Castro-Gómez in this volume).

3   There is no reader of Garcilaso de la Vega who does not immediately detect his command of Renaissance letters and his brilliant maneuvers to harness the Renaissance recovery of classical Greece and Rome in order to make the Inca civilization understandable to Europe's first modernity (see Durand 1976, Zamora 1988, Rabasa 2000).

4   See the entry on "discourse" in *Key Concepts in Post-colonial Studies*. There the editors note that discourse as used in postcolonial theory is "specifically derived from Foucault" (Ashcroft, Griffiths, and Tiffin 1998, 70). The entry goes on to say that "for Foucault discourse is a strongly bounded area of social knowledge, a system of statements within which the world can be known. The key feature of this is that the world is not simply 'there' to be talked about, rather it is through discourse itself that the world is brought into being. . . . It is the 'complex of signs and practices which organizes social existence and social production' " (71).

5   Of course the problem of the writing of history entails many more concerns than the three touched on here, and both Mariátegui and postcolonial theory address them in complex and multiple ways, many of which have yet to be explored fully and which of course I cannot even begin to list here.

6   I do not have here the space to enter into the question of suppressed languages and subalternized knowledges in relation to education and the formation of the national subject, but I think that some aspects of the problematic will at least be touched on at a glance in the section on literature.

7   For an in-depth study of intellectuals in Cuzco at the time when Mariátegui wrote, see Tamayo Herrera 1980; for a history of indigenismo in Cuzco in the twentieth century, see Cadena 2000; for an assessment on the survival and transformación of indigenous culture in Peru, see Flores Galindo 1987 and Burga 1988. See also Castro-Klaren 2003.

8   See specially parts 1, 2, and 4, where in separate essays critics such as Jenny Sharp, Vijay Mishra and Bob Hodge, Ann McClintock and Anja Looma take up the apparent disconnection and disregard of certain aspects of postcolonial theory and the need for liberation from oppression of colonialism in the world. See Williams and Chrisman 1994. Of course, the most charged and sustained critique of postcolonial theory is Aijaz Ahmad's *In Theory: Classes, Nations, Literatures* (1992).

9   This question is addressed, in a different context, by Sklodowska in reviewing Antonio Benítez Rojo's literary treatment of religiosity and myth (see her essay in this volume).

10   For an extensive discussion of how Bhabha's concept of mimicry as quite different from Garcilaso's idea of cultural mestizaje and sense of a post conquest navigation (in a double registry which does not necessarily imply the Lacanian idea of self betrayal, fear and suspicion of the other), see Castro-Klaren (1999).

11   See Mazzotti's essay in this volume.

12   See Arguedas 1992, Rama 1982, and Moreiras 1997.

UNFORGOTTEN GODS:
POSTCOLONIALITY AND REPRESENTATIONS OF HAITI
IN ANTONIO BENÍTEZ ROJO'S "HEAVEN AND EARTH"
Elzbieta Sklodowska

The remarkably vast and diverse domain of the Caribbean does not lend itself to easy overviews, and
even the stylistic and thematic coordinates shared by
national literatures—such as the colonial legacy of slavery, the African-based cultural heritage, or the nation-
building experiences of modernity—should not cause
us to deemphasize local differences, nor should these
affinities obliterate voices that have been subjected
to "hybridization" or "transculturation" with European
elements in the crucible of the plantation economy.
Michel-Rolph Trouillot has stressed the difficulty of
theorizing the Caribbean by calling it an "undisciplined
region," whose "multiracial, multilingual, stratified
and, some would say, multicultural" nature combined
with "inescapable" historicity call for equally idiosyncratic methodologies (1992, 21). Given the cultural
diversity of the Caribbean steeped in the violent past,
it is not surprising that postcolonial approaches have

resonated with great force among the scholars from or of the region. In fact, it has become commonplace within literary criticism to state that Caribbean writings lend themselves almost by default to postcolonial approaches.

Postcolonialism's unique combination of a sociocultural awareness with a deconstructive imprint provides, indeed, a much-needed angle for the (re)articulation of subaltern and "hyphenated" identities based on "the conviction of necessity of deconstructing the absolutism of European culture and its hegemonization of other, 'lower' culture" (Ippolito 2000, 10). The extent to which postcolonial thinking has laid the groundwork for the recasting of the Caribbean is tangible, and as a critical force it has to be reckoned with. For one, postcolonial approaches continue to shape the gradual unraveling of the repositories of Caribbean collective memory, an endeavor that has become the order of the day for scholars, writers, and literary critics interested in drawing a distinction between exoticized versions of African cultures and representations better attuned to an African-based consciousness.

Faced with the vexing problem of ever-changing methodologies—some of which are deemed obsolete as soon as they gain widespread acceptance in the intellectual marketplace—a critic may be tempted, indeed, to "expedite" his or her writing by forgoing the painstaking process of sociohistorical research and textual analysis in favor of the theoretical fad du jour, applied indiscriminately to texts at hand. However, while it may be illuminating to carefully unravel textual complexities through a prism of postcolonial criticism, it can be even more beneficial to tame theory just a bit, especially when it imposes itself with predictable and schematic obviousness.

My point in this essay is not so much to disengage myself from postcolonial theory as to gain insight into a specific text—Antonio Benítez Rojo's short story "Heaven and Earth" (1967)—by focusing on the interface of textual analysis and sociocultural research. I hope to avoid excessive reliance on theoretical tools furnished by postcolonial approaches without relinquishing the postcolonial wisdom of reading "against the grain." In view of the totality of Benítez Rojo's work—historically minded, traversed by a web of inter-Caribbean connections, and never blinded by the glare of theory—it seems worthwhile to open the door to textual exploration that reckons with some of the clues provided by the writer himself.

Much as we can learn from the existing critical bibliography on the works of Benítez Rojo, in-depth studies of individual narrative texts are still scarce. "Heaven and Earth" is something of an exception, having been a subject of illuminating readings by Roberto González Echevarría (1985), María Zielina

(1992), Lidia Verson Vadillo (1999), Julio Ortega (1973a, 1973b), and Eugenio Matibag (1996). However, contrary to those critics who have seen "Heaven and Earth" as part of a vogue of magical realism, I argue that this masterful short story fits better under the sign of "undisciplined" Caribbean poetics. Insofar as "Heaven and Earth" defies all formulas—to the point of having been criticized for its "undisciplined" structure (Llopis 1970)—it also repays a close, contextualized reading.[1] The only rival to its aesthetic challenge is the multilayered complexity of the constant, albeit shadow presence of history and the symbolic resonance of popular beliefs.

I explore in particular the story's articulation of Haitian subtext within the framework of Cuban prerevolutionary and postrevolutionary society. I will show that Benítez Rojo's narrative highlights Haitian culture as a distinctive cultural and political force identified primarily with African-based spirituality. Even though Vodou—a syncretic religion derived from West African Yoruba tradition most commonly practiced in Haitian communities—is mentioned by name only a couple of times, "Heaven and Earth" is replete with references to Vodou rituals and beliefs (houngan, possession, zombification), deities (bon Dieu, Oggun Ferraille, Legba), and connections between Vodou and the Haitian past (Mackandal).[2] Marc McLeod attributes the lasting Haitian presence in Cuba to the cementing power of Vodou and to the adaptability of this religion whose strength resides in its "symbiotic" and "decentralized" nature, its "portability" and flexibility.[3] According to Marc McLeod, "Haitianos were forced to rely upon closed, rural communities which kept them on the margins of Cuban society but out of the hands of Cuban authorities. Whether in Caidije, Guanamaca, or numerous other Haitian villages, in many ways they lived as modern-day maroons" (1998, 614). On a more general level, if we bear in mind Patrick Taylor's statement that, as a form of mythical narrative, Vodou "always remained bound to the drama of colonialism and its neocolonial aftermath" (1989, 95), some of the threads running through postcolonial thinking may be, after all, well-suited for unveiling the marks of Caribbean identity inscribed by Haiti in Cuba.[4]

When Pedro Limón, the story's main protagonist and occasional narrator, returns home to the Cuban province of Camagüey after seven years of revolutionary involvement—the Sierra, the Bay of Pigs—he is introduced as a Haitian because of the linguistic reference to Creole: "Pedro Limón said good-bye to Pascasio and told him in Creole—so that he'd know that in spite of all the time between them he was still one of them" (190). While the deliberate use of Creole certainly denotes otherness in Cuba, it does not necessarily point to a well-defined identity. According to the Haitian writer

René Depestre, the problem of "self" in Creole still awaits serious study and articulation (quoted in Dayan 1993a, 141).

In the reenactment of Pedro's conversation with his childhood friend, Pascasio, other signs of Haitian culture embedded in the context of post-revolutionary Cuba quickly emerge, this time in the form of explicit references to Vodou: "And Ti-Bois was fine, grumbling when he wasn't communicating with the greatest *voudoun* spirits . . . preaching to the old hags that Fidel Castro was crazy and had shaken up the whole island, taking for himself the land that the *bon Dieu* had given to the Cubans" (190). To further accentuate cultural difference Ti-Bois is identified as *houngan*—"the sorcerer Ti-Bois, as the whites called him, Pascasio's and Aristón's grandfather" (191)—and the Creole name denoting his status is italicized. According to Laënec Hurbon, *houngan* (or, alternatively, *oungan*) is "the man to whom a person turns in all circumstances, a man who is able to make himself heard by the spirits. As the head of a brotherhood, he reports to nobody. . . . He combines the functions of priest, healer, exorcist, magician, head of the chorus, and organizer of activities. The *oungan* also occupies a very high position in the social echelons of the peasant world" (1992, 788).

It bears repeating that from its opening lines "Heaven and Earth" associates the presence of Haiti in Cuba with otherness. This textual clue constitutes an important analytical point of departure, and it takes us directly to a vast array of postcolonial approaches which, over the last three decades or so, have submitted the image of the other to a serious scrutiny across a range of disciplines in the humanities and social sciences (Johannes Fabian 1983; Shohat and Stam 1994; Taussig 1984). And since perceptions of the other are most powerfully manifested in the domain of ethnicity, along with the emphasis on the "constructed" or "invented" nature of ethnic categories, we have also become alerted to the cross-over between ethnicity, class, gender, and sexuality (Mason 1990). As anthropologists are quick to tell us, two distinct attitudes emerge when approaching the other: on one hand, we may find an attempt to "translate" the "anomalous" alien into the familiar; on the other, we may encounter the exoticizing of the other through emphasis on difference and strangeness. In a well-known argument Johannes Fabian asserts that, by and large, Western anthropological discourse tends to place the images of the other in a mythical time frame, outside the time of historical representation, thus transforming him or her into a timeless archetype of primitivism. In his study of postslavery writings George Handley, on the other hand, points to a constant hesitation "between speaking from within lived historical experience or speaking to it as an isolated outsider" (2000,

115). Handley draws on J. Hillis Miller's essay "The Two Relativisms," in which Miller argues "that this tension reflects the dynamic between the taboos against too much difference—implied in the notion of miscegenation —and too much sameness, implied in incest" (quoted in ibid.). In Latin America and the Caribbean in particular otherness, according to Beatriz González Stephan, is part of the paradigm of civilization and barbarism whereby the modernizing power of the city (law, culture, reason) is meant to control the uncivilized inhabitants of the rural areas (anarchy, nature, irrationality). Otherness, continues González Stephan, assumes "legal *penalty,* inquiry, judgment, and exclusion, ethical and cultural *degradation* ('filthy,' 'repugnant,' 'uncivil,' 'unpleasant,' 'vicious') and social and economic failure" (2003, 198). In any case, otherness harbors the notion of the monstrous and the primitive.

All these perspectives certainly provide suggestive paths of inquiry when approaching what I call the "inscription" of Haitian otherness onto Cuban imaginary as recast in "Heaven and Earth." It is equally important, however, to bear in mind the extent to which the deep-seated fear associated with Haiti went far beyond the geographic confines of the Caribbean. Trouillot traces some of these associations to the era of the Haitian Revolution, when "making zombies and vodoun a trope for 'barbaric' Haiti was a favorite strategy of the 'civilized' world once the former French colony of Saint Domingue became the first Black Republic in 1804" (quoted in Dayan 1993b, 165). By focusing on the bizarre, so goes Trouillot's argument, the West was able to easily achieve the effacement of the unprecedented accomplishments of the Haitian Revolution of 1791–1804: " 'The more Haiti appears weird, the easier it is to forget that it represents the longest neocolonial experiment in the history of the West' " (ibid.). Small wonder, then, that, as Trouillot has shown elsewhere, "when we are being told over and over again that Haiti is unique, bizarre, unnatural, odd, queer, freakish, or grotesque, we are also being told, in varying degrees, that it is unnatural, erratic, and therefore unexplainable" (ibid.). In more recent history the occupation of Haiti by U.S. forces (1915–34) reinforced the racial stereotypes of Haitians—"black magic, frightful zombies, evil sorcerers, cannibalism" (Patrick Taylor 1992, 815)—providing "much fodder" not only for North American popular culture (ibid., 812) but also for "high" literature (e.g., William Faulkner's *Absalom, Absalom* [1936]).

In the very beginning the rhetoric of the Haitian Revolution might have played some role in fueling these fears and images. It is not without significance, for example, that Boisrond Tonnerre, secretary to General Jean-Jacques Dessalines, is largely remembered (and often quoted) for the chilling words in which he described the task of drafting the Haitian Act of Independence: "Pour dresser l'acte de indépendance, il nous faut la peau d'un blanc pour parchemin, son crâne pour encrier, son sang pour encre et une baïonnette pour plume" [In order to prepare the independence act all we need is the skin of a white man for parchment, his skull for a desk, his blood for ink, and bayonet for a pen] (Laroche 1977, 1, my translation).

The Haitian Revolution had a particularly deep impact on the Spanish portion of the island baptized by the Spaniards as Hispaniola. In the Dominican Republic the threat of "Africanization" and the contempt for the "savage" neighbors was magnified by prolonged Haitian occupation of the Spanish part of the island (1822–44). Subsequently, Haitian Africanness became vilified and demonized as part of the Dominican nation-building process.[5] One look at the literature of the Dominican Republic reveals racial stereotypes ciphered onto a vast repertory of texts, mirroring the process of nationalist self-affirmation in terms that either excluded the presence of African cultures or relegated it to the undesirable "influence" of marginalized immigrants from neighboring Haiti or the English-speaking Antilles (Coulthard 1962, 38).

It is commonplace to hear, in contrast, that the postslavery nationalist discourse in Cuba (cubanidad) has tended toward the incorporation rather than rejection of cultural formations of African descent (transculturation, mestizaje).[6] According to Aviva Chomsky, "Today it is almost a truism that Cuban nationalism has historically been based on an anti-racist ideology, and harked back to the words of José Martí, that 'to be Cuban is more than being black, more than being white'" (2000, 417). While canonical literary works—like the late-nineteenth-century novel Cecilia Valdés exemplified the dilemmas of Cuban nationalists whose visions of cubanidad assumed a gradual whitening of the population through miscegenation and integration, for an average Cuban Villaverde's mulatto heroine continues to be an immensely popular figure embodying the nation's mixed ethnic heritage. Alejo Carpentier's novel Écue-Yamba-O (1933)—subtitled "novela afrocubana" —was, in turn, reduplicating the nationalist ideology of Afro-Cubanism of the 1920s "that saw national identity as residing in Cuba's African heritage" (Aviva Chomsky 2000, 425). Écue-Yamba-O also recognized the emergence of a significant Haitian community of migrant workers and their cultural impact in Cuba.[7] Carpentier's bewilderment and his awkward mediating position between the representation of African-based cultures and the reader was clearly enmeshed in what Amy Emery has called "ethnographic surrealism" based on the technique of virtuoso bricolage (Emery 1996, 8–9).

The novel's experimental nature notwithstanding, the author himself contended in retrospect that *Ecué-Yamba-O* suffered from an excessive cultural distance toward African-based cultures, and he proceeded to remedy these shortcomings in *El reino de este mundo* (*The Kingdom of This World*) (1949) by highlighting the uniqueness of Latin America and the Caribbean, which he attributed to the idiosyncratic blend of transculturated myth, magic, and irrational excess.[8] Epitomized by the spiritual impact of Vodou on the Haitian Revolution and the history of the region, Carpentier's theory of *lo real maravilloso americano* opened up the door to worldwide recognition of Latin American writings steeped in magic, myth, and fantasy.[9] It is far from obvious that Vodou provided a blueprint for some of the narrative techniques commonly associated with magical realism, such as the blurring of the boundaries between life and death and a peculiar treatment of time. Nevertheless, as Deslauriers has argued, "Voodoo is a system that undermines any familiar Western rational understanding of the notion of reality, where the boundary between the worlds of the living and the dead is nonexistent or unclear, and where time is transcended, for the living live as if they were living in the world of the dead, and the dead live in eternity. . . . To a geographer, voodoo seems to establish a particular relationship between time and space . . . where space is shared by the living and the dead" (2001, 338, 343).

To be sure, Carpentier was not the only Cuban intellectual to reckon with the extraordinary impact of Haiti in the Caribbean and beyond.[10] Ever since the 1791 revolution Haiti has remained in Cuban imaginary a source of constant anxiety, bewilderment, and fascination. Cuban nation-building, literary, and popular discourses are certainly more ambivalent in their perception of the neighboring nation than the blatantly anti-Haitian construct of "dominicanness." Some scholars have questioned, however, what Aline Helg has called "the myth of Cuban racial equality" (1995, 247), documenting long-standing racist prejudice that has been difficult to erase even with the changes brought by the revolution of 1959. As McLeod demonstrated in his in-depth study of Antillean immigrant workers in the first third of the twentieth century, ethnic stigmatization of Haitians in Cuba went hand in hand with discriminatory labor practices, whereas British West Indian immigrants tended to be treated more fairly. According to McLeod, stereotypes of "Haitian witchcraft and proclivity for revolt, of Antillean criminality, disease, and immorality in general" were very strong among Cubans (1998, 602). Research done by the authors of *El Vodú en Cuba* confirms the stereotype of Haitian as a malevolent sorcerer (James Figarola, Millet, and Alarcón 2000, 79–83).

These views correspond quite neatly to the paradigm evoked by González Stephan (2003), in which law, culture, and reason are used to control "the primitive" through cultural degradation ("filthy," "repugnant," "sick," "criminal"). In prerevolutionary Cuba, opposition to Haitian immigration was often phrased in terms of national rather than strictly ethnic identities as these foreign, noncitizen, black, exploited, potentially rebellious workers replicated the "dangers" associated with African slaves (Aviva Chomsky 2000, 433–34). Inasmuch as Cuba's and Haiti's African-based cultures and plantation economies suggest a shared legacy, the racist register of Haitian otherness has been particularly persistent. Linked to what Helg has called the three main "icons of fear" among Cubans—black revolution, black religion, and black sexuality (15)—Haitian otherness, not surprisingly, resurfaces also at the time of revolutionary change captured by Benítez Rojo in "Heaven and Earth."

Haitian identity as depicted by Benítez Rojo epitomizes both the tantalizing richness of the Caribbean and the region's resistance to theory. In defiance of rigid classifications "hyphenated" names or terms are often created in the Caribbean so as to account for unstable and multicultural identities. In "Heaven and Earth" Pedro Limón—in one of several attempts at self-definition—refers to himself as "a Marxist-Leninist Haitian" (199). In the Spanish original, Pedro Limón uses the term *pichón* ("[un] pichón de haitiano marxistaleninista" (22), which designates a Haitian born in Cuba.[11] The Spanish term not only evokes a movement between cultural identity and political ideology, but it also marks the particular relevance of cultural and ethnic heritage (Haitian) for an expatriate whose sense of belonging (Haitian born in Cuba) does not translate into full-fledged citizenship. Nasser Hussein's comment on hyphenation as a space of liminality is particularly astute: "Hyphens are radically ambivalent signifiers, for they simultaneously connect and set apart; they simultaneously represent both belonging and not belonging. What is even more curious about a hyphenated pair of words is that meaning cannot reside in one word or the other, but can only be understood in movement" (1990, 10).

The hyphenated, "neither-nor" identity of belonging and exclusion (Haitian-Cuban) is further exacerbated by equating Pedro Limón with the fearful image of a zombie. According to Haitian beliefs, a zombie "is a human being whom a sorcerer has killed, raised from the dead, and restored to bodily form; the soul and will of the zombie are completely controlled by the sorcerer" (Patrick Taylor 1989, 101).[12] This description bears an uncanny resemblance to the portrayal of Pedro Limón, and the reader has to deal with the symbolic equivalence between the protagonist and a zombie: "Initially Pascasio hadn't recognized him, behind the face that'd been pasted together bit by bit in the hospital; the sad face that burned through to the bone on muggy nights and that, according to the doctor, had turned out all right" (190). Pedro Limón, as we see, was almost literally "raised from the dead" after having suffered a disfiguring injury from "the shrapnel that struck him in the face during the Bay of Pigs invasion" (190–91). Brought back from the dead and "restored to bodily form" through a series of surgeries, Pedro Limón ends up losing his Haitian soul (*bon ange*) and identity to the "sorcerers" of the revolution: "Me, afraid. It infuriates me. I'm tough. A man of blood and fire. A Marxist-Leninist Haitian. A cadre of the revolution. Lies. All lies. I am afraid of Guanamaca, afraid to inaugurate the school and have none show up, afraid of failure, that they won't want to see me because of the Ariston thing and that they'll throw the presents in my face. At this face of mine. Now I'm nothing more than a frightened schoolteacher with the face of a zombie" (198–99).

If zombification is, as Wade Davis has claimed, "a community-sanctioned judicial process whereby individuals who break communal norms of reciprocity and solidarity are deprived of their right to participate in the community" (quoted in Patrick Taylor 1992, 813), then Pedro Limón's fear of his people and his self-perception as a zombie clearly overlap with his guilt-ridden conscience for having contravened community values and rules. The elusive reference to "the Ariston thing" becomes clarified later in the story when we learn how Pedro Limón was chosen to participate in the firing squad which executed Ariston, his closest friend. Charged with having killed a fellow soldier who had offended him with racist and homophobic insults, Ariston remains convinced of his own invulnerability, which he believes has been bestowed on him by the gods of Vodou: "When the Habanero pronounced the sentence, he stalled a bit. Later he explained carefully, as he always did, why things had to happen that way. But no one wanted to be on the firing squad, no one. Then Ariston raised his head, smiled, and asked permission to choose the men, and I was the first. 'Pedro Limón,' he said, and then he named the others. 'Don't worry,' he said to me in Creole as they tied his hands. 'If you're with me nothing can happen'" (204). It is not a coincidence that Ariston's sense of immunity is deeply grounded in ancestral beliefs. According to Patrick Taylor, "Religious symbolism, myth, and ritual unified the slave community against its owners and induced slaves to believe that they could not be harmed by bullets or that they would return to Africa if they died on the battlefield. The transformative dimension of Vaudou reached its peak in the Haitian Revolution" (1989, 109).[13]

Pedro Limón's fear of being ostracized (zombified) by his community after having played a tragic role in Aristón's death is linked to the horror of becoming a faceless, soulless entity. Consequently, Pedro's predicament should be read within a broader cultural framework of Haitian culture. It is interesting to note, following Dayan, that one of Haiti's leading intellectuals and writers, René Depestre—who, incidentally, during his exile in Cuba worked at Casa de las Américas at the same time as Benítez Rojo—has displayed "pervasive concern" with the theory of zombies and argued repeatedly that the Haitian people can be seen as a collective zombie.[14] Depestre believes that "zombification replaces the theory of alienation in Haiti. It is the concrete form of the alienation of a people. In Haiti, zombification tells the same story that one finds in other societies, but it is the colonial form of the impoverishment of being" (quoted in Dayan 1993a, 146). For Depestre, "Obsession with the zombi is perhaps the most interesting fact in cultural life in Haiti. And further, it corresponds to a reality which is the state of the Haitian people. . . . Haiti is a zombified country, a country that has lost its soul. Political and colonial history has plunged Haiti into an unrelenting state of total alienation" (ibid., 147). An author who, as Dayan points out, has grappled in his writings with "the poetic usages of Creole, the voice of the Haitian people, as well as with vodoun, their collective historical and religious experience" (1993b, 160), Depestre has also attempted to come to grips with his experience in revolutionary Cuba. In Dayan's view Cuba becomes part of the rhetoric of zombification in Depestre's novel Hadriana dans tous mes rêves whose protagonist, Patrick, describes himself as "zombified by Cuba."[15] Dayan sees Patrick as a semiautobiographical projection of the author himself, both having undergone "years of exile, culminating in what he describes as his 'false death' in Cuba, where his 'body and soul' were bled to death by socialism" (1993b, 173–74).

These theoretical interpretations notwithstanding, connections between zombification and rebellion, community sanctions and individual transgression are as evident in "Heaven and Earth" as the association between zombification and humiliation that appears to be passed along from generation to generation among Haitians. In several instances, when reminiscing about his childhood, Pedro Limón refers to his father's passive suffering. Pedro remembers, for example, how a dishonest Cuban truck driver robbed the itinerant Limón family of their meager possessions. After the incident, while one of the women "gets up and casts a spell on the driver that can't miss" (193), Pedro's distraught father is completely paralyzed, likened to "the juif that we burned last year during the carnival" as he stands in the middle of the road, quiet and sad, "with his arms outstretched" (193). After Aristón's death, Pedro's internalized guilt culminates in a self-deprecating comparison to his father: "I am just like my father, a poor bastard of a Haitian not worth shit" (199). It is certainly possible to see Pedro Limón's reaction to Aristón's death in the light of Freud's meditation on mourning and melancholia, since at least some of the "symptoms" of zombified Pedro fit Freud's definition of melancholia (Freud 1953–74, vol. 14, 237–58). However, what resonates in Pedro Limón's self-deprecating language is also the stereotypical view of a Haitian peasant as uneducated and gullible, an easy prey for savvier and more "urban" Cubans. This opposition is reaffirmed by another episode from Pedro Limón's youth, when a friend returns home from a shopping expedition: "Julio Maní, a distant grandson of Ti-Bois, appears with a box of shoes. He calls everyone around to see them, he wants to amaze them, they are two-tone shoes, an American brand. . . . Now he breaks the string and opens the box, but there are no shoes. They have cheated him and inside there is only a brick" (195). Even in Haiti, as Dayan has shown, the hierarchy of rural versus urban often goes beyond issues of color, class, or income (1995, 78–79).

It should be clear by now that Vodou holds many clues to various layers of meaning embedded in the story, and pursuing some of the additional references to Haitian beliefs should be critically productive. The story of Pedro Limón is, for the most part, a predicament of zombification, whereas the trajectory of his friend, Aristón, who embraces the heroic tradition of the Haitian people, appears to be the reverse of Pedro's plight. Aristón's transformation in the course of the story hinges on his possession by the god of war, Oggun: "I'll be a greater *houngan* than Ti-Bois. Oggun Ferraille protects me, Oggun the Captain, Oggun of Iron, Oggun of War. I aammm Oggunnn."[16] The mention of Oggun Ferraille is both historically and symbolically important. According to Patrick Taylor, there is a link between the Oggun family of deities and revolutionary movements "because of its connection with the waging of war and, hence, with the processes of social and political transformation" (1989, 115). When tracing the revolutionary tradition of Haiti, Taylor underscores the role of Oggun in the movement "from secrecy to rebellion," which follows the strategy of guerrilla struggle (1989, 114).

It is significant that in Benítez Rojo's story Aristón decides to join the rebels of Sierra Maestra and to take Pedro Limón along because of Oggun's orders. At the same time, an explicit link between the legacy of the Haitian Revolution and Fidel Castro's anti-Batista movement serves as a catalyst for Aristón's and Pedro's involvement in the rebellion: "Oggun says that I have to fight, to set the earth on fire, that I have to fight at your side, that you're my protection, and that the bullets won't do me no harm if you're there. They won't do you no harm too. . . . Fight or I kill you. Choose. . . . We were going to war because Oggun had demanded it; we were going to fight against the tanks and cannons of Batista that rolled down the highway; against the airplanes, the ships, and the army, we, who hadn't meddled in the white's things for a long time, were fighting. . . . Ti-Bois said that Touissant L'Ouverture's soul was with us and he gave us sweets to offer to Papa Legba, the Lord of the Roads" (199, 200).

Both Pedro and Aristón—subject, respectively, to zombification and possession—are vehicles of powerful external forces that exert their hold on each of them. Whereas Aristón becomes empowered by the ancestral forces that inhabit his body, Pedro's zombification by Marxist ideology carries negative connotations that imply dispossession. According to Janice Boddy, in many societies the ritual of possession serves—along with divination and dreams—as a vehicle to communicate the desires of a vast array of deities and spirits (1994, 407).

Within the framework of Haitian cultural presence in Cuba, zombification and possession are powerful symbols that serve to dramatize the perception of otherness. Possession in particular "appears dramatically and intransigently exotic" (Boddy 1994, 407) because of its reason-defying power "destabilizing scholarly assumptions about objectivity and rationality" (ibid., 425). Also important, however, is the fact that zombification and possession in "Heaven and Earth" are recognized as external manifestations of Vodou spirituality, and they become powerful catalysts that generate tension between the modernizing project of the Cuban Revolution and African-based ancestral spirituality.

To be sure, tensions and paradoxes always tend to emerge at the interface between modernity and spirituality, and in the Caribbean the cultural force of spirituality and the power of social revolution derived from African-based religions are part and parcel of modernity. If modernity is, indeed, as Charles Taylor has argued, "that historically unprecedented amalgam of new practices and institutional forms (science, technology, industrial production, urbanization), of new ways of living (individualism, secularization, instrumental rationality) and of new forms of malaise (alienation, meaninglessness, a sense of impending social dissolution)" (2002, 91), then we should also bear in mind Brendbekken's dictum that "many of these phenomena formed part of the experiences of New World populations subjugated to slavery and colonial rule" (2002, 18).

The project of the Cuban Revolution, as depicted in "Heaven and Earth," aligns itself with secular rationalism by disengaging itself at the same time from the repository of collective memory.[17] Such an approach is consistent with what Michael Taussig has seen as a common trend among Marxist ideologues in general, who have opted for rationalism as the foundation of their modernization project and rejected the potential force of popular imagination, fantasy, and myth. The Left, according to Taussig, "had abandoned this terrain where the battle had to be fought and whose images contained the revolutionary seeds which the soil ploughed by Marxist dialectics could nourish and germinate" (1984, 89). In the context of the Caribbean in particular, where the pragmatic role of myth, ritual, and spirituality in concrete social situations is not subject to dispute, disregarding such practices or reducing them to "the psychopathology of the individual" (Patrick Taylor 1989, 100) is likely to be a political mistake.

In "Heaven and Earth" cultural practices commonly associated with Haitian Vodou—witchcraft, possession, zombification, sorcery, spells, invocations, metamorphoses—are perceived by the official representative of the revolution, the Habanero, with a certain degree of uneasiness, since they are competing forms of control and power. At the same time, these spiritual forces stand in contrast with the revolution, since they go against the grain of its modernizing practices, which are embodied in rationalism, education, and technological progress. Throughout the story, books, manuals, machines, and newly acquired technical skills and trade titles among previously disenfranchised and illiterate characters are visible forms of the empowerment of the Haitian community in postrevolutionary Cuba and external symbols of the modernizing move beyond and away from magic, sorcery, and enchantment. When Pedro Limón returns to Guanamaca, we quickly find out that he has been sent by the government to inaugurate a new school. After a seven-year hiatus, he finds his childhood friend Pascasio "working in the sugar refinery, taking apart machines and reading engineering manuals" (190). Other references to Pascasio's newly acquired status further highlight a keen awareness of rapid, modernizing change brought by the revolution: "And now Pascasio had moved to the factory compound and was an assistant mechanic and was studying—he pointed to the book with boiler diagrams on the cover" (191).

Judging by these and other details about Guanamaca interspersed throughout "Heaven and Earth," Benítez Rojo must have done extensive research in its history, economy, and topography when crafting his short story. In an article published in 1966 in *Etnología y Folklore*—an important journal, published by the Cuban Academy of Science—the sociologist Alberto Pedro Díaz offered an interesting picture of "Guanamaca, una comunidad haitiana" [a Haitian community] which might have served as a point of reference or inspiration for Benítez Rojo's fictional rendering of this *batey*, which is situated "a media hora poco más o menos, en automóvil, de Esmeralda, la ciudad más cercana" [more or less half an hour away, driving from Esmeralda, the nearest city] (Díaz 1966, 25). In his article, Díaz describes pre-revolutionary Guanamaca as a migrant community of sugar-cane workers, who after each *zafra* would leave for Oriente in search of temporary employment harvesting coffee: "Antes de que comenzara el tiempo muerto se producía un verdadero éxodo hacia los cafetales de Oriente" [A true exodus to the coffee plantations of Oriente took place every year before the onset of dead time between harvests] (ibid.). In Benítez Rojo's story, Pedro Limón's recollection of his childhood describes this experience in poignant detail: "The harvest was over and they were going to Oriente. . . . [T]hey were going to the mountains near Guantánamo, to fill coffee cans on the land of Monsieur Bissy Porchette, honorary consul of the Haitian republic. . . . Monsieur Bissy Porchette didn't need more people. . . . He kept saying no and Adelaide screamed into his face that he must have been lying to say he was a Haitian. We returned to Guanamaca on foot. That summer we went hungry and my sister Georgette died" (192–93).

Glimpses of pre-revolutionary Guanamaca flash throughout the story and serve as a counterpoint to the modernizing efforts of the revolution. In one particularly dramatic passage Pedro Limón refers to the forced deportation of Haitians, "the law that the Cubans had created to throw us out of their country, so that we could no longer work for less pay and not take jobs away from anyone" (194). This episode appears to be grounded, once again, in thorough historical research. According to McLeod, lacking strong diplomatic support and facing racial prejudice, *haitianos* in Cuba encountered their most severe challenge during the forced repatriation movement in the 1930s, which was linked to the economic decline. In 1937 Cuban authorities stepped up forced deportations, banishing nearly 25,000 Haitians. The process was brutal and arbitrary: soldiers and members of the rural guard descended on unsuspecting villagers, rounding up Haitians who had been working in Cuba for years and herding them onto ships. Not surprisingly, adds McLeod, many Haitians tried to remain in Cuba by going into hiding in isolated communities of Camagüey and Oriente (including Guanamaca). According to the testimonies compiled by researchers in *El vodú en Cuba*, "Esa repatriación está vinculada a nuestra historia, en primer lugar, con el robo y con el atropello, y, en segundo lugar con el genocidio. La historiografía no ha recogido de manera oficial esos hechos. No hay documentos para poder recogerlos. Pero sí existen testimonios orales. Hubo muchos barcos cargados de negros haitianos cuya repatriación se pagaba en los puertos . . . a tantos reales o a tantas pesetas por cabeza de repatriado. Estos nunca llegaban a las costas haitianas sino que eran, sencillamente, sus cargazones humanas" (James, Millet, and Alarcón 1992, 59).

Benítez Rojo's rendition of the horror of repatriation is as succinct as it is dramatic, reminiscent of the tragedy of the Middle Passage and of the experience of slavery.

> "The ships have crossed the Windward Passage. They are in Santiago de Cuba's harbor. They are waiting for us," said the spirit of President Dessalines through Ti-Bois's mouth. And the next day the rural police came with their long machetes in hand. Inside his hat the mulatto corporal carries a list of the families that must leave. Without dismounting, he goes from cabin to cabin shouting the names that Cubans have given us, the names that appear on the plantation's payroll because the French surnames are too difficult, the names that complicated any transaction, José Codfish, Antonio Pepsicola, Juan First, Juan Second, Andrés Silent, Julio Papaya, Ambrosio Limón, Ambrosio Limón! . . . We are a proud race. We've a history. We're a race of warriors that defeated Napoleon's army and conquered Santo Domingo. But now something is wrong. They are crowding us into the center of the compound. They do a head count. They whip and herd us to the refinery train. The boats are waiting in Santiago de Cuba. (194–95)

While "Heaven and Earth" paints a uniformly grim picture of the predicament of Haitian workers in pre-revolutionary Cuba, the duality between ancestral values and the modernizing forces of the revolution is not devoid of ambiguities. Violent and destructive, Oggun/Aristón stands at the crossroads between tradition and progress. Oggun, as scholars tell us, is a complex deity, since he "kills and he creates" (Barnes 1989, 16). According to Sandra Barnes and Paula Ben-Amos, Oggun's Promethean nature is the brighter side of his destructive demeanor (1989, 57). In the figure of Aristón, the metaphoric representation of creativity and historical transformation is inextricably linked with destruction and death: "It was curious watching him fight. Just before the first gunshot, Oggun would take possession of him. . . . Oggun Ferraille, the merciless god. The Lord of War" (201). Curiously enough, the very premise of Western understanding of modernity —destroy in order to build—appears to be inscribed in Oggun's/Aristón's ambivalent identity. This ambivalence is complicated even further by his unwillingness to relinquish his ancestral beliefs. Clinging to his faith in Vodou, Aristón dies in front of the firing squad, whereas Pedro—aspiring perhaps to become Che Guevara's "new man" of the revolution—opts for a more down-to-earth approach, and survives.

Once again, however, there is much more to the story than a simple opposition between life and death, survival and defeat, rationalism and traditional spiritual practices. Benítez Rojo places his protagonists—literally and symbolically—at the crossroads between life and death, the rational and the irrational, the African spiritual heritage and the European-based ideology. Patrick Taylor reminds us that in Vodou the crossroads is the point of ambiguity, the meeting place between order and disorder, the point of intersection between the visible and the invisible, the living and the ancestors (1989, 106). The crossroads is also the point of choices and decisions. Pedro's survival is marked by the guilt, fear, and humiliation that accompany his self-perceived "zombification." On the other hand, Aristón's death in front of the firing squad can be interpreted as a triumph, if we choose to believe Pedro Limón's testimony that Aristón might have been resurrected in the form of a snake: " 'Fire!' He bounced against the tree. He made a sound like a cough and let out a mouthful of blood; he slipped slowly down the trunk; he sighed and sank into the thicket. . . . I don't know what kind of snake it was, but immediately after the captain fired his pistol, an ashen wisp ran through his legs and lost itself up in the hill. It wasn't my imagination. We all remained looking up at the slope of the hill" (205).

The parallel between this scene and the well-known episode from Carpentier's The Kingdom of This World describing the 1757 execution/resurrection of a rebellious slave leader, Mackandal, is difficult to miss (The Kingdom 35–36). Carpentier's novel was inspired by the legend of the slave Mackandal, who, according to Taylor, was a houngan who in 1757 organized a plot among a group of maroons in Saint Domingue to poison the masters, their water supplies, and their animals. The movement spread, until the secret of Mackandal was extracted under torture from a slave. According to the eighteenth-century French historian Moreau de Saint-Méry, "Mackandal persuaded the slaves that he was the mouthpiece of a loa, that he was immortal, and that he should be worshipped. When he was caught and burned, many slaves refused to believe that he had perished. Popular tradition relates that he was possessed by a loa, and escaped" (quoted in Patrick Taylor 1989, 110).

Narrative renditions of both executions—in Carpentier's novel and in Benítez Rojo's short story—deal with the difficulty of accounting for a variety of different perspectives and of making credible what, from the "scientific" point of view, appears to be impossible or fantastic. In Carpentier's novel the reality of the slaves does not overlap with the reality of the masters: while the slaves believe they have witnessed the resurrection of Mackandal, the narrator is quick to rectify this perception. Carpentier's novel, as we all know, was intended to epitomize his theory of lo real maravilloso americano, based on the premise that in modern Europe "the marvelous" has to be artificially created, whereas in Latin America it is an integral part of everyday reality because of the syncretic hybridity that remains at the core of its culture. Benítez Rojo's representation of conflicting (in)versions of the execution, on the other hand, clearly goes beyond the transculturated poetics of magical realism. In fact, I would argue that it is possible to read the story's ambivalent rendition of Aristón's death/resurrection as a tacit critique of two major trends of Latin American literature: magical realism and testimonio. "Heaven and Earth" underscores the premeditated manipulation and political eradication of difference by focusing on those parts of discourse which, almost by tacit agreement, remain "offstage" in mediated testimonies—namely, the "hidden transcript" of the original oral exchange between the witness and the editor/interviewer, which then gets effaced from the final, written version of the account (Pedro's letter written by the Habanero). Benítez Rojo traces the process of (re)creation of history in what amounts to a cautionary tale of reckoning with past and present political suppression of difference. A curious link emerges between mediated testimonials and the dispossession of the witness on one hand and the process of zombification—seen as a spiritual dispossession—on the other.

"Heaven and Earth" is a text built around numerous ambiguities and contradictions that resist resolution within the logic of binary oppositions. While Benítez Rojo points to Vodou as a system that determines the perception of Haitian culture in Cuba in terms of otherness, he also persists in suggesting the need for cultivating the spiritual realm within the material world of postrevolutionary Cuba. Aristón's dead body—adorned with beaded necklaces of Vodou and yellow, white, and black scarves reminiscent of Mackandal's prophecy and bearing the religious memorabilia taken from the enemies—defies not only the idea of transculturation but even the most hyphenated labels of postcolonialism: "Ready! yelled the captain and I cocked my Springfield. Aristón was, as usual, cheerful, with his rural police hat, the rim pinned up with the religious medals of the Virgin that he'd taken from the dead, placed sideways on his kinky hair, dirty with earth. I looked at him to imprint him in my memory, in case Oggun turned him into an owl or something. I saw that he wore the two beaded necklaces, and I'd always thought that there'd been more, and the colors of Adelaide's scarves were yellow, white, and black, like Mackandal's handkerchiefs" (205).

Placed at the crossroads of history, Aristón and Pedro Limón replicate the twins of Vodou beliefs—a somewhat mysterious set of forces, which in Vodou embodies basic contradictions of human existence. Pressed by the Habanero to choose between the material and the spiritual realm—"because in life men have always had to decide between heaven and earth, and it was about time that I did so" (205)—Pedro Limón makes his choice, just like Aristón made his, but he is unable to reconcile the different worlds that inhabit him. In a deeply moral and symbolic sense, at the story's closure Pedro Limón remains at the crossroads. And the reader of "Heaven and Earth" cannot help but paraphrase Shakespeare's famous dictum and admit that there are more things in heaven and earth than are dreamt of in post-colonial theory.

NOTES

Translated quotations from Benítez Rojo's "La tierra y el cielo" are taken from the English translation "Heaven and Earth" by James Maraniss. Other English translations from Spanish are my own.

1   On the connection between magical realism and postcolonialism, see the Chanady intervention in this volume.

2   According to Arthur and Dash, "A definition of Vodou is problematic. The tenets of the faith do not exist in a written form, and instead are passed on by word of mouth from one generation to another" (1999, 256). Wyrick provides the following explanation of the various spellings of *Vodou* (Vodou, Vodun, Vadoun, Voodoo): "Vodou studies have a long tradition of orthographic and terminological disputes centering on the fact that, until recently, Haitian Creole was an oral language (it still has no comprehensive, definitive dictionary covering the Vodou lexicon) with varying pronunciations and transcription histories. Most scholars preface their works with a note on orthography" (1999, para. 15).

3   Pierre Deslauriers sees several reasons for Vodou's successful survival in a variety of settings. For one, while Vodou provided "a needed, parallel social structure" to slaves who had no access to European social order, it also allowed its practitioners to avail themselves of the opportunities to "selectively exchange or interchange their pantheon of deities with Roman Catholic hagiology" (2001, 341).

4   According to René Depestre, "Vodoun is the kernel of the Haitian imaginary" (quoted in Dayan 1993a, 140). While historians have been trying to separate facts from myth when studying the link between Vodou and the Haitian Revolution, the subversive force of Vodou is underscored by most scholars. Marit Brendbekken quotes several studies to support his view that Vodou is a product

of the "resistant accommodation" of Dominican and Haitian slaves and peasants in response to ongoing political and socioeconomic oppression. Patrick Taylor echoes this view by saying that "African-based religions were at the heart of resistance and rebellion against a plantation society founded on violence. In colonial Saint Domingue, voudou contributed in a vital way to the only slave rebellion in the Americas completely to overturn the colonial plantation order and achieve both emancipation and national independence" (1989, 95).

5 In Marit Brendbekken's words, "The demonization campaign launched by Dominican ruling elites against Haitians, especially after the third declaration of the Dominican Republic's independence in 1865, was sharpened and by various means institutionalized during the long Trujillo regime. Ruling elites suppressed any recognition of the African contribution to Dominican societal and cultural formation. Vodou was exclusively attributed to Haitians, who were conceptualized as evil and powerful but defeated African barbarians and sorcerers who posed a major threat to the Dominican nation, the latter being praised as civilized, Hispanic and Catholic, and born out of relatively peaceful Taino-Spanish mestizaje" (2002, 2). In October 1937 the Dominican dictator Rafael Leonidas Trujillo Molina ordered the killings of Haitians living in the Dominican Republic's northwestern region. The massacre (referred to as El Corte by Dominicans) resulted in the deaths of approximately 15,000 ethnic Haitians, many of whom were either born in the Dominican Republic or had lived in the country for several generations. Many were forcibly deported, and hundreds were killed in the southern frontier region (Turtis 2002, 589).

6 Even the regionalist literary and artistic trends of the 1920s and 1930s based on the affirmation of African-based traditions—negrismo and its Francophone counterpart, négritude—were less prominent in the Dominican Republic than in other Caribbean countries.

7 In Écue-Yamba-O Carpentier describes the altar that apparently belongs to Vodou worship in terms that underscore its links with witchcraft, as he lists "un cráneo en cuya boca relucían tres dientes de oro," "cornamentas de buey y espuelas de aves," "collares de llaves oxidadas, un fémur y algunos huesos pequeños" (1968 [1933], 53).

8 According to Graciela Limón, in The Kingdom of this World "gone is the self-conscious concentration on folklore and customs, on the exotic, and on religious practice. In its place, Carpentier penetrates the core of African mysticism-voodoo—showing how Haitian slaves drew from it a source of self identity and ultimately political freedom" (1993, 195).

9 As is well known, Carpentier's theory evolved into a style in its own right, publicized as "magical realism." First coined by the German art critic Franz Roh after World War I, the original term became transposed and intertwined with the concept of Latin American marvelous reality (lo real maravilloso americano) proposed by Carpentier in his prologue to The Kingdom of This World.

10 See González Echevarría 1990a for an excellent analysis of the broader context in which Écué-Yamba-O appeared, including references to Haiti.

11 Local informants interviewed in Guanamaca by Alberto Pedro Díaz in the early

1960s explain that the term *pichón* does not carry negative connotations, unlike *codaso*, which describes "un haitiano o haitiana que no habla español correctamente, no sabe realizar compras y que no sabe nada de nuestras costumbres" (1966, 30). Diaz concludes that "codaso ha servido para diferenciar al miembro del grupo nacido en Haití del nacido en Cuba, llamándosele a este último por el nombre de pichón" (ibid.).

12 Dayan mentions the historical figure of a mulatto, Jean Zombi, who accompanied Dessalines in the massacre of the French in 1801 and who epitomizes evil spirit among Haitians (1995, 84).

13 According to Patrick Taylor, "The archival and oral based reconstruction of the role of vaudou in the revolution remain hypothetical, but they tell a relatively consistent story of loa participating in the struggle for emancipation and independence" (1989, 117). In the postindependence period, continues Taylor, Vodou was perceived as a process of accommodation to the oppressive neocolonial regimes, to the extreme of being co-opted in the interest of the oppressive state (Duvalier's regime).

14 Dayan offers the following commentary: "The zombi has always mattered for Depestre. From his early *Minerai noir*, which retells the conversions of humans into slaves, identities crushed in brutal commodification, to the wild promise of the 'human future' captured in 'Cap'tain Zombi' in *Un Arc-en-ciel pour l'occident chrétien*, to his perceptive theoretical writings, Depestre evokes the zombi as the most powerful emblem of anonymity, loss, and neocolonialism. The business of capital made possible what Depestre had described in *Bonjour et adieu a la négritude* as this 'fantastic process of reification and assimilation' that 'means the total loss of my identity, the psychological annihilation of my being, my zombification' " (1993b, 174).

15 "Something happened to Depestre's sense of vodoun and treatment of the gods once he left Cuba. Without a certain kind of struggle, a specific history, it seems that the gods lost a context that could resist their conversion into décor or exotica. In Haiti the appearance of the gods depends upon their involvement in a social world: the spirits respond to the demands of quite specific sociopolitical situations" (Dayan 1993b, 159–60).

16 Without making a specific connection to zombification, Dayan's more overarching argument seems to detect a similar duality between dispossession of slave communities and the ritual of possession: "The dispossession accomplished by slavery became a model for possession in vodou, for making man not into a thing but into a spirit" (1995, 83). The role of possession in Vodou is underscored by Patrick Taylor, who states, "Unlike the mythology of many peoples, Haitian mythology is not generally related in the form of stories. As Alfred Métraux indicates, there are few actual myths to be heard in Haiti. This is because of the disruption brought about by the Middle Passage. Haitian mythology remains implicit; the center of its presentation is the ritual process itself, particularly possession" (1989, 99).

17 We should be careful to hedge any blanket statements about the role of religion after the Cuban Revolution. Ivor L. Miller's commentary provides an insightful

caveat regarding this problem: "The 1959 Revolution that radically transformed Cuba's government and economic systems did not alter the use of religious symbolism by politicians. The use of religious symbolism early in the Cuban Revolution clearly demonstrates that deeply rooted cultural practices are more resistant to change than are bureaucracies. . . . In the early 1960s, Castro became linked with the Abakuá, a mutual aid society for men. . . . Abakuá uphold strict requirements for entry into their society, and some groups refuse to admit white members. For Abakuá to select Castro as a member was a tremendous coup for his political career, and these ceremonies were broadcast on Cuban television in 1959" (2000, 36–37).

PART THREE

OCCIDENTALISM, GLOBALIZATION, AND THE GEOPOLITICS OF KNOWLEDGE

The theoretical essays in this section elaborate on problems related to the paradigms that have traditionally defined Western culture and on the power systems that perpetuate coloniality in peripheral Latin America. In this section we gather some of the foundational studies of the Latin American critique of colonialism in which the notions of coloniality, transmodernity, social classification, and colonial difference interplay. For Aníbal Quijano, both social classification —the distribution of world populations into areas of privilege or subalternization on the basis of the colonial concept of "race"—and the hegemony of global capitalism are the dominant features of modernity. Quijano analyzes the emergence of Western Europe as a new historic-cultural entity after the industrial revolution, as well as the emergence of the dualism center/periphery as the diagram used to refer to dominant and subjugated populations. His insightful elaboration on European political philosophies imposed as distinct forms of universal rationality provide the background for his groundbreaking concept "coloniality of power," which has been widely utilized across the disciplines. From this perspective, Walter Mignolo's concept of "colonial difference" contributes to the analysis of the "modern/colonial world system," which benefits from, among others, Emmanuel Wallerstein's and Paul Braudel's historical studies. Mignolo's goal is to make coloniality visible as a constitutive part of modernity, and not just as its aftermath. Coloniality and the colonial difference are, then, loci of enunciation, that is to say, spaces of intelligibility ("epistemic locations") that provide a cultural, ideological, and political standpoint for the interpretation of power structures and cultural paradigms.

Santiago Castro-Gómez draws attention to the idea that Latin American specificity can only be appreciated in contrast with categories and elaborations offered by "central" postcolonial theories. He analyzes Marxist social theory and Edward Said's *Orientalism* in order to illuminate some of the blind spots of Marxism, particularly with regard to the issue of colonialism. Castro-Gómez's study also interweaves the contributions of Latin American scholars such as Enrique Dussel and Aníbal Quijano to the study of peripheral coloniality, making special mention of many authors who have contributed to the "destruction of the myth of modernity."

Eduardo Mendieta also offers a thorough account of some of the directions that have reshaped the field of Latin American studies. For Mendieta, "Latinamericanism is the name for forms of knowledge, ideological attitudes, and spectral mirrors." He identifies four types of Latinamericanism since the end of the nineteenth century, examining in this context the accomplishments of studies dealing with postcolonialism, Occidentalism, globalization, and so on. He is particularly concerned about the ways in which we can establish the "space of theory" and "a place for criticism" in a "saturated theoretical market" which, for the most part, maintains European modernity on a pedestal.

Ramón Grosfoguel undertakes a thorough and polemic critique of dependency theory vis-à-vis developmentalist ideology and what the author calls "feudalmania," as part of the *longue durée* of Latin America's modernity. He explores the ways in which "many dependentistas were caught in . . . developmentalism" and examines, in particular, Fernando Henrique Cardoso's version of dependency theory. Finally, Grosfoguel considers the dependentistas' concept of culture. In Grosfoguel's opinion, "dependentistas underestimated the coloniality of power in Latin America, which obscured the ongoing existence of the region's racial/ethnic hierarchies," which then led to "Eurocentric assumptions about technical progress and development. This contributes to an understanding of the current complicity of many old dependentistas with the recent dominant neoliberal global designs in the region."

COLONIALITY OF POWER, EUROCENTRISM, AND LATIN AMERICA

Aníbal Quijano

What is termed globalization is the culmination of a process that began with the constitution of America and colonial/modern Eurocentered capitalism as new global powers. One of the fundamental axes of this model of power is the social classification of the world's population around the idea of race, a mental construction that expresses the basic experience of colonial domination and pervades the more important dimensions of global power, including its specific rationality: Eurocentrism. The racial axis has a colonial origin and character, but it has proven to be more durable and stable than the colonialism in whose matrix it was established. Therefore, the model of power that is globally hegemonic today presupposes an element of coloniality. In what follows, my primary aim is to open up some of the theoretically necessary questions about the implications of coloniality of power regarding the history of Latin America.[1]

AMERICA AND THE NEW MODEL OF GLOBAL POWER

America was constituted as the first space/time of a new model of power of global vocation, and both in this way and by it became the first identity of modernity.[2] Two historical processes associated in the production of that space/time converged and established the two fundamental axes of the new model of power. One was the codification of the differences between conquerors and conquered in the idea of "race," a supposedly different biological structure that placed some in a natural situation of inferiority to the others. The conquistadors assumed this idea as the constitutive, founding element of the relations of domination that the conquest imposed. On this basis, the population of America, and later the world, was classified within the new model of power. The second process involved the constitution of a new structure of control of labor and its resources and products. This new structure was an articulation of all historically known previous structures of the control of labor—slavery, serfdom, small independent commodity production, and reciprocity—around and on the basis of capital and the world market (see Quijano and Wallerstein 1992).

RACE: A MENTAL CATEGORY OF MODERNITY

The idea of race, in its modern meaning, does not have a known history before the colonization of America. Perhaps it originated in reference to the phenotypic differences between conquerors and conquered.[3] However, what matters is that soon it was constructed to refer to the supposed differential biological structures between those groups.

Social relations founded on the category of race produced new historical social identities in America—Indians, blacks, and mestizos—and redefined others. Terms such as *Spanish* and *Portuguese* and, much later, *European*, which had until then indicated only geographic origin or country of origin, acquired from then on a racial connotation in reference to the new identities. Insofar as the social relations that were being configured were relations of domination, such identities were considered constitutive of the hierarchies, places, and corresponding social roles, and consequently of the model of colonial domination that was being imposed. In other words, race and racial identity were established as instruments of basic social classification.

As time went by, the colonizers codified the phenotypic trait of the colonized as color, and they assumed it as the emblematic characteristic of racial category. That category was probably first established in the area of Anglo-

America. There, so-called blacks were not only the most important exploited group, since the principal part of the economy rested on their labor; they were also, above all, the most important colonized race, since Indians were not part of that colonial society. Why the dominant group calls itself "white" is a story related to racial classification.[4]

In America the idea of race was a way of granting legitimacy to the relations of domination imposed by the conquest. After the colonization of America and the expansion of European colonialism to the rest of the world, the subsequent constitution of Europe as a new id-entity needed the elaboration of a Eurocentric perspective of knowledge, a theoretical perspective on the idea of race as a naturalization of colonial relations between Europeans and non-Europeans. Historically, this meant a new way of legitimizing the already old ideas and practices of relations of superiority and inferiority between dominant and dominated. From the sixteenth century on, this racial principle has proven to be the most effective and long-lasting instrument of universal social domination, since the much older principle—gender or intersexual domination—was encroached on by inferior-superior racial classifications. So the conquered and dominated peoples were situated in a natural position of inferiority, and as a result, their phenotypic traits as well as their cultural features were likewise considered inferior.[5] In this way, race became the fundamental criterion for the distribution of the world population into ranks, places, and roles in the new society's structure of power.

CAPITALISM: THE NEW STRUCTURE FOR THE CONTROL OF LABOR

In the historical process of the constitution of America, all forms of control and exploitation of labor and production, as well as the control of appropriation and distribution of products, revolved around the capital-salary relation and the world market. These forms of labor control included slavery, serfdom, petty-commodity production, reciprocity, and wages. In such an assemblage, each form of labor control was no mere extension of its historical antecedents. All of these forms of labor were historically and sociologically new: in the first place, because they were deliberately established and organized to produce commodities for the world market; in the second place, because they did not merely exist simultaneously in the same space/time, but each one of them was also articulated to capital and its market. Thus they configured a new global model of labor control and in turn a fundamental element of a new model of power to which they were historically structurally dependent. That is to say, the place and function, and therefore the historical movement, of all forms of labor as subordinated points of a totality belonged to the new model of power, in spite of their heterogeneous specific traits and their discontinuous relations with that totality. In the third place, and as a consequence, each form of labor developed into new traits and historical-structural configurations.

Insofar as that structure of control of labor, resources, and products consisted of the joint articulation of all the respective historically known forms, a global model of control of work was established for the first time in known history. And while it was constituted around and in the service of capital, its configuration as a whole was established with a capitalist character as well. Thus emerged a new, original, and singular structure of relations of production in the historical experience of the world: world capitalism.

COLONIALITY OF POWER AND GLOBAL CAPITALISM

The new historical identities produced around the foundation of the idea of race in the new global structure of the control of labor were associated with social roles and geohistorical locations. In this way, both race and the division of labor remained structurally linked and mutually reinforcing, in spite of the fact that neither of them were necessarily dependent on the other in order to exist or change.

In this way, a systematic racial division of labor was imposed. In the Hispanic region, the Crown of Castilla decided early on to end the enslavement of the Indians in order to prevent their total extermination. They were instead confined to serfdom. For those that lived in communities, the ancient practice of reciprocity—the exchange of labor force and labor without a market—was allowed as a way of reproducing the labor force. In some cases, the Indian nobility, a reduced minority, was exempted from serfdom and received special treatment owing to their roles as intermediaries with the dominant race; they were also permitted to participate in some of the activities of the non-noble Spanish. Blacks, however, were reduced to slavery. As the dominant race, Spanish and Portuguese whites could receive wages, be independent merchants, independent artisans, or independent farmers— in short, independent producers of commodities—but only nobles could participate in the high-to-midrange positions in the military and civil colonial administration.

Beginning in the eighteenth century, in Hispanic America an extensive and important social stratum of mestizos (those born of Spanish men and

Indian women) began to participate in the same offices and activities as non-noble Iberians. To a lesser extent, and above all in activities of service or those that required a specialized talent (music, for example), the more "whitened" among the mestizos from the union of black women and Spanish or Portuguese had an opportunity to work. But they were late in legitimizing their new roles, since their mothers were slaves. This racist distribution of labor in the interior of colonial/modern capitalism was maintained throughout the colonial period.

In the course of the worldwide expansion of colonial domination on the part of the same dominant race (or, from the eighteenth century onward, "Europeans"), the same criteria of social classification were imposed on all of the world population. As a result, new historical and social identities were produced: yellows and olives were added to whites, Indians, blacks, and mestizos. The racist distribution of new social identities was combined, as had been done so successfully in Anglo-America, with a racist distribution of labor and of the forms of exploitation inherent in colonial capitalism. This occurred, above all, through a quasi-exclusive association of whiteness with wages and, of course, with the high-order positions in the colonial administration. Thus each form of labor control was associated with a particular race. Consequently, the control of a specific form of labor could be, at the same time, the control of a specific group of dominated people. A new technology of domination/exploitation, in this case race/labor, was articulated in such a way that the two elements appeared naturally associated. To this day, this strategy has been exceptionally successful.

COLONIALITY AND THE EUROCENTRIFICATION OF WORLD CAPITALISM

The privileged positions conquered by the dominant whites for the control of gold, silver, and other commodities produced by the unpaid labor of Indians, blacks, and mestizos (coupled with an advantageous location in the slope of the Atlantic through which, necessarily, the traffic of these commodities for the world market had to pass) granted whites a decisive advantage to compete for the control of worldwide commercial traffic. The progressive monetization of the world market that the precious metals from America stimulated and allowed, as well as the control of such extensive resources, made possible the control of the vast preexisting web of commercial exchange that included, above all, China, India, Ceylon, Egypt, Syria— the future Far and Middle East. The monetization of labor also made it possible to concentrate the control of commercial capital, labor, and means of production in the whole world market.

The control of global commercial traffic by dominant groups headquartered in the Atlantic zones propelled in those places a new process of urbanization based on the expansion of commercial traffic between them and, consequently, the formation of regional markets increasingly integrated and monetarized due to the flow of precious metals originating in America. A historically new region was constituted as a new geocultural id-entity: Europe —more specifically, Western Europe.[6] A new geocultural identity emerged as the central site for the control of the world market. The hegemony of the coasts of the Mediterranean and the Iberian Peninsula was displaced toward the northwest Atlantic coast in the same historical moment.

The condition Europe found itself in as the central site of the new world market cannot by itself alone explain why Europe also became, until the nineteenth century and almost until the worldwide crisis of 1870, the central site of the process of the commodification of the labor force, while all the rest of the regions and populations colonized and incorporated into the new world market under European dominion basically remained under non-waged relations of labor. And in non-European regions wage labor was concentrated almost exclusively among whites. Of course, the entire production of such a division of labor was articulated in a chain of transference of value and profits whose control corresponded to Western Europe.

There is nothing in the social relation of capital itself, or in the mechanisms of the world market in general, that implies the historical necessity of European concentration first (either in Europe or elsewhere) of waged labor and later (over precisely the same base) of industrial production for more than two centuries. As events after 1870 demonstrated, Western European control of wage labor in any sector of the world's population would have been perfectly feasible and probably more profitable for Western Europe. The explanation ought to lie, then, in some other aspect of history itself.

The fact is that from the very beginning of the colonization of America, Europeans associated nonpaid or nonwaged labor with the dominated races because they were "inferior" races. The vast genocide of the Indians in the first decades of colonization was not caused principally by the violence of the conquest or by the plagues the conquistadors brought, but because so many American Indians were used as disposable manual labor and forced to work until death. The elimination of this colonial practice did not end until the defeat of the *encomenderos* in the middle of the sixteenth century. The subsequent Iberian colonialism involved a new politics of population reorganization, a reorganization of the Indians and their relations with the colonizers. But this did not advance American Indians as free and waged laborers. From then on, they were instead assigned the status of unpaid serfs. The serfdom of the American Indians could not, however, be compared with feudal serfdom in Europe, since it included neither the supposed protection of a feudal lord nor, necessarily, the possession of a piece of land to cultivate instead of wages. Before independence, the Indian labor force of serfs reproduced itself in the communities, but more than one hundred years after independence, a large contingent of the Indian serfs was still obliged to reproduce the labor force on its own.[7] The other form of unwaged or, simply put, unpaid labor—slavery—was assigned exclusively to the "black" population brought from Africa.

The racial classification of the population and the early association of the new racial identities of the colonized with the forms of control of unpaid, unwaged labor developed among the Europeans the singular perception that paid labor was the whites' privilege. The racial inferiority of the colonized implied that they were not worthy of wages. They were naturally obliged to work for the profit of their owners. It is not difficult to find, to this very day, this attitude spread out among the white property owners of any place in the world. Furthermore, the lower wages that "inferior races" receive in today's capitalist centers for the same work done by whites cannot be explained as detached from the racist social classification of the world's population—in other words, as detached from the global capitalist coloniality of power.

The control of labor in the new model of global power was constituted thus, articulating all historical forms of labor control around the capitalist wage-labor relation. This articulation was constitutively colonial. First, it was based on the assignment of all forms of unpaid labor to colonial races (originally American Indians, blacks, and, in a more complex way, mestizos) in America and, later on, to the remaining colonized races in the rest of the world, olives and yellows. Second, labor was controlled through the assignment of salaried labor to the colonizing whites.

The coloniality of labor control determined the geographic distribution of each one of the integrated forms of labor control in global capitalism. In other words, it determined the social geography of capitalism: capital, as a social formation for control of wage labor, was the axis around which all remaining forms of labor control, resources, and products were articulated. But, at the same time, capital's specific social configuration was geographically and socially concentrated in Europe and, above all, among Europeans in the whole world of capitalism. Through these measures, Europe and the European constituted themselves as the center of the capitalist world-economy.

When Raúl Prebisch coined the celebrated image of center and periphery to describe the configuration of global capitalism since the end of World War II, he underscored, with or without being aware of it, the nucleus of the historical model for the control of labor, resources, and products that shaped the central part of the new global model of power, starting with America as a player in the new world-economy (see Prebisch 1959, 1960; on Prebisch, see Baer 1962). Global capitalism was, from then on, colonial/modern and Eurocentered. Without a clear understanding of those specific historical characteristics of capitalism, the concept of a "modern world-system"—developed principally by Immanuel Wallerstein (1974–89; Hopkins and Wallerstein 1982), but based on Prebisch and on the Marxian concept of world capitalism—cannot be properly or completely understood.

THE NEW MODEL OF WORLD POWER AND
THE NEW WORLD INTERSUBJECTIVITY

As the center of global capitalism, Europe not only had control of the world market but was also able to impose its colonial dominance over all the regions and populations of the planet, incorporating them into its world-system and its specific model of power. For such regions and populations, this model of power involved a process of historical reidentification; from Europe, such regions and populations were attributed new geocultural identities. In that way, after America and Europe were established, Africa, Asia, and eventually Oceania followed suit. In the production of these new identities, the coloniality of the new model of power was, without a doubt, one of the most active determinations. But the forms and levels of political and cultural development, and more specifically intellectual development, played a role of utmost importance in each case. Without these factors, the category "Orient" would not have been elaborated as the only one with sufficient dignity to be the other to the "Occident," although by definition inferior, without some equivalent to "Indians" or "blacks" being coined.[8] But this omission itself puts in the open the fact that those other factors also acted within the racist model of universal social classification of the world population.

The incorporation of such diverse and heterogeneous cultural histories into a single world dominated by Europe signified a cultural and intellectual intersubjective configuration equivalent to the articulation of all forms of labor control around capital, a configuration that established world capital-

ism. In effect, all of the experiences, histories, resources, and cultural products ended up in one global cultural order revolving around European or
Western hegemony. Europe's hegemony over the new model of global power
concentrated all forms of the control of subjectivity, culture, and especially
knowledge and the production of knowledge under its hegemony.

During that process, the colonizers exercised diverse operations that
brought about the configuration of a new universe of intersubjective relations of domination between Europe and the Europeans and the rest of the
regions and peoples of the world, to whom new geocultural identities were
being attributed in that process. In the first place, they expropriated those
cultural discoveries of the colonized peoples that were most apt for developing capitalism to the profit of the European center. Second, they repressed as
much as possible the colonized forms of knowledge production, models of
the production of meaning, symbolic universe, and models of expression and
of objectification and subjectivity. As is well known, repression in this field
was most violent, profound, and long-lasting among the Indians of Ibero-
America, who were condemned to be an illiterate peasant subculture stripped
of their objectified intellectual legacy. Something equivalent happened in
Africa. Doubtless, the repression was much less intense in Asia, where an
important part of the history of the intellectual written legacy has been
preserved. And it was precisely such epistemic suppression that gave origin
to the category "Orient." Third, in different ways in each case, the Europeans
forced the colonized to learn the dominant culture in any way that would be
useful to the reproduction of domination, whether in the field of technology
and material activity or of subjectivity, especially Judeo-Christian religiosity.
All of those turbulent processes involved a long period of the colonization of
cognitive perspectives, modes of producing and giving meaning, the results
of material existence, the imaginary, the universe of intersubjective relations
with the world: in short, colonization of the culture (see Stocking 1968;
Robert Young 1995; Quijano 1992c, 1997; and Gruzinski 1988).

The success of Western Europe in becoming the center of the modern
world-system, according to Wallerstein's suitable formulation, developed
within the Europeans a trait common to all colonial dominators and imperialists: ethnocentrism. But in the case of Western Europe, that trait had a
peculiar formulation and justification: the racial classification of the world
population after the colonization of America. The association of colonial
ethnocentrism and universal racial classification helps to explain why Europeans came to feel not only superior to all the other peoples of the world
but, in particular, naturally superior. This historical instance is expressed

through a mental operation of fundamental importance for the entire model of global power, but above all with respect to the intersubjective relations that were hegemonic, among other reasons because of the production of knowledge: the Europeans generated a new temporal perspective of history and relocated colonized populations, along with their respective histories and cultures, in the past of a historical trajectory whose culmination was Europe (Mignolo 1995; Blaut 1993; Lander 1997). Notably, however, they were not in the same line of continuity as the Europeans, but in another, naturally different category. The colonized peoples were inferior races and in that manner were the past vis-à-vis the Europeans.

That perspective imagined modernity and rationality as exclusively European products and experiences. From this point of view, intersubjective and cultural relations between Western Europe and the rest of the world were codified in a strong play of new categories: East-West, primitive-civilized, magic/mythic-scientific, irrational-rational, traditional-modern—Europe and not Europe. Even so, the only category with the honor of being recognized as the other of Europe and the West was "Orient"—not the Indians of America and not the blacks of Africa, who were simply "primitive." For underneath that codification of relations between Europeans and non-Europeans, race is, without doubt, the basic category.[9] This binary, dualist perspective on knowledge, particular to Eurocentrism, was imposed as globally hegemonic in the same course as the expansion of European colonial dominance over the world.

It would not be possible to explain the elaboration of Eurocentrism as the hegemonic perspective of knowledge otherwise. The Eurocentric version is based on two principal founding myths: first, the idea of the history of human civilization as a trajectory that departed from a state of nature and culminated in Europe; second, a view of the differences between Europe and non-Europe as natural (racial) differences and not consequences of a history of power. Both myths can be unequivocally recognized in the foundations of evolutionism and dualism, two of the nuclear elements of Eurocentrism.

THE QUESTION OF MODERNITY

I do not propose to enter here into a thorough discussion of the question of modernity and its Eurocentric version. In particular, I will not lengthen this piece with a discussion of the modernity-postmodernity debate and its vast bibliography. But it is pertinent for the goals of this essay, especially for the following section, to raise some questions.[10]

The fact that Western Europeans will imagine themselves to be the culmination of a civilizing trajectory from a state of nature leads them also to think of themselves as the moderns of humanity and its history, that is, as the new and, at the same time, most advanced of the species. But since they attribute the rest of the species to a category by nature inferior and consequently anterior, belonging to the past in the progress of the species, the Europeans imagine themselves as the exclusive bearers, creators, and protagonists of that modernity. What is notable about this is not that the Europeans imagined and thought of themselves and the rest of the species in that way—which is not exclusive to Europeans—but the fact that they were capable of spreading and establishing that historical perspective as hegemonic within the new intersubjective universe of the global model of power.

Of course, the intellectual resistance to that historical perspective was not long in emerging. In Latin America, from the end of the nineteenth century and above all in the twentieth century, especially after World War II, it happened in connection with the development-underdevelopment debate. That debate was dominated for a long time by the so-called theory of modernization.[11] One of the arguments most frequently used, from opposing angles, was to affirm that modernization does not necessarily imply the Westernization of non-European societies and cultures, but that modernity is a phenomenon of all cultures, not just of Europe or the West.

If the concept of modernity only, or fundamentally, refers to the ideas of newness, the advanced, the rational-scientific, the secular—that is, the ideas normally associated with it—then one must admit that modernity is a phenomenon possible in all cultures and historical epochs. With all their respective particularities and differences, the so-called high cultures (China, India, Egypt, Greece, Maya-Aztec, Tawantinsuyu) prior to the current world-system unequivocally exhibit signs of that modernity, including rational science and the secularization of thought. In truth, it would be almost ridiculous at these levels of historical research to attribute to non-European cultures a mythical-magical mentality, for example, as a defining trait in opposition to rationality and science as characteristics of Europe. Therefore, apart from their symbolic contents, cities, temples, palaces, pyramids or monumental cities (such as Machu Picchu or Borobudur), irrigation, large thoroughfares, technologies, metallurgy, mathematics, calendars, writing, philosophy, histories, armies, and wars clearly demonstrate the scientific development in each one of the high cultures that took place long before the formation of Europe as a new id-entity. The most that one can really say is that the present period has gone further in scientific and technological developments and has made major discoveries and achievements under Europe's hegemonic role and, more generally, under Western hegemony.

The defenders of the European patent on modernity are accustomed to appeal to the cultural history of the ancient Greco-Roman world and to the world of the Mediterranean prior to the colonization of America in order to legitimize their claim on the exclusivity of that patent. What is curious about this argument is, first, that it obscures the fact that the truly advanced part of the Mediterranean world was Islamo-Judaic. Second, it was the Islamo-Judaic world that maintained the Greco-Roman cultural heritage, cities, commerce, agricultural trade, mining, textile industry, philosophy, and history, while the future Western Europe was being dominated by feudalism and cultural obscurantism. Third, very probably, the commodification of the labor force—the capital-wage relation—emerged precisely in the Islamo-Judaic area, and its development expanded north toward the future Europe. Fourth, starting only with the defeat of Islam and the later displacement by America of Islam's hegemony over the world market north to Europe did the center of cultural activity also begin to be displaced to that new region. Because of this, the new geographic perspective of history and culture, elaborated and imposed as globally hegemonic, implies a new geography of power. The idea of Occident-Orient itself is belated and starts with British hegemony. Or is it still necessary to recall that the prime meridian crosses London and not Seville or Venice? (see Robert Young 1995).

In this sense, the Eurocentric pretension to be the exclusive producer and protagonist of modernity—because of which all modernization of non-European populations, is, therefore, a Europeanization—is an ethnocentric pretension and, in the long run, provincial. However, if it is accepted that the concept of modernity refers solely to rationality, science, technology, and so on, the question that we would be posing to historical experience would not be different than the one proposed by European ethnocentrism. The debate would consist just in the dispute for the originality and exclusivity of the ownership of the phenomenon thus called modernity, and consequently everything would remain in the same terrain and according to the same perspective of Eurocentrism.

There is, however, a set of elements that point to a different concept of modernity that gives an account of a historical process specific to the current world-system. The previous references and traits of the concept of modernity remain relevant. But they belong to a universe of social relations, both in its material and intersubjective dimensions, whose central question and, consequently, whose central field of conflict is human social liberation as a historical interest of society. In this article, I will limit myself to advancing, in a brief and schematic manner, some propositions to clarify these issues (Quijano 2000d).

The current model of global power is the first effectively global one in world history in several specific senses. To begin with, it is the first where in each sphere of social existence all historically known forms of control of respective social relations are articulated, configuring in each area only one structure with systematic relations between its components and, by the same means, its whole. Second, it is the first model in which each structure of each sphere of social existence is under the hegemony of an institution produced within the process of formation and development of that same model of power: thus, in the control of labor and its resources and products, it is the capitalist enterprise; in the control of sex and its resources and products, the bourgeois family; in the control of authority and its resources and products, the nation-state; in the control of intersubjectivity, Eurocentrism.[12] Third, each one of those institutions exists in a relation of interdependence with each one of the others. Therefore, the model of power is configured as a system.[13] Fourth, finally, this model of global power is the first that covers the entire population of the planet.

In this fourth sense, humanity in its totality constitutes today the first historically known global *world-system*, not only a world, as was the case with the Chinese, Hindu, Egyptian, Hellenic-Roman, Aztec-Mayan, or Tawantinsuyan. None of those worlds had in common only one colonial/imperial dominant. And though it is a sort of common sense in the Eurocentric vision, it is by no means certain that all the peoples incorporated into one of those worlds would have had in common a basic perspective on the relation between that which is human and the rest of the universe. The colonial dominators of each one of those worlds did not have the conditions or, probably, the interest for homogenizing the basic forms of social existence for all the populations under their dominion. On the other hand, the modern world-system that began to form with the colonization of America has in common three central elements that affect the quotidian life of the totality of the global population: the coloniality of power, capitalism, and Eurocentrism. Of course, this model of power, or any other, can mean that historical-structural heterogeneity has been eradicated within its dominions. Its globality means that there is a basic level of common social practices and a central sphere of common value orientation for the entire world. Consequently, the hegemonic institutions of each province of social existence are universal to the population of the world as intersubjective models, as illustrated by the nation-state, the bourgeois family, the capitalist corporation, and the Eurocentric rationality.

Therefore, whatever it may be that the term *modernity* names today, it involves the totality of the global population and all the history of the last five hundred years, all the worlds or former worlds articulated in the global model of power, each differentiated or differentiable segment constituted together with (as part of) the historical redefinition or reconstitution of each segment for its incorporation to the new and common model of global power. Therefore, it is also an articulation of many rationalities. However, since the model depicts a new and different history with specific experiences, the questions that this history raises cannot be investigated, much less contested, within the Eurocentric concept of modernity. For this reason, to say that modernity is a purely European phenomenon or one that occurs in all cultures would now have an impossible meaning. Modernity is about something new and different, something specific to this model of global power. If one must preserve the name, one must also mean another modernity.

The central question that interests me here: what is really new with respect to modernity? And by this I mean not only what develops and redefines experiences, tendencies, and processes of other worlds, but also what was produced in the present model of global power's own history. Enrique Dussel (1993b, 1999, 2002) has proposed the category "transmodernity" as an alternative to the Eurocentric pretension that Europe is the original producer of modernity. According to this proposal, the constitution of the individual, differentiated ego is what began with American colonization and is the mark of modernity, but it has a place not only in Europe but also in the entire world that American settlement configured. Dussel hits the mark in refusing one of the favorite myths of Eurocentrism. But it is not certain that the individual, differentiated ego is a phenomenon belonging exclusively to the period initiated with America. There is, of course, an umbilical relation between the historical processes that were generated and that began with America and the changes in subjectivity or, better said, the intersubjectivity of all the peoples that were integrated into the new model of global power. And those changes brought the constitution of a new intersubjectivity, not only individually but collectively as well. This is, therefore, a new phenomenon that entered history with America and in that sense is part of modernity. But whatever they might have been, those changes were not constituted from the individual (nor from the collective) subjectivity of a preexisting world. Or, to use an old image, those changes are born not like Pallas Athena from the head of Zeus, but are rather the subjective or intersubjective expression of what the peoples of the world are doing at that moment.

From this perspective, it is necessary to admit that the colonization of America, its immediate consequences in the global market, and the formation of a new model of global power are a truly tremendous historical change and that they affect not only Europe but the entire globe. This is not a change in a known world that merely altered some of its traits. It is a change in the world as such. This is, without doubt, the founding element of the new subjectivity: the perception of historical change. It is this element that unleashed the process of the constitution of a new perspective about time and about history. The perception of change brings about a new idea of the future, since it is the only territory of time where the changes can occur. The future is an open temporal territory. Time can be new, and so not merely the extension of the past. And in this way history can be perceived now not only as something that happens, something natural or produced by divine decisions or mysteries as destiny, but also as something that can be produced by the action of people, by their calculations, their intentions, their decisions, and therefore as something that can be designed and, consequently, that can have meaning (Quijano 1988b).

With America an entire universe of new material relations and intersubjectivities was initiated. It is pertinent to admit that the concept of modernity does not refer only to what happens with subjectivity (despite all the tremendous importance of that process), to the individual ego, to a new universe of intersubjective relations between individuals and the peoples integrated into the new world-system and its specific model of global power. The concept of modernity accounts equally for the changes in the material dimensions of social relations (i.e., world capitalism, coloniality of power). That is to say, the changes that occur on all levels of social existence, and therefore happen to their individual members, are the same in their material and intersubjective dimensions. And since "modernity" is about processes that were initiated with the emergence of America, of a new model of global power (the first world-system), and of the integration of all the peoples of the globe in that process, it is also essential to admit that it is about an entire historical period. In other words, starting with America, a new space/time was constituted materially and subjectively: this is what the concept of modernity names.

Nevertheless, it was decisive for the process of modernity that the hegemonic center of the world would be localized in the north-central zones of Western Europe. That process helps to explain why the center of intellectual conceptualization will be localized in Western Europe as well, and why that version acquired global hegemony. The same process helps, equally, to explain the coloniality of power that will play a part of the first order in the

Eurocentric elaboration of modernity. This last point is not very difficult to perceive if we bear in mind the way in which the coloniality of power is tied to the concentration in Europe of capital, wages, the market of capital, and finally, the society and culture associated with those determinations. In this sense, modernity was also colonial from its point of departure. This helps explain why the global process of modernization had a much more direct and immediate impact in Europe.

In fact, as experiences and as ideas, the new social practices involved in the model of global, capitalist power, the concentration of capital and wages, the new market for capital associated with the new perspective on time and on history, and the centrality of the question of historical change in that perspective require on one hand the desacralization of hierarchies and authorities, both in the material dimension of social relations and in its inter-subjectivity, and on the other hand the desacralization, change, or dismantle-ment of the corresponding structures and institutions. The new individu-ation of subjectivity acquires its meaning only in this context, because from it stems the necessity for an individual inner forum in order to think, doubt, and choose—in short, the individual liberty against fixed social ascriptions and, consequently, the necessity for social equality among individuals.

Capitalist determinations, however, required also (and in the same his-torical movement) that material and intersubjective social processes could not have a place except within social relations of exploitation and domina-tion. For the controllers of power, the control of capital and the market were and are what decides the ends, the means, and the limits of the process. The market is the foundation but also the limit of possible social equality among people. For those exploited by capital and, in general, those dominated by the model of power, modernity generates a horizon of liberation for people of every relation, structure, or institution linked to domination and exploita-tion, but also the social conditions necessary to advance in the direction of that horizon. Modernity is, then, also a question of conflicting social inter-ests. One of these interests is the continued democratization of social exis-tence. In this sense, every concept of modernity is necessarily ambiguous and contradictory (Quijano 1998b, 2000d).

It is precisely in the contradictions and ambiguities of modernity that the history of these processes so clearly differentiates Western Europe from the rest of the world, as it is clear in Latin America. In Western Europe the concentration of the wage-capital relation is the principal axis of the tenden-cies for social classification and the correspondent structure of power. Eco-nomic structures and social classification underlay the confrontations with the old order, with empire, with the papacy during the period of so-called competitive capital. These conflicts made it possible for nondominant sectors of capital as well as for the exploited to find better conditions to negotiate their place in the structure of power and in selling their labor power. It also opens the conditions for a specifically bourgeois secularization of culture and subjectivity. Liberalism is one of the clear expressions of this material and subjective context of Western European society. However, in the rest of the world, and in Latin America in particular, the most extended forms of labor control are nonwaged (although for the benefit of global capital), which implies that the relations of exploitation and domination have a colonial character. Political independence, at the beginning of the nineteenth century, is accompanied in the majority of the new countries by the stagnation and recession of the most advanced sectors of the capitalist economy and therefore by the strengthening of the colonial character of social and political domination under formally independent states. The Eurocentrification of colonial/modern capitalism was in this sense decisive for the different destinies of the process of modernity in Europe and in the rest of the world (Quijano 1994).

COLONIALITY OF POWER AND EUROCENTRISM

The intellectual conceptualization of the process of modernity produced a perspective of knowledge and a mode of producing knowledge that gives a very tight account of the character of the global model of power: colonial/ modern, capitalist, and Eurocentered. This perspective and concrete mode of producing knowledge is Eurocentrism. The literature on the debate about Eurocentrism is growing rapidly.[14]

Eurocentrism is, as used here, the name of a perspective of knowledge whose systematic formation began in Western Europe before the middle of the seventeenth century, although some of its roots are, without doubt, much older. In the following centuries this perspective was made globally hegemonic, traveling the same course as the dominion of the European bourgeois class. Its constitution was associated with the specific bourgeois secularization of European thought and with the experiences and necessities of the global model of capitalist (colonial/modern) and Eurocentered power established since the colonization of America.

This category of Eurocentrism does not involve all of the knowledge of history of all of Europe or Western Europe in particular. It does not refer to all the modes of knowledge of all Europeans and all epochs. It is instead a

specific rationality or perspective of knowledge that was made globally hegemonic, colonizing and overcoming other previous or different conceptual
formations and their respective concrete knowledges, as much in Europe as
in the rest of the world. In the framework of this essay I propose to discuss
some of these issues more directly related to the experience of Latin America, but, obviously, they do not refer only to Latin America.

CAPITAL AND CAPITALISM

First, the theory of history as a linear sequence of universally valid events
needs to be reopened in relation to America as a major question in the social-
scientific debate. More so when such a concept of history is applied to labor
and the control of labor conceptualized as modes of production in the
sequence precapitalism-capitalism. From the Eurocentric point of view, reciprocity, slavery, serfdom, and independent commodity production are all
perceived as a historical sequence prior to commodification of the labor
force. They are precapital. And they are considered not only different, but
radically incompatible with capital. The fact is, however, that in America
they did not emerge in a linear historical sequence; none of them was a mere
extension of the old precapitalist form, nor were they incompatible with
capital.

Slavery, in America, was deliberately established and organized as a commodity in order to produce goods for the world market and to serve the
purposes and needs of capitalism. Likewise, the serfdom imposed on Indians, including the redefinition of the institutions of reciprocity, was organized in order to serve the same ends: to produce merchandise for the global
market. Independent commodity production was established and expanded
for the same purposes. This means that not only were all the forms of labor
and control of labor simultaneously performed in America, but they were
also articulated around the axis of capital and the global market. Consequently, they were part of a new model of organization and labor control. Together these forms of labor configured a new economic system: capitalism.

Capital, as a social relation based on the commodification of the labor
force, was probably born in some moment around the eleventh or twelfth
century in some place in the southern regions of the Iberian and/or Italian
Peninsulas and, for known reasons, in the Islamic world (see Wallerstein
1983; Arrighi 1994). Capital is thus much older than America. But before the
emergence of America, it was nowhere structurally articulated with all the
other forms of organization and control of the labor force and labor, nor

was it predominant over any of them. Only with America could capital consolidate and obtain global predominance, becoming precisely the axis around which all forms of labor were articulated to satisfy the ends of the world market, configuring a new pattern of global control of labor, its resources, and products: world capitalism. Therefore, capitalism as a system of relations of production, that is, as the heterogeneous linking of all forms of control of labor and its products under the dominance of capital, was constituted in history only with the emergence of America. Beginning with that historical moment, capital has always existed, and continues to exist to this day, as the central axis of capitalism. Never has capitalism been predominant in some other way, on a global and worldwide scale, and in all probability it would not have been able to develop otherwise.

EVOLUTIONISM AND DUALISM

Parallel to the historical relations between capital and precapital, a similar set of ideas was elaborated around the spatial relations between Europe and non-Europe. The Eurocentric version of modernity's foundational myth is the idea of the state of nature as the point of departure for the civilized course of history whose culmination is European or Western civilization. From this myth originated the specifically Eurocentric evolutionist perspective of linear and unidirectional movement and changes in human history. Interestingly enough, this myth was associated with the racial and spatial classification of the world's population. This association produced the paradoxical amalgam of evolution and dualism, a vision that becomes meaningful only as an expression of the exacerbated ethnocentrism of the recently constituted Europe; by its central and dominant place in global, colonial/ modern capitalism; by the new validity of the mystified ideas of humanity and progress, dear products of the Enlightenment; and by the validity of the idea of race as the basic criterion for a universal social classification of the world's population.

The historical process is, however, very different. To start with, in the moment that the Iberians conquered, named, and colonized America (whose northern region, North America, would be colonized by the British a century later), they found a great number of different peoples, each with its own history, language, discoveries and cultural products, memory and identity. The most developed and sophisticated of them were the Aztecs, Mayas, Chimus, Aymaras, Incas, Chibchas, and so on. Three hundred years later, all of them had become merged into a single identity: Indians. This new identity was racial, colonial, and negative. The same happened with the peoples forcefully brought from Africa as slaves: Ashantis, Yorubas, Zulus, Congos, Bacongos, and others. In the span of three hundred years, all of them were Negroes or blacks.

This resultant from the history of colonial power had, in terms of the colonial perception, two decisive implications. The first is obvious: peoples were dispossessed of their own and singular historical identities. The second is perhaps less obvious, but no less decisive: their new racial identity, colonial and negative, involved the plundering of their place in the history of the cultural production of humanity. From then on, there were inferior races, capable only of producing inferior cultures. The new identity also involved their relocation in the historical time constituted with America first and with Europe later: from then on, they were the past. In other words, the model of power based on coloniality also involved a cognitive model, a new perspective of knowledge within which non-Europe was the past and, because of that, inferior, if not always primitive.

On the other hand, America was the first modern and global geocultural identity. Europe was the second and was constituted as a consequence of America, not the inverse. The constitution of Europe as a new historic entity/identity was made possible, in the first place, through the free labor of the American Indians, blacks, and mestizos, using their advanced technology in mining and agriculture, and using their products such as gold, silver, potatoes, tomatoes, and tobacco (Viola and Margolis 1991). It was on this foundation that a region was configured as the site of control of the Atlantic routes, which became in turn, and for this very reason, the decisive routes of the world market. This region did not delay in emerging as . . . Europe. So Europe and America mutually produced themselves as the historical and the first two new geocultural identities of the modern world.

However, the Europeans persuaded themselves, from the middle of the seventeenth century, but above all during the eighteenth century, that in some way they had self-produced themselves as a civilization, at the margin of history initiated with America, culminating an independent line that began with Greece as the only original source. Furthermore, they concluded that they were naturally (i.e., racially) superior to the rest of the world, since they had conquered everyone and had imposed their dominance on them.

The confrontation between the historical experience and the Eurocentric perspective on knowledge makes it possible to underline some of the more important elements of Eurocentrism: (1) a peculiar articulation between dualism (capital-precapital, Europe–non-Europe, primitive-civilized, traditional-modern, etc.) and a linear, one-directional evolutionism from some state of nature to modern European society; (2) the naturalization of the cultural differences between human groups by means of their codification with the idea of race; and (3) the distorted-temporal relocation of all those differences by relocating non-Europeans in the past. All these intellectual operations are clearly interdependent, and they could not have been cultivated and developed without the coloniality of power.

HOMOGENEITY/CONTINUITY AND HETEROGENEITY/DISCONTINUITY

As it is visible now, the radical crisis that the Eurocentric perspective of knowledge is undergoing opens up a field full of questions. I will discuss two of them. First is the idea of historical change as a process or moment in which an entity or unity is transformed in a continuous, homogeneous, and complete way into something else and absolutely abandoning the scene of history. This process allows for another equivalent entity to occupy the space, and in such a way that everything continues in a sequential chain. Otherwise, the idea of history as a linear and one-directional evolution would not have meaning or place. Second, such an idea implies that each differentiated unity (for example, "economy/society," or "mode of production" in the case of labor control of capital or slavery, or "race/civilization" in the case of human groups) subjected to the historical change is a homogeneous entity/identity. Even more, each of them is perceived as a structure of homogeneous elements related in a continuous and systemic (which is distinct from systematic) manner.

Historical experience shows, however, that global capitalism is far from being a homogeneous and continuous totality. On the contrary, as the historical experience of America demonstrates, the pattern of global power that is known as capitalism is, fundamentally, a structure of heterogeneous elements as much in terms of forms of control of labor-resources-products (or relations of production) as in terms of the peoples and histories articulated in it. Consequently, such elements are connected between themselves and with the totality by means that are heterogeneous and discontinuous, including conflict. And each of these elements is configured in the same way.

So, any relation of production (as any other entity or unity) is in itself a heterogeneous structure, especially capital, since all the stages and historic forms of the production of value and the appropriation of surplus value are simultaneously active and work together in a complex network for transferring value and surplus value. Take, for example, primitive accumulation, absolute and relative surplus value, extensive or intensive—or in other no-menclature, competitive—capital, monopoly capital, transnational or global capital, or pre-Fordist capital, Fordist capital, manual or labor-intensive capital, capital-intensive value, information-intensive value, and so on. The same logic was at work with respect to race, since so many diverse and heterogeneous peoples, with heterogeneous histories and historic tenden-cies of movement and change, were united under only one racial heading, such as American "Indians" or "blacks."

The heterogeneity that I am talking about is not simply structural, based in the relations between contemporaneous elements. Since diverse and het-erogeneous histories of this type were articulated in a single structure of power, it is pertinent to acknowledge the historical-structural character of this heterogeneity. Consequently, the process of change of capitalist totality cannot, in any way, be a homogeneous and continuous transformation, either of the entire system or of each one of its constituent parts. Nor could that totality completely and homogeneously disappear from the scene of history and be replaced by any equivalent. Historical change cannot be lin-ear, one-directional, sequential, or total. The system, or the specific pattern of structural articulation, could be dismantled; however, each one or some of its elements can and will have to be rearticulated in some other structural model, as it happened with some components of the precolonial model of power in, for instance, Tawantinsuyu.[15]

THE NEW DUALISM

Finally, it is pertinent to revisit the question of the relations between the body and the nonbody in the Eurocentric perspective, because of its importance both in the Eurocentric mode of producing knowledge and to the fact that modern dualism has close relations with race and gender. My aim here is to connect a well-known problematic with the coloniality of power.

The differentiation between body and nonbody in human experience is virtually universal in the history of humanity. It is also common to all histori-cally known "cultures" or "civilizations," part of the co-presence of both as inseparable dimensions of humanness. The process of the separation of these two elements (body and nonbody) of the human being is part of the long history of the Christian world founded on the idea of the primacy of the soul above the body. But the history of this point in particular shows a long and unresolved ambivalence in Christian theology. The soul is the privileged object of salvation, but in the end, the body is resurrected as the culmination of salvation. The primacy of the soul was emphasized, perhaps exaggerated, during the culture of the repression of Christianity, which resulted from the conflicts with Muslims and Jews in the fifteenth and sixteenth centuries, during the peak of the Inquisition. And because the body was the basic object of repression, the soul could appear almost separated from the inter-subjective relations at the interior of the Christian world. But this issue was not systematically theorized, discussed, and elaborated until Descartes's writing (1963–67) culminated the process of bourgeois secularization of Christian thought.[16]

With Descartes, the mutation of the ancient dualist approach to the body and the nonbody took place.[17] What was a permanent co-presence of both elements in each stage of the human being, with Descartes came a radical separation between reason/subject and body. Reason was not only a secular-ization of the idea of the soul in the theological sense, but a mutation into a new entity, the reason/subject, the only entity capable of rational knowledge. The body was and could be nothing but an object of knowledge. From this point of view the human being is, par excellence, a being gifted with reason, and this gift was conceived as localized exclusively in the soul. Thus, the body, by definition incapable of reason, does not have anything that meets reason/subject. The radical separation produced between reason/subject and body and their relations should be seen only as relations between the human subject/reason and the human body/nature, or between spirit and nature. In this way, in Eurocentric rationality the body was fixed as object of knowledge, outside of the environment of subject/reason.

Without this objectification of the body as nature, its expulsion from the sphere of the spirit, the "scientific" theorization of the problem of race (as in the case of the Comte de Gobineau [1853–57] during the nineteenth cen-tury) would have hardly been possible. From the Eurocentric perspective, certain races are condemned as inferior for not being rational subjects. Being objects of study, they are, consequently, bodies closer to nature. In a sense, they became dominatable and exploitable. According to the myth of the state of nature and the chain of the civilizing process that culminates in European civilization, some races—blacks, American Indians, or yellows—are closer to nature than whites.[18] It was only within this peculiar per-spective that non-European peoples were considered objects of knowledge and domination/exploitation by Europeans virtually to the end of World War II.

This new and radical dualism affected not only the racial relations of domination but the older sexual relations of domination as well. Women, especially the women of inferior races ("women of color"), remained stereotyped together with the rest of the bodies, and their place was all-the-more inferior for their race, so that they were considered much closer to nature or (as was the case with black slaves) directly within nature. It is probable (although the question remains to be investigated) that the modern androcentric idea of gender was elaborated after the new dualism of the Eurocentric cognitive perspective in the articulation of the coloniality of power.

Furthermore, this dualism was amalgamated in the eighteenth century with the new mystified ideas of "progress" and of the state of nature in the human trajectory: the foundational myths of the Eurocentric version of modernity. The peculiar dualist/evolutionist historical perspective was linked to the foundational myths. Thus, all non-Europeans could be considered as pre-European and at the same time displaced on a certain historical chain from the primitive to the civilized, from the rational to the irrational, from the traditional to the modern, from the magic-mythic to the scientific. In other words, from the non-European/pre-European to something that in time will be Europeanized or modernized. Without considering the entire experience of colonialism and coloniality, this intellectual trademark, as well as the long-lasting global hegemony of Eurocentrism, would hardly be explicable. The necessities of capital as such alone do not exhaust, could not exhaust, the explanation of the character and trajectory of this perspective of knowledge.

EUROCENTRISM AND HISTORICAL EXPERIENCE IN LATIN AMERICA

The Eurocentric perspective of knowledge operates as a mirror that distorts what it reflects, as we can see in the Latin American historical experience. That is to say, what we Latin Americans find in that mirror is not completely chimerical, since we possess so many and such important historically European traits in many material and intersubjective aspects. But at the same time we are profoundly different. Consequently, when we look in our Eurocentric mirror, the image that we see is not just composite but also necessarily partial and distorted. The tragedy is that we have all been led, knowingly or not, wanting it or not, to see and accept that image as our own and as belonging to us alone. In this way, we continue being what we are not. And as a result we can never identify our true problems, much less resolve them, except in a partial and distorted way.

EUROCENTRISM AND THE "NATIONAL QUESTION": THE NATION-STATE

One of the clearest examples of this tragedy of equivocations in Latin America is the history of the so-called national question: the problem of the modern nation-state in Latin America. I will review some basic issues of the national question in relation to Eurocentrism and the coloniality of power, which, as far as I know, is a perspective that has not been fully explored (Quijano 1994, 1997). State formations in Europe and in the Americas are linked and distinguished by coloniality of power.

Nations and states are an old phenomenon. However, what is currently called the "modern" nation-state is a very specific experience. It is a society where, within a space of domination, power is organized with a significant degree of democratic relations (as democratic as possible in a power structure), basically in the control of labor, resources, products, and public authority. The society is nationalized because democratized, and therefore the character of the state is as national and as democratic as the power existing within such a space of domination. Thus, a modern nation-state involves the modern institutions of citizenship and political democracy, but only in the way in which citizenship can function as legal, civil, and political equality for socially unequal people (Quijano 1998b).

A nation-state is a sort of individualized society between others. Therefore, its members can feel it as an identity. However, societies are power structures. Power articulates forms of dispersed and diverse social existence into one totality, one society. Every power structure always involves, partially or totally, the imposition by some (usually a particular small group) over the rest. Therefore, every possible nation-state is a structure of power in the same way in which it is a product of power. It is a structure of power by the ways in which the following elements have been articulated: (1) the disputes over the control of labor and its resources and products; (2) sex and its resources and products; (3) authority and its specific violence; (4) intersubjectivity and knowledge.

Nevertheless, if a modern nation-state can be expressed by its members as an identity, it is not only because it can be imagined as a community (Benedict Anderson 1991). The members need to have something real in common. And this, in all modern nation-states, is a more or less democratic participation in the distribution of the control of power. This is the specific manner of homogenizing people in the modern nation-state. Every homogenization in the modern nation-state is, of course, partial and temporary and consists of common democratic participation in the generation and management of the institutions of public authority and its specific mechanisms of violence. This authority is exercised in every sphere of social existence linked to the state and thus is accepted as explicitly political. But such a sphere could not be democratic (involving people placed in unequal relations of power as legally and civilly equal citizens) if the social relations in all of the other spheres of social existence were radically undemocratic or antidemocratic.[19]

Since every nation-state is a structure of power, this implies that the power has been configured along a very specific process. The process always begins with centralized political power over a territory and its population (or a space of domination), because the process of possible nationalization can occur only in a given space, over a prolonged period of time, with the precise space being more or less stable for that period. As a result, nationalization requires a stable and centralized political power. This space is, in this sense, necessarily a space of domination disputed and victoriously guarded against rivals.

In Europe, the process that brought the formation of structures of power later configured as the modern nation-state began, on one hand, with the emergence of some small political nuclei that conquered their space of domination and imposed themselves over the diverse and heterogeneous peoples, identities, and states that inhabited it. In this way the nation-state began as a process of colonization of some peoples over others that were, in this sense, foreigners, and therefore the nation-state depended on the organization of one centralized state over a conquered space of domination. In some particular cases, as in Spain, which owes much to the "conquest" of America and its enormous and free resources, the process included the expulsion of some groups, such as the Muslims and Jews, considered to be undesirable foreigners. This was the first instance of ethnic cleansing being exercised in the coloniality of power in the modern period and was followed by the imposition of the "certificate of purity of blood."[20] On the other hand, that process of state centralization was parallel to the imposition of imperial colonial domination that began with the colonization of America, which means that the first European centralized states emerged simultaneously with the formation of the colonial empires.

The process thus has a twofold historical movement. It began as an internal colonization of peoples with different identities who inhabited the same territories as the colonizers. Those territories were converted into spaces of internal domination located in the same spaces of the future

nation-states. The process continued, simultaneously carrying on an imperial or external colonization of peoples that not only had different identities
than those of the colonizers but inhabited territories that were not considered spaces of internal domination of the colonizers. That is to say, the
external colonized peoples were not inhabiting the same territories of the
future nation-state of the colonizers.

If we look back from our present historical perspective to what happened
with the first centralized European states, to their spaces of domination of
peoples and territories and their respective processes of nationalization, we
will see that the differences are very visible. The existence of a strong central
state was not sufficient to produce a process of relative homogenization of a
previously diverse and heterogeneous population in order to create a common identity and a strong and long-lasting loyalty to that identity. Among
these cases, France was probably the most successful, just as Spain was
the least.

Why France and not Spain? In its beginnings, Spain was much richer and
more powerful than its peers. However, after the expulsion of the Muslims
and Jews, Spain stopped being productive and prosperous and became a
conveyor belt for moving the resources of America to the emergent centers
of financial and commercial capital. At the same time, after the violent and
successful attack against the autonomy of the rural communities and cities
and villages, it remained trapped in a feudal-like seigniorial structure of
power under the authority of a repressive and corrupt monarchy and church.
The Spanish monarchy chose, moreover, a bellicose politics in search of an
expansion of its royal power in Europe, instead of hegemony over the world
market and commercial and finance capital, as England and France would
later do. All of the fights to force the controllers of power to allow or
negotiate some democratization of society and the state were defeated, notably the liberal revolution of 1810–12. In this way the combined internal
colonization and aristocratic patterns of political and social power proved to
be fatal for the nationalization of Spanish society and state, insofar as this
type of power proved to be incapable of sustaining any resulting advantage
from its rich and vast imperial colonialism. It proved, equally, that the monarchy was a very powerful obstacle to every democratizing process, and not
only within the space of its own domination.

On the contrary, in France, through the French Revolution's radical democratization of social and political relations, the previous internal colonization evolved toward an effective, although not complete, "frenchification"
of the peoples that inhabited French territory, originally so diverse and his-

torically and structurally heterogeneous, as were those under Spanish domination. The French Basque, for example, are in the first place French, just like the Navarrese. Not so in Spain.

In each one of the cases of successful nationalization of societies and states in Europe, the experience was the same: a considerable process of democratization of society was the basic condition for the nationalization of that society and of the political organization of a modern nation-state. In fact, there is no known exception to this historical trajectory of the process that drives the formation of the nation-state.

THE NATION-STATE IN AMERICA: THE UNITED STATES

If we examine the experience of America in its Spanish and Anglo areas, equivalent factors can be recognized. In the Anglo-American area, the colonial occupation of territory was violent from the start. But before independence, which was known in the United States as the American Revolution, the occupied territory was very small. The Indians did not inhabit occupied territory—they were not colonized. Therefore, the diverse indigenous peoples were formally recognized as nations, and international commercial relations were practiced with them, including the formation of military alliances in the wars between English and French colonists. Indians were not incorporated into the space of Anglo-American colonial domination. Thus, when the history of the new nation-state called the United States of America began, Indians were excluded from that new society and were considered foreigners. Later on, they were dispossessed of their lands and almost exterminated. Only then were the survivors imprisoned in North American society as a colonized race. In the beginning, then, colonial/racial relations existed only between whites and blacks. This last group was fundamental for the economy of the colonial society, just as it was during the first long moment of the new nation. However, blacks were a relatively limited demographic minority, while whites composed the large majority.

At the foundation of the United States as an independent country, the process of the constitution of a new model of power went together with the configuration of the nation-state. In spite of the colonial relation of domination between whites and blacks and the colonial extermination of the indigenous population, we must admit, given the overwhelming majority of whites, that the new nation-state was genuinely representative of the greater part of the population. The social whiteness of North American society included the millions of European immigrants who arrived in the second half of the nineteenth century. Furthermore, the conquest of indigenous territories resulted in the abundance of the offer of a basic resource of production: land. Therefore, the appropriation of land could be concentrated in a few large states, while at the same time distributed in a vast proportion of middling and small properties. Through these mechanisms of land distribution, the whites found themselves in a position to exercise a notably democratic participation in the generation and management of public authority. The coloniality of the new model of power was not canceled, however, since American Indians and blacks could not have a place at all in the control of the resources of production or in the institutions and mechanisms of public authority.

About halfway through the nineteenth century, Tocqueville (1835, chaps. 16–17) observed that in the United States people of such diverse cultural, ethnic, and national origins were all incorporated into something that seemed like a machine for national reidentification; they rapidly became U.S. citizens and acquired a new national identity, while preserving for some time their original identities. Tocqueville found that the basic mechanism for this process of nationalization was the opening of democratic involvement in political life for all recently arrived immigrants. They were encouraged toward an intense political participation, but given a choice about whether or not to take part. But Tocqueville also noticed that two specific groups were not allowed participation in political life: blacks and Indians. This discrimination expressed the limit of the impressive and massive process of modern nation-state formation in the young republic of the United States of America. Tocqueville did not neglect to advise that unless social and political discrimination were to be eliminated, the process of national construction would be constrained. A century later, another European, Gunnar Myrdall (1944), saw these same limitations in the national process of the United States, when the source of immigration changed and immigrants were no longer white Europeans but, for the most part, nonwhites from Latin America and Asia. The colonial relations of the whites with the new immigrants introduced a new risk for the reproduction of the nation. Without doubt, those risks are increasing to this very day insofar as the old myth of the melting pot has been forcefully abandoned and racism tends to be newly sharpened and violent.

In sum, the coloniality of the relations of domination/exploitation conflict between whites and nonwhites was not, at the moment of the constitution of a new independent state, sufficiently powerful to impede the relative, although real and important, democratization of the control of the means of production and of the state. At the beginning control rested only among the whites, true, but with enough vigor so that nonwhites could claim it later as well. The entire power structure could be configured in the trajectory and orientation of reproducing and broadening the democratic foundations of the nation-state. It is this trajectory to which, undoubtedly, the idea of the American Revolution refers.

LATIN AMERICA: THE SOUTHERN CONE AND THE WHITE MAJORITY

At first glance, the situation in the countries of the so-called Southern Cone of Latin America (Argentina, Chile, and Uruguay) was similar to what happened in the United States. Indians were not, for the most part, integrated into colonial society, insofar as they had more or less the same social and cultural structure of the North American Indians. Socially, both groups were not available to become exploited workers, not condemnable to forced labor for the colonists. In these three countries, the black slaves were also a minority during the colonial period, in contrast with other regions dominated by the Spanish or Portuguese. After independence, the dominants in the Southern Cone countries, as was the case in the United States, considered the conquest of the territories that the indigenous peoples populated, as well as the extermination of these inhabitants, to be necessary as an expeditious form of homogenizing the national population and facilitating the process of constituting a modern nation-state "a la europea." In Argentina and Uruguay this took place in the nineteenth century, and in Chile during the first three decades of the twentieth century. These countries also attracted millions of European immigrants, consolidating, in appearance, the whiteness of the societies of Argentina, Uruguay, and Chile and the process of homogenization.

Land distribution was a basic difference in those countries, especially in Argentina, in comparison with the case of North America. While in the United States the distribution of land happened in a less concentrated way over a long period, in Argentina the extreme concentration of land possession, particularly in lands taken from indigenous peoples, made impossible any type of democratic social relations among the whites themselves. Instead of a democratic society capable of representing and politically organizing into a democratic state, what was constituted was an oligarchic society and state, only partially dismantled after World War II. In the Argentinean case these determinations were undoubtedly associated with the fact that colonial society, above all on the Atlantic coast (which became hegemonic over the rest), was lightly developed, and therefore its recognition as seat of a viceroyalty came only in the second half of the eighteenth century. Its rapid transformation in the last quarter of the eighteenth century as one of the more prosperous areas in the world market was one of the main forces that drove a massive migration from southern, eastern, and central Europe in the following century. But this migratory population did not find in Argentina a society with a sufficiently dense and stable structure, history, and identity to incorporate and identify themselves with it, as occurred in the United States. At the end of the nineteenth century, immigrants from Europe constituted more than 80 percent of Buenos Aires's population. They did not imme-diately enforce the national identity, instead preferring their own European cultural differences, while at the same time explicitly rejecting the identity associated with Latin America's heritage and, in particular, any relationship with the indigenous population.[21]

The concentration of land was somewhat less strong in Chile and in Uruguay. In these two countries, especially in Chile, the number of European immigrants was fewer. But overall they found a society, a state, and an identity already sufficiently densely constituted, to which they incorporated and identified themselves much sooner and more completely than in Argen-tina. In the case of Chile territorial expansion at the expense of Bolivia's and Peru's national frontiers allowed the Chilean bourgeoisie the control of resources whose importance has defined, since then, the country's history: saltpeter, first, and copper a little later. From the middle of the nineteenth century, the pampas saltpeter miners formed the first major contingent of salaried workers in Latin America; later, in copper mines, the backbone of the old republic's workers' social and political organizations was formed. The profits distributed between the British and Chilean bourgeoisie allowed the push toward commercial agriculture and urban commercial economy. New classes of salaried urbanites and a relatively large middle class came together with the modernization of an important part of the landed and commercial bourgeoisie. These conditions made it possible for the workers and the middle class to negotiate the conditions of domination, exploitation, and conflict with some success and to struggle for democracy in the condi-tions of capitalism between 1930 and 1935. In this way, the power could be configured as a modern nation-state—of whites, of course. The Indians, a scant minority of survivors inhabiting the poorest and most inhospitable lands in the country, were excluded from such nation-states. Until recently they were sociologically invisible; they are not so much today as they begin to mobilize in defense of these same lands, which are at risk of being lost in the face of global capital.

The process of the racial homogenization of a society's members, imagined from a Eurocentric perspective as one characteristic and condition of modern nation-states, was carried out in the countries of the Southern Cone not by means of the decolonization of social and political relations among the diverse sectors of the population, but through a massive elimination of some of them (Indians) and the exclusion of others (blacks and mestizos). Homogenization was achieved not by means of the fundamental democratization of social and political relations, but by the exclusion of a significant part of the population, one that since the sixteenth century had been racially classified and marginalized from citizenship and democracy. Given these original conditions, democracy and the nation-state could not be stable and firmly constituted. The political history of these countries, especially from the end of the 1960s until today, cannot be explained at the margins of these determinations.[22]

INDIAN, BLACK, AND MESTIZO MAJORITY: THE IMPOSSIBLE "MODERN NATION-STATE"

After the defeat of Tupac Amaru and of the Haitian Revolution, only Mexico (since 1910) and Bolivia (since 1952) came along the road of social decolonization through a revolutionary process, during which the decolonization of power was able to gain substantial ground before being contained and defeated. At the beginning of independence, principally in those countries that were demographically and territorially extensive at the beginning of the nineteenth century, approximately 90 percent of the total population was composed of American Indians, blacks, and mestizos. However, in all those countries, those races were denied all possible participation in decisions about social and political organization during the process of organizing the new state. The small white minority that assumed control of those states sought the advantage of being free from the legislation of the Spanish Crown, which formally ordered the protection of colonized peoples or races. From then on the white minority included the imposition of new colonial tribute on the Indians, even while maintaining the slavery of blacks for many decades. Of course, this dominant minority was now at liberty to expand its ownership of the land at the expense of the territories reserved for Indians by the Spanish Crown's regulations. In the case of Brazil, blacks were slaves and Indians from the Amazon were foreigners to the new state.

Haiti was an exceptional case in that it produced a national, social, and racial revolution—a real and global decolonization of power—in the same historical movement. Repeated military interventions by the United States brought about its defeat. The other potentially national process in Latin America took place in the Viceroyalty of Peru in 1780, under the leadership of Tupac Amaru II, but was defeated quickly. Thereafter, the dominant group in all the rest of the Iberian colonies successfully avoided social decolonization while fighting to gain independent status.

Such new states could not be considered nations unless it could be admitted that the small minority of colonizers in control were genuinely nationally representative of the entire colonized population. The societies founded in colonial domination of American blacks, Indians, and mestizos could not be considered nations, much less democratic. This situation presents an apparent paradox: independent states of colonial societies.[23] The paradox is only partial and superficial, however, when we observe more carefully the social interests of the dominant groups in those colonial societies and their independent states.

In Anglo-American colonial society, since Indians were a foreign people living outside the confines of colonial society, Indian serfdom was not as extensive as in Ibero-America. Indentured servants brought from Great Britain were not legally serfs, and after independence, they were not indentured for very long. Black slaves were very important to the economy, but they were a demographic minority. And from the beginning of independence, economic productivity was achieved in great part by waged laborers and independent producers. During the colonial period in Chile, Indian serfdom was restricted, since local American Indian servants were a small minority. Black slaves, despite being more important for the economy, were also a small minority. For these reasons, colonized racial groups were not as large a source of free labor as in the rest of the Iberian countries. Consequently, from the beginning of independence an increasing proportion of local production would have to be based on wages, a reason why the internal market was vital for the pre-monopoly bourgeoisie. Thus, for the dominant classes in both the United States and Chile, the local waged labor and the internal production and market were preserved and protected by external competition as the only and the most important sources of capitalist profits. Furthermore, the internal market had to be expanded and protected. In this sense, there were some areas of common national interest of waged laborers, independent producers, and the local bourgeois. With the limitations derived from the exclusion of blacks and mestizos, this was a national interest for the large majority of the population of the new nation-state.

INDEPENDENT STATES AND COLONIAL SOCIETY:
HISTORICAL-STRUCTURAL DEPENDENCE

In certain Ibero-American societies, then, the small white minority in control of the independent states and the colonial societies could have had neither consciousness nor national interests in common with the American Indians, blacks, and mestizos. On the contrary, their social interests were explicitly antagonistic to American Indian serfs and black slaves, given that their privileges were made from precisely the dominance and exploitation of those peoples in such a way that there was no area of common interest between whites and nonwhites and, consequently, no common national interest for all of them. Therefore, from the point of view of the dominators, their social interests were much closer to the interests of their European peers, and consequently they were always inclined to follow the interests of the European bourgeoisie. They were dependent.

They were dependent in this specific way not because they were subordinated by a greater economic or political power. By whom could they have been subordinated? Spain and Portugal were by the nineteenth century too weak and underdeveloped, unable to exercise any kind of neocolonialism like the English and French were able to do in certain African countries after the political independence of those countries. In the nineteenth century the United States was preoccupied with the conquest of Indian territory and the extermination of the Indian population, initiating its imperial expansion on parts of the Caribbean, without the capacity yet for further expanding its political or economic dominance. England tried to occupy Buenos Aires in 1806 and was defeated.

The Latin American white seigniors, owners of political power and serfs and slaves, did not have common interests with those workers that were the overwhelming majority of the populations of those new states. Actually, they were exactly antagonistic. And while the white bourgeoisie expanded the capitalist social relation as the axis of articulation of the economy and society in Europe and the United States, the Latin American seigniors could not accumulate abundant commercial profits to pay for a salaried labor force precisely because that went against the reproduction of their dominion. The white seigniors' commercial profits were allotted for the ostentatious consumption of commodities produced in Europe.

The dependence of the seigniorial capitalists of the new Ibero-American nation-states had an inescapable source: the coloniality of their power led to the perception of their social interests as the same as other dominant whites in Europe and the United States. That coloniality of power itself, however, prevented them from really developing their social interests in the same direction as those of their European peers, that is, converting commercial capital (profits produced either by slavery, serfdom, or reciprocity) into industrial capital, since that involved liberating American Indian serfs and black slaves and making them waged laborers. For obvious reasons, the colonial dominators of the new independent states, especially in South America after the crisis at the end of the eighteenth century, could not be in that configuration except as minor partners of the European bourgeoisie. When much later it was necessary to free the slaves, freedom was not a transformation of labor relations, but a reason to substitute slaves with immigrant workers from other countries, European and Asiatic. The elimination of American Indian serfdom is very recent. There were no common social interests with colonized and exploited workers, nor was there an internal market that would have included the wage laborer, since no such internal market was in the interest of the dominators. Simply put, there was no national interest regarding seigniorial bourgeoisie.

The dependence of the seigniorial capitalists did not come from national subordination. On the contrary, this was the consequence of the community of racialized social interests with their European peers. We are addressing here the concept of historical-structural dependence, which is very different from the nationalist proposals conceptualized as external or structural dependence (Quijano 1967). Subordination came much later, as a consequence of dependence and not the inverse: during the global economic crisis of the 1930s, the bourgeoisie, holding most of Latin America's commercial capital (that of Argentina, Brazil, Mexico, Chile, Uruguay, and, to a certain extent, Colombia), was forced to produce locally its conspicuous consumption of imported products. This period was the beginning of the peculiar system followed by Latin American dependent industrialization: imported goods for ostentatious consumption (by the seignior class and their small groups of middle-class associates) took the place of local products intended for that same consumption. For that reason, it was not necessary for Latin America to globally reorganize the local economies, to massively liberate and pay wages to serfs and slaves, to produce its own technology. Industrialization through the substitution of imports is, in Latin America, a defining case of the implications of the coloniality of power (Quijano 1993a).

In this sense, the process of independence for Latin American states without decolonizing society could not have been, and it was not, a process toward the development of modern nation-states, but was instead a rearticulation of the coloniality of power over new institutional bases. From then on, for almost two hundred years, workers and critical intellectuals have

been concerned with the attempt to advance along the road of nationalization, democratizing our societies and our states. In no Latin American country today is it possible to find a fully nationalized society, or even a genuine
nation-state. The national homogenization of the population could only
have been achieved through a radical and global process of the democratization of society and the state. That democratization would have implied, and
should imply before anything else, the process of decolonizing social, political, and cultural relations that maintain and reproduce racial social classification. The structure of power was and even continues to be organized on
and around the colonial axis. Consequently, from the point of view of the
dominant groups, the construction of the nation, and above all of the central state, has been conceptualized and deployed against American Indians,
blacks, and mestizos. The coloniality of power still exercises its dominance,
in the greater part of Latin America, against democracy, citizenship, the
nation, and the modern nation-state.

From this perspective, four historical trajectories and ideological lines
can be distinguished today in the problem of the nation-state.

1   A limited but real process of decolonization/democratization through radical
     revolutions, such as in Mexico and Bolivia. In Mexico the process of the
     decolonization of power was slowly limited from the 1960s, until finally enter-
     ing a period of crisis at the end of the 1970s. In Bolivia the revolution was
     defeated in 1965.
2   A limited but real process of colonial (racial) homogenization, as in the South-
     ern Cone (Chile, Uruguay, Argentina), by means of a massive genocide of the
     aboriginal population. A variant of this line is Colombia, where the original
     population was almost exterminated and replaced with blacks during the
     colonial period.
3   An always frustrated attempt at cultural homogenization through the cultural
     genocide of American Indians, blacks, and mestizos, as in Mexico, Peru,
     Ecuador, Guatemala, Central America, and Bolivia.
4   The imposition of an ideology of "racial democracy" that masks the true
     discrimination and colonial domination of blacks, as in Brazil, Colombia, and
     Venezuela. It is with difficulty that someone can recognize with seriousness a
     true citizen of the population of African origin in those countries, although the
     racial tensions and conflicts are not as violent and explicit as those in South
     Africa or the southern United States.

These trajectories show that there is, without doubt, an element that
radically impedes the development and culmination of the nationalization of

society and state, insofar as it impedes their democratization, since one cannot find any historical examples where modern nation-states are not the result of a social and political democratization. What is, or could be, that element?

In the European world, and therefore in the Eurocentric perspective, the formation of nation-states has been theorized—imagined, in truth—as the expression of the homogenization of the population in terms of common historic subjective experiences. *Nation* is an identity and a loyalty, especially for liberalism. At first sight, the successful cases of nationalization of societies and states in Europe seem to side with that focus. The homogenizing seemingly consists basically of the formation of a common space for identity and meaning for the population. However, this, in all cases, is the result of the democratization of society that can be organized and expressed in a democratic state. The pertinent question, at this stage of the argument, is why has that been possible in Western Europe and, with some well-known limitations, in all the world of European identity (Canada, the United States, Australia, and New Zealand, for example)? Why has it not been possible in Latin America until today, even in a partial and precarious way?

To begin with, would social and political democratization have been possible—for instance in France, the classic example of the modern nation-state—if the racial factor had been included? It is very unlikely. To this very day it is easy to observe in France the national problem and the debate produced by the presence of nonwhite populations originating from France's former colonies. Obviously, it is not a matter of ethnicity, culture, or religious beliefs. It is sufficient to remember that a century earlier, the Dreyfus affair showed the French capacity for discrimination, but its conclusions also demonstrated that for many French people, the identity of origin was not a requisite determinant to be a member of the French nation, as long as your "color" was French. The French Jews today are more French than the children of Africans, Arabs, and Latin Americans born in France, not to mention what has happened with Russian and Spanish immigrants whose children, having been born in France, are French.

This means that the coloniality of power based on the imposition of the idea of race as an instrument of domination has always been a limiting factor for constructing a nation-state based on a Eurocentric model. Whether to a lesser extent, as is the case in North America, or in a decisive way, as in Latin America, the limiting factor is visible in both cases. The degree of limitation depends on the proportion of colonized races within the total population and on the density of their social and cultural institutions. Because of all of this, the coloniality of power established on the idea of race should be accepted as a basic factor in the national question and the nation-state. The problem is, however, that in Latin America the Eurocentric perspective was adopted by the dominant groups as their own, leading them to impose the European model of nation-state formation for structures of power organized around colonial relations. All the same, we now find ourselves in a labyrinth where the Minotaur is always visible, but with no Ariadne to show us the exit we long for.

EUROCENTRISM AND REVOLUTION IN LATIN AMERICA

A final note of this tragic disjuncture between our experience and our Eurocentric perspective of knowledge is the debate about, and practice of, revolutionary projects. In the twentieth century the vast majority of the Latin American Left, adhering to historical materialism, has debated two types of revolution: bourgeois-democratic or socialist. Competing with that Left, between 1925 and 1935, the movement called "Aprista" proposed an anti-imperialist revolution.[24] It was conceived as a process of purification of the character of the economy and society, eliminating feudal adherences and developing its capitalist side, as well as encouraging the modernization and development of society by means of the national-state control of the principal means of production as a transition toward a socialist revolution. The major theorist of the Revolutionary Anti-imperialist Popular Alliance (APRA), which made such proposals, was the Peruvian Victor Raúl Haya de la Torre. From the end of World War II, that project has become a sort of social liberalism and has been exhausted.[25]

In a brief and schematic but not arbitrary way the Latin American debate about the democratic-bourgeois revolution can be presented as a project in which the bourgeoisie organized the working class, peasants, and other dominated groups in order to uproot the feudal aristocrats' control of the state and organize society and the state in terms of their own interest. The central assumption of that project was that in Latin America society is fundamentally feudal or, at the most, semifeudal, since capitalism is still incipient, marginal, and subordinate. The socialist revolution, on the other hand, is conceived as the eradication of bourgeois control of the state by the industrial working class heading a coalition of the exploited and the dominated classes in order to impose state control on the means of production and to construct a new society through the state. The assumption of that proposition is, obviously, that the economy and, therefore, society and state in Latin

America are basically capitalist. In its language, that implies that capital as a social relation of production is already dominant and that consequently the bourgeoisie is also dominant in society and state. It admits that there are feudal remnants and democratic-bourgeois tasks in the trajectory of the socialist revolution. In fact, the political debate of the past half century in Latin America has been anchored in whether the economy, society, and state were feudal/semifeudal or capitalist. The majority of the Latin American Left, until recently, adhered to the democratic-bourgeois proposition, following all the central tenets of "real socialism" with its head in Moscow or Peking.

In order to believe that in Latin America a democratic-bourgeois revolution based on the European model is not only possible but necessary, it is essential to recognize in America and more precisely in Latin America three things: (1) the sequential relation between feudalism and capitalism; (2) the historical existence of feudalism and consequently the historically antagonistic conflict between feudal aristocracy and the bourgeois; (3) a bourgeoisie interested in carrying out similar revolutionary business. We know that in China at the beginning of the 1930s Mao proposed the idea of a new type of democratic revolution because the bourgeoisie was neither interested in nor capable of carrying out that historical mission. In this case, a coalition of exploited/dominated classes under the leadership of the working class should substitute for the bourgeoisie and undertake the new democratic revolution.

In America, however, for five hundred years capital has existed as the dominant axis of the total articulation of all historically known forms of control and exploitation of labor, thus configuring a historical-structurally heterogeneous model of power with discontinuous relations and conflicts among its components. In Latin America there was not an evolutionist sequence between modes of production; there was no previous feudalism detached from and antagonistic to capital; there was no feudal seignior in control of the state whom a bourgeoisie urgently in need of power would have to evict by revolutionary means. If a sequence existed, it is without doubt surprising that the followers of historical materialism did not fight for an antislavery revolution prior to the antifeudal revolution, prior in turn to the anticapitalist revolution. In the greater part of this hemisphere (including the United States, all of the Caribbean, Venezuela, Colombia, Brazil, and the coasts of Ecuador and Peru), slavery has been more extensive and more powerful. But, clearly, slavery had ended before the twentieth century, and the feudal seigniors had inherited power. Isn't that true?

Therefore, an antifeudal, democratic-bourgeois revolution in the Eurocentric sense has always been a historical impossibility. The only democratic revolutions that really occurred in America (apart from the American Revolution) have been the Mexican and Bolivian, popular revolutions—nationalist, anti-imperialist, anticolonial, that is, against the coloniality of power and oligarchies, against the control of the state by the seigniorial bourgeois under the protection of the imperial bourgeoisie. In the majority of the other countries, the process has been one of gradual and uneven purification of the social character, society, and state. Consequently, the process has always been very slow, irregular, and partial. Could it have been any other way?

All possible democratization of society in Latin America should occur in the majority of these countries at the same time and in the same historical movement as decolonization and as a radical redistribution of power. The reason underlying these statements is that social classes in Latin America are marked by color, any color that can be found in any country at any time. This means that the classification of people is realized not only in one sphere of power—the economy, for example—but in each and every sphere. Domination is the requisite for exploitation, and race is the most effective instrument for domination that, associated with exploitation, serves as the universal classifier in the current global model of power. In terms of the national question, only through the process of the democratization of society can the construction of a modern nation-state, with all of its implications, including citizenship and political representation, be possible and successful. But under the ongoing process of reconcentration of power at a global scale, that perspective may well not be feasible any longer and a process of democratization of society and public authority may require some quite different institutional structure.

With respect to the Eurocentric mirage about "socialist" revolutions (as control of the state and as state control of labor/resources/product), it should be emphasized that such a perspective is founded in two radically false theoretical assumptions. First, the idea of a homogeneous capitalist society, in the sense that capital exists only as social relation and therefore that the waged industrial working class is the majority of the population. But we have just seen that this has never been so in either Latin America or the rest of the world, and that it will most assuredly never occur. Second, there is the assumption that socialism consists in the state control of each and every sphere of power and social existence, beginning with the control of labor, because from the state a new society can be constructed. This assumption puts history, again, on its head, since even in the crude terms of historical materialism, the state, a superstructure, becomes the base of construction of society. By the same token, it hides the reconcentration of the control of power, which necessarily brings total despotism of the controllers, making it appear to be radical redistribution of the control of power. But socialism, if the word still has some effective meaning, cannot be something other than the trajectory of a radical return of the control over labor/resources/product, over sex/resources/products, over authorities/institutions/violence, and over intersubjectivity/knowledge/communication to the daily life of the people. This is what I have proposed since 1972 as the socialization of power (Quijano 1972, 1981b).

In 1928 José Carlos Mariátegui was, without a doubt, the first to begin to see (and not just in Latin America) that in his space/time, the social relations of power, whatever their previous character, existed and acted simultaneously and together in a single and whole structure of power. He perceived that there could not be a homogeneous unity, with continuous relations among its elements, moving itself in a continuous and systematic history. Therefore, the idea of a socialist revolution by historical necessity had to be directed against the whole of that power. Far from consisting of a new bureaucratic reconcentration of power, it could have meaning only as a redistribution among the people, in their daily lives, of the control over their conditions of social existence.[26] After Mariátegui, the debate was not taken up again in Latin America until the 1960s, and in the rest of the world it began with the worldwide defeat of the socialist camp.

In reality, each category used to characterize the Latin American political process has always been a partial and distorted way to look at this reality. That is an inevitable consequence of the Eurocentric perspective, in which a linear and one-directional evolutionism is amalgamated contradictorily with the dualist vision of history, a new and radical dualism that separates nature from society, the body from reason, that does not know what to do with the question of totality (simply denying it like the old empiricism or the new postmodernism) or understands it only in an organic or systemic way, making it, thus, into a distorted perspective, impossible to be used, except in error.

It is not, then, an accident that we have been defeated, for the moment, in both revolutionary projects, in America and in the entire world. What we could advance and conquer in terms of political and civil rights in a necessary redistribution of power (of which the decolonization of power is the presupposition and point of departure) is now being torn down in the process of the reconcentration of the control of power in global capitalism and of its management of the coloniality of power by the same functionaries. Consequently, it is time to learn to free ourselves from the Eurocentric mirror where our image is always, necessarily, distorted. It is time, finally, to cease being what we are not.

Translated by Michael Ennis

NOTES

I want to thank Edgardo Lander and Walter Mignolo for their help in the revision of this article. Thanks also to an anonymous reviewer for useful criticisms of a previous version. Responsibility for the errors and limitations of the text is mine alone.

1   On the concept of the coloniality of power, see Quijano 1992b.

2   Even though for the imperialist vision of the United States of America the term *America* is just another name for that country, today it is the name of the territory that extends from Alaska in the north to Cape Horn in the south and includes the Caribbean archipelago. But from 1492 until 1610, America was exclusively the space/time under Iberian (Hispanic Portuguese) colonial domination. This included, in the northern border, California, Texas, New Mexico, Florida (conquered in the nineteenth century by the United States), and the Spanish-speaking Caribbean area, and extended south to Cape Horn—roughly, the space/time of today's Latin America. The Eurocentered, capitalist, colonial/ modern power emerged then and there. So, although today America is a very heterogeneous world in terms of power and culture and for descriptive purposes could be better referred to as "the Americas," in regards to the history of the specific pattern of world power that is discussed here, "America" still is the proper denomination.

3   On this question and the possible antecedents to race before America, see Quijano 1993b.

4   The invention of the category "color"—first as the most visible indication of race and later simply as its equivalent—as much as the invention of the particular category "white," still requires a more exhaustive historical investigation. In every case, such categories were most likely Anglo-American inventions, since there are no traces of them in the chronicles and other documents from the first hundred years of Iberian colonialism in America. For the case of Anglo-America, an extensive bibliography exists. Allen 1994 and Jacobson 1998 are among the most important works on this topic. However, this kind of scholarship ignores what happened in Iberian America, and thus we still lack sufficient information on this specific problem for that region. Therefore, the invention of color is still an open question. It is very interesting to note: despite the fact that from the time of the Roman Empire those who would in the future be deemed "Europeans" recognized and tended to see the future "Africans" as a different category—as did the Iberians who were more or less familiar with Africans much earlier than the conquest—they never thought of them in racial terms before the colonization of America. In fact, race as a category was applied for

the first time to Indians, not to blacks. In this way, race appeared much earlier than color in the history of the social classification of the global population.

5   The idea of race is literally an invention. It has nothing to do with the biological structure of the human species. Regarding phenotypic traits, those that are obviously found in the genetic code of individuals and groups are in that specific sense biological. However, they have no relation to the subsystems and biological processes of the human organism, including those involved in the neurological and mental subsystems and their functions. See Mark 1994 and Quijano 1999d.

6   Western Europe is the location on the Atlantic coast to the west of the large peninsula protruding from the continental mass that Europeans named Asia. Fernando Coronil (1996) has discussed the construction of the category "Occident" as part of the formation of a global power.

7   This is precisely what Alfred Métraux, the well-known French anthropologist, found at the end of the 1950s in southern Peru. I found the same phenomenon in 1963 in Cuzco: an Indian peon was obliged to travel from his village, in La Convención, to the city in order to fulfill his turn of service to his patrons. But they did not furnish him lodging or food or, of course, a salary. Métraux proposed that that situation was closer to the Roman *colonato* of the fourth century B.C. than to European feudalism.

8   On the process of the production of new historical geocultural identities, see O'Gorman 1991 [1958]; Rabasa 1993; Dussel 1995c; Mudimbe 1988; Tilly 1990; Said 1994a [1978]; and Coronil 1996.

9   Around the categories produced during European colonial dominance of the world there exist a good many lines of debate: subaltern studies, postcolonial studies, cultural studies, and multiculturalism are among the current ones. There is also a flourishing bibliography, too long to be cited here, lined with famous names such as Ranajit Guha, Gayatri Spivak, Edward Said, Homi Bhabha, and Stuart Hall.

10   Of my previous studies, see principally Quijano 1992b, 1998b.

11   A summary of the vast literature on this debate can be found in Quijano 2000c.

12   On the theoretical propositions of this conception of power, see Quijano 1999a.

13   I mean "system" in the sense that the relations between parts and the totality are not arbitrary and that the latter has hegemony over the parts in the orientation of the movement of the whole. But not in a systematic sense, as the relations of the parts among themselves and with the whole are not logically functional. This happens only in machines and organisms, never in social relations.

14   See Amin 1989 for a different (although somewhat related) position than the one that orients this article.

15   On the origin of the category of historical-structural heterogeneity, see Quijano 1966, 1977, 1988b.

16   I have always wondered about the origin of one of liberalism's most precious propositions: ideas should be respected, but the body can be tortured, crushed, and killed. Latin Americans repeatedly cite with admiration the defiant phrase spoken while a martyr of the anticolonial battles was being beheaded: "Barbarians, ideas cannot be beheaded!" I am now sure that the origin of the idea can be found in the new Cartesian dualism that made the body into mere "nature."

17 Bousquié 1994 asserts that Cartesianism is a new radical dualism.

18 The fact that the only alternative category to the Occident was, and still is, the Orient, while blacks (Africa) or Indians (America before the United States) did not have the honor of being the other to Europe, speaks volumes about the processes of Eurocentered subjectivity.

19 See Quijano 1998b and 2000d for a full discussion of the limits and conditions of democracy in a capitalist structure of power.

20 "Purity of blood" is probably the closest antecedent to the idea of "race" produced by Spaniards in America. See Quijano 1993b.

21 Even in the 1920s, as in the whole twentieth century, Héctor Murena, an important member of the Argentinean intelligentsia, proclaimed, "We are Europeans exiled in these savage pampas." See Imaz 1964. During Argentina's social, political, and cultural battles in the 1960s, *cabecita negra* was the nickname for racial discrimination.

22 Homogenization is a basic element of the Eurocentric perspective of nationalization. If it were not, the national conflicts that emerge in European nations every time the problem of racial or ethnic differences arises could not be explained or understood. Nor could we understand the Eurocentric politics of settlement favored in the Southern Cone or the origin and meaning of the so-called indigenous problem in all of Latin America. If nineteenth-century Peruvian landowners imported Chinese workers, it was because the national question was not in play for them except as naked social interests. From the Eurocentrist perspective, the seigniorial bourgeoisie, based in the coloniality of power, has been an enemy of social and political democratization as a condition of nationalization for the society and state.

23 In the 1960s and 1970s many social scientists within and outside of Latin America, including myself, used the concept of "internal colonialism" to characterize the apparently paradoxical relationship of independent states with respect to their colonized populations. In Latin America, Pablo González Casanova (1965b) and Rodolfo Stavenhagen (1965) were surely the most important among those who dealt with the problem systematically. Now we know that these problems concerning the coloniality of power go further than the institutional development of the nation-state.

24 Some of the movements include the Revolutionary Anti-imperialist Popular Alliance (APRA) in Peru, Democratic Action (AD) in Venezuela, the Nationalist Revolutionary Movement (MNR) in Bolivia, the Movement for National Liberation (MLN) in Costa Rica, and the Authentic Revolutionary Movement (MRA) and the orthodoxy in Cuba.

25 Eurocentric myopia (not only in European and American studies but in Latin America as well) has spread and nearly imposed the term *populism* on movements and projects that have little in common with the movement of the Russian *narodniks* of the nineteenth century or the later North American populism. See Quijano 1998b.

26 It is this idea that gives Mariátegui his major value and continued validity as a critic of socialisms and their historical materialism. See, above all, the final chapter in Mariátegui 1928b, as well as Mariátegui 1928a and 1929.

THE GEOPOLITICS OF KNOWLEDGE AND
THE COLONIAL DIFFERENCE

Walter D. Mignolo

In December 1998 I had the good fortune to be one of the commentators in the workshop "Historical Capitalism, Coloniality of Power, and Transmodernity," featuring presentations by Immanuel Wallerstein, Aníbal Quijano, and Enrique Dussel.[1] Speakers were asked to offer updates and to elaborate on the concepts attributed to them. Reflecting on "transmodernity," Dussel made a remark that I take as a central point of my argument. According to Dussel, postmodern criticism of modernity is important and necessary, but it is not enough. The argument was developed by Dussel in his recent short but important dialogue with Gianni Vattimo's work, which he characterized as a "Eurocentric critique of modernity" (Dussel 1999b, 39). What else can there be, beyond a Eurocentric critique of modernity and Eurocentrism? Dussel has responded to this question with the concept of transmodernity, by which he means that modernity is not a strictly European but a planetary phenomenon, to which the "excluded barbarians" have contributed, although their contribution has not been acknowledged. Dussel's argument resembles, then, the South Asian Subaltern Studies Group, although it has been made from the legacies of earlier colonialisms (Spanish and Portuguese). Transmodernity also implies—for Dussel—a "liberating reason" (razón liberadora) that is the guiding principle of his philosophy and ethic of liberation. The dialogues between Dussel and Wallerstein, between philosophy of liberation (Dussel 1994b [1987]) and world-system analysis (Wallerstein 1987), and between philosophy of liberation (Dussel 1996b, 1999b; Apel 1996) and opening the social sciences (Wallerstein 1996a, 1999) have two things in common. First, both are critical of capitalism, the neoliberal market, and formal democracy. Second, both (and Quijano as well) conceive of modernity as unfolding in the sixteenth century with capitalism and the emergence of the Atlantic commercial circuit. However, there is a break between Wallerstein, on one hand, and Dussel and Quijano, on the other: they stand at different ends of the colonial difference. To explain this intuition is the main thrust of this essay.

Dussel's remarks can also be applied to Wallerstein's conception of historical capitalism, in that it is defined as a Eurocentric criticism of capitalism (Wallerstein 1983). By introducing the notion of colonial difference, I will be able to expand on Dussel's notion of transmodernity and Quijano's coloniality of power. I will be able also to compare the three in their approach to Eurocentrism and to introduce Slavoj Žižek's take on "Eurocentrism from the left."[2] My first step, then, will be to distinguish two macronarratives, that of Western civilization and that of the modern world (from the early modern period [i.e., the European Renaissance] until today). The first is basically a philosophical narrative, whereas the second is basically the narrative of the social sciences. Both macronarratives have their positive and negative sides. While Western civilization is celebrated by some, its logocentrism is criticized by others. Similarly, modernity has its defenders as well as its critics. Dussel is located between the two macronarratives, but his criticism diverges from both the criticism internal to Western civilization and the critique internal to the modern world, as in world-system analysis (Wallerstein 1987, 1997a). As a philosopher, Dussel is attuned to the first macronarrative, the macronarrative of Western civilization and its origins in ancient Greece. As a Latin American philosopher, he has been always attentive to the historical foundation of the modern/colonial world in the sixteenth century. He shares these interests with Wallerstein and Quijano, both of whom are sociologists. However, Quijano and Dussel share the Latin American colonial experience or, rather, a local history of the colonial difference. Wallerstein, instead, is immersed in the imperial difference that distinguishes the philosophical critique of Western civilization in Europe and the sociological critique of modernity in the United States. In essence, the geopolitics of knowledge is organized around the diversification, through history, of the colonial and the imperial differences. Let me specify further these distinctions.

The following argument is built on the assumption (which I cannot develop here) that the history of capitalism as told by Fernand Braudel, Wallerstein, and Giovanni Arrighi and the history of Western epistemology as it has been constructed since the European Renaissance run parallel to and complement each other (Braudel 1992 [1979]; Wallerstein 1983; Arrighi 1994). The expansion of Western capitalism implied the expansion of Western epistemology in all its ramifications, from the instrumental reason that went along with capitalism and the industrial revolution, to the theories of the state, to the criticism of both capitalism and the state. To make a long story short, let me quote a paragraph by Sir Francis Bacon, written at the beginning of the seventeenth century. The passage reveals a conceptualization of knowledge that began to move away from Renaissance epistemology grounded on the trivium and the quadrivium and strongly dominated by rhetoric and the humanities. Bacon replaced rhetoric with philosophy, and the figure of the Renaissance humanist began to be overtaken by the figure of the philosopher and the scientist that contributed to and further expanded from the European Enlightenment. According to Bacon, "The best division of human learning is that derived from the three faculties of the rational soul, which is the need of learning. History has reference to the Memory, Poesy to the Imagination and Philosophy to the Reason. . . . Wherefore from these three fountains, Memory, Imagination and Reason, flow these three emanations, History, Poesy and Philosophy, and there can be no others" (Bacon, Novum organum 1875 [1620], 292–93). The three "emanations" were expanded and modified in the subsequent years. However, the assertion that "there can be no others" persisted. And at the moment when capitalism began to be displaced from the Mediterranean to the North Atlantic (Holland, Britain), the organization of knowledge was established in its universal scope. "There can be no others" inscribed a conceptualization of knowledge to a geopolitical space (Western Europe) and erased the possibility of even thinking about a conceptualization and distribution of knowledge "emanating" from other local histories (China, India, Islam, etc.).

WESTERN CIVILIZATION AND THE MODERN/
COLONIAL WORLD-SYSTEM

The concept and image of modernity are not equivalent to those of the modern world-system. There are several differences between the two. First, modernity is associated with literature, philosophy, and the history of ideas, whereas the modern world-system is associated with the vocabulary of the social sciences. Second, this first characterization is important if we remember that since the 1970s both concepts have occupied defined spaces in academic as well as public discourses. During the Cold War, the social sciences gained ground within cultures of scholarship, in the United States particularly in regard to the relevance purchased by area studies (Fals-Borda 1971; Wallerstein 1997b; Lambert 1990; Rafael 1994). Consequently, post-modernity is understood both as a historical process in which modernity encountered its limits and as a critical discourse on modernity that was housed in the humanities, even though social scientists were not deaf to its noise (Seidman and Wagner 1992). Third, modernity (and, obviously, post-modernity) maintained the imaginary of Western civilization as a pristine development from ancient Greece to eighteenth-century Europe, where the bases of modernity were laid out. In contrast, the conceptualization of the modern world-system does not locate its beginning in Greece. It underlines a spatial articulation of power rather than a linear succession of events. Thus, the modern world-system locates its beginning in the fifteenth century and links it to capitalism (Braudel 1995 [1949], 1992 [1979]; Wallerstein 1974–89, vol. 1; Arrighi 1994). This spatial articulation of power, since the sixteenth century and the emergence of the Atlantic commercial circuit, is what Quijano theorizes as "coloniality of power" (Quijano and Wallerstein 1992, 549; Mignolo 2000d).

Borrowing the word *paradigm* for pedagogical convenience, I would say that modernity and the modern world-system are indeed two interrelated, although distinct, paradigms. The advantage of the latter over the former is that it made visible the spatiality of Western history in the past five hundred years, along with the need to look at modernity and coloniality together. Modernity places the accent on Europe. Modern world-system analysis brings colonialism into the picture, although as a derivative rather than a constitutive component of modernity, since it does not yet make visible coloniality, the other (darker?) side of modernity. It is indicative of Quijano's merit that he has shown coloniality to be the overall dimension of modernity, thereby distinguishing coloniality from colonialism. It is also to his merit to have brought to light the fact that the emergence of the Atlantic circuit during the sixteenth century made coloniality constitutive of modernity. If modernity is chronologically located in the eighteenth century, coloniality becomes derivative. Thus the Iberian foundational period of capitalistic expansion and coloniality is erased or relegated to the Middle Ages as the Black Legend, to which the Enlightenment construction of the "South" of Europe testifies.[3] In this scenario, if modernity comes first, then colonialism and coloniality become invisible. Quijano and Dussel make it possible not only to conceive of the modern/colonial world-system as a sociohistorical structure coincident with the expansion of capitalism but also to conceive of coloniality and the colonial difference as loci of enunciation. This is precisely what I mean by the geopolitics of knowledge and the colonial difference (Mignolo 2000d, 2000e).

The eighteenth century (or more exactly, the period between approximately 1760 and 1800) was dominated by two distinctive shifts. First, there was the displacement of power in the Atlantic circuit from the south to the north. Second, the main concern in Europe, from the Peace of Westphalia (1648) until the end of the eighteenth century, was nation-state building rather than colonialism (Perry Anderson 1975). England, France, and Germany were not yet colonial powers in the sixteenth and seventeenth centuries, and when they became so, they mutually reinforced nation building with colonial expansion, particularly starting in the nineteenth century. However, the strong preoccupation in the north with the Europe of nations placed colonialism on the back burner, so to speak. Colonialism was a secondary concern for nations such as England and France, whose presence in the Americas was geared toward commerce rather than conversion, like the project of Spain and Portugal. At that point, France and England did not have a civilizing mission to accomplish in the Americas, as they would have in Asia and Africa after the Napoleonic era. Current conceptualizations of modernity and postmodernity are historically grounded in that period. The second stage of modernity was part of the German restitution of the Greek legacy as the foundation of Western civilization.

Although there is a discussion as to whether the world-system is five hundred or five thousand years old, I do not consider this issue to be relevant. What is relevant, instead, is that the modern/colonial world-system can be described in conjunction with the emergence of the Atlantic commercial circuit and that such a conceptualization is linked to the making of colonial difference(s) (Mignolo 2000d). The colonial difference is a connector that, in short, refers to the changing faces of colonial differences throughout the history of the modern/colonial world-system and brings to the foreground the planetary dimension of human history silenced by discourses centering on modernity, postmodernity, and Western civilization.

THE LIBERATION OF PHILOSOPHY AND THE DECOLONIZATION OF THE SOCIAL SCIENCES

Dependency theory has not yet lost its posture, although it has been severely criticized. It is capable of holding its own in the middle of a critical tempest because its critics addressed the conceptual structure of dependency, not its raison d'être. The fact that dependency at large was and is the basic strategy in the exercise of coloniality of power is not a question that needs lengthy and detailed argumentation. Even though in the current stage of globalization there is a Third World included in the First, the interstate system and the coloniality of power organizing it hierarchically have not vanished yet. It is also not the point here whether the distinction between center and periphery was as valid at the end of the twentieth century as it was in the nineteenth century. If dependency in the modern/colonial world-system is no longer structured under the center-periphery dichotomy, this does not mean that dependency vanishes because this dichotomy is not as clear today as it was yesterday. On the other hand, *interdependency* is a term that served to restructure the coloniality of power around the emergence of transnational corporations (MacNeill, Winsemius, and Yakushiji 1991). What Quijano terms "historico-structural dependency" should not be restricted to the center-periphery dichotomy (Quijano 1997). Rather, it should be applied to the very structure of the modern/colonial world-system and capitalistic economy.

Dependency theory was more than an analytic and explanatory tool in the social sciences (Cardoso and Faletto 1969; Cardoso 1976). While world-system analysis owes its motivating impulse and basic economic, social, and historical structure to dependency theory (Dussel 1990a; Grosfoguel 1997, 200), it is not and could not have served as the political dimension of dependency theory. Dependency theory was parallel to decolonization in Africa and Asia and suggested a course of action for Latin American countries some 150 years after their decolonization. World-system analysis operates from inside the system, while dependency theory was a response from the exteriority of the system—not the exterior but the exteriority. That is to say, the outside is named from the inside in the exercise of the coloniality of power. Dependency theory offered an explanation and suggested a course of action for Latin America that could hardly have been done by a world-system analysis. World-system analysis in its turn did something that the dependency analysis was not in a position to accomplish. That is, world-system analysis introduced a historical dimension and a socioeconomic frame (the modern world-system) into the social sciences, thus displacing the origin of history and cultures of scholarship from ancient Greece to the modern world-system. The emergence of the social sciences in the nineteenth century was indeed attached to the epistemic frame opened by the second modernity (the French Enlightenment, German Romantic philosophy, and the British industrial revolution) (Foucault 1966; Wallerstein et al. 1996). World-system analysis responded to the crisis of that frame in the 1970s, when decolonization took place in Africa and Asia and the changes introduced by transnational corporations brought to the foreground the active presence of a world far beyond Western civilization. The irreducible (colonial) difference between dependency theory and world-system analysis cannot be located in their conceptual structures but in the politics of their loci of enunciation. Dependency theory was a political statement for the social transformation of and from Third World countries, while world-system analysis was a political statement for academic transformation from First World countries. This difference, implied in the geopolitics of knowledge described by Carl E. Pletsch (1981), is indeed the irreducible colonial difference—the difference between center and periphery, between the Eurocentric critique of Eurocentrism and knowledge production by those who participated in building the modern/colonial world and those who have been left out of the discussion.[4] Las Casas defended the Indians, but the Indians did not participate in the discussions about their rights. The emerging capitalists benefiting from the industrial revolution were eager to end slavery that supported plantation owners and slaveholders. Black Africans and American Indians were not taken into account when knowledge and social organization were at stake. They—Africans and American Indians—were considered patient, living organisms to be told, not to be heard.

The impact of dependency theory on the decolonization of scholarship in Latin America was immediate and strong. In 1970 the Colombian sociologist Orlando Fals-Borda published an important book titled *Ciencia propia y colonialismo intelectual* (Intellectual colonialism and our own science), which today echoes a widespread concern in cultures of scholarship in Asia and Africa. The scenario is simple: Western expansion was not only economic and political but also educational and intellectual. The Eurocentric critique of Eurocentrism was accepted in former colonies as "our own" critique of Eurocentrism; socialist alternatives to liberalism in Europe were taken, in the colonies, as a path of liberation without making the distinction between emancipation in Europe and liberation in the colonial world. Quite simply, the colonial difference was not considered in its epistemic dimension. The foundation of knowledge that was and still is offered by the history of Western civilization in its complex and wide range of possibilities provided the conceptualization (from the Right and the Left) and remained within the language frame of modernity and Western civilization. Fals-Borda's book is still valid because it keeps in mind a current dilemma in cultures of scholarship. In fact, Fals-Borda's early claims for the decolonization of the social sciences echoes the more recent claims made by Boaventura de Sousa Santos (1998) from Portugal in his argument "toward a new common sense." Granted, Santos is not focusing on Colombia or Latin America. However, the marginality of Portugal, as the south of Europe, allows for a perception of the social sciences different from that which one might find in the north.

While Wallerstein argues for the opening of the social sciences, assuming the need to maintain them as a planetary academic enterprise, Fals-Borda's concerns are with the very foundation of the social sciences and other forms of scholarship. In other words, the planetary expansion of the social sciences implies that intellectual colonization remains in effect, even if such colonization is well intended, comes from the Left, and supports decolonization. Intellectual decolonization, as Fals-Borda intuited, cannot come from existing philosophies and cultures of scholarship. Dependency is not limited to the Right; it is created also from the Left. The postmodern debate in Latin America, for example, reproduced a discussion whose problems originated not in the colonial histories of the subcontinent but in the histories of European modernity.

An indirect continuation of Fals-Borda's argument for intellectual decolonization is the project that Enrique Dussel has been pursuing since the early 1990s (Dussel 1994a, 1996b). Philosophy of liberation, as conceived by Dussel since the late 1960s, is another consequence of dependency theory and the intellectual concerns that prompted its emergence. One of Dussel's main concerns was and still is a philosophical project contributing to social liberation. His latest book is the consequence of a long and sustained philosophical, ethical, and political reflection (Dussel 1999b). Fals-Borda's argument was concerned not just with a project in the social sciences for the liberation of the Third World; rather, it concerned also a project of intellectual liberation from the social sciences. In the case of Dussel, liberation is thought with regard to philosophy. Here again is the irreducible colonial (epistemic) difference between a leftist social-sciences project *from the First*

World and a liberation *of* the social sciences (and philosophy) from the Third World (Lander 2000b). The logic of this project, from the standpoint of the colonial difference, has been formulated in Dussel's confrontations between his own philosophy and ethic of liberation and that of Gianni Vattimo (Dussel 1999b). In one short but substantial chapter (" 'With Vattimo?': 'Against Vattimo?' ") Dussel relates Vattimo's philosophy to nihilism and describes nihilism as a "twilight of the West, of Europe, and of modernity" (ibid., 34). In closing this section (and immediately after the preceding description), Dussel adds, "Has Vattimo asked himself the meaning that his philosophy may have for a Hindu beggar covered with mud from the floods of the Ganges; or for a member of a Bantu community from sub-Saharan Africa dying of hunger; or for millions of semi-rural Chinese people; or for hundreds of thousands of poor marginalized in suburban neighborhoods like Nezahualcoyotl or Tlanepantla in Mexico, as populated as Torino? Is an aesthetic of 'negativity,' or a philosophy of 'dispersion as final destiny of being,' enough for the impoverished majority of humanity?" (ibid).

At first glance, and for someone reading from the wide horizon of continental philosophy, this paragraph could be interpreted as a cheap shot. It is not, however. Dussel is naming the absent location of thinking, obscured by the universalizing of modern epistemology and its parallelism and companionship with capitalism, either as justification or as internal critique, such as Vattimo's. Indeed, what is at stake in Dussel's argument is not just being but the coloniality of being, from whence philosophy of liberation found its energy and conceptualization. It is simply the colonial difference that is at stake. Dussel's point comes across more clearly in the second section of his article on Vattimo, when Dussel underlines the discrepancy between the starting point in both projects. As is well known, a room looks altered if you enter it from a different door. Furthermore, of the many doors through which one could have entered the room of philosophy, only one was open. The rest were closed. One understands what it means to have only one door open and the entrance heavily regulated. Dussel notes that the starting point for a "hermeneutic ontology of the twilight" (Vattimo 1963, 179–84) and the "philosophy of liberation" are quite different. Dussel framed this distinction in terms of the geopolitics of knowledge: the first is from the north; the second, from the south. The south is not, of course, a simple geographic location but a "metaphor for human suffering under global capitalism" (Boaventura de Sousa Santos 1995, 506). The first discourse is grounded in the second phase of modernity (industrial revolution, the Enlightenment). The second discourse, that of philosophy of liberation, is grounded in the first phase of modernity and comes from the subaltern perspective—not from the colonial/Christian discourse of Spanish colonialism but from the perspective of its consequences, that is, the repression of American Indians, African slavery, and the emergence of a Creole consciousness (both white/ mestizo mainly on the continent and black in the Caribbean) in subaltern and dependent positions. From this scenario, Dussel points out, while in the north it could be healthy to celebrate the twilight of Western civilization, from the south it is healthier to reflect on the fact that 20 percent of the earth's population consumes 80 percent of the planet's income.

It is no longer possible, or at least it is not unproblematic, to "think" from the canon of Western philosophy, even when part of the canon is critical of modernity. To do so means to reproduce the blind epistemic ethnocentrism that makes difficult, if not impossible, any political philosophy of inclusion (Habermas 1998). The limit of Western philosophy is the border where the colonial difference emerges, making visible the variety of local histories that Western thought, from the Right and the Left, hid and suppressed. Thus, there are historical experiences of marginalization no longer equivalent to the situation that engendered Greek philosophy and allowed its revamping in the Europe of nations, emerging together with the industrial revolution and the consolidation of capitalism. These new philosophies have been initiated by thinkers such as Frantz Fanon, Rigoberta Menchú, Gloria Anzaldúa, Subramani, Abdelkhebir Khatibi, and Edouard Glissant, among others. Consequently, two points should be emphasized.

The first is the ratio between places (geohistorically constituted) and thinking, the geopolitics of knowledge proper. If the notion of being was invented in Western philosophy, coloniality of being cannot be a continuation of the former. Because of coloniality of power, the concept of being cannot be dispensed with. And because of the colonial difference, coloniality of being cannot be a critical continuation of the former (a sort of postmodern displacement), but must be, rather, a relocation of the thinking and a critical awareness of the geopolitics of knowledge. Epistemology is not ahistorical. But not only that, it cannot be reduced to the linear history from Greek to contemporary North Atlantic knowledge production. It has to be geographical in its historicity by bringing the colonial difference into the game.[5] The densities of the colonial experience are the location of emerging epistemologies, such as the contributions of Franz Fanon, that do not overthrow existing ones but that build on the ground of the silence of history. In this sense Fanon is the equivalent of Kant, just as Guamán Poma de Ayala in colonial Peru could be considered the equivalent of Aristotle (see R. Adorno 1986). One of the reasons why Guamán Poma and Fanon are not easily

perceived as equivalents of Aristotle and Kant is time. Since the Renaissance
—the early modern period or emergence of the modern/colonial world—
time has functioned as a principle of order that increasingly subordinates
places, relegating them to before or below from the perspective of the holders (of the doors) of time. Arrangements of events and people in a timeline is
also a hierarchical order, distinguishing primary sources of thought from
interesting or curious events, peoples, or ideas. Time is also the point of
reference for the order of knowledge. The discontinuity between being and
time and coloniality of being and place is what nourishes Dussel's need to
underline the difference (the colonial difference) between continental philosophy (Vattimo, Jürgen Habermas, Karl-Otto Apel, Michel Foucault) and
philosophy of liberation.

Dussel's insistence on the *punto de partida diferente* (distinct starting point),
in relation to Vattimo, could be supported by arguments made by the Native
American lawyer and intellectual Vine Deloria Jr. and by Robert Bernasconi,
an expert in continental philosophy. Deloria's reflections on space and time
(sacred places and abstract and symbolic time) touch on and make visible
the irreducible colonial difference that Dussel emphasizes in his philosophy
of liberation. In both Deloria and Dussel there is a need to establish the
limits of Western cosmologies. Although this is done from the experience of
a Native American and from a descendant of European immigrants in Latin
America, the colonial difference is entrenched in their distinct experiences.
Of course, European immigrants in former colonial worlds, such as Argentina, do not have the same experiences as Native Americans. However, both
groups experience the colonial difference that can be either narcotized or
revealed. They both choose to reveal and think from it.

Deloria makes a simple, albeit fundamental, point: "Conservative and
liberal, terms that initially described political philosophies, have taken on
the aspect of being able to stand for cultural attitudes of fairly distinct
content. Liberals appear to have more sympathy for humanity, while conservatives worship corporate freedom and self-help doctrines underscoring
individual responsibility. The basic philosophical differences between liberals and conservatives are not fundamental, however, because both fit in
the idea of history a thesis by which they can validate their ideas" (1994
[1972], 63). One could add *socialist* to *conservative* and *liberal*, thus completing
the political-ideological tripartite distribution of the late-nineteenth-century
North Atlantic political and ideological spectrum. These three varieties of
secular political ideologies are also in the same frame of Christianity. For all
of them, time and history are the essence of their cosmology.

Furthermore, Deloria adds, when the domestic (i.e., in the United States) ideology "is divided according to American Indian and Western European immigrant, however, the fundamental difference is one of great philosophical importance" (1994 [1972], 62). The "fundamental difference" is indeed the "colonial difference," since it is not just a case of incommensurable cosmologies or worldviews but a difference articulated by the coloniality of power. Consequently, the two are historically and logically linked to each other in a relation of dependency. This is a dependency related to the universality attributed to time, in domestic ideology, and the particularity attributed to place in the same movement. Place, of course, is not naturally particular but historically so, according to the location attributed to place by hegemonic discourses assuring the privilege of time and history.

I am not proposing here that some merging of time and space—which we could term *spacetime* from one side of the domestic ideology (either the Western European immigrants or the social sciences)—will solve the problems created by a hegemonic discourse of time, history, progress, and development. The terrain of epistemology is not far removed from the map Deloria traced from the domestic political ideology (e.g., liberals and conservatives, to which I added socialists). Wallerstein has traced the map of modern epistemology, which was first divided between science and philosophy (and the humanities), or in effect between the two cultures. Later this division was bridged in conflictive ways by the emergence of the social sciences, with some of the disciplines leaning toward the sciences (economy, sociology, and political sciences) and others toward the humanities (cultural anthropology and history). Wallerstein described two basic concepts of spacetime in the social sciences: the "geopolitical or episodic spacetime" and "eternal spacetime" (1991, 66–94). The first concept alludes to the explanation of the present and particular. The second alludes to what is valid across time and space. After indicating the limitations of these two types of spacetime, Wallerstein underlined other dimensions that the social sciences have left out of consideration. These include the "cyclical-ideological spacetime," the "structural spacetime," and the "transformational spacetime" (Wallerstein 1997b). Arguing in favor of including these new dimensions in the future of the social sciences, Wallerstein advanced the arguments, and the hope, for a "new unifying epistemology" that will overcome the classic divorce between the sciences and philosophy (or the humanities), leaving the social sciences in an uncomfortable middle ground. If this is possible, what will be left out? In this case it would be the entire space of the colonial difference to which Wallerstein, like Vattimo, is blind.

Let me begin my explanation by quoting Deloria: "Western European peoples (and of course later U.S. people) have never learned to consider the nature of the world discerned from a spatial point of view" (Deloria 1994 [1972], 63). The consequences of such a statement, which once again under-lines the colonial difference, are enormous for religion, epistemology, and international relations. Time and history allowed global designs (religious, economic, social, and epistemic) to emerge as responses to the need of a given place that were assumed to have universal value across time and space. The experience, in which global designs emerged, is emptied when a given global design is exported and programmed to be implanted over the experi-ence of a distinct place. However, this project (that was the project of moder-nity from Renaissance Christianity to the contemporary global market) is no longer convincing. "Space generates time, but time has little relationship with space" (ibid., 71). Consequently, the universal ideology of disincorpo-rated time and history has reached the point in which space and place can no longer be overruled. The world, therefore, is not becoming, nor can it be conceived of as, a global village. Instead, it is a "series of non-homogeneous pockets of identity that must eventually come into conflict because they represent different historical arrangements of emotional energy" (ibid., 65). Therefore, the question is no longer a new conceptualization of spacetime within a Kantian paradigm, with space and time as invariants, but their discontinuity on the other side of the colonial difference. I am thinking here of spacetime without such a name (e.g., Pachakuti among the Aymara peo-ple in the Andes) on the other side of the colonial difference that the Kantian model made invisible.[6] Wallerstein's reconceptualization of spacetime re-mains within the domestic ideology of Western cultures of scholarship, with the assumption of their universal scope, valid for all time and all societies. Deloria's radical conceptualization of time and place situates the discussion elsewhere, beyond the social sciences, looking not for an epistemology that will unify the two cultures but for an epistemology that will be built on the irreducible colonial difference. The consequence is the right to claim episte-mic rights from the places where experiences and memories organize time and knowledge.

Dussel's dialogue with Vattimo's philosophy goes in the same direction, albeit from different motivations. There is a partial agreement between Vat-timo and Dussel, as one could imagine a similar partial agreement between Deloria and Wallerstein. The important question, however, is that of the irreducible epistemic colonial difference on which Deloria and Dussel build their claims for the future of ethics, politics, and epistemology, which can no longer be built on categories and premises of Western philosophy and social sciences. While Deloria's argument could be taken as an indirect argument to decolonize (and not just to open) the social sciences (as claimed in Latin America by the Colombian sociologist Fals-Borda in the early 1970s), Dussel's argument is a direct claim for decolonizing philosophy. According to Dussel, "An Ethic of Liberation, with planetary scope ought, first of all, 'to liberate' [I would say decolonize] philosophy from Helenocentrism. Otherwise, it cannot be a future worldly philosophy, in the twenty-first century" (Dussel 1998a, 57).

The irreducible colonial difference that I am trying to chart, starting from Dussel's dialogue with Vattimo, was also perceived by Robert Bernasconi in his account of the challenge that African philosophy puts forward to continental philosophy. Simply put, Bernasconi notes that "Western philosophy traps African philosophy in a double bind. Either African philosophy is so similar to Western philosophy that it makes no distinctive contribution and effectively disappears; or it is so different that its credentials to be genuine philosophy will always be in doubt" (1997, 188). This double bind is the colonial difference that creates the conditions for what I have elsewhere called "border thinking."[7] I have defined border thinking as an epistemology from a subaltern perspective. Although Bernasconi describes the phenomenon with different terminology, the problem we are dealing with here is the same. Furthermore, Bernasconi makes his point with the support of the African American philosopher Lucius Outlaw in an article titled "African 'Philosophy': Deconstructive and Reconstructive Challenges" (1987). Emphasizing the sense in which Outlaw uses the concept of deconstruction, Bernasconi at the same time underlines the limits of Jacques Derrida's deconstructive operation and the closure of Western metaphysics. Derrida, according to Bernasconi, offers no space in which to ask the question about Chinese, Indian, and especially African philosophy. Latin and Anglo-American philosophy should be added to this. After a careful discussion of Derrida's philosophy, and pondering possible alternatives for the extension of deconstruction, Bernasconi concludes by saying, "Even after such revisions, it is not clear what contribution deconstruction could make to the contemporary dialogue between Western philosophy and African philosophy" (1997, 187). Or, if a contribution could be foreseen, it has to be from the perspective that Outlaw appropriates and that denaturalizes the deconstruction of the Western metaphysics from the inside (and maintains the totality, à la Derrida). That is to say, it has to be a deconstruction from the exteriority of Western metaphysics, from the perspective of the double bind that Bernasconi detected in the interdependence (and power relations) between Western and African philosophy. However, if we invert the perspective, we are located in a particular deconstructive strategy that I would rather call the decolonization of philosophy (or of any other branch of knowledge, natural sciences, social sciences, and the humanities). Such a displacement of perspective was already suggested by the Moroccan philosopher Abdelkhebir Khatibi (see Mignolo 2000d). However, certainly Bernasconi will concur with Khatibi in naming decolonization as the type of deconstructive operation proposed by Outlaw, thus maintaining and undoing the colonial difference from the colonial difference itself—that is to say, maintaining the *difference* under the assumption that "we are all human" although undoing the *coloniality of power* that converted differences into values and hierarchies. "The existential dimension of African philosophy's challenge to Western philosophy in general and Continental philosophy in particular is located in the need to decolonize the mind. This task is at least as important for the colonizer as it is for the colonized. For Africans, decolonizing the mind takes place not only in facing the experience of colonialism, but also in recognizing the precolonial, which established the destructive importance of so-called ethnophilosophy" (Bernasconi 1997, 191). The double bind requires also a double operation from the perspective of African philosophy, that is, an appropriation of Western philosophy and at the same time a rejection of it grounded in the colonial difference. Bernasconi recognizes that these, however, are tasks and issues for African philosophers. What would be similar issues for a continental philosopher? For Europeans, Bernasconi adds, "decolonizing the colonial mind necessitates an encounter with the colonized, where finally the European has the experience of being seen as judged by those they have denied. The extent to which European philosophy championed colonialism, and more particularly helped to justify it through a philosophy of history that privileged Europe, makes it apparent that such a decolonizing is an urgent task for European thought" (ibid., 192).

My interest in developing at length Bernasconi's position is not, of course, that of repeating the authoritative gesture of a North Atlantic philosopher validating the claims of African philosophers. Quite the contrary, it is Bernasconi's humble recognition of the limits of continental philosophy, from inside continental philosophy itself, in which I am interested. By recognizing the colonial difference, Bernasconi breaks with centuries of European philosophical blindness to the colonial difference and the subalternization of knowledge. Credit should be given to African philosophers for successfully raising the issue and projecting a future, taking advantage of the epistemic potential of thinking from the colonial difference. Credit should also be given to Bernasconi for recognizing that here we are in a different ball game, where the contenders, although in sportive friendship, have different tasks and goals.

This is precisely the point that Dussel has been trying to make since his early polemic dialogue with Apel, Paul Ricoeur, Habermas, and, more recently, Vattimo (Dussel 1994a). However, Dussel is in a position more similar to the one defended by African philosophers than to the position articulated by Bernasconi. Like Outlaw and others, Dussel calls for a double operation of deconstruction-reconstruction or, better yet, decolonization (to use just one word that names both operations and underlines the displacement of perspectives, tasks, and goals) (Outlaw 1987). Dussel's is a claim made from an epistemic subaltern position in which Latin American philosophy has been located by Western philosophy. His preference for a philosophy of liberation is both a liberation of philosophy and an assertion of philosophy as an instrument of decolonization. Dussel is clearly underscoring Vattimo's blindness to the other side of modernity, which is coloniality: the violence that Vattimo (or Nietzsche and Heidegger) attributed to modern instrumental reason, the coloniality of power forced on non-European cultures that have remained silenced, hidden, and absent. The colonial difference is reproduced in its invisibility. Dussel's claim for decolonization, for an ethic and philosophy of liberation, is predicated on a double movement similar to the strategy of African philosophers. On one hand, there is an appropriation of modernity and, on the other, a move toward a transmodernity understood as a liberating strategy or decolonization project that, according to Bernasconi, includes everybody, the colonizer and the colonized (Dussel 1998a, 39; Bernasconi 1997, 191).

I have highlighted philosophy, but what I said about it applies to the social sciences as well. It is a commendable move to open the social sciences but, as Dussel said about Vattimo, it is not enough. Opening the social sciences implies that the social sciences will remain in place, will be exported to places whose experiences do not correspond or correspond only partially, and overlooks the fact that modernity revealed its other side, coloniality, in non-European locations. As in the case of philosophy analyzed by Bernasconi, social sciences in the First World trap the social sciences of the Third World in a double bind. Either the social sciences are similar to North Atlantic social sciences all over the planet and thus do not make any distinctive contributions, or they are not social sciences and social knowledge is not being recognized. Social scientists from the Third World have not raised their voices as loudly as philosophers have. Yet they have not been silenced either, as the examples of Fals-Borda and Quijano in Latin America and the South Asian Subaltern Studies Group illustrate. We may not subscribe today to the recommendations made by Fals-Borda in the 1970s. However, the solution that Fals-Borda suggested should not be an excuse to dismiss the problem he raised. Or, if you wish, the solution suggested could be read as a way of raising the problem rather than as a solution that would be expected to be valid today. The belief that social scientists with goodwill toward social transformation will be endorsed by "the people," whose interest the social scientist claims to defend, would be difficult to sustain today. First, this is because the people (e.g., social movements of all kind) do not need intellectuals from outside to defend their interests. Second, the transformation of knowledge (and social transformation, of course), to which the social scientist could contribute, is located not so much in the domain of the people as in learned institutions and the mass media. Certainly, there is a wealth of knowledge that has been subalternized by modernity/coloniality, but that knowledge is not necessarily in the minds or the interests of the people, whose interests, in turn, may not coincide with those of the social scientist.

In any case, Fals-Borda's perception of the double "diaspora of brains" in the Third World remains valid today. Brains are not being stolen when a social scientist leaves a country in which there are limited research conditions and moves to a country and institution with better resources. Instead, this happens when the social scientist remains in a country under limited research conditions and reproduces or imitates the patterns, methods, and, above all, the questions raised by the social sciences under different historical and social experiences. This is another version of the double bind in which North Atlantic scholarship and sciences placed the production of knowledge and which reproduces the coloniality of power. If opening the social sciences is a good step but hardly enough, "indigenous sociology" is also an important contribution, yet it does not carry the radical force articulated by African philosophers or by the philosophy of liberation (Akiwowo 1999). Insofar as it remains indigenous, sociology solves only part of the problem. In order to be decolonized, sociology and the social sciences must be submitted to the double movement of appropriation and radical criticism from the perspective of the indigenous to the point of revealing the colonial difference in the social sciences. Sociology, even with its opening, cannot do the job (Wallerstein et al. 1996). Like Derrida's deconstruction, North Atlantic social sciences are reaching the limits of the colonial difference, the space where alternatives to philosophy and the social sciences are necessary.

HISTORICAL CAPITALISM AND
COLONIALITY OF POWER

The frame and stage are now set for a shorter treatment of historical capitalism and coloniality of power in relation to transmodernity. Wallerstein's concept of historical capitalism (introduced in the early 1980s) complements his earlier key notion of the modern world-system. Instead of the structure and the law of capital accumulation studied by Marx, Wallerstein focuses on its historical expansion and transformations. Wallerstein characterizes the economic system identified as capitalism by its purpose: capital accumulation and, as a necessary consequence, self-expansion. The second aspect is its historical emergence, which Wallerstein locates somewhere in fifteenth-century Europe. These first two features presuppose that (1) until the fifteenth century, in Europe and the rest of the world, there existed economic systems that were not capitalist, and (2) the emergence of capitalism supplanted and erased all other previous economic organizations. Consequently, Wallerstein's first characterization of historical capitalism is hampered by the conceptions of linear time and newness, which are two basic presuppositions of capitalistic ideology and modern epistemology. In other words, the assumption that once something new emerges, everything preceding it vanishes does not leave much room for maneuvering beyond current market philosophy.

The linear conception of time (logically necessary for the notion of progress) that Wallerstein identifies as a third basic characteristic of historical capitalism, along with its newness, works toward an image of capitalism as a totality that erased all other existing economic alternatives from the face of the earth. In a sense, it is true that capitalism began to overpower all other alternative economic organizations it encountered in the history of its expansion, from the fifteenth century to the end of the twentieth. On the other hand, it is not true that overpowering also means erasure. What is missing in Wallerstein's conception of historical capitalism is exteriority of capitalism, that moment in which "living labor" is transformed into "capitalist labor," the exploitation of the plus-value (Dussel 1994b [1987]; Saénz 1999, 213–48; Mignolo 2000e). By exteriority I do not mean the outside, but the space where tensions emerge once capitalism becomes the dominant economic system and eliminates all the possibilities of anything outside it, but not its exteriority. Wallerstein's conceptualization of historical capitalism presupposes a totality without exteriority. I would say that transmodernity and coloniality of power are to historical capitalism what Levinas's philosophical reflections on being are to Heidegger's being and time. The analogy is appropriate because of Dussel's translation of Emmanuel Levinas's exteriority to the colonial experience (Dussel 1975b). The analogy is also relevant because of the parallels between the fracture in the narrative of Western civilization between Greek and Jewish philosophical traditions, on the one hand, and the fracture between modernity and coloniality in the narrative of the modern/colonial world-system, on the other.

Wallerstein's frame for historical capitalism, as well as Arrighi's, allows us to tell the story of imperial conflicts and, consequently, to identify the imperial difference (i.e., the difference in the interiority) of the system (Arrighi 1994; Wallerstein 1983, chap. 2). However, it leaves the colonial difference out of sight, in the very obscurity in which capitalistic expansion placed it and where capitalistic expansion goes with violence, physical as well as epistemic. Consequently, Wallerstein's notion of historical capitalism goes with his criticism of the social sciences and his predisposition to open them. Yet it maintains the social sciences in an overarching epistemic totality that parallels the overarching totality of capitalism. Alternative economies in tension with capitalism as well as alternatives to capitalism have no place in Wallerstein's conception of the social sciences, in which the very notion of historical capitalism is founded. Since the colonial difference is blurred in Wallerstein's notion of historical capitalism, it is impossible to foresee the possibility of thinking from it or of thinking the tensions between capitalism and other economic organizations as well as the alternatives to capitalism from subaltern perspectives.

There are several possibilities open to the future, of which I would only underline some, with the purpose of making visible the colonial difference, its epistemic potential, and the alternative futures it allows us to imagine. Otherwise, the more refined analysis of historical capitalism will contribute to reproduce the idea that the power of capitalism and the desire for expansion and accumulation eliminate all possible difference. This is the risk of opening the social sciences without questioning and replacing their very foundations, as Fals-Borda and Santos have been arguing (Fals-Borda 1971; Boaventura de Sousa Santos 1995, 1998). I suspect also that Dussel's and Quijano's arguments point toward decolonizing rather than opening the social sciences.

Could we say that capitalism puts alternative economies into a double bind, similar to what continental philosophy did to African philosophy? Could we say that alternative economies shall be either similar to capitalism (and disappear) or be condemned to remain so different that their credentials as genuine economies will be in doubt? I think that the analogy can be defended and that there are several grounds on which the argument can be built. First, there is the survival, through five hundred years, of American Indian economies in which the goals are not accumulation and expansion but accumulation and reciprocity. When accumulation goes with reciprocity its meaning changes (Quijano 1998b). The final orientation is accumulation for the well-being of the community rather than for the well-being of the agents of accumulation and expansion without regard to the interests of the community. Remembering the emergence of capitalism as an economic system, as outlined by Wallerstein, may help make this idea more concrete. Capitalism emerged as an economic system from a subaltern perspective: the commercial bourgeois class felt constrained by the power of the church and landlords. The French Revolution, which Wallerstein highlights so much as the moment in which the geoculture of the modern world-system (and historical capitalism) finds its moment of consolidation, was indeed a bourgeois revolution. Therefore the Russian Revolution, as its counterpart, remained within the logic of capital accumulation and expansion and proposed that the ruling agents be the workers rather than the bourgeoisie. The struggle for power between liberalism and socialism concluded with the victory of the former. Socialism was not able to replace the desire that nourishes and makes capitalism work. The desire for accumulation and possession is stronger than the desire for distribution that was the socialist alternative, although within the logic of capitalism. The colonial difference remained equally valid for an expansive capitalism under the name of liberalism and civilization or socialism and liberation. Socialism, therefore, was not placed in a double bind by capitalism, as African philosophy was by continental philosophy, since socialism emerged as an alternative within an alternative that changed the content of the conversation and maintained the terms of capitalistic production.

If the analogy between philosophy and economy can be maintained, it is necessary to look for economic organizations that have not been cornered by the capitalist expansion and that today can offer alternatives to capitalism. When I say economic organizations, I am not referring to a different logic of economic organization as much as to a different principle and philosophy of economic production and distribution. The problem, therefore, is not so much a technical one generated by the industrial revolution as it is the principles and goals that generated the industrial revolution. Consequently, if changes in the principles and goals are possible, they would have to start from the appropriation and twisting of the uses of technology rather than from its reproduction, which is in the hands of those who will not voluntarily relinquish control. For that, a fundamental reorientation of philosophy is necessary. At this point, it is easy to understand the analogy between philosophy and capitalism, as far as we leave open the space between economy and capitalism and are constantly aware of the colonial difference that capitalism erases by establishing equivalence between the two. In reality both capitalism and economy presuppose different principles. Originally economy meant administration of scarcity, while capitalism implies accumulation of wealth.

Historical capitalism, as conceived of by Wallerstein and narrated by Arrighi, occludes the colonial difference and, even more, the necessity of looking at capitalism from the other end, that is, from its exteriority (Wallerstein 1983, Arrighi 1994). This is an exteriority that cannot only be narrated from the interiority of the system (as Wallerstein does very well) but that needs its own narrative from its own exteriority. At this point, opening and exporting the social sciences to analyze historical capitalism will no longer do, since such a move will reproduce the occlusion of the colonial difference and, with it, the possibility and necessity of looking at capitalism otherwise. Quijano's notion of coloniality of power offers this opportunity. Yet, before focusing on the coloniality of power, I would like to make a few comments about racism and universalism, conceived of by Wallerstein as substantial aspects of historical capitalism. In this argument Wallerstein touches on the epistemic colonial difference. In revealing the links between universalism and racism (and sexism) as justifications for the exploitation of labor, Wallerstein makes an important statement about the social structure. However, the statement falls short in revealing that the complicity between universalism, racism, and sexism also framed the principles of knowledge under which Wallerstein made his critique. If epistemology runs parallel to the history of capitalism, epistemology cannot be detached from or untainted by the complicity between universalism, racism, and sexism. Here the epistemic colonial difference comes into the foreground.

Wallerstein's integration of racism and universalism into the picture of historical capitalism is perhaps the most radical aspect of his conceptualization. Racism, said Wallerstein, "has been the cultural pillar of historical capitalism," and "the belief in universalism has been the keystone of the ideological arch of historical capitalism" (1983, 80, 81). How are racism and universalism related? The ethnicization of the world in the very constitution of the modern/colonial world-system has had, for Wallerstein, three major consequences. First, the organization and reproduction of the workforce that can be better illustrated by the link, in the modern/colonial world, of blackness with slavery, which was absent, of course, in Aristotle, the reading of whom went through a substantial transformation in sixteenth-century theological and legal discussions. Second, Wallerstein considers that ethnicization provided a built-in training mechanism for the workforce, located within the framework of ethnically defined households and not at the cost of the employers or the state. But what Wallerstein considers crucial is the third consequence of the ethnicization of the workforce. This is institutional racism as the pillar of historical capitalism.

> What we mean by racism has little to do with the xenophobia that existed in various prior historical systems. Xenophobia was literally fear of the *stranger*. Racism within historical capitalism had nothing to do with *strangers*. Quite the contrary. Racism was the mode by which various segments of the work-force within the same economic structure were constrained to relate to each other. Racism was the ideological justification for the hierarchization of the work-force and its highly unequal distributions of reward. What we mean by racism is that set of ideological statements combined with that set of continuing practices which have had the consequence of maintaining a high correlation of ethnicity and work-force allocation over time. (ibid., 78, emphasis added)

Universalism, as the ideological keystone of historical capitalism, is a faith as well as an epistemology, a faith in the real phenomenon of truth and the epistemology that justifies local truth with universal values.

> Our collective education has taught us that the search for truth is a disinterested virtue when in fact it is a self-interested rationalization. The search for truth, proclaimed as the cornerstone of progress, and therefore of well-being, has been, at the very least, consonant with the maintenance of a hierarchical, unequal, social structure in a number of specific respects. The process involved in the expansion of the capitalist world-economy . . . involved a number of pressures at the level of culture: Christian proselytization; the imposition of European language; instruction in specific technologies and mores; changes in the legal code. . . . That is that complex processes we sometimes label "westernization," or even more arrogantly "modernization," and which was legitimated by the desirability of sharing both the fruits of and faith in the ideology of universalism. (ibid., 82)

It cannot be said of Wallerstein that he, like Vattimo or Habermas, is blind to colonialism. Unlike continental thinkers, Wallerstein is not imprisoned in the Greco-Roman–modern European tradition. The politics of location is a question valid not just for minority epistemology. On the contrary, it is the keystone of universalism in European thought. Cornel West's perception and analysis of the "evasion of American philosophy" (1989) speaks to that politics of location that is not a blind voluntarism but a force of Westernization. Although the United States assumed the leadership of Western expansion, the historical ground for thinking was not, and could not have been, European. The "evasion of American philosophy" shows that tension between the will to be like European philosophy and the impossibility of being so (West 1993). The logic of the situation analyzed by West is similar to the logic underlined by Bernasconi vis-à-vis African philosophy. The variance is that the evasion of American philosophy was performed by Anglo-Creoles displaced from the classical tradition instead of by native Africans who felt the weight of a parallel epistemology.

The social sciences do have a home in the United States as well as in Europe, which is not the case for philosophy. But the social sciences do not necessarily have a home in the Third World. Therefore, while opening the social sciences is an important claim to make within the sphere of their gestation and growth, it is more problematic when the colonial difference comes into the picture. To open the social sciences is certainly an important reform, but the colonial difference also requires decolonization. To open the social sciences is certainly an important step, but it is not yet sufficient, since opening is not the same as decolonizing, as Fals-Borda claimed in the 1970s. In this sense Quijano's and Dussel's concepts of coloniality of power and transmodernity are contributing to decolonizing the social sciences (Quijano) and philosophy (Dussel) by forging an epistemic space from the colonial difference. Decolonizing the social sciences and philosophy means to produce, transform, and disseminate knowledge that is not dependent on the epistemology of North Atlantic modernity—the norms of the disciplines and the problems of the North Atlantic—but that, on the contrary, responds to the need of the colonial differences. Colonial expansion was also the colonial expansion of forms of knowledge, even when such knowledges were critical to colonialism from within colonialism itself (like Bartolomé de las Casas) or to modernity from modernity itself (like Nietzsche). A critique of Christianity by an Islamic philosopher would be a project significantly different from Nietzsche's critique of Christianity.

COLONIALITY OF POWER, DEPENDENCY, AND EUROCENTRISM

Wallerstein, Quijano, and Dussel have in common their debt to dependency theory.[8] They are apart (although not enemies) because of the epistemic colonial difference. Quijano's concepts of coloniality of power and historic-structural dependency emphasize this complicity, similar to Dussel's arguments with and against Vattimo (Dussel 1999b).

To understand Quijano's coloniality of power, it is first necessary to accept coloniality as constitutive of modernity and not just as a derivative of modernity—that is, first comes modernity and then coloniality. The emergence of the commercial Atlantic circuit in the sixteenth century was the crucial moment in which modernity, coloniality, and capitalism, as we know them today, came together. However, the Atlantic commercial circuit did not immediately become the location of Western hegemonic power. It was just one more commercial circuit among those existing in Asia, Africa, and Anahuac and Tawantinsuyu in what would later become America (Abu-Lughod 1989; Wolf 1982; Mignolo 2000d). Modernity/coloniality is the moment of Western history linked to the Atlantic commercial circuit, the transformation of capitalism (if we accept from Wallerstein and Arrighi that the seed of capitalism can be located in fifteenth-century Italy), and the foundation of the modern/colonial world-system (Wallerstein 1983; Arrighi 1994).

I have purposely mixed two macronarratives. One I will call the Western-civilization macronarrative and the other the modern/colonial world-system narrative. The first emerged in the Renaissance and was consolidated during the Enlightenment and by German philosophy in the early nineteenth century. As such, this macronarrative is tied to historiography (the Renaissance) and philosophy (the Enlightenment). The second macronarrative emerged during the Cold War as it is linked to the consolidation of the social sciences. The first macronarrative has its origin in Greece, the second in the origin of the Atlantic commercial circuit. Both macronarratives are founded in the same principles of Western epistemology, and both have their own double-personality complex (double side). For instance, the narrative of Western civilization is at the same time celebratory of its own virtues and critical of its own failings. In the same vein modernity is often celebrated as hiding coloniality and yet is critiqued because of coloniality, its other side. Both macronarratives can also be criticized from the inside (Nietzsche, Heidegger, Derrida, Wallerstein, Gunder Frank, etc.) and from the exteriority of the colonial difference (Dussel 1995a, 1998a; Quijano 1992a, 1997). Both coloniality of power and historicostructural dependency are key concepts in Quijano's critique of these macronarratives from the exteriority of the colonial difference.

Quijano singles out Latin America and the Caribbean as places where a double movement constitutes their history: a constant and necessary process of "re-originalization" that goes with the process of their repression. The double process indicated by Quijano is the inscription of the colonial difference and the consequence of the coloniality of power. Coloniality of power should be distinguished from colonialism, which is sometimes termed the colonial period. Colonialism is a concept that inscribes coloniality as a derivative of modernity. In this conception modernity occurs first, with colonialism following it. On the other hand, the colonial period implies that, in the Americas, colonialism ended toward the first quarter of the nineteenth century. Instead coloniality assumes, first, that coloniality constitutes modernity. As a consequence, we are still living under the same regime. Today coloniality could be seen as the hidden side of postmodernity and, in this respect, postcoloniality would designate the transformation of coloniality into global coloniality in the same way that postmodernity designates the transformation of modernity into new forms of globalization. Or it could designate a critical position of modernity from the perspective of coloniality and the colonial difference, similar to postmodernity understood as a critique of modernity from inside modernity itself. In brief, colonialism could be removed from the picture after the first (United States, Haiti, and Latin American countries) and second (India, Algeria, Nigeria, etc.) waves of decolonization, whereas coloniality is alive and well in the current structure of globalization. Thus Quijano observes,

> En el momento actual ocurren fenómenos equivalentes [a aquellos ocurridos desde el siglo XVI]. Desde la crisis mundial de los 70s se ha hecho visible un proceso que afecta a todos y a cada uno de los aspectos de la existencia social de las gentes de todos los paises. El mundo que se formó hace 500 años está culminando con la formación de una estructura productiva, financiera y comercial que tiende a ser más integrada que antes. Con una drástica reconcentración del control de poder político y de recursos.

> [Today we are witnessing similar phenomena [to those that took place in the sixteenth century]. Since the world crisis of the 1970s, a process has been becoming visible that affects everyone, as well as every aspect of the social existence of the people of every country. The social world that began to be structured five hundred years ago is arriving at its closure through an economic, financial, and commercial organization much more integrated than in the past. And that means a far-reaching reconcentration of political power and of economic resources.] (Quijano 1997, 113)

Changes did not encroach equally on diverse societies and local histories. Modernity/coloniality and capitalism went through different phases in their common history. However, coloniality of power is the common thread that links modernity/coloniality in the sixteenth century with its current version at the end of the twentieth century. For Quijano, coloniality of power is a principle and strategy of control and domination that can be conceived of as a configuration of several features.

The idea of race—or purity of blood, as it was expressed in the sixteenth century—became the basic principle for classifying and ranking people all over the planet, redefining their identities, and justifying slavery and labor. In this manner a matrix of power constituted several areas.

1   The existence and reproduction of geohistorical identities, of which Kant's ethnoracial tetragon (Africans are black, Americans are red [Kant was thinking of the United States], Asians are yellow, and Europeans are white) (see Kant 1875) was the eighteenth-century version of early Spanish classifications of Moors, Jews, American Indians, black Africans, and the Chinese.

2   The hierarchy established between European and non-European identities, as Kant's example so eloquently illustrates.

3   The need to transform and design institutions that would maintain the coloniality of power structured and implemented in the sixteenth century, which became an internal aspect of modernity and capitalism—and that internal aspect was precisely the coloniality of power.

Consequently, modernity/coloniality or, if you wish, the constitution and history of the modern/colonial world-system is at the same time a structure in which the historicostructural dependency, as a structure of domination, is the visible face of the coloniality of power. Not only is such a historico-structural dependency economic or political; above all, it is epistemic.

En el contexto de la colonialidad del poder, las poblaciones dominadas y todas las nuevas identidades, fueron también sometidas a la hegemonia del eurocentrismo como manera de conocer, sobre todo en la medida que algunos de sus sectores pudieron aprender la letra de los dominadores. Así, con el tiempo largo de la colonialidad, que aún no termina, esas poblaciones fueron atrapadas entre el patrón epistemológico aborigen y el patrón eurocéntrico que, además, se fue encauzando como racionalidad instrumental o tecnocrática, en particular respecto de las relaciones sociales de poder y en las relaciones con el mundo en torno.

[Coloniality of power means that all dominated populations and all the newly created identities were subjected to the hegemony of Eurocentrism understood as a way of conceiving of and organizing knowledge, above all, when some sectors of the dominated population had the opportunity and the chance to learn the writing system [la letra] of the colonizer.] (Quijano 1997, 117)

Coloniality of power worked at all levels of the Western-civilization and modern world-system macronarratives. The colonized areas of the world were targets of Christianization and the civilizing mission as the project of the narrative of Western civilization, and they became the target of development, modernization, and the new marketplace as the project of the modern world-system. The internal critique of both macronarratives tended to present itself as valid for the totality, in the sense that it was configured by the program of Western civilization and the modern world-system. The insertion of the word *colonial*, as in *modern/colonial world-system*, makes visible what both macronarratives previously obscured: that the production of knowledge and the critique of modernity/coloniality from the colonial difference is a necessary move of decolonization. Otherwise, opening the social sciences could be seen as a well-intentioned reproduction of colonialism from the Left. Similarly, a critique of Western metaphysics and logocentrism from the Arabic world may not take into account the critical epistemic legacy and the memory of epistemic violence inscribed in Arabic language and knowledge. Historicostructural dependency, in the narrative of the modern/colonial world-system, presupposes the colonial difference. It is, indeed, the dependency defined and enacted by the coloniality of power. Barbarians, primitives, underdeveloped people, and people of color are all categories that established epistemic dependencies under different global designs (Christianization, civilizing mission, modernization and development, consumerism). Such epistemic dependency is for Quijano the very essence of coloniality of power (Quijano 1997).

Both Quijano and Dussel have been proposing and claiming that the starting point of knowledge and thinking must be the colonial difference, not the narrative of Western civilization or the narrative of the modern world-system. Thus transmodernity and coloniality of power highlight the epistemic colonial difference, essentially the fact that it is urgently necessary to think and produce knowledge from the colonial difference. Paradoxically, the erasure of the colonial difference implies that one recognize it and think from such an epistemic location—to think, that is, from the borders of the two macronarratives, philosophy (Western civilization) and the social sciences (modern world-system). The epistemic colonial difference cannot be erased by its recognition from the perspective of modern epistemology. On the contrary, it requires, as Bernasconi clearly saw in the case of African philosophy, that epistemic horizons open beyond Bacon's authoritarian assertion that "there can be no others." The consequences of this are gigantic not only for epistemology but also for ethics and politics.

EUROCENTRISM AND THE GEOPOLITICS OF KNOWLEDGE

I have mentioned that Wallerstein, Quijano, and Dussel have dependency theory as a common reference, and I have suggested that while Wallerstein brought dependency theory to the social sciences as a discipline, Quijano and Dussel followed the political and dialectical scope of dependency theory.

The epistemic colonial difference divides one from the other. Of course, this does not place one against the other but underlines the colonial difference as the limit of the assumed totality of Western epistemology. That is why to open the social sciences is a welcome move, but an insufficient one. It is possible to think, as Quijano and Dussel (among others) have, beyond and against philosophy and the social sciences as the incarnation of Western epistemology. It is necessary to do so in order to avoid reproducing the totality shared by their promoters and their critics. In other words, the critiques of modernity, Western logocentrism, capitalism, Eurocentrism, and the like performed in Western Europe and the United States cannot be valid for persons who think and live in Asia, Africa, or Latin America. Those who are not white or Christian or who have been marginal to the foundation, expansion, and transformation of philosophy and the social and natural sciences cannot be satisfied with their identification and solidarity with the European or American Left. The criticism of Christianity advanced by Nietzsche (a Christian) cannot satisfy the criticism of Christianity and colonization advanced by Khatibi (a Muslim and Maghrebian). It is crucial for the ethics, politics, and epistemology of the future to recognize that the totality of Western epistemology, from either the Right or the Left, is no longer valid for the entire planet. The colonial difference is becoming unavoidable. Greece can no longer be the point of reference for new utopias and new points of arrival, as Slavoj Žižek still believes, or at least sustains (Žižek 1998).

If Wallerstein, Quijano, and Dussel have dependency theory as a common reference, they also share a critique of Eurocentrism (Wallerstein 1997a; Dussel 1995a, 1998a; Quijano 1992a, 1997). However, their motivation is different. Quijano's and Dussel's critiques of Eurocentrism respond to the overwhelming celebration of the discovery of America, which both scholars read not only as a Spanish question but also as the beginning of modernity and European hegemony. Both concur that Latin America and the Caribbean today are a consequence of North Atlantic (not just Spanish and European) hegemony. Wallerstein's critique of Eurocentrism is a critique of the social sciences: "Social sciences has been Eurocentrism throughout its institutional history, which means since there have been departments teaching social science within a university system" (1997a, 93). Thus, Wallerstein's critique of Eurocentrism is one of epistemology through the social sciences. Quijano's and Dussel's critiques come to Western epistemology through coloniality of power from the colonial difference.

Clearly dissatisfied with recent criticism of Eurocentrism, Žižek made a plea for Eurocentrism from the Left. I do not think that Žižek had Waller-

stein, Quijano, and Dussel in mind. Wallerstein is a social scientist, and
Žižek seems more concerned with poststructuralist (philosophical and psychoanalytic) debates. Quijano and Dussel are thinkers from Latin America
who write primarily in Spanish, and Žižek has not given any signs of being
interested in or even familiar with them. In fact, he seems more concerned
with the United States and identity politics, which for him is the negation of
politics proper. Consequently he asks, "Is it possible to imagine a leftist
appropriation of the European political legacy?" (Žižek 1998, 988; 1999, 171–
244). I will not discuss here whether identity politics is the end of politics or
whether there are arguments that can justify a plea from the Left for identity
politics parallel to the plea for Eurocentrism performed by Žižek. For the
time being, I prefer to concentrate on his argument about universalism and
globalization to justify his leftist appropriation of the European political
legacy and to invent new forms of repoliticization after the crisis of the Left
and of identity politics filled the gap. "The political (the space of litigation in
which the excluded can protest the wrong or injustice done to them) fore-
closed from the Symbolic then returns in the Real in the guise of new forms
of racism" (Žižek 1999, 97). Racism, however, is not returning, as it has
been the foundation of the modern-colonial world, to which the modern-
postmodern political has been blind, which is obvious in the arguments
developed by Wallerstein and Etienne Balibar (1991 [1988]). In this respect
Frantz Fanon's famous example can help us understand what is at stake
here. For a "Negro who works on a sugar plantation," says Fanon, "there is
only one solution: to fight. He will embark on this struggle, and will pursue
it, not as the result of a Marxist or idealistic analysis but quite simply because
he cannot conceive of life otherwise than in the form of a table against
exploitation, misery and hunger" (1967 [1952], 224). Of course this is simply
because he or she is a "Negro." We know that the equation "Negro = Slave"
is a feature of the modern/colonial world and that this equation was part of
a larger frame in which the ethnoracial foundation of modernity was established. The basic events were Christianity's victory over the Moors and
the Jews, the colonization of the American Indians, and the establishment
of slavery in the New World. One could argue that "postmodern racism
emerges as the ultimate consequence of the postpolitical suspension of the
political, of the reduction of the state to a mere police agent servicing the
(consensually established) needs of market forces and multiculturalist, tol-
erant humanitarianism" (Žižek 1999, 97). Or one could argue that the postcolonial, after the 1970s, reinstalled the political in terms of ethnic-antiracial
struggles, in the United States as well as in Europe.

Since Žižek sees in multiculturalism and racism the end of the political, he looks for an argument that would point out the path for a return to the political. His argument cannot avoid globalization, and he makes a move to distinguish globalization from universality. This is precisely where the leftist appropriation of the European legacy takes place. Žižek alerts us to avoid two interconnected traps brought about by the process of globalization. First, "the commonplace according to which today's main antagonism is between global liberal capitalism and different forms of ethnic/religious fundamentalism"; second, "the hasty identification of globalization (the contemporary transnational functioning of capital) with universalization" (Žižek 1999, 107). Žižek insists that the true opposition today is "rather between globalization (the emerging global market, new world order) and universalism (the properly political domain of universalizing one's particular fate as representative of global injustice)" (ibid.). He adds that "this difference between globalization and universalism becomes more and more palpable today, when capital, in the name of penetrating new markets, quickly renounces requests for democracy in order not to lose access to new trade partners" (ibid.). One must agree with Žižek on this point. The problem lies in the projects that we embark on to resist and to propose alternatives to capitalist universalism. Žižek has one particular proposal, which is preceded by a lengthy analogy between the United States today and the Roman Empire.

Žižek describes the opposition between universalism and globalization, focusing on the historical reversal of France and the United States in the modern/colonial world-system (although, of course, Žižek does not refer to world-system theory per se). French republican ideology, Žižek states, is the "epitome of modernist universalism: of democracy based on a universal notion of citizenship. In clear contrast to it, the United States is a global society, a society in which the global market and legal system serve as the container (rather than the proverbial melting pot) for the endless proliferation of group identities" (1999, 109). Žižek points out the historical paradox in the role reversal of the two countries: while France is being perceived as an increasingly particular phenomenon threatened by the process of globalization, the United States increasingly emerges as the universal model. At this point Žižek compares the United States with the Roman Empire and Christianity: "The first centuries of our era saw the opposition of the global 'multicultural' Roman empire and Christianity, which posed such a threat to the empire precisely on account of its universal appeal" (ibid.). There is another perspective from the past that could be taken: France as an imperial European country, and the United States as a decolonized country that takes a leading role in a new process of colonization. This perspective emphasizes the spatial order of the modern/colonial world-system instead of the linear narrative that Žižek invokes by going back to the Roman Empire and locating it in "the first century of our era." To whose era is he referring? This is not an era that can be claimed without hesitation by Wallerstein, Quijano, or Dussel, for example, not to mention American Indian and African American intellectuals. However, what matters here is that in Žižek's argument what is really being threatened by globalization is "universality itself, in its eminently political dimension." The consequences, manifested in several contradictory arguments and actions, are countered by Žižek with a strong claim for sustaining the political (struggle) in place of the depoliticization that is the challenge globalization poses to universality. Here is Žižek's triumphal claim of the "true European legacy": "Against this end-of-ideology politics, one should insist on the potential of democratic politicization as the true European legacy from ancient Greece onwards. Will we be able to invent a new mode of repoliticization questioning the undisputed reign of global capital? Only such a repoliticization of our predicament can break the vicious cycle of liberal globalization destined to engender the most regressive forms of fundamentalist hatred" (ibid.). Žižek here identifies the "true European legacy," and a few pages earlier he refers to "the fundamental European legacy." However, he also alludes to "forms of fundamentalist hatred" as if the "fundamental European legacy" were excused and excluded from any form of "fundamentalism." Žižek's plea totally ignores the colonial difference and blindly reproduces the belief that whatever happened in Greece belongs to a European legacy that was built during and after the Renaissance —that is, at the inception of the Atlantic commercial circuit and the modern/colonial world. In fact, all the examples Žižek quotes in his arguments are consequences of the emergence, transformation, and consolidation of the modern/colonial world (the formation and transformation of capitalism and occidentalism as the modern/colonial world imaginary). However, Žižek reproduces the macronarrative of Western civilization (from ancient Greece to the current North Atlantic) and casts out the macronarrative of the modern/colonial world in which the conflict between globalization and universality emerged. Since he does not see beyond the linear narrative of Western civilization, he also cannot see that "diversality" rather than universality is the future alternative to globalization.

Let me explain. I see two problematic issues in Žižek's proposal. One is that Greece represents only a European legacy, not a planetary one. If we agree that solutions for contemporary dilemmas can be found in Greek moral and political philosophy, we cannot naturally assume that "from Greece onwards" is linked only to the European legacy. The first issue here would be to de-link the Greek contribution to human civilization from the modern (from the Renaissance on, from the inception of the modern/ colonial world) contribution. Thus, the Greek legacy could be reappropriated by the Arabic/Islamic world, which introduced Greece to Europe, and also by other legacies—Chinese, Indian, sub-Saharan African, or American Indian and Creole in Latin America and the Caribbean—that do not exist as a European legacy but as a discontinuity of the classical tradition (Mignolo 1995, pt. 1). One of the consequences of this perspective would be diversality, that is, diversity as a universal project, rather than the reinscription of a "new abstract universal project" such as Žižek proposes. I no longer feel like enrolling (or requesting membership) in a new abstract universal project that claims a fundamental European legacy. I assume that there are several good alternatives to the increasing threat of globalization, and of course the fundamental European legacy is one of them. I am not talking about relativism, of course. I am talking about diversality, a project that is an alternative to universality and offers the possibilities of a network of planetary confrontations with globalization in the name of justice, equity, human rights, and epistemic diversality. The geopolitics of knowledge shows us the limits of any abstract universal, even from the Left, be it the planetarization of the social sciences or a new planetarization of a European fundamental legacy in the name of democracy and repoliticization.

CONCLUDING REMARKS

The main thrust of my argument has been to highlight the colonial difference, first as a consequence of the coloniality of power (in the making of it), and second as an epistemic location beyond Right and Left as articulated in the second modernity (i.e., liberal, neoliberal; socialism, neosocialism). The world became unthinkable beyond European (and, later, North Atlantic) epistemology. The colonial difference marked the limits of thinking and theorizing, unless modern epistemology (philosophy, social sciences, natural sciences) was exported or imported to those places where thinking was impossible (because it was folklore, magic, wisdom, and the like). Quijano's "coloniality of power" and Dussel's "transmodernity" (and the critique of Eurocentrism from this perspective) imprint the possibilities both of thinking from the colonial difference and of opening new perspectives from and to the Left. Quijano and Dussel move beyond the planetarization of the social sciences (Wallerstein) or the reinscription of a new abstract universality (Žižek) and contribute to the making of diversality as a universal project. As such, they join forces with South Asian subaltern studies (Chakrabarty 1992), with "negative critique" as proposed by African philosophers (Eze 1997; Bernasconi 1997), and with Khatibi's "double critique" (Mignolo 2000d), that is, of Islamic and Western fundamentalism at the same time. The *tertium datur* that Žižek is seeking can be found not by Khatibi "in reference to the fundamental European legacy" but in an other thinking, an other logic that cannot avoid the planetarization of the European legacy but that also cannot rely only on it.[9] An other logic (or border thinking from the perspective of subalternity) goes with a geopolitics of knowledge that regionalizes the fundamental European legacy, locating thinking in the colonial difference and creating the conditions for diversality as a universal project.

NOTES

Unless otherwise indicated, English translations are my own.

1   For a discussion of Dussel's concept of transmodernity, see Maldonado in this volume.

2   See Dussel 1995a, 1998a; Wallerstein 1997a; Quijano 1997, 2000b; and Žižek 1998.

3   Boaventura de Sousa Santos 1998, 161–92, 369–454; Cassano 1995. The Black Legend refers to the denigrating stories told in France and England, particularly in the eighteenth century, against the colonial violence practiced by Spaniards in the colonization of the Indias Occidentales (today's Latin America). Curiously enough, British and French intellectuals grounded their arguments against the Spaniards in Bartolomé de Las Casas's relentless internal critique of Spanish colonialism. The Black Legend, in other words, was the northern imperial legitimization against the empires of the south (mainly Spain, but also Portugal). The Reformation and the Counter-Reformation as well as the new centers of mercantile capitalism (Amsterdam and London) were good enough reasons to enact demeaning narratives against the competition.

4   I have been referring mainly to Dussel and Quijano because of the very structure of the workshop I am referring to. I could easily mention other similar examples, chiefly among them Frantz Fanon (see Gordon 1995, Sekyi-Otu 1996).

5   David Harvey has made an important contribution in this direction in his reading of the geographical dimension of Karl Marx's and Friedrich Engels's *Communist Manifesto*, an important contribution that, however, falls short of the colonial difference. Harvey's geographical reading of capitalism (2000) remains within the geopolitical structure of the power of capitalism and the conditions it created for the hegemony of modern epistemology.

6   See, for instance, Medina 1992, 41–61; Bouysse-Cassagne and Harris 1987; Deloria 1994 [1972]; and Mignolo 2000b.

7   I have been asked on several occasions whether this is a privilege of African philosophy or of a similar epistemic geopolitical structure established and inherited by the coloniality of power in the formation of the modern/colonial world. Rather than a privilege, I would say, it is a potential, the potential of "double consciousness" translated into epistemic geopolitics of knowledge.

8   Connections between dependency theory and postcolonial theory are also developed by Coronil and Grosfoguel in this volume.

9   During the final revision of my original article I had the opportunity to read Žižek's *The Fragile Absolute, or, Why Is the Christian Legacy Worth Fighting For?* (2000), which I cannot discuss here. However, it is worth mentioning in relation to my argument the fact that he opens the book with an interesting and intriguing meditation on the "Balkan Ghost" and devotes the last forty or so pages of the argument to justifying the subtitle. The Christian legacy indirectly reinforces his previous argument about the Greek legacy. Between both legacies, one imagines, a veil is floating over the Balkans. The veil is fixed to a pole that is grounded in Slovenia and has two satellite dishes on top, one pointing toward Greece and Rome and the other toward Paris.

(POST)COLONIALITY FOR DUMMIES: LATIN AMERICAN PERSPECTIVES ON MODERNITY, COLONIALITY, AND THE GEOPOLITICS OF KNOWLEDGE

Santiago Castro-Gómez

According to the taxonomy recently proposed by John Beverley, the field of cultural studies over the past ten years can be divided into four distinct albeit not complementary categories: studies on politics and cultural practice spearheaded by Néstor García Canclini, George Yúdice, Jesús Martín Barbero, and Daniel Mato; cultural criticism (deconstructivist or neo-Frankfurtian) led by figures such as Alberto Moreiras, Nelly Richard, Beatriz Sarlo, Roberto Schwarz, and Luis Britto García; subaltern studies with notables such as Beverley himself, Ileana Rodríguez, and the members of the Latin American Subaltern Studies Group; and finally postcolonial studies with Walter Mignolo and the "Coloniality of Power" group, which includes Edgardo Lander, Aníbal Quijano, Enrique Dussel, Catherine Walsh, Javier Sanjinés, Fernando Coronil, Oscar Guardiola, Ramón Grosfoguel, Freya Schiwy, and Nelson Maldonado, along with myself (Beverley 2002, 49–

50). It is not my intent to discuss, as others do, the heuristic pertinence of this taxonomy, as that yields a rather arbitrary selection and exclusion process. I would, nonetheless, like to refer to the final of the four categories in an attempt to explain, in a quasi-pedagogical way, the types of debates seminal to the theoretical configuration of the Latin American Coloniality Group.[1] Rather than initiating the presentation with analytical categorizations ("transmodernity," "coloniality," "colonial difference," "border gnosis," "epistemic communities," etc.), which have by now become a sort of *koiné* for the group, or listing the publications we compiled over four years of collaboration (1999–2002), I will refer to the way in which our discussions are framed within the broader discursive context which academia has termed postcolonial theory.[2] In adopting this theory I intend not to position our debates as mere reception to "mainstream" theorists such as Edward Said, Homi Bhabha, Gayatri Spivak, but rather to illustrate that the specificity of the Latin American debate can only be appreciated in contrast to the discourse which has been discussed elsewhere under this rubric.

I will proceed, then, by attempting first to demonstrate the ways in which Marxist social theory has envisioned colonialism, citing Karl Marx's own works as an example, then examine Said's *Orientalism*, which puts into perspective some of the "blind spots" of Marxist theory, reconstructing in this manner coloniality as a "problem." After demonstrating that metropolitan postcolonial theory is not enough to envision the specificity of colonialism in Latin America, I will examine how the problem of coloniality and its relationship to modernity has been approached differently by Latin American social theory.

MARX'S BLIND SPOT

In *The Communist Manifesto* Marx stated that the bourgeoisie was the first truly revolutionary class in history. Never before had there been a social group with the capacity to restructure the entirety of social relations. Ways of living that had remained unchanged for centuries, legitimized by the power of religion and force of habit, had to concede to the flood of the bourgeoisie. The old had been uprooted by the new, giving way to a world that even the most fanciful poet could not have imagined: "The bourgeoisie cannot exist without constantly revolutionizing the instruments of production, and thereby the relations of production, and with them the whole relations of society. . . . All fixed, fast frozen relations, with their train of ancient and venerable prejudices and opinions, are swept away, all new-formed ones become antiquated before they can ossify. All that is solid melts into air, all that is holy is profaned, and man is at last compelled to face with sober senses his real condition of life and his relations with his kind" (Marx 1930, 32).

According to Marx, two elements facilitated the ascent of the bourgeoisie: an upsurge in global markets and the development of industry. Beginning with the discovery of America and the subsequent trade with the colonies, European nations were able to administrate an international system of commerce that broke into a thousand pieces the delimitations of feudal organization. The new markets created new necessities for consumption that could no longer be satisfied by national products, generating a demand for the introduction of merchandise from the most diverse and remote regions of the world. On the other hand, the opening of these new markets provided for an unprecedented impulse toward scientific and technological advancements. Steam-powered engines, locomotives, the electric telegraph, and the use of industrial machines revolutionized the ways in which man was submitted to the forces of nature and generated new sources of wealth. For Marx, the relationship between these two elements—the global market and industry—is not casual but, rather, dialectical: the global market stimulates the surge in industry and this, in turn, expands the global market.[3]

Nonetheless, in spite of the fact that the "bourgeoisie spans the entire world" thanks to the surge of global markets, Marx seems skeptical in considering the development of the bourgeoisie in non-European societies. Noncapitalist societies, economically dependent and colonized, which today in *grosso mondo* we call the Third World, are regarded by Marx, from the perspective of modern European society, to have achieved an entirely capitalist development. Therefore, when Marx states in his Manifesto that the "bourgeoisie have given a cosmopolitan character to production and consumption in every country" (1930, 8, 9), he seems to be referring to a European—and particularly British—bourgeoisie, which due to its dominance over international commerce had been able to establish nuclei of capitalist production throughout its colonies. Even in his later works, published after his death under the title of *The Eastern Question* and dealing specifically with the European periphery (Russia, Ireland, and Spain), Marx identifies a considerable "ascent" in the bourgeois class in these regions.[4] As far as Latin America is concerned, Marx never bothered to study the development of capitalism in that part of the world. The reason for the notable absence of the "Latin American question" in the works of Marx seems to be, according to José Aricó and Leopoldo Zea, the influence of G. W. F. Hegel's verdict on Latin America (Aricó 1980, 97–99; Zea 1988, 235–36). In his *Lessons on a*

Philosophy of a Universal History Hegel still considers the Americas to be "outside of history." Hegel felt this because they had not yet developed the political institutions and philosophical thought that would have allowed them to incorporate themselves into the progressive movement toward liberty characteristic of his Universal History. In Hegel's view, while the United States of America had already begun to develop a thriving industry and republican social institutions, the fledgling Latin American nations continued to be oppressed beneath the weight of a "rigorous social hierarchy," the unyieldingness of a secular clergy, and the "vanity" of a ruling class whose primary interest was dominance and wealth through prestige of public office, titles, and degrees.

The Hegelian thesis of "peoples without history" inherited by Marx enables us to understand why he viewed it as a continent not yet capable of developing a socioeconomic structure that would allow it to be incorporated into a global revolutionary process with any measure of success. Latin America was, it seemed to Marx, a grouping of semi-feudal societies governed by large landowners that wielded their despotic power without any organized structure. The act of independence would have been a revolt by a handful of separatist Creoles with the support of the English bourgeoisie and without the backing of the popular masses.

It is for this reason that in his 1857 article on Simón Bolívar for the *New York Daily Tribune* Marx refers to the Venezuelan hero as a typical representative of a reactionary class with a vested interest in establishing a Bonaparte-like monarchy on the Latin American continent.[5] The 1848 defeat of the workers in Paris, the general distaste for the French monarchy, as well as the coronation of Maximilian as emperor of Mexico, seemed only to substantiate his argument. Due to the semifeudal relation among social classes and the dominance of the aristocracy in the ruling classes (as represented by Bolívar), Latin American societies seemed to be an enclave of counterrevolution on a global scale.

In Marx's analysis Bolívar was not a bourgeois revolutionary, but rather an aristocrat with aspirations of power who sought to construct a geopolitical regime in which the masses would have no representation whatsoever. This aristocratic distaste for the popular was clearly revealed in the proposal Bolívar presented to the Congress of Angostura, whereby he suggested a constitution comprised of a hereditary senate and a life-term president. In other words, for Marx, there was nothing in Bolívar reminiscent of the revolutionary tendencies of the bourgeoisie to break "with all things stratified and stagnate," which he had described ten years earlier in his manifesto. On the contrary, Bolívar as a representative of Creole nobility in Latin America favored conserving the "old regime" and was opposed not only to the interests of the small, liberal bourgeoisie but also to those of the as-of-yet unconscious within the popular masses.

From Marx's perspective, colonialism is not a phenomenon in and of itself, but rather it holds a distinct and separate place on the periphery of the bourgeoisie—the only class able to change the crisis in the feudal order of production. Colonialism was a collateral effect of global European expansion and was in this sense a necessary route toward the advent of communism. This is why what interests Marx is class struggle, to the exclusion of other struggles (ethnic conflicts, for example), which he deemed less important than the "trajectory of universal history." It is for this reason that Marx considers ethnic and racial discrimination a "precapitalist" phenomenon, limited to societies where a bourgeoisie had not yet emerged and where theological and stratified rule prevailed, and characteristic of the old regime. The text wherein Marx describes the assassination attempt on Bolívar in Bogotá is latent proof of his position on colonialism: "An attempt to assassinate him in his own bedroom in Bogota, from which he was saved only because he jumped over a balcony in the middle of the night and stayed there crouched under a bridge, permitted him to exercise a sort of military terror for some time. Bolívar, however, took care not to lay a hand on Santander, even though he had participated in the attempt, yet he had General Padilla killed, because although the latter's culpability had not been fully demonstrated, as a man of color he could offer no resistance" (Marx 2001, 71).

The fact that Bolívar had not "laid a hand" on the Creole Santander—in spite of their political rivalry—but had instead chosen to perpetrate violence against the black admiral Padilla could be explained, according to Marx, by the "absence of modernity" in Latin American societies. In those societies a bourgeois revolution had not yet taken place, feudal relations of production were still predominant, and political power was held by caudillos such as Simón Bolívar. Vested with such political power, they were able to impose their will on the more ignorant masses—since the modern social classes of the bourgeoisie and the proletariat had not yet emerged. Honorable bloodlines and ethnic privilege still constituted the fundamental criteria for honor and distinction. But as this precapitalist order disappeared and the bourgeoisie finally appropriated the means of production, when these forces of production were fully developed, when everything solid had dissolved into air, only then would colonialism be a thing of the past. For Marx, colonialism was nothing more than the past of modernity and would disappear altogether with the global crisis that would give rise to communism.

The global markets were thus "prepared for the discovery of America" and impelled by European colonial expansion. Marx remains steadfast to a teleological and Eurocentric vision of history in which colonialism is merely an additive to modernity and not a constituent of it. What truly constitutes modernity is capitalism, which expands from Europe to the rest of the world, so that to Marx, it seems as if colonialism is an "effect" related to the consolidation of a global market. In Marx there is not a clear sense that colonialism might be seminal to the foundations of the ideological practices of a society—scientific practice, for example—much less that it might play the primary role in the emergence of capitalism and modern subjectivity. For Marx, therefore, an explanation of colonialism is exhausted in the use of philosophical categories ("false conscience"), economic categories ("modes of production"), and sociological categories ("class struggle").

This is precisely what begins to change with the emergence of postcolonial and subaltern studies toward the end of the twentieth century. What theorists from former European colonies of Asia and the Middle East—such as Said, Bhabha, Spivak, Gyan Prakash, Partha Chatterjee, Ranajit Guha, Dipesh Chakrabarty, and others—begin to demonstrate is that colonialism is not simply an economic or political phenomenon. It possesses an epistemological dimension relating to the emergence of the human sciences as much in the center as in the periphery. In this sense we ought to discuss coloniality before colonialism in order to distinguish the cognitive and symbolic phenomenon to which we make reference. Nearly all of the above-mentioned authors have argued that the humanities and modern social sciences created an imaginary with respect to the social world of the "subaltern" (the Orientals, the blacks, the Indians, the peasants) that not only served to legitimize imperial dominance on a political and economic level but also helped to create epistemological paradigms within these sciences, as well as to generate the (personal and collective) identities of the colonizers and the colonized. Seen in this way, coloniality ceases to be a collateral phenomenon in the development of modernity and capitalism, as Marx had believed.

THE "ORIENTALIZATION" OF THE ORIENT

This is not the place for me to enter into a detailed presentation on postcolonial theory, and in particular its development in North America. To exemplify my point about the cultural and epistemological dimension of colonialism, I will concentrate solely on Said, especially on his most distinguished work: Orientalism.

The central argument of Orientalism is that the imperial domination of

Europe over its Asian and Middle Eastern colonies during the nineteenth and twentieth centuries necessarily implies an institutionalization of a certain image or representation of the "Orient" and the "Oriental." According to Said, one of the characteristics of colonial power in modernity is that dominance (Herrschaft) is not only achieved through killing and forced subjugation but also requires an ideological or "representational" element; in other words, without a discourse on the "Other" and without the incorporation of this discourse into the habitus of both the dominators and the dominated, Europe's political and economic power over its colonies would have been impossible. In this manner Said begins to show what still constituted Marx's "blind spot": the centrality of two "superstructural" elements—knowledge and subjectivity—for the consolidation of Europe's imperial domain. The European dominator constructs the other as an object of knowledge ("Orient") and constructs an image of his own locus of enunciation ("Occident") in the very process of exercising his dominance.

> The Orient is not only adjacent to Europe; it is also the place of Europe's greatest and richest and oldest colonies, the source of its civilizations and languages, its cultural contestant, and one of its deepest and most recurring images of the Other. In addition, the Orient has helped to define Europe (or the West) as its contrasting image, idea, personality, experience. Yet none of this Orient is merely imaginative. The Orient is an integral part of European *material* civilization and culture. Orientalism expresses and represents that part culturally and even ideologically as a mode of discourse with supporting institutions, vocabulary, scholarship, imagery, doctrines, even colonial bureaucracies and colonial styles. . . . Orientalism is a style of thought based upon an ontological and epistemological distinction made between "the Orient" and (most of the time) "the Occident." Thus a very large mass of writers, among whom are poets, novelists, philosophers, political theorists, economists, and imperial administrators, have accepted the basic distinction between East and West as the starting point for elaborate theories, epics, novels, social descriptions, and political accounts concerning the Orient, its people, customs, "mind," destiny, and so on. (Said 1994a [1978], 1–3)

The representations, the "conceptions of the world," and the formation of subjectivity within those representations are, then, the fundamental elements in establishing colonial dominance. Without the construction of an imaginary of "East" and "West," not as geographical locations but rather as ways of life and of thinking capable of generating concrete subjectivities, any explanation (economic or sociological) of colonialism would be incomplete. Obviously, Said indicates, such ways of living and thinking are not only found in the habitus of social actors, they are anchored in objective structures: the laws of the state, commercial codes, school curricula, institutionalized forms of cultural consumption, and so on. For Said, Orientalism is not a matter of "conscience" (whether it be false or true) but the experience of an objective materiality.

Of particular interest is the role Said assigns science in the construction of this colonial imaginary. From the early nineteenth century, Orientalism found its place in metropolitan academia with the foundation of academic positions on "ancient civilizations" and within the framework of the new-found interest then generated by the study of Eastern languages. Said affirms that it was Great Britain's dominion over India that granted scholars unrestricted access to the texts, the languages, and the religions of the Asian world, which until that time had remained unknown to Europe (Said 1994a [1978], 77). The magistrate William Jones, an employee of the East India Company and member of the British colonial bureaucracy, with his vast knowledge of Arabic, Hebrew, and Sanskrit, was among the first to elaborate a theory on Orientalism. In a 1786 conference of the Asiatic Society of Bengal, Jones stated that the classic European languages (Latin and Greek) evolved from a common lineage that could be traced to Sanskrit. This thesis generated unprecedented enthusiasm within the European scientific community and stimulated the development of a new humanistic discipline: philology.[6]

The central point of this argument is that the study of ancient Asian civilizations obeys a strategy in the construction of a European colonial present. In the study of the Asiatic world's past there was a search for the origins (the "roots") of triumphant European civilization. Philology seemed somehow to "scientifically prove" what philosophers like Hegel had been suggesting since the end of the eighteenth century: Asia was none other than the grandiose past of Europe. While civilization may have "begun" in Asia, its fruits were harvested only by Greece and Rome, which constituted the most recent cultural referent for modern Europe. As Hegel would have said, civilization follows the same path as the sun: emerging and arcing in the East but not reaching its telos, its final destination, until it reaches the West. European dominance over the world required "scientific" legitimacy, and it is during the Enlightenment that the nascent humanistic sciences such as philology, archaeology, history, ethnology, anthropology, and paleontology began to play a prominent role. In exploring the past of ancient Eastern civilizations these disciplines actually began to "construct" a European colonial present.

Said's reflections on the humanistic sciences point to a theme which will comprise the central Latin American debate on coloniality: the critique of epistemological Eurocentricism. *Orientalism* showed that the present of Asia had nothing to do with the present of Europe, since these postulations had been deemed "old" and had been "replaced" by modern civilization. Scholars were only interested in the past of Asiatic culture inasmuch as it was relevant as a "preparation" for the emergence of modern European rationalities. From the perspective of the Enlightenment, all other cultural voices are "traditional," "primitive," or "pre-modern" and are thus situated outside of a "Universal History." It follows that the Orientalist imaginary, the Eastern world—with Egypt perhaps being the best example—is directly associated with the exotic, the mysterious, the magical, the esoteric, the originary—in other words, with "pre-rational" cultural manifestations. The "many forms of knowledge" are situated in this way in a conception of history that delegitimizes its spatial coexistence and organizes them according to a teleological scheme of temporal progression. The diverse forms of knowledge developed by humanity throughout the course of history would lead gradually toward the only legitimate way of knowing the world: the way that is elaborated by the technicoscientific rational of modern Europe.

In establishing a genetic relationship between the birth of the humanistic sciences and the birth of modern colonialism, Said indicates the inevasible connection between power and knowledge, as pointed out by authors like Michel Foucault. With regard to the dominant belief that the scientist could transcend social and political conditioning in order to capture the inherent "truth" in his object of study, Said states,

> What I am interested in doing now is suggesting how the general liberal consensus that "true" knowledge is fundamentally non-political (and conversely, that overtly political knowledge is not "true" knowledge) obscures the highly if obscurely organized political circumstances obtaining when knowledge is produced. . . . Therefore, Orientalism is not a mere political subject matter or field that is reflected passively by culture, scholarship, or institutions; nor is it a large and diffuse collection of texts about the Orient; nor is it representative and expressive of some nefarious "Western" imperialist plot to hold down the "Oriental" world. It is rather a *distribution* of geopolitical awareness into aesthetic, scholarly, economic, sociological, historical, and philological texts; it is an elaboration not only of a basic geographical distinction (the world is made up of two unequal halves, Orient and Occident) but also of a whole series of "interests" which, by such means as scholarly discovery, philological reconstruction, psychological

analysis, landscape and sociological description, it not only creates but also maintains; it is, rather than expresses, a certain will or intention to understand, in some cases to control, manipulate, even to incorporate, what is a manifestly different (or alternative and novel) world. . . . Indeed, my real argument is that Orientalism is—and does not simply represent—a considerable dimension of modern political-intellectual culture, and as such has less to do with the Orient than it does with "our" world. (Said 1994a [1978], 10, 12)

In other words, the geopolitical nexus between knowledge and power which created the East is the same as that which has sustained the Western cultural, economic, and political hegemony over the rest of the world since the Enlightenment. In fact, one of Said's most interesting arguments is that coloniality is a constituent of modernity, in that it represents itself, from an ideological point of view, on the belief that the geopolitical division of the world (centers and peripheries) is legitimate because it is founded on an ontological division. On one side is "Western culture," represented as the active originator and distributor of knowledge, whose mission is to disseminate modernity throughout the world. On the other side are the other cultures (the Rest), represented as passive elements, receptors of knowledge, whose mission is to welcome the progress and civilization coming from Europe. The characteristics of the "West" would be rationality, abstract thought, discipline, creativity, and science; other cultures, on the contrary, are perceived as pre-rational, empirical, spontaneous, imitative, and dominated by myth and superstition.

Said's great merit, then, is to have seen that the discourse in the humanistic sciences, which had constructed the triumphant image of "historical progress," is sustained on the geopolitical machinery of knowledge/power that has subalternized other voices of humanity from an epistemological point of view. That is to say, it has declared "illegitimate" the existence of other simultaneous cultural "voices" and forms of producing knowledge. With the birth of the humanistic sciences in the eighteenth and nineteenth centuries, we witness the gradual invisibilization of the epistemic simultaneity of the world. Europe implemented a territorial as well as an economic expropriation of the colonies (colonialism), which corresponds to an epistemological expropriation (coloniality) that condemned the knowledge produced therein to be merely "the past of modern science." But although Orientalism convincingly stated the geopolitical connections between the Enlightenment, colonialism, and the humanistic sciences, from the field of Latin American studies a theory of coloniality has evolved which not only complements but also adds new elements to Said's postcolonialism.

THE DESTRUCTION OF THE MYTH OF MODERNITY

Colonial criticism already boasts a great tradition in Latin American social theory, from the works of Edmundo O'Gorman, Rodolfo Stavenhagen, and Pablo González Casanova in Mexico, to the contributions of Agustín Cuevas in Ecuador, Orlando Fals-Borda in Colombia, and Darcy Ribeiro in Brazil, to the prolific works of Aníbal Pinto, Ruy Mauro Marini, Fernando Henrique Cardoso and other theorists, not to mention José Carlos Mariátegui, Víctor Raúl Haya de la Torre, José Martí, Rodó, and other "classic" Latin American thinkers. Nonetheless, and with the notable exception of O'Gorman's *Invention of America* and Fals-Borda's *Science and Colonialsm*, there are very few works which have focused specifically on the epistemic dimension of colonialism. In fact, the majority of these works concentrate on the economic, historical, political, and social aspects of colonialism, approached basically from the disciplinary paradigms of the humanistic sciences without touching on what we have termed coloniality.

It is from Latin American philosophy that a critique of colonialism that emphasizes its epistemic nucleus begins to emerge. I am referring concretely to the works of the philosopher Enrique Dussel, and particularly to those the specific focus of which is the critique of Eurocentrism. In fact, the critique of epistemological Eurocentrism, a focal point of postcolonial theory, had always been one of the pillars in Dussel's philosophy of liberation (see Dussel in this volume). In the 1970s Dussel set out to demonstrate that modern philosophy on the subject materializes in the praxis of conquest. Taking Martin Heidegger's critique of Western metaphysics as a point of departure, Dussel states that none of modern European thinking, including that of Marx, recognizes that thinking is vitally linked to quotidian life (the "world of life") and that relations between people cannot be seen as relations between one rational subject and one object of knowledge (Dussel 1995b, 92, 107). It is precisely this subject-object relationship created by modern thought that explains, according to Dussel, the "totalization" of Europe, since that relationship from the onset denies the possibility of an exchange of knowledge, and forms of producing knowledge in different cultures. Between the "subject" and the "object" of knowledge there can exist only a relationship founded on exteriority and asymmetry. For this reason the "ontology of totality," a characteristic central to European civilization, views everything that does not belong to it ("exteriority") as "absence of being" and "barbarity," in other words raw nature, in need of being "civilized." In this manner, the elimination of alterity—including epistemic alterity—constituted the "totalizing logia" that began to impose itself on the indigenous and African populations from the sixteenth century, as much by the Spanish conquistadors as by their Creole descendants (ibid., 200–204).

The first great task of critically liberating postcolonial thought is the "destruction"—in a Heideggerian sense—of the ontology that made possible the colonial dominance of Europe over the rest of the world. Only "from the ruins of totality," states Dussel, "could the possibility of a Latin American philosophy emerge" (1995b, 111). In the late 1970s the Argentine philosopher formulated his project.

> It is necessary first to destroy something in order to build something new, and Latin American philosophy, for some time, has had to destroy the wall of Eurocentrism so that a new historical process can make its way through the breach. . . . In order to discover new categories with which to make thinking about ourselves possible, we must begin by talking like Europeans, and from that perspective reveal their limitations and overcome Eurocentric thought in order to make room for something new. Therefore, for a long time to come we will have to converse with Europe and acquaint ourselves with their thoughts in greater depth. Otherwise we will pass them by without succeeding in breaking the wall. (ibid., 138–39)

Nonetheless, in more recent times Dussel has begun creatively reformulating his theory. The necessary "wall" in need of demolition is no longer conceived of in terms of "ontological totality" in the vein of Heidegger—which would have extended from the time of the Greeks to the present—but rather as a "paradigm" assigned a specific name: the Eurocentric myth of modernity. This myth, in Dussel's opinion, emerged with the discovery of America and has since dominated, in varied forms, our theoretical and practical understanding of what modernity means. This point interestingly parallels Said's thought. Like Said, Dussel attempts to explain modern colonialism as departing from a "structure of thought" that originated in Greece and extends seamlessly throughout Western history. Dussel later abandons this metahistory—to elaborate a historical analysis of modern colonialism from an ethical and epistemological perspective.

Dussel's new thesis states that from the eighteenth century modernity began to develop a vision of itself, a myth of its own origins that possesses a clearly Eurocentric character (1999a, 147). According to this myth, modernity was an exclusively European phenomenon that originated during the Middle Ages and then, through inter-European experiences such as the Italian Renaissance, the Protestant Reformation, and the French Revolution, inevitably spread throughout the world. According to this paradigm, Europe

possessed unique internal qualities that permitted the development of technicoscientific rationality, which explains its cultural superiority above all
others. The Eurocentric myth of modernity would thus have been the aspiration that identified European particularism with universality as such. This is
why the myth of modernity entails what Dussel calls the "developmental
fallacy," according to which all of the cities on earth ought to follow the
"levels of development" set forth by Europe, with the goal of obtaining
social, political, moral, and technological emancipation. European civilization constitutes the "*telos*" of world history (Dussel 1992, 21–34).

To counter this hegemonic interpretation, Dussel proposes an alternative
model which he calls the "planetary paradigm": modernity is nothing more
than the "central" culture of the world-system and emerges as a result of the
administration of that centrality by various European nations between the
sixteenth and nineteenth centuries. This means that modernity is not a
European but rather a global phenomenon, whose precise date of birth is
12 October 1492. Dussel explains.

> Modernity is not a phenomenon that can be predicated on a Europe considered as
> if it were an independent system, but only about Europe if it is conceived as a
> center. This simple hypothesis completely transforms the concept of modernity,
> its origin, development, and contemporary crisis, and consequently it also trans-
> forms the content of late and post-modernity. In addition, I would like to in-
> troduce another idea that qualifies the former: Europe's centrality within the
> world-system is not the result of an internal superiority accumulated during the
> European Middle Ages about and against other cultures. It is instead a basic effect
> of the discovery, conquest, colonization, and integration (submission) of Amer-
> india. This simple fact gave Europe the comparative and determinant advantage
> over the Ottoman-Islamic world, India and China. Modernity is the result of
> these events, not their cause. Therefore, it is the administration of that centrality
> within the world-system that would allow Europe to become something like "the
> reflexive consciousness" (the modern philosophy) of world history. . . . Even
> capitalism is the result and not the cause of this conjunction between European
> expansion around the world and the centralization of the world-system. (Dussel
> 1995c, 148–49)

This alternative paradigm clearly challenges the dominant vision, according to which the conquest of America was not a constituent element of
modernity, since it was considered one of those purely intra-European phenomena like the Protestant Revolution, the emergence of a new science, or
the French Revolution. Spain and its transoceanic colonies would have re-

mained outside of modernity since none of these phenomena took place there. Dussel, modeling Immanuel Wallerstein, demonstrates that European modernity was built on materiality, which had been specifically created after Spain's sixteenth-century territorial expansion. This generated the opening of new markets, the incorporation of new resources of raw materials and a workforce that allowed for what Marx called the "originary accumulation of capital." The modern world-system begins with the simultaneous synthesis of Spain as a "center" and Hispanic America as its "periphery." Modernity and colonialism are then a mutually dependent phenomenon. There is no modernity without colonialism and no colonialism without modernity. After all, Europe could only be conceived as the center of the world-system at the moment when its transatlantic colonies became the periphery.

Up to this point Dussel seems to be closely following the analysis of the world-system set forth by Wallerstein. Nevertheless, a more detailed inspection reveals that Dussel is not simply "inscribing" his critique of colonialism within the parameters of Wallerstein's theory of a world-system. On the contrary, he is "reading" Wallerstein from the philosophy of liberation, which has important consequences for the Latin American debate on coloniality. Perhaps Dussel's most prominent "departure" from Wallerstein is the thesis that the incorporation of America as the first periphery of the world-system not only represents the possibility of an "originary accumulation" in central countries but also generates the first cultural manifestations of a global order; in other words, it is what Wallerstein himself terms a "geoculture." This means that the first geoculture of world-modernity, extended as a system of ritual, cognitive, judicial, political, and ethical symbols belonging to the expanding world-system, has its epicenter in Spain.[7] What the Hispano-American world of the sixteenth and seventeenth centuries contributes to the world-system is not only physical labor and raw materials, as Wallerstein believes, but also the epistemic, moral, and political foundations of modernity.

In fact, Dussel identifies two modernities (1992, 156). The first emerged during the sixteenth and seventeenth centuries and corresponds to the humanist Renaissance Christian ethos that flourished in Italy, Portugal, Spain and their respective American colonies. This modernity was globally administered by Spain, the first hegemonic power of the world-system, and it generated not only the first critical theory on modernity but also the first form of modern-colonial subjectivity.[8] Dussel conceptualizes this subjectivity in very philosophical terms (adapted from Emmanuel Levinas), describing a "conqueror self," a warrior and aristocrat that establishes with the "other" (the native, the black, and the mestizo-American) an exclusionary relationship of domination.[9] The *ego conquiro* of the first modernity, states Dussel, constitutes the protohistory of the ego cogito of the second modernity (ibid., 67). The second modernity, which presents itself as the only modernity, only begins to emerge at the end of the seventh century with the geopolitical collapse of Spain and the emergence of new hegemonic powers (Holland, England, and France). The administration of the centrality of the world-system now takes place elsewhere and responds to imperatives of efficacy, biopolitics, and rationalization, as admirably described by Max Weber and Foucault. The subjectivity that evolves then corresponds to the emergence of the bourgeoisie and the formation of capitalist methods of production (ibid., 158).

THE DISCOURSE OF RACIAL PURITY

Dussel's philosophy of liberation initiates a critical dialogue with Wallerstein's analysis of the world-system in an attempt to integrate the critique of colonialism within a global perspective. Nevertheless, the primary way that both projects diverge from each other, namely Dussel's idea regarding the emergence of a modern Hispano-Catholic geoculture prior to the French Revolution, merits a deeper elaboration. This work was done for the most part by the Argentine semiologist Walter Mignolo, who developed an explicit critique of Wallerstein's thesis in consideration of Dussel's reflections on the emergence of a modern—though not bourgeois—subjectivity in the Hispanic world.

Mignolo recognizes the importance of Wallerstein's monumental book *The Modern World-System* in the epistemological displacement that arose in social theory during the 1970s. In relating the contributions of the theory of dependence with Braudel's works on the Mediterranean, Wallerstein is able to analyze the centrality of the Atlantic circuit in the formation of the modern world-system in the sixteenth century (Mignolo 2001c, 11). As such, the Mediterranean ceases to be the axis of world history as Hegel had suggested, and Europe begins to be "provincialized" by social theory.[10] What becomes important is not the study of Europe per se, but rather the world-system in all its structural diversity (centers, peripheries, and semiperipheries). Nevertheless, Wallerstein's project conceives the peripheries in terms of geohistorical and geoeconomic units, but not as geocultural ones (Mignolo 2001c, 12). Although Wallerstein does point out that the modern world-system emerges around 1500, he still holds a Eurocentric perspective. He believes that the first geoculture of this system—liberalism—arises only in the eighteenth century, as a result of the globalization of the French Revolution. For this reason, Mignolo believes that Wallerstein is still held captive by the myths constructed by the philosophers of the Enlightenment, according to whom the second modernity (of the eighteenth and nineteenth centuries) is the only modernity (Mignolo 2000a, 56–57). The geoculture of the first modernity is rendered invisible from this perspective.

In his book *Local Histories/Global Designs* Mignolo states that the conquest of America not only meant the creation of a new "world-economy" (with the emergence of a commercial circuit unifying the Mediterranean and the Atlantic) but also the formation of the first great "discourse" (in terms of Said and Foucault) of the modern world. Debating Wallerstein, Mignolo argues that the universalizing discourse legitimizing the global expansion of capital did not emerge during the eighteenth and nineteenth centuries on the basis of the bourgeois revolutions in Europe, but instead evolved much earlier, with the development of the modern/colonial world-system (2000d, 23). The first universalist discourse of modern times, then, is not related to the liberal bourgeois mentality but rather, pedagogically, to the aristocratic Christian mentality. It is, according to Mignolo, the discourse of racial purity. This discourse was the first classification scheme of the global population. Although it did not arise until the sixteenth century, it began to evolve during the Christian Middle Ages. The discourse of racial purity became a "global" one as a result of Spain's commercial expansion across the Atlantic and the beginning of European colonization. Thus, a classifying matrix that belonged to a local history (Medieval European Christian culture) became, by virtue of the global hegemony acquired by Spain during the sixteenth and seventeenth centuries, a global design that served to classify populations according to their position in the international division of labor.

As a cognitive scheme of social classification, the discourse of racial purity is not a product of the sixteenth century. Its roots are grounded in the tripartite division of the world as suggested by Herodotus—and accepted by some of the most prominent thinkers of antiquity: Erastothenes, Hiparco, Estrabon, Pliny, Marino, and Ptolemy. The world was viewed as a great island (*orbis terrarum*) divided into three vast regions: Europe, Asia, and Africa.[11] Although some assumed that in the antipodes, to the south of the orbis terrarum, there could be other islands inhabited perhaps by other species of men, the interest of the ancient historians and geographers centered on the world they knew and the types of peoples inhabiting its three principal regions. In this manner the territorial division of the world became a social division of a hierarchical and qualitative kind. In this hierarchy Europe occupied the most prominent place, since its inhabitants were considered to be more educated and civilized than those in Asia and Africa, who were considered by the Greeks and Romans to be "barbarians" (O'Gorman 1991 [1958], 147).

Christian intellectuals of the Middle Ages appropriated this scheme of social classification, but not without introducing some modifications. Thus, for example, the Christian dogma of the fundamental unity of the human race (all men being descendants of Adam) forced St. Augustine to recognize that if there were to exist other islands on the orbis terrarum, its inhabitants, if there were any, could not be categorized as "men," since the potential inhabitants of the "City of God" could only be found in Europe, Asia, or Africa (O'Gorman 1991 [1958], 148). In the same manner, Christianity rein-terpreted the ancient hierarchical division of the world. For reasons now theological, Europe continued to occupy a privileged place above Asia and Africa.[12] These three geographic regions were regarded as the places where Noah's three sons had settled after the flood and for this reason they were inhabited by three completely different types of people. The sons of Sem, Ham, and Jafet inhabited Asia, Africa, and Europe, respectively. This meant that the three regions of the known world were hierarchically classified according to ethnic differentiation: Asians and Africans—descendants of those sons who, according to the Bible, had fallen into disgrace in the eyes of their father—were viewed as racially and culturally inferior to the direct descendants of Jafet, Noah's beloved son.

Mignolo points out that Christianity redefined the ancient scheme of social division, transforming it into an ethnic and religious taxonomy of the population, whose practical dimension became evident in the sixteenth cen-tury (1995, 230).[13] Columbus's voyages had proven that the Americas were a geographic entity, distinct and separate from the orbis terrarum, which immediately sparked a great debate surrounding the nature of its inhabitants and their territory. If only the "isle of earth"—that portion of the globe comprising Europe, Asia, and Africa—had been assigned to man by God as the land he must inhabit after his expulsion from Eden, what legal statute did the newly discovered territories possess? Were these lands that would fall under the universal sovereignty of the pope and that could, as such, be legitimately occupied by a Christian king? If only the sons of Noah could be considered direct descendants of Adam, the father of humanity, what an-thropological statute did the inhabitants of these new lands possess? Did they lack a rational soul, and could they thus be legitimately enslaved by the

Europeans? Following O'Gorman, Mignolo states that the new territories and their populations were not viewed ontologically as different from Europe, but rather as its natural extension—the "New World."

> During the sixteenth century, when "America" became conceptualized as such not by the Spanish crown but by intellectuals of the North (Italy and France) . . . , it was implicit that America was neither the land of Shem (the Orient) nor the land of Ham (Africa), but the enlargement of the land of Japheth. There was no other reason than the geopolitical distribution of the planet implemented by the Christian T/O map to perceive the planet as divided into four continents; and there was no other place in the Christian T/O map for "America" than its inclusion in the domain of Japheth, that is, in the West (Occident). Occidentalism, in other words, is the overarching geopolitical imaginary of the modern/colonial world system. (Mignolo 2000a, 58–59)

Mignolo's point is that the belief in the ethnic superiority of Europe over the colonized populations was inherent in the cognitive scheme of the tripartite division of the global population and the imaginary Orbis Universalis Christianis. This vision of American territories as extensions of the land of Jafet made the exploitation of its natural resources and the subjugation of its inhabitants "just" and "legitimate" because it was only Europe that could shed the light of God. Evangelization was the state imperative that determined the only reason that the "old Christians"—in other words, those who were not mixed with Jewish, Moorish, and African populations (descendants of Cam and Sem)—could travel and establish themselves legitimately on American territory. The New World became a natural stage for the extension of the white Europeans and their Christian culture. The discourse of ethnic purity—in accordance with Mignolo's interpretation, the first geocultural imaginary of the world-system that is incorporated into the habitus of the European immigrant population—legitimized at once the ethnic division of labor and exchange of personal goods and capital on a global scale. Mignolo's reading possesses both a continuity and a difference with Said's postcolonial theory. Like Said, and contrary to Marx, Mignolo knows that without the constructs of a discourse that could be incorporated into the habitus of the dominators as well as the dominated, European colonialism would have been impossible. By contrast, Mignolo does not identify this discourse as Orientalism but rather as Occidentalism, emphasizing in this way the need to inscribe postcolonial theory with the consideration of specific colonial legacies (in this case, the Hispanic legacy).[14]

With Orientalism posited as colonial discourse par excellence, Said seems not to realize that discourse regarding the other generated by France and the British Empire corresponds to a second modernity. As such, Said is not only unaware of the geocultural and geopolitical hegemony of Spain during the sixteenth and seventeenth centuries, but ends up legitimizing the eighteenth-century (Eurocentric) imaginary of modernity denounced by Dussel. On this matter Mignolo states,

> I have no intention of ignoring the tremendous impact and the scholarly transformation Said's book has made possible. Nor do I intend to join Aijaz Ahmad (1992) and engage in a devastating critique of Said because the book doesn't do exactly what I want it to. However, I have no intention of reproducing the enormous silence that Said's book enforces: without Occidentalism there is no Orientalism, and Europe's "greatest and richest and oldest colonies" are not the "Oriental" but the "Occidental": the Indias Occidentales and then the Americas. "Orientalism" is the hegemonic cultural imaginary of the modern world system in the second modernity when the image of the "heart of Europe" (England, France, Germany) replaces the "Christian Europe" of the fifteenth to mid-seventeenth century (Italy, Spain, Portugal). . . . It is true, as Said states, that the Orient became one of the recurring images of Europe's Other after the eighteenth century. The Occident, however, was never Europe's Other but the difference within sameness: Indias Occidentales (as you can see in the very name) and later America (in Buffon, Hegel, etc.) was the extreme West, not its alterity. America, contrary to Asia and Africa, was included as part of Europe's extension and not as its difference. That is why, once more, without Occidentalism, there is no Orientalism. (Mignolo 2000a, 57–58)

In all and despite their differences, the theoretical projects of Said and Mignolo share common ground on the importance designated to coloniality in explaining the phenomenon of colonialism. Both Said's Orientalism and Mignolo's Occidentalism are seen above all as cultural imaginaries, discourses whose objective is not only to function as disciplinary "apparatuses" (laws, institutions, colonial bureaucracy) but are translated into concrete forms of subjectivity. Orientalism and Occidentalism are not simply ideologies (in Marx's restricted sense), but rather ways of life, structures (constructs) of thought and action. Within this symbolic cognitive environment, the category of "coloniality" refers to the ethnic identities of the actors.

Mignolo in this way reinforces Dussel's argument: the subjectivity of the first modernity has nothing to do with the emergence of the bourgeoisie but is instead related to the aristocratic imaginary of whiteness. It is the identity founded on ethnic distinction in contrast to the other that characterizes the first geoculture of the modern/colonial world-system. It assumes not only the superiority of some men over others but also the superiority of one form of knowledge over another. In fact, Mignolo affirms that the key to understanding the emergence of scientific epistemology during the eighteenth century is the separation that European geographers had previously established between the ethnic and geometric centers of observation (Mignolo 1995, 233–36). In almost all of the known maps until the sixteenth century, the geometric and ethnic centers were one and the same. In this way Chinese cartographers, for example, generated spatial representations in which the emperor's palace occupied the center and was surrounded by its imperial dominion. The same is true for Christian maps of the Middle Ages, in which the world appears to be laid out around the city of Jerusalem. In Arab maps of the thirteenth century Islam is featured as the center of the world. In all of these instances the "center was mobile," because the observer was not concerned with his own point of observation and was excluded from representation. On the contrary, it was clear to the observer that the geometric center would logically coincide with the ethnic and religious center that served as his point of reference (in Chinese, Jewish, Arab, Christian, Aztec cultures, etc.). Nevertheless, something different begins to happen with the conquest of America and the need to represent with precision the new territories under the imperative of the colonizers' control and delimitation. Cartography incorporates the mathematics of perspective, which at that time revolutionized pictorial practice in Mediterranean Catholic countries (especially Italy). Perspective implies the adoption of a fixed and unique point of view, in other words, the adoption of a sovereign gaze external to the representation. Perspective is an instrument through which one can see but, at the same time, cannot be seen. Perspective thus provides the possibility of having a point of view about which it is not possible to adopt a point of view.

This completely revolutionizes the scientific practice of cartography. In making the point of observation invisible, the geometric center no longer coincides with the ethnic center. Instead, cartographers and European navigators who now possess precise instruments of measurement, begin to believe that a representation made from the ethnic center is prescientific, since it is related to a specific cultural particularity.

Truly scientific and "objective" representation is that which can remove itself from its point of observation and generate a "universal point of view." It is precisely this gaze that attempts to articulate itself independent of its ethnic and cultural center of observation, which here I will call *the hubris of zero degrees.*

Closely following what Dussel and Mignolo have elaborated, one can then say that the hubris of zero degrees, with its pretense of being objective and scientific, does not emerge with the second modernity but has its roots, rather, in the geoculture of the first modernity. It is not an effect of the Copernican revolution or of bourgeois individualism; rather, it results from the Spanish state's need to exercise control over the Atlantic domain—against their European competitors—and to eradicate in the periphery the old belief systems that were considered "idolatries." Different worldviews could no longer coexist; instead, they had to be taxonomized according to a hierarchy of space and time. From the sovereign point of view of the unobserved observer, world maps of the sixteenth and seventeenth centuries organize space in greater units called "continents" and lesser units called "empires" which are completely irrelevant to physical geography. These maps are geopolitical constructions that, as such, are organized according to extrascientific imperatives. Europe—as it had already happened with the T/O map of Isidoro de Sevilla—continues to function as the central producer and distributor of culture, while Asia, Africa, and America are held as sites of "reception." This continental and geopolitical separation of the world would become the epistemological base that gave rise to the anthropological, social, and evolutionist theories of the Enlightenment. Mignolo reinforces this thesis: "Colonization of space (of language, of memory) was signaled by the belief that differences could be measured in values and values measured in a chronological evolution. Alphabetic writing, Western historiography, and cartography became part and parcel of a larger frame of mind in which the regional could be universalized and taken as a yardstick to evaluate the degree of development of the rest of the human race" (1995, 256–57).

It is here where the geopolitics of knowledge becomes a pertinent category, broadly utilized by Mignolo. One of the consequences of the hubris of the zero degrees is the invisibilization of a particular place of enunciation, which is then converted into a place without a place, into a universal. The tendency to convert local history into global design runs parallel to the process of establishing that particular place as a center of geopolitical power. To the centrality in the world-system of Spain, later France, Holland, and England, and now the United States corresponds the intention to convert their own local histories into a unique and universal point of enunciation and production of knowledge. Knowledge that is not produced in the centers of power or in the circuits controlled by them is declared irrelevant and "prescientific." The history of knowledge, as it is represented from zero degrees, has a place on the map, a specific geography. Asia, Africa, and Latin America, as in the T/O map of Isidoro de Sevilla, remain outside of this cartography and are not viewed as producers but rather as consumers of knowledge generated by the centers.

5. THE COLONIALITY OF POWER

Along with Dussel and Mignolo, it is necessary to study the contributions of the sociologist Aníbal Quijano in the construction of a critical theory of coloniality. Beginning with his studies in the 1970s and the emergence of Cholo identity in Peru, as well as in his works in the 1980s on the relationship between cultural identity and modernity, Quijano established that the cultural tensions of the continent ought to be studied from the starting point of European colonial domination over America. Nevertheless, during the 1990s, Quijano broadened his perspective, affirming that colonial power cannot be reduced to economic, political, and military domination of the world by Europe, but that it involves also and primarily the epistemic foundations that supported the hegemony of European models of production of knowledge in modernity. It is here where the Peruvian sociologist positions himself critically with respect to the project of the Enlightenment regarding a "Science of Man" (*Cosmópolis*) along lines similar to the ones identified in Said, Dussel, and Mignolo. For Quijano, the critique of colonial power must necessarily entail the critique of its epistemic nucleus (Eurocentrism), that is, a critique of the type of knowledge that contributed to the legitimization of European colonial domination and its pretenses of universal validation.

Like Mignolo, Quijano affirms that colonial power has its epistemic roots in the hierarchical classification of populations already established since the sixteenth century, but it found its primary legitimacy with the use of physiocratic and biological models in the eighteenth and nineteenth centuries, respectively. These taxonomies divided the world population into diverse "races" assigning each one a fixed and immobile place within the social hierarchy. Although the idea of race was already evolving during the time of the war of reconquest in the Iberian Peninsula, it was only with the formation of the world-system in the sixteenth century that it became the epistemic base of colonial power (Quijano 1999a, 197). The idea that by "nature" there exist superior and inferior races functioned as one of the pillars on which Spain consolidated its dominance over America during the sixteenth and seventeenth centuries, and it served as "scientific" legitimacy of European colonial power in the following centuries. In order to explain this phenomenon Quijano develops his notion of the coloniality of power.

In fact, the coloniality of power is a category of analysis that makes reference to the specific structure of domination imposed on the American colonies since 1492. According to Quijano, Spanish colonizers established a relationship of power with the colonized based on ethnic and epistemic superiority of the former over the latter. This matrix of power did not only entail militarily subjugating the indigenous peoples and dominating them by force (colonialism); it also attempted to radically change their traditional knowledge of the world, to adopt the cognitive horizon of the dominator as their own (coloniality). According to Quijano, the coloniality of power "consists, in the first place, of a colonization of the imaginary of dominated peoples, in other words, it acts within that imaginary. . . . The repression was imposed, above all, on the ways of knowing, producing knowledge, producing perspectives, images, and systems of images, symbols, modes of signification; upon the resources, models, and instruments of formalized visual or intellectual expression. . . . The colonizers also imposed a mystified image of their own models of production of knowledge and meaning" (1992a, 438).

According to this, the first characteristic of the coloniality of power, the most general of all, is the domination by means not exclusively coercive. It was not only about physically repressing the dominated populations but also about getting them to naturalize the European cultural imaginary as the only way of relating to nature, the social world, and their own subjectivity. We are confronted with the sui generis project of attempting to radically change the volition as well as the cognitive and affective structures of the dominated, in other words, to transform him into a "new man," made in the image and likeness of the Western white man. In order to achieve this civilizing goal, the Spanish State created the encomienda, whose function was to integrate the Indian to the cultural model of the dominant ethnic group. The role of the encoméndero was to diligently care for the "integral conversion" of the Indian through systematic evangelization and hard corporal labor. Both of these instruments were directed toward the transformation of intimacy, attempting to liberate the Indian of his condition as "minor" and finally have access to the modes of thought and action characteristic of civilized life.

The coloniality of power makes reference to the way in which Spanish domination attempted to eliminate the "many forms of knowledge" of native populations and to replace them with new ones more appropriate for the civilizing purposes of the colonial regime. It thereby indicates the epistemological violence exercised by the first modernity over other forms of production of knowledge, images, symbols, and forms of signifying. Nevertheless, the category has another complementary meaning. Although these other forms of knowledge were not completely eliminated but were, at most, deprived of their ideological legitimacy and subsequently subalternized, the European colonial imaginary exercised a constant fascination over the desires, aspirations, and will of subaltern populations. Quijano formulates the second characteristic of the coloniality of power: "European culture became a seduction; it gave access to power. After all, besides repression, seduction is the main instrument of all power. Cultural Europeization turned into an aspiration. It was a means of participating in colonial power" (1992a, 439).

This aspiration of cultural Europeization was part of a structure of power that was shared both by dominators and dominated peoples and that constituted the basis on which the Enlightenment project of Cosmópolis was implanted in New Granada, beginning at the end of the eighteenth century. In unifying Quijano's and Mignolo's theses we could say that the imaginary of whiteness, produced by the discourse of racial purity, was an aspiration that all social sectors internalized in colonial society and that functioned as the axis around which the subjectivity of all social actors was built. To be "white" was not so much related to the color of the skin as to the personal mise-en-scène of a cultural imaginary constituted by religious beliefs, forms of dress, customs, and, more important for us, forms of producing and disseminating knowledge. The ostentation of those cultural signs of distinction that were associated with the imaginary of whiteness was a sign of social status, a form of acquiring, accumulating, and transmitting symbolic capital.

In addition to making reference to a hegemonic type of subjectivity (whiteness), the coloniality of power also makes reference to a new type of knowledge production that I have called the hubris of zero degrees. I refer to a form of human knowledge that entails the pretense of objectivity and scientificity, and takes for granted the fact that the observer is not part of what is being observed. This pretense can be compared to the sin of hubris that Greeks identified with the arrogance of men who wanted to elevate themselves to the level of gods. To place oneself in the zero degrees is equivalent to having the power of a *Deus absconditus* that can see without being seen and can observe the world without having to prove to anybody, not even to himself, the legitimacy of that observation. It is equivalent to instituting a vision of the world recognized as valid, universal, legitimate, and supported by the state. It yields to the necessity first of the Spanish State (and later to all of the other hegemonic powers of the world-system) of eradicating any belief system that did not favor the capitalist vision of *homo oeconomicus*. No longer could different "worldviews" coexist—they had to be classified according to a hierarchy of time and space. All other forms of knowledge were declared to belong to the "past" of modern science, as the "doxa" that fooled the senses, as "superstitions" that created obstacles in the path to a "coming of age." From the perspective of zero degrees, all human knowledge is arranged on an epistemological scale that goes from the traditional to the modern, from barbarism to civilization, from the community to the individual, from tyranny to democracy, from the individual to the universal, from East to West. We face an epistemic strategy of domination, which, as we well know, continues to thrive. Coloniality is not the past of modernity; it is simply its other face.

Translated by Rosalia Bermúdez

NOTES

English translations from Spanish works have been made by Rosalia Bermúdez. This chapter benefited from the editing of Juliet Lynd.

1   Obviously, my presentation here reflects my personal affiliation with the Latin American coloniality group, and only reflects my own perspective.

2   See Castro-Gómez, Guardiola-Rivera, Millán 1999; Lander 2000b; Castro-Gómez 2000b; Walsh 2001; Mignolo 2001a; Walsh, Schiwy and Castro-Gómez 2002; Grosfoguel 2002.

3   "Industry had created a global market that was already prepared for the discovery of America. The global market prodigiously accelerated the development of commerce, navigation and travel by land. This development influenced the surge in industry and as industry, commerce, navigation and travel expanded, so developed the bourgeoisie" (Marx 1930, 29).

4   The book was published at the end of the nineteenth century (London, 1897). These works appear in a later publication with Engels titled *Gesammelte Schriften von Karl Marx und Friedrich Engels, 1852 bis 1862* (Stuttgart, 1916). In Spanish they initially appeared under the title *Sobre el colonialismo* (Mexico City, 1978).

5   "Bolivar never denied his despotism, in proclaiming the Bolivian Code—a remediation of the Napoleonic Code. He sought to apply the code in Bolivia and Peru and later in Colombia and keep the former in line with Colombian troops. . . . Bolivar wanted to unify Latin America into a federal republic, with himself as dictator" (Marx 2001, 67, 69).

6   The same can be said of the development of other disciplines, such as archaeology, for example, which was impelled by the study of ancient Egyptian civilization and made possible by the Napoleonic invasion (Said 1994a [1978], 87).

7   This does not mean that prior to 1492 the process of cultural modernization was not already well under way in some parts of Europe. Dussel is clear in this respect: "According to my central thesis, 1492 is the date of the 'birth' of modernity, although its gestation involves a preceding period of 'intrauterine' growth. The possibility of modernity originated in the free cities of Medieval Europe

which were centers of tremendous creativity, but modernity as such was 'born' when Europe was in a position to compare itself to an other, when, in other words, Europe could constitute itself as a unified ego, exploring, conquering, colonizing an alterity that could reflect its image upon itself" (2001a, 58).

8   Dussel has written a great deal on this topic. His central argument is that in his polemic with Ginés de Sepúlveda around the mid-sixteenth century Bartolomé de Las Casas discovers for the first time the irrationality of the myth of modernity, in spite of using the philosophical tools of the previous paradigm. Las Casas proposes the idea—which Dussel assumes as his own—of "modernizing" the other without destroying his alterity; adopting modernity without legitimizing its myth: modernity arising from alterity and not from "sameness" of the system (Dussel 1992, 110–17).

9   "The *Conquistador* is the first practical, active, modern man to impose his 'violent' individuality upon other people. . . . The subjectivity of the Conquistador, constituted itself and evolved slowly in praxis. . . . The poor *hidalgo* from Extremadura [Cortés] is now the '*general*.' The modern ego was constituting itself" (Dussel 1992, 56, 59).

10   It is worth noting Hegel's famous comments: "The Old World consists of three parts. . . . These divisions are not fortuitous, but the expression of a higher necessity which accords with the underlying concept. The whole character of its territories is composed of three distinct elements, and this tripartite division is not arbitrary but spiritual, for it is essentially based on determinations of nature. The three continents of the Old World are, therefore, essentially related, and they combine to form a totality. . . . The Mediterranean is the focus of the whole of World History. . . . The Mediterranean Sea is the axis [Mittelpunkt] of World History. . . . We cannot conceive of the historical process without the central and unifying element of the sea" (1997, 120, 121).

11   In characterizing the orbis terrarum I will basically follow the arguments on the social division of the world as outlined by the Mexican philosopher and historian Edmundo O'Gorman in his book *The Invention of America*. Mignolo also bases his arguments on O'Gorman's text (Mignolo 1995, 17).

12   Although certainly Europe did not represent the most perfect form of civilization—from technical, economic, scientific, and military perspectives, it was an impoverished "periphery" in relation to Asia and Northern Africa—it was regarded by many as the only society in the world founded on true faith. This made it a representative of the imminent destiny and transcendence of humanity. Western Christian civilization set the standard by which to judge all other cultural forms on the planet (O'Gorman 1991 [1958], 148).

13   Mignolo makes explicit reference to the famous T/O map of Isidoro de Sevilla. This map, used to illustrate the book *Etimologiae* by Isidoro de Sevilla (560–636 E.C.), represents a circle divided in three by two lines that formed a T. The upper part, occupying half of the circle, represents the Asiatic continent (the East) inhabited by the descendants of Sem, while the other half of the circle is divided in two sections: the left represents the European continent, populated by Jafet's descendants; the right represents the African continent, populated by Cam's descendants (Mignolo 1995, 231).

14 "I attempt to emphasize the need to make a cultural and political intervention by inscribing postcolonial theorizing into particular colonial legacies: the need, in other words, to inscribe the 'darker side of the Renaissance' into the silenced space of Spanish/Latin America and Amerindian contributions . . . to postcolonial theorizing" (Mignolo 1995, xi).

REMAPPING LATIN AMERICAN STUDIES: POSTCOLONIALISM, SUBALTERN STUDIES, POST-OCCIDENTALISM, AND GLOBALIZATION THEORY

Eduardo Mendieta

When we think about Latin America from the perspective of the United States, we cannot help it but to think of a series of pivotal dates: 1848 and the Mexican American War; 1898, the Spanish-American War; 1916, the Mexican Revolution; 1945, the end of World War II; 1959, the Cuban Revolution; 1973, Pinochet and the assassination of Allende; 1979, the Nicaraguan revolution; 1989, the end of the Sandinista government; 1994, the North Atlantic Free Trade Agreement going into effect and the Zapatista uprising in the south of Mexico, in the Lacandonian jungle. These are very recent historical events, but they have in very decided ways shaped the way the United States and Latin America have related. I want to suggest that these events have determined four axes around which four types of Latinamericanisms have emerged. Furthermore, I want to suggest that these events in Latin American history are related to general ruptures in the fabric of knowledge as it has been woven over the last 200 years or so. Simultaneously, when we think *about* Latin America, we must realize that we think *from* a particular locus, as I do now, for instance, on the eastern coast of the United States, from within New York's state-university system. Thinking in time requires that we think the space of our timing, the becoming space of time. Latin America, no less than any other geopolitical signifier, is always the detritus of temporalizing and spatializing regimes that write the maps of world history. The tables of chronology are always accompanied by the maps of empires and nations (Mendieta 2001b). I will first discuss the four types of Latinamericanisms that have emerged since the late nineteenth century. Next, I will turn to the crises of knowledge in the last century that have fractured and given impetus for structuring new epistemic matrices. The point is to discern on what grounds, on what new chronotope, we can begin to develop a new form of Latinamericanism, one which perhaps seeks to bridge postcolonialism and post-Occidentalism.

LATINAMERICANISMS

Latinamericanism is the name for forms of knowledge, ideological attitudes, and spectral mirrors.[1] Latinamericanism as a form of knowledge has assumed different forms, as we will see, hence the plural in the title of this section. Analogously, Latinamericanism is plural because it has been about how Latin America has been portrayed by at least four major agents of imagination: Latin America itself, the United States, Europe, and, most recently, Latinos. There are many Latin Americas, and not solely because of the waxing and waning of its boundaries and shifting place in the Western imaginary, as Arturo Ardao (1993) has documented so excellently, but also because it has been imagined differently by different social actors. Finally, Latinamericanism has to do with the specters that haunt the rise of the West to global dominance, and because in it (the imagined Latin America) we also find reflected the dreams of an alternate "America" and possibly a different West. The four types of Latinamericanism register not just a particular chronology but also the shifting of the location, or geopolitical place, of the imaging agent.

The first type of Latinamericanism to emerge did so in part as a response to the events of both 1848 and 1898. This Latinamericanism juxtaposed the United States with Latin America in terms of their distinctive and opposite cultural and spiritual outlooks. One is depicted as crass, materialistic, utilitarian, soulless, and without cultural roots, while the other is characterized as the true inheritor of the European spirit of culture, civilization, and ideal-istic principles grounded in love and tradition. These distinctions can be found in the work of someone like José Enrique Rodó, but we also find them in the work of José Martí. This opposition was influential for generations of thinkers in Latin America, even when they did not share the original set of terms or animus. In the work of some Mexican thinkers like José Vascon-celos and even Leopoldo Zea, we find these kinds of differentiations. An-other source of the first Latinamericanism was the Latin American affirma-tion of its identity vis-à-vis Europe, also for the reasons that Latin America sought to differentiate itself from the United States, namely, imperialism, war, and putative patrician cultures of disdain for the colonized and the racially mixed. Yet not all intellectuals rejected unequivocally Latin America's relationship to Europe. For some, in fact, the problem was that Latin Amer-ica was not enough like Europe. This is a view that we find expressed in the work of Domingo Sarmiento, who basically established a whole school of thought based on the opposition between "civilization" and "barbarism." This first type of Latinamericanism, then, was one that descended from the era of the colonial and imperialistic expansion of the United States and from Latin America's affirmation of its distinctive cultural traditions. This Latin-americanism was based on a geopolitics of culture, and one may therefore correctly characterize it as a *Kulturkampf* Latinamericanism, one which juxta-posed the spirit of an imperialistic modernity with the promise of a human-istic and pluralistic form of modernization that, in the words of Pedro Henriquez Ureña, was embodied in the idea of America as the fatherland of justice.

The second type of Latinamericanism is the one that emerged after World War II and the onset of the Cold War in the United States. More precisely, we should date the rise of this type of Latinamericanism with the U.S. National Defense Education Act of 1958, which determined that it was a priority of national security to invest in the educational programs that could contribute to the defense of the nation (Noam Chomsky et al. 1997). Guided by such national-security and defense goals, area-studies programs were developed that sought to parcel the world in terms of areas of strategic interest. Clearly, Latin America was a major area of geopolitical strategic interest, and thus arose what I will call area-studies Latinamericanism, which had as its goal to gather and disseminate knowledge about "Third World" countries. This Latinamericanism treated Latin America like any other foreign land, al-though there was from its inception an ambiguity about treating Latin Amer-ica in the same terms as Asia and Africa. There were some fascinating debates, including the Eugene Bolton debates, for instance, which argued that Latin America should be studied in the same way that the United States and Canada should be studied. Nonetheless, Cold War knowledge interests dictated the research model. Area-studies Latinamericanism thus offered a way to think or represent Latin America from the standpoint of the North American academy. But, to be fair, one should note that area-studies Latinamericanism could be said to have two foci: one involving Latin America as the land of underdevelopment, bringing in tow all that this entails, that is, lack of proper stages of modernization, weak public spheres, lack of technological innovations, and so on; the other being a Latinamericanism of Third Worldism, or a form of First World romanticization and exoticization of the Latin American. But the latter is merely the inverse of the former. It is the second form of Latinamericanism that explains the fetishization of the Latin American novel. And it is these two types of Latinamericanisms reacting to each other that gives rise to the collapse of the epistemological and aesthetic with respect to Latin America that Román de la Campa points out in his book *Latin Americanism* (1999).

After the Cuban Revolution in 1959 and the 1968 Conference of Latin American Bishops at Medellín, which essentially made official the Christian Ecclesial Base Communities and Liberation Theology, a third type of Latinamericanism emerged: critical Latinamericanism.[2] This sets Latin America in opposition to the United States, but now in terms of an anti-imperialist and anticapitalist stand that is accompanied by a thorough critique of the epistemological regimes that permitted the theorization of Latin America. It appears in the works of Orlando Fals-Borda, Darcy Ribeiro, Zea, Sebastián Salazar-Bondy, Gustavo Gutiérrez, and Enrique Dussel. This is a Latinamericanism developed in Latin America to explain the Latin American situation to Latin Americans and to the United States. In many ways, it also emerged to counter the ideological effects of the area-studies Latinamericanism, as developed by the epistemological apparatus of the U.S. Cold War establishment during the 1950s, 1960s, and 1970s.

Finally, a fourth type of Latinamericanism has begun to develop over the last two decades and is linked to the aftermath of the Latino diaspora in the United States and the emergence of a critical consciousness in that Latino population as it came to be expressed in the Chicano and Puerto Rican movements of the 1960s. This is a transnational, diasporic, and postcultural Latinamericanism that brings together critical Latinamericanism and the homegrown epistemological and social critique that identity movements develop simultaneously but separately. Thus, this Latino Latinamericanism has two foci and loci of enunciation and enactment, and it operates at various levels of critique: it is critical of the West but also of how Occidentalism was deployed in order to normalize and regulate the very internal sociality of the West in the Americas. The thinkers that give expression to this are trans-American intellectuals like Juan Flores, Roberto Fernández Retamar, Román de la Campa, Subcomandante Marcos, Lewis Gordon, José Saldívar, Walter Mignolo, and Santiago Castro-Gómez.[3]

ON THE RELATIONSHIP BETWEEN GEOPOLITICS AND KNOWLEDGE PRODUCTION

In a 1981 essay entitled "The Three Worlds, or the Division of Social Scientific Labor, circa 1950–1975" Carl E. Pletsch looked at the emergence of the threefold division of the world into "first, second and third world." He looked at the ideological context of the emergence of these now suspect distinctions, but, more important, he looked into their conceptual matrix in order to discern some fundamental epistemological categories that belong to the most elemental aspects of Western thought, or what today we call logocentrism. The distinctions among First, Second, and Third World allowed Western social scientists to develop a disciplinary division of labor that nonetheless permitted them to assume a privileged place in the order of things. Talk of three worlds was based on a pair of abstract and always reinscribable binary oppositions that in turn were underwritten by the ontology of history, or teleology of history. The first binary was modern versus traditional; that is, the world was divided into those societies that were modern and those that were traditional (un-modern, pre-modern, or on the way to becoming modern). The second binary, moved ahead in the implicit temporal continuum, referred to the opposition between "communist" (or socialist) and "free" (or democratic). While "communist" stood for authoritarian, "free" stood for liberal, constitutional, and under the rule of law. Freedom was seen as the natural and logical outcome of societies that have overcome and superseded an earlier stage of unenlightened, or even enlightened, despotism. In this way the social semantics of the three worlds cashed out into a cultural semantics that assigned the following invidious distinctions to each world: "The third world is the world of tradition, culture, religion, irrationality, underdevelopment, overpopulation, political chaos, and so on. The second world is modern, technologically sophisticated, rational to a degree, but authoritarian (or totalitarian) and repressive, and ultimately inefficient and impoverished by contamination with ideological preconceptions and burdened with an ideologically socialist elite. The first world is purely modern, a haven of science and utilitarian decision making, technological, efficient, democratic, free—in short, a natural society unfettered by religion or ideology" (Pletsch 1981, 574). While the cultural semantics—the way in which words carry a whole conceptual package that allows one to see only certain things while overlooking others—operated due to a prior commitment to modernization theory, this was but an expression of a more-deep-seated belief in a *telos* of history, or an ontology of history. In this way the cultural semantics of First, Second, and Third Worlds allowed social scientists to make distinctions between degrees of economic and technological "development," on the one hand, and between kinds of "mentalities," on the other. These distinctions were deployed from the standpoint of the blind spot of those who thought they were granted by the logic of history the right to look on those that were headed toward where they now stood. On the basis of this cultural semantics, there emerged a division of labor that assigned to the Third World and the Second World the ideographic sciences, while assigning to the First World the nomothetic sciences. While the Third World was studied by anthropology and ethnography, the Second was approached as a case study in the emergent spheres of economic, social, and political theory that nomothetic sciences examine in the First World.

THE SPACE OF THEORY

Having briefly looked at Pletsch's very insightful and critical approach to the crises of the social sciences, I find it inadequate not just because it is bereft of any constructive suggestions but also because it fails to give an account of its own theoretical position that does not presuppose what it is ultimately criticizing, namely, the epistemological primacy of an ontology of history, or what we generally call a triumphalist teleology of the West. Pletsch presupposes the existence of a historical soil of theory when he criticizes the conceptual matrix of twentieth-century social science; that is, he is able to criticize what stands before his eyes because he stands at the most forward moment in the historical continuum he seeks to criticize. But in what way can I engage in a criticism of a conceptual apparatus without at some level presupposing the very elements that constitute the normativity of that apparatus? In order to be aware of one's own blind spot—or, in other words, to be able to justify one's criticism without occluding the place from which one enunciates that criticism—one must engage in a doubling operation. One observes oneself in the act of observing. If one cannot see the place from which one observes, one can at least observe what it is that one observes and how it is that one observes it. The language is that of systems analysis, or complex systems, but the intent is different. The goal is to make sense of the plethora of theories that are now available in the marketplace of ideas. I am interested in making sense of this theoretical cacophony not because I think that theoretical diversity is a sign of the decay or obsolescence of theory. The opposite is more true: the plurality of theoretical wares in the marketplace of ideas reflects the very level of commodification of theory that is necessary for the healthy exchange of ideas as the exchange of a cultural semantics that imposes a certain type of social semantics. I am interested in how theories operate in the circulation of cultural wealth and how they grease the wheels of a global market in which what is traded is a product whose use-value is as important as its exchange-value, wherein cultural and theoretical capital stand on the same level as commercial and technological capital. At the same time, I am interested in how in this uncircumventable situation of extreme commodification and reification of the theoretical, of its coagulation into theory, we might nonetheless discover a place of criticism. I will begin by laying out criteria for the development of typology of theories. In contrast to Pletsch, who wanted to get to the conceptual matrix of social theory writ large, I am interested in the ways in which in a saturated theoretical market we might begin to differentiate between theories and their effects.

First criteria: we must determine what is the epistemograph or ontograph that is inscribed by a group of theories or theory. This is the language of Gayatri Spivak (1999), but it is a terminology that one can claim descends also from Henri Lefebvre and David Harvey. But by ontograph or epistemograph, I mean that every theory, whether consciously or unconsciously, is determined by a spatial imaginary. This spatial imaginary operates both at a macrolevel and at microlevels. The classic example is G. W. F. Hegel with his idea that Europe is the privileged center for the substantialization of reason. Another example is how Immanuel Kant, as Spivak and LeDouff have shown, inscribes the categories of cognition within a particular geography of the imagination. In Dussel's language every philosophy participates in a geopolitical locus, not only in the sense that philosophy is determined by its place of enunciation, but also in the sense that philosophy also projects a certain image of the planet, the ecumene, and the polis as the space of what is the civilized, or the place of civilization, which may or may not be besieged by the barbarians. Philosophy enacts an act of spatialization at the very same time that it is spatialized by its locus of enunciation. Every philosophy, again, inscribes an ontos or epistemograph.

Second criteria: we have to make explicit the locus of the instantiation of the social. Every theory offers one or a group of structures and social processes that are the privileged locus for the substantialization of the reason or logos. In other words, reason materializes in certain social structures in a form and, some might claim, in a normative way. It is for this reason, for instance, that Hegel could undertake a phenomenology of the spirit as an analysis of sociality, or society. Clearly, the relation between reason and social structure is what allows someone like Jürgen Habermas, for example, to speak of modernity as the process of the rationalization of the systems level and the life-world. A theory of rationality in turn becomes a theory of social differentiation, which in turn becomes a theory about the modernity (read, rationality) of certain forms of society, a theory that results in a differential hierarchy in which some societies are primitive, and others premodern, and still others modern. Conversely, in this view there are social spheres that have not been rationalized or have been insufficiently rationalized. For this criterion the central question is: what is the institutional focus of a group of theories or theory?

The third criteria refers to what is taken to be the normative criteria or criteria of evaluation that allows one to adjudicate on whether a society has achieved what is putatively taken to be the actualization of reason in the social world. In other words, what is normative for each group of theories or theory? In some theories of modernity the criteria of whether societies are modern is dependent on whether a society has obtained a high level of bureaucratization, formalization, institutionalization of abstract universality, self-reflexivity, or even contextual uncoupling (as one can say that both Anthony Giddens [1990] and Habermas [1987] argue). And what is the operating evaluative norm when one says that societies are globalized or have been globalized or should be globalized: that a society has accepted the austere policies of the World Bank, that national economies have been liberalized and are open to the onslaught of transnationals?

Fourth criteria: what are the political consequences of an epistemological project? That is, in what ways does a certain ontograph or epistemograph turn into an actual political project? Every theory has a political impact: it contributes toward sanctioning or legitimating and thus normalizing certain forms of social violence. Conversely, a theory or group of theories contributes to the demystification of the supposed naturalness of certain social processes and thus can call into question the impact of certain forms of social violence that are tolerated and neglected because naturalized. What political projects are sanctioned when certain processes, loci of materialization of reason, epistemograph or ontographs are theoretically defended and articulated?

Fifth, and final, criteria: this whole form of articulating criteria could be stylized and formalized by asking, Who is the subject who thinks what object? And, more acutely still, where is this subject, and how does it project and localize its object of knowledge? Who speaks for whom and who speaks over or about whom? This is a way of asking questions about the production of theory and the position of theoretical agents, that is, agents who produce theory. It is a form of looking at the production of theory that makes explicit that there are subjects who are authorized to make theoretical pronouncements, while there are other "subjects" who are just spectators and who are relegated to being mere objects of knowledge. Some subjects are credible epistemic and theoretical witnesses, while others are from the outset suspect and illegitimate subjects of credible theoretical reflection. This all concerns the practices of partitioning, of parceling, or, as one might say in Mexico, of *fraccionamientos*, and what we in the United States might call theoretical gerrymandering or gentrification. Who speaks, or who is authorized to speak, about and for others occupies a privileged epistemological place, which is in turn made available by the theories and epistemological practices that are used by theorists. There is what Mignolo (1994b, 2000d) calls a locus of enunciation and a practice of *enactment*. Theorizing, or philosophizing is a habitus that is always accompanied or framed by a configuration of both social and imaginary space. (All space is imaginary and social, and the social is always conditioned by a certain imaginary.) To think our locus of epistemological privilege, or to think the place of our epistemological scorn and segregation—this is what Raymond Pannikar (1988) has called a "plurotopic hermeneutics."

The goal of this type of analysis, which I am profiling with the help of Spivak, Pannikar, Dussel, and Mignolo, and which I am formalizing in terms of a set of criteria of discernment, is to supersede the cybernetic and systems-theoretical proposals of thinkers, such as Niklas Luhmann, who juxtapose the mere observer with the solely observed, on one side, and with the observer who is observed, on the other. In other words, Luhmann juxtaposes what merely observes objects with the observing observer, or subjects that look at other subjects. The second type of observation is what Luhmann (1995) calls "second order observation." Analogously, it is necessary to go beyond the distinction that Habermas makes—translating Luhmann's points into the language of hermeneutics and the philosophy of language—between the first-person and third-person perspectives. The position of the first person is that of the participant in a community of communication that is at the same time one of interpretation; such a participant for this reason is thoroughly soaked by a hermeneutical immersion. The position of the second person is that of the one who observes, but in an objectifying manner. This position is allegedly of someone who can objectify because she is not a participant of the life-world which she observes. In fact, the grammar of the observer and the observed, the participant and the nonparticipant is much more complicated than these two types of distinctions allow. We are always already—immer schon, as Martin Heidegger would say—and simultaneously, both observer and observed. We are observed observators and observers who observe themselves. The gaze is not monological, but always mediated by a third. In the language of semiology we could say that observation is always a triadic relation: there is always a gazing of an observer who is in turn observed in his very act of gazing. Who is observed can always return the gaze: the observed can gaze back, can look back. Using Mignolo's language, I would say that we always speak about something, or someone, from a given perspective, and when we do so, we are enacting, performing, deploying certain forms of knowledge-power. What this type of analysis allows us to make explicit are the power dimensions or the dimensions of coercion and epistemological violence that every knowledge pronouncement entails. At the same time, it also allows us to unmask the form in which allegedly universal propositions and formulations—pronouncements that are putatively not contaminated and damaged by the subjective or the local—are in fact made possible by an epistemological machine that has specific goals and functions. Behind every theory there is what, echoing Michel Foucault, we could call an apparatus of knowledge-power, what he called specifically a dispositif: an apparatus of coercion and control.

With these criteria, we can turn to a comparative analysis of the theories that are on display and up for sale on the global marketplace of ideas. Theories of modernity, looked at from afar and as types of theories, are forms of theorizing that think from the ontograph of Europe. These are theories that are primordially about how Europe is the locus classicus for the actualization of reason. Europe is their subject of preoccupation, and furthermore, the world must mimic Europe. In this way the object of study is not the world, but an entirely ideological construct. The institutional locus of analysis for theories of modernity is society understood as the unfolding of a social and state logic, on one side, and scientific logic, on the other. Thus, the institutional locus is the sociopolitical bureaucracies, such as the rule-of-law state or the economy supposedly rationalized through abstract economic exchange mediated by money. Thus, state logic, on one hand, but on the other is the idea that technology is institutionalized as sociostate project. This is science at the service of the state and society. The normative criteria of evaluation are formalization, the imposition of self-reflexivity (through science), and, most important, whether political, economic, and scientific institutions are sufficiently formalized in order to be spatially translated. This is what Giddens calls the uncoupling of institutions (1990), meaning that these institutions can be translated to different contexts. It is worth noting that one of the evaluation criteria is that the most modern structures and institutions are those that are most simply and rapidly exportable and translatable. The political consequences already begin to be observable. The goal of these theories is to legitimate certain historical violences. Once processes of conquest, once the institutionalization of certain forms of science, are naturalized, then culpability, responsibility, and the possibility of calling cultures to account for genocide are neutralized and disallowed. These theories, viewed from an epistemological angle, impose an epistemological blindness and an ethical silence. Finally, these theories are about a subject purified of all alterity, a subject that speaks for and about others. This subject is in a place that is different than that of its object of knowledge. In this type of theory one encounters the classic instance of what Spivak diagnosed as speaking for, and thus silencing, the subaltern.

Postmodern theories do not digress or divert too much from this epistemograph. The ontograph continues to be Europe, and the locus of reason or rationalization continues to be the Euromodern institutions, but now as those that have been exhausted or that have arrived at their logical extremes. The normative focus is the critique of the ontoteleology of the homogenizing and suicidal logos of modernity. As a critique of the rational project of modernity and its violent univocity, postmodern theories become the celebration of and reverence for alterity, which includes all that is most singular, all that belies the triumph of Max Weber's iron cage of modernity. However, this other that is supposedly placed on a pedestal is merely the other face of the self-sameness of modernity's "I conquer," which Dussel has studied and unmasked so eloquently. Politically, the consequences are that all projects of emancipation are pronounced exhausted at best or totalitarian at worst. Every project of social transformation that would be designed and projected from out of the matrix of modernity is deemed failed and genocidal. Here we have the same phenomenon of the impossibility for the other to speak for himself or herself. The future is closed. Since the West has arrived at its own exhaustion, then it is impossible to conceive of the future in any different form. In this way, and once again, criticism is neutralized and silenced. Responsibility for the other is recognized, but this is unfulfillable because the great narratives of modernity that supported the possibility of being responsible for the other have been extinguished. Clearly, we have here a subject that abrogates for itself the authority of speaking for others and, furthermore, that says that not even they are able to speak, since the languages of liberation and responsibility have become anachronisms. The locus of enunciation thus lies in the very same institutions, academic as well as of quotidian life, of the modern countries, which also announce that no other path is acceptable. For subjects located in this *locus enunciationis*, the end of modernity has become the end of history tout court.

I have discussed chronologically a series of theories and have offered a diagnosis, an analysis that looks at how these theories have power-knowledge effects. If I were to continue following this chronological line, I would next address globalization theories. But a whole host of theories that compete with globalization have emerged, a competition that can be expressed thus: where are localized the discourses about globalization with respect to the discourses of modernity and postmodernity, on the one hand, and discourses of postcolonialism and post-Occidentalism, on the other? With regard to nomenclature, the distinction between one group of theories or discourses is not just chronological but is fundamentally related to the place from which and about which they theorize. Insofar as the discourses of globalization seem to have become the discourses of a *pax Americana*, that is, insofar as they are discourses about the celebration of the triumph of so-called democracy and the defeat of the Soviet project and, therefore, the triumph of neoliberalism, and insofar as the discourses of globalization are understood primarily from an economic, technological, and even political perspective (that is, insofar as globalization is understood as the planetarization of an economic, technological, and political system), then we have to see that these discourses are principally about whom the West globalizes (that is, who "modernizes" the world). Again, if we accept the discourses of White House and Pentagon apologists, à la Samuel P. Huntington and Francis Fukuyama, then the discourses on globalization represent the renewal of the triumphalist discourses of modernity. Globalization thus becomes a modernized modernity, an actualized and updated modernity, and a second modernity, to use Ulrich Beck's term. Globalization is the new name for modernity, but now seen from the perspective of the United States, which has inherited the Western project. If Europe modernized, the United States globalizes. The goal, the means, and the justification are the same. For this reason, a radiography of globalization will make evident how this is a theorization that continues to trace and map the same epistemograph or ontograph that modernity traced. Europe, along with the United States, is the vortex of globalization. Evidently, positions like those of Néstor García-Canclini have shown how globalization is as much the projection of the local as it is the acculturation of the global, and for this reason it is more appropriate to talk of *glocalization*. García-Canclini, furthermore, has shown how the supposedly pre-modern or so-called traditional is an investure, a form of fitting and appropriating transnational, modernizing, and globalizing projects. Using the language of Eric Hobsbawm, the pre-modern and the traditional are inventions of the modern—the modern can not be defined without inventing that which is its opposite (see also Wolf 1982). And as García-Canclini shows, it is for this reason that hybridity is an already globalized strategy to enter modernity, or a modern strategy to access globality. Yet both García-Canclini and Robertson illustrate exactly what it is that I am circling around, namely, the need to shift the epistemological locus of enunciation. For in order to accept García-Canclini's and Robertson's corrections requires that we see globalization as a global process in which there is not one agent, one society that globalizes, or one catalyst that inaugurates or accelerates an allegedly inevitable process, but a plurality of agents, both cultural and social that transform in unexpected ways the directions and telos of globalization.

The difference between globalization and modernity is that the first seems to have abandoned all strong universalistic claims and pretensions, as was fundamental to modernity. While modernity operated on the logic of an ontoteleology, globalization transfers its alibi to a naturalized history of social development. History is the realm of contingency and chaos, but it also abides by the rules of selection and elimination that control the organic world. What survives is selected out. If it has survived, it is because it has been selected by nature. In fact, globalization presents itself as a second nature, as something that is inevitable. Globalization will happen, regardless of whether we want it or not. The formulation is that we are already globalized or, rather, that he who does not want to be globalized will be despite his own desires. Globalization, then, is a new philosophy of history that tells us not that the telos that guides everything is in the future, but that the future is already here. There is no future, because we are already in the future. According to Habermas's expression, one might say that globalization constitutes a closure of the horizon of the future. There are no other futures, since we already live in it. And this is precisely what Microsoft, for example, suggests when it asks in its commercials, "Where do you want to go today?" Everything is at our disposal and within our reach. Postmodern cynicism is synthesized with the plenipotentiary and absolutist logic of modernity, and thus we have the discourses of globalization. Turning to our criteria, we could say that the institutional locus is Euro-North American politics, economics, and technology. It is obvious that neither Indian, African, Nicaraguan, nor even French technology can globalize. Politically, the effect once again is the neutralization of all critique. Who would want to stand in the way of the inevitable and logical path of social development? Of course, there are resistances, but these are caricaturized as a type of anti-modern romanticism limited to Luddites and countermoderns. There is one difference with respect to both modernity and postmodernity: the discourses of globalization pretend to situate themselves beyond the borders of Europe and the United States. In this they share certain preoccupations and methodologies with the postcolonial and post-Occidentalist theories. Globalization theories pretend to think the world from the perspective of the other. However, all that they can see or think is themselves. That is, they go to the other in order to see only themselves. In this form the locus of enunciation is the world, as a horizon of knowledge and concern, but what it enacts is a negation of this very locus of enunciation—for the world is not one of cultural, social, and technological heterogeneity, but of a mere tabula rasa for the actualization of one global design.

Postcolonial theories began as a methodological critique of Marxism, and they were first elaborated in former European colonies. Seen through this optic, postcolonial theories participate in a general discontent and disenchantment with Western culture, which discredited itself so thoroughly and irreversibly with the massacres of the two world wars, the genocides that took place in the concentration camps, and the communist gulags. Postcolonial theories attempt to rescue certain Marxist-inspired methods of analysis for postcolonial societies. For this reason the Indian subaltern group was launched initially as an internal critique to Marxism, which because of its focus on European industrial capitalism cannot understand or appreciate the logic and originality of revolutionary movements that have nothing to do with the revolutionary logic of late capitalism as was diagnosed by Marx, Engels, and Lenin. Eventually, this methodological critique became an epistemological revolution, even a paradigm revolution. The goal was no longer to transform historical materialism and the cultural studies inaugurated by

Raymond Williams and E. P. Thompson, in order to acculturate and adapt them to the historical reality of the Indian world. On the contrary, the goal was now to abandon these methods, for their epistemological as well as ontohistorical presuppositions were what hindered the possibility of understanding Indian reality in its own terms.

What is the relationship between postcolonial theory and subaltern studies? Is one a subset of the other, or are both different faces of the same coin? One way in which we can understand the relationship between postcolonial theory and subaltern studies is to think of the former as the theorizing of the horizon of historical praxis as seen from the standpoint of social agents and the institutions that frame their modes of actions, while the latter is the questioning of the modalities of subjectivity and agency as seen from the standpoint of lived experience and "the psychic life of power," to use Judith Butler's wonderful phrase (1997). Postcolonial theory is to subaltern studies what historical materialism is to psychoanalytic, or Freudian, Marxism, or what Hegel's *Lectures on the Philosophy of World History* are to his *Phenomenology of Spirit*, or what Marx's *Grundrisse* is to his *1844 Manuscripts*; but perhaps more aptly, postcolonial theory is to subaltern studies what Edward Said's *Orientalism* is to Homi Bhabha's *The Location of Culture*. What is at stake on one side is to think from the larger canvas of history, not assuming the givenness of this canvas, but precisely to question the existence and nature of that canvas as the very condition of the possibility of painting something like the scene of history, that is, not just how history happens, but why history is required in order to think the very possibility of agency at a macrolevel, as the agency of social ensembles. On the other side, what is at stake is to think the space of subjectivity as one that is already occupied by the sociohistorical, to think how the subjectivities of the master and the slave are co-determined and co-determining. In this way we may think of subaltern studies as an ensemble of investigations into modes of subjection, an analytics not of *dasein* but of subjected and revolted agency, an analytics in which one is not only and always the subaltern of another, but in which this one is also an insurrected and resisting other. Subaltern studies thus always imply a theory of insurrected agencies, agencies that inaugurate and disclose new modalities and horizons of praxis, or social action.

We can thus surmise that while postcolonial theories are an epistemological and ontohistorical revolution that put in question all the science that is made, written, and exported by the Euro-North American pedagogical and ideological machine, subaltern studies are a sociopsychological deconstruction of the allowed theories of agency and subjectivity. For this reason, postcolonial theories and subaltern studies change the epistemograph and the ontograph. The world requires many chronotopographs—different historical and geographical maps (Spivak and Chakrabarty). In addition, there are different ways of being historical and contemporary with the modern project—there are different ways of being modern. There are many ways in which agency and subjectivity have been and will continue to be lived beyond the shadow of the master's sovereignty. Dussel makes a distinction between modernity understood as a project that is supposedly accomplished only by Europe and modernity as a global or planetary project, one which is the horizon of possibility for both René Descartes and Kant (Dussel 1996b, 1998c). The normative criterion is enunciated in the negative: theories that negate, reject, and occlude the contribution, real or potential, of all cultures to an emergent planetary human culture are unacceptable. Modernity is the product of the globality or *mundialidad* of humanity, and it would be hubristic to negate most or any contributions to such a project. The political consequences of this form of theories are evident. They are a critique of all forms of Eurocentrism, Americanism, and ethnocentrism. The subject is at the same time the object of study, and its locus of enunciation is the locus of enactment and actualization. Here the other speaks about itself from its own place: from its quotidianity. The question "Can the subaltern speak?" is provisionally answered with no, so long as the same onto-epistemological-historical categories of the Euro-North American project of modernity and globalization continue to be used (Derrida has written "theo-onto-epistemology," and I accept this neologism if we also accept how theo-ontology masks and harbors an entire philosophy of history).

I am using the word *post-Occidentalism* to refer to those theories that emerged in Latin America during the 1960s (Mignolo 2000a, Lander 2001). This is a paradigm of Latin American thinking that gathers and synthesizes many theoretical currents: theories of dependence, the sociology of liberation, the philosophy of liberation, Paulo Freire's pedagogy of the oppressed, including the works on history by Darcy Ribeiro, Samuel Ramos, Edmundo O'Gorman, and Octavio Paz. Methodologically, post-Occidentalism emerges not only from a confrontation with historical materialism but also from a synergistic synthesis and transformation of the existential ontology of Heidegger, the historicism of José Gaos and José Ortega y Gasset, and a symbolics, or cultural semantics and hermeneutics in the tradition of Ricoeur. I mention all of these precedents because I want to underscore how there is also an epistemological revolution in Latin American thought that is similar but anterior to that which took place within Indian thought and within

Marxist thought in England in the late 1960s and early 1970s. To look at Latin American thought from the perspective of postcolonial theory allows us to appreciate the innovation and originality of Latin American thought. One, and only one, of the many critical foci of post-Occidentalism is a critique of Eurocentrism and European ethnocentrism, a critique that is carried from within. The central tenet of post-Occidentalism is that Europe constitutes itself through a political economy of alterization of its others (as masterfully discussed by Said). The logic of alterization creates others, but only in order to define that which must remain unsoiled, pristine, which is the same, the identical. The grammar of abjection that determines the entire text of modernity in its relation to its others is not criticized from outside, but from within. What is threatening, what is vile and possibly contaminating is within. Thus, the post-Occidentalist critique begins by discovering the abject alterity within. The figure is not the despised and feared Moor or the despotic Byzantium. The figure is now of Caliban cursing Prospero. The civilizing project, justified and imposed by a sanctified teleology but disguised behind the mantle of a historical reason, shipwrecks on the shoals of indigenous and mestizo culture, the Amerindian and the American slave. From its inception, the Occidentalist project begins its failure, but it is nonetheless continued and perpetuated, in the form of management of those others that it produces but that it must at the same time quarantine. Formulaically put, already the Amerindians, the slaves of the new world, the mestizos and mulattos that were born with the modern project knew, in their flesh and in their sequestered and quarantined sociality, what the postcolonial thinkers began to discover after the 1960s and 1970s in light of a process of decolonization begun in the aftermath of World War II.

It is evident that there has been a change in the locus of enunciation. It is no longer admissible to permit a subject to speak for others, to epistemologize about them, without allowing them in turn to speak or to make knowledge claims. Nor is it acceptable to suppose that there is another who is silent and merely known. Post-Occidentalist thought is that in which the other answers and responds back in his and her polluted and vulgar tongues. This speaking subaltern confronts the master with his own voice and answers back: I do not recognize myself in your caricatures of me. The goal is to acknowledge that we are always objects of a fantasy of control and that this control materializes if we agree to live under the fictions of the master and his discourse. In short, post-Occidentalism is what Luhmann (1995) would call a second-order observation, an observation of observations. In this way, post-Occidentalism contributes to a critique of the modernist disciplines that occlude their political dimensions behind the curtains of scientization. Thus, post-Occidentalism, in a manner analogous to that of postcolonial theories, is a critique of the political economy of knowledge.

There are fundamental differences between post-Occidentalism and post-Orientalism, however. Post-Occidentalism is a tradition that is socio-theoretical critique as much as it is philosophical critique, and which has behind it five hundred years of experience and accumulated work. Yet post-colonialism elaborates a critique of European colonialism in the epoch of its last stage. It is a critique that for that reason is focused on the more re-cent and visible consequences of the colonial-modern project (as Mignolo thinks we should write it) in its second stage (the first stage being when the colonial-modern project was inaugurated with the discovery of the New World and when Spanish hegemony was established in synchrony with the expulsion of the Jews and the Moors from the Iberian Peninsula). In con-trast, the post-Occidentalist critique is articulated synchronically and dia-chronically. Post-Occidentalism is a look that gazes back from the inaugura-tion of the Western or Occidental project, which is prior to the Orientalist project and which, due to geopolitical and historical-cultural reasons, inevi-tably analyze from within the third and most recent stage of the colonial-modern project. This latest stage has to be understood as the continuation of the civilizing project by the United States, under the flag of the war against all wars that is benignly called the crusade for human rights and its condi-tion of possibility, globalization. This convergence among the transfer of flags, the exacerbation of the violence of the civilizing project that is masked by the fiscal and banking policies imposed by the G-7 and backed by the NATO armies, and the crisis of this rationalized irrationality that is given voice by the thinkers of the center (to echo the economic philosopher Franz Hinkelammert [1999]) requires that we opt for a long-term view that post-colonialism, which is so young, can neither admit nor provide. Alternatively, the postcolonial critique is only able to criticize the effects of colonialism once this mutates into the projects of nation building. It is for this reason that postcolonialism seems fastidiously obsessed with the question of na-tionalism and its alter ego, the nation, whether this be thought in terms of its fragments, its shadow, its agony, its absence, its failure, or its noncon-vergence with the space of a people's culture. While postcolonialism con-tinues to focus on the nation, even in its absence, it also continues to be overdetermined by questions of class and the last instance of social relations as being epiphenomenal to a mode of production. And in this way it "narco-tizes," to use Mignolo's expression, against the geopolitics of location and the localizing, or mapping, of the world-historical. But in the age of the symbolic reproduction of the system of production, what is needed is a political-economic critique of the sign, or the production of the symbolic that conditions what is desirable as commodity—that is, how the local of the nation is a metonym of the global and how the global is produced from and through the local.

At a more elemental level, when we try to decipher the categories that allow postcolonial criticism, we are faced with an ambiguity or indeterminacy that seems to plague and render suspect the proposals of postcolonial criticism. Postcolonial theory advocates in favor of the subaltern, but who is the subaltern? How is the social, political, economic locus of the subaltern determined? How can one determine conceptually the theoretical locus of the subaltern? The subaltern sometimes appears to be part of the social system; at other times, it seems to be beyond the system. As Spivak writes, "Subalternity is the name that I grant to the space that is outside any serious contact with the logic of capitalism and socialism" (qtd. in Moore-Gilbert 1997, 101). In other words, the category of the subaltern is outside any historical determination. But this indeterminacy becomes an empty space and an inaccessible and intransigent opacity at the very moment that it turns into the cancellation of the ethical response. To clarify: faced with the challenge of the subaltern, the one who dominates—the hegemonic "I" of the ruling system—only has two options: either respect absolutely and without reservation the alterity of the other and in this way leave the status quo totally intact; or open up, respond to the other without trying to assimilate him (Spivak, qtd. in Moore-Gilbert 1997, 102). This type of paradox is confronted directly in the philosophical corpus that animates the post-Occidentalist critique. And to put it more concretely, the challenge of the encounter with the other and of having to formulate an answer that is neither adulatory nor sacralizing, neither assimilating nor devastating, is the central theme of the work of the ethics of liberation that is at the center of so much post-Occidentalist work. A philosophy of alterity (the regimes of the production of otherness would be more apt) is fundamental to the critiques of Occidentalism and Orientalism. What may be interpreted perhaps ungenerously as the philosophical poverty of postcolonialism is nonetheless justifiable: it is an epistemological critique that is inaugurated by a methodological crisis; it is critique in the aftermath of running up against that limit in which historical narrative is turned into logic, to paraphrase Spivak.[4] The critique of the political economy of knowledge that is developed by post-Occidentalism proceeds *further* by stepping back *farther* since it seeks to begin from the crisis of reason itself at the moment of its inception, before the thrust to turn narrative into ontological ineluctability is even launched. It does this by moving from "representation to enactment, from text to action, from the enunciated to the enunciation, from the belief that space and territories are *places* where interaction is enacted, to the belief that it is interaction as enactment that creates the idea of places, territories and regions" (Mignolo 1994b, iii–iv). In the post-Occidentalist critique, in short, we discern a post-philosophical strategy that seeks to think the spacing of time, and the timing of space, which are generative of reason; that is, the mapping of world-historical time and the temporalizing of geolocalities, which become the chronotope against which, or onto which, the narratives may be thought as logos, and logos as space, that is, the time of the modern and the space of civilization.[5] The universal logos of Western philosophy is the trace, the cipher, of time/space, one which is always a particular time/space that projects itself as universal. In this way, post-Occidentalism is a critique of Western rationality, unmasking it as a hubristic and blind chronotope, in favor of a reason that announces a universality yet to be, one that is enunciated from and out of the heterochronotopology of a world that is many, that is only one in its plurality. It is a critique of reason from within its own hybridity and insufficiency.

NOTES

1 The following discussion of Latinamericanism has been elaborated further in my forthcoming essay "The Emperor's Map: Latin American Critiques of Globalism."

2 Michael Löwy's article in this volume expands on Enrique Dussel's overview, attempting to include other aspects of liberation theology, and provides elements relating to the genealogy of the movement. He proposes "Christianity of Liberation" to describe a wider array of contemporary political and social movements.

3 For a more developed version of Latino Latinamericanism, see Mendieta 2003.

4 After Spivak's *A Critique of Postcolonial Reason: Toward a History of the Vanishing Present* (1999), no one can accuse postcolonial theory of philosophical weakness. Yet Spivak and Bhabha are the main theorists of subaltern studies and postcolonial theory who have performed extended studies of what I call the analytics of subjection and insurrection. In the post-Occidentalist canon, this has been a persistent question in works by Fernández Retamar, Dussel and Ribeiro, Mignolo, Castro-Gómez, and González Stephan.

5 This phrasing echoes Jacques Derrida's definition of *différance*: "*Différer* in this sense is to temporize, to take recourse, consciously or unconsciously, in the temporal and temporizing mediation of a detour that suspends the accomplish-

ment or fulfillment of 'desire' or 'will,' and equally effects this suspension in a mode that annuls or tempers its own effect. . . . [T]his temporization is also temporalization and spacing, the becoming-time of space and the becoming-space of time, the 'originary constitution' of time and space, as metaphysics of transcendental phenomenology would say, to use the language that here is criticized and displaced" (1982, 8).

DEVELOPMENTALISM, MODERNITY, AND DEPENDENCY THEORY IN LATIN AMERICA

Ramón Grosfoguel

The Latin American *dependentistas* produced a knowledge that criticized the Eurocentric assumptions of the *cepalistas*, including the orthodox Marxist and the North American modernization theories. The dependentista-school critique of stagism and developmentalism was an important intervention that transformed the imaginary of intellectual debates in many parts of the world. However, I will argue that many dependentistas were still caught in the developmentalism, and in some cases even in the stagism, that they were trying to overcome. Moreover, although the dependentistas' critique of stagism was important in denying the "denial of coevalness" that Johannes Fabian (1983) describes as central to Eurocentric constructions of "otherness," some dependentistas replaced it with new forms of denial of coevalness. In this essay I discuss developmentalist ideology and what I call "feudalmania" as part of the *longue durée* of modernity in Latin America, the dependentistas' developmentalism, Fernando Henrique Cardoso's version of dependency theory, and the dependentistas' concept of culture.

DEVELOPMENTALIST IDEOLOGY AND FEUDALMANIA AS PART OF THE IDEOLOGY OF MODERNITY IN LATIN AMERICA

There is a tendency to present the post-1945 development debates in Latin America as unprecedented. In order to distinguish continuity from disconti-nuity, we must place the 1945–90 development debates in the context of the longue durée of Latin American history. The 1945–90 development debates in Latin America, although seemingly radical, in fact form part of the longue durée of the geoculture of modernity that has dominated the modern world-system since the French Revolution in the late eighteenth century.

Before I can elaborate this further, I must, however, clarify some histori-cal and conceptual points. The idea that anything new is necessarily good and desirable because we live in an era of progress is fundamental to the ideology of modernity (Wallerstein 1992a, 1992b). This idea can be traced to the eighteenth-century Enlightenment, which asserted the possibility of a conscious rational reform of society, the idea of progress, and the virtues of science vis-à-vis religion. The modern idea that treated each individual as a free, centered subject with rational control over his or her destiny was ex-tended to the nation-state level. Each nation-state was considered to be sovereign and free to rationally control its progressive development. The further elaboration of these ideas in classical political economy produced the grounds for the emergence of a developmentalist ideology.

Developmentalism is linked to liberal ideology and to the idea of prog-ress. For instance, one of the central questions addressed by political econo-mists was how to increase the wealth of nations. Different prescriptions were recommended by different political economists, some of whom were free-traders and others neomercantilist. In spite of their policy disagree-ments, they all believed in national development and in the inevitable prog-ress of the nation-state through the rational organization of society. The main bone of contention was how to ensure more wealth for a nation-state. According to Immanuel Wallerstein, "This tension between a basically pro-tectionist versus a free trade stance became one of the major themes of policy-making in the various states of the world-system in the nineteenth century. It often was the most significant issue that divided the principal political forces of particular states. It was clear by then that a central ideological theme of the capitalist world-economy was that every state could, and indeed eventually probably would, reach a high level of national income and that conscious, rational action would make it so. This fit very well with the underlying Enlightenment theme of inevitable progress and the teleological view of human history that it incarnated" (1992b, 517).

Developmentalism became a global ideology of the capitalist world economy. In the Latin American periphery these ideas were appropriated in the late eighteenth century by the Spanish Creole elites, who adapted them to their own agenda. Since most of the elites were linked to, or part of, the agrarian landowner class, which produced goods through coerced forms of labor to sell for a profit in the world market, they were very eclectic in their selection of which Enlightenment ideas they wished to utilize. Free trade and national sovereignty were ideas they defended as part of their struggle against the Spanish colonial monopoly of trade. However, for racial and class reasons, the modern ideas about individual freedom, rights of man, and equality were underplayed. There were no major social transformations of Latin American societies after the independence revolutions of the first half of the nineteenth century. The Creole elites left untouched the colonial noncapitalist forms of coerced labor as well as the racial/ethnic hierarchies. White Creole elites maintained after independence a racial hierarchy wherein Indians, blacks, mestizos, mulattoes, and other racially oppressed groups were located at the bottom. This is what Aníbal Quijano (1993a) calls "coloniality of power."

During the nineteenth century, Great Britain had become the new core power and the new model of civilization. The Latin American Creole elites established a discursive opposition between Spain's "backwardness, obscurantism and feudalism" and Great Britain's "advanced, civilized and modern" nation. Leopoldo Zea, paraphrasing José Enrique Rodó, called this the new "northernmania" (nordomanía), that is, the attempt by Creole elites to see new "models" in the North that would stimulate development while in turn developing new forms of colonialism (Zea 1986, 16–17). The subsequent nineteenth-century characterization by the Creole elites of Latin America as "feudal" or in a backward "stage" served to justify Latin American subordination to the new masters from the North and is part of what I call "feudalmania," which would continue throughout the twentieth century.

Feudalmania was a device of "temporal distancing" (Fabian 1983) to produce a knowledge that denied coevalness between Latin America and the so-called advanced European countries. The denial of coevalness created a double ideological mechanism. First, it concealed European responsibility in the exploitation of the Latin American periphery. By not sharing the same historical time and by existing in different geographical spaces, each region's destiny was conceived as unrelated to that of the others. Second, living different temporalities, where Europe was said to be at a more advanced stage of development than Latin America, reproduced a notion of European superiority. Thus Europe was the "model" to imitate and the developmentalist goal was to "catch up." This is expressed in the civilization-barbarism dichotomy seen in figures such as Domingo Faustino Sarmiento in Argentina.

The use of both neomercantilist and liberal economic ideas enabled the nineteenth-century Ibero-American elites to oscillate between protectionist and free-trade positions depending on the fluctuations of the world-economy. When they were benefiting from producing agrarian or mining exports in the international division of labor dominated at the time by British imperialism, liberal economic theories provided them with the rational justification for their role and goals. But when foreign competition or a world economic crisis was affecting their exports to the world market, they shifted production toward the internal markets and employed neomercantilist arguments to justify protectionist policies. In Chile, Argentina, and Mexico there were neomercantilist and economic-nationalist arguments that anticipated many of the arguments developed one hundred years later by the Prebisch-CEPAL school and by some of the dependentistas (Potasch 1959; Andre Gunder Frank 1970; Chiaramonte 1971).[1] For example, the 1870s developmentalist debate was the most important economic debate in Argentina during the nineteenth century and one of the most important in Latin America. An industrial-development plan using protectionist neomercantilist policies was proposed. This movement was led by a professor of political economy at the University of Buenos Aires and member of the Cámara de Diputados, Vicente F. López. López's group was supported by the agrarian landowners, artisans, peasants, and incipient industrial capitalists. Although all of them were protectionists, not all were economic nationalists. The protectionist position of the agrarian landowners was due to the 1866 and 1873 world economic crises, which had negatively affected export prices on wool, Argentina's major export item at the time. Thus, López promoted the development of a national cloth industry as a transitional solution to the world depression. The movement ended once the wool producers shifted to cattle raising and meat exports.

Influenced by the late-1830s Argentinean romantic generation (e.g., Juan Bautista Alberdi, Esteban Echevarría), López defended a historicist/idiographic approach against the universalism of liberal political economists (Chiaramonte 1971, 128–29, 133–34). According to López, the idea of free trade is not an absolute principle; rather, its application depends on the particular conditions of each country. If free trade was beneficial for the industrial development of foreign countries, in the Argentinean case, where different industrial and economic structures were present, free trade was not a solution. In the first phase of industrial development, industries need protection from foreign competition. As one of the protectionist-group members, Lucio V. López, said in 1873, "It is a mistake to believe that political economy offers and contains immutable principles for all nations" (ibid., 129–30). This critique of the nomothetic/universalist approach of core state intellectuals is even stronger in the thesis of one of Vicente F. López's disciples, Aditardo Heredia, who attacked European intellectuals' social conceptions as ahistorical and metaphysical. Heredia criticized in particular the European Enlightenment thinkers for aspiring to develop a social science guided by universal and inflexible principles, similar to geometric theorems or algebraic formulas, without attention to the peculiar historical conditions of each nation (ibid., 130). Carlos Pellegrini, one of the leading protectionist deputies, said as early as 1853 that Adam Smith's beautiful deductions did not pay enough attention to an aspect that influences all human institutions: time (ibid., 133). The debate was a classical nomothetic-idiographic confrontation. The Argentinean scholars opposed a theory based on a concept of an eternal time/space with more particularistic and historicist arguments.

The originality of their arguments was to articulate an economic policy in support of a nationalist industrialization project in the periphery of the world-economy and to identify relations with England as part of the source of Argentina's underdevelopment. The economic nationalism of Vicente F. López and his group offered a critique of the dependent relations of Argentina with England and other European centers as early as the 1870s (Chiaramonte 1971, 192–93). Regarding this point, we can quote the following statements made by this protectionist group, which can show some similarities with certain CEPAL-dependentista positions one hundred years later.

> It is very beautiful . . . to speak of free trade. . . . [T]his word *freedom* . . . is so beautiful! But we must understand freedom. For the English who favor free trade, freedom is to allow English factories to manufacture the foreign products, to allow the English merchant to sell the foreign product. This type of freedom transforms the rest of the world into tributary countries; while England is the only nation that enjoys freedom, the remainder are tributary nations; but I do not

understand free trade in this manner. By *free trade* I understand an exchange of finished goods for finished goods. The day our wool can be exported not in the form of a raw material, but rather as a finished frock coat in exchange for England's iron needles or clock strings, then I would accept free trade, that is, a finished product from our country for a finished product from England. But if free trade consists of sending our wool . . . so England may wash it (when I speak of England I also mean Europe and the rest of the world), manufacture it, and sell it to us through English merchants, brought on English ships and sold by English agents, I do not understand; this is not free trade, this is making a country that does not possess this industry a tributary country. Thus, let's follow the path of protectionism, given that if we see the history of the manufacturing countries, we will find that their progress is due to protectionism. (Speech by Finance Minister. Rufino Varela in the legislature in 1876, cited in Chiaramonte 1971, 182–83)

In the English Parliament, one of the illustrious defenders of free trade said that he would like, upholding his doctrine, to make of England the factory of the world and of America the farm of England. He said something very true . . . that to a great extent has been realized, because in effect we are and will be for a long time, if we do not solve this problem, the farm of the great manufacturing nations. (Speech by Carlos Pellegrini at the Cámara de Diputados in 1875, ibid., 189)

It is impossible to be independent when a country is not self-sufficient, when it does not have all it needs to consume. . . . I know well what the remedies are: they are to have capital to pay ourselves for the elaboration of products and their adaptation for consumption. Only in this way would the country have independence and credit and be saved through its own efforts. (Speech by Vicente F. López at the Cámara de Diputados in 1875, ibid., 27)

It has been recognized that political independence cannot exist without industrial and mercantile independence. (Speech by a protectionist deputy in 1874, ibid., 192)

[It is not necessary] to be permanently dependent on foreign capital. . . . I am completely opposed to the establishment of companies with foreign capital. (Deputy Seeber in 1877, ibid., 185)

Although this nationalist group was questioning the tenets of traditional liberal political economy and the location of Argentina within the world division of labor (Chiaramonte 1971, 193), it is important to indicate that they were committed to a nationalist liberalism. They defended protectionism as a transitory, although necessary, stage to direct the country toward economic liberalism. They criticized the supporters of the free-market doctrine because this policy maintained the subordination of Argentina to England. They wished to restrict momentarily the full implementation of economic liberalism as a means of achieving it later: the newborn industries needed protection, but once they grew, free markets should be encouraged (ibid., 1971, 191). This doctrine is very close to that of the German political economist Frederich List, who also promoted protectionism against England as a necessary developmental stage. However, although their names were mentioned several times during the 1870s parliamentary debate (ibid., 135), the dominant influence on the Argentinean protectionists in the 1870s came from their own intellectual tradition (ibid., 134–35). In sum, they were committed to national capitalist development through the formation of a local industrial bourgeoisie.

Other countries in Latin America, such as Mexico (Potasch 1959) and Chile (Andre Gunder Frank 1970), had similar debates during the nineteenth century. Probably the most extreme case in terms of the free-trade and protectionist debates was nineteenth-century Paraguay, where a protectionist regime led by Dr. Francia and the López family was destroyed by a military intervention of Brazil, Uruguay, and Argentina, aided by the British, to install a free-trade regime. Six out of seven Paraguayan males were killed in the Triple Alliance War. This war was a turning point for the triumph of the free-trade doctrine, which dominated in Latin America during the nineteenth century, the period of British hegemony. Agrarian and mining capitalists profited from selling raw materials or crops to, and buying manufactured products from, the British, rather than attempting to compete with them through industrialization.

By the end of the nineteenth century, Spencerian evolutionism and Comtian scientism joined forces to form the Latin American version of positivism, which provided ideological justification for both the economic subordination to the "empire of free trade" and the political domination of the dictatorships of "order and progress." Scientism, progress, truth, property, evolutionary stagism, and order were all Enlightenment themes reproduced in Auguste Comte's positivist and Herbert Spencer's evolutionary doctrines. They were both used in the Latin American periphery to justify the penetration of foreign capital investments and to promote economic liberalism against "backwardness" and "feudalism." Evolutionary stagism, inevitable progress, and optimism in science and technology combined to form a teleological view of human history that strengthened the basis of developmentalist ideology. As a result of the U.S. military invasions in the region, the Mexican Revolution in 1910, and the disillusionment with liberalism during World War I, a new wave of nationalism emerged among Latin American elites. Once again, after World War I, there was a radical questioning of economic liberalism, this time focused against the new *hegemon* in the region, the United States of America.

The nationalists promoted protectionist policies and state intervention, while the positivists defended free-market policies. Yet between the nationalist ideology of the Mexican revolutionaries and the positivism of Porfirio Díaz's dictatorship, there were more continuities than is commonly accepted. Both promoted the feudalmania ideology and believed that the implementation of the proper policies would move the country away from its backwardness and toward progress. Both nationalism and positivism asserted faith in progress and science and in the rational control and development of the national economy through a strong nation-state. Both shared a developmentalist ideology. Each made use of feudalmania's representation of past regimes as backward and barbaric to gain legitimation.

Similar debates emerged from the world's revolutionary experiences in the 1910s, anticipating once again some of the arguments developed in the post-1945 debates. The most important was that between Victor Raúl Haya de la Torre and José Carlos Mariátegui in Peru during the 1920s. The influence of Marxist ideas following the Russian Revolution set the terms of the debate. This time the problematic of development was centered around the character of the revolution. The belief in accelerating the historical processes toward progress through revolutionary upheavals could be found in Latin American elites since the nineteenth century (Villegas 1986, 95). But it was twentieth-century Leninism that popularized the idea of a rational revolution enlightened by a scientific theory and implemented by a revolutionary party.

Both Haya de la Torre and Mariátegui reproduced some of the nineteenth century's favorite liberal concepts (e.g., the feudal character of Peru), but with a Marxist flavor. The revolution was a radical means to achieve the project of modernity: national development, a rational control of society through a scientific theory (Marxism), the eradication of ignorance and "feudal" backwardness. They both condemned imperialism and the landlord class, favoring agrarian reform and industrialization as a solution for Peru.

Haya de la Torre, applying his particular version of Marxism, concluded that capitalism in Latin America did not follow the same trajectory that it had in Europe, due to the "feudal" backwardness created by centuries of Spanish colonialism. If imperialism was the last stage of capitalism in Europe, it was just the first stage in Latin America. Thus, the Aprista revolution should pursue the constitution of an anti-imperialist nationalist capitalism allied to an independent bourgeoisie and led by the petite bourgeoisie (Villegas 1986, 96–97).[2] Due to the weakness of the national bourgeoisie, Haya de la Torre proposed the need for a strong, interventionist anti-imperialist state to lead economic development.

Mariátegui believed that the feudal *latifundio* and capitalist relations form part of a single capitalist international system, opposing Haya's dualism (Quijano 1981a; Vanden 1986). Accordingly, there could be no progressive role for capitalism in Peru. Capitalism as a system would not allow the development of an independent national capitalism. Moreover, international capitalism was linked to and reproduced the precapitalist relations in Peru. This was the first Latin American attempt to break with the denial of coevalness within the Marxist tradition. Rather than characterizing semifeudal forms of labor as part of a backward and underdeveloped mode of production, Mariátegui conceptualized them as produced by the international capitalist system. In this conceptualization, semifeudal forms are not a residual from the past, but a labor form of the present world capitalist system.

Mariátegui proposed a socialist revolution as the only solution for Peru's underdevelopment. It was through the Indians' *ayllu* (communal property) that Peru could skip the capitalist stage and make a direct transition from feudal forms to socialism. The revolution should be organized by a broad alliance between workers, peasants, and revolutionary intellectuals led by a proletarian party. The so-called national bourgeoisie had no revolutionary role to play.

This debate would again reappear in quite similar terms between some communist parties and dependentista intellectuals during the 1960s and 1970s. The Haya-Mariátegui debate had profound effects on the dependentista positions and on the political programs of many political parties in Latin America.

In sum, contemporary developmentalist choices between free trade and protectionism have a long history in Latin America. These debates have emerged several times in the last two hundred years with different programs and political projects. The dependentista school was a radical version of the protectionist program in Latin America. Their solution for dependency was to delink from the capitalist world-system and to organize a socialist society insulated from the influence and control of metropolitan capitalism. The dependentista school reproduced a particular version of developmentalist ideology. Needless to say, nineteenth-century developmentalist themes continue to be very much alive today.

DEPENDENTISMO **AND** *CEPALISMO:*
SAME DEVELOPMENTALIST ASSUMPTIONS?

Three important events in the early 1960s provided the social context for the emergence of the dependency school: (1) the crisis of the import-substitution industrialization (ISI) strategy in Latin America; (2) the Cuban Revolution; and (3) the concentration of an important generation of exiled left-wing intellectuals in Santiago due to the wave of military coups that began in 1964 with the Brazilian coup.

First, the import-substitution industrialization crisis initiated a debate questioning some of the sacred principles of the CEPAL school. All the problems that the ISI strategy was supposed to solve had been aggravated instead. Rather than importing consumer goods, Latin America started importing capital goods in the early 1950s. The latter were more expensive than the former. Moreover, most of the new industries were created by multinational corporations in search of Latin America's local markets. As a result, by the early 1960s, after a decade of import-substitution industrialization, balance of payments deficits, trade deficits, increased marginalized populations, and inflation continued to affect the region.

Second, the Cuban Revolution transformed the political imaginary of many Latin Americans. The communist parties had been arguing for years that Latin America's feudal character required a capitalist revolution under the leadership of the local bourgeoisie. Following that logic, communist parties supported populist regimes such as that of Getúlio Dornelles Vargas in Brazil and dictators like Fulgencio Batista and Anastasio Somoza. Castro ignored the orthodox communist dogmas. In spite of how we may conceptualize the Cuban Revolution today, at the time it was considered a socialist revolution. For many, Cuba was living proof of the possibility for an alternative path of development "outside the world capitalist system." This provided the political basis for questioning the characterization by the Communist parties of the region as "feudal." Instead, the new leftist movement claimed that Latin America's priority should be not to develop capitalism in alliance with the "national bourgeoisie," as the communist parties alleged, but to start immediately armed struggles for the socialist revolution. Guerrilla movements proliferated all over the region, attempting to repeat the Cuban experience.

Third, due to the military coups in the region, a young generation of left-wing intellectuals were exiled in Santiago where they worked at the CEPAL and in Chilean universities. This generation, critical of the communist parties' orthodox version of Marxism and influenced by the new leftist ideas inspired by the Cuban Revolution, contributed to the critical revision of the CEPAL's doctrine. This generation of intellectuals came to be known world-wide as the dependency school.

The dependency school waged a political and theoretical struggle on three fronts: against the neodevelopmentalist ideology of the CEPAL, against the orthodox Marxism of the Latin American communist parties, and against the modernization theory of U.S. academicians. Though these three traditions were diverse, they shared a dualistic view of social processes. Accordingly, the problem of Latin American societies was understood to be the archaic, traditional, and feudal structures that needed to be overcome in order to become more advanced, modern, and capitalist. This "time distanciation" reproduced the nineteenth-century Eurocentric feudalmania. Latin America was purportedly lagging behind the United States and Europe due to its "archaic" structures.

In contrast to the cepalistas, the dependentistas criticized the import-substitution industrialization model and the role of the "national" bourgeoisie. Prior to 1950, Latin American anti-imperialist movements struggled for the industrialization of the region as a so-called solution to the subordination to the capitalist centers. The imperialist alliance between foreign capital and the local landed oligarchy was an obstacle to the industrialization of Latin America. The peripheral role assigned to Latin America in the international division of labor was to export primary products to the centers. However, as of 1950, with the proliferation of multinationals and a "new international division of labor," industrialization to produce goods for the internal markets of Latin America was not in contradiction with the interest of international capital. The protectionist tariffs of the import-substitution industrialization strategy and the search for cheaper labor costs increased foreign industrial investments in the Latin American periphery. Thus, the nature of dependency was not any longer an industrial dependency, but a technological dependency. The problems with the balance of payments that the import-substitution industrialization attempted to solve were dramatically aggravated due to the technological dependence on the centers. Rather than importing consumer goods, Latin Americans were forced to import machinery, new technologies, patents, and licenses for which they needed to pay still more. The "national" bourgeoisie became associated with multinational corporations. They were dependent on foreign capitalists for technology, machinery, and finance. Thus, according to the dependentistas, the national bourgeoisie did not represent a progressive or reliable ally to dismantle the structures of the world capitalist system that reproduced "under-development" in the periphery.

The dependentistas challenged the orthodox communist parties' portrayal of Latin America as feudal. According to the orthodox Marxist dogma, all societies had to pass through successive fixed stages to achieve socialism. It followed that Latin America, to the degree that it was not yet capitalist, had to first reach the capitalist stage of development. It could do so by an alliance of the working classes with the national bourgeoisie in order to eradicate feudalism and create the conditions for capitalism, after which the struggle for socialism might begin. This theory assumed an eternal time/space framework by generalizing the purported stages of national development of European countries to the rest of the world. Rather than stimulate capitalism, dependency scholars prescribed a radical and immediate transformation of the social structures toward socialism. According to their analysis, if the region's underdevelopment was due to the capitalist system, more capitalism was not a solution. The solution would be to eradicate capitalism through a socialist revolution.

The dependentistas also criticized the modernization theories. Although this is not the place for a detailed exposition of the modernization approach to development, it is important to introduce some of its most influential authors. Modernization theorists such as Bert F. Hoselitz (1960) and Walt W. Rostow (1960) assumed the Eurocentric denial of coevalness. They divided societies into modern and traditional sectors. Hoselitz, using Parsonian pattern variables, developed a classificatory schema to define each sector. In modern societies relationships tend to be universalistic, functionally specific, and people are evaluated by their achievements. In traditional societies, relationships are particularistic, functionally diffused, and people are evaluated by ascribed status. Accordingly, development consists of changing cultural values from the latter to the former.

In Rostow's schema (1960) development is a five-stage process from traditional to modern society. Using the metaphor of an airplane, Rostow's stages are as follows: stationary (traditional society), preconditions for take-off, takeoff, drive to maturity, and high mass-consumption society (modern society). In terms of my topic Rostow and Hoselitz universalized what they considered to be the cultural features or the more advanced stages of development of the United States and Western European countries. Thus, similar to the orthodox mode of production theory of the communist parties, the modernization theorists assumed an eternal/universal time/space notion of stages through which every society should pass. Moreover, they assumed the superiority of the "West" by creating a time/space distanciation between the "advanced" modern societies and the "backward" traditional societies.

The struggle between the modernization and the dependentista theories was a struggle between two geocultural locations. The "locus of enunciation" (Mignolo 1995) of the modernization theorists was North America. The Cold War was a constitutive part of the formation of the modernization theory. The ahistorical bias of the theory was an attempt to produce a universal theory from the experience and ideology of the core of the world-economy. On the other hand, the dependentistas developed a theory from the loci of enunciation of the Latin American periphery. The attempt was not to universalize but to produce a particular theory for this region of the world.

Five important dependentista authors developed an extensive and detailed critique of modernization theory, namely, Fernando Henrique Cardoso (1964, chap. 2), Fernando Henrique Cardoso and Enzo Faletto (1969, 11–17), Andre Gunder Frank (1969b, pt. 2), Aníbal Quijano (1977), and Theotonio dos Santos (1970). These intellectuals raised the following critiques to the modernization theory.

1   Development and underdevelopment are produced by the center-periphery relationships of the capitalist world-system. Dependentistas contended that development and underdevelopment constituted each other through a relational process. This is contrary to the modernization theories' conceptualization of each country as an autonomous unit that develops through stages.

2   The modern-traditional dichotomy is abstract, formal, and ahistorical. This modernization-theory dichotomy does not characterize correctly or explain adequately the social processes underlying development and underdevelopment. The modern-traditional opposition refers to descriptive categories (cultural or economic) at the national level that obscure structures of domination and exploitation at the world level.

3   The foreign penetration, diffusion, and acculturation of modern values, techniques, and ideas from the centers to the periphery do not necessarily produce development. In most of the cases this process contributes to the subordination of the underdeveloped countries to the centers.

4   Dependentistas consider incorrect the assumption that equates development to passing through the same "stages" of the so-called advanced societies. Since historical time is not—as the modernization theories presuppose—chronological and unilinear, the experience of the metropolitan societies cannot be repeated. Underdevelopment is a specific experience that needs to be analyzed as a historical and structural process. Development and underdevel-

opment coexist simultaneously in historical time. The coevalness of both processes is overtly recognized.

5 Dependency is an approach that attempts to explain why Latin American countries did not develop similarly to the center. Dependency is understood as a relation of subordination in the international capitalist system, rather than as a result of archaic, traditional, or feudal structures. The latter is a result of the modern, capitalist structures. Thus, underdevelopment involves an interrelation of "external" and "internal" elements.

6 The correct approach to explain the underdevelopment of Latin America is not the structural-functionalist method, but the historical-structural methodology.

Dependency writers basically agreed on these points. They all criticized the universalistic, eternal time/space framework of the modernization theories. The interesting questions for our topic are: did the dependentistas break completely with the Eurocentric premises of time distanciation and denial of coevalness presupposed by the modernization and mode of production theories? Did they successfully overcome developmentalism as a geoculture of the world-system?

One of the major weaknesses of the dependentista approach was that their solution for eliminating dependency was still caught in the categories of developmentalist ideology. The boundaries of the questions asked limit the answers found. Dependency questions were trapped in the problematic of modernity: what are the obstacles to national development? How to achieve autonomous national development? Dependency assumed the modernist idea that progress was possible through a rational organization of society, where each nation-state could achieve an autonomous national development through the conscious, sovereign, and free control of its destiny.

The main difference between the developmentalist ideas of cepalistas and dependentistas was that for the former, autonomous national development could be achieved within capitalism, while for the latter, it could not be achieved under the capitalist world-system. The establishment of socialism in each nation-state was the dependentista prescription for the rational organization of autonomous national development. The "national" bourgeoisie, allied to foreign capital interests, represented a reactionary force, as opposed to the exploited classes, which would purportedly lead the revolutionary struggle for socialism. The Cuban Revolution became the myth of socialist national development. Thus, for the dependentistas, the major obstacle to autonomous national development was the capitalist system, and the solution was to delink and build socialism at the level of the nation-state.

This position is summarized by the Brazilian radical dependentista Vania Bambirra. Here Bambirra responds to Octavio Rodriguez's cepalist critique of the dependentistas' denial of autonomous national development under capitalism: "None of the [dependentista] authors 'analyzed' by Rodriguez deny the possibility of autonomous national development, since that would be absurd. Yet they do demonstrate that autonomous national development cannot be led by the dependent bourgeoisie. This leads them to the logical conclusion, implicit in some, explicit in others, that the historical necessity for the development of the productive forces in Latin America be impelled by a superior socioeconomic system, that is, socialism" (1978, 88). He continues, "The struggle for socialism in countries such as those of Latin America is within the framework of the struggle for autonomous national development that capitalism cannot achieve" (ibid., 99).

Dependency ideas must be understood as part of the longue durée of modernity ideas in Latin America. Autonomous national development has been a central ideological theme of the modern world-system since the eighteenth century. Dependentistas reproduced the illusion that rational organization and development could be achieved from the control of the nation-state. This contradicted the position that development and underdevelopment were the result of structural relations within the capitalist world-system. The same contradiction is found in Andre Gunder Frank. Although Frank defined capitalism as a single world-system beyond the nation-state, he still believed it was possible to delink or break with the world-system at the nation-state level (Frank 1970, 11, 104, 150; Frank 1969b, chap. 25). This implied that a revolutionary process at the national level could insulate the country from the global system. However, as we know today, it is impossible to transform a system that operates on a world scale by privileging the control or administration of the nation-state (Wallerstein 1992a). No "rational" control of the nation-state would alter the location of a country in the international division of labor. Rational planning and control of the nation-state contributes to the developmentalist illusion of eliminating the inequalities of the capitalist world-system from a nation-state level.

In the capitalist world-system, a peripheral nation-state may experience transformations in its form of incorporation to the capitalist world-economy, and a minority of them might even move to a semiperipheral position. However, to break with or transform the whole system from a nation-state level is completely beyond the range of possibilities for peripheral nation-states (Wallerstein 1992a, 1992b). Therefore, a global problem cannot have a national solution. This is not to deny the importance of political interventions at the nation-state level. The point here is not to reify the nation-state but to understand the limits of political interventions at this level for the long-term transformation of a system that operates at a world scale. The nation-state, although still an important institution of historical capitalism, is a limited space for radical political and social transformations. Collective agencies in the periphery need a global scope in order to make an effective political intervention in the capitalist world-system. Social struggles below and above the nation-state are strategic spaces of political intervention that are frequently ignored when the focus of the movements privileges the nation-state. The social movements' local and global connections are crucial for effective political intervention. The dependentistas overlooked this, due in part to their tendency to privilege the nation-state as the unit of analysis. This had terrible political consequences for the Latin American Left and the credibility of the dependentista political project. The political failure contributed to the demise of the dependentista school. The decline of this school enabled the reemergence of old developmentalist ideas in the region. Although the problem was shared by most dependentista theorists, some dependentistas reproduced new versions of the Eurocentric denial of coevalness. Cardoso's version of dependency theory is a good example.

CARDOSO'S DEVELOPMENTALISM

Fernando Henrique Cardoso and Enzo Faletto together developed a typology to understand the diverse national situations of dependency. They make an analytical distinction between autonomy-dependency relationships, center-periphery relationships, and development-underdevelopment (Cardoso and Faletto 1969, 24–25). *Dependency* refers to the conditions of existence and function of the economic and political systems at the national level and can be demonstrated by drawing out their internal and external linkages. *Periphery* refers to the role underdeveloped economies play in the international markets without addressing the sociopolitical factors implied in the situations of dependency. *Underdevelopment* refers to a developmental stage of the productive system (forces of production) rather than to the external (e.g., colonialism, periphery of the world market) or internal (e.g., socialism, capitalism) control of the economic decision making. Thus, the dependent-autonomous continuum refers mostly to the political system within the nation-state; the center-periphery continuum addresses the roles played in the international market; and the development-underdevelopment continuum refers to the developmental stages of the economic system. These analytical distinctions allow Cardoso to state that a nation-state can develop its economic system, even to the extent of producing capital goods, despite not having an autonomous control over the decision-making process—that is, while being dependent. This is what he calls "dependent development." The reverse is also possible—that is, autonomous underdeveloped nation-states. This schema serves as the basis for the following typology of national societies.

1. Autonomous-Developed (centers): the United States and Western Europe, for example.
2. Dependent-Developed (peripheral): Brazil and Argentina, for example.
3. Autonomous-Underdeveloped (nonperipheral): Algeria, Cuba, and China, for example.
4. Dependent-Underdeveloped (peripheral): Central America, the Caribbean, Bolivia, and Peru, for example.

The countries at levels 2 and 4 are peripheral because they are still subordinated to the central economies in the international capitalist system. The social mechanism for this subordination is the internal system of domination or the internal relations of forces that produce dependency rather than autonomy in the political system. If, through a reformist or revolutionary process, a country achieves autonomous decision making at the nation-state level, then it can stop being a peripheral country in the capitalist world-economy, even if it still continues being a one-crop export economy. The difference among dependent societies is whether they are developed (industrialized) or underdeveloped (agrarian), and this is related to processes internal to the nation-state in terms of who controls the main productive activities (enclave economies vs. population economies) and of the "stage of development" of the productive system. The countries at level 3 are non-dependent because they have broken their links with particular internal systems of domination through revolutionary processes that, according to Cardoso, have liberated them from being incorporated to an imperialist system of domination. Although they are still economically underdeveloped because they have not industrialized, they enjoy autonomous decision making over their economic system. Thus, these countries are nonperipheral in that they are not politically dominated and economically subordinated by the metropolitan centers in the international market. For Cardoso, nation-states can achieve an autonomous decision making and a nonperipheral location in the international system without yet achieving development (level 3 countries). The reverse is also possible: nation-states can be dependent and peripheral, and still achieve development (level 2 countries). Level 1 nation-states are the centers because they are in the only group of countries with developed economic systems together with autonomous political systems. This enables the centers to have a dominant and powerful position in the international market.

Since all Latin American societies, with the exception of Cuba, are classified in levels 2 and 4, Cardoso's and Faletto's book concentrates on the different situations of dependency among these countries. They have developed another typology for the bifurcation of dependent societies' trajectories between those that industrialized and those that remain primary producers (agricultural or mining).

Enclave economies are those wherein the production for export is directly controlled by foreign capital (financial dependency), originating the capital accumulation externally. Nationally controlled export economies are those wherein the production for export is controlled by "national" capital (commercial dependency), originating capital accumulation internally. New dependency is the post-1950 form of dependency wherein the multinational corporations invest directly in the industrialization of the periphery, not for exports but to conquer their internal market (financial and/or industrial dependency or technological dependency). Although capital accumulation often originates, similar to the enclaves, in the exterior, there is a major difference: most of the industrial production is sold in the internal markets. These diverse forms of dependency articulate with the "external" phases of capitalism in the centers, such as competitive capitalism, monopolistic capitalism, industrial capitalism, or financial capitalism (Cardoso 1973, 96; Cardoso 1985, 141–42).

The dependent societies that industrialized were those with nationally controlled peripheral economies. According to Cardoso and Faletto, they industrialized during the 1930s world depression when a developmentalist alliance emerged due to the crisis of the agrarian oligarchy. The local capitalists spontaneously developed an import-substitution industrialization program. However, after 1950, once the centers recovered from the world crisis, these same countries were dominated by multinational capital. The latter established alliances with the state and factions of local capitalists to control Latin American internal markets. According to Cardoso, only at this phase can we talk of an international capitalist mode of production; before this phase, there was only an international capitalist market (Cardoso 1985, 209). The diverse forms of dependency (enclave, nationally controlled export economies, new dependency) are not stages, but characterizations of national social formations (ibid., 147). Sometimes, these three forms can coexist with a hierarchical articulation within a nation-state; that is, one form dominates and subordinates the others. For Cardoso, it is the internal processes of the nation-state and not the cultural or structural location in the international division of labor that determines if a country is peripheral, dependent, and underdeveloped. The propositions that an autonomous decision-making process at the nation-state level is possible for every country to achieve, that dependency is mainly an internal relation of forces in favor of foreign actors, and that underdevelopment is a backward stage of the productive system lead Cardoso to developmentalist premises. For Cardoso, development and underdevelopment are defined in terms of the advanced or backward technology in the productive system within a nation-state. European and American standards of industrialization are what serve as a parameter for development and underdevelopment. The deficiencies of capitalist development and the presence of precapitalist forms of production within the boundaries of the nation-state are what prevent Latin American societies from completing the expanded reproduction of capital (ibid., 50). These deficiencies contribute to a subordinate position in the international division of labor. Thus, the explanation is centered on the political dynamics internal to the nation-state, not in the global or international capitalist system.

Accordingly, for Cardoso, there are three ways of achieving development for dependent societies. The first path to development is when a dependent nation-state achieves an autonomous decision-making process and reorganizes its economy in a nonperipheral way. This could be done through a revolution or a political reform that transforms the internal relation of forces creating the possibilities for advancing the stages of development. The second path is when nationally controlled, export-oriented dependent economies generate an internal capital accumulation that allows them to industrialize. Although they may experience trade dependency, still there is some process of "national" capitalist accumulation that fosters industrialization. The third path of development is when a country that is dependent (meaning being nonautonomous in the decision-making processes internal to the nation-state) and peripheral (meaning economically subordinate in the international market) achieves development by the industrial expansion and investments of multinational corporations. This new character of dependency comes through the control and creation of new technologies by multinational enterprises, which ensures them a key role in the global system of capitalist accumulation (Cardoso 1973, 117; Cardoso 1985, 210–11). In this manner, for Cardoso, peripheral industrialization depends on the centers for new technologies and advanced machinery. However, in his opinion, this new character of dependency is equivalent to development because it contributes to the expansion of industrial capitalism (i.e., growth of wage-labor relations and development of the productive forces).

In Cardoso's view the inequalities and "underdevelopment" of the productive process at the national level foster the inequalities and dependency at the international level. The capitalist world market is conceptualized as an international (multiple national social formations) unequal structure of dominant and subordinate nations wherein the centers' capital penetrates dependent societies. Thus, although for Cardoso capitalism has laws of motion that remain constant in the centers and the periphery, a single capitalist social system in which every country forms an integral part does not exist. There are as many capitalist systems (or capitalist social formations) as there are nation-states in the world. The trade and capital investments among different nations and corporations with uneven levels of capitalist development are responsible for an "inter-national," unequal capitalist market. For Cardoso, the main goal is to achieve development, meaning to industrialize. Cardoso's proposition of stages of development of the productive forces assumes a denial of coevalness. There are advanced and backward stages of development internal to a nation-state. This is related to Euro-centric premises where the models of so-called advanced societies are the United States and Europe, while the rest of the world is conceived as backward. Cardoso replaced the old stagism of both modernization and mode-of-production theory with a new form of denial of coevalness based on the technology used in the productive system within a nation-state.

DEPENDENTISTAS' UNDERESTIMATION OF CULTURE

Dependentistas developed a neo-Marxist political-economy approach. Most dependentista analysis privileged the economic and political aspects of social processes at the expense of cultural and ideological determinations. Culture was perceived as instrumental to capitalist accumulation processes. In many respects dependentistas reproduced some of the economic reductionism that had been criticized in orthodox Marxist approaches. This led to two problems: first, an underestimation of the Latin American colonial/racial hierarchies; and second, an analytical impoverishment of the complexities of political-economic processes.

For most dependentistas, the "economy" was the privileged sphere of social analysis. Categories such as "gender" and "race" were frequently ignored, and when used they were reduced to class or to an economic logic. Aníbal Quijano is one of the few exceptions to this. He has developed the concept of "coloniality of power" to understand the present racial hierarchies in Latin America. According to Quijano, the social classification of peoples in Latin America has been hegemonized by white Creole elites throughout a long historical process of colonial/racial domination. Categories of modernity such as citizenship, democracy, and national identity have been historically constructed through two axial divisions: (1) between labor and capital; (2) between Europeans and non-Europeans (Quijano 1993a); and, I will add, (3) between men and women. White male elites hegemonized these axial divisions. According to the concept of coloniality of power developed by Quijano, even after independence, when the formal juridical and military control of the state passes from the imperial power to the newly independent state, white Creole elites continue to control the economic, cultural, and political structures of the society (ibid.). This continuity of power relations from colonial to postcolonial times allows the white elites to classify populations and to exclude people of color from the categories of full citizenship in the imagined community called the "nation." The civil, political, and social rights that citizenship provides to the members of the nation are never fully extended to colonial subjects such as Indians, blacks, zambos, and mulattoes. "Internal colonial" groups remain as "second-class citizens," never having full access to the rights of citizens. Coloniality is a sociocultural relationship between Europeans and non-Europeans that is constantly reproduced as long as the power structures are dominated by the white Creole elites and the cultural construction of non-European peoples as "inferior others" continues.

What is implied in the notion of coloniality of power is that the world has not fully decolonized. The first decolonization was incomplete. It was limited to the juridicopolitical "independence" from the European imperial states. The "second decolonization" will have to address the racial, ethnic, sexual, gender, and economic hierarchies that the first decolonization left in place. As a result, the world needs a second decolonization different and more radical than the first one.

Many leftist projects in Latin America following the dependentista underestimation of racial/ethnic hierarchies have reproduced, within their organizations and when controlling state power, white Creole domination over non-European people. The Latin American "Left" never radically problematized the racial/ethnic hierarchies built during the European colonial expansion and still present in Latin America's coloniality of power. For instance, the conflicts between the Sandinistas and the Misquitos in Nicaragua emerged as part of the reproduction of the old racial/colonial hierarchies (Vila 1992). This was not a conflict created by the CIA, as Sandinistas used to portray it. The Sandinistas reproduced the historical coloniality of power between the Pacific coast and the Atlantic coast in Nicaragua. The white Creole elites on the Pacific coast hegemonized the political, cultural, and economic relations that subordinated blacks and Indians on the Atlantic coast. The differences between the Somocista dictatorship and the Sandinista regime were not that great when it came to social relations with colonial/racial others.

No radical project in Latin America can be successful without dismantling these colonial/racial hierarchies. This requirement affects not only the scope of "revolutionary processes" but also the democratization of the social hierarchies. The underestimation of the problems of coloniality has been an important factor contributing to the popular disillusionment with leftist projects in Latin America. The denial of coevalness in developmentalist dependency discourses reinforces the coloniality of power within the nation-state by privileging white Creole elites in the name of technical progress and superior knowledge. Poor and marginalized regions within the nation-state—where black, mulatto, and Indian populations frequently live—are portrayed by left-wing regimes as "backward" and "underdeveloped" due to the "laziness" and "bad habits" of these regions' inhabitants. Thus *coloniality* refers to the long-term continuities of the racial hierarchies from the time of European colonialism to the formation of nation-states in the Americas. When it comes to the coloniality of power in Latin America, the difference between the left-wing and right-wing regimes is not that great. Today there is a coloniality of power in all of Latin America even when colonial administrations have disappeared.

The second problem with the dependentistas' underestimation of cultural and ideological dynamics is that it impoverishes their own political-economy approach. Symbolic/ideological strategies, as well as Eurocentric forms of knowledge, are constitutive of the political economy of the capitalist world-system. Global symbolic/ideological strategies are an important structuring logic of the core-periphery relationships in the capitalist world-system. For instance, core states develop ideological/symbolic strategies by fostering "Occidentalist" (Mignolo 1995) forms of knowledge that privilege the "West over the rest." This is clearly seen in developmentalist discourses, which has become a "scientific" form of knowledge in the last fifty years. This knowledge privileged the West as the model of development. Developmentalist discourse offers a recipe about how to become like the West.

Although the dependentistas struggled against universalist or Occidentalist forms of knowledge, they perceived such knowledge as a superstructure or an epiphenomenon of some economic infrastructure. Dependentistas never perceived this knowledge as constitutive of Latin America's political economy. Constructing peripheral zones such as Africa and Latin America as regions with "problems" in their stages of development concealed European and Euro-American responsibility in the exploitation of these continents. The construction of "pathological" regions in the periphery, as opposed to the "normal" development patterns of the West, justified an even more intense political and economic intervention from imperial powers. By treating the other as underdeveloped and backward, metropolitan exploitation and domination were justified in the name of the civilizing mission.

Moreover, the Euro-American imperial state has developed global symbolic/ideological strategies to showcase peripheral regions or ethnic groups, as opposed to challenging peripheral countries or ethnic groups. These strategies are material and constitutive of global political-economic processes. They are economically expensive because they entail the investment of capital in unprofitable forms such as credits, aid, and assistance programs. Nevertheless, symbolic profits could translate into economic profits in the long run.

How to explain the so-called Southeast Asian miracle without an understanding of global ideological and cultural strategies? Since the 1950s, the United States has showcased several peripheral countries in different regions of the world where communist regimes represented a challenge, such as Greece vis-à-vis Eastern Europe, Taiwan vis-à-vis China, South Korea vis-à-vis North Korea; in the 1960s, Nigeria vis-à-vis Tanzania, Puerto Rico vis-à-vis Cuba; and in the 1980s, Jamaica vis-à-vis Grenada, Costa Rica vis-à-vis Nicaragua. Other showcases in the region include Brazil in the 1960s (the so-called Brazilian miracle) and, more recently, Mexico and Chile in the 1990s as post–Cold War neoliberal showcases. Compared to other countries, all of these showcases received disproportionately large sums of U.S. foreign aid and favorable conditions for economic growth, such as flexible terms for paying their debts, special tariff agreements that made commodities produced in these areas accessible to the metropolitan markets, and/or technological transfers. Most of these showcases' success lasted for several years, but subsequently failed. However, they were crucial to produce an ideological hegemony over Third World peoples in favor of pro-U.S. developmentalist programs. Developmentalist ideology is a crucial constitutive element in the hegemony of the West. The capitalist world-system gains credibility by developing a few successful semiperipheral cases. These are civilizational and cultural strategies to gain consent and to demonstrate the "superiority" of the West.

It would be extremely difficult to answer the following questions without an understanding of global symbolic/ideological strategies: why did U.S. officials in Taiwan and South Korea implement, finance, support, and organize a radical agrarian reform in the early 1950s, while in Guatemala a much milder agrarian reform put forward by the Arbenz administration during the same years met with a CIA-backed coup d'état? Why did the U.S. government support an agrarian reform in Puerto Rico that forced U.S. corporations to sell all land in excess of five hundred acres (Dietz 1986)? Why was the U.S. government willing to sacrifice its corporate economic interests in Taiwan, South Korea, and Puerto Rico, but not its economic interests in Chile or Guatemala? Why did the import-substitution industrialization in Japan, Taiwan, and South Korea not lead to deficits in balance of payments as it did in Latin America? An economic reductionist approach to political economy simply cannot answer these questions. Dependentista analysis, by not taking into consideration global symbolic/ideological strategies, has impoverished the political-economy approach.

CONCLUSION

Developmentalism, the denial of coevalness, and the concealment of coloniality of power in Latin America are three conceptual limitations of the dependentista school. These three conceptual processes are historically interrelated in the geoculture of the capitalist world-system. The construction of the other as inhabiting a distant space and a past time emerged simultaneously with the formation of a "modern/colonial capitalist world-system" (Mignolo 2000d) with its colonial/racial hierarchies. This created the historical conditions of possibility for the emergence of developmentalism, proposing that the solution to backwardness in time is to develop, to catch up with the West.

Dependentistas form part of the longue dureé of the ideology of modernity in Latin America. Dependentistas were caught up in developmentalist assumptions similar to the intellectual currents they attempted to criticize. By privileging national development and the control of the nation-state, they reproduced the illusion that development occurs through rational organization and planning at the level of the nation-state. This emphasis contributed to overlooking alternative and more strategic antisystemic political interven-

tions below (local) and above (global) the nation-state. Moreover, dependentistas underestimated the coloniality of power in Latin America. This
obscured the ongoing existence of the region's racial/ethnic hierarchies.
Power relations in the region are constituted by racial/ethnic hierarchies that
have a long colonial history. Leftist movements influenced by the dependentista paradigm, have reproduced white Creole domination when in control of the nation-state. Thus there can be no radical project in the region
without decolonizing power relations.

Finally, both the developmentalist assumptions and the underestimation
of coloniality of power, together with the production of new forms of denial
of coevalness, has led some dependentistas, such as Fernando Henrique
Cardoso, to Eurocentric assumptions about technical progress and development. This contributes to an understanding of the current complicity of
many old dependentistas with the recent dominant neoliberal global designs
in the region.

NOTES

Unless otherwise indicated, all English translations are my own.

1   CEPAL was the Comisión Económica para América Latina (ECLA), created by
    the United Nations in 1948. Raúl Prebisch was an Argentinean economist, the
    first director of CEPAL, and a leading theorist of the first school of economic
    thought in the periphery, known worldwide as the Prebisch-CEPAL school
    (Grosfoguel 1997).

2   Alianza Popular Revolucionaria Americana (APRA) was the party founded by
    Victor Raúl Haya de la Torre in Peru.

PART FOUR

RELIGION, LIBERATION, AND THE NARRATIVES OF SECULARISM

The authors in this section elaborate on a particular articulation of modernity and coloniality in Latin America. Enrique Dussel, one of the most prominent scholars of the philosophy of liberation, relates this field to the postmodern debate and to the agenda of Latin American studies in order to map the transformation of Latin Americanism and its particular interactions with European philosophy. According to Dussel, "The philosophy of liberation could be considered an expression of postmodern thought avant la lettre, a truly transmodern movement that appreciates postmodern criticism but is able to deconstruct it from a global peripheral perspective in order to reconstruct it according to the concrete political demands of subaltern groups."

In a similar critical direction, Michael Löwy expands on Dussel's overview in an attempt to include other aspects of liberation theology, and he analyzes elements relating to the genealogy of this movement. He proposes the concept "Christianism of liberation" as a denomination that could embrace "both religious culture and social network, faith and praxis. Liberation theology in the strict sense is only one aspect (though an important one) of this broad socioreligious reality." As "a preferential option for the poor," liberation theology strengthens in response to both Latin American social conditions and the proliferation of dictatorships in the 1970s. According to Löwy, it is with the Peruvian Gustavo Gutiérrez's publication of *Liberation Theology: Perspectives* (1971) that liberation theology is born. From this perspective, the poor are not considered just passive recipients of charitable work, but rather agents of their own liberation. Exploring the connections between liberation theology, modernity, and secularism—in other words, between religion and politics—Löwy concludes that "at the institutional level, separation and autonomy are indispensable; but in the ethical-political domain, compromised engagement becomes the essential imperative."

Nelson Maldonado explores "how secularism creatively reproduces imperial discursive structures that have been historically embedded in European Christianity." For Maldonado, secularism—the invitation to leave the past behind, "*to live in the century*," by embracing "new standards of meaning and rationality"—"has become in many ways the religion of the modern world." His study evaluates "the contributions of contemporary Latin American and Latina/o criticism for an overcoming of the limits of secular discourse" in the context of new elaborations on modernity, postmodernity, and postcolonial theory. He examines the intersections between theological discourse, the humanities, and social sciences, particularly dependency theory. In an insightful overview of modern European philosophy, from Kant to Vattimo, Maldonado approaches the question "Is postcolonialism postsecular?" He finds some of the answers in Dussel's concept of transmodernity, thereby adding a new dimension to the study of the topics addressed in this volume.

PHILOSOPHY OF LIBERATION, THE POSTMODERN DEBATE, AND LATIN AMERICAN STUDIES

Enrique Dussel

The operative theoretical framework that was constructed in the late 1990s, as much within Latin America as by Latin American scholars in the United States (philosophers, literary critics, and anthropologists, as well as historians, sociologists, etc.), has diversified and acquired such complexity that it has become necessary to map a topography of these positions in order to deepen the debate. In other words, the perspectives, the categories, the planes of "localization" of subjects within theoretical and interpretative discourse have changed so much that it has become difficult to continue the Latin American debate without a preliminary understanding of its theoretical and conceptual basis. The old Latin Americanism seems to have become a museum object rather than an obligatory reference point. Let us briefly look at the topography of the debate, knowing that it offers only "one" possible interpretation.

"LATIN AMERICAN THOUGHT": FROM THE END OF THE
SECOND EUROPEAN–NORTH AMERICAN WAR

In the mid-1940s, toward the end of the second European–North American War, a group of young philosophers (Leopoldo Zea in Mexico, Arturo Ardao in Uruguay, Francisco Romero in Argentina, to name a few) returned to the problematic debate of "our (Latin) America" ("Nuestra América"), which had begun in the nineteenth century with Alberdi, Bello, and Martí, and was continued into the early part of the twentieth century with Mariátegui, Vasconcelos, and Samuel Ramos, among many others. In response to North American pan-Americanism there emerged an interpretation of Latin America that was distinct and not to be confused with the Ibero-Americanism of Franco's Spain.

The members of the "institutionalized" academic philosophy—in the pre-war era, according to periodization proposed by Francisco Romero—had begun to forge contacts throughout the Latin American continent. They sought to understand the "history" of Latin American thought, forgotten thanks to the focus on Europe and the United States. Leopoldo Zea's *America en la Historia* (1957) exemplifies the ideas of this era. The theoretical framework of this generation was influenced by philosophers such as Husserl, Heidegger, Ortega y Gasset, and Sartre, or historians such as Toynbee. The young philosophers revisited the heroes of the emancipation from the beginning of the nineteenth century (so as not to recover the colonial era), in order to rethink its ideal of freedom with respect to the United States, which had established its hegemony in the West since 1945, at the beginning of the Cold War. Contemporaneously in Africa, Placide Tempels published *La philosophie bantoue* (1949). In Asia and India Mahatma Gandhi was rediscovering "Hindu thought" as an emancipatory catalyst for the former British colony. The postwar era culminated around 1968, a time of great political uprising for students and intellectuals, one marked by the 1966 Cultural Revolution in China and echoed in the 1968 "May Movement" in France, in the Vietnam War demonstrations in the United States, in Mexico's Tlatelolco, and in the 1969 Cordobazo in Argentina.

MODERNITY/POSTMODERNITY IN EUROPE
AND THE UNITED STATES

In the 1970s the atmosphere of European philosophy began to change. The student uprisings had exhausted a portion of the Left (which had in part abandoned the Marxist tradition), while others had become bureaucratized (constituting "standard" Marxism, including Althusserian "classism"). The gradual emergence of a critique of universalism and dogmatism from non-traditional positions began. Michel Foucault, a protagonist of the student protests that took place in Nanterre in 1968, posited a critique of the meta-physical and ahistorical positions of standard Marxism (the proletariat as a "Messianic subject," the idea of history as a necessary progression, the concept of macrostructural power as the only existent power, etc.).[1] Gilles Deleuze, Jacques Derrida, and Jean-François Lyotard in France and Gianni Vattimo in Italy—all of them with very different viewpoints—rose up against "modern reason," a concept that Emmanuel Levinas approached through the category of "totality" (in *Totalité et infini*, published in the Phaenomeno-logica collection by Nijhoff, 1971).[2] Lyotard's *The Postmodern Condition* (1979) reads like a manifesto. In the third line of the introduction he states that "the word [*postmoderne*] is in current use on the American continent among so-ciologists and critics" and that "it designates the state of our culture follow-ing the transformations which, since the end of the nineteenth century, have altered the game rules for science, literature, and the arts. The present study will place these transformations in the context of the crisis of narratives" (Lyotard 1984, xxiii).[3]

From Heidegger, with his critique of the subjectivity of the subject, and even more from Nietzsche, with his critique of the subject, of current values, truth, and metaphysics, the "postmodern" movement is not only opposed to standard Marxism but also demonstrates that universalism has the same connotations of epistemological violence that we find, on a larger scale, in modern rationality (Dussel 1974 [1969]). In contrast to the unicity of the dominant being, the concepts of *différance*, multiplicity, plurality, fragmen-tation, as well as the process of deconstruction of all macronarratives, start to develop.

In the United States, Fredric Jameson's *Postmodernism, or, The Cultural Logic of Late Capitalism* (1991) outlines a new stage in this process. As for Richard Rorty, he is, in my opinion, a more anti-foundationalist and skeptical intel-lectual, who only collaterally could be considered part of the "postmodern" tradition.

In Latin America the reception of the postmodern movement emerged in the late 1980s. Hermann Herlinghaus's and Monika Walter's *Postmodernidad en la periferia: Enfoques latinoamericanos de la nueva teoria* (1997)[4] and the articles compiled by John Beverley, Michael Aronna, and José Oviedo in *The Postmod-ernism Debate in Latin America* (1995) include a wide range of contributions to this topic, the earliest dating from the mid-1980s.[5]

In general, these publications give evidence of a generation that is experiencing a certain disenchantment at the close of an era in Latin America, disenchantment not only with populism but also with all of the promise that was stirred by the Cuban Revolution in 1959, then confronted by the fall of socialism in 1989. This generation attempts to confront the cultural hybridity of a peripheral modernity that no longer believes in utopian change. They seek to evade the simplification of the dualities of center-periphery, progress-underdevelopment, tradition-modernity, domination-liberation, and they operate, instead, within the heterogeneous plurality and the fragmentary and differential conditions that characterize urban, transnational cultures. Now it is the social anthropologists (particularly Néstor García Canclini's *Culturas híbridas* [1989]) and the literary critics who are producing a new interpretation of Latin America (see Follari 1991; Arriarán 1997; Maliandi 1993).

The work of Santiago Castro-Gómez is of great interest since it represents a good example of a postmodern philosophy produced from Latin America.[6] His criticism is geared against progressive Latin American thought, in contrast to Adolfo Sánchez Vázquez, Franz Hinkelammert, Pablo Guadarrama, Arturo Roig, Leopoldo Zea, Augusto Salazar-Bondy, and so on.[7] In all of these cases, including my own, the argument is as follows: according to Castro-Gómez, these philosophers, under the pretense of criticizing modernity, in not being conscious of the "localization" of their own discourse, and for not having had the Foucauldian tools to undertake an epistemic archaeology, which would have permitted a reconstruction of the modern theoretical framework, have in one way or another fallen back into modernity (if they had strayed from it). To speak of the subject, of history, of domination, of external dependence, of the oppression of social classes, using categories such as totality, exteriority, liberation, hope, is to fall back into a moment that does not take seriously the "political disenchantment" that has impacted current culture so deeply. To speak in terms of macro-institutions such as the state, the nation, or the city, or about epic heroic narratives, results in the loss of meaning of micro, heterogeneous, plural, hybrid and complex realities. According to Castro-Gómez, "The other of totality is the poor, the oppressed, the one who, by being located outside the system, becomes the only source of spiritual renewal. There, in the exterior of the system, in the ethos of oppressed societies, people have values that are very different from those that prevail in the center. . . . With this, Dussel creates a second reduction: that of converting the poor in some kind of transcendent subject, through which Latin American history will find its meaning. This is the opposite side of postmodernity, because Dussel attempts not to de-centralize the Enlightened subject, but to replace it by another absolute subject" (1996, 39–40).[8]

What Castro-Gómez does not state is that Foucault criticizes certain forms of the subject but relegitimizes others; he criticizes certain forms of making history that depart from a priori and necessary laws, but reemphasizes a genetic-epistemological history. Often Castro-Gómez is seduced by the fetishism of formulaic thought, and he does not take into consideration that a certain criticism of the subject is necessary in order to reconstruct a deeper vision of it: one must recognize that it is necessary to criticize the external causes of Latin American underdevelopment in order to integrate it into a more comprehensive interpretation, that it is necessary to not dismiss micro-institutions (forgotten by the descriptions of the macro) in order to connect them to these macro-institutions, that power is mutually and relationally constituted between social subjects, but that, in any case, the power of the state or the power of a hegemonic nation (such as the United States) continues to exist. When one criticizes one unilaterality with another, one falls into that which is being criticized. From a panoptical postmodern criticism some critics return to the claim of universalism that was characteristic of modernity. According to Eduardo Mendieta, "Postmodernity perpetuates the hegemonic intention of modernity and Christianity, by denying other peoples the possibility to name their own history and to articulate their own self-reflexive discourse" (Castro-Gómez and Mendieta 1998, 159).

In Europe, on the other hand, a certain universalist rationalism such as that of Karl-Otto Apel or Jürgen Habermas, which distrusts fascist irrationalism (of the German Nazi era), posits that the objective is to "complete the task of modernity" as a critical/discursive and democratic form of rationality. The intent is to defend the significance of reason against the opinion of skeptical intellectuals, such as Richard Rorty. To sum up, in the North the debate was established between the pretense of universal rationality and the affirmation of difference, that is, the negation of the subject, the deconstruction of history, progress, values, metaphysics, and so on.

THE EMERGENCE OF CRITICAL THOUGHT IN THE POSTCOLONIAL PERIPHERY: THE PHILOSOPHY OF LIBERATION

In 1970 Ranajit Guha initiated a theoretical transformation that would later serve as the foundation of subaltern studies.[9] Through a "situated" reading of Foucault, and coming from a previous position of standard Marxism, Guha began to deviate from the trodden paths of the past toward the study of mass popular culture and the culture of groups or subaltern classes in India. This movement was later enriched with the participation of intellectuals such as Gayatri Spivak (1987, 1988a [1985], 1993), Homi Bhabha (1994a),

Gyan Prakash, Dipesh Chakrabarty, and many others.[10] All of them, without abandoning Marxism, were informed by the epistemologies of Foucault and Lacan. Now equipped with new instruments of critical analysis, they could engage in issues of gender, culture, and politics and in critiques of racism.

In *Orientalism: Western Conceptions of the Orient* (1978) Edward Said posits a critical analysis of European studies on Asia. With respect to Africa, Tempels's position is criticized, three decades after his work is published, in Paulin Hountondji's *Sur la philosophie africaine: Critique de l'ethnophilosophie* (1977). Throughout the periphery (Africa, Asia, and Latin America) there began to emerge critical movements that utilized their own regional reality as a point of departure, and in some cases a revitalized Marxism as a point of theoretical reference.

I estimate that the Philosophy of Liberation in Latin America—which also emerged around 1970 (at roughly the same time that the first works of Guha emerged in India), and which was likewise influenced by a French philosopher, in this case Levinas—is framed by the same sorts of discoveries.[11] Nevertheless, these discoveries may be misinterpreted if the originary situation is not taken into account and, consequently, the theoretical perspective is distorted. The philosophy of liberation was never simply a mode of "Latin American thought," nor a historiography of such. It was a critical philosophy self-critically localized in the periphery, within subaltern groups. In addition, for more than twenty years (since 1976 in some cases) it has been said that the philosophy of liberation has been exhausted. Yet it seems that the opposite is true, since it was not until the late 1990s that it was actually discovered and further delved into in order to provide a South-South—and in the future a North-South—dialogue.

The originary intuition for the philosophy of liberation—a philosophical tradition that (in contrast to other movements in the fields of anthropology, history, and literary criticism) was influenced by the events of 1968—emerged from a critique of modern reason—the Cartesian subject on Heidegger's ontological criticism—which in part permitted it to sustain a radical critical position. It was also inspired by the Frankfurt School (Horkheimer, Adorno, and especially Herbert Marcuse's *One-Dimensional Man* [1964]), which illuminated the political meaning of said ontology, allowing it to be more thoroughly understood (including the Heideggerean position in its relation to Nazism). In *Para una destrucción de la historia de la ética* (1969) I quoted Heidegger: "What do we mean by world when we talk about the darkening of the world? The worldly darkening implies the weakening of spirit itself, its dissolution, consumption, and false interpretation. The dominant dimension is that of extension and numbers. . . . All of this is later on intensified in America and Russia" (Heidegger 1966, 34–35). I concluded by stating that it is necessary to say, "No to the modern world whose cycle is done, and yes to the New Man that today lives in the time of his conversion and transformation (Kehre)" (Dussel 1974 [1969], 126 n. 170).

But at the same time it was through works like Frantz Fanon's The Wretched of the Earth that we became positioned on the horizon of the struggles for liberation in the 1960s. In Argentina at that time the masses battled against the military dictatorships of Onganía, Levingston, and Lanusse. As philosophers and scholars, we assumed critical and theoretical responsibility in that process (Dussel 1994c). We endured bomb threats, expulsion from our universities and our countries, and some (like Mauricio López) were tortured and assassinated. Theoretical and practical processes were highly articulated. Critical categories began to emerge in response to modern subjectivity. Historical access was fundamental for the destruction of modernity. The genealogy of modern categories was being undertaken from a global perspective (metropolis/colony). In situating our discourse from within the world-system (which neither Foucault, Derrida, Vattimo, nor Levinas could really access), we discovered that the "I" used by the emperor king of Spain to sign his documents in 1519 was the same "I" used by Hernán Cortés when he said "I conquer" in 1521, long before Descartes produced his "ego cogito" in Amsterdam in 1637. It was not merely a matter of exploring the epistemologies of France's "Classical Age," but rather of considering how modernity has developed in the world for the past five hundred years.

The "myth of Modernity" (Dussel 1992)—that is, the idea of European superiority over the other cultures of the world—began to be sketched out five hundred years ago. Ginés de Sepúlveda was certainly one of the first great ideologists of Occidentalism (the Eurocentrism of modernity) and Bartolomé de Las Casas the creator of the first "counterdiscourse" of modernity, established from a global, center-periphery perspective.

The "excluded," the individual "being watched" in the madhouses and "classical" French panoptical prisons, had long before been anticipated by Indians who were "watched" in the "reservations" (reducciones) and "excluded" from the Latin American towns and doctrines since the sixteenth century.[12] The blacks, who were watched in the "senzala" next to the "casa grande," already existed in Santo Domingo by 1520, when the exploitation of gold in the rivers had ended and the production of sugar began. Levinas's "Other"—which in 1973, having carefully read Derrida, I termed distinto (because "di-fference" was defined as the counterpart of "id-entity")—is, in general or in abstract terms, what Foucault calls the "excluded" and the one "being watched" when making reference to the insane person who is kept in the madhouse or to the criminal who is kept in prison.[13] To see in "exteriority" merely a modern category is to distort the meaning of this Levinasian critical category, which in the philosophy of liberation is "reconstructed"—though not without the opposition of Levinas himself, who was only thinking of Europe (without even noticing) and of the pure ethical "responsibility" for the other. The philosophy of liberation soon deviates from Levinas, because it ought to consider, from a critical standpoint, its responsibility regarding the vulnerability of the other in the process of constructing a new order (with all of the ambiguities that implies). The philosopher of liberation neither represents anybody nor speaks on behalf of others (as if this were his sole vested political purpose), nor does he undertake a concrete task in order to overcome or negate some petit-bourgeois sense of guilt. The Latin American critical philosopher, as conceived by the philosophy of liberation, assumes the responsibility of fighting for the other, the victim, the woman oppressed by patriarchy, and for the future generation which will inherit a ravaged Earth, and so on—that is, it assumes responsibility for all possible sorts of alterity. And it does so with an ethical, "situated" consciousness, that of any human being with an ethical "sensibility" and the capacity to become outraged when recognizing the injustice imposed on the other.

To "localize" (in Homi Bhaba's sense) its discourse has always been the intent of the philosophy of liberation. It has sought to situate itself on the periphery of the world-system from the perspective of dominated races, from the point of view of women in a patriarchal system, from the standpoint of disadvantaged children living in misery.[14] It is clear that the theoretical tools ought to be perfected, and for that, the postmodern approach needs to be taken into consideration. But the philosophy of liberation has also assumed the categories of Karl Marx, Sigmund Freud, the hermeneutics of Paul Ricoeur, the ideas of discursive ethics, and all of the other movements that could contribute categories that are useful but not alone sufficient for formulating a discourse that could contribute to a justification of the praxis of liberation.

If it is true that there is a Hegelian story, an all encompassing and Eurocentric "master narrative," it is not true that the victims only need fragmentary microstories to represent them (see Dussel 1992, chap. 1). On the contrary, Rigoberta Menchú, the Zapatistas, black Americans, Hispanics living in the United States, feminists, the marginalized, the working class of global transnational capitalism, and so on need a historical narrative to reconstruct their memories and make sense of their struggle. A "struggle for recognition" of new rights (as Axel Honneth would put it) needs organization, hope, and an epic narrative to yield new horizons. Despair makes sense for a while, but the hope of humanity, its production, reproduction, and development is a "will to live"—which Arthur Schopenhauer—though not Nietzsche —was opposed to.

The simplistic dualisms of center-periphery, development-underdevelopment, dependence-liberation, and exploiters-exploited, all levels of gender, class, race that function in the bipolarity of dominator-dominated, civilization-barbarism, universal principles-incertitude, and totality-exteriority, should be overcome, if they are used in a superficial or reductive manner. But to overcome does not imply "to decree" its inexistence or its epistemic uselessness. On the contrary, Derridean deconstruction proposes that a text could be read from a totality of possible current-meanings, from the exteriority of the other (the latter is what permits deconstruction). These dual dialectical categories should be placed on concrete levels of greater complexity and articulated with other mediating categories on a microlevel. Nonetheless, to assume that there are no dominators and dominated, no center and periphery, and the like is to lapse into dangerously utopian or reactionary thought. The time has come in Latin America to move on to positions of greater complexity, without the fetishism or the linguistic terrorism that, without any particular validation, characterize as "antiquated" or "obsolete" positions that are expressed in a language that the speaker does not like. Class struggle will never be overcome, but it is not the only struggle; it is one among many others (those of women, environmentalists, ethnic minorities, dependent nations, and so on) and in certain conjunctures other struggles might become more urgent and of greater political significance. If the "proletariat" is not a "metaphysical subject" for all eternity, this does not mean that it is no longer a collective or intersubjective subject, one that might appear and disappear in certain historical periods. Forgetting its existence would be a grave error.

LATIN AMERICAN STUDIES IN THE UNITED STATES

Over the past three decades, in part due to the Latin American diaspora in the United States that resulted from military dictatorships, and in part due to the poverty in Latin America that was a result of the exploitation of transnational capitalism, many Latin American intellectuals (as well as many already integrated as "Hispanics" in the United States) have completely renewed the interpretive theoretical framework in the field of Latin American studies (LASA was founded in 1963), particularly within the field of literary criticism, which assumed the study of "Latin American thought," which had been, in previous decades, the terrain of philosophers. This is partially due to the fact that much of the Marxist Left, expelled from its positions in departments of philosophy, migrated toward departments of literary criticism, comparative literature, or romance languages (French in particular), a phenomenon that contributed to a theoretical sophistication never seen before, neither in the United States nor in Europe. The preponderant use of French philosophers (Sartre, Foucault, Derrida, Lyotard, Baudrillard, etc.) is also explained by the fact that this theoretical movement was born in French departments (and not in the usually more traditional and conservative departments of English).[15]

If we then add cultural studies, particularly in the United Kingdom, which also benefits from the contributions of the Latin American diaspora (for example, Stuart Hall, of Jamaican origin, and Ernesto Laclau), we can see that the panorama has indeed broadened a great deal.

The field of subaltern studies, coming from India as well as from the Afro-American and Afro-Caribbean "thought" and "philosophy," which currently are in a process of expansion, allowed for a productive discussion of the innovative hypothesis of postcolonial reason, which emerged in Asia and Africa following the emancipation of many of the nations on these continents after World War II.[16] But then it becomes evident that Latin American thought and the philosophy of liberation had already raised many of the questions that comprise the current debate in Asia and Africa. A "subaltern Latin American study" returns to many of the topics previously addressed in the Latin American philosophical tradition of the 1960s, which has apparently been forgotten (in part because the specialists in literary criticism were not the protagonists in the philosophical discussions of that era).

For this reason, Alberto Moreiras explains the necessity of a critique of the first Latin Americanism (as much of Latin American studies in the United States as of Latin American thought on the continent itself), as well as of a neo-Latin Americanism. The task of the second Latin Americanism would be "to produce itself as an anti-conceptual, anti-representational apparatus, whose main function would be to disturb the tendency of epistemic representation to advance towards its total cancellation."[17]

In response to the interpretation of Said's Orientalism, a certain Occidentalism is also discovered (the modern self-recognition of Europe itself) and consequently a post-Occidentalism, theorized by Roberto Fernandez Retamar and Fernando Coronil. According to Coronil, "Occidentalism is thus the expression of a constitutive relationship between Western representations of cultural difference and worldwide Western dominance. Challenging Occidentalism requires that it be unsettled as a mode of representation that produces polarized and hierarchical conceptions of the West and its Others" (1997, 14–15). Coronil's postcolonialism is thus the sort of transmodernity that we are proposing in other works. The postmodern is still European, Western. The post-Occidental or transmodern goes beyond modernity (and postmodernity) and is more closely related to the Latin American situation, whose "Westernization" is greater than that experienced in Africa and Asia. Latin America's distant emancipation makes the term *postcolonialism* less than adequate to describe its particular condition (Mignolo 1998b).

FINAL REFLECTIONS

All of the above mentioned direction of study has been in part intuited by the philosophy of liberation since its inception, and if not it can at least be gleaned from, incorporated into, and reconstructed from its discourse. Nevertheless, and with respect to new epistemic proposals, the philosophy of liberation continues to hold its own position, as much in the centers of study in Latin America as in the United States and Europe. In the first place, it is a "philosophy" that can enter into a dialogue with literary criticism and assimilate itself thereto (and to postmodernism, subaltern studies, cultural studies, postcolonial reason, metacriticism of Latin Americanism such as Moreiras's, etc.). As a critical philosophy, the philosophy of liberation has a very specific role: it should study the more abstract, general, philosophical, theoretical framework of "testimonial" literature. (I prefer to refer to it as an "epic" narrative, as a creative expression related to new social movements that impact civil society.) In the third place it should analyze and set the basis for a method, for general categories, and for the very theoretical discourse of all of these critical movements, which, having been inspired by Foucault, Lyotard, Baudrillard, Derrida, and so on, should be reconstructed from a global perspective (since they, for the most part, speak Eurocentrically). In this process of reconstruction, the need to articulate an intercultural dialogue (if there were one) within the parameters of a globalizing system should be taken into consideration. The dualism globalization-exclusion (the new aporia that ought not be fetishistically simplified) frames the problem presented by the other dimensions.

It would still be possible to reflect on anti-foundationalism, of the Rortyian sort, for example, which is accepted by many postmodernists. Anti-foundationalism is not merely a defense of reason for reason itself. It is about defending the victims of the present system, defending human life in danger of collective suicide. The critique of modern reason does not allow the philosophy of liberation to confuse it with a critique of reason as such, or with particular types or practices of rationality. On the contrary, the critique of modern reason is made in the name of a differential rationality (the reason used by feminist movements, environmentalists, cultural and ethnic movements, the working class, peripheral nations, etc.) and a universal rationality (a practical/material, discursive, strategic, instrumental, critical form of reason) (Dussel 1998c). The affirmation and emancipation of difference is constructing a novel and future universality. The question is not difference or universality but rather universality in difference and difference in universality.

In the same manner, the group of anti-foundationalist thinkers opposes universal principles, the incertitude or fallibility that are natural to human finitude, which seems to open a struggle for an a priori unresolvable hegemony.[18] The philosophy of liberation can assess the incertitude of the pretense of goodness (or justice) of human acts, knowing the unavoidable fallibility of practice, while at the same time being able to describe the universal conditions or the ethical principles of said ethical or political action. Universality and incertitude permit precisely the discovery of the inevitability of victims, and it is from here that critical liberating thought originates.

Thus, I believe that the philosophy of liberation has the theoretical resources to face present challenges and in this manner to incorporate the tradition of the Latin American thought of the 1940s and 1950s within the evolution that took place in the 1960s and 1970s, which prepared it to enter into new, vital, and creative dialogues in the critical process of the following decades. Along with Imre Lakatos we could say that a program of research (such as the philosophy of liberation) is progressive as long as it is capable of incorporating old and new challenges. The "hard nucleus" of the philosophy of liberation, its ethics of liberation, has been partially criticized (by Horacio Cerruti, Ofelia Schutte, Apel, and others), but, in my opinion, it has responded creatively as a totality, thus far.

In fact, we face urgent tasks in the twenty-first century. For more than twenty years, Cerruti and other scholars (some since 1976) have been announcing the exhaustion of the philosophy of liberation. Yet the contrary seems to be true. Since the year 2000, new perspectives in the South-South dialogue have begun to emerge, in preparation for a North-South dialogue which includes Africa, Asia, Latin America, Eastern Europe, and all the minorities from the "center." In addition, we have the "transversal" dialogue of difference: the possibility of relating to one another the critical thinking of feminist movements; environmentalists; anti-discriminatory movements focused on different races, peoples, or indigenous ethnicities; movements concerned with marginalized social sectors; immigrants coming from impoverished countries; the elderly; children; the working class and migrant workers; the countries that belong to what used to be called the Third World; the impoverished nations on the periphery; and the "victims" (using Walter Benjamin's term) of modernity, colonization, and transnational and late capitalism. The philosophy of liberation seeks to analyze and define the philosophical metalanguage of all of these movements.

I believe that the philosophy of liberation was born in this critical environment and as a result it has, from the beginning, taken these problems into account with the resources it has had and within the limits of its time and historical location. Metacategories such as totality and exteriority continue to be valid as abstract and global references that should be mediated by the microstructures of power, which are disseminated at every level and for which everybody is responsible.

Toward the end of the 1960s, the philosophy of liberation was already a postmodern philosophy emerging from the global periphery. It overcame the limitations of the ontology (the *Überwindung*) inspired by the misery in Latin America and by the Levinasian concept of alterity. It was criticized by standard Marxism, by irrationalist populism, by liberalism and conservatism, by repetitive philosophies (analytical, hermeneutical, academic, etc.), and today by young (Eurocentric?) postmodern Latin Americans, who perhaps have not yet discovered that the philosophy of liberation is itself a postmodern movement avant la lettre, a truly transmodern movement that appreciates postmodern criticism but is able to deconstruct it from a global peripheral perspective in order to reconstruct it according to the concrete political demands of subaltern groups.

Translated by Rosalia Bermúdez

NOTES

This chapter benefited from the editing of Juliet Lynd.

1 See Foucault (1966, 1969, 1972, 1975, 1976, 1984, 1986). As Didier Eribon (1989) explains, in *The History of Madness* Foucault shows that the excluded are not allowed a voice (as in his critique of psychiatry), while in *The History of Sexuality* (since *La voluntad de saber*) the notion of Power proliferates and the excluded has the last word (against psychoanalysis). Foucault's intent is a liberation of the subject arising from originary negation and establishes the possibility of a

differential voice. The "order" (the system) of disciplinary discourse (the repressor), exercises a power that at first either legitimizes or prohibits. Nevertheless, at a later point the "repressed" finds a voice. Foucault is an intellectual of the "differential," whereas Sartre elaborates on the "universal." It is necessary to learn how to connect both tendencies.

2   See Deleuze 1983, 1991; Deleuze and Guattari 1972. See also the early works of Derrida (1964, 1967a, 1967b); and the works of Vattimo (1968, 1985, 1988, 1989a, 1989b, 1998a).

3   Welsch shows that the historical origin of the term is earlier (1993, 10).

4   Besides Herlinghaus's and Walter's essays, the volume *Postmodernidad en la periferia* includes work by José Joaquín Brunner, Jesús Martín-Barbero, Nestor García Canclini, Carlos Monsiváis, Renato Ortiz, Norbert Lechner, Nelly Richard, Beatriz Sarlo, and Hugo Achúgar.

5   Besides Beverley's, Aronna's, and Oviedo's essays, *The Postmodernism Debate in Latin America* includes work by Xavier Albó, José J. Brunner, Fernando Calderón, Enrique Dussel, Martin Hopenhayn, N. Lechner, Aníbal Quijano, Nelly Richard, Beatriz Sarlo, Silviano Santiago, and Hernán Vidal.

6   See Castro-Gómez 1996. See also Castro-Gómez and Mendieta 1998, which includes contributions by Walter Mignolo, Alberto Moreiras, Ileana Rodríguez, Fernando Coronil, Erna von der Walde, Nelly Richard, and Hugo Achugar.

7   On this issue, see Castro-Gómez 1996, 18, 19. It is worth mentioning that both Arturo Andres Roig and Leopoldo Zea are often criticized. On Augusto Salazar Bondy, see ibid., 89–90: "Salazar Bondy believes that psychological schizophrenia is just an expression of economic alienation" (ibid., 90). Castro-Gómez has the irritating inclination to simplify the position of others too much.

8   Castro-Gómez does not take into consideration that Horacio Cerutti criticized my position in the name of the working class (the proletariat as a metaphysical category that I could not accept as a dogmatic concept) and also in the name of Althusserianism, due to the improper use of the concepts of "the poor" and "the people," which, as I will show, constitute a very Foucauldian way to refer to the "excluded" (the insane in madhouses, the criminal in prisons, those "Others" that wander outside of the panoptic perspective of the French "totality" in the classic era). Levinas had radicalized topics that Foucault approached later on.

9   Guha 1988a, 1988b. As one might suppose, this current is opposed to a mere "historiography of India," traditional in the Anglo-Saxon world. The difference between the two lies in its critical methodology, informed by the works of Marx, Foucault, and Lacan. It is in this aspect that its similarity to the Philosophy of Liberation becomes evident.

10   According to Said, Bhabha's work "is a landmark in the exchange between ages, genres, and cultures; the colonial, the post-colonial, the modernist and the postmodern" (blurb on cover of Bhabha's *Location of Culture*), and is situated in a fruitful location: the "in-between(ness)." It overcomes dichotomies without unilaterally denying them. It operates within tensions and interstices. Bhabha does not deny either the center or the periphery, either gender or class, either identity or difference, either totality or alterity (he frequently makes reference to the "otherness of the Other," with Levinas in mind). He explores the fecundity

of "being-in-between," in the "border-land" of the earth, of time, of cultures, of lives, as a privileged and creative location. He has overcome the dualisms, but he has not fallen into their pure negation. The Philosophy of Liberation, without denying its originary intuitions, can learn a lot from Bhabha and can also grow beyond Bhabha. Bhabha assumes the simplistic negation of Marxism, as many postmodern Latin Americans do, falling into conservative and even reactionary positions without even noticing.

11 See Dussel 1996a [1977], 1996b.

12 The panopticon could be observed in the design of clear and square spaces, with the church in the middle, in towns designed with the rationality of the Hispanic Renaissance. At the same time, this rationality managed to "discipline" bodies and lives by imposing on all individuals a well-regulated hourly schedule, beginning at 5 a.m. These rules were interiorized through a Jesuitical "self-examination," like a reflexive "ego cogito" discovered well before Descartes. This was implemented in the utopian socialist reducciones in Paraguay, among Moxos and Chiquitos in Bolivia, and among Californians in the north of Mexico (in the territory that is today part of the United States).

13 In Para una ética de la liberación latinoamericana (1973) I was speaking of "Différance" as a "Difference" that was not just the mere "difference" in identity. In Filosofía de la liberación (1977) I pointed out on several occasions the contrast between "difference" and "Dis-tinction" of the other. In all modesty, in the prologue of Filosofía de la liberación I stated (two years before Lyotard) that this line of reasoning constituted a "postmodern" philosophy.

14 Hermann Cohen (1914) explains that the ontic method begins by assuming the position of the poor.

15 The situation begins to undergo a radical transformation only when Asiatic, African, and Caribbean intellectuals start thinking about the "commonwealth," along similar lines as the philosophy of liberation.

16 With excellent descriptions, Moore-Gilbert (1997) demonstrates the presence of critical thought within the post-colonial periphery in Departments of English in U.S. universities.

17 See Castro-Gómez and Mendieta (1998, 59–83). The North American Latin Americanism practiced within the field of area studies in U.S. universities counts on the massive migration of Latin American intellectuals, in a hybrid condition, and inevitably rooted out. Nonetheless solidarity is possible. "The politics of solidarity must be conceived, in this context, as a counter-hegemonic response to globalization, and as an opening into the traces of Messianism in a global world" (ibid., 70). The only question, then, would be whether poverty and domination of the masses in peripheral nations does not exclude them from the process of globalization. In other words, it does not seem clear that "today civil society cannot conceive itself outside global economic and technological conditions" (ibid., 71).

18 This is the position of Ernesto Laclau (1977, 1985, 1990, 1996). An article of mine will soon be published offering a critical account of this crucial Latin American thinker.

THE HISTORICAL MEANING OF CHRISTIANITY OF LIBERATION IN LATIN AMERICA

Michael Löwy

What is Christianity of Liberation? I am not speaking of Liberation Theology, a well-known collection of texts produced since 1971 by a wide array of Latin American Christian thinkers.[1] Liberation Theology was but the visible tip of an iceberg. More precisely, it is the expression of a vast social movement which appeared at the beginning of the 1960s—well before the appearance of the new theological works. This movement comprises significant sectors of the church: priests, religious orders, bishops; "lay" religious movements: Catholic Action, Christian university organizations, young Christian workers; pastoral commissions, including Pastoral Commission for Workers, Pastoral Commission for the Land, and Pastoral Commission for Indigenous peoples; and Ecclesial Base Communities (Comunidades Eclesiales de Base, or CEBs). It also influences popular nonreligious organizations, such as neighborhood associations, women's groups, labor unions, peasant organizations, primary-education move-ments, and even political parties. Without the praxis of this social move-ment, one cannot understand the social and historic phenomena as impor-tant in recent Latin American history (for thirty years or so) as the rise of revolution in Central America (Nicaragua, El Salvador) or the emergence of a new workers and peasants movement in Brazil.

At times the phenomenon of liberation theology is referred to as "the Church of the Poor," but in fact this social movement, which of course includes members of the clergy, stretches well beyond the limits of church institutions. I propose calling it "Christianity of Liberation" (*christianisme de la libération*), since such a concept would be more capacious than employing the terms *theology* or *church*. Christianity of Liberation embraces both re-ligious culture and social network, faith and praxis. Liberation theology in the strict sense is only one aspect (though an important one) of this broad socioreligious reality.

Liberation Christianity, and in particular the CEBs (which include mil-lions of practitioners in Latin America), does not hearken back either to the paradigm of the church nor to that of sect, as defined in Ernst Troeltsch's sociology of religion. Rather, it bears more resemblance to what Max Weber called the communitarian salvation religion, that is, a typical ideal form of religiosity founded on the religious ethic of brotherhood, the source of which is the ancient economic ethic of neighborliness, which can lead, in certain cases, to a "communism of fraternal love" (*brüderlicher Liebeskom-munismus*) (Max Weber 1986, 11–12).

This socioreligious orientation influences but a minority of Latin Ameri-can churches; in the majority of them the predominant tendency remains conservative or moderate. But its impact is far from negligible, especially in Brazil where the Episcopalian Conference, despite the insistent pressure coming from the Vatican, has always refused to condemn liberation theol-ogy. Among the most well-known bishops and cardinals of this movement, there is D. Helder Câmara (Brazil), D. Paulo Arns (Brazil). Monseñor Ro-mero (El Salvador), Monseñor Mendez Arceo (Mexico), and Monseñor Sam-uel Ruiz (Mexico).

If we had to formulate the central idea of liberation Christianity, we could refer to the expression coined by the Conference of Latin American Bishops in Puebla (1979): "a preferential option for the poor."

What's new about all this? Hasn't the church always been charitably inclined toward the suffering of the poor? The important difference is that for liberation Christianity, the poor are no longer perceived as mere objects

—objects of aide, compassion, charity—but rather as subjects of their own history, as subjects of their own liberation. The role of socially engaged Christians is to participate in the "long march" of the poor toward the "promised land"—freedom—while contributing to their self-organization and social emancipation.

Not all the bishops present in Puebla shared this radical interpretation, but a certain consensus was established regarding the "preferential option for the poor," with considerable leeway of personal interpretation.

The concept of "poor" clearly has a profound religious reverberation in Christianity. But it also corresponds to an essential social reality in Latin America: the existence of an immense mass of dispossessed people, both in urban as well as rural areas, not all of whom are proletariat or workers. Certain Latin American Christian unionists (syndicalists) speak of the "pooretarian" (*pobretariado*) to describe this disenfranchised class. Simply put, they are the victims not only of exploitation but especially of social exclusion.

The radicalization process in Latin American Catholic culture, which culminated in the formation of liberation theology, does not start from the summit of the church and irrigate downward to its base, nor does it flow from the base toward the summit—the two versions often proposed by sociologists and historians of the phenomenon—but rather it moves from the periphery to the center. The social categories or sectors within the religious-ecclesiastical field, which would become the rejuvenating force, are in one way or another marginal or peripheral with regard to the institution: the lay apostolate and its chaplains, the lay experts, foreign priests, the religious orders. In certain cases the movement seizes the "center" and influences the Episcopal conferences (notably in Brazil); in others it remains blocked in the "margins" of the institution.

We can trace the date of birth of liberation Christianity in 1960, when the Brazilian Juventude Universitária Católica (JUC), influenced by the progressive French Catholic culture (Emmanuel Mounier and the journal Esprit, Father Lebret and the Economy and Humanism movement, the "Thought of Karl Marx" by the Jesuit J. Y. Calvez), formulated for the first time, in the name of Christianity, a radical proposition of social transformation. Throughout the 1960s a process of radicalization of certain Christian milieus took place not only in Brazil and Chile, where the Christians for Socialism movement originated, but also within the clergy and in the lay sectors. In diverse forms analogous events unfolded in other countries. The most well known is of course the case of the Colombian priest Camilo Torres, a former student of the Catholic University of Louvain, who, after organizing a popular combative movement, joined the ranks of the National Liberation Army

(ELN), a Castroist Colombian guerilla army, in 1965; he was killed in a confrontation with soldiers in 1966, and his martyrdom has had a profound emotional and political impact on Latin American Christians.

All of this commotion in the context of the renewal that followed the Second Vatican Council (1962–65) had the effect of agitating the ensemble of the church apparatus in the continent. When the Latin American Episcopal Conference of Medellín took place, in 1968, new resolutions were adapted which for the first time not only denounced existing structures as founded on injustices, violations of the fundamental rights of the people and the institutionalized violence, but which also recognized in certain circumstances the legitimacy of the revolutionary insurrection and expressed solidarity with the people aspiration for "liberation from all servitude."

It is within this context that liberation theology was born. From the end of the 1960s, the topic of liberation began to preoccupy the most advanced Latin American theologians, who were frustrated with the "theology of development," then predominant in Latin America. Hugo Assmann, a Brazilian theologian educated in Frankfurt, played a pioneering role in elaborating in 1970 the first elements of a Christian and liberational critique of *desarrollismo*. But it was in 1971, with the publication of *Teologia de la liberación: Perspectivas* by Gustavo Gutiérrez, a Peruvian priest and former student at the Catholic universities of Louvain and Lyon, that liberation theology was truly born. In this work Gutiérrez advanced a certain number of contestatory ideas which went on to profoundly upset church doctrine. He insisted, for example, on the necessity of a break with the dualism inherited from Greek thought: there are not two realities, one "temporal" and the other "spiritual," nor are there two histories, one "sacred" and the other "profane." There is only one history, and it is within this temporal and human history that redemption must take place, the Kingdom of God. It is not a matter of awaiting salvation from above: Exodus had shown us "the construction of man by man within the historical-political struggle" (700). Man becomes as well the model not for a private and individual salvation but one that is communitarian and "public," in which the stakes are not the individual soul as such, but rather the redemption and liberation of an entire subjected people. The poor, within this perspective, are no longer an object of pity or charity, but rather, like the Hebrew slaves, the agents of their own liberation.

As for the church, according to Gutiérrez, it must cease being a cog in the wheel of domination: following the great tradition of biblical prophets and the personal example of Jesus Christ, its role is to oppose the powerful and denounce social injustice.

Although significant divergences exist among theologians, one finds in the majority of their writings several fundamental themes that constitute a radical departure from the established traditional doctrines of Protestant and Catholic churches.

1   An implacable moral and social imperative against capitalism as an unjust, iniquitous system, even as a form of structural sin.
2   The use of Marxism as a way of understanding the causes of poverty, the contradictions of capitalism, and the forms of class struggle.
3   The preferential option in favor of the poor and solidarity with their struggle for social self-emancipation.
4   The development of CEBs among the poor as a new form of the church and as an alternative to the individualist way of life imposed by the capitalist system.
5   The struggle against idolatry (not atheism) as the principal enemy of religion; that is, against the new idols of death worshiped by the new pharaohs, Caesars, and Herods: Mammon, wealth, power, national security, the state, military force, and Western Christian civilization.

Throughout the 1960s and 1970s, military regimes were established in many Latin American countries: Brazil, Chile, Argentina, and so on. The militants of liberation Christianity participated actively in the resistance to these dictatorships and largely contributed to their decline beginning in the 1980s. They were an important and at times decisive factor in the democratization of these nations. During the 1970s in Brazil, the Church of the Poor surfaced as the principal enemy of the dictatorship in the eyes of civil society and the military leaders themselves and was considered more powerful (and radical) than the tolerated and docile parliamentary opposition. Many Christians—both the clergy and secular—paid with their lives for their commitment to the resistance to the authoritarian regimes in Latin America, or simply for the denunciation of torture, assassination, and violations of human rights.

On the other hand, the CEBs, because of the democratic slant, had much to contribute to the new social and political movements that they themselves nurtured: since they were rooted in the daily life of popular sectors and because of their humble and concrete preoccupations, they contributed an encouragement to the base organization, a distrust of political manipulation and the paternalism of the state.

It was thought that with the end of these military dictatorships the *engagés* Christians would withdraw from the political and social arena. This was indeed the case in certain countries, but in others their commitment has continued under new guises. The conservative offensive by the Vatican, with its nomination of bishops openly hostile to liberation theology, and the spectacular rise of Pentecostal "churches" or "sects" have without doubt weakened liberation Christianity.

Nevertheless, many of the most important activists and cadre leaders of the most important social movements in Latin America since 1990 are profoundly rooted in liberation Christianity. Let's take for example the Movement of Landless Peasants (Movimento dos Trabalhadores Rurais Sem Terra, or MST), one of the most important movements in the contemporary history of Brazil for its capacity for mobilization, its radicalness, its political astuteness, and its popularity. The majority of leaders and activists in the MST were originally from the CEBs from the Pastoral Commission for the Land. Their religious, moral, social, and even, in a certain sense, political formation took place within the ranks of the Church of the Poor. Nevertheless, since its origin in the 1970s, the MST has considered itself a secular movement, autonomous and independent with regard to the church. The majority of its adherents are Catholic, but some are evangelical and (a few) others are nonbelievers. The (socialist!) doctrine and the culture of the MST make no reference to Christianity, but we could go so far as to say that the militant style, the faith in the cause, and the predisposition toward the sacrifice of its adherents (many have become victims of assassinations or even collective massacres in the last few years) probably spring from a religious source.

The same could be said, to some degree, about the other movements in Latin America: the Indigenous National Confederation of Ecuador (CONAIE), the Unitary Peasant Confederation (CUC) in Guatemala, and so on. A similar reasoning can be applied even to political parties, such as the Brazilian Workers' Party, whose candidate Luis Inacio "Lula" da Silva, a former labor activist who came from a pastoral commission for workers, was elected president of Brazil in October 2002. There are also insurgent movements, such as the Mexican Zapatista Army, which has no ties to the church, but whose majority of indigenous combatants were formed by liberation Christianity.

In certain cases, the Christian militants abandoned their participation in the CEBs or in the church pastoral commissions in order to commit fully to their social and political activity. But many have remained attached to their original socioreligious communities and continue to practice their faith.

In the context of our debates, two issues need to be addressed specifically: the relationship that liberation Christianity has with modernity, on the one hand, and with secularism, on the other. Liberation theologians have often articulated a critique of the neoliberal economic model. Should we see in the critique of economic liberalism and capitalism articulated by the liberation theologians an instance of the old doctrine of conservative social Catholicism?

As Max Weber suggested in his sociology of religion, there exists as well traditionally a "profound aversion" within the Catholic ethos/ethic to the spirit of modern capitalism—an economic system which, because of its impersonal character, offered little possibility for ethical intervention on the part of the church.[2] But whereas in the history of the church anticapitalism usually took on an antiliberal regressive form (the Syllabus!), in liberation Christianity, without losing any of its ethical intransigence, anticapitalism became modern.

The critique of the capitalist system or of neoliberalism articulates here a moral rejection with a modern (notably Marxist) economic analysis of exploitation; it replaces charity with social justice; and especially, it refuses to idealize the patriarchal past and proposes as an alternative not a return to pre-modern hierarchies, but rather an egalitarian and socialist economy.

Certain liberation theologians associated with the Department of Ecumenical Research (DEI) of Costa Rica—Hugo Assmann, Franz Hinkelammert, and Pablo Richard—combined a (modern) Marxist critique of commodity fetishism with the (traditional) *veterotestamentaire* prophetic denunciation of idolatry, in order to combat capitalism as a false religion: idolatry of money, capital, and the market.

Contrary to church tradition, the most advanced liberation theologians do not limit themselves to a moral critique of capitalism: they call for its abolition.

One might ask the same sort of question regarding modern individualism, another object of radical critique from liberation Christianity. Does it add up to a rejection of modernity?

According to Gutiérrez, "Individualism is the most important aspect of modern ideology in bourgeois society. In the modern mind set, man is the absolute beginning, an autonomous center of decisions. Initiative and individual interests are the point of departure and the engine of economic activity" (1986, 187). Gutiérrez does not hesitate to use, in this context, the work of the Marxist sociologist Lucien Goldman, who has shown the opposition between religion as a system of transindividual values and the strictly individualist problematic of Enlightenment and the market economy (ibid., 172–73).

For the liberation theologians and the agents of the Pastoral Commission for Workers in the basic communities, one of the most negative aspects of urban-industrial modernity in Latin America (from a social and ethical point of view) is the destruction of the traditional community links. Entire populations have been uprooted from their communities into the periphery of the great urban centers, where they find an individualist atmosphere of unleashed competition.

In a study of CEBs, Marcello Azevedo, a Brazilian Jesuit theologian, blames modernity for the rupture of the links between individual and group and interprets the CEBs as a concentrated expression of a double attempt to revive the idea of community in society and in the church (1986, 1).

One of the main activities of pastoral commissions, such as the Pastoral Commission for the Land and the Pastoral Commission for the Indigenous Peoples, is the defense of traditional (peasant or indigenous) communities threatened by the voracity of the vast agroindustrial enterprises or by the grand projects of state modernization. Within the chaotic periphery of the urban centers, it is a matter of reconstructing, through the CEBs, communitarian life by relying on the traditions of a rural past which are still present within the collective memory: customs of neighborliness, solidarity, and mutual assistance. An attentive observer of the CEBs, the North American theologian Harvey Cox, suggests that through them the poor populations "re-appropriate an array of histories and a moral tradition that have survived the devastating attack of capitalistic modernization and which are beginning to furnish an alternative to the established system of values and significations" (1984, 103). Latin American Christianity has "an organizational style which privileges the community over the individualism and organic modes of life over mechanical ones" (ibid., 215).

Are we dealing here, then with a return to the pre-modern, traditional community, the organic Gemeinschaft described by Ferdinand Tönnies? Yes and no. Yes, insofar as, in the face of a modern society which, according to Leonardo Bloff, "engenders an atomization of existence and a generalized anonymity of people," it is a question of creating "communities in which people know and recognize one another," characterized by "direct relationships, by reciprocity, by profound brotherhood, mutual assistance and communion within the evangelical ideas and the equality of its members" (1978, 7–21). No, since these communities are not simple reconstitutions of the premodern social relations.

Here, too, liberation Christianity and the CEBs are innovative: as Harvey Cox has pertinently observed, they contain the typically modern aspect of the individual choice allowing for new forms of solidarity that no longer have any resemblance to the archaic urban structures (Cox 1984, 127). It is not a matter of reconstituting traditional communities, that is to say, closed and authoritarian structures, with a system of norms and obligations imposed on the individual from his birth (by the family, the tribe, the locality of the religious group). Rather, it is now a question of the formation of a new type of community that necessarily incorporates some of the most important "modern liberties," beginning with the free choice of adhesion. Through this modern aspect, one might consider the CEBs as voluntary utopic groups, in the sense that Jean Séguy attributes to this concept; that is, grouping within which the members participate of their own free will and who aim (implicitly or explicitly) to radically transform existing global systems (Séguy 1999, 117, 218). What the CEBs wish to retain from the communitarian traditions are the "primary" personal relations, the practices of mutual assistance and communion which revolve around a shared faith.

There is still the question of the secularism and the separation between the church and the state. Liberation Christianity does not accept the privatization of faith and political abstention. In a critique of liberal theologies, Gutiérrez writes, "By attributing excessive attention to the demands of bourgeois society, those theologians accepted the place within which this society had confined them: the sphere of the private conscience" (1986, 187).

Insofar as their methodology effectively implies a "re-politicization" of religion and a religious intervention in the political sphere, liberation theologians have been accused by certain liberals (Ivan Vallier) of mounting obstacles to modernization (Vallier 1972, 17–23). This simplistic analysis certainly misses its mark, but nevertheless liberation Christianity refuses to limit itself to the "ecclesiastical sphere" by allowing economic and political matters to follow their "autonomous" development. From this point of view we can trace a parallel between it and the "intransigente" tradition, with its refusal of the modern separation of spheres.[3]

As Juan Carlos Scannone observes, liberation theology does not accept the principle of temporal autonomy defended by modern rationalism, or the reassuring separation of temporal and spiritual struggle declared by liberal progressivism (Scannone 1975).

Nevertheless, this orientation is not necessarily in opposition to secularism. In fact, liberation Christianity situates itself in polar opposition to clerical conservatism by preaching the total separation of the church and the state, and a rupture of the traditional complicity between the clergy and the powerful; by rejecting the idea of a Catholic party of syndicate and by acknowledging the necessary autonomy of popular political and social movements; by rejecting all idea of a return to an acritical "political Catholicism" and its illusion of a "new Christianity"; and by favoring the participation of Christians within secular popular parties or movements.

For liberation theology, there is no contradiction between this demand for modern, secular society and the committed engagement of Christians within the political domain. It is a matter of two different levels of approach to the question of the relationship between religion and politics: at the institutional level, separation and autonomy are indispensable; but in the ethical-political domain, compromised engagement becomes the essential imperative.

Translated by Paul B. Miller

NOTES

1   The most well-known texts are by Gustavo Gutiérrez (Peru), Rubem Alves, Hugo Assmann, Carlos Mesters, Leonardo et Clodovis Boff (Brazil), Jon Sobrino, Ignacio Ellacuria (El Salvador), Segundo Galilea, Ronaldo Munoz (Chile), Pablo Richard (Chile, Costa Rica), José Miguel Bonino, Juan Carlos Scannone (Argentina), Enrique Dussel (Argentina, Mexico), and Juan-Luis Segundo (Uruguay). On the philosophy of liberation and its connection to Latin American studies, see Dussel in this volume.

2   The expression *tiefe Abneigung* appeared in Weber's *Wirtschaftgeschichte* (*General Economic History*) (1923, 305). This problematic is also addressed in his *Wirtschaft und Gesellschaft* (*Economy and Society*) (1922, 335).

3   See Hervieu-Léger and Champion 1986, 299.

SECULARISM AND RELIGION IN THE MODERN/ COLONIAL WORLD-SYSTEM: FROM SECULAR POSTCOLONIALITY TO POSTSECULAR TRANSMODERNITY

Nelson Maldonado-Torres

Secularism has become in many ways the religion of the modern world.[1] Not only modern nation-states but also the modern academy has been very much imprinted with its mold. Latin America is not an exception to the rule. Like many other contexts it has had its enormous share of patriots, liberators, scholars, and scientists who have aimed to exorcize the public sphere from the allegedly irrational and regressive forces of religious life. It is almost ironical that one of the most influential intellectual productions in the continent is a theological methodology, liberation theology—perhaps only superseded in recognition by the literature of the boom. Liberation theology came up with creative ways of intersecting theological discourse with the humanities and the social sciences, particularly with European philosophy and Latin American dependency theory. The humanities and social sciences, however, have not done much to meet liberation theology halfway.[2] In some respects at least, humanists and social scientists have been less willing to investigate the foundations of their disciplines than theologians. One of the reasons for this is that at least for the last two hundred years theologians have not been able to take for granted the epistemic status of their discourse. Humanists and social scientists, on the other hand, rely on the bedrock of secularism, which undergirds not only their disciplines but also, as I will argue, European imperial visions as well.

My account of the imperial character of secular discourse is informed by world-system analysis, particularly by the concept of the modern/colonial world-system. The concept of the modern/colonial world-system may be in some respects viewed as an important transformation of Latin American dependency theory. World-system analysis can be seen as dependency theory adopting a global framework and integrating a *longue durée* concept of history. The concept of the modern/colonial world-system introduces a refashioned concept of dependency—coloniality—into the concept of the capitalist world-system, one that cannot be reduced to the logics of capitalist exploitation. This is a collective contribution of Aníbal Quijano, Enrique Dussel, and Walter Mignolo to Immanuel Wallerstein's account of the history and transformation of the capitalist world-economy and world-system.[3]

The historical and sociological exploration in the first section of this essay informs a phenomenological description of secularism in the second. With *phenomenological description* I refer to an elucidation of some of secularism's most typical features. I show in this section how secularism creatively reproduces imperial discursive structures that have been historically embedded in European Christianity. I then trace these structures in influential representatives of modern and postmodern thought. Modern and postmodern complicity with the imperial features of secularism leads me to examine the contributions of postcolonial theory. In the third and final section of this essay I explore the extent to which the evasion of secularism is coextensive with the concept of the postcolonial. I will critically evaluate the work of some postcolonial theorists and outline the contributions of contemporary Latin American and Latina/o criticism for an overcoming of the limits of secular discourse.

SECULARISM FROM A WORLD-SYSTEM PERSPECTIVE

According to the traditional and widely accepted conception of secularism, the birth of secularism is contemporaneous with the emergence of modern philosophy and with the first decisive steps of modern science (e.g., René

Descartes and Galileo Galilei). A new rationality was claiming a space of its own in a world mostly understood and defined according to the teleological and metaphysical views of European Christianity. Secularism, as its literal meaning conveys, became in this context a call "to live in the century," that is, a call to leave the past behind and conform to the new standards of meaning and rationality. This temporal reference made secular discourse useful for the articulation of the transition from the pre-modern (metaphysical and religious) world of feudalism and aristocracy to the modern world of capitalism and the bourgeoisie. Secularism was thus intrinsically linked with the legitimization of a split or historical divide in reference to which the criteria of modernity, civility, and rationality could be clearly established. The need for a clear historical divide emerged out of the very ideals and values that undergird the unconditional defense of modernity and rationality, that is, the ideas of progress and development. The subject of the progress and development in question is certainly none other than European societies. Modernity, civility, and secularism gradually came to be seen as the present of Europe and as the possible future of everyone else. Part of the claim of modernity and secularism is that the future is already here among us, that the future has found a place in the present. Secularism thus rests on a discourse that merges temporality and spatiality in innovative ways. A critical investigation of secularism needs to begin by challenging the conception of space and time on which it rests.

In what might arguably be referred to as one of the most important essays in twentieth century social science—"Societal Development, or Development of the World System?"—Immanuel Wallerstein questions the most fundamental theses on which the traditional conception of European modernity stands (1991, 64–79). Wallerstein demystifies the connection between progress, development, and particular spatial configurations. For him the subject of development is an interstate system with global dimensions, and not particular societies and nations. The fixation on societies and nations ultimately functions to sustain a more encompassing systemic totality. This means that what from the point of view of the "dominant historical myth of modern European history" is seen as the "future" in the present, from the point of view of world-system analysis it becomes simply a particular kind of present, that is, a present moment of the world-system. From this point of view, the typical picture of a radical discontinuity between modern capitalist Europe and a European feudal world appears rather limited in perspective. For Wallerstein, the transition from feudalism to capitalism can be seen as a controlled process in which "the old-upper strata were able to preserve their dominance in a new and improved form" (ibid., 23–24). The argument is, in a nutshell, that "the concept of the rise of a bourgeoisie, which somehow overthrew an aristocracy, is more or less the opposite of what really happened, which is that the aristocracy reconverted itself into a bourgeoisie in order to salvage its collective privilege" (ibid., 73). From this point of view, then, despotism was not eliminated by capitalism; it just found new and more efficient ways to continue previously existing forms of subjugation.

Wallerstein argues that while the economic basis of the modern capitalist world-system can be traced back to the "long sixteenth century" (roughly from 1450 to 1640), its cultural and ideological bases are not solidified until after the French Revolution. Before the French Revolution, "there existed no social consensus, even a minimal one, about such fundamental issues as whether the states should be secular; in whom the moral location of sovereignty was invested; the legitimacy of partial corporate autonomy for intellectuals; or the social permissibility of multiple religions (Wallerstein 1995, 128). If secularism was on the scene in the world-system at least as early as the seventeenth century, it took a dominant form only after 1789 when the French Revolution and its Napoleonic continuation worked as catalyzing events that fomented the ideological transformation of the capitalist world-economy into a world-system (Wallerstein 1991, 13). Ideologies like liberalism emerged and were gradually spread in the world-system. Liberalism, indeed, became the dominant ideology and gave rise to institutions and political principles that were destined to deal with the idea of the normality of change and the moral sovereignty of the people (Wallerstein 1995, 131). Liberalism promoted the idea of a normal but controlled political change predicated on the progressive acceleration and sophistication of the system and the need to keep at bay the uneasy demands posed by the principle of moral sovereignty. From here that liberalism took extremely paradoxical forms. As Wallerstein notes, "Liberalism, far from being a doctrine that was antistate in essence, became the central justification for the strengthening of the efficacy of the state machinery. This was because liberals saw the state as essential to achieving their central objective—furthering the modernity of technology while simultaneously judiciously appeasing the 'dangerous classes'" (1995, 132). Liberalism became the geoculture of the world-system because it allowed and still allows for continuity in patterns of subordination in a world where political change has asserted itself as natural. The liberal political principles of suffrage, the welfare state, and national identity share a fundamental ambiguity that can be traced to a strong interest in maintaining the "unabashed classes" and demands for popular sovereignty under control. These principles became extremely effective in exerting a politics of simultaneous inclusion and exclusion from the spheres of political power. The case of national identity is particularly striking since it ultimately leads to nationalism and racism. As Wallerstein puts it,

> The political project of nineteenth-century liberalism for the core countries of the capitalist world-economy was to tame the dangerous classes by offering a triple program of rational reform: suffrage, the welfare state, and national identity. The hope and assumption was that ordinary people would be contented by this limited devolution of reward and therefore would not in fact press for the fullness of their "human rights." The propagation of the slogans—human rights, or freedom, or democracy—was itself part of the process of taming the dangerous classes. The thinness of the social concessions bestowed upon the dangerous classes might have become more salient except for two facts. One, the overall living standards of the core countries were benefiting from the effective transfer of surplus from the peripheral zones. And the local nationalisms of each of these states was complemented by a collective nationalism of the "civilized" nations vis-à-vis the "barbarians." Today, we call this racism, a doctrine explicitly codified in just this period in just these states, which came to permeate profoundly all the social institutions and public discourse. At least, this was true until the Nazis brought racism to its logical conclusion, its ne plus ultra version, and thereby shamed the Western world into a formal, but only partial, theoretical repudiation of racism. (1995, 152–53)

Wallerstein sheds light on the nature and contradictions of liberalism and its three political principles, yet he does not seem to be so interested in elucidating the nature and possible inherent contradictions of a concomitant reality, the secular project. This is particularly regretful because secularism is not only part of liberalism. Secularism was also central for Marxism, liberalism's fierce competing ideology. Secularism is more pervasive than any of the modern ideologies by themselves. The lack of a critical reflection on secularism also raises the question of the extent to which Wallerstein's own world-system analysis may subscribe to a secular point of view. Wallerstein's silence in regard to secularism notwithstanding, his analysis of the alleged transition from feudalism to capitalism and his account of the ambiguities of liberalism provide important clues for a renewed understanding of secularism. For if secularism is understood in terms of the world-system's long patterns of development, then its dominance after the French Revolution may be understood not as a radical break with a mythical and religious past, but as a response to a needed transition to more sophisticated ideological components for the sustenance and development of the capitalist world-economy. The question is now to characterize this transition and to show in what ways secularism provided more effective tools to maintain the capitalist world-system.

SECULARISM IN THE
MODERN/COLONIAL WORLD-SYSTEM

Walter Mignolo has recently questioned Wallerstein's idea that the world-system did not have a geoculture prior to the French Revolution. Mignolo refers to Occidentalism as "the imaginary of the Atlantic commercial circuit, which is extended, and thus includes what Wallerstein calls "geoculture," to the end of the twentieth century and is resemantized by the market and the transnational corporations" (Mignolo 2000d, 24). According to Mignolo, Christianity represented this imaginary from the sixteenth to the eighteenth centuries. For Mignolo, the imperial enterprise of what Enrique Dussel calls the first modernity, which roughly coincides with Wallerstein's long sixteenth century, needed a macronarrative to give sense and meaning to the imperial efforts of the emerging center (Dussel 1998c, 59–60). While Wallerstein highlights how popular demands for political change in the second modernity (from 1789 onward) called for ideological formations, Mignolo puts the accent elsewhere: for him, ideology is needed to legitimize and promote the sort of relationships that ensue between Europe and the colonial peoples. He argues that Christianity provided the ideological backup that made possible a justification of the emergent capitalism and the foundation of the necessary interstate system of commercial exchange and surplus value. Christianity was not merely a religion in the first modernity. It was the organizing narrative that defined imperial purpose and that shaped in different ways the institutions and subjectivities of colonized peoples. Mignolo takes this insight from particular fields of scholarly expertise. He specializes in colonial literature and has studied carefully the interactions between European and indigenous peoples in the first modernity. From his point of view it becomes patently clear that nobody could escape from Christianity in Latin America during the first modernity, just as nobody could escape liberalism and its related concept of secularism during the second.

There is a second important insight that derives from Mignolo's considerations. If coloniality is intrinsic to modernity, as Mignolo, following Aníbal Quijano, claims, then one should be able to explain the transition from Christianity to secularism in reference to their role in the promotion of imperial power and colonial relations (Quijano 2000b, 2001). A good indication of this is that defenders of secularism have invested more time passionately attacking religion than critiquing the forms of subjugation that are constitutive of the modern state. To be sure, this step would have required a substantial amount of self-criticism. It would also have demanded more appreciation of the diversity of religious life, particularly of the ways in which religious practices and institutions sometimes play a progressive political role. The fixation on religion as dogma could be interpreted as an evasive strategy, which aims to make less obvious the appearance of new forms of domination and social control at both the national and the geopolitical levels. What is clear is that while in the post-1789 period the acceptance of political change and the increasing demands of the popular will challenged the religious configuration of imperial power, coloniality, racism, and sexism were to be sustained by all means. The aristocrats could easily become bourgeois but certainly not anticolonials. It is not a coincidence that the second modernity saw in the actions of England and France a renovation of the imperial gesture later in the nineteenth century. Everything happened just as if the modern/colonial system needed to reaffirm imperialism under a more complex configuration of power. The first modernity, with its imperial project baptized by religion, now had to give space to the second modernity, with its scientifically based racism and with the notion of "civility" as its main slogan. The discourse of secularism was needed both to maintain popular groups at bay through a clear differentiation between the civic space and the public or private, and to legitimize colonization. Colonization found a justification in secular discourse because, ultimately, the colonial others were conceived as primitives living in stages where only religion or tradition dominated their customs and ways of being. The critical gesture of the imperialism of the second modernity against the inefficacy of the imperialism of the first—the former based on secularism, the latter on religion—is extended to other places or locations where religion is supposedly still dominant. The defense of secularism and the critique of religion in the core nations of the world-system simultaneously advocate the emancipation from tradition and the continued subjugation of colonial peoples under the auspices of reason and civilization. This is the dreadful ambivalence of the predominance of secularism in the second modernity.

What I am suggesting here is not only that liberalism and its political principles had their antecedents in an imperial religiosity, but also that the confrontation between European Christianity and modern European secular discourse may be understood as an intra-imperial event, inserted in the logic of the management of the modern/colonial world-system. That is the reason why secularism takes primarily posttraditional and postmetaphysical dimensions, but rarely ever a consistently post-imperial form. In this light it appears that if secularism opposed itself to religion it was not because religion was imperial, but simply because it was just not imperial enough. The secular definition and opposition to religion hide more than they reveal. They hide how secularism legitimizes colonial structures of meaning and institutions, and how it is able to do this precisely by taking on prominent aspects of certain religiosities. These religious dimensions must not be understood in terms of intrinsic phenomenological features of some abstract entity called Religion. Religions, as we find them, are always inflected by social interests and cannot be detached from a context where struggles for recognition take place. With the idea of imperial features of religion I refer to the point where imperial interests and imperial modes of recognition merge with particular dimensions of a certain religiosity. It was Christianity which provided the imperial grammar to the first modernity. The continuity of coloniality between the first and the second modernity suggest fundamental points of contact between Christianity and the seemingly opposite but equally influential point of view in the second modernity, secularization. An elucidation of the points of contact between Christianity and secularism demands the articulation of a phenomenology of the secular.

PHENOMENOLOGY AND CRITIQUE OF THE SECULAR

Phenomenology is a description of the most stable forms and aspects of a phenomenon.[4] It brackets metaphysical commitments, but it can never be done in a vacuum. Its descriptions are always informed by subjective commitments and historical points of view. The modern/colonial world-system informs my description of the ties between Christianity and secularism. The description has a double relevance: it offers a fresh perspective into a familiar phenomenon, and it adds force to the history and genealogy behind the concept of the modern/colonial world-system. I will highlight two features of secularism: its reliance on the divide between the sacred and the profane, and its creative use of the Christian conception of the relation between Christianity and Judaism.

Secularism takes on the role of legitimating and articulating discursive mechanisms to create a civic space needed to make of national civilized citizens the central (at least ideologically) generator of power in modern societies. In order to do this secularism has to engage in a constant purification of the public space from nonnational, noncivilized, and alien interventions. Secularism secures the space of a new lord or a new master who, like the previous one, does not tolerate mixture and "disorder." The secular space has thus to be secured by interdictions. Reason and civility have to flee from religion and barbarianism. Interestingly enough, secularism adopts features usually associated with what for some becomes the central and most primitive element of religion, the notion of the sacred. The following assertions on the sacred made early in the twentieth century by the sociologist Émile Durkheim may very well be applied to the secular space.

> All that is sacred is the object of respect, and every sentiment of respect is translated, in him who feels it, by movements of inhibition. In fact, a respected being is always expressed in the consciousness by a representation which, owing to the emotion it inspires, is charged with a high mental energy; consequently, it is armed in such a way as to reject to a distance every other representation which denies it in whole or in part. Now the sacred world and the profane world are antagonistic to each other. They correspond to two forms of life which mutually exclude one another, or which at least cannot be lived at the same time with the same intensity. . . . This is because the representation of a sacred thing does not tolerate neighbors. But this psychic antagonism and this mutual exclusion of ideas should naturally result in the exclusion of the corresponding things. If the ideas are not to coexist, the things must not touch each other or have any sort of relations. This is the very principle of the interdict. Moreover, the world of sacred things is, by definition, a world apart. Since it is opposed to the profane world by all the characteristics we have mentioned, it must be treated in its own peculiar way. (1947, 317)

To understand the full implications of this passage for a critique of secularism we should compare it with the following description of contexts marked by imperialism and coloniality. In his *Wretched of the Earth* Frantz Fanon writes, "A world divided into compartments, a motionless, Manicheistic world, a world of status: the statue of the general who carried out the conquest, the statue of the engineer who built the bridge; a world which is sure of itself, which crushes with its stones the backs flayed by whips: this is the colonial world. The native is a being hemmed in; apartheid is simply one form of the division into compartments of the colonial world. The first thing which the native learns is to stay in his place, and not to go beyond certain limits" (1991, 51–52). Secularism, with its emphasis on civility and civilization, transforms the structure of the difference between the sacred and the profane and reinscribes on it an imperialist intentionality. The sacred is found and identified, in this religious form of secularism, with the privileged space of the civilized, while the profane turns out to be located in the space where the colonized and racialized subjectivities live. Racial segregation and colonial geopolitical formations are promoted by ideals of order and civility that find expression in the notion of secularity. According to this logic, even religion falls within the confines of the profane. Indeed, religion becomes in the second modernity a most efficient form of subalternation of knowledges and peoples. For this reason, Western societies have come to rapidly recognize the religious element in non-Western or colonized societies, but not the emergence of particularly theoretical or philosophical productions. As religion becomes equivalent with fanaticism and irrationality, the concept also serves to legitimize vigilance, policing, control, and war. Secularism thus simply inverts and then properly modernizes the imperial dimension found in the radical dichotomy between the sacred and the profane.

The radical division between the sacred and the profane forms part of Christianity. The intolerable opposition between the two dimensions justifies an order where lords have direct dominance over "subjects." Since we find this structure of power in the so-called Middle Ages, it is possible to say that the imperial dimension of Christianity existed long before it took the role of geoculture in the world-system.[5] One of the features that facilitated Christianity's role as an imperial ideology from early on and that later became fundamental for the articulation of secularism is the hierarchical distinction between Christianity and Judaism. According to this centuries-old conception, Christianity represents, as it were, the self-overcoming of Judaism. This self-conception largely defines Christianity's approach to other cultural formations in which promises of salvation are made. Similar to the way in which Judaism represents for Christianity a one-sided element of religious experience, that is, a strict legalism, other religions come to represent equally one-sided and limited dimensions of the human—for example, Islam is represented as the religion of violence, and Asian and South Asian religions would be seen as purely mystical. The world is thereby mapped according to a misguided phenomenology of religious experience. Only in Europe one finds the last and more complete expression of the religious, out of which a properly rational civilization can emerge.

Secularism behaved with Christianity in ways similar to the ones in which Christianity behaved with Judaism and other religions. Christianity was simultaneously demonized and glorified by some of the more influential ideologues of the new secular order. It was demonized because it was identified with a configuration of power that inhibited the full expression of the potentialities of capitalism; it was glorified because it was thought that only

Christianity could have led to the formation of a properly secular world where freedom (of market and of opinion) reigned. "Christianity could be a demon, but it is decidedly our demon, and a better demon than anyone else's," or so went the theme. The battle against Christianity thus becomes at the same time the apology of Christianity. What is searched for in this process is simply the justification of the idea that secularism is and could not be but a European achievement. Secularism is something that can be explained in reference to internal virtues or distortions of European humanity.

The particularly Christian logic of secularism is evinced in an array of European thinkers from Immanuel Kant to those of the present. A brief exploration of the record shows not only that there are significant continuities between the geocultures of the first and second modernities but also that coloniality remains firm in some of the most influential modern and postmodern philosophical visions. The very debate between defenders of modernity and postmodernity could be seen in this light, much like dominant forms of the confrontation between Christianity and liberalism, as an intra-imperial affair. I will take a brief look at the ways in which some European thinkers have continued this imperial legacy.

SECULARISM FROM A MODERN AND
POSTMODERN POINT OF VIEW

In his well-known definition and celebration of the Enlightenment, Kant argues that the Enlightenment represents mankind finally getting to a stage of maturity (1990). "Dare to know" became the slogan of the new ideological configuration. Religions were seen, to be sure, as signs of immaturity, and among these Judaism rated fairly low, to the extent of becoming for Kant more a political ideology than a religion. Kant went so far as even articulating a view about the so-called euthanasia of Judaism, which meant, as Nathan Rotenstriech notes, "not a death out of merciful attitude, but a disappearance out of the inner factors or forces of the entity in question" (1984, 5). Here is Kant's recipe for the "euthanasia" (as it appeared in *Strife of the Faculties*): "The Jews should publicly adopt the 'religion of Jesus' and study the New Testament in addition to the Old, but interpret them both in the spirit of modern morality and the Enlightenment, and thus actually transcend both religions. Only in this way, said Kant, could the Jews acquire civil rights and at the same time overcome historical religion in favor of the religion of reason" (Yovel 1998, 20). Maturity entails for Kant a process of Christianization. Thus, when Kant argued in his answer to the question "What is Enlightenment?" that peoples who have not reached a stage of maturity are guilty, he clearly was legitimating the old-style imperialism of the Christianization of mankind (see on this Dussel 1995c, 19–20).

Later in the nineteenth century Hegel gave to the idea of subsumption of one culture, religion, or system into another a stronger role. The idea of dialectic in Hegel's speculative system introduces the notion of progress as a process of gradual sublimation that goes from the particular to the universal, and from the implicit to complete awareness. For Hegel Christianity represents, at the level of religion, a progressive step in the actualization of the idea of freedom and universality—that is, over the ethnic Judaism and over polytheism. Christianity is indeed for Hegel the perfect religion. "Christianity is the outcome and expression of the eternal dialectic immanent in God's own being as it works itself out under the conditions of time and space" (Reardon 1977, 59). In Christianity God reveals himself to himself, becoming thus totally manifest. But this manifestation is still articulated in figurative language, resorting to feelings and the imagination. Only in philosophy can the Absolute show itself up in concepts and the Idea. Philosophy is in this respect superior to religion, but since the concept and the Idea fails to satisfy the living spirit, what Hegel calls "the concrete human soul," then it is clear that we still need religion—not any religion, but the highest religion, Christianity. For this reason Hegel recruits his own system in the attempt to mediate between Christianity and a secular world dominated by a scientific frame of mind. Christianity is limited but absolutely necessary as a step both in the unfolding of Spirit—a step that leads to secularism—and in the satisfaction of fundamental human needs. Christianity, and only Christianity, is to be both subordinated and preserved in the new European social world.

The logic of subordination and preservation of Christianity found its ultimate challenge in Friedrich Nietzsche who took the idea of the links between secularism and Christianity to its limits. He argued that the destiny of Christianity consisted in its formal disappearance as a doctrine in the brave new world of science. The will to truth, the imperative to tell the truth by all means even if it is not beneficial, is what caused European Christian peoples to engage in a process of inquiry which ended up eroding the very basis of Christian faith (see Nietzsche's *The Will to Power* [1968]). The "death of God" represented for Nietzsche one of the last steps in this logic of self-evisceration. It was still, however, not the last step. Nietzsche argued that Christian morality remained alive in the new scientific discipline. An ascetic spirit still dominated Europe in its incessant search for the truth—a truth to be found at all costs. Something interesting happens in Nietzsche's account:

he reverses the logic of Christian privilege; Christianity now becomes not the highest but the poorest and more perverse type of religiousness ever. Christianity gives a unique and highly sophisticated expression to the instinct of the weak, the poor, and the slave. It takes Jewish subordination to the law and elevates it to the highest expression by integrating its spirit in the conscience of the individual. Now we not only obey the law, but go beyond the formality of the law and come to desire whatever denies life and inflicts suffering. "The Christian conception of God . . . is one of the most corrupt conceptions of the divine ever attained on earth. It may even represent the low-water mark in the descending development of divine types. God degenerated into the *contradiction* of life, instead of being its transfiguration and eternal Yes!" (Nietzsche 1954, 585). Christianity for Nietzsche is the paradigmatic religion of decadence. Now, note that only out of this decadence could scientism and secularism have emerged. Nietzsche still operates with the idea of subsumption characteristic of Kant and Hegel, and elevates Christianity and Europe to a special status. It is in Europe, then, that another humanity can be born. To Christianity Nietzsche opposes the anti-Christ or overman. The overman is born out of a European crisis of meaning. From here the philosophies of crisis that followed, like Husserl's and Heidegger's, for example, tended to be strongly Eurocentric.

Where Nietzsche saw a sign of depravity, Jürgen Habermas, that late hero of modernity and the Enlightenment, sees, along with Durkheim, the traces of a progressive achievement in abstraction and communicative rationality. The Christian God, with a kingdom that is not of this world, paves the way for a radical disassociation of nature from the divine and thus for a new and more independent mode of justification. Gradually, language and not religious authority becomes the medium of social integration. The sacred gives up its primary function to communicative processes.[6] In modernity, science, ethics, and aesthetics emerge as spheres of culture where claims for validity or for truthfulness can be only adequately thematized. Modern Europe becomes in this way the highest expression of human rationality at a world-historical level. So again, Christianity carries the torches of reason and gives itself up to European modernity. In this context the contradictions in Habermas's call for a dominant European Union become evident. Consider the following:

> In this context, our task is less to reassure ourselves of our common origins in the European Middle Ages than to develop a new political self-consciousness commensurate with the role of Europe in the world of the twenty-first century. Hitherto, history has granted the empires that have come and gone but *one* appearance

on the world stage. This is just as true of the modern states—Portugal, Spain, England, France, and Russia—as it was for the empires of antiquity. By way of exception, Europe as a whole is now being given a *second* chance. But it will be able to make use of this opportunity not on the terms of its old-style power politics but only under the changed premises of a nonimperialistic process of reaching understanding with, and learning from, other cultures. (Habermas 1996, 507)

Habermas's call for a non-imperialistic process of reaching understanding does not hide the perverse dimensions of his nostalgia for the greatness of empire. For it is not clear in his work how a country other than Europe could be capable of reaching the stage of non-imperial communication. That is, it is difficult to see how in Habermas's premises cultures dominated by other religions (like Islam or Confucianism) could practice the sort of dialogue that Habermas considers to be rational. The end result is clear: when reaching understanding renders itself impossible, given the inadequacies in the culture and religion of a certain society or nation, it will be legitimate to intervene by force and, in the process, try to form institutions that foment a truly rational form of communication. Violence, war, and intervention will be justified in the light of the other's intrinsic fundamentalism and intolerance. In short, Habermas would like Europe to become the United States of the twenty-first century.

In Gianni Vattimo, another contemporary figure, member of the European Parliament and former Distinguished Visiting Fellow at Stanford University, we find an equally or even more dangerous conception of secularism. Vattimo is perhaps the best-known student of Hans-Georg Gadamer. Faithful to his philosophical roots he has tried to develop a hermeneutics of culture in the line of Nietzsche and Martin Heidegger. In his work Vattimo aims to formulate a positive conception of nihilism, identified with the end of metaphysics. He argues that the postmodern condition represents a consistent expression of nihilism where ultimate principles or ideas of the real are eviscerated in the name of difference, playfulness, appearance, and spectacle. Postmodernism then represents the end of metaphysics and the event where Being gives itself. Vattimo has labeled his position "weak thought." Recently, Vattimo, a Catholic by birth, has returned to his religious roots and attempted to provide a definition of Christianity compatible with his view of the end of metaphysics and weak thought. He argues not only that there is an intrinsic link between Christianity and postmodern secularism but that postmodern secularism is the highest and most complete expression of Christianity. He focuses on the idea of the kenosis, or incarnation, which for him gives expression to his own conception of the weakening of thought (from

God the father to God the son). In Vattimo's account Heidegger, whose work calls for the end of metaphysics and for the self-revelation of Being, appears much like the last apostle of Jesus Christ. In Vattimo's own words, "The incarnation, that is, God's abasement to the level of humanity, what the New Testament calls God's kenosis, will be interpreted as the sign that the non-violent and non-absolute God of the post-metaphysical epoch has as its distinctive trait the very vocation for weakening of which Heideggerian philosophy speaks" (1999, 39). That Heidegger, a self-declared participant of national socialism in Germany, someone who considered only Greek and German as the authentic languages of philosophical thinking, and whose conception of the end of metaphysics was defined as a return to early Greek thinking (read, not to Judaic sources), represents for Vattimo the representative of Christianity in the modern world gives much to think about. But Vattimo does not entirely agree with Heidegger: for him postmodern secularism itself represents the moment of the weakening of Being, and this is to be traced back not to early Greek thinking but to the New Testament itself. It is, in fact, our embeddedness in a culture that emanates of Christianity that according to Vattimo accounts for the fact of the "return" to the religious in the postmodern world. Vattimo's idea is that, since secular postmodernism is an emanation from Christianity and can be accounted for and understood in Christian concepts, the most consistent form of religiosity in postmodern times is Christianity. Vattimo sometimes refers to the "Hebraic-Christian" tradition, but in line with his predecessor (Heidegger) he does not see something altogether positive in Judaism itself. The God of the Judaic scriptures, the God of the Old Testament for Vattimo, represents the principles of a violent metaphysics. For Vattimo, the Judaic scriptures are obsolete and only Christianity promotes the principles of the weakening of thought and culture. Vattimo goes so far as to explain what he calls the regressive character of Emmanuel Lévinas's philosophical project in terms of Lévinas's indebtedness to Judaic scriptures: "If the God that philosophy rediscovers is only God the Father, little headway is made beyond the metaphysical thinking of foundation—indeed, it may be that one takes a step or two backwards. . . . Only in the light of the Christian doctrine of the Incarnation of the son of God does it seem possible for philosophy to think of itself as a reading of the signs of the times without this being reduced to a purely passive record of the times" (Vattimo 1998b, 92). Vattimo's conception of philosophy and postmodern secularism takes the relation between Christianity and the secular world to new levels: not only is Christianity necessary to arrive to an authentically secular order, but it is itself positively that secular order. In a postmodern world where conceptions of enlightened rationality are weakened and the door for the advent of the religious is opened once more again religion returns. But only one religion can claim legitimacy in the postmodern world: a nonviolent and postmetaphysical Christianity. Postmodern secularism comes from Christianity and is essentially Christian.

We see that for more than two hundred years some of Europe's most influential thinkers have kept reproducing the idea that gave legitimacy and impetus to the imperialism of the first modernity. Christianity supersedes Judaism and becomes the highest religious form. Kant applies this logic to Christianity itself in relation to the Enlightenment, while Vattimo applies it to the Enlightenment in relation to postmodernism. What remains constant is the idea of the superiority of Europe in regard to every nation and every society on earth. The missionary spirit of the imperial church is transferred to the self-conception of a new invigorated Europe. The imperative of domination simultaneously leads to a relative subordination of Christianity and to an even more reductionistic conception of non-Christian religions. At the end it becomes clear that with or without metaphysics imperialism and domination continues. If modern and postmodern thought do not appear to be so useful in overcoming the imperial effects of secularity, would postcolonial theory be any better? In certain ways postcolonial theory, particularly in the Saidian vein, relates to the problem of the secular-religious divide.

SECULARISM FROM A POSTCOLONIAL POINT OF VIEW: IS POSTCOLONIALISM POSTSECULAR?

As we have seen, the imperial logic of secularism has been largely unchallenged by defenders of modernity and postmodernity alike. Unfortunately, the most influential postcolonial theorists have not done much better in this regard. It is well known how Edward Said unabashedly defends secularism and condemns religion while also relegating it to the private sphere. For Said, "In the secular world—our world, the historical and social world made by human effort—the intellectual has only secular means to work with; revelation and inspiration, while perfectly feasible as modes for understanding in private life, are disasters and even barbaric when put to use by theoretically minded men and women. Indeed I would go so far as saying that the intellectual must be involved in a lifelong dispute with all the guardians of sacred vision or text, whose depredations are legion and whose heavy hand brooks no disagreement and certainly no diversity" (Said 1994b, 88–89). Said's definition of intellectual activity in terms of secular criticism does not seem to consider the ways in which secularism has been used to justify colonization. It is true that Said's foremost interest is the defense of what most intellectuals won't be opposed to—the freedom of speech and critical inquiry—yet by categorically describing these virtues as secular Said reproduces a divide that has been instrumental for the closure of the voices of the religious other, which is coextensive in many cases, with the colonial sub-other. Instead of challenging the logic that identifies the religious with dogma, Said makes of religion the quintessential source of all evils. He detects religion wherever there is a menace to free inquiry. There is religion in nationalism and in imperialism as well. He goes as far as to compare Orientalism to religious discourse. For him, each "serves as an agent of closure, shutting off human investigation, criticism, and effort in deference to the authority of the more-than-human, the supernatural, the otherworldly" (Said 1983, 290).

Said's comparison between religion and Orientalism is somewhat ironical, for there is a sense in which the dichotomous juxtaposition between the religious and the secular suggests, as William Hart has indicated, that religion may be for Said his own Orient. Through a close examination of an extensive collection of Said's writings Hart shows that Said's discourse presupposes a transhistorical and transcultural view of religion that posits it as "dogmatic, deferential to authority, otherworldly, subservience-compelling, and violence-producing" (Hart 2000, 45). For Hart, "Said orientalizes religion. . . . The Orientalist-inspired othering that Said criticizes looks much like his religious-secular distinction, which resembles if not mimes the East-West distinction. The religious-secular distinction is Said's *Orientalism*, the way he produces otherness for his own uses" (ibid., 86). As Hart points out, this puts Said in a contradictory position since he produces Manichean oppositions in the very effort of dismantling them. Although Said has questioned the logics of imperialism more than any of the modern and postmodern thinkers discussed above, he still continues a legacy that has been instrumental for the justification of colonialism. To use Hart's own expression, when it comes to religion, Said does not do much more than to enact "the perspective of an enlightened, rational, non-dogmatic, secular (European!) consciousness" (ibid.).

Said's style of postcolonial criticism has influenced more nuanced accounts of religion and the secular. In *Outside the Fold: Conversion, Modernity, and Belief* (1998) Gauri Viswanathan applies and mildly modifies Said's counterpunctual writing of history to elucidate the intricate relations between secular and religious culture in Britain and India. Viswanathan focuses on the phenomenon of conversion and, more particularly, on "the deliberate adoption of a religion defined as a 'minority' or 'other' " (1998, 33). Conversion, Viswanathan notes, can often be seen as a site of contestation, as an act whereby subjects critique and aim to reform their cultures. Although Viswanathan's approach to conversion seems to defy Said's conception of the religious, she rather points to the way in which "religious dissent" may be likened to Said's concept of secular criticism. She goes as far as to state that it is precisely in "the historical move . . . from an established to a dissenting ecclesiastical tradition" that "the full complexities of practicing secular criticism in the Saidian sense can be most sharply discerned" (ibid., 46). Viswanathan's statement is inventive and generous, yet I do not think that it represents an accurate portrayal of Said's concept of secular criticism. For the "transition from an established to a dissenting ecclesiastical tradition" is rarely disassociated from those sources that Said condemns: visions and sacred scriptures. However creatively a tradition may use those sources, they often remain as anchor points. While it would be possible from a Saidian point of view to praise certain critical aspects in this transition, still the horizon of critique seems to be defined by a disavowal of the sacred sources. That is to say, for religious people to become authentically critical they would have to turn secular. Hart is certainly right when he comments that Said's view of religion, just like Freud's or Marx's, is simply not dialectical enough (Hart 2000, 38).

The accuracy or inaccuracy of Viswanathan's interpretation of Said's secular criticism surely does not determine the quality of her work. She indeed does better work than Said in exploring the links between the political and the religious. Yet at the same time one notes a limitation in her work that connects precisely with a Saidian view of religion. She disagrees with Said, but never too much. This proves to be a problem when Said's view of religion and secularism are concerned. Viswanathan asserts that religion could become critical, but only or primarily when radical changes like conversion are at stake. It is difficult to discern if for Viswanathan religions are also able to become critical when they are more stable. It does not transpire in her work how religious epistemologies could challenge the liberal order that often marginalizes them to the private sphere of individual practice and consciousness—the same liberal order that has accompanied Western imperialism for a couple of centuries now. Traditions and the project of retrieving ideas from traditions seem to be fundamentally irrelevant to or even at odds with the postcolonial project. This is what transpires when Viswanathan explicates her focus on conversion by clarifying that "at certain moments conversion has less to do with retrieving tradition than with bringing about attitudinal changes in England toward its minority populations" (1998, 33). Religion seems to be important for the postcolonial critic when it challenges the imperial configuration according to the clear logics of political opposition, a logic that can be easily understood by secular minds. Religion becomes relevant when the act of conversion, for instance, can be easily interpreted as a "deliberate adoption of a religion defined as a 'minority' or 'other' " (ibid., 32). That is, conversion is considered to be critical when it obeys a political strategy that may as well be articulated in secular terms. Conversion presents itself to the analyst as something to be dissected. There seems to be no epistemological challenges brought forward by it, at least to the analyst who studies it. The analyst is in control and can easily unveil a "grammar of dissent." The analyst controls the criteria that decide what is sufficiently critical and what is not. The postcolonial critic is never destabilized in this picture or challenged by narratives that bring forth alternative ideas of political relationships or other kinds of human interactions. There is never an authentic engagement with conversion.

Viswanathan's approach remains within the shapes of the Saidian mold. The grammar of dissent can be informed by religious expressions like conversion; nonetheless, it fundamentally remains in her hands a secular grammar. The postcolonial project remains thus *modern* in these expressions, and by *modern* I mean caught up in the ideological framework of the modern/ colonial world-system. Anouar Majid has made a similar point about Said and other postcolonial intellectuals. Majid, who studies Islam and frequently engages the intellectual contributions of Muslim scholars, complains that "the secular premises of scholarship have . . . increased the remoteness of Islam" (2000, 3). For Majid, postcolonial theorists like Said and Gayatri Spivak have contributed to make Islam more opaque and to occlude the voices of intellectuals "whose project is precisely to theorize Islamic alternatives to Western hegemony" (ibid., 28). This occlusion is not accidental. When religion is understood to be antithetic to critical thinking and theory, there is no real need to seriously engage ideas articulated from religious perspectives. If the subaltern happens to be religious, then the postcolonial theorist herself makes sure that she will never speak. At the same time, European discourse gains more strength as it clearly dominates the field of secular ideas and theoretical formulations. My point is not that secularism is purely the West's invention, but that more often than not the accent on the secular helps to maintain the West's epistemic hegemony. The secular postcolonial critic therefore becomes an ally of the West. It is this situation that leads Majid to assert that "as long as the secular premises of Western

scholarship are not interrogated, it is unlikely that the discursive interventions of a few highly talented Third World critics can effectively contribute to the emancipation of all Third World peoples. No matter how
insightful and liberating Western self-critique can be, it still partakes from
the secular assumptions of the liberal tradition and cannot persuasively
intervene in any discourse without accepting the limitations of this condition" (ibid., 29–30).

A critique of the colonizing effects of secular discourse should at least be
able to offer some ideas about the way to overcome the limits of secularism.
For Majid, an important step in this regard would be to accept the idea that
"the cultural rights of Others must be presented even if they are radically at
odds with secular premises" (2000, 30). Majid is not inviting us here to
embark in a fantastic voyage of nostalgic returns to pre-colonial cultures.
Nor is he simply defending a vulgar form of relativism. He is, rather, interested in the task of epistemic decolonization, which involves the search for
alternatives to capitalist forms of production and forms of life. His defense
of "Muslims' rights to their identities and memories is motivated exclusively
by [their] strong belief that only secure, progressive, indigenous traditions,
cultivated over long spans of time, can sustain meaningful global diversities
and create alternatives to the deculturing effects of capitalism" (ibid., vii).
Like Viswanathan, Majid seems to be entirely clear about what terms like
secure and *progressive* mean. It seems that a secular brand of social criticism
informs his work and gives meaning to his normative statements. On the
other hand, for him, religions and cultures have more than ecstatic visions,
dogmas, and conversions to offer. Cultures and religions are repositories of
knowledge and sources of theory. He refers to Islam as a cultural epistemology. Religion is typically considered to be and effectively occupies in
the imaginary of the modern/colonial world-system the other side of the
secular. The notion of cultural epistemology, on the other hand, challenges
the divide between culture and theory so distinctive of European epistemic
colonialism.

Majid is not alone in making the point that paying attention to the epistemic dimension of cultures or religions is an important step in overcoming
the secular pitfalls of postcolonial discourse. In his book *Orientalism and
Religion* Richard King claims that "the introduction of a variety of indigenous
traditions is, in my view, the single most important step that postcolonial
studies can take if it is to look beyond the Eurocentric foundations of its
theories and contest the epistemic violence of the colonial encounter. This
challenge requires engagement with the knowledge-forms and histories of

those cultures that have been colonized by the West and, somewhat ironically, provides a role for disciplines such as Indology in the questioning
of Western hegemonies and regimes of epistemic violence" (1999, 199).
King laments that the terms of the debate in which postcolonial discourse
has tended to define itself and its discourse is "narrowly Eurocentric." He
wishes to open up the intellectual horizon of postcolonial discourse. For
this, he gives examples of ways in which "Buddhist philosophical culture"
presents alternatives to the poststructuralist and humanist conception of
reality and the human. His aim is not to prove the superiority of a philosophical culture over another. His interest, rather, lies in inducing others to
recognize that Buddhist thought is "significantly *different*." The same would
go for "traditional Islamic notions of 'brotherhood,'" for instance. One
could investigate the extent to which they represent "an alternative to the
autonomous subject of Enlightenment humanism" (ibid.). King's purpose
is "to transgress the limits set up by the opposition of humanism and anti-
humanism and thereby to highlight the lacunae in much contemporary
postcolonial theorizing—as if the European framings of the debate were the
only options available to the postcolonial critic" (ibid.).

For Majid and King, the postcolonial thinker appears to be a secular-all-
too-secular critic. They challenge one to recognize and engage the epistemic
resources of non-European cultural philosophies, and to dialogue with contemporary reformist anti-imperial thinkers, whose grammar of dissent may
not be all too recognizable to a secular mind. It is not simply multiculturalism that they are advocating. Their goal is, rather, the decolonization of
epistemic sources and the pluralization of ways of thinking. In a way the task
becomes twofold: the location of knowledges, which provides fresh conceptions of the body, experience, intersubjectivity, social life, and so on, and the
decolonization of Western expertise, which does not mean its rejection in
toto but its reshaping in light of its limits.

It is possible to find similar insights in the Americas. Therefore, it is not
strange to find that both Majid and King consider traditions and sources that
have emerged in the two continents. Majid, for instance, discusses Latin
American liberation theology as a progressive Christian movement that,
along with a progressively defined Islam, "could address the injustices of the
modern capitalist system and provide alternatives to failed Eurocentric models for social, economic, and political arrangements" (2000, 150). Liberation
theology provides a good counterpoint to Said's secular criticism. Liberation
theology is theological discourse that aims to transform itself into a critical
theory, but without abandoning its own religious affiliations. For liberation

theologians Christianity is a betrayal without criticism. That does not mean, though, that secular people cannot be critical or that they would have to *convert* in order to become authentically critical. Critique follows as many different paths as orthodoxy and dogmatism. It is possible to say—echoing Mignolo (1995; 2000d, 273)—that critique is pluritopic and di-versal, not monotopic and universal.

King has found Mignolo's reflections on knowledge production and loci of enunciation useful. In a recent presentation in the American Academy of Religion King discussed Mignolo's concept of border gnosis and presented it as an idea that signals the overcoming of the limits of philosophy of religion and postcolonial discourse.[7] For Mignolo, gnosis is "knowledge in general, including *doxa* and episteme" (2000d, 11). *Border gnosis* refers to the intellectual production of subaltern subjects who critically engage the premises and foundations of the modern/colonial world-system. Gnosis comprehends episteme and doxa while at the same time questions the analytical power of these concepts. Gnosis also dissolves the opposition between the secular and the religious. The exploration of border gnosis is important because, as Mignolo points out and King quotes with approval, "alternatives to modern epistemology can hardly come only from *modern* (Western) epistemology itself" (Mignolo 2000d, 9). Border gnoseology aims to locate different forms of knowledge and decolonizing forms of critique that offer alternatives to modernity. The suspicion of modernity and Eurocentrism is what leads Mignolo to articulate a discourse that aims to evade the limits of the secular-religious divide.

The move toward a postsecular discourse is found in several other contemporary figures, particularly in the work of a diverse group of women of color.[8] Their work on spirituality addresses the need of presenting images of the human being beyond the mind-body and the secular-religious divides. The decolonizing work of women of color also provides models for innovative forms of critical engagement with modernity/coloniality. Muslim women, for instance, have provided models of how to engage critically traditional Islam as well as Western modernity.[9] Feminist work in this line is particularly relevant because it shows the limits of progressive movements whose critiques of imperialism are still dominated by male oriented perspectives, like, for instance, the very Latin American theology of liberation that seems to be as progressive in other points.[10] Racialized women have also highlighted the relevance of subject positioning for decolonization, not only geopolitical and cultural difference. This is evinced in the work of womanist theologians like Kelly Brown Douglas and postsecular

thinkers like Gloria Anzaldúa.[11] Postsecularism won't go very far without these and so many other important voices.

CONCLUSIONS: FROM MODERNITY/COLONIALITY TO
TRANSMODERN POSTSECULAR THINKING

I have argued here that main trends in modern, postmodern, and postcolonial theory share a secular thrust that reflect either a commitment or a
complicity with modernity/coloniality. The intellectual genealogies that can
be traced from Kant to Habermas and from Nietzsche to Vattimo consistently sustain an imperial logic of power premised on the ideas of the religious and the secular. Postcolonial theory, for its part, particularly in the
Saidian vein, has shown us more than any other of the above-mentioned
intellectual positions some of the imperial underpinnings of modernity. It
has also called attention to the ways in which modernity is the result of the
impact and counter-impact of cultures, with, to be sure, certain hegemony
on Europe's part. Yet insofar as postcolonial theory has remained bound
by secularism it has left one of the stronger expressions of modernity/
coloniality untouched.

I mentioned that there are similar problems with Wallerstein's world-
system analysis. Wallerstein fails to examine critically enough the role of
secularism in the geoculture of the world-system. He cannot therefore see
the ways in which secularism continues the logics of imperial Christendom.
This observation may have led him to realize that the discontinuities between the first and the second modernities (pre-1789 and post-1789) are
even less than he imagines. As Mignolo has pointed out, the continuities
occur both at the economic and the imaginary levels. Secularism inherits
from imperial Christianity a fundamental impetus either to convert, to control, or to radically domesticate other epistemes (or gnoseological forms, if
one uses Mignolo's expression). The secular-religious divide has come to
work in ways similar to the Christian-pagan divide. The lack of a radical
critique of secularism surreptitiously serves to maintain the superiority of
Western cultural epistemologies intact. One can find this in Wallerstein's
work. As I have pointed out elsewhere, Wallerstein exclusively registers
progressive epistemic change in the European sciences (Maldonado-Torres
2002). He is not attentive to the decolonizing effects of cultural epistemologies and ways of thinking that do not entirely share the premises of Western
modernity. We see thus that while Wallerstein is able to move himself away
from the national-centered mode of analysis of the nineteenth-century social

sciences, he remains bound by its secularistic premises. The tasks for a social science for the twenty-first century should therefore consist not only in overcoming the fixation with the nation as the unit of analysis, but also in becoming postsecular. In order to do this it has to combine at least two activities: to locate different forms of knowledge and to decolonize the expertise of those who do the locating and their disciplines. These activities are neither modern nor postmodern, but transmodern in character.

The notion of the transmodern derives from Dussel's concept of transmodernity. For Dussel, transmodernity refers to the self-affirmation of cultures that have been occluded by Western modernity (Dussel 2002). He has in mind the critical renovation of cultures that define themselves in several ways beyond the horizon of modernity/coloniality. While transmodernity refers to the response by a variety of cultural epistemologies to the challenge of modernity, a transmodern form of thinking names the theories that make visible such kinds of defiance to modern and postmodern paradigms as well as to secularizing postcolonial postures. Transmodern thought is postsecular and, therefore, postreligious as well. It is inspired by the recognition that religion is a modern concept that can never subsist without its opposite, modern secularism. Transmodern thought also recognizes that what is often referred to as religion can be as colonizing as secularism itself. It takes this insight from the way in which coloniality worked together with Christianity in the first modernity and from the efforts of subjects who criticize their own religious traditions as well as secularistic point of views in the second modernity. In this sense transmodernity may be better understood as the transgression of the limits and imperial visions of the first and the second modernities, and as the effective proposal of alternative visions for the present and the future. Transmodernity transgresses and transcends. While the first task may be more strictly defined as decolonization, the second indicates the emergence of a transmodern way of thinking. Transmodernity could be thus defined as the complex reality that comes into being through decolonizing processes and transmodern proposals. Transmodernity designates a future beyond the pitfalls of modernity/coloniality. This is the future that a transmodern way of thinking would aim to promote.

NOTES

1   Michael Löwy examines the role of secularism and the modern separation of the spheres of religion and politics, as well as its connections to liberation theology and liberation Christianity. See his essay in this volume.

2   Theologians and social scientists frequently meet in the Departamento de Estu-

dios Ecuménicos in San José, Costa Rica, to discuss the ways in which their disciplines intersect and enrich each other. The research center is an exception to the typical rule which dictates a split of theology from other fields of expertise and vice versa.

3   The transformation of the capitalist world-economy and world-system and its relation to coloniality is a concern that traverses all articles included in part 3 of this volume.

4   For an exposition of the philosophical bases of phenomenology, see Husserl 1965, 1982.

5   On this point see Peter Iver Kaufman's extraordinary account of religion and politics in early and medieval Christianity (1990).

6   For an exposition of the theory of the linguistification of the sacred, see Habermas 1984–87, vol. 2.

7   King's presentation on philosophy of religion and postcolonial discourse took place in November 2003, Toronto, Canada.

8   See, among others, Anzaldúa and Keating 2002; Kirk-Duggan 1997; Wade-Gayles 1995.

9   See, for instance, miriam cooke's account of multiple critique (2000). Muslim feminist voices occupy an important part in Majid's account of polycentrism, as outlined in the chapter "Women's Freedom in Muslim Spaces" in Unveiling Traditions (2000, 99–131).

10 See Vuola 1997. For feminist engagement with other traditions, see Donaldson and Pui-lan 2002.

11 See, among other works, Gloria Anzaldúa's Borderlands: The New Mestiza—La frontera (1987) and Interviews/Entrevistas (2000); and Kelly Brown Douglas's The Black Christ (1993).

PART FIVE

COMPARATIVE (POST)COLONIALISMS

The contributors in this section probe the connection between the generalizing assumptions of postcolonial theory and the specificity of the region, in order to evaluate possible articulations within this relatively new field of study. In this direction, both Peter Hulme and Fernando Coronil propose a general critique of the theoretical scope that has characterized the postcolonial debate, particularly of Edward Said's essential contributions to the configuration of the field. The question posed by Peter Hulme is "Just *when* is postcolonialism?" According to the British critic, one of the issues that has been disregarded in this theorization is "the time-depth of imperialism," that is, the recognition of the early stages of Spanish and Portuguese colonial domination as a foundational period in which issues such as racism and slavery, which are crucial for the understanding of modern coloniality, emerge in their current discursive and political configuration. In a similar manner, Coronil indicates that "the inclusion of Latin America in the field of postcolonial studies expands its geographical scope and also its temporal depth." "In the spirit of a long tradition of Latin American transcultural responses to colonialism and 'digestive' appropriation of imperial cultures," Coronil proposes to speak of a "tactical postcolonialism." For Coronil, who is concerned about the shift from Eurocentrism to globalcentrism, "Critical responses to colonialism from different locations take different but complementary forms. While from an Asian perspective it has become necessary to 'provincialize' European thought . . . , from a Latin American perspective it has become indispensable to globalize the periphery."

Hulme also argues against the notion of Latin America's exceptionalism that is often utilized when approaching the case of Latin America (J. Jorge Klor de Alva, Roleno Adorno), an argument that often results in the exclusion of this region from central debates. In his interpretation "nothing in the word 'postcolonial' implies an achieved *divorce* from colonialism; rather, it implies the *process* of breaking free from colonialist ways of thinking." In particular, Hulme makes reference to the Caribbean—the literary representation of race and the right of indigenous peoples to recuperate the land, as elaborated in the rewritings of *The Tempest* by Aimé Cesaire, Kamau Brathwaite, Roberto Fernández Retamar, and others—as an illuminating discursive and political counterpoint to general postcolonial theories.

Amaryll Chanady's comparative approach is another attempt at "bringing marginalized participants into the debate." Her essay focuses on the production by Latin American writers whose works give testimony of a cultural difference which resists being channeled through metropolitan models. According to Chanady, paradoxically, postcolonial theories, which cover a broad scope of historical phenomena, face the risk of producing a homogenizing effect that can be counteracted by bringing other actors and cultural experiences into the general discussion through the implementation of comparative analyses. At the same time, the debate has stereotyped roles (subject positions) in such a way that "the postcolonial subject has become interesting . . . only insofar as s/he writes back to the center." Chanady elaborates on the topics of Latin American exceptionalism, ambivalence, transculturation, and the like, as well as on literary-based concepts such as magical realism, in order to study the insertion of the particular into the universal, of local differences into the realm of dominant critical and theoretical paradigms.

Román de la Campa also focuses on "the question of literature," particularly on the role of *testimonio* in the context of the postcolonial debate. According to de la Campa, "The question . . . is not whether *postcolonial* applies to Latin America in some general or metaphoric sense, but rather whether the term can sustain the latter's rich and varied modern/colonial history without imploding or erasing more than it unearths." Elaborating further on the question of the locus of enunciation for the production of critical discourses, de la Campa explores the interconnections between an "autochthonous sphere of Latin American theory" (e.g., transculturation, theology, and dependency theory) and Euro-American or South Asian scholarship. The interpretation of *testimonio*—a paradigmatic and engaged form of writing in which postmodernity meets subalternism—has been the object of diverse and often divergent critical approaches.

For Mary Louise Pratt, "The postcolonial project requires some decolonizing of its own." She wonders, "Do we live in a postcolonial era? Is 'postcoloniality' a state which has been achieved, or one to which we aspire? In a statement like that, who is the 'we'? Are some of 'us' more postcolonial than others? Or does the term describe a planetary 'state of the system,' a *coyuntura* which is being lived out in myriad ways, in myriad subject positions and a vast array of geopolitical contexts?" Pratt elaborates a critique of postcolonial theory that recuperates concepts often neglected or minimized in central debates, such as neocolonialism, peripheral modernity, and imperialism, "a category [that] draws together colonialism, neocolonialism, and other forms of expansion and intervention that continue to shape the world today." Pratt's piece offers insightful references to the contributions of Simón Bolívar, Aimé Césaire, Horacio Quiroga, Alejo Carpentier, Mario de Andrade, José María Arguedas, and others to the definition of a cultural identity that incorporates (neo)coloniality in a creative way without adhering to the script of otherness imposed on Latin American cultures from outside and above.

POSTCOLONIAL THEORY AND THE REPRESENTATION OF CULTURE IN THE AMERICAS

Peter Hulme

There are only two controversial parts to the word *postcolonial*—one is the word *post*, and the other is the word *colonial*—so let me start with some tentative definitions. I'm *not* speaking about some vague cultural phenomenon called "postcolonialism," and I'm only speaking secondarily about the political state of "postcoloniality," or about "postcolonial literatures." I'm mainly speaking about "postcolonial theory," using that term as a way of describing a body of work which attempts to break with the colonialist assumptions that have marked many of the projects of political and cultural criticism launched from Europe and the United States, while learning from and frequently refiguring those theoretical projects in the interests of an analysis of and resistance to the networks of imperial power which continue to control much of the world. *Postcolonial theory* may not be a wonderful term, but it seems to me a perfectly adequate starting point and to do as much as one could reasonably expect a single term to do. It's certainly helped put questions of colonialism and imperialism onto the agenda of cultural studies, for which many of us have reason to be grateful.

Patrick Williams's and Laura Chrisman's *Colonial Discourse and Post-Colonial Theory* (1994), which is the first postcolonial reader but not the last, reprints thirty-one articles, twenty-one of which have some clear geocultural reference point: eight relate to Africa, five to India, four to the Middle East, two to the United States, one to the Caribbean, and one to Latin America. This is probably not an inaccurate map of how postcolonial theory as currently understood has developed, and of the bits of the world to which it has paid attention, in part through the major influence of Edward Said. America—in a continental sense—hardly features on this map at all.

To put "postcolonial" theory and "the Americas" into the same title is, then, immediately to exacerbate some of the problems that accrue to the very idea of postcolonial theory. And it's just those problems that I want to examine. Postcolonial theory is obviously still in the process of consolidation. My remarks are aimed *from* within a basic sympathy to the project marked by that term at certain tendencies to consolidate in the wrong places or too quickly or too unthinkingly: "America" is the spoon I stir with, in order to keep the debate fluid.

There are perhaps three separate problems here, though they tend to interfere with one another. First off, there's the problem of the time-depth of imperialism. In his recent book *Culture and Imperialism* Edward Said only recognizes the age of high imperialism, ignoring the earlier colonial period altogether: Said discusses Jane Austen's *Mansfield Park* (published in 1814) as a work from the "pre-imperialist age." Now, the relationship between "imperialism" and "colonialism" could be the subject for a paper in itself. Generally speaking, however, *imperialism* is taken as the broader term, so Said can—and does—discuss the phenomenon of postcolonial theory within a wider discussion of the relationship between "culture" and "imperialism." Fair enough. In practice, though, the field studied in the new book is not significantly broader than what was studied in *Orientalism*. The geographical fulcrum of *Culture and Imperialism* is very similar to that of *Orientalism*: the Middle East, with a stretch east to India and west to Algeria. The temporal fulcrum of the book is 1902—the year of *Heart of Darkness*—with about ninety years on either side given any real weight of analysis. The temporal limitation explains the geography of the book given the disposition of the British and French empires at the beginning of the twentieth century, but the temporal limitation has itself no *obvious* explanation given that these empires both began in the seventeenth century, in America. One consequence of all this is that issues of slavery and racism, so inextricably associated with European culture and empire, only make the briefest of appearances in Said's work—which is one reason why we have to acknowledge *Orientalism* (1994a [1978]) as one important, but *not the only* progenitor of postcolonial theory.

The second problem—still with *Culture and Imperialism* in mind—is Said's failure to recognize the United States as a colonial and imperial power from its inception, not just from the end of the Second World War. What happens in *Culture and Imperialism*, as it had in *Orientalism*, is that the United States— which Said casually but unforgivably refers to as "America"—appears on the scene to assume the imperial mantle after the Second World War, but without any substantial consideration of the country's own origins as a set of British, Spanish, and French colonies, nor of its own imperial beginnings in the Pacific during the mid-nineteenth century, nor of its own history of "internal colonialism," nor of its own genocidal wars against the indigenous population of North America, nor of its own twentieth-century adventurism in Central America and the Caribbean. Said's insistence on placing U.S. foreign policy within a discussion of imperial projects is entirely salutary, but his analysis of U.S. imperialism lacks the historical and cultural time-depth he brings to the European material. Such an analysis would inevitably have brought America onto his map.

The third problem revolves around a difficult question which underlies the other two: "just *when* is postcolonialism?" Williams and Chrisman date the formal dissolution of the colonial empires to 1947, which is not unconventional. That date allows us to gather together a group of anticolonial writers who can become Said's precursors as postcolonial theorists—Fanon, Césaire, James, Antoninus, Guha; but it still leaves most of the American continent out of the equation. Just where and *when do* the United States, Canada, and most of the countries of Latin America and the Caribbean fit into this picture?

What I've said so far has tended to suggest that America's absence from the debate has been accidental: Said's work was the inaugurator of the discourse and he focused on the Middle East; postwar struggles against the colonial empires have been in Africa and the Indian subcontinent, therefore the most prominent postcolonial theorists have come from those places. However, Rolena Adorno's argument, in her *Latin American Research Review* piece (1993b), is that the Latin American countries simply don't fit into the postcolonial paradigm that has been implicitly applied to them, especially in the series of books that Patricia Seed originally reviewed under the general heading "Colonial and Postcolonial Discourse."

Adorno addresses her remarks to the notion of "colonial discourse," perhaps the analytic phrase most usually associated with postcolonial theory. She argues that the need for a lingua franca in an age of specialisms led to the idea of "colonial discourse," and that it's now time to start registering some differences. That would be fine. Except that her argument—which is based upon some provocative but not very systematic remarks by the anthropologist Jorge Klor de Alva (1992a)—seems to suggest *exceptionalism* rather than *difference*. I can't go into this in detail but basically Klor de Alva argues—in a nice twist to the postcolonial debate—that the very notions of colonialism and imperialism came from the modern experiences of the non-Hispanic colonial powers, and were only subsequently and improperly imposed on the Spanish American experience from the sixteenth to the mid-eighteenth centuries. If this argument were correct, then certainly Latin America, and probably the whole of the continent, would fall outside the terms of this discussion. Said's oversights would turn out to be intuitively correct emphases.

However, the argument seems to me fundamentally flawed. Klor de Alva wants to separate off America altogether on the grounds that the wars of independence were not primarily fought by people who were colonized against the people who had colonized them. This is undoubtedly true in a sense, but the real question is: why take *that* model of colonialism and decide that since America doesn't fit you can't talk about decolonization or colonial discourse or postcolonial theory? If you're going to make distinctions, and we should, then there are plenty of important distinctions to be made—as Anne McClintock and Ella Shohat and others have demonstrated —without removing America from the colonial picture. For one thing, the etymology of the word *colony* doesn't suggest that you had to colonize *people*; *land*, as so often, is the crucial issue: the *requerimiento* and John Locke's *Second Treatise* were both justifications of the appropriation of land which stand as classic documents of colonial discourse from an indigenous perspective, irrespective of whether or not the invaders who justified their actions by the arguments in such documents saw themselves as colonists in any sense acceptable to Klor de Alva or Rolena Adorno. To say, rightly, that the wars of independence were followed by wars of extermination against the indigenous populations of north and south America does not entail calling subsequent discourses justifying such extermination noncolonial; it just means that from the indigenous perspective colonialism is not over when a particular state becomes in that formal sense "postcolonial." Everything can become an exception if you look at it hard enough. We need to look hard, but we also need to hold on to our hard-won generalities, of which "colonial discourse" is one of the most important.

Now the *post* in postcolonial theory is not, as I see it, principally a temporal marker, although there is an obviously closely related use of the word *postcolonial* in that formal political register to refer to nations that have once been colonies. I think we have to grasp the nettle: in this second sense of the word the United States becomes a postcolonial nation in 1776 and its early literature is marked by this fact and therefore quite properly described as postcolonial—Melville is a good example, as is a significant amount of mid-nineteenth-century Latin American literature, which doesn't stop the United States and Argentina, for example, from becoming immediately themselves colonizing powers with respect to the native populations of the continent whose lands and resources they covet, and doesn't stop the postcolonial writers of the continent struggling, sometimes unsuccessfully, to formulate a postcolonial discourse which might be adequate to the geocultural realities of the newly independent nations in their complex relationships with each other, with indigenous and African populations, and with the world of European writing and politics. The real advantage of considering such unlikely figures as Ralph Waldo Emerson and Andrés Bello as postcolonial writers is that we are provoked into rereading them in a way which might make them seem new to us. Then again, it might not.

Where, then, within this postcolonial America can we look for signs of an American postcolonial theory? I'll suggest a few, but let me preface the suggestions with a caveat. One of the most frequent ways of misunderstanding the term *postcolonial* is by imagining that the term itself somehow misleadingly suggests that "colonialism" has been completely left behind, whereas we all know that we live in a world marked by neocolonialism. This seems to me a linguistically incorrect reading of the prefix *post*. Let me give a personal example. I was a post–Second World War baby, born three years after the end of the war, but I could be called a "postwar baby" because everything about my upbringing was marked by the aftermath of that war. I was also born "post" the French Revolution and "post" the English Civil War and "post" the decline of the Roman Empire—and no doubt my early years were in some distant sense marked by those events, but the generation to which I belong was not called "post–Roman Empire." You can perhaps see the point I'm making. Nothing in the word *postcolonial* implies an achieved *divorce* from colonialism; rather, it implies the *process* of breaking free from colonialist ways of thinking. If and when "newness" is achieved, the word *postcolonial* will become as irrelevant as "post–Roman Empire."

Some American locations, then. Frantz Fanon is increasingly recognized as an absolutely key figure, but still more for *The Wretched of the Earth* than for *Black Skin, White Masks*: questions of nationalism tend to be emphasized over questions of race, revolutionary violence over psychology, class analysis over language, Algeria over Martinique, Africa over America. I don't want to reverse the polarities, just to give them equal emphasis.

In the middle part of the twentieth century much American postcolonial theory and criticism clustered around readings of Shakespeare's play *The Tempest*. Particularly in Aimé Césaire's powerful rewriting of the play, the dominant relationship came to be seen as that between Prospero and Caliban, colonizer and colonized, a model taken from the Caribbean to Africa and grounded in anticolonial struggle by Fanon himself. In this reading the key words of the play are "This island's mine," spoken by Caliban: an assertion of his rights to the land that has been taken from him by Prospero's usurpation. I remain committed to the continuing valency of this model and to the relevance of Caliban's words. However much we might want to complicate the picture—and I'm going to try to complicate it myself—that claim to land rights is still fundamental to indigenous groups throughout the world, and nowhere more so than on the American continent.

But the conflict between Prospero and Caliban cannot be definitive of the colonial situation. Caliban is an overdetermined figure that can be read as either American or African, but his compacted character obviously can't suggest the triangular relationship—the white, the red, and the black—that defines so many parts of the continent during the colonial period. In addition, feminist critics have rightly pointed out that the marginalization of Miranda and Sycorax within the anticolonial criticism and appropriations of *The Tempest* has tended to deliver an entirely masculine world of heroic struggle inadequate both to historical realities and to postcolonial ideals. Aphra Behn's *Oroonoko*, set in Surinam, and recently and provocatively called the first American novel in English, has been discussed by several critics (i.e., Spengemann 1984) as offering a more complex and perhaps ultimately more fruitful paradigm for the study of colonial relationships; although it has to be said that *The Tempest* still has some life left in it, judging by the exciting ways it has been reworked in two of the best English novels of the last few years, Barry Unsworth's *Sacred Hunger* and Marina Warner's *Indigo*.

To my mind the limitation of *The Tempest* for this sort of work comes from the very clarity with which it articulates one of the most powerful fears running at least through English America: here in the interdiction that Prospero puts on what might have been seen as the "natural" or an any rate "inevitable" relationship between Caliban and Miranda. One reading of the play would see Prospero's willingness to lose his beloved Milanese kingdom through Miranda's marriage to the heir of Naples as indicative of the high price he is willing to pay to avoid miscegenation. Ultimately, The Tempest turns it back on what at one, perhaps unconscious level, the play is aware will become one of the defining factors of American culture: mestizaje.

One of the ironies of Said's lack of attention to America in Culture and Imperialism is that the word which does most work for Said in establishing the kinds of connections he wants to make between "culture" and "imperialism" is the term counterpoint. Now counterpoint obviously has a long history within musical terminology, but within postcolonial theory, it has a very precise origin in Fernando Ortiz's Contrapunteo cubano, published in 1940, the book which also introduced the term transculturación. This is an irony rather than an oversight: there's no reason why Said's already encyclopedic knowledge and range of references should extend to the Caribbean. But I do want to make a larger point out of the irony.

All the American examples I've given so far come from the Caribbean. Apart from Fanon and Césaire and Ortiz, that relatively small area has produced postcolonial theorists of the significance of Edouard Glissant, George Lamming, Roberto Fernández Retamar, C. L. R. James, to name just a few. Now, whether the Caribbean has been exceptionally endowed with writers who can with hindsight be seen as developing the lineaments of a postcolonial theory is a matter which I'm not competent to judge. It does seem to me, however, that one reason for the wealth of this kind of writing in the Caribbean is the fact that all theorizing in the Caribbean is articulated across— even if it often ignores—the genocide of the area's native population. Native is always a fraught term, certainly so in Algeria and India, which often provide the paradigms for the colonizer-colonized relationship; equally so, no doubt, in Mexico and Peru. The Caribbean is perhaps exceptional inasmuch as no discourse (with minor and recent exceptions) can claim to embody a genuinely native point of view, however much indigenismo of various colors can be a political or cultural card to play at certain junctures. So what I'm suggesting is that this lack of a native positionality in the debate has put Caribbean theorists in the forefront of the articulation of a conceptual vocabulary which can make sense of at least certain sorts of cultural developments during and after the colonial period.

As we reread, we need also to pay attention to periodization, which might look very different when approached with a postcolonial eye. There is certainly no easy correlation between the formal ending of a colonial relationship and the production of theoretical work that can be regarded as "postcolonial"; but what was written in Haiti in the early nineteenth century could certainly do with more attention. If, however, I were pressed to identify a "beginning" moment in the Saidian sense of the word, then increasingly it seems to me that that moment would be 1898, a seismic year for the Caribbean, the beginning, perhaps, of its modernity. Ortiz will, I'm sure, be increasingly read as the great theorist of the cultural *consequences* of 1898. The great figure on the other side of that dividing year is José Martí, from whose work may yet be drawn the bases for a genuinely American postcolonial theory.

I'll end with a very open-ended remark. One of the concerns of postcolonial theory has been with identifying the *locatedness* of European theoretical vocabulary as a way of challenging the easy and false universal claims made by that theory. To *ground* conceptual language is to make it work harder to grasp the world beyond its locality. Similarly, postcolonial theory is slowly putting together its own conceptual repertory drawn from its own places and localities, its own cultural resources. The Caribbean has been a fertile ground for these, and—as it happens—a ground seemingly in tune with the dominant notes of postcolonial theory: the language of transculturation and counterpoint, of Creolization and *métissage*, sits quickly and comfortably alongside hybridity and ambivalence, migration and diaspora. Whether, however, the Caribbean *should* stand as a metonym for America as a whole is a difficult question I'm happy to leave unanswered: some theory undoubtedly travels well, but we don't as yet understand much about the cultural baggage that all terms inevitably carry with them. It's tempting to think that we can make words mean what we want them to mean; but that was Humpty Dumpty's theory, and look what happened to him.

ELEPHANTS IN THE AMERICAS?
LATIN AMERICAN POSTCOLONIAL STUDIES AND
GLOBAL DECOLONIZATION

Fernando Coronil

G iven the curiously rapid rise to prominence of postcolonial studies as an academic field in Western metropolitan centers since the late 1980s, it is to be expected that its further development would involve efforts, like this one, to take stock of its regional expressions. Yet, while the rubric "Latin American postcolonial studies" suggests the existence of a regional body of knowledge under that name, in reality it points to a problem: there is no corpus of work on Latin America commonly recognized as "postcolonial." This problem is magnified by the multiple and often diverging meanings attributed to the signifier *postcolonial*, by the heterogeneity of nations and peoples encompassed by the problematical term *Latin America*, by the thoughtful critiques that have questioned the relevance of postcolonial studies for Latin America, and by the diversity and richness of reflections on Latin America's colonial and postcolonial history, many of which, like most nations in this region, long predate the field of postcolonial studies as it was developed in the 1980s. How, then, to identify and examine a body of work that in reality does not appear to exist? How to define it without arbitrarily inventing or confining it? How to treat it as "postcolonial" without framing it in terms of the existing postcolonial canon and thus inevitably colonizing it?

These challenging questions do not yield easy answers. Yet they call attention to the character of postcolonial studies as one among a diverse set of regional reflections on the forms and legacies of colonialism, or rather, *colonialisms*. In light of the worldwide diversity of critical thought on colonialism and its ongoing aftermath, the absence of a corpus of Latin American postcolonial studies is a problem not *of* studies on Latin America, but *between* postcolonial and Latin American studies. I thus approach this discussion of Latin American postcolonial studies—or, as I prefer to see it, of postcolonial studies in the Americas—by reflecting on the relationship between these two bodies of knowledge.

While its indisputable achievements have turned postcolonial studies into an indispensable point of reference in discussions about old and new colonialisms, this field can be seen as a general standard or canon only if one forgets that it is a regional corpus of knowledge whose global influence cannot be separated from its grounding in powerful metropolitan universities; difference, not deference, orients this discussion. Rather than subordinating Latin American studies to postcolonial studies and selecting texts and authors that may meet its standards and qualify as postcolonial, I seek to establish a dialogue between them on the basis of their shared concerns and distinctive contributions. This dialogue, as with any genuine exchange even among unequal partners, should serve not just to add participants to the postcolonial discussion but also to clarify its assumptions and transform its terms.

My discussion is divided into four sections: the formation of the field of postcolonial studies; the place of Latin America in postcolonial studies; responses to postcolonial studies from Latin Americanists; and open-ended suggestions for deepening the dialogue between postcolonial and Latin American studies. By focusing on exchanges between these fields, I have traded the option of offering close readings of selected texts and problems for the option of engaging texts that have addressed the postcolonial debate in terms of how they shape or define the fields of postcolonial and Latin American studies.

POSTCOLONIAL STUDIES

Despite a long history of critical reflections on modern colonialism originating in reaction to the conquest and colonization of the Americas, *postcolonialism* as a term and as a conceptual category originates in discussions about the decolonization of African and Asian colonies after World War II. At that time, *postcolonial* was used mostly as an adjective by sociologists and political scientists to characterize changes in the states and economies of former colonies of the "Third World," a category that was also created at that time. This regional focus was already present in the French sociologist George Balandier's analysis of "the colonial situation" (1951) as well as in later debates about the "colonial" and "postcolonial state" (Alavi 1972; Chandra 1980), the "colonial mode of production" (Alavi 1972), or the "articulation of modes of production" (Wolpe 1980; Berman and Lonsdale 1992). Although Latin America was considered part of the Third World, because most of its nations had achieved political independence during the first quarter of the nineteenth century, it was only tangentially addressed in these discussions about decolonization that centered on the newly independent nations of Africa and Asia.

As a label for "old" postcolonial nations that had faced the problem of national development for a long time, the key word in Latin American social thought during this period was not *colonialism* or *postcolonialism*, but *dependency*. This term identified a formidable body of work developed by leftist scholars in the 1960s, designed to understand Latin America's distinct historical trajectory and to counter modernization theory. Riding atop the wave of economic growth that followed World War II, modernization theory presented capitalism as an alternative to socialism and conditioned the achievement of modernity to overcoming obstacles inhering in the economies, cultures, and subjective motivations of the peoples of the "traditional" societies of the Third World. W. W. Rostow's *The Stages of Economic Growth* (1960), revealingly subtitled "A Non-Communist Manifesto," was a particularly clear example of modernization theory's unilinear historicism, ideological investment in capitalism, and teleological view of progress.

In sharp contrast, dependency theorists argued that development and underdevelopment are the mutually dependent outcomes of capitalist accumulation on a world scale. In their view, since underdevelopment is the product of development, the periphery cannot be modernized by unregulated capitalism but through an alteration of its polarizing dynamics (see, on this issue, Grosfoguel in this volume). This basic insight about the mutual constitution of centers and peripheries was rooted in the Argentinian economist Raúl Prebisch's demonstration that unequal trade among nations leads to their unequal development. Formulated in the 1940s, Prebisch's critique of unequal exchange has been considered "the most influential idea about economy and society ever to come out of Latin America" (Love 1980, 46). His insights were integrated into "structural" reinterpretations of social and historical transformation in Latin America by Fernando Henrique Cardoso, Enzo Faletto, Aníbal Quijano, Theotonio Dos Santos, Rui Mauro Marini, and many other "dependency" theorists; as Cardoso (1977) noted, their work was "consumed" in the United States as "dependency theory" associated with the work of Andre Gunder Frank.

The worldwide influence of dependency declined after the 1970s. Dependency theory was criticized for its one-dimensional structuralism and displaced by the postmodern emphasis on the textual, fragmentary, and indeterminate; its Eurocentric focus on state-centered development and disregard of racial and ethnic divisions in Latin American nations has been a focus of a recent critique (Grosfoguel 2000). Despite its shortcomings, in my view the dependency school represents one of Latin America's most significant contributions to postcolonial thought within this period, auguring the postcolonial critique of historicism and providing conceptual tools for a much-needed postcolonial critique of contemporary imperialism. As a fundamental critique of Eurocentric conceptions of history and of capitalist development, dependency theory undermined historicist narratives of the "traditional," "transitional" and "modern," making it necessary to examine postcolonial and metropolitan nations in relation to each other through categories appropriate to specific situations of dependency.

Starting around three decades after World War II, the second usage of the term *postcolonial* developed in the Anglophone world in connection with critical studies of colonialism and colonial literature under the influence of postmodern perspectives. This change took place during a historical juncture formed by four intertwined worldwide processes: the increasingly evident shortcomings of Third World national-development projects; the breakdown of really existing socialism; the ascendance of conservative politics in Britain (Thatcherism) and the United States (Reaganism); and the overwhelming appearance of neoliberal capitalism as the only visible, or at least seemingly viable, historical horizon. During this period, postcolonial studies acquired a distinctive identity as an academic field, marked by the unusual marriage between the metropolitan location of its production and the anti-imperial stance of its authors, many of whom were linked to the Third World by personal ties and political choice.

In this second phase, while historical work has centered on British colonialism, literary criticism has focused on Anglophone texts, including those from Australia and the English-speaking Caribbean. The use of postmodern and poststructuralist perspectives in these works became so intimately associated with postcolonialism that the *post* of postcolonialism has become identified with the *post* of postmodernism and poststructuralism. For instance, a major postcolonial reader argues that "postcolonial studies is a decidedly new field of scholarship arising in Western universities as the application of post-modern thought to the long history of colonising practices" (Henry Schwarz 2000, 6).

In my view, equally central to postcolonialism has been the critical application of Marxism to a broad spectrum of practices of social and cultural domination not reducible to the category of "class." While marked by idiosyncratic traces, its identifying signature has been the convergence of these theoretical currents—Marxist and postmodern/poststructuralist—in studies that address the complicity between knowledge and power. Edward W. Said's integration of Gramscian and Foucauldian perspectives in his path-breaking critique of *Orientalism* (1994a [1978]) has been widely recognized as foundational for the field. A similar tension between Marxism and post-structuralism animates the evolving work of the South Asian group of historians associated with subaltern studies, the strongest historiographical current of postcolonial studies.

Postcolonial critique now encompasses problems as different as the formation of minorities in the United States or African philosophy. But while it has expanded to new areas, it has retreated from analyzing their relations within a unified field; the fragmentary study of parts has taken precedence over the systemic analysis of wholes. Its critique of the grand narratives of modernity has led to skepticism toward any grand narrative, not always discriminating between Eurocentric claims to universality and the necessary universalism arising from struggles against worldwide capitalist domination (Amin 1989; Lazarus 1999).

As the offspring of a tense marriage between anti-imperial critique and metropolitan privilege, postcolonial studies is permeated by tensions that also affect its reception, provoking sharply different evaluations of its significance and political implications. While some analysts see it as an academic commodity that serves the interests of global capital and benefits its privileged practitioners (Dirlik 1994), others regard it as a paradigmatic intellectual shift that redefines the relationship between knowledge and emancipatory politics (Robert Young 2001). This debate helps identify what in my view is the central intellectual challenge postcolonial studies has raised: to develop a bifocal perspective that allows one, on the one hand, to view colonialism as a fundamental process in the formation of the modern world without reducing history to colonialism as an all-encompassing process and, on the other hand, to contest modernity and its Eurocentric forms of knowledge without presuming to view history from a privileged epistemological standpoint.

In this light, the apparently simple grammatical juxtaposition of *post* and *colonial* in *postcolonial studies* serves as a sign to address the murky entanglement of knowledge and power. The *post* functions both as a temporal marker to refer to the problem of classifying societies in historical time and as an epistemological sign to evoke the problem of producing knowledge of history and society in the context of imperial relations.

POSTCOLONIAL STUDIES AND LATIN AMERICAN STUDIES

Given this genealogy, it is remarkable but understandable that debates and texts on or from Latin America do not figure significantly in the field of postcolonial studies as it has been defined since the 1980s. As Peter Hulme (1996) has noted, Said's canonical *Culture and Imperialism* (1993) is emblematic of this tendency: it centers on British and French imperialism from the late nineteenth century to the present; its geographical focus is limited to an area stretching from Algeria to India; and the role of the United States is restricted to the post–World War II period, disregarding this nation's origin as a colonial settlement of Britain, Spain, and France, the processes of internal colonialism through which Native Americans were subjected within its territory, and its imperial designs in the Americas and elsewhere from the nineteenth century to the present.

The major readers and discussions on postcolonial studies barely take Latin America into account. One of the earliest attempts to discuss postcolonial literatures as a comprehensive field, *The Empire Writes Back: Theory and Practice in Post-Colonial Literatures* (Ashcroft, Griffiths, and Tiffin 1989), acknowledges a focus on Anglophone literatures. Even so, its extensive sixteen-page bibliography, including "all the works cited in the text, and some additional useful publications" (224), fails to mention even a single text written on Latin America or by a Latin American author. The book treats Anglophone literatures, including those produced in the Caribbean, as if these literatures were not cross-fertilized by the travel of ideas and authors across regions and cultures—or at least as if the literatures resulting from the Iberian colonization of the Americas had not participated in this exchange.

This exclusion of Latin America was clearly reflected in the first general anthology of postcolonial texts, *Colonial Discourse and Postcolonial Theory* (Williams and Chrisman 1994), whose thirty-one articles include no author from Ibero-America. Published two years later, *The Post-Colonial Studies Reader* (Ashcroft, Griffiths, and Tiffin 1995) reproduces the Anglocentric perspective that characterizes their earlier *The Empire Writes Back*, but this time without the justification of a topical focus on English literatures. The reader features eighty-six texts divided into fourteen thematic sections, including topics such as nationalism and hybridity, which have long concerned Latin American thinkers. While some authors are repeated under different topics (Bhabha appears three times, Spivak twice), the only author associated with Latin America is José Rabasa, whose contribution is a critical reading of Mercator's *Atlas*, a topic relevant but not specific to Latin America.

The marginalization of Latin America is reproduced in most works on postcolonialism published since then. For example, Leela Gandhi's *Postcolonial Theory: A Critical Introduction* (1998) does not discuss Latin American critical reflections or include even a single reference to Latin American thinkers in its extensive bibliography. While *Relocating Postcolonialism* (Goldberg and Quayson 2002) "relocates" the postcolonial through the inclusion of such topics as the cultural politics of the French radical right and the construction of Korean-American identities, it maintains the exclusion of Latin America by having no articles or authors associated with this area. This taken-for-granted exclusion appears as well in a dialogue between John Comaroff and Homi Bhabha that introduces the book. Following Comaroff's suggestion, they provide a historical frame for "postcoloniality" in terms of two periods: the decolonization of the Third World marked by India's independence in 1947; and the hegemony of neoliberal capitalism signalled by the end of the Cold War in 1989 (ibid., 15).

In contrast, two recent works on postcolonialism include Latin America within the postcolonial field, yet their sharply different criteria highlight the problem of discerning the boundaries of this field. In an article for a book on the postcolonial debate in Latin America, Bill Ashcroft (whose coedited book basically excludes Latin America) presents Latin America as "modernity's first born" and thus as a region that has participated since its inception in the production of postcolonial discourses (1999). He defines postcolonial discourse comprehensively as "the discourse of the colonized" produced in colonial contexts; as such, it does not have to be "anti-colonial" (ibid., 14–15). He presents Menchú's *I, Rigoberta Menchú* and Juan Rulfo's *Pedro Páramo* as examples that reveal that "the transformative strategies of postcolonial discourse, strategies which engage the deepest disruptions of modernity, are not limited to the recently colonized" (ibid., 28). While his comprehensive definition of the field includes Latin American discourses from the conquest onward, his examples suggest a narrower field defined by more discriminating but unexamined criteria.

The second text is Robert Young's *Postcolonialism: An Historical Introduction* (2001). While Young (like Ashcroft) had not discussed Latin America in a previous work (*White Mythologies* [1990]), in his new book he gives such foundational importance to Latin America and to the Third World that he prefers to name the field "tricontinentalism," after the tricontinental conference held in Havana in 1966 (2001, 57). Young recognizes that postcolonialism has long and varied genealogies, but he finds it necessary to restrict it to anticolonial thought developed after formal political independence has been achieved: "Many of the problems raised can be resolved if the postcolonial is defined as coming after colonialism and imperialism, in their original meaning of direct-rule domination" (ibid.). Yet Young distinguishes further between the anticolonial thought of the periphery and the more theoretical thought formed at the heart of empires "when the political and cultural experience of the marginalized periphery developed into a more general theoretical position that could be set against western political, intellectual and academic hegemony and its protocols of objective knowledge" (ibid., 65). Thus, even successful anticolonial movements "did not fully establish the equal value of the cultures of the decolonised nations." "To do that," Young argues, "it was necessary to take the struggle into the heartlands of the former colonial powers" (ibid.).

Young's suggestive discussion of Latin American postcolonial thought leaves unclear the extent to which its anticolonialism is also "critical" in the sense he ascribes to metropolitan reflections. Young discusses Latin American postcolonial thought in two brief chapters. The first, "Latin America I: Mariátegui, Transculturation and Cultural Dependency," is divided into four sections: "Marxism in Latin America," an account of the development of communist parties and Marxist thinkers in the twentieth century, leading to the Cuban Revolution; "Mexico 1910," a presentation of the Mexican revolution as precursor of tricontinental insurrections against colonial or neo-colonial exploitation; "Mariátegui," a discussion of Mariátegui's role as one of Latin America's most original thinkers, highlighting his innovative interpretation of Peruvian reality; and "Cultural Dependency," an overview of the ideas of some cultural critics which, for brevity's sake, I will reduce to a few names and to the key concepts associated with their work: the Brazilian

Oswaldo de Andrade's "anthropophagy" (the formation of Latin American identity through the "digestion" of worldwide cultural formations); the Cuban Fernando Ortiz's "transculturation" (the transformative creation of cultures out of colonial confrontations); the Brazilian Roberto Schwarz's "misplaced ideas" (the juxtaposition in the Americas of ideas from different times and societies); and the Argentinian Néstor García Canclini's "hybrid cultures" (the negotiation of the traditional and the modern in Latin American cultural formations).

Young's second chapter, "Latin America 2: Cuba: Guevara, Castro, and the Tricontinental," organized around the centrality of Cuba in the development of postcolonial thought, is divided into three sections: "Compañero: Che Guevara" focuses on Guevara's antiracism and radical humanism; "New Man" relates Guevara's concept of "the new man" to José Martí's proposal of cultural and political independence for "Our America" and to Roberto Fernández Retamar's Calibanesque vision of *mestizaje*; and "The Tricontinental" presents the Tricontinental Conference of Solidarity of the Peoples of Africa, Asia and Latin America" held in Havana in 1966 as the founding moment of postcolonial thought—in Young's words, "Postcolonialism was born with the *Tricontinental*" (2001, 213).

While Young's selection is comprehensive and reasonable, its organizing criteria are not sufficiently clear; one can easily imagine a different selection involving other thinkers and anticolonial struggles in Latin America. And despite the significance he attaches to theoretical reflections from metropolitan centers, Young makes no mention of the many Latin Americanists who, working from those centers or from shifting locations between them and Latin America, have produced monumental critiques of colonialism during the same period as Said, Bhabha, and Spivak—for example, Enrique Dussel, Aníbal Quijano, and Walter Mignolo, among others.

The contrasting positions of Ashcroft and Young reveal the difficulty of defining postcolonial studies in Latin America. At one extreme, we encounter a comprehensive discursive field whose virtue is also its failing, for it must be subdivided to be useful. At the other extreme, we encounter a restricted domain that includes an appreciative and impressive selection of authors, but that needs to be organized through less-discretionary criteria. But whether one adopts an open or a restricted definition of Latin American postcolonial studies, what is fundamental is to treat alike, with the same intellectual earnestness, all the thinkers and discourses included in the general field of postcolonial studies, whether they are produced in the metropolitan centres or in the various peripheries, writing or speaking in English or in other imperial and subaltern languages. Otherwise, the evaluation of postcolonial thought risks reproducing within its midst the subalternization of peoples and cultures it claims to oppose.

LATIN AMERICAN STUDIES AND POSTCOLONIAL STUDIES

Given this genealogy, it is understandable that the reception of postcolonial studies among Latin Americanists has been mixed. Many thinkers have doubted the appropriateness of postcolonial studies to Latin America, claiming that postcolonial studies responds to the academic concerns of metropolitan universities, to the specific realities of Asia and Africa, or to the position of academics who write about, not from, Latin America and disregard its cultural traditions (Achugar 1998; Colás 1995; Klor de Alva 1992a, 1995; Moraña 1998a; Pérez 1999; and Yúdice 1996). Klor de Alva has presented the most extreme critique, arguing that colonialism and postcolonialism are "(Latin) American mirages," for these terms, "as they are used in the relevant literature," or "as commonly understood today," properly apply only to marginal populations of indigenes, not to the major non-Indian core that has formed the largely European and Christian societies of the American territories since the sixteenth century. For him, its wars of independence were not anticolonial wars, but elite struggles inspired in European models that maintained colonial inequalities.

This argument, in my view, has several problems: it takes as given the standard set by discussions of the Asian and African colonial and postcolonial experiences; it assumes too sharp a separation between indigenous and non-indigenous peoples in America; it adopts a restricted conception of colonialism derived from a homogenized conception of Northern European colonialism and an idealized image of the effectiveness of its rule; it disregards the importance of the colonial control of territories in Iberian colonialism; it pays insufficient attention to the colonial control of populations in the high-density indigenous societies of Mexico, Peru, and Central America and in plantations run by imported slave labor in the Caribbean and Brazil; and it fails to see the similarity between the wars of independence and the decolonizing processes of Asia and Africa, which also involved the preservation of elite privilege and the reproduction of internal inequalities (what Pablo González Casanova [1965b] and Rodolfo Stavenhagen [1965] have theorized for Latin America as "internal colonialism"). Rather than presenting one set of colonial experiences as its exclusive standard, a more productive option would be to pluralize colonialism—to recognize its multiple forms as the product of a common historical process of Western expansion.

An influential debate on colonial and postcolonial studies in a major journal of Latin American studies was initiated by Patricia Seed, a historian of colonial Latin America, who presented the methods and concepts of colonial and postcolonial discourse as a significant breakthrough in social analysis. According to Seed (1991), postcolonial studies' critique of conceptions of the subject as unitary and sovereign, and of meaning as transparently expressed through language, recasts discussions of colonial domination that are simplistically polarized as resistance versus accommodation by autonomous subjects. Two years later in the same journal, three literary critics questioned her argument from different angles. Hernán Vidal expressed misgivings about "the presumption that when a new analytic and interpretative approach is being introduced, the accumulation of similar efforts in the past is left superseded and nullified," which he called "technocratic literary criticism" (1993, 117). Rolena Adorno (1993b), echoing Klor de Alva's argument, argued for the need to recognize the distinctiveness of Latin America's historical experience, suggesting that colonial and postcolonial discourse may more properly apply to the historical experience of Asia and Africa. And Walter Mignolo (1993) argued for the need to distinguish among three critiques of modernity: postmodernism (its internal expression), postcolonialism (its Asian and African modality), and post-Occidentalism (its Latin American manifestation). Yet far from regarding postcolonialism as irrelevant for Latin America, Mignolo suggested that we treat it as liminal space for developing knowledge from our various loci of enunciation. He has developed his ideas of post-Occidentalism (building on its original conception by Fernandez Retamar [1976] and on my own critique of Occidentalism [Coronil 1996]) in his pathbreaking *Local Histories/Global Designs* (2000d), a discussion of the production of non-imperial knowledge that draws on wide-ranging Latin American reflections, in particular Quijano's notion of the "coloniality of power" (2000a) and Dussel's critique of Eurocentrism (1995c).

Subaltern studies has been widely recognized as a major current in the postcolonial field. While historians developed subaltern studies in South Asia, literary theorists have played a major role in the formation of subaltern studies on Latin America. Around the time of the Seed debate, the Latin American Subaltern Studies Group was founded at a meeting of the Latin American Studies Association in 1992. Unlike its South Asian counterpart, after which it was named, it was initially composed of literary critics, with the exception of Seed and two anthropologists who soon thereafter left the group. Its "Founding Statement" offered a sweeping overview of major stages of Latin American studies, rejecting their common modernist foundations and celebrating the South Asian critique of elitist representations of the subaltern. But unlike the South Asian group, formed by a small group of historians organized around a coherent historiographical and editorial project centered on rewriting the history of India, this group, mostly composed of literary critics, was characterized by its diverse and shifting membership and the heterogeneity of their disciplinary concerns and research agendas. While the publications of its members have not fit within traditional disciplinary boundaries, they have privileged the interpretation of texts over the analysis of historical transformations. The group's attempt to represent the subaltern has typically taken the form of readings of texts produced by authors considered subaltern or dealing with the issue of subalternity. In its decade-long life (I myself participated in the second half of it), the group stimulated efforts to rethink the intellectual and political engagements that had defined the field of Latin American studies.

While centered on literary studies, subaltern studies has been considered a major source of postcolonial historiography in Latin America. In a thoughtful discussion titled "The Promise and Dilemma of Subaltern Studies: Perspectives from Latin American History," published in a forum on subaltern studies in a major history journal, historian Florencia Mallon (1994) examines the consumption and production of subaltern studies in Latin America and evaluates the tensions and prospects of this field. Her account focuses on historical works, making explicit reference to the contributions of scholars based on the United States who have made significant use of the categories or methods associated with subaltern studies. She highlights Gil Joseph's pioneering use of Guha's work on India's peasantry in his examination of banditry in Latin America, noting that it moved discussion beyond simplistic oppositions that reduced bandits to either resisters or reproducers of given social orders.

In her review Mallon does not address subaltern studies on literary and cultural criticism (perhaps because she does not find this work properly historical), but she does offer a critique of the Latin American Subaltern Studies Group's "Founding Statement," noting its ungrounded dismissal of historiographical work on subaltern sectors in Latin America. She makes a similar critique of the more substantial article by Seed, the one historian of the group. Objecting to Seed's presentation of members of the "subaltern studies movement" as leaders of the "postcolonial discourse movement," Mallon offers ample references to recent historical work on politics, ethnicity, and the state from the early colonial period to the twentieth century that "had begun to show that all subaltern communities were internally differentiated and conflictual and that subalterns forged political unity or consensus in painfully contingent ways" (1994, 1,500).

Mallon's erudite discussion expands the scope of subaltern studies, but it does not sufficiently clarify why certain historical works should be considered part of the subaltern or postcolonial movement. Since studies on the social and cultural history of subaltern sectors ("history from below") and subaltern/postcolonial studies share subalternity as a subject matter and employ similar theories and methods, the lines separating them are sometimes difficult to define. Yet South Asian subaltern historiography has sought to distinguish itself from social and cultural history by attaching singular significance to the critique of historicist and Eurocentric assumptions, problematizing the role of power in fieldwork and in the construction of archives, and interrogating such central historiographic categories as the "nation," the "state," "consciousness," and "social actors." The historiographical subaltern project has been marked by the tension between its constructivist aim, which necessarily involves the use of representational strategies not unlike those of social and cultural history, and its deconstructivist strategy, which entails questioning the central categories of historical research and interrupting the powerful narratives of the powerful with those expressed by subaltern actors.

Mallon casts the "dilemma" of Latin American subaltern studies in terms of the tension between (Gramscian) Marxist and postmodern perspectives (a tension frequently noted in discussions about South Asian subaltern studies). She proposes to solve this dilemma by placing the Foucauldian and Derridean currents of postmodern criticism "at the service of a Gramscian project" (1994, 1,515). Perhaps her subordination of deconstruction, so central to subaltern history, to the Gramscian project, so fundamental to social and cultural history, helps account for her insufficient attention to the difference between these fields.

This difference is central for John Beverley, one of the founders of Latin American Subaltern Studies Group, who in his writings argues for the superiority of subaltern perspectives over nonsubalternist studies of the subaltern (1993, 1999, 2000). Deploying criteria that for him define a subalternist perspective, he criticizes Mallon's *Peasant and Nation: The Making of Postcolonial Mexico and Peru* (1995), arguing that despite her intentions, she appears as an omniscient narrator engaged in a positivist representational project that uses subaltern accounts to consolidate rather than interrupt the biographies of the nation, reinscribing rather than deconstructing the official biographies of these nations.

In a sophisticated discussion of subaltern studies and Latin American history, the Ecuadorian historian Guillermo Bustos (2002) uses Mallon and Beverley as a focal point to assess the relation between these two bodies of knowledge. While sympathetic to Mallon's discussion of this topic in "The Promise and Dilemma of Subaltern Studies," Bustos notes the Anglocentric and metropolitan focus of her discussion and suggests the inclusion of a more representative sample of work produced in Latin America; Mallon's only reference is to the Andeanist historian Flores Galindo, which Bustos complements by mentioning three related Andeanists: Assadourian, Colmenares, and Rivera Cusicanqui. Like Beverley, Bustos recognizes the need to distinguish between social history and subalternist perspectives. But while Beverley uses this distinction to evaluate Mallon's work in terms of the standards of subaltern studies, Bustos uses it to caution against assuming the superiority of a subaltern perspective, recalling Vidal's critique of "technocratic literary criticism."

Bustos's proposal is to turn claims about the theoretical and political superiority of any perspective into questions answerable through concrete analysis. He exemplifies this option through a subtle reading of Mallon's *Peasant and Nation* that demonstrates the complexity of her narrative, including her attempt to engage in dialogical relation with her informants and fellow historians. While distancing himself from Beverley's critique, Bustos endorses Tulio Halperin Donghi's observation that Mallon's presentation of other perspectives does not stop her from the common practice of assuming the superiority of her professional account. His point is thus neither to criticize nor to defend Mallon's work, but to refine the dialogue between subaltern studies and Latin American historiography. He develops his argument by discussing other texts, including related attempts to break away from accounts organized as "the biography of the nation-state" based on the critical use of multiple voices and sources (Coronil 1997; Thurner 1997). In agreement with the Italian historian Carlo Ginzburg, Bustos proposes that we meet the postmodern challenge not by making "evidence" impossibly suspect, but by following, as Paul Ricoeur suggests, the "traces that left from the past, take its place and represent it" (Bustos 2002, 15). Needless to say, the challenge remains how to retrieve and interpret these traces.

Postcolonial historical studies also received attention in Latin America in a book published in Bolivia, *Debates post-coloniales: Una introducción a los estudios de la subalternidad* (Postcolonial debates: An introduction to studies of subalternity) (1997), edited by the historians Silvia Rivera Cusicanqui and Rossana Barragán and composed of translations of a selection of nine essays by South Asian authors. In their introduction Rivera Cusicanqui and Barragán make only tangential reference to the Latin American Subaltern Studies Group, and none to the work of its members. They are critical of its "Founding Statement" for reducing the contributions of the South Asian group to an assortment of ethnographic cases that "exemplify from the South the theory and the broad conceptual guidelines produced in the North" (ibid., 13). And they criticize Mallon's article on subaltern studies both for its inattention to a long Latin American tradition of critical work on colonialism and postcolonialism and for reducing South Asian subaltern studies "to a questionable Gramscian project on behalf of which one should place the whole postmodern and poststructuralist debate" (ibid.).

Their own interpretative effort is centered on underlining the significance of South Asian subaltern studies for Latin American historiography, emphasizing the innovative importance of the poststructuralist perspectives informing the South Asian scholarship. Their brief discussion of Latin American work highlights three critical currents: the Argentinean school of economic history represented by Enrique Tandeter, Carlos Sempat Assadourian, and Juan Carlos Garavaglia, and distinguished by its transformation of Marxist and Gramscian categories through a confrontation with the specificities of Indian labour in the Potosí area; the studies of peasant insurgency and oligarchic rule carried out by the *Taller de Historia Oral Andina* (Andean workshop of oral history) and by such influential scholars as Alberto Flores Galindo and Rene Zavaleta; and the studies of "internal colonialism" initiated by the Mexican sociologist Pablo Gonzalez Casanova in the 1960s (and, I should add, Rodolfo Stavenhagen). Their call for a South-South dialogue at the same time avoids a dismissal of the North, warning against the danger present in "certain academic Latin American circles" to adopt new theories and discard "our own intellectual traditions—and Marxism is one of them—for this impoverishes and fragments the Latin American debate" (Rivera Cusicanqui and Barragán 1997, 19). Their horizontal dialogue establishes a common ground between postcolonial studies and Latin American historiography on colonialism and postcolonialism, yet presents subaltern studies as the product of an "epistemological and methodological rupture" (ibid., 17). If subaltern studies is postcolonial, its *post* is the *post* of postmodernism and poststructuralism.

A variant of this view is presented by the philosophers Eduardo Mendieta and Santiago Castro-Gómez in their thoughtful introduction to an important book of essays written by Latin Americanists published in Mexico under the title *Teorías sin disciplina: Latinoamericanismo, postcolonialidad y globalizacion en debate* (Theories without discipline: Latinoamericanism, postcoloniality and globalization in debate) (1998). Focusing on the relationship between critical thought and the historical context of its production, Castro-Gómez and Mendieta seek to determine the specific character of postcolonial studies. They draw a distinction between "anti-colonial discourse," as produced in Latin America by Las Casas, Guamán Poma de Ayala, Francisco Bilbao, and José Enrique Rodó, and "postcolonial discourse," as articulated by Said, Spivak, and Bhabha. For them, anticolonial discourse is produced in "traditional spaces of action," that is, "in situations where subjects formed their identities in predominantly local contexts not yet subjected to intensive processes of rationalization" (as described by Weber or Habermas); they argue that postcolonial theories, in contrast, are produced in "post-traditional contexts of action," that is, "in localities where social subjects configure their identities interacting with processes of global rationality and where, for this reason, cultural borders become porous" (Castro-Gómez and Mendieta 1998, 16–17). For them, this distinction has political implications: while anticolonialist discourse claims to speak for others and seeks to dismantle colonialism deploying colonial categories, postcolonial discourse historicizes its own position, not to discover a truth outside interpretation, but to produce truth effects that unsettle the field of political action. It follows that radical politics lies not in anticolonial work that defines struggles with the categories at hand, thus confirming the established order, but in intellectual work that deconstructs them in order to broaden the scope of politics. From this perspective, the *post* of postcolonialism turns out to be an anti anticolonial *post*, at the service of decolonizing decolonization.

This position has the merit of offering a clear definition of postcolonialism. In my view, it raises several questions. Its distinction between anticolonial and postcolonial discourse risks reproducing the tradition-modernity dichotomy of modernization theory, turning the convulsed and rapidly changing social worlds of Las Casas, Guamán Poma, or Bilbao into stable "traditional" societies of limited rationality, in contrast to the globally rational worlds that engender postcolonial theorists and their superior discourses. By treating deconstruction as a theoretical breakthrough that supersedes previous critical efforts—now relegated to less-rational traditional contexts—this position also risks becoming an expression of Vidal's "technocratical literary criticism." Spivak's dictum that "Latin America has not participated in decolonization" (Vidal 1993, 57) is perhaps an extreme expression of this risk. While they acknowledge the "irritation" of those who recognize that Latin American thinkers have "long shown interest on the examination of colonialism," they seem to accept this risk as an inevitable consequence of the radical theoretical and methodological novelty of post-colonial studies (Goméz and Mendieta 1998, 20).

By contrast, the Cuban public intellectual Roberto Fernández Retamar's discussion of Latin American decolonizing struggles, originally offered as a lecture for a course on Latin American thought in Havana, can be seen in part as a response to Spivak's dictum, which, according to him, wins the prize for epitomizing the problem of Latin America's exclusion from post-colonial studies (Fernández Retamar 1996). It is impossible to summarize his already tight synthesis, organized around thirteen interrelated themes identified by key phrases or ideas that embody political and intellectual movements, such as "Independence or death." Suffice it here to indicate that his presentation links together political struggles and intellectual reflections as part of a single process of decolonization. Thus he joins the Haitian Revolution, the wars of independence, the Mexican Revolution, the Cuban Revolution, and the movements of the Zapatistas and the Madres de la Plaza de Mayo with such diverse intellectual struggles as literary modernism, theology and philosophy of liberation, dependency theory, pedagogy of the oppressed, Latin American historiography, and *testimonio*. His wide selection of authors and texts celebrates the originality and heterogeneous sources informing self-critical reflections from the Americas. His examples are too numerous to mention here, but they include Venezuelans Simón Rodríguez and Andrés Bello, Mexicans Leopoldo Zea and Octavio Paz, Brazilians Oswald de Andrade and Darcy Ribeiro, and Cubans José Martí and Fernando Ortiz. He highlights the contemporary importance of Rigoberta Menchú and Subcomandante Marcos as articulating in new ways the decolonizing projects of indigenous and national sectors in Guatemala and Mexico. Fernández Retamar is not concerned with defining or erasing the boundaries between Latin American and postcolonial critical thought, but with appreciating their shared engagement with decolonization.

The difference between Mendieta/Castro-Gómez and Fernández Retamar, like that between Ashcroft and Young, reveals the difficulty of defining the relation between postcolonial and Latin American reflections on colonialism and its aftermath. As in Bustos's discussion of the Mallon-Beverley exchange, a dialogue between these intellectual traditions requires not only clearer classificatory efforts but also closer reading of texts, in order to refine the criteria that define these fields. A treatment of authors who are not considered part of the postcolonial canon as postcolonial thinkers may help us appreciate different modalities of critical reflexivity, as Sandra Castro-Klaren has done through her subtle reading of Guamán Poma and of the Inca

Garcilaso de la Vega (1999; 2001). Or perhaps, as Hulme suggests, "the real advantage of considering distant figures like Ralph Waldo Emerson or Andrés Bello as postcolonial writers is that this leads us to read them as if they were new" (1996, 6). A particularly productive option is to engage the postcolonial debate through studies of specific postcolonial encounters, as in the pioneering integration of theoretical reflection and detailed historical case studies of U.S.-Latin American relations in the collection edited by Gilbert Michael Joseph, Catherine LeGrand, and Ricardo Donato Salvatore (1998).

ELEPHANTS IN THE AMÉRICAS?

This discussion has made evident how difficult it is to define "Latin American postcolonial studies." As in the well-known parable of the elephant and the wise blind scholars (each of whom visualizes the elephant as a different creature by the part he or she feels), this field, like the wider field of postcolonial studies itself, can be represented in as varied a manner as there are different perspectives from which it can be "seen." If this parable shows that knowledge of reality is always partial and inconclusive, its use to reflect on Latin American postcolonial studies raises two more fundamental points.

First, the peculiar object of postcolonial studies is not a natural entity, like an elephant, or even a social subject regarded as sharing the cultural world of the observer, but one formed as a colonized object, an inferior and alien "Other" to be studied by a superior and central "Self." Since the "elephant" can speak, the problem is not just to represent it but to create conditions that would enable it to represent itself. From the perspective of postcolonial studies, analysis should involve not just self-reflection (an inherent dimension of any serious intellectual enterprise) or granting subjectivity to the social subject studied (as anthropologists and cultural historians have typically sought to do), but the integration of these two analytical endeavours into one unified intellectual project directed at countering this unequal, colonizing relationship. Its epistemology is not just representational but transformative; it uses representational strategies to counter the hierarchies and assumptions that turn some subjects into objects of knowledge of allegedly superior subjects.

Second, insofar as postcolonial studies appears as the most evolved critique of colonialism, it tends to invalidate or diminish the significance of reflections on colonialism developed from other locations and perspectives. If the wise scholars were to act wisely, they would not privilege their respective views of the elephant or isolate it from other creatures. As a reflection on the relationship between postcolonial and Latin American studies, the parable appears as a literal story, the absence of indigenous elephants in the Americas justifying the identification of postcolonial studies with scholarship on Africa and Asia.

If we take the parable literally, since the only elephants that exist in the Americas are imported ones, artificially confined in zoos or circuses so as to protect them from an inhospitable terrain, we may have the desire to see only those rare creatures who have managed to mimic their Asian or African counterparts—our Latin American "elephants." Refusal is another option. Following thinkers who justifiably object to the ease with which metropolitan ideas become dominant in Latin America, or who unjustifiably see Latin America as a self-fashioned and bounded region and argue in defense of its autochthonous intellectual productions (but doing so typically in metropolitan languages and with arguments supported by theories which were once considered "foreign"), one could reject the attempt to define Latin American postcolonial studies, restricting postcolonial studies to other continents and regarding it as an imperial "import" that devalues "local" Latin American knowledge.

In my opinion, the view that restricts postcolonial reflexivity to certain currents of Western intellectual theory, as well as the position that treats postcolonial studies as another foreign fad that undermines local knowledge, reinforces both the field's theoretical and ethnographic provincialism and its de facto exclusion of Latin America. These two sides of a protected parochial coin prevent us from taking advantage of the global circulation of postcolonial studies as a potent intellectual currency for the exchange and development of perspectives on colonialism and its legacies from different regions and intellectual traditions.

The problem is not simply, as some Latin American critics of postcolonialism have suggested, that Latin Americanists should be drawing on Kusch or Jorge Luis Borges as much as on Said or Derrida, but that knowledge should be global and acknowledge the worldwide conditions of its production. Just as Kusch drew on Heidegger, and Derrida was inspired by Jorge Luis Borges, Said and Ortiz developed independently of each other, fifty years apart, a contrapuntal view of the historical formation of cultures and identities that disrupts the West-rest dichotomy (Coronil 1995). Critical responses to colonialism from different locations take different but complementary forms. While from an Asian perspective it has become necessary to "provincialize" European thought (Chakrabarty 2000), from a Latin American perspective it has become indispensable to globalize the periphery: to recognize the worldwide formation of what appears to be self-generated modern metropolitan centers and backward peripheries.

As it has been defined so far, the field of postcolonial studies tends to neglect the study of contemporary forms of political domination and economic exploitation. Recognized by many as one of the field's founders, Edward Said has distanced himself from it, saying that he does not "belong to that" and arguing that "postcolonialism is really a misnomer" that does not sufficiently recognize the persistence of neocolonialism, imperialism, and "structures of dependency" (2002, 2). Said's concerns, so central to Latin American thought, highlight the importance of expanding postcolonial studies by building on Latin American critical traditions.

If the relationship between colonialism and modernity is the core problem for both postcolonial and Latin American studies, the fundamental contribution of Latin American studies is to recast this problem by setting it in a wider historical context. The inclusion of Latin America in the field of postcolonial studies expands its geographical scope and also its temporal depth. A wider focus, spanning from Asia and Africa to the Americas, yields a deeper view, revealing the links between the development of modern colonialism by Northern European powers and its foundation in the colonization of the Americas by Spain and Portugal. This larger frame modifies prevailing understandings of modern history. Capitalism and modernity, so often assumed both in mainstream and in postcolonial studies to be a European process marked by the Enlightenment, the dawning of industrialization, and the forging of nations in the eighteenth century, can be seen instead as a global process involving the expansion of Christendom, the formation of a global market, and the creation of transcontinental empires since the sixteenth century. A dialogue between Latin American and postcolonial studies ought not to be polarizing, and might range over local histories and global designs, texts and their material contexts, and subjective formations and structures of domination.

This dialogue should bring to the forefront two interrelated areas of significant political relevance today: the study of postcolonialism itself, strictly understood as historical transformations after political independence, and the analysis of contemporary imperialism. Ironically, these two areas, so central to Latin American thought, have been neglected by postcolonial studies. At the juncture of colonialism's historical dusk and the dawn of new forms of imperial domination, the field tends to recollect colonialism rather than its eventualities. Building on a long tradition of work on post-independence Latin America, I have argued for the need to distinguish "global" from "national" and "colonial" imperialism as a phase characterized by the growing abstraction and generalization of imperial modes of political and economic control (Coronil 2003). And drawing on postcolonial studies, I have proposed to understand what I call Occidentalist representations of cultural difference under global imperialism as involving a shift from "Eurocentrism" to "globalcentrism." I see globalcentrism as entailing representational operations that: dissolve the "West" into the market and crystallize it in less-visible transnational nodules of concentrated financial and political power; lessen cultural antagonisms through the integration of distant cultures into a common global space; and emphasize subalternity rather than alterity in the construction of cultural difference. In an increasingly globalized world, U.S. and European dominance is achieved through the occlusion rather than the affirmation of radical differences between the West and its others (Coronil 2000c, 354).

This dialogue should also redefine the terms of postcolonial studies. Postcolonialism is a fluid and polysemic category, whose power derives in part from its ability to condense multiple meanings and refer to different locations. Rather than fix its meaning through formal definitions, I have argued that it is more productive to develop its significance through research and analysis on the historical trajectory of societies and populations subjected to diverse modalities of imperial power (1992, 101). In the spirit of a long tradition of Latin American transcultural responses to colonialism and "digestive" appropriation of imperial cultures, I thus opt for what I call "tactical postcolonialism." While Spivak's notion of "strategic essentialism" serves to fix socially constructed identities in order to advance political ends, tactical postcolonialism serves to open up established academic knowledge toward open-ended liberatory possibilities. It conceives postcolonialism not as a fenced territory but as an expanding field for struggles against colonial and other forms of subjection. We may then work not so much *within* this field, as *with it*, treating it with Ortiz as a "transcultural" zone of creative engagements, "digesting it" as Andrade may playfully do, approaching it as a liminal locus of enunciation as Mignolo suggests, in order to decolonize knowledge and build a genuinely democratic world, "a world which would include many worlds," as Subcomandante Marcos and the Zapatistas propose.

NOTE

This text reflects the lively discussions of a postgraduate seminar on postcolonialism and Latin American thought that I taught during the summer of 2002 at the Universidad Andina Simón Bolívar, Ecuador. My gratitude to all. Thanks also to Genese Sodikoff and Julie Skurski for help with editing it.

Unless otherwise indicated, all English translations are my own.

THE LATIN AMERICAN POSTCOLONIALISM DEBATE IN A COMPARATIVE CONTEXT

Amaryll Chanady

Situating postcolonialism "in a comparative context" may seem like a curious endeavor, since most postcolonial criticism involves precisely that—the comparison of societies that often seem to have little in common. In fact, the scope of postcolonial studies is so ambitious that it has frequently been criticized for producing superficial knowledge about an extremely broad field, leading to an inevitable homogenization of entirely different phenomena. Arun Mukherjee, for example, has pointed out the "absurdity of our being saddled with the responsibility of teaching about two-thirds of the world" (1990, 7). This "overburdening" of the academic has often produced discussions of complex cultural and political practices in terms of reductive binaries such as colonizer and colonized and center and periphery, in which internal differences dissolve. What also disappears is the study of the interaction between particular discourses within a single society, as the postcolonial subject has become interesting to us only insofar as s/he writes back to the center. As Mukherjee argues, Indian literatures are "not in conversation with a distant outsider but with those at home. They are, like any other literature, in a 'dialogic' . . . relation with other social discourses that circulate in the Indian society" (6). Finally, critics outside the West sometimes see postcolonial theory as yet another paradigm imported from hegemonic centers of knowledge production that marginalizes local knowledges in a new avatar of epistemic violence. In short, one may come to the conclusion that Latin Americanists seem to have little to learn from this fashionable new import, which is criticized by intellectuals coming from the very country (India) that has produced several authors of the most prestigious postcolonial theories in the West.

Many of these criticisms are certainly justified, with the result that scholars have deconstructed the binary categories of early postcolonial criticism as well as the homogenization of the postcolonial other to take into account internal conflict and subaltern groups. Some of Mukherjee's remarks are thus less pertinent today, as postcolonial theory has demonstrated great interest in complex subject positions and previously "silenced voices." Important problems remain, however, and continue to elicit widespread unease at the application of postcolonial theory to Latin America. I wish to examine the extent to which we can further reorient postcolonial criticism by transforming the traditional terms of comparison and bringing marginalized participants into the debate. In other words, instead of studying Latin America exclusively according to concepts introduced by theorists such as Bhabha, Spivak, and Guha, we should also look at postcolonial debates in more peripheral areas, such as the settler societies of Canada or Australia. The purpose of this new comparative context is not to find new concepts to apply to Latin America, but to escape what many consider to be a new orthodoxy and enter into a broader dialogue with critics in societies that may at times have greater relevance to the postcolonialism debate in Latin America, in spite of appearances to the contrary.

Both English settler societies and Latin America share certain uneasiness toward postcolonial criticism because of their problematic inclusion in the category of the postcolonial. Although they have gained political independence from Europe, they were not "colonies of intervention" like India. As Bill Ashcroft, Gareth Griffiths, and Helen Tiffin pointed out in their influential introductory study on postcolonial literatures, there are major differences between "colonies of intervention and exploitation" (1989, 26) such as India and the African nations, from which most of the colonizers departed when the indigenous population succeeded in their struggle for independence, the predominantly white diasporic settler societies such as Canada and Australia, in which the descendants of the European colonizers eventually formed a new society and broke off from the metropole, colonies populated largely by former slaves in the Caribbean, and the South Africa of apartheid.

Latin America is not included in this classification, since the authors are mainly interested in the former British colonies. However, there are certain obvious parallels between Latin America and other settler societies, in spite of the important differences between them (see Mazzotti in this volume). These differences may at first make any comparison seem superficial. While English settler societies are generally considered part of the developed world, have not seen widespread miscegenation, and have a very small percentage of native peoples, Latin American nations are often relegated to the periphery of the industrialized world and continue to struggle with debilitating external debts and the constant threat of foreign intervention, in addition to numerous internal conflicts based on race, class, and ethnicity. Both English-speaking and Spanish-speaking former colonies, however, are uneasily situated between colony and postcolony, and any attempt to conceptualize them as simply postcolonial inevitably leads to simplifications. It is therefore interesting to compare these societies with respect to the ambiguity of their postcolonial status and the subsequent hesitations of many critics to study their society according to traditional paradigms of postcolonial theory.

In his criticism of the application of the concepts of colonialism and postcolonialism to Latin America, Klor de Alva has pointed out not only that this paradigm has evolved relatively recently in the English-speaking world and thus cannot rightfully be applied to the Latin American colonial experience several hundred years ago. He has also argued that certain native sectors have never been colonized, while the descendants of colonizers and the legacy of Western hegemonic institutions are still in place. Latin America has thus been only partly colonized and, in other areas, never decolonized. It is useful to situate this observation in the context of the postcolonialism debates in other settler societies. Many postcolonial theorists are as uneasy as Klor de Alva about the attribution of postcolonial status to countries such as Canada and Australia, and question the legitimacy of placing colonies of intervention, such as India and the countries of Africa, in the same category as predominantly Western settler colonies. Mukherjee, now living in Canada, criticizes the erasure of differences based on race, arguing that India was not "colonized in the same way" (1990, 2) as white settler societies were, since the latter were seen as the daughters of empire and treated differently. Furthermore, native peoples in Canada and Australia have never been decolonized but live in marginalized and economically disadvantaged enclaves.

The Canadian critic Stephen Slemon thus refers to Canada as part of the "Second World," which is the "neither/nor territory of white settler-colonial writing" and embodies the "radical ambivalence of colonialism's middle ground" (1990, 30, 34). However, he does not argue against the use of postcolonial criticism in Canada. On the contrary, he criticizes the general *exclusion* of settler cultures from the category of the postcolonial, which has been conflated with the Third and Fourth world. In a position diametrically opposed to that of Mukherjee, Slemon argues that postcolonial criticism should be "concerned with identifying a social force, colonialism, and with the attempt to understand the resistances to that force, *wherever* they lie" (ibid., 32). He believes that the exclusion of settler societies from postcolonial studies is based on a "remarkably purist and absolutist" conception that reinforces the "binarism of Europe and its Others, of colonizer and colonized, of the West and the Rest" (ibid., 33, 34). In an interesting echo of the denunciations of postcolonial criticism's ignorance of Latin American critical traditions and anticolonial discourses, Slemon complains about this "forgetfulness, of overlooking the Second World entirely as though its literature and its critical tradition didn't even exist. . . . [W]hat *really* remains 'virtually ignored'—in a gesture so common as to be symptomatic of much of the US-based, First-World 'post-colonial' critical practice—is the body of critical works, published in Second-World critical journals by scholars such as Diana Brydon and Chantal Zabus. . . . [T]he academic star-system of First-World criticism inscribes itself wholesale into post-colonial studies" (ibid., 34).

While this objection to being marginalized in the global market of hegemonic critical practices could be voiced by any intellectual writing outside dominant cultural centers, Slemon's comments on ambivalence concern the specific status of settler societies. He argues that while critics such as Bhabha stress the ambivalence, mediation, and in-between nature of colonial resistance, settler cultures are excluded by that same postcolonial criticism precisely because of their ambivalence. Not only does he consider this to be a singularly contradictory gesture, but he believes that the ambivalent status of settler cultures has never permitted the simple binary distinctions between colonizer and colonized that have characterized many postcolonial approaches to Third World countries: "[T]he ambivalence of literary resistance itself is the 'always already' condition of Second-World settler and post-colonial literary writing" since its "anticoloniaIst resistance has *never* been directed at an object or a discursive structure which can be seen as purely external to the self" (1990, 38). Because of the inevitable but ambivalent complicity with colonial practices and the resulting "internalization of the self/other binary of colonialist relations" (ibid., 39), Slemon believes that postcolonial theory has much to learn from Second World practices.

Ambivalence is an important characteristic of Latin American discourses and practices as well, and much interesting work has been done in this area. But I would argue that this ambivalence should not always be considered in terms of resistance, but in terms of the quest for identity. The autonomization of a settler society is a complex and contradictory process in which the return to a supposed indigenous past is even more illusory than in colonies of intervention. Strategies of identity construction take numerous forms, and a dialogue between different settler societies reveals interesting resemblances, as well as important differences. While many intellectuals felt like exiles in a wasteland (a common theme in both Latin America and English-speaking settler societies) and were unable to identify with the new society, others developed a sense of belonging based on these strategies of identity construction. The symbolic identification with indigenous peoples has inspired many identitarian discourses in Latin America, for example, whereas this was seldom the case in English-speaking settler societies, although many settlers there also deplored the "absence of history" in the new land and inscribed the native past in its topography.

Such comparative studies would involve extensive dialogue between critics in these societies and problematize what is often considered as the imposition of a homogenizing metropolitan theoretical paradigm on the periphery (or vice versa—Arif Dirlik, for example, criticizes Indian historiographers for projecting their local observations globally [1994, 341]). Dirlik's negative conception of institutionalized postcolonial criticism, which often has little to do with dialogue between critics in settler societies and the metropolitan centers, is shared by many critics in Latin America. While Dirlik sees it as an expression of "newfound power" by prominent "Third World intellectuals who have arrived in First World academe" and seek to constitute the world in their self-image, thus giving rise to a "new orthodoxy" (ibid., 339, 330), Latin American intellectuals criticize the marginalization and devalorization of local knowledge and critical traditions brought about by what they consider as the latest version of epistemic violence and "intellectual colonization" (Mignolo 1993, 130). In an article entitled

"Colonial and Postcolonial Discourse: Cultural Critique or Academic Colonialism," Walter Mignolo also questions the innovative nature of postcolonial approaches to Latin America, where local historians such as Edmundo O'Gorman, who wrote long before the advent of poststructuralism, had a "similar foundation and perspective" (Mignolo 1993, 122). Finally, English-speaking postcolonial critics are faulted for ignoring Latin America in their work. While Slemon criticizes postcolonialism's marginalization of Canadian studies on the subject, Sara Castro-Klaren criticizes its "lack of awareness of a previous, major, if not modular, colonial period and Post-Colonial experience which is enormously relevant to many of its concerns," and gives as examples the "sub-altern subject, cultural translations, oral and written traditions, margin-centre relations, the question of authenticity, modalities of excess, hybridization and transgression" (1995, 45). She is particularly critical of Bill Ashcroft for not making any reference to Latin American resistance in writing and the debate on *mestizaje* in his own discussions of hybridity, concluding that much contemporary theorizing of postcolonial issues has already existed in Latin America, whose intellectuals questioned the foundations and assumptions of philosophy and history (ibid., 46). She argues that Guamán Poma and Garcilaso, in particular, "managed to produce a critique of European modes of representation when this colonial discourse was in full power/knowledge ascendance" (ibid., 53; also Castro-Klaren in this volume). In reaction to such criticism, Ashcroft published a conciliatory article titled "Modernity's First Born: Latin America and Postcolonial Transformation," in which he explains the Latin American resistance to postcolonial theory partly by the reductive understanding of it as a product of poststructuralism. He argues that the "postcolonial begins from the moment of colonization" and that "postcolonial analyses have been a feature of Latin American intellectual life at least since the 1950s" (ibid., 15, 10). He adds that the Latin American experience of colonization, hybridity, and contestation "all radically widen the scope of postcolonial theory" (ibid., 12) and underlines the importance of the *testimonio*.

On the other side of the debate stand critics such as Fernando de Toro, who criticize Walter Mignolo, Roberto Fernández Retamar, Angel Rama, Carlos Rincón, Beatriz Sarlo, and Beatriz Pastor for establishing simplistic and anachronistic binary distinctions between "them" and "us," for their "fervent nationalism" and even "Latin Americanist fundamentalism" (1999, 112, 118, 129). He argues that many Latin American critics "attempted to use Western theoretical inquiry as tools to look at a variety of texts and cultures, not to colonize them, but to be able to understand them better, to understand texts which are discursive constructions, texts which carry a culture, texts that talk in more ways than one, texts which are in contact with an international circulation of knowledge and cultural production" (ibid., 116). Alfonso de Toro also argues that postcolonial theory,provides essential conceptual and analytical tools that have brought about a genuine "change of paradigm" in Latin American cultural thought. He adds that empirical analyses, although useful, do not create new theoretical models. Postcolonial criticism is not just a matter of sophisticated jargon, but the "result of a serious epistemological reflection" (ibid., 63).

The debate over postcolonial approaches to Latin America is extensive, and must be situated within a long tradition of discussions between advocates of national or continental knowledge and those in favor of "imported" models and paradigms. A particularly interesting intervention in this debate is made by Santiago Castro-Gómez (1999), who attempts to avoid the frequently polemical and simplistically binary nature of the debate by reexamining the notion of "modernity." Instead of rejecting it as the emanation of European cultural hegemony, epistemic violence, and intellectual colonialism, or, on the other hand, touting it as the only way to intellectual progress, he questions the reductive juxtaposition of the human and social sciences with the instrumental knowledge of the bureaucratic and administrative apparatus of capitalism and imperialism. He argues that the rejection of the knowledge of experts as "imperial reason" destructive of local knowledge removes the very foundations of subaltern criticism of the system, since globalization also provides the reflexive tools for contesting this system (ibid., 91, 93).

Drawing on the work of Enrique Dussel, Immanuel Wallerstein, and especially Anthony Giddens, Castro-Gómez explains that modernity is not simply a regional process that radiated outward from Europe, but that is it a phenomenon created by a Western expansion leading to a "*global* network of interactions" [red *global* de interacciones] (1999, 94). It is the very constitution of this global system that has created modernity. As the face-to-face relationships of local interaction based on presence are replaced by impersonal determinations that are distant in time and space, thought becomes reflexive and abstract. And these abstract systems are not the exclusive privilege of the elite, but also allow other social agents to perceive themselves and work toward transforming social practices: it is "a phenomenon inherent in the structure of the world system in which everyone is involved" [un fenómeno inherente a la estructura del sistema-mundo en el que todos estamos involucrados] (ibid., 95). Expert knowledges thus provide local groups with the "reflexive competence" to reterritorialize the abstract in the local and develop self-reflexive and resistant practices leading to new subjectivity formations and social and political action. Castro-Gómez argues that Latin American thought has always been reflexive, owing to its situation within the global system, and has constituted itself as a subject of knowledge through enlightenment philosophy, romanticism, positivism, Marxism, structuralism, and cultural studies. He stresses that what is important is the way in which global reflexivity has been inscribed in local contexts (and subaltern groups) and how "social self-observation" [auto-observación social] (ibid., 96) has emerged through deterritorialization and reterritorialization (see also Castro-Gómez in this volume).

Castro-Gómez emphasizes the importance of what he calls the "recycling" (ibid., 95) of the social sciences. This emphasis on rewriting discourses emanating from hegemonic centers of culture echoes not only the proclamations of the Brazilian anthropophagy movement in the 1920s but also numerous English-speaking postcolonial critics who analyze "appropriation" or "interpolation" (the term favored by Ashcroft, who defines it as the way in which "the colonized culture interpolates the dominant discourse in order to transform it in ways that release the representation of local realities" [ibid., 18]). But Castro-Gómez's concept of global knowledge production goes beyond the Brazilian modernists' concept of anthropophagy, in which the devouring of the other leads to the emergence of new cultural forms, or postcolonial criticism's emphasis on the parodic reworking of colonial discourses. When he observes that excluded subjects examine their own practices and "compare them with those practices of subjects distant in time and space" [compararlas con las prácticas de sujetos distantes en el tiempo y el espacio] (ibid., 97), he introduces a new dimension, which suggests other possibilities to us, although he does not develop this in his article. We could add that marginalized subjects do not just rewrite the discourses of the center, just as the fringes of empire do not only write back. Global networks allow them to enter into a complex interdiscursive and intercultural field occupied by many actors (not just the empire and its subjects or the center and its peripheries), who can establish a polyphonic exchange.

In this more complex model, the one-way action of devouring a Western other is replaced by the mutual discursive interaction between numerous others. This departs not only from the potentially binary model of the margins recycling the center, but also from that of the appropriation by the West of non-Western cultural objects or that of Western theorizing about the non-

West as a perpetually silent object of knowledge. The Indian critic Viney Kirpal has argued in the context of Indian literature that the "third-world novelist . . . also draws upon his traditional literary forms to create one that can suitably express his own modern experience" (1988, 148), and that it is thus essential to situate this literature within these forms as well as with respect to more "universal" ones. This echoes many Latin American critics of Western appropriations of their literature in Western theoretical paradigms such as postmodernism and metafiction that erase local context and literary traditions. Postcolonial criticism must thus enter a dialogue with "local" critics, who, in turn, would enter into dialogue with other "local" critics.

There are several examples of interaction between Latin American theoretical or critical paradigms and knowledge production in other societies, mainly postcolonial. An obvious one is magical realism, which has been applied to Canadian, African, and Indian literatures, since it provided a suggestive and innovative way of describing new literary forms in societies with continuing indigenous traditions. Another Latin American concept that stimulated theoretical discussions elsewhere is that of transculturation, introduced by Fernando Ortiz and further developed by Angel Rama. This concept was considered particularly relevant by intellectuals of Italian origin in the Canadian francophone province of Quebec, who tried to develop new paradigms of subject formation for trilingual immigrants who felt integrated in the new society while retaining a sense of difference.

A more recent critical paradigm, that of "foundational fictions," developed by Doris Sommer in the context of Latin America, has been used to analyze a canonical Canadian novel in innovative ways departing both from traditional Canadian critical models and simple postcolonial colonizer-colonized binaries. In an essay on the novel The Diviners, by Margaret Laurence, Neil ten Kortenaar (1996) refers to Sommer's work on Latin American foundational novels in his own rereading of the Canadian novel as a national romance. After characterizing it in Fredric Jameson's terms as a national allegory and calling it a rewriting of Shakespeare's Tempest, he stresses the novel's "celebration of creolization, the blending of different cultures in an indigenous mix" (ibid., 13). In this national romance, in which "nation is rewritten in terms of the family," the orphaned protagonist Morag "rejects an identification with the imperialist and identifies with the indigenous, the dispossessed, and the land of her birth" (ibid., 26, 13). She finally marries a métis, with whom she has a child "who carries in her veins the blood of both settlers and indigenes" and is nourished with "stories of both sides of the racial divide" (ibid., 14–15). These three concepts—magical realism, transculturation, and foundational fictions—which were developed to conceptualize complex cultural strategies in Latin America, have thus pointed the way to an increasing dialogue between critics in societies that are different in many respects, but which consider themselves to be in an ambiguous in-between situation at odds with many postcolonial models developed in Asia.

Furthermore, there is no reason to limit this dialogue to the West and the formerly colonized. Interesting theoretical work has emerged recently from Japanese intellectuals, whose knowledge of their culture as well as of Western theoretical paradigms have led to challenging studies of identity constructions in Japan that bear a certain resemblance to those in formerly colonized societies. Naoki Sakai, for example, has developed the concept of "cofiguration," which he defines as follows: "The *self* of the Japanese is always posited as the *other* of the Chinese, Indian, or the European. In other words, the determinations of those *others* serve reflectively to postulate the self of the Japanese in specularity" (1997, 144). Arguing that "the obsession with one's own ethnicity or nationality would not make much sense except in relation to its opposite," he stresses the "essentially 'imaginary' nature of the comparative framework . . . in the sense that it is a sensible image on the one hand, and practical in its ability or evoke one to act toward the future on the other" (ibid., 50, 52). Even if there was no unified social group in the past, a Japanese spirit is postulated and projected into the past, and this represses hybridity (ibid., 61). Japanese thought in the past is also very different from that of today, but its continuity is assumed, with the result that it is not considered as foreign to contemporary Japanese.

Although we think of Japan as a particularly homogeneous society, and one without the colonial history of Latin America, Sakai's remarks remind us of anticolonial constructions such as the revalorized Caliban of Fernández Retamar (an obvious cofiguration with the negative Prospero figure), or Martí's "nuestra América mestiza" (in opposition to a racist North), as well as Argentine constructions of an authentic (gaucho) identity. Sakai's discussion of "subjective technologies," which he defines as "the political (or subjective) *techné* as to how to manufacture and effectively institute the desire to 'want to be a nation'" is quite relevant to Latin American identitarian discourses through which the subject of the nation produces itself by representing itself (1997, 63, 67).

His discussion of cultural difference is particularly interesting. Sakai stresses the "enunciative positionality of the observer" that creates its object and explains that observation is at the same a practice through which "the description of cultural difference produces and institutes cultural difference" (1997, 118, 120). The feeling of anxiety produced by cultural otherness "must be *articulated* in enunciation and be repressed so as to be perceived as *determined* cultural difference, as an identifiable difference between entities" (ibid., 121). This process of signification is thus forgotten, since the practical relation (the act of instituting) is reduced to the epistemic, as the distinction between the "articulatory function of the enunciation of cultural difference" and the "representation of cultural difference in cultural essentialism" (ibid., 215) disappears. At the same time, the constructed particularity (of nations, etc.) replaces the singularity of exchanges between individuals (ibid., 149).

Although Sakai's study concentrates on Japan, his work illuminates strategies of identity formation in settler societies, where one of the most serious cultural predicaments after independence was the perceived lack of an autonomous, authentic tradition distinguishable from that of the European colonizers and not considered as a second-rate imitation. Their cofiguration (to use Sakai's term) as Europe's opposite was problematic, owing to the transfer of cultural paradigms during colonization and the domination of European languages and practices in administration, religion, and politics. This problem is faced by all settler societies, which cannot look back to an indigenous cultural tradition to which they can supposedly return, since the ruling elites are of European origin. Although every society figures cultural differences with respect to its various others, settler societies feel a stronger lack of cultural autonomy, and the search for identity becomes an ever-present problem. Differences must be created in order to legitimate independence, and in many cases new paradigms must be found with which the heterogeneous population can identify, to legitimate a particular government. While many Latin American intellectuals looked to the indigenous civilizations of the Aztecs and the Incas for self-valorization in an act of symbolic identification, novelists of the second half of the twentieth century sought to develop new forms of writing specific to their culture. This quest was intended to create a sense of identity, but also cultural value in a global context in which Latin America persistently hovered on the margins of power.

The role of cultural mediators in the construction of Latin America as an imaginary community is particularly important. Familiar with European philosophy, political debates and discourses on the non-Western other, Latin American authors who traveled to Europe provided some of the most striking figurations of the continent. The Cuban novelist Alejo Carpentier, for example, developed the idea of Latin America as a marvelous world in opposition to Europe in a very influential cofiguration that has not yet disappeared in spite of its obvious shortcomings. The following rereading of Carpentier stresses the dynamic process of figuring the continent in a powerful, albeit ambivalent construction of the collective self in the context of the search for specificity and value in a settler society.

The expression lo real maravilloso, or marvelous reality, was coined by Carpentier in his frequently quoted prologue to the first edition in 1949 of the novel The Kingdom of This World (El reino de este mundo), in which he recounts the vicissitudes of the black independence struggles on the island of Hispaniola since the end of the eighteenth century. He initially applied the expression to Haiti, which he had visited in 1943, and where he was inspired by the imposing dimensions of the ruins of La Ferriere, the fortress built by the black king Henri Christophe after the country's independence in 1804. As he explained in his prologue, the syncretic conjunction of voodoo beliefs and Catholic rites, the European garb of Christophe and his courtiers, and the faith of the black slaves in the lycanthropic powers of their leader Mackandal and various African divinities, inspired him to consider Haitian reality as marvelous. Further on in the prologue he extends the concept to include Latin American reality in general, because of the impact of its relatively recent discovery by Europeans in 1492, its impressive geography, the presence of diverse racial groups, and a series of "extraordinary" historical events.

Carpentier describes marvelous reality both in phenomenological and in ontological terms: his statement that "the feeling of the marvelous presupposes faith" suggests that what is involved in considering Latin American reality as marvelous is a particular disposition in the contemplating subject or a specific type of perception, while the rhetorical question of the concluding sentence of the prologue points to an ontological consideration of the essence of Latin America: "But what is the history of all of America if not a chronicle of marvelous reality?" (1967 [1949], 17).

Several critics have examined the European sources of Carpentier's conception of the New World. Emir Rodriguez Monegal has discussed Carpentier's debt to the French surrealists; Roberto González Echevarría has pointed to the influence of Spengler's The Decline of the West; and Irlemar Chiampi has meticulously documented the parallels between Le miroir du merveilleux (The Mirror of the Marvelous) (1940), by the French surrealist Pierre Mabille, and Carpentier's 1949 prologue to the novel The Kingdom of This World, in which he developed the notion of lo real maravilloso. Without explicitly criticizing Carpentier for the derivative nature of his theory, Chiampi emphasizes the importance of the surrealists' influence on the theories and literary practices of the Cuban writer (who in fact collaborated with the surrealists in Paris), in spite of his ostensible rejection of their influence and categorical denial of any significant similarities between the Latin American real maravilloso and French surrealism. In his prologue, Carpentier virulently attacks surrealist techniques of free association, the creation of an artificial marvelous, and the use of literary stereotypes such as vampires and ghosts, arguing that the genuine marvelous is not invented but found on the Latin American continent. He refers to the latter's luxuriant vegetation, imposing geography, ethnic diversity, the mixture of architectural styles, and the fact that explorers and conquistadors have frequently projected mythological paradigms on the New World (El Dorado, the sirens, the fountain of eternal youth).

It is interesting to note that while Carpentier attacks the surrealists in an attempt to distinguish his literary practice from theirs, even though he points out in 1964 that surrealism was widely imitated in Latin America, the Guatemalan novelist Miguel Angel Asturias, who studied ethnology in Paris and first read Mayan indigenous texts in French translation, openly asserts that his own magical realist fiction, which, he believes, represents the "original mentality" of the Indians, "is similar to what the surrealists around Breton wanted" (Asturias 1967, 58). Chiampi demonstrates that the Cuban author's rejection of dominant surrealist practices echoes criticism voiced within the group of French surrealists by members such as Pierre Mabille, who, in *Le miroir du merveilleux*, had already distinguished between the "authentic" and "inauthentic" marvelous, and considered primitive cultures, and specifically that of Haiti, as an example of the authentic marvelous. Napoleon Sanchez also attributes Carpentier's attack on the surrealists at least partly to the influence of those who rebelled against the fetishization of Lautreamont's *Songs of Maldoror* and the regimentation of the surrealists by the dictatorial Breton, while other critics point to Antonin Artaud's idealization of Mexican autochthonous cultures as a source for Carpentier's theories (Müller).

However, while Carpentier's reading of the surrealists, which is really a productive misreading, can be considered as a symbolic parricide in which, to quote de Man, the "effort of the late poet's revisionary reading is to achieve a reversal in which lateness will become associated with strength instead of with weakness" (1983, 274), his textual practice is not oedipal in the individual sense. The apparent psychologization of Carpentier's misreading of and verbal attack on the surrealists need not necessarily entail a bracketing of the wider perspective of cultural interaction between Europe and Latin America, as well as questions of ideology, hegemony, and resistance. The Cuban author is very much aware of his continent's belatedness or chronological "mismatch" (*desajuste*), explaining fifteen years after the publication of his prologue that "surrealism is imitated in America, when, at the original source, it is in a process of disintegration" (1964, 29). It is against the hegemony of metropolitan cultural centers, beside which cultural practices in the "periphery" appear derivative, that Carpentier attempts to valorize Latin American culture and contribute to its development in a manner that is presented as different from that of the metropole.

Harold Bloom's term misprision is particularly apt in the context of Carpentier's reading of the surrealists in his development of a proto-poetics of Latin American writing. It implies, even more than the term intertextuality or influence, a dynamic relationship between subjects, whether individual or collective. Paul de Man's discussion of Bloom, however, in which he emphasizes the "structural pattern of the misprisions" and defines influence as a "metaphor that dramatizes a linguistic structure into diachronic narrative," implies a purely textual and structuralist conceptualization of literary interaction that ignores the immersion of textual production in wider cultural and political configurations and processes (1983, 274, 276). We cannot follow de Man's recommendation when he exhorts us to ignore the "intentional schemes by means of which Bloom dramatizes the 'causes' of the misreading" (ibid., 274), especially in the case of Carpentier, whose parricidal impetus in representing the metropolitan other as artificial is an essential aspect of the constitution of an imaginary Latin American community.

The implications of the marvelous are quite different for the French surrealists than they are for Carpentier. The former indicted dominant Western rational paradigms such as positivism and empiricism, advocated a more "authentic" relation between man and nature in which the emotions and subjective perception are not restricted by the scientific observation of the world, criticized hegemonic moral and esthetic norms, and sought a utopian escape in "primitive" societies. In Carpentier's translation of the term from the French *merveilleux* to the Spanish *lo real maravilloso*, his insistence on the importance of faith for the perception of the marvelous, and his valorization of indigenous societies, while due to a large extent to the influence of the surrealists, must be situated with respect to cultural self-affirmation, the rejection of the colonial civilizing mission, and the symbolic construction of differences between Europe and Latin America. For the

French surrealists and for Carpentier, non-Western societies are seen as other, since the cultural milieu of the erudite and Europeanized Carpentier is just as different from the African American rural communities of Haiti as that of urbanized Europeans is from "primitive" cultures. For the European surrealists, however, discourses on the "primitive" are a pretext for self-criticism or an incursion into exoticism, whereas for Carpentier, natives and African Americans are a "marker of difference" essential for the affirmation of Latin American specificity in contrast to the metropole. The other is in fact a part of the imaginary community in Latin America, whereas it stands in opposition to it in Europe, even if the discursive construction of this other draws partly from the same sources.

In his prologue Carpentier insists on the "authenticity" of the Latin American literary treatment of the marvelous, based on aspects of reality "impossible to situate in Europe" (1964, 16). These assertions are not original, since, as Chiampi has demonstrated, they echo Mabille's condemnation of the inauthentic marvelous and his valorization of the authentic marvelous of societies such as Haiti. However, Carpentier deliberately neglects to mention the surrealist whom he knew well and with whom he had many affinities, while representing surrealist practice in terms of superficial literary technique and passing over the axiological and epistemological implications of the major surrealist theoretical writings. He thereby legitimizes Latin American literary practice as original and different from that of a metropole he devalorizes and presents as sterile and decadent. In the prologue to his novel The Kingdom of This World he thus implicitly argues for his own novel's uniqueness and its resulting literary and cultural value.

The progressive substitution of the term lo real maravilloso by that of the baroque, especially in his 1964 essay on Latin American fiction in which Carpentier claims that the "legitimate style of the contemporary Latin American novelist is the baroque" (43), suggests that his rejection of the surrealists and his insistence on Latin American specificity is not merely an attempt to extol his own novels for representing the authentic marvelous, but also a desire to initiate a literary mode that could be considered as specifically Latin American and thus contribute to the construction of cultural identity and the development of an adequate form for figuring Latin America. In his 1964 essay entitled "De lo real maravillosamente americano [sic]" Carpentier argues that a Latin American style has progressively emerged throughout its history (127) and that surrealism is no longer generally imitated: "We are left with lo real maravilloso which is of a very different nature, constantly more palpable and discernible, which is starting to proliferate in the narrative of some young novelists of our continent" (129). The ambiguous term lo real maravilloso cannot be translated in this text as "marvelous reality," since it is explicitly contrasted with a particular literary practice, namely surrealism, and thus would be more correctly rendered by "marvelous realism," a term that Irlemar Chiampi adopts in her study of Carpentier. Instead of denoting, as it did in the 1949 prologue, a particular perception of reality, expressed in ontological and phenomenologial terms, lo real maravilloso has come to designate a literary style, technique, and thematic emphasis that supposedly characterize contemporary Latin American narrative.

In his essay "Problemática de la actual novela latinoamericana," Carpentier further develops his ideas on the necessity for Latin America to develop an autonomous and unique literary language. He argues that Latin American novelists must recreate their reality in a language that is both specific and at the same time accessible to the European reader. Latin American fauna and flora, for example, should not be designated by indigenous terms and explained in footnotes or glossaries, as was often the case in regionalist novels, but by words belonging to what he calls a universal vocabulary, that is, standard (or rather metropolitan) Spanish. Carpentier advocates a new and original textualization of the continent that would ensure that Latin American literature would no longer be considered as a marginalized regional production: "Now we Latin American novelists must name everything—everything that defines us, envelops us, and surrounds us: everything that operates with the energy of context—in order to situate it in the universal" (1964, 42).

His replacement of the term lo real maravilloso by that of the baroque in his comments on the necessity of naming a "previously unnamed" reality partly reflects his realization that what is at stake is not so much an ontological difference between Latin America and Europe, or even a particular perception, but a difference in literary practice, seen as the authentic expression of its people. Conscious of the belatedness of Latin American culture (1964, 29–30), he identifies marvelous realism (my translation of lo real as realism instead of reality reflects the semantic transformation undergone by the term in Carpentier's writings, although the later meaning is already implied in his 1949 essay) with the birth of an original and mature literary production, attesting to a specific cultural identity. Further on in the same essay, he emphasizes the necessity for Latin Americans to develop their own epic (ibid., 46). Since this genre has always been closely affiliated with the constitution of national identity, it is obvious that Carpentier is very concerned with developing what Sakai calls a "subjective technology" designed to foster a sense of collective identity in a heterogeneous and conflict-driven continent. What may be considered as an external and exoticist perspective inspired by a rereading of European discourses on the New World and the "primitive" thus becomes instrumental in a self-representation intended to include the other within Latin America. But the importance of the global context is never absent, since the creation of an "authentic voice" also creates cultural capital. The celebration of an autonomous literature pervades the writings of numerous Latin American critics, and several consider lo real maravilloso as a "modality of contemporary Latin American narrative" (Bravo 1978, 6) that allows it to acquire the status of world literature.

Other Latin American critics deplore the fact that many Europeans and North Americans equate Latin American literature with magical realism, of which Gabriel García Márquez is considered to be the most celebrated exponent. However, the Colombian Nobel Prize winner has helped maintain that perception by his own literary endeavor as well as by essays such as "Fantasía y creación artística en América Latina y el Caribe" (1979), in which he claims that the Latin American continent is more marvelous than any fiction, and this attribute becomes the basis for a cofiguration of the New World as Europe's opposite. In a desire for specificity, the affirmation of difference sometimes leads to the proclamation of a total incommensurability between Latin America and other cultures, as in the following passage by the Guatemalan novelist Asturias:

> For a translator really to put himself into my books is as difficult as for a European who has never seen America to understand *our landscape. Our landscape* is alive in a way *entirely different* from his, which makes *our reality different*. One has to be very intimate with *our cosmic world*, this world of terrestrial battles in which one still has to struggle simply in order to live. . . . I don't doubt that most translators do speak excellent Spanish, but they do not speak *our Spanish* and therefore do not have *our feelings and our spirit*. Thus, they are likely to make strict Castilian translations of our books. They translate them as if they had been written in a Spanish province that is very foreign to *our temperament* and *our life*, to *our character* and *our way of speaking*. (Asturias 1967, 58; emphasis added)

The repetitive nature of this passage, in which the possessive adjective "our" recurs eleven times, demonstrates an almost obsessive desire for difference, culminating in the image of a culture that is intrinsically distinct and absolutely inaccessible to readers and translators outside Latin America. At the same time, Asturias seems unaware of his own subjectivity in translating (and interpreting) indigenous culture in his novels written for non-indigenous readers, assuming a situation of total transparence between him-self, the university-educated Spanish-speaking Guatemalan, and the rural native communities. His claim that he represents the "original mentality" of the Indians (ibid.) obscures the fact that his portrayal of indigenous culture constitutes it as a specific, bounded, and identifiable object which can be represented in a successful act of communication within Latin America. In spite of the enormous cultural differences between educated, Spanish-speaking Latin Americans and native communities in which indigenous languages are the only means of communication for many, Asturias sees his role as cultural mediator in terms of what Sakai has called a "homolingual address," in which one takes for granted reciprocal and transparent com-munication between unitary communities of two single languages (Sakai 1997, 3–4). The translation of his own novels into other languages, by contrast, inevitably involves failed communication between cultures consid-ered as incommensurate (in spite of their common European origins). His admission that his fiction resembles what the French surrealists had in mind, however, emphasizes the importance of European discourses in his own subjective figuration of an indigenous culture seen as central to a specific Latin American identity.

Rereading Carpentier in dialogue not only with the Western critical tradi-tion, Latin American debates, and postcolonial concepts of ambivalence, but also with discussions on identity in English-speaking peripheral settler so-cieties and Sakai's reflections on Japan is only a first step in a broader comparative project that seeks to broaden the postcolonial critical paradigm. In conclusion, studies of postcolonial cultures should be reduced neither to a dialogue between metropolitan intellectuals about the non-Western "Other," nor to one between those "Others," but include voices from the institutionalized postcolonial discourse decried by Dirlik and the local dia-logues advocated by Mukherjee, while remaining open to debates from other sources, such as Sakai's analyses of identity construction in Japan and, in the case of Latin America, studies of other settler societies marginalized by the postcolonial canon.

NOTE

Unless otherwise indicated, all English translations are my own.

POSTCOLONIAL SENSIBILITY, LATIN AMERICA, AND THE QUESTION OF LITERATURE

Román de la Campa

Postcolonial research issues from a wide-ranging body of theoretical insights and historical temporalities easily abridged by singular definitions and widespread usage. As with other critical paradigms, its conditions of possibility—a dynamic but conflictive plural—are all too often shunted by the pull of academic mainstreaming and marketing. Due to the postcolonial's current status as an established practice with seemingly unlimited range, restoring its contested terrain may require closer attention to pivotal questions that continue to snare its inner workings. One involves its understanding of literature, an intricate problematic that Peter Hallward's *Absolutely Postcolonial* (2001), for example, has recently essayed with particular intensity. Briefly put, it seems pertinent to ask if the postcolonial emphasis on localized histories offers new ways of engaging the specificity of literature, or if it unwittingly revives the notion and practice of representational art.[1]

Equally urgent is differentiating postcolonial models, historical as well as literary, as they pertain to English and Spanish, the two vast colonial traditions that crisscross the Americas, a contentious and difficult task that has begun to concern scholars on both sides of the Atlantic. Guided by these underlying queries, this essay will outline a plane of distinctions based on various modes of engagement that cut across the terrain of postcolonialism. My aim is not to argue the grounds of legitimacy of one version over another, but rather to explore the growing scope of postcolonial usage, and its moving cartography on the ground, its varying modes of application as they pertain to the Latin American theoretical and literary realm.

The postcolonial is often invoked as a historical marker that speaks for itself, a sense of time with no greater specificity than "the period following" colonial or neocolonial rule anywhere or at any time since the onset of modernity. *Postcolonial* thus found its way into our vocabulary, particularly in the English-speaking world, with even greater ease than the once favored *postmodern*. It is not difficult to identify reasons for this. One could be the slow release of repressed irony. After centuries of denial, academic disciplines now recognize that colonialism, or colonial logic, persists in many forms, not only in nation-states caught up in truncated modernities, but perhaps everywhere, including developed nations such as the United States. This is welcome news for most practitioners, especially younger generations of scholars eager to infuse politics into their academic practice at a time of generalized quietude. Another explanation may be a sort of collective nostalgia for periodization, for the postcolonial invokes a yearning for localized time-framing otherwise denied by global synchronicity, a spatial imaginary that engulfs all temporalities.

Postcolonial sensibility fills a void, even though its application to former Third World societies remains largely unspecified and steeped in layers of conceptual contradiction often premised on an intrinsic failure (inability to enter into nationhood) according to a model of state formation (the Western republic) that is itself now in question, albeit bereft of empirical alternatives. Basic postcolonialism also supplants the notion of "Third World," now in apparent disfavor, with a term thoroughly caught up in the morphology of "post-ing," while aiming to retain most if not all of the old term's historical force. As such, the postcolonial occupies a rhetorical space vacated but not quite emptied, a tacit refutation of the premise that global capital has turned the corner on historical inequities across the planet, or eliminated history and ideology. Yet, it could also be said that widespread use of *postcolonial* bespeaks a sort of semantic attrition in which "colonial" and "neocolonial" historical formations, as well as their corresponding critiques, lose their specificity as stand-alone categories. The same could be said for the category of imperialism and its corresponding analysis, often bypassed by the postcolonial stress on internal chain of causation as the main story explaining the rule of local elites and their national failures. Then again, one cannot possibly deny, or easily dismiss, the arrival of postcolonial thinking in the critical imaginary, even if its politics often resort to deconstructive utopias or get snared in the constant renaming and repackaging that permeates academic criticism, a site of production conditioned by a growing nexus of conceptual and marketing impulses.

In Latin America the postcolonial sensibility must contend with a vast multinational legacy of truncated modernities as well as thick layers of highly codified literature, a combination that must not be forgotten or written off. Traversing such an intricate web of locations and articulations seems like a tall order for any epochal construct. Each period has left an indelible mark in what is known as Latin America, an area that encompasses more than twenty nations and various distinct civilizational groupings, each with its respective modes of hybridization. Yet, it must also be said that coloniality retained its force in the region throughout all these historical periods, as the renowned critic Angel Rama argued in La ciudad letrada (1984). The question, therefore, is not whether postcolonial applies to Latin America in some general or metaphoric sense, but rather whether the term can sustain the latter's rich and varied modern/colonial history without imploding or erasing more than it unearths.

Latin America remains, by and large, a sphere of pseudorepublics, as José Martí mapped it at the end of the nineteenth century in his classic essay "Our America." In that sense, the area seems as ripe for postcolonial critique as the commonwealth grouping of nations. Then again, if one takes into consideration that Latin American postcolonial history antedates the end of Anglo-American colonial rule by more than a century and that it includes a rich legacy of anticolonial critique articulated by scholars representing a wide-ranging body of academic disciplines, as well as by creative artists, it becomes immediately clear why the two temporalities, as well as the sensibilities they invoke, seem highly incommensurable. Then there is the question of contemporary Latin American literature and its attendant periodicity, often strung by signifiers such as modernism, avant-garde, neobaroque, Boom, and post-Boom, all of which correspond to artistic movements that the postcolonial tends to codify, perhaps uneasily, either as defeating mimicry (of Western cosmopolitanism) or misplaced conceit (that of ruling Creole aestheticism), thereby linking modern literature and national failure in almost deterministic fashion.

Postcolonial readings of Latin American literature must therefore answer a fundamental set of questions: can they attend to the area's deep colonial traces while simultaneously distinguishing modern and postmodern temporalities? Will they yield instead to a mode of representational aesthetics in which literature can only stand for the false consciousness of ruling elites, a mask for their political defeat? The literary implications of this second critique deserve further attention: do they mask a nostalgic but conflicted yearning for the area's national bourgeois republics in the nineteenth century and the lost socialist imaginaries in the twentieth? If not, how would the dictum of "modern failures" specifically account for such a rich history throughout the differing regions of Latin America? Most important, in the absence of historical and theoretical distinctions, the notion of generalized failure all too easily leads the constellation of Latin American nation-states into a theoretical cul-de-sac in which forced accommodation to global market imperatives is the only way to access alternative projects, including those of civil society. In that context, the overwhelming force of the present exhausts all utopian pursuits except those driven by negative theoretical critique, a political imaginary that may itself conceal an elite mask of sorts.

Much has been said about the category of "the aesthetic," particularly as regards its abandonment of an authoritarian hermeneutic tradition laden with universal value claims that often went unquestioned. One must also note, however, that little attention is paid within humanistic endeavors, even those concerned with cultural studies, to the ways in which market-driven cultural production discerns quality and value. Choices of that nature continue to be made, but one must ask if a domain so driven by consumption can in any way sustain artistic detachment and deliberative language. With respect to literary studies, or any alternative discourse imbued by the distinct practice of verbal exploration and polysemy, it seems unclear what role they could have in the contemporary cultural domain. This, one gathers, ought to concern postcolonial theory at its deepest level, for it should aspire to interrogate simultaneously both the old aesthetic of universal claims and the new realm of aesthetic critique occupied by discourses all too willing to blur the distinction between politics and culture.[2]

Historically speaking, if one follows its linguistic footprints, the postcolonial breaks into our imaginary with a belated but vigorous critique of the rule of English. Edward Said, Homi Bhabha, Gayatri Spivak, though widely different in their approaches, fashioned a long-awaited deconstruction of

Anglo-American hegemony in their own terms. The incursion of India and Palestine into high French theory brought a new style of English prose that applied poststructuralist critique to the Third World, with more cultural nuance than traditional Marxism and more political specificity than postmodernism. With varying degrees of success and specificity, these writers set the diasporic subject to the work of theory, while studiously distancing themselves from any essentialist claims to the Third World that inspired them. Though highly celebrated by the academy, they saw their work as at odds with that of the disciplines, as if doomed to the fate of uninvited guest in the house of English and theory. In time, Ranajit Guha's emphasis on historical grounding shifted the focus somewhat from discursive transgression to Third World subaltern communities, a turn that has inspired various strands of Latin American postcolonial critiques and debates, but the stamp of the three diasporic pioneers continues to mark the postcolonial enterprise, its adherents as well as its critics and reformers.

The early English substratum of postcolonialism shares its temporality with a less precise but more powerful construct known simply as globalization; indeed, the two now seem to shadow each other, for English turned into the lingua franca of globalization at the time when postcolonial theory seemed to engulf its academic imaginary, both in the First World and among the diasporic multitudes connected by its geopolitical and linguistic traditions. In that context, Asian American, U.S. Latino, and Latin American intellectuals working in the United States posed a new challenge for postcoloniality, with rather significant implications for Spanish as well. Both colonial (and modern) traditions of language and literature in the Americas, English and Spanish, now had to recast their transatlantic contours in wholly new terms, for their respective Wasp, Catholic, or syncretic traditions of monolingualism no longer sufficed.

The postcolonial sensibility was particularly relevant to this moment, which called for a new order of knowledge production, driven less by interests such as national defense and more in concert with a globalized cultural sphere. The vast Cold War apparatus of American research institutions, in many ways outmoded by the end of the 1980s, responded to this challenge in various ways. Andreas Huyssen, a noted German scholar of comparative literature, explains this moment of adjustment and shifting boundaries as one in which European aesthetics and Western history, otherwise known as humanism, were replaced by a new realm of cultural studies and postmodernity largely framed in the United States.[3] Postcolonial critique derives from this new political economy of knowledge production, a new logic of symbolic capital in which disciplines function less as guardians of the past than as lines of flight, in constant movement amid linguistic, political, and cultural traditions.[4]

English turned into the language of empire—in Hardt and Negri's sense (2000)—at the same time that the links connecting language, literature, and nation came into question as never before. In this new code of production and consumption, English-language literature had to account for an increasing body of recognized authors who write in English, but whose cultural and national bearings reside elsewhere, not only in former British colonies and settler societies but also in the Asian and Latino communities of the United States. One may think of such new authorship as the growing voice of those who have become native speakers of English as a second language. In that contradictory terrain, Spanish also awakens to an enlarged but uncertain destiny in the United States, in spite of this country's deep-seated antipathy toward foreign languages, a sentiment that has only intensified in recent decades. This uncharted—one might call it subaltern—bilingual condition contributes to a global sense of Spanish in which Spain has found an unexpected reentry of sorts, one not defined by a sense of national or linguistic colonial empowerment, but rather by the opportunities for investment in cultural and linguistic dissemination, a sort of postnational Spanish marketing that is intrinsically transnational, with its main theater of consumption in the Americas.[5]

Millions of English-dominant speakers of Spanish now come knocking on the doors of both Spanish and English departments in the U.S. academy, a site whose influence has grown to unprecedented hegemonic status, in no small part because its institutional framework still affords vast numbers of research-level positions in the humanities and the lettered social sciences. Spanish departments must therefore not only brave the fragmentation of their traditional discipline but also come to grips with the opportunities implicit in these rising entanglements. These administrative units of academic capital, once the guardians of Hispanism (the study of Spanish as a European foreign language and literature), first shifted their focus toward Latin America during the Cold War amid a set of contradictory stimuli. These included area studies, an enterprise largely driven by the defense interests of the United States, which happened to coincide, in contradictory fashion, with socialist revolutionary struggles and pockets of capitalist development in the area. Now, in the post–area studies moment, both schools of U.S. Hispanic studies, the Iberian and the Latin American, must ask what it means—culturally, linguistically, and theoretically—to live and work amid forty million Latinos and Hispanics, with a buying power projected to approach $1 trillion by the end of this decade.[6] No longer the cultural embassies of Hispanism in U.S. academia, Spanish departments now rehearse the possibilities of an unexpected global realm with uncertain but profound implications for the potential links between English and Spanish.

Postcolonial Latin Americanist work in the United States at times takes stock of these new challenges, but generally speaking its focus remains on nations with large indigenous populations ignored by the modern tradition, as one would expect.[7] An exception might be found in the attempt to bring together indigenous Latin American peoples and U.S. Latinos under the banner of Latin American postcolonialism, which seems both opportunistic and contradictory. On the one hand, it opens the field to a transnational understanding of colonial traditions in the Americas, identifying key moments of geopolitical conflict ripe for postcolonial critique, such as the 1848 Treaty of Guadalupe Hidalgo and the 1898 Spanish-American War. On the other hand, bracketing Latinos and Amerindian populations as mirror images of postcolonial logic risks imposing a formulation in which Latinos are exclusively cast as the floating component at the postmodern "border," and indigenous groups are made the testimonial, historical, and pre-modern "root." Such narrow casting, while suggestive, eludes modern history as such, most particularly evading the need for a differential engagement with how each group bears on the broader non-indigenous, non-Latino communities of Latin America and the United States.

As one might expect, this mode of mapping presents a series of difficulties for Latin America, in part due to the avalanche of critical frameworks that have occupied the space of literary studies in just a few decades, a theoretical boom in which postcolonialism has figured prominently, as have the respective inflections brought about by multiculturalism, feminism, and cultural studies. This new impetus, largely articulated in U.S. universities, flooded the market of discourses pertaining to Latin American literary and artistic culture, a disciplinary sector that, unlike the social sciences, had remained largely bound to the influence of national or regional Latin American articulations during the Cold War. True to form, the spread of "metropolitan" theory intensified a debate that has shadowed cultural Latin Americanism since the nineteenth century, notwithstanding the fact that, for the most part, postcolonialism was first enunciated by Latin Americans, and that poststructuralism implied, from the outset, an immanent but deep critique of Eurocentric modes of thinking.

It goes without saying that all contexts have their needs and economies of value, but it seems particularly relevant to emphasize that the institutional expansiveness and wealth of the North American academy makes possible humanistic discourses that ignore the local. Indeed, those of us working in the United States may be more prone to conceive of our object of study as a transnational community of discourses able to absorb all difference through theoretical practice alone. At the same time, it must be said that distinctions largely based on location—the old use-value concept, for example—always entail significant risks. Should one judge the validity of theory, history, or literature based on the locus of its enunciation? How does one define such a concept, by nation of origin, language of expression, place of work, political inclination, or some arbitrary combination of these elements depending on one's need at the time? Similarly, how far can one go in asserting that transculturation, liberation theology, and dependency theory constitute an autochthonous sphere of Latin American theory shortchanged by U.S.-bound critics who favor scholarship that is Euro-American or South Asian (with the latter's British accentuation)? Are such Latin American discourses devoid of European theoretical traces, elite masks, and neocolonialist residues?

Most critics concede that globalization impacts different nations differently, but few scholars take such complications to heart. Piecing together the influence of the post–Cold War period on theory has been a challenging task, as one can plainly see in two of the most frequently cited attempts to address the matter, Jacques Derrida's *Specters of Marx* (1994) and Michael Hardt and Antonio Negri's *Empire* (2000). The most pressing question one draws from both, after thirty years of deconstructive work, is whether deconstruction can critically address the post-1989 global scene, or at least draw a clear line of resistance from postcapitalism, that other source of radical designification. Postcolonialism belongs to this new scene, even while insisting on more specific, localized mapping of the past. Its logic must attend not only to the global and the local, but also to the past and the present. As such, it puts critics and their disciplines to the test, not only those who opt to remain exclusively within literature but also those who seem to have abandoned it altogether. The same could be said for scholars who seek a way out of this dilemma by shifting the lyrical force of literary training into a theoretical enterprise far removed from the here and now of Latin America.

At stake here is the role of the academic intellectual in the research university, particularly in the United States, an institutional space that has radically changed during the past decade or so, as intellectuals are increasingly subject to market pressures, which obviously can affect how they address their objects of study. Whether we choose to dispense with tradition or to learn new ways of reading it, our own subjectivity is rehearsed in the process. Yet postcolonial scholarship, like that of postmodern and cultural studies, continues to emanate from scholars with literary training who have ventured into the brave new world of global culture somewhat lightheartedly. We seem to bank on our symbolic capital, particularly our command of theory, to guarantee our claims about film, television, architecture, music, and above all, epistemology, a new discursive genre cultivated largely within the academy. But we remain bound to a type of textual analysis—literary, historical, and epistemological—that calls for little if any exploration of the forms of technomediatic culture and everyday experiences. Needless to say, such an approach may still yield new and refreshing work, but one wonders if it is sufficient to meet its own claims and aspirations.

A LATIN AMERICAN STORY

There are many ways of avoiding the valuable links between literary studies and the lettered social sciences. Both sides, at least within Latin Americanism, have grown fond of casting each other as governed either by relativism or factualism. Freeing oneself of this old habit may be easier said than done, as Florencia Mallon (2001) spelled out in an essay challenging Latin American subaltern historians and literary critics to move beyond disciplinary limitations. An equally important task is revisiting the inherent heterogeneity of poststructural theory, a body of work that galvanized the reach and ambition of humanistic disciplines for decades. Latin American literary and cultural studies figured prominently in this enterprise at the outset, especially regarding the question of postmodernity, largely defined by the extraordinary influence of Jorge Luis Borges and the new Latin American novel (i.e., the product of the "Boom"). In just a few decades, however, the postmodern turned into a fertile matrix of theoretical and applied work redefined in many disparate ways, particularly after 1989, with the near absolute demise of left-wing state projects and the institution of neoliberal political order throughout the continent. At that moment, Latin American literary studies suddenly found itself caught in a discursive vacuum it had never quite imagined.

The ambitious repertory of semiosis, deconstruction, and metanarrative critiques, otherwise known as poststructuralism, took high theory far beyond the realm of literature, even while retaining a debt to it, one often forgotten by critics now ready to forego literary questions altogether. Indeed, the Foucauldian debt to Edward Said, Ranajit Guha, Gyan Prakash, and Partha Chatterjee, among others whose work has deeply inspired Latin American subaltern studies, belongs to this diverse body of discourse. Even the more recent rereading of liberation theology and dependency theory inspired by Immanuel Wallerstein's world-systems theory largely constitutes, within Marxism and the social sciences, a correlative response to the poststructural turn's impact on the postcolonial. In Latin American literature, however, poststructuralism first came into play through literary studies in perhaps the deepest sense. It was claimed by Boom, post-Boom, neobaroque, magical realism, testimonio, feminist writing, and postmodernity before postcolonialism and subaltern studies came on the scene. This chronology does not by itself constitute a privileged point of origination, but it warrants careful consideration, for it has left an anxiety of influence that looms large in current theory.

The now common reference to Latin America's dual "modern/colonial" condition amply enacts the mirroring of two seemingly opposite periodicities, with their corresponding posts. Indeed, postmodern and postcolonial approaches mirror—some might say, shadow—each other, in spite of their alleged differences. Each generates its own modes of unremitting designification of modern traditions as well as ways of remapping the cultural landscape of Latin America largely on the basis of epistemological critique. Together they have redefined Latin American literary studies, leading to a nimble archive of theoretical metaphors and epistemic exploration, a language (grammar and poetics) of criticism especially able to adjust to ebbs and flows in the new market of academic production. As such, both constitute forms of academic realignment within the neoliberal moment.[8]

For Latin American literary studies, the postcolonial began as a questioning of the postmodern, an apparatus constructed around a few Boom novelists—generally all male—from a predictable set of nations whose indigenous past was minimally regarded or totally repressed. Later this inflection claimed an emphasis on coloniality as such, broadly defined as a logic that lingered after the onset of modernist aesthetics and developmental models designed by social scientists. But Latin American postcolonialism has since moved toward the topic of subalternity, as well as to a revision of the area's long-lasting tradition of neocolonial critique, including liberation theology through the work of Enrique Dussel and dependency theory through that of Aníbal Quijano. In short, in order to distinguish itself from Western postmodernism, English Commonwealth postcolonialism, and South Asian subalternism, the Latin American postcolonial inflection has had to take a much closer look at the post-independence period otherwise understood as Latin American "modernity."

Various strands of postcolonial critique converge around this problematic, all of them first articulated in the United States, but with the increasing collaboration of Latin American scholars. One, much closer to Immanuel Wallerstein's systems theory and social science than to literature, places coloniality at the center of Latin American studies, with a renewed interest in vindicating earlier discourses such as liberation theology and dependency theory, but emphasizing race and ethnicity rather than social class, and shifting the focus from cosmopolitan Latin America to Amerindian cultures.[9] Another strand, closer to literature but only as the anteroom for philosophical deconstruction, looks on modern Latin America through the theoretical lens of "negative alterity," a critique imbued by notions of "impossibility" and "ungovernability" that are not meant to articulate new social or political programs, but rather to capture the course of subalternity as the never-ceasing logic of excess inherent to the links between epistemology and discourse production.[10] A third strand combines the first two positions, simultaneously mapping historical subjects such as indigenous movements through the deconstructive lens, but with an eye toward identifying subaltern movements as concrete new subjects for both history and postliterary studies.[11]

These strands converge in the unconditional critique of the Latin American modern paradigm, particularly as codified by the fin de siècle modernist tradition and its subsequent postmodern Boom period. This particularized, if not exclusive, focus leads to various important considerations. One involves the lineaments of theory itself.[12] We have all learned that there is theory in every text, but perhaps one should also take a closer look at the text in every theory, that is, the storylines, drama, and rhetorical force internal to the work of theory itself. One of these narratives, perhaps the most telling, is that of testimonio, whose basic chronology is widely known. The genre dawned in the 1960s, with texts such as *Autobiography of a Runaway Slave*, by Miguel Barnet (1973 [1966]), and then steadily rose through the 1970s and 1980s, reaching worldwide attention with the publication of *I, Rigoberta Menchú* (1984). Since then, however, a series of theoretical pursuits, often embedded in storylines that read like novels, have overshadowed it.

Testimonio appeared on the literary scene as a sign of promise, not so much within the new Latin American canon, but rather as an articulation of new realist or anthropological alternatives to the Boom and the promise of national emancipation. Now, after the Cold War and under the negative-alterity paradigm, many of these same texts stand as epistemological registers of disillusionment, both within literature as well as toward the possibilities of Latin American state formation. One hastens to add that the postcolonial umbrella also provided an important new forum for Latin Americanists dedicated to colonial studies proper. Indeed, the influential work of scholars such as Rolena Adorno, Mercedes López Baralt, and Mary Louise Pratt during this period attests to the fact that colonial Latin American literature, a discipline not long ago considered part of the Spanish Golden Age, has earned a larger and much deserved profile as a result. That body of work, conversant with, but independent of, postcolonial theory, has brought new depth and specificity to Latin American colonial literary studies. One could also trace alternative storylines for testimonio's rise, U.S. as much as Latin American. Indeed, many renowned specialists have worked significantly on the topic, including Elzbieta Sklodowska, Doris Sommer, and George Yúdice, but I will follow here the plotline that is perhaps most recognizable to the U.S. academy.

Testimonio literature may have presaged a realist alternative to the Boom, but the enthusiasm afforded by such a reading waned considerably with the demise of the Central American revolution. It came as a surprising irony that testimonio criticism should turn, for its own survival, to deconstructive theory, the very source that the "Left" had largely stigmatized up to this moment, a body of theory that, for two decades, had thoroughly imbued its literary antithesis, the postmodern Boom paradigm. The turn came, in part, by way of the subaltern studies approach of Ranajit Guha, who had successfully coupled poststructuralism with a critique of British colonial history. Working from the suppositions of John Beverley, Latin American testimonio moved toward Guha's construct, sometimes buttressed by the deconstructive insights of Alberto Moreiras, sometimes by the focus on Andean indigenous gnosis pursued by Walter Mignolo, and at other times indistinctly combining all three articulations.

In time, these divergent notions of subalternity came to be understood as a posthumanist literary corpus capable of opening a new left-wing stance on postmodernity's colonial deficit through a complex fusion of critical and theoretical strategies for the 1990s. Roughly speaking, the new framework issued from a set of interrelated presuppositions, of which the following seem preeminent: to rescue deconstruction, semiosis, history of the language, systems theory, and other discursively oriented practices by moving them beyond modern literature toward the colonial logic underlying Latin

American cultural history; to recast canonical discourses of Latin American state formation and modernist aesthetics as a categorical negative otherwise understood as the failed New World Creole utopia; to specify the work of postcoloniality through subaltern theory, fashioning the latter as the new, or perhaps exclusive, paradigm of resistance to modern and postmodern colonial logic.[13]

Again, this story emerged at a moment of exhaustion for Latin American revolutionary movements, a tradition fully committed to the early reading of testimonio as realist literature. The subaltern turn consequently demanded a series of valuations in the space of postmodern theory and Latin American studies. Politically speaking, the role of testimonio as an ideal discursive form for national emancipation movements had vanished; understanding this bitter truth led many to reread all of Latin American literature as the story of the failure of the state and its intellectual classes. Theoretically speaking, the turn to subalternity opened a conduit for regrouping, a sort of poststructuralist alternative to Latin Americanist politics through negative alterity, an anti-aesthetic of impossibility applicable to state projects, regardless of whether they emerged through coups, electoral regimes, or revolutions.[14]

There remain deeper literary issues pertaining to subaltern testimonio that bear closer attention, given that this approach negates and reaffirms the importance of literature at the same time. Subaltern studies often focuses on the Boom period, but it aims to deconstruct all official literature, which constitutes, by implication, the entire modern Latin American tradition. Testimonio thus moves toward the notion of a "postliterary" form, as the once frequent debates on the literary nature of the genre give way to a reflection on its indigenous historicity, understood as colonial practices, flows, and traces ignored by the state and its modernist aesthetics, a legacy understood to be synonymous with the self-referential postmodernity championed by the Boom.[15] Subalternity thus shifted the weight of Latin American textuality from a literary to a culturalist matrix, say, from Gabriel García Márquez to Rigoberta Menchú, or from Juan Rulfo to Gloria Anzaldúa. As such, its immediate range of political involvement seemed to draw closer to the curricular debates in the United States, a nation-state deeply caught in its own denial of indigenous history and the growing presence of cultural, racial, and ethnic minorities. In that sense, Latin American subalternity, having left the Latin American "nation" as a lost cause, and having turned its attention primarily to ethnic struggles, acquired a much more active role in the cultural practices of the U.S. Left, even if its implications for Latin America itself remained open to debate and further specification.

COMPARATIVE POSTCOLONIAL

It should surprise no one that scholars in Latin America appropriate "post-ing" (modern or colonial) in radically different ways, when they do, or that they have widely varying takes on the future of the nation-state and its literature, which obviously reflect different ways of dealing with disillusion-ment without outright foreclosing of possibility. Unlike in the U.S. academy, postmodernity in Latin America has not been articulated mainly by literary theorists, nor has multiculturalism been tailored by a global marketing interest, nor has postcolonialism been caught in a binary of ethnic assimi-lation and minority contestation. This means not that Latin America has found an answer to these entanglements, but that it responds to them through differing modalities difficult to synthesize into any one theoretical model. It also explains why Latin America has always been skeptical of, if not resistant to, literary and philosophical frameworks enshrined by the U.S. academy, perhaps even more than those of European provenance, which inform the work of theorists in the United States at the deepest levels. Reasons abound for this contradictory disposition beyond the hazy debate surrounding loci of enunciation. We may gain broader perspective on the issue by focusing on the work of disciplines and their respective attitudes toward interdisciplinary work on both sides of the Rio Grande.

It may seem obvious to say that the Cold War legacy of area studies left its imprint on disciplinary work in the U.S. academy, or that it was followed by the current nexus of theoretical speculation and disciplinary lines of flight otherwise understood as border studies (among other new concentrations). But what remains almost untouched are the intricate counterpoints between European theory and academic work in the United States and Latin America. Such a contrast seems particularly relevant if one recognizes that both post-modernity and postcoloniality largely derive from a transnational hybridiza-tion of epistemology difficult to contain within disciplinary, linguistic, and national boundaries. Social scientists in Latin America, such as Néstor Gar-cía Canclini, generally find more invested readers among literary critics in the United States, whereas literary critics working in the U.S. academy, such as Walter Mignolo, are now largely engaged by social scientists in Latin America. Yet García Canclini and Mignolo share not just their nation of origin, but a penchant for interdisciplinary research acquired during their formative years in Europe, later redefined by their respective work on Latin American topics. Their research methods and specific conclusions remain widely different, but their refusal to commit to the U.S. academy's disciplin-ary divide is an important point of convergence.

The issue of racial imaginaries in the Americas also remains relatively unexplored as a comparative field, even though Latin American postcolonialism relies heavily on ethnicity. It seems fair to say that a thorough engagement with African American scholarship as well as with U.S. Latino cultural forms awaits subalternity, as does a deeper awareness of racial diversity in Latin America.[16] Latinos, a century-old migratory flow of Latin Americans to the United States, have increased their numbers exponentially during the past two decades, a presence that calls for a comparative focus for postcolonial studies in the United States and Latin America. It is often observed, for example, that concepts such as *mestizaje* and transculturation have lent themselves to racialist myths in modern Creole Latin America, even though these terms are often embraced—and at times celebrated—by postcolonialists when they are deployed by Latino scholars such as Gloria Anzaldúa and Guillermo Gómez Peña. At the same time, a simultaneous critique of the "melting pot" narrative and the "construction of whiteness" found in the United States seldom comes into play as the basis for deconstruction by Latin Americanists of the links between national literature and U.S. state formation. It would be ironic if Latin American postcolonialism unwittingly exempted European and North American literary history from the critique that brackets modernist aesthetics and national identity so easily in Latin America.[17]

Comparative theory could bring a much-needed new focus to these positions, which can no longer advance by following ready-made binaries such as here versus there, autochthonous versus foreign, or relativism versus facticity. Difference will only be served if we fully recognize the differing sites of production, consumption, and legitimization that simultaneously claim Latin America, the United States, and in-between populations such as U.S. Latinos. It is not difficult to find imaginative books on Latin American postmodernity based on Argentine or Cuban literature, for example, or new postcolonial critiques based on Bolivian or Ecuadorian cultural traditions, but few map Latin America transnationally with sufficient rigor to account for different modern/colonial hybrid formations within each area. The stakes have risen for Latin Americanist scholarship largely bound to the one-nation or one-region perspectives that continue to drive production, even in feminist research, a paradigm that by definition cuts across all others. If there is a common theme in many of the new approaches discussed thus far, perhaps it can be found in their multifarious—at times perhaps even capricious—attempts to accommodate deconstructive theory, which became an anchor of sorts for subaltern critiques after the socialist debacle. Obviously, the sense of closure that entered utopian thinking after

1989 had a role in this turn of events, but the preeminence of poststructural theory in the humanities, established prior to 1989—particularly in literary studies—also required important readjustments.

Initially, subaltern notions of literature, like cultural studies, may have been aimed less at literature than at widening the reach of deconstructive insights that had been confined to postmodernism in its strict artistic sense. By now, however, many of these theoretical insights unwittingly converge with what might be understood as the lived experience of global capital and neoliberal order. After all, the latter largely look on the nation-state structure as an obstacle, and their cultural imperative has replaced the formative role of literature with a radical dimension of audiovisual performance and wired subjectivity, not to speak of the power of redemptive autobiography and local specificity. One wonders, therefore, how negative alterity, or colonial historicity, will map the future of multitudes as global capital unleashes its own process of decentering at a time devoid of national emancipation narratives. Will the neoliberal utopia converge or silently collude with a subaltern critique content to elaborate the exhaustion, if not end, of the possibilities of the modern nation-state? Will the call for a postnational theory of Latin America satisfy subjects who hope for national reconstruction?

The storyline I have drawn thus far, limited no doubt by its exclusions and oversights, as all stories tend to be, envisions a new Latin Americanism whose ways of mapping the area's literary and cultural referents must increasingly respond to transnational dimensions. The latter have been deeply felt in North American academia (that of the United States and Canada, in different ways), not only through testimonio and the Latino diaspora but also through feminist approaches. In Latin America the unraveling or splitting of modern states has become the norm rather than the exception. Many different types of crises have enveloped the area—Chiapas, Venezuela, Colombia, and Argentina, for example—not to mention what it means for more than ten Latin American nations to have permanent communities of considerable size residing in the United States, whose remittances to their countries of origin constitute a leading source of revenue for their former nations. In short, Latin American texts, literary and otherwise, evince an array of postnational entanglements that demand our critical attention and call for more thorough ways of reading, theorizing, and representing the region as an object of study.

These concerns have yet to fully capture the attention of literary and cultural specialists. *The Real Thing* (Gugelberger 1996), a widely quoted anthology of essays substantially dedicated to testimonio, provides a telling sample. Many of its entries demonstrate a complex understanding of Latin American literary postmodernity and subalternity, while others offer an imaginative catalog of the practice of Latin Americanism in curricular debates within the United States. One should note, however, that few venture into the comparative terrain of cultural differences within Latin America or entertain the question of how such specific knowledge would affect subaltern theoretical models largely framed in the United States, rather than the other way around. Indeed, the notion of "posthumanist" literature, together with the subaltern remapping it encompasses, seems to beg for a specific awareness of how it applies to the widely different cultures that pertain to Latin America. Without that level of specificity and without the onus of a comparative optic, Latin America folds into a neatly synchronized global domain in which negative alterity becomes readily applicable to all nations and regions at once and from a distance, perhaps signaling an unwitting return to the universalizing tendencies traditionally associated with modern aesthetics.

In their book on the literary politics of the Central American revolutionary movements during the 1980s John Beverley and Marc Zimmerman (1990) observed that Rubén Darío, an end-of-the-nineteenth-century poet known for his refined, if not aristocratic tastes, took on a completely new meaning for the peasants involved in the Nicaraguan insurgency. Following the logic of such fortuitous allegorical destinies, one might be thus tempted to question any attempt to consign the symbolic value of writers like Gabriel García Márquez to the dustbin of modern, failed, Creole, Latin American discourses. Indeed, one could surmise that such a sweeping brushstroke inadvertently creates its own subaltern object—the existing masses of mestizos and Creoles in Latin America whose lives continue to nurture an ontology and an aesthetic sense that communicates a cultural and political reality as well as an understanding of literature. These effects—as with Darío's poetry, or Borges's aesthetics—may be subject to critique, but they continually resurface as unexpected combinations and contradictions in Latin America.

Envisioning an end to the symbolic order—like declaring the end of history or ideology—may well be a symptom of global capitalist logic, thoroughly charged with symbolism. If modernity equated state formation with national literature, postmodernity (like its postcolonial shadow) equates the postnational with postliterature, perhaps privileging the globalizing tendencies of those few states that are able to absorb, and even promote, epistemic crises from a position of stability rare in regions like Latin America. That difference may be one way to understand the lingering, and often untheo-rized, distinctions between First and Third World, different modernities caught up in categories such as globalization, postcoloniality, postmoder-nity, *maquiladora* states, and narcocapitalist states, among the many other formations that compete for financial, human, and symbolic capital.

CASE STUDY

An unsuspected illustration of postnational anxiety revealed itself with Har-old Bloom's (1994) call for a new "Western" literary canon, a global model in which English and the U.S. institutional apparatus of research universities are called to function as the only exchange currency capable of reconstitut-ing literary values.[18] Bloom speaks of preserving the Western canon from the onslaught of cultural studies, but beneath that heartfelt concern lies the deeper question of the links between literature and the nation-state at the end of the twentieth century. In this case it materializes not as critique but rather as nostalgia for the primacy of humanist aesthetics in English and in the United States, even for those who privilege experimental literature once viewed as inherently avant-garde and transgressive. For that reason, Bloom's famous call for a new canon suggests the need for further thinking into the role of literature and criticism during global reordering, all the more so for languages other than English and states with less stability than the United States.

Calls for a new literary order, a symptom worthy of study, therefore require many clarifications and distinctions. One major example is to the literature of Borges, for many a model of the postsymbolic imaginary. His short stories first sought to provoke the literary establishment of the first half of the twentieth century, a tradition all too willing to surrender individ-ual texts to the tedium of literary history. A few decades later, his oeuvre took on a new symbolic meaning as it turned into a point of reference for late-modern and even postmodern aesthetics. Then, ultimately, it has been asked to stand as symbol for a restoration of humanist literary values that aim beyond Western to perhaps global appreciation, as Bloom's inclusion of Borges in his new Western canon suggests. One can only surmise that Borges's universally recognized mastery resides precisely in having taken literature to an aesthetic plane able to probe its own making, and that such a state of immanence has shown itself eminently capable of renewing the metaphysical needs of Borges's readers at different points of history.[19]

It therefore seems pertinent to ask what kind of mapping evolves from an undifferentiated critique of modern metanarratives inspired by negative alterity, a construct shared by both postcolonial and postmodern modes of criticism.[20] Is this construct only a symptom of the disillusionment that overcame many Latin Americanist critics working in the United States after the demise of revolutionary projects in Latin America, or has it become a constitutive element of deconstructionist work as a whole? Might the changing relationship between nation, literature, and culture across the Americas profit from a more differential body of theory? As I understand them, these questions, which obviously have multiple answers, can only be addressed within a framework that is more comparative than the one currently prevailing in Latin American literary and cultural studies, on both sides of the continental divide. In order to illustrate this point and develop it a bit further, it might be useful to explore a different reading of testimonio, in this case one derived from a Latin American site of theoretical and literary production. I will therefore turn to the perspective offered by Nelly Richard (1994a), formulated within the context of the Chilean postdictatorship cultural scene.

Richard has argued that privileging testimonio as a model of postmodern discourse relegates Latin American texts to a use-value imposed by "metropolitan" (read, U.S.) centers of academic power. Her critique evokes a bit of the old center-periphery debate, but her primary concern resides elsewhere. She aims to unveil the hierarchy of values within postmodernism, particularly the pull of institutional frameworks whose influence cannot help but totalize knowledge production, even while claiming a commitment to decentering it. Richard's approach thus engages deconstruction within Chilean culture while questioning its use in the United States, suggesting that the latter's institutional power cannot help but overwhelm, even vitiate, that influential body of theory. Her elaboration of these premises were first articulated in *La estratificación de los márgenes* (1989), with subsequent elaboration and intensification in *La insubordinación de los signos* (1994b) and *Residuos y metáforas* (1998b). Together these books encompass feminism, literature, and the visual arts—a significant part of the Chilean postdictatorship national imaginary. Yet, Richard's mapping of testimonio as "metropolitan use-value" seems to overlook the earlier identification of Latin American postmodernism with the Boom novel, precisely the body of texts the postcolonial perspective aims to isolate for its critique. The Boom was, and in many respects continues to be, a much more influential and perhaps even more hegemonic paradigm; indeed, it could be argued that the subaltern proposal, at least in its initial stages, was a direct response to it.

By now, we have all grown accustomed to using Benedict Anderson's metaphor of imagined communities to explain nationalism in general, but I believe the latter can be further specified in terms of the relationship between intellectuals and their objects of study, a *patria chica* of sorts. In this sense, scholars in Latin America are not the only ones whose imagining of the region is influenced by their national communities: the "national" finds its way into the work of Latin Americanists in the United States as well. Diasporic Latin Americans naturally work the field from their own national frameworks, even when these are veiled in broader regional or even continental constructs. But it could be said that working in the United States, regardless of one's national origin, also leads to a predictable set of interests, such as the conception of the field as a community of discourses able to absorb difference through theoretical paradigms that dispense all too easily with layers of history and culture within national bearings, even while one calls for more localized specificity. That could be one way of recognizing the "national" inherent to an academic culture solely driven by exchange, the sort of postdialectic concept of value that Jean Baudrillard began theorizing in *For a Critique of the Political Economy of the Sign* (1981).

As Richard suggests, all contexts have their internal forms and needs, even if her own understanding of the United States as a metropolitan center precludes a greater awareness of the pulls that direct comparative Latin Americanism, a perspective that might lead away from such strictures. One obviously cannot deny that the cultural wars in the U.S. academy revolved, to a considerable degree, around Rigoberta Menchú's *testimonio*. In this sense, Latin American subalternity rehearsed its increasingly U.S. positionality. But it could additionally be said that the post-NAFTA indigenous rebellions in Latin America, beginning in 1994 with the uprising in Chiapas, are also pertinent to the symbolic order conjured by Menchú's text. In that sense, there is another side of the *testimonio* story that pertains to a postcolonial Latin America in the deepest sense, even if Richard's otherwise probing critique leaves it unmentioned.

By and large, Richard's work remains at arm's length from prominent postcolonial points of engagement such as indigenous texts or cultures and Latin American diasporas in the United States; yet it could be argued that her Chilean-based critique has broad implications for Latin American and perhaps even American studies. That relevance comes from what could be seen as an inherent contradiction: her deployment of metropolitan theory—deconstruction and negative alterity—within a distinctly Latin American perspective that breaks down the more facile "here versus there" attempts to map points of theoretical articulation. Her work aims to deconstruct the metaphors that sustained Chilean national culture from their discursive frames, be they military, economic, political, or, most important, academic, given the close relationship between disciplinary discourses and the pursuit of epistemic power.[21] Richard's argument gains force from its imaginative theorizing of the local and from the fact that Richard's discourse does not issue directly from academia, but rather from the cosmopolitan cluster of scholars, writers, and visual and performing artists to which she belongs. Their work suggests a different understanding of cultural studies than the one prevalent in the United States, something closer to cultural critique and lived experience through the arts, involving theory but remaining close to artistic forms, rather than reducing art to theory or submitting it to a cultural-studies domain indistinguishable from the logic of mass culture.

Richard's refusal to look back nostalgically at the Allende period, or any moment of Chile's national past, is another debatable but important aspect of her critique, even though she focuses on the Pinochet regime, and most particularly on its aftermath. This approach to national deconstruction specifically comes into play in her reading of El padre mío, by the Chilean novelist Diamela Eltit (1989). Richard reads this text as a counterexample to the model of subaltern testimonio inspired by Rigoberta Menchú's life story. Eltit's protagonist is a deranged, apparently incomprehensible homeless man, whose life story seems like it could inspire little but nausea and disgust. But his insanity somehow provides a very clear picture of national unraveling. His speech acts are filled with the names of historical periods and well-known public figures, but they are all mingled, precisely because his aphasia prevents him from placing them in their "proper" order, leading him to confuse the chronology of Allende and Pinochet. He cannot speak about any topic differentially, no matter how trivial the circumstance. The decomposition of Chilean history and grammar is thus acted out in the words of this loathsome paternal figure, a most disturbing and articulate critique, one that offers an understanding of subalternity bound not to specific subjects or demands for historical redress but to the realist pretenses of testimonio discourse itself.

The contrast with the traditional subaltern hero could not be clearer, but Eltit also seeks distinctions in terms of form. The customary testimonio preface, in which the role of the recorder, transcriber, and compiler of the other's story is revealed, gets a complicated, if not disturbing treatment in El padre mío. Eltit presents a disjunctive object-subject relationship between herself as editor and her informant, with whom she eventually loses contact. She claims not to understand him or even know how to find him. By clearly establishing her distance from her informer, Eltit provides a clear critique of anthropological "othering," so reliant on proximity and voicing over, as exhibited by Elizabeth Burgos in the production of Menchú's text. But Eltit's distance also suggests literary construction, including the possibility of a total work of fiction. Indeed, her introduction, a highly stylized theoretical piece prefacing El padre mío's "own discourse," tips its hand a bit when it explains that the only way to construe her protagonist's story as an image of contemporary Chile would be to see it as a negative, a technique first deployed by Julio Cortázar in his own literary testimonio, "Apocalypse at Solentiname."[22]

Of course, flirting with the possibility of total fiction may actually provide the ultimate deconstruction of testimonio's claim to realist representation, particularly if one understands testimonio (as Richard does) as a canonical expression of Latin America in the United States, which, as I have argued, may be subject to question. But restoring testimonio to literature also entails risks. In that case, Eltit's counter-testimonio, transgressive though it seems, could be easily read as a return to a symbolic form of estrangement well established in contemporary literary history by such Latin American Boom novelists as the Cuban Severo Sarduy, whose body of work explored the limits of linguistic saturation and national designification since the 1970s, most particularly in reference to authoritarian regimes. This Latin American context, however, does not factor in Richard's reading of Eltit, or in her strictly Chilean-based method of deconstruction.

Eltit's text may also pose an even more important question, one it may not have intended, or one that lies beyond the grasp of Richard's astute reading: how does the Latin American scholar juggle such contrastive readings of testimonio as the two developed in this essay, one anchored in the U.S. academy, the other in Chilean cultural praxis, yet both, in their own way, imbued by the theoretical archive of negative alterity? It would be hard to find more distinct readings of postmodernity, subalternity, and the possibilities of literature at this moment of uncertainty for Latin American nation-states. How does the Latin American scholar—here, there, everywhere—approach the implicit disconnection between these and other valuable projects? One might expect the market to provide direction on this matter, given the growing number of theoretical monographs, critical anthologies, and symposia on Latin Americanism during the past decade. But these differences have shown their capacity to coexist, if not flourish, without clear definition or acknowledgment of their inherent disparity. Instead of critical discernment, the reader discovers the imperative of continuous production and cultural *insiderism* at play in the academy.

It seems to me that Latin American literary and cultural studies would be well served if we conceived of comparative frameworks able to distinguish across the spectrum of postmodern, postcolonial, feminist, and other approaches, as well as the growing disconnect between the humanities and the social sciences. The question of difference seems paramount here. Latin American studies, particularly after the Cold War period that engendered area studies, requires a mapping of multiple contradictory textual and cultural practices difficult to encompass from national paradigms, or singular epochal constructs. That realization, however, may require new thinking about national contexts, not their outright dismissal. Postmodern and postcolonial mapping will only gain from a deeper understanding of the relationship between literatures and cultures, one that neither conflates the two nor dissolves their differences through theoretical immanence. Needless to say, such a problematic is unlikely to release scholars from the need to simultaneously study both I, *Rigoberta Menchú* and *El padre mío* in their contradictory richness.

NOTES

1   In the same venue Mary Louise Pratt and Amaryll Chanady in this volume recognize the relevance of literature as a field for symbolic representation of postcolonial sensibilities and of the importance of comparative innovative rereadings.
2   For a fuller discussion of this tendency within postcolonialism, see Hallward 2001, 45.
3   Huyssen (2002) makes a significant attempt to establish the dates of the first state of postmodernism and to distinguish it from the contemporary moment.
4   The extent of this phenomenon has become quite evident in England, where a new national emphasis has been placed on studying the future of English studies. See Showalter 2003.
5   Néstor García Canclini (2003) details how Spain has strategically positioned itself in the new cultural economy of globalization, while Latin American governments have failed to do so.
6   This figure comes from television-industry calculations, as reported in Navarro 2002.
7   See in particular two new anthologies that bring both elements together in challenging ways: Lao-Montes and Dávila 2001; and Poblete 2003.
8   The original debate on the postcolonial topic published in *Latin American Research Review* 28, no. 3 (1993) remains highly informative. See also my discussion of the problems and possibilities of postcolonial studies in de la Campa 1996.
9   This strand, roughly speaking, is outlined and summarized in Mignolo 2000d.

10 Alberto Moreiras's *The Exhaustion of Difference* (2001) provides a detailed illustration of this approach.

11 This approach corresponds to the work of John Beverley (1999) and Ileana Rodríguez (2001a), among others.

12 It seems pertinent to recall here Nietzsche's assertion that "every great philosophy is the personal confession of its author and a kind of involuntary and unconscious memoir" (1968, 203). For a fuller discussion of this topic, see Romano 2004.

13 The first full iteration of this approach came in Beverley and Zimmerman 1990. Needless to say, the scholarship on testimonio is both vast and varied. I am here placing a special focus on the ongoing evolution, since the early 1990s, of the subaltern perspective. This later evolved into a subaltern critique of the state, within which there are many different, at times even opposing, perspectives often conflated as one.

14 An important example in this context is Rabasa 1997.

15 A counterposition has been articulated by Roberto González Echevarría (1990b), who argues that testimonio amounts to a step backward in comparison to the boom as far as Latin American literary development is concerned. Indeed, he sees its return to a realist domain as closer to earlier literary moments, such as the *novela de la tierra* of the 1940s, thus finding testimonio potentially more naïve (221).

16 The dossier in *Nepantla: Views from South* 4, no. 2 (2003) dedicated to the work of Cornel West begins an important dialogue. The dossier includes a number of essays on the subject, among them de la Campa 2003b.

17 For a broader exploration of this problematic link, see de la Campa 2001.

18 A brief discussion of the issues and authors discussed in this section will appear in de la Campa forthcoming.

19 Alberto Moreiras (1994) offers an impassioned argument for the centrality of Borges and the value of postsymbolic theory.

20 Idelber Avelar (1999) argues for a new understanding of Latin American postmodernity largely imbued by negative alterity.

21 For a discussion of knowledge production and academic power in Chile, see Richard 1996.

22 This short story by Cortázar appeared in *Nicaragua, tan violentamente dulce* (1984). For a fuller discussion of the negative as literary medium, see chapter 2 of de la Campa 1999.

IN THE NEOCOLONY: DESTINY, DESTINATION, AND THE TRAFFIC IN MEANING

Mary Louise Pratt

"**M**e gustó su piel blanca" [I liked his white skin], said the young Colombian *guerrillera*, explaining why in April 1999 she had fled into the jungle with one of the captured soldiers she had been assigned to guard.[1] For five days she had guided her lover and his partner through the forest to an army post where she laid down her arms. Her betrayal was not without cause. She had not, she said, joined the guerrillas by solidarity; she had been sold by her mother to a guerrilla commander when she was ten years old. The story appeared in a Mexican newspaper with the headline "New Romeo and Juliet." The Shakespearean image was striking, mostly because the much more obvious parallel lay in Mexico's own mythology, in the story of La Malinche. Shakespeare, and his current Hollywood revival, however, trumped the hemispheric imaginary.

In the so-named postcolonial era, when the last European colonies have become independent and globalization is widely seen as having replaced Western imperialism, white skins continue to seduce, brown-skinned daughters continue to be sold, and imperial myths continue to generate meanings, desires, and actions. In what sense, then, do we live in a postcolonial era? Is "postcoloniality" a state which has been achieved, or one to which we aspire? In a statement like that, who is the "we"? Are some of "us" more postcolonial than others? Or does the term describe a planetary "state of the system," a *coyuntura* which is being lived out in myriad ways, in myriad subject positions and a vast array of geopolitical contexts?

Graciela Montaldo has said that in Latin America in general, postmodernism "serves primarily as a way of thinking about the scope of our modernity" (1977, 628). The analogous point might be made for the term *postcolonial*. Perhaps it is most useful as a way of thinking about the scope of one's coloniality. If so, the prefix *post* refers to the fact that the workings of colonialism and Euro-imperialism are now available for reflection in ways they were not before. But the *post* is also used to suggest the opposite: that colonialism and Euro-imperialism are behind us, no longer important determinants of the contemporary world. A similar ambiguity seems to me to characterize all the *post* categories as they proliferated in the 1990s. *Post-X* can be used to mean either X is available for reflection in ways it was not before, or X is no longer a vital historical dynamic and can now be studied as a thing of the past. The ambiguity was functional, one suspects, creating spaces of tolerance which could be cohabited by people of very different ideological orientations and historical visions. This essay takes the first position. The *post* prefix is used here to call forth not a subject paralyzed between nostalgia and cynicism in a Fukiyaman "end of history," but a subject newly capacitated to read the present in light of a broadened more discerning reading of the past. This subject is oriented not toward a future frozen in a post-progress eternity but toward a renewed anti-imperial, decolonizing practice. The decolonization of knowledge is, I believe, one of the most important intellectual challenges of our time.

The postcolonial project requires some decolonizing of its own. While it corrects what Edward Said calls the "massive avoidance" of imperialism in the study of European history (1993, xv), at the same time, as Ella Shohat, Anne McClintock, and others observe, the postcolonial optic continues to colonize to the degree that it identifies everything with respect to European-dominated power relations, as if coloniality were the only axis along which ex-colonial or colonial places could be known (Shohat 1993; McClintock 1994). The object of knowledge gets defined and easily monopolized by its relation to the dominant. Against the continuing Occidentalism of scholarship and theory, Fernando Coronil has called for the development of "nonimperial geo-historical categories" (1996, 51) by which I believe he means not necessarily categories where imperial dynamics are bracketed out, but categories which do not describe those dynamics from the point of view of the imperial metropoles and do not award them interpretive monopoly.

The postcolonial critic, as Gayatri Spivak underscores repeatedly in her *A Critique of Postcolonial Reason* (1999), faces the complex intellectual challenge of apprehending imperial dynamics in their continuing adjustments, transformations, and permutations. If one seeks simply to establish the continuity across time of a "colonial legacy" one will fail to explain the processes by which this "legacy" has been and continues to be ongoingly renewed and reintegrated into a changing world through continuing permutations of its signifying powers, administrative practices, and forms of violence. Today the terms *modernization* and *industrialization* define projects different from those they defined thirty years ago under national development and import-substitution policies, or eighty years ago before the First, Second, and Third Worlds had come into being. The imperial character of contemporary neoliberalism was obscured for a time by the language of free trade and open markets. When Spain in the 1990s began inviting Argentinians to repopulate its empty rural interior, the gesture was a mutation of Argentina's search in the nineteenth century for immigration that would sustain whiteness against darker others. When the collapse of Argentina's economy sent hundreds of thousands of Argentines "back" to Spain and Italy, the process had meaning precisely as a mutant reversal of colonial and neocolonial emigration patterns.

POSTCOLONIALITY AND THE AMERICAS

The postcolonial inquiry has been dominated by dialogues mainly among scholars from Britain and North America, India and parts of Africa and the Middle East—the former British and French empires. Most of the participants are now based in European and North American universities. The inquiry has thus engaged only a subset of those parties involved in the decolonization of history and knowledge, and often distinguishes itself from explicitly anticolonial and anti-imperial voices.[2] With respect to Latin America the postcolonial endeavor suffers from a number of distortions that are both unnecessary and overdetermined. Interventions from Latin America are the only way to correct these.

To begin with, postcolonial studies have been based overwhelmingly on the second wave of Euro-imperial expansion, especially the late-nineteenth-century interventions in Africa and Asia. The insistence on overlooking the first imperial wave in the Americas, from the fifteenth century to the eighteenth, seems almost obsessive, particularly because the second wave can obviously not be understood without the first. The failure of metropolitan scholars to learn Spanish or Portuguese is a factor, and it is also a symptom of the neocolonial dimensions of the postcolonial project.

Second, by focusing specifically on the colonial, postcolonial studies elide the intricately related phenomenon of neocolonialism, which is of course central to the historical experience of the Americas. Postcolonial criticism has shown a remarkable disinterest in the obvious convergences between the colonial process in Africa and Asia and the neocolonial process in Latin America. Despite volumes written on colonial discourses, the mapping of neocolonial discourses has yet to be proposed. Yet such a mapping would be of the greatest interest to the study of peripheral modernities.

Even more troubling perhaps is the systematic elision in postcolonial studies of the term *imperialism*. This category draws together colonialism, neocolonialism, and other forms of expansion and intervention that continue to shape the world today (such as the American-British occupation of Iraq, during which this essay was written). In metropolitan circles intellectuals who, like Said, insist on imperialism as the primary object of study and critique are quite rare. For Said, "The real potential of post-colonial liberation is the liberation of all mankind from imperialism" and "the reconceiving of human experience in non-imperialist terms" (1993, 274, 276).

The focus on a limited time frame and a limited range of cases at times leads postcolonial criticism to attribute a deceptive homogeneity to its object of study. The rare occasions when distinctions are drawn between types and forms of colonialism are important. One such distinction critical for the Americas is that between settler colonialism, which was deployed in the Americas, and administrative colonialism, deployed in Africa and India. Among the many differences between these two systems, one of the most important is the form decolonization takes in each case. As McClintock (1994) points out, in the case of settler colonialism, decolonization (independence) consists of a takeover of power by the Creole settler class from the external colonial authorities. In all other respects, social and economic relations do not decolonize, nor does the cultural relation with the metropolis. This was the case in both North and South America following independence processes between 1776 and 1820. In both instances the decolonization of the imagination, especially among the Creole ruling classes, was a long, slow process.

Hence the richly discussed coloniality of American modernities. Independence struggles, though conducted within ideologies of liberation, served to relegitimize and refunctionalize colonial hierarchies and the practices and institutions that sustained them. White supremacy and Christianity are conspicuous examples; the European linguistic and cultural referent is another. In Latin America independence consisted in this process of partial decolonization and inaugurated the era of European neocolonialism followed at the end of the century by U.S. imperialism. To the architects of independence in the Americas, it was not fully apparent that their efforts were producing a partial decolonization and a refunctionalizing of colonial social relations, nor has this perception become commonplace since. Alongside the brilliantly studied foundational fictions of the Americas, then, there are foundational silences that await our attention, silences without which nineteenth-century narratives of emancipation would not have been possible. This would seem to be one fruitful point of entry for postcolonial inquiry in the Americas.

I noted above the elision of the terms *neocolonialism* and *imperialism* in the postcolonial vocabulary. When the Americas are factored into the account, neocolonialism comes into view as one of the main strategies of nineteenth-century British and French imperialism. Spanish American independence was won only with the support of British and French troops, some of whom were hired mercenaries and others state-sponsored emissaries. From a north European point of view, "independence" and "decolonization" in Spanish America meant nothing more or less than access for French and British capital, commodities, and technology to Spanish American markets, raw materials, and financial collaborators. That is, the same process of breathlessly expanding productivity and capital accumulation that drove the colonialist scramble for Africa drove independence struggles and nonterritorial neocolonialism in the Americas.

Indeed the two intersected constantly. The twenty-three-volume *Description de l'Egypte* (Jomard 1809–28) that resulted from Napoleon's famed expedition of 1798 coincides exactly with the thirty-volume *Voyages aux Régions equinoxiales du Nouveau Continent* (1805–34) that resulted from Alexander von Humboldt and Aimé Bonpland's 1799–1804 expedition to South America. The co-incidence is not a coincidence. Humboldt's and Bonpland's original plan had been to travel to Egypt, and they were poised to leave Marseilles when they were turned back by Napoleon's invasion—the invasion that produced the *Description*. They made a right-hand turn and carried their torch to the Americas instead. The last decades of the nineteenth century are familiar as a colonizing moment when Europe's partition of African territory got under way. In the Americas it was a neocolonial moment. In the 1880s Peru's economy was turned over to Lloyd's Bank of London, who administered it for nearly a decade. This occurred as a result of a disastrous war which Chile and Peru fought over possession of the guano coast—Conrad's Costaguana —that is, over the neocolonial exchange of raw materials for cash and commodities. Peru lost the war and Chile won, but England won on both fronts —it got the guano *and* the Peruvian national treasury.

Though Conrad's *Nostromo* is often read in colonial studies through the discourses on African colonialism, the real link between *Heart of Darkness* and *Nostromo* is surely between British colonialism in Africa and British neocolonialism in Spanish America. The common denominator is modern imperialism and its motor, capitalist expansion. Introducing his masterful reading of *Nostromo* in *Culture and Imperialism*, Said finds Conrad prophetic when he said in 1902 that governing Spanish American republics is like plowing the sea (Said 1993, xvii), yet, as Said also observes, Conrad was quoting Simón Bolívar who had made the observation some eighty years before. Why, then, is Conrad the prophet? And why is Bolívar absent from the genealogy of postcolonial thought? Similarly Said's fascinating treatment of Fanon, James, Rodney, and Césaire vis-à-vis the Europe-Africa axis needs to be complemented by an analysis that links them to the prior history of colonialism, resistance, and independence in the Americas and to national liberation movements. The dynamics of independence–nation building–neocolonialism that shaped Spanish America in the nineteenth century were clear, if often depressing, antecedents for independence struggles of the 1950s and 1960s in Africa and Asia. The Americas were the crucible for neocolonial ideologies of progress, for experiments in nationalism, and for supranational anticolonial visions like Bolívar's dream of a united Gran Colombia. A cultural history of imperialism will require recovering these American genealogies.

The American postcolony, then, is a neocolony. It is internally self-administering and charged with developing and maintaining its own institutions. It occupies an economic circuit in which it is a producer/exporter of raw materials, and a consumer/importer of manufactured goods. It is prevented from industrializing and is continually operated on by the exported expertise of the metropole. It is expected to act as a political ally of its metropolitan partners. It develops and sustains two forms of cultural capital: the local/national and the metropolitan/universal. The relation between these is that of minor to major. The normative cultural referent is that of the metropole, which establishes the minor status of the local. This relation is sustained by the cultural and educational practices of the Creole elite, whom the metropole supplies with higher education for their young. Among that elite, the neocolony tends to produce split subjectivities: one's lived reality lacks significance; the "*real*" *real* is elsewhere, and it owns you much more than you own it. The neocolony is seen as the receiving end of a diffusion of polished knowledge and processed goods. In the next few pages I briefly examine a series of Latin American literary texts reading through this category of neocoloniality.[3] In these texts, I suggest, the writers are working with, working on, and working through the configuration of relationships that is the neocolony. This working through, a decolonizing operation, is a distinctive, energizing aspect of Latin American modernisms. The focus of these readings is on mobility and travel, specifically on how writers work with and on the patterns of movement that configure the neocolony.

ESTHETICS IN THE NEOCOLONY: DESTINATION AS DESTINY

In 1928 Horacio Quiroga, a high modernist if there ever was one, published his famous short-story collection *Los desterrados y otros textos*, set in Misiones, a remote area in the Argentine-Brazilian interior where Quiroga homesteaded for a number of years. The stories are populated by a motley set of eccentrics, mainly stranded Europeans who have washed up here at the margins of the margins, one by one over twenty or thirty years. There is the Frenchman Rivet, an industrial chemist who, after twenty years in Argentina and a successful industrial career, appears without explanation and eventually dies drinking lamp alcohol with his Argentine friend Juan Brown, who having come "un par de horas, asunto de ver las ruinas" [for a couple of hours to see the ruins] was still there fifteen years later (Quiroga 1990, 231).[4] There is a Flemish explosives expert named Van Houten and nicknamed "Lo-que-queda-de-Van Houten" [what's left of Van Houten] because he had lost "an eye, an ear and three fingers of his right hand" (ibid., 221) in accidents. There is the Swedish biologist Dr. Else, once a member of a team of European experts contracted by the Paraguayan government to organize hospitals, schools, and laboratories, who, fifteen years later, shows up inexplicably in Misiones wearing "bombachas de soldado paraguayo, zapatillas sin medias y una mugrienta boina blanca terciada sobre el ojo" [Paraguayan soldier's pants, shoes with no socks, and a filthy beret cocked over one eye] (ibid., 269). In an alcoholic delirium Else shoots his only daughter, thinking she is a rat. His excess is the result of his collaboration in a failed distilling experiment with the one-armed engineer Luisser, whose prize possession is two volumes of Diderot's Encyclopédie. Misiones is a parody of cosmopolitanism at the periphery, which is also the heart of the neocolonial order.

These are figures from the American neocolony, Europeans trapped at the terminus of empire's reach by an American world that has devoured their will. They bear in them the norms of metropolitan modernity, but cannot put them into operation here. Quiroga's narrator refers to them as *ex-hombres* (ex-men), a term that, along with their alcoholism and damaged bodies, points to the breakdown of the relations of travel, empire, masculinity, agency and citizenship, center and periphery that compose the modernizing neocolonial order. Defeating the teleology of modernity itself, the tropics extract from them "el pesado tributo que quema como en alcohol la actividad de tantos extranjeros, y el derrumbe no se detiene ya" [the heavy tribute which burns up as if in alcohol the activity of so many foreigners, in an unstoppable collapse] (ibid., 270). Travel is reduced to the pathetic challenge (fatal in the case of Van Houten and Rivet) of getting home drunk at night from the bar. The book does contain one epic journey, a heart-stopping day-and-night marathon through rain and floods by the local municipal clerk, who is determined to turn in his records on time. But this epic, too, turns into a parable of peripheral modernity. Triumphing over nature the bureaucratic hero is greeted with mockery for having taken the deadline seriously.

Quiroga's ex-hombres are among the travelers who will not write travel books, like Humboldt's partner Bonpland. It is not their relation to travel writing that I wish to consider here, however, but the narrator's. The narrator of Los desterrados is writing from the reception end of European travel and travel writing, from the position of the people and places traveled to.[5] I do not mean this in the trivial sense that the stories are told from South America and that many Europeans went there. I mean European travel and travel writing are part of the immediate context of the writing; they are among the determinants of the narrator's, and Quiroga's, subject positions. As the title Los desterrados suggests, Misiones is brought into being not as a location, but as a destination and as a place able to disrupt the circular paradigm of departure and return that produces travel literature. The narrator of Los desterrados depicts, from the reception end, a socioeconomic order constructed out of the impropriety and improvisation, the discontinuity and unaccountability, the imposed receptivity, that define the presence of these people in this place. It is a failed order. The native oranges are not sweet enough to produce liqueur that meets the standards of the city; no one survives to old age; there are no women.

In modern Latin American writing the position of destination and re-ceptor is a continuous point of reference for the negotiation of identity and the representation of self. It is less a position than a relation between the neocolony and the metropole: each is a destination for the other, but each receives the other's emissaries differently. Scholars are now familiar with the flood of northern European travelers and traveler-writers whose writings in the wake of independence textualized the neocolony. The let-tered elites of the new republics drew on their discourses to found ex-(and neo-)colonial national imaginaries. The status of destination was built in. A self-awareness as destination for the metropole has remained a constantly evolving dynamic in Latin American letters. Metropolitan discourses of oth-erness remain part of the raw material with which Latin American writers and artists negotiate, interact, and create. In *Los desterrados* Macondo, for example, is brought into being as a destination and a receptor. From the opening encounter with the mysterious block of ice brought by the gypsies, it is a place where history and time are marked by the uncontrollable, un-predictable arrivals of people, things, institutions, meanings from else-where. Indeed, Macondo can be read (and a very readerly construction it is) as the underside of the whole corpus of European travel writing about Amér-ica. In *A Small Place* (1988) Jamaica Kincaid constructs a decidedly unmagical account of her native Antigua from the point of view of the destination-receptor. Hers is a reverse-travel book about a place called on to produce itself for travelers in the framework of neocolonial relations and the tourist industry. More recently still, the main character of Ricardo Piglia's *La ciu-dad ausente* (1997) is introduced in the opening lines as a descendant of nineteenth-century English travelers who "abandoned their families and friends to tour regions where the industrial revolution had not yet arrived. Solitary and nearly invisible, they had invented modern journalism because they had left their personal histories behind" (9). The genealogy turns out to be a key image of the impossibility of belonging and the irrecoverability of history that are the novel's main themes. For the neocolonial lettered sub-ject, metropolitan travel writing and the identity of destination are condi-tions of existence and of writing.

Most serious students of Latin American literature have read Alejo Car-pentier's essay "De lo real maravilloso americano" (On the American mar-velous real). It is easy to forget that the essay is written as a travel account, a conscientiously dysfunctional one that marks the neocolonial difference

between the American traveler and his (gendering intended) European counterpart. Carpentier opens the essay describing his travels to China, a catalog
of wonders, which, he concludes, he did not understand.

> He visto muchas cosas profundamente interesantes. Pero no estoy seguro de
> haberlas entendido. Para entenderlas realmente . . . hubiese sido necesario cono-
> cer el idioma, tener nociones claras acerca de una de las culturas más antiguas del
> mundo.[6]

> [I saw many highly interesting things. But I am not sure I understood them. To
> really understand them . . . it would have been necessary to know the language, to
> have a clear ideas about one of the most ancient cultures in the world.] (1987, 67)

What he lacked in particular, he said, was book knowledge: "un entendi-
miento de los textos." He went to the Middle East, he continued, and felt
nothing more acutely than "la gran melancolía de quien quiso entender y
entendió a medias" [the great melancholy of one who wished to understand
and only half-understood]. Here again, lettered knowledge is the lack, "al-
gún antecedente literario, de la filosofía" [some antecedent from literature
or philosophy] (ibid., 68). For the traveler from the neocolony, unlike his
metropolitan counterpart, ignorance is apparently not sanctioned. When he
got to Russia, Carpentier went on, the universe became intelligible. He
found place names he had heard of, buildings whose images he had seen,
points of historical contact with the Americas. And in Prague, the stones
spoke to him, of Schiller, Kepler, Kafka.

In contrast with the metropolitan traveler, Carpentier records this familiar universe in *experiences of recognition*, but not in *acts of representation*. That is,
he does not attempt to create evocative word-pictures of what he sees; he
records his recognition of sights familiar from prior travels or from the
"antecedentes literarios." Though he possesses cultural capital, he does not
claim (or possess) the European's cultural authority to represent, nor perhaps the motivation to do so: who in the 1940s would read a travel book
about China by a Cuban? It is interesting to see this distinction arise in
Carpentier, because among Latin American modernists he is often criticized
for being *europeizante* (Europeanizing). He is, but in an undeniably American and, it would seem, neocolonial way. The absolute insistence on book
knowledge as an essential credential is something one does not find in
European travel texts, and it reflects the situation of the peripheral intellectual for whom reality and history have been lived as somewhere else. Behind
Carpentier's traveler one discerns the ex- and neocolonial autodidact whose
personal library is the basis for his claim to belonging in modernity.

The experience of travel as discovery begins for Carpentier on his return to Cuba where he discovers . . . Cuba. He gives us his famous line: "Vuelve el latinoamericano a lo suyo y empieza a entender muchas cosas" [The Latin American returns home and begins to understand many things] (1987, 72). After Carpentier's travels abroad, postcolonial América comes into view as a self-creation, rather than a reflection of Europe, and as a place sometimes ahead of rather than behind the metropole.

> Arrastra el latinoamericano una herencia e treinta siglos, pero . . . debe reconocerse ue su estilo se va afirmando a través de su historia, aunque a veces ese estilo puede engendrar verdaderos monstruos.

> [The Latin American drags behind him a legacy of thirty centuries, but . . . it must be recognized that his style is expressed in his own history, though at times it can engender monsters.] (ibid., 73)

With this act of recognition the beginnings of a decolonizing optic emerge, a neocolonial one fettered to the European antecedent. Describing a visit to the fort of King Henri Christophe in Haiti, and guided by the figure of Napoleon's Caribbean wife Pauline, Carpentier observes:

> "Vi la posibilidad de traer ciertas verdades europeas a las latitudes que son nuestras actuando a contrapelo de quienes, viajando contra la trayectoria del sol, quisieron llevar verdades nuestras adonde, hace todavía treinta años, no había capacidad de entendimiento ni de medida para leerlas en su justa dimensión."

> [I saw the possibility of bringing certain European truths to our latitudes, against the grain of those who, traveling against the sun, tried to take our truths where even thirty years ago there was no ability to understand them or to measure their just dimensions.] (ibid.)

The local begins to take shape as cultural capital. In a gesture problematic to contemporary readers, this new cultural authority culminates by affirming the authentic "marvelous real" of the Américas over the "agotante pretensión de suscitar" [exhausting attempt to revive] the marvelous by the European surrealists (ibid., 74). What makes América authentically marvelous, in Carpentier's formulation, is its unmodernized European component, the persistence in popular culture of medieval forms of the marvelous destroyed in Europe by the Weberian disenchantment of the world. Carpentier's readers are not wrong to be disturbed by this conclusion. Even at his decolonizing moment, Carpentier "belongs" to Europe. Indeed, more than once, he identifies with the conquistador. Disparaging Lautréamont's line about adolescents who find pleasure in raping the corpses of beautiful women, Carpentier remarks that "lo maravilloso sería violarlas vivas" [the marvelous would be in raping them alive] (ibid., 75). The colonial unconscious is never far away, coded in gender ideologies that cross the imperial divide.

Carpentier proposes a simultaneously decolonizing and neocolonial epistemological matrix in which the metropolitan makes the local knowable as it was not knowable before. *Vuelve el latinoamercano a lo suyo y empieza a entender muchas cosas.* In Carpentier's cosmos this does not mean that the Caribbean cultural world in which he lived was mysterious or opaque to him. It means something like the opposite: it had not been brought into existence for him as an object of knowledge, as something to be reflected on. It had to be discovered as such, through travel—on an itinerary that went not around but through the metropole, and back. Latin American literature is punctuated by such decolonizing manifestos of return, from *Cahier d'un retour au pays natal* to *Rayuela* to *Canto general* and Octavio Paz's "Vuelta" (Return), written on his return to Mexico in 1968 after the massacre at Tlatelolco.

Carpentier's gesture in "Sobre lo real maravilloso" is to claim the home space as a destination, and a destiny, of his own. Latin American modernists often perform the same gesture through internal travel. Internal national or regional travel writing is an important corpus in the archive of Latin American modernism, and an important instrument in creating one of the two kinds of cultural capital that the neocolony is required to develop and sustain. This may be one reason why, in sharp contrast with Europe, the category of the national has a central place in American (including North American) modernisms and avant-gardes, and they develop on rural as well as urban axes. In the 1930s and 1940s Gabriela Mistral wrote an extensive work called El poema de Chile (Poem of Chile), a work of travel made up of over three hundred compositions, in which the poetic "I" moves through the Chilean landscape in the company of an indigenous child. The work is vehemently rural. It, too, is staged as a return and rediscovery in which the poet returns to her homeland from elsewhere, as a ghost. Gender has everything to do with this ghostly status.[7]

In an extraordinary novel from the same period, *Yawar fiesta* (Blood feast) (1947), the Peruvian Jose María Arguedas explicitly substitutes the outside traveler with the local returnee. Set in the Andes and published within a few years of Mistral's text, the novel opens with an arrival scene on the one hand familiar to any reader of travel writing, and on the other hand unlike anything that reader has read before. For the arriving subjectivity is an Andean not a European or cosmopolitan one, and the world it renders (this is Arguedas's artistry) is decipherable to metropolitan subjectivity but arises from another cosmos in which place is mapped not by land formations, but by water. Here are the opening sentences:

> Entre alfalfares, chacras de trigo, de habas y debada, sobre una lomada desigual, está el pueblo.
>
> Desde el abra de Sillanayok' se ven tres ricahuelos que corren, acercándose poco a poco, a medida que van llegando a la quebrada del río grande. Los riachuelos bajan de las punas corriendo por un cauce brusco, pero se tiende después en una pampa desigual donde hay hasta una lagunita; termina la pampa y el cauce de los ríos se quiebra otra vez y el agua va saltando de catarata en catarata hasta llegar al fondo de la quebrada.
>
> El pueblo se ve grande, sobre el cerro siguiendo la lomada. (1980, 19)

The English translation fails to capture the oral and regional quality of the Spanish.

> Amid fields of alfalfa and patches of wheat, broad beans and barley, on a rugged hillside lies the town.
>
> From the Sillanayok' Pass one can see three streams that flow closer and closer together as they near the valley of the great river. The streams plunge down out of the punas through steep channels, but then spread out to cross a plain uneven enough to hold a small lake; the plain ends, the river's course is broken again, and the water goes tumbling down from one waterfall to another until it reaches the bottom of the valley.
>
> The town looks big as it follows the slope of the mountain.

Only after this Andean arrival has been performed is the voice of the outside traveler, *el viajero*, heard, designating the place with its disparaging travelee's name: *pueblo indio* (Indian town). "Pueblo indio," the narrator tells us, is what los viajeros say when they cross the pass and see the town, Puquio, below them. "Unos hablan con desprecio; tiritan de frío en la cumbre los costeños, y hablan '!Pueblo indio!'" (ibid., 20). But, the narrator replies, these travelers are from lowlands; they have never seen their own towns from a distant mountain pass; they do not know the highlander's "la alegría del corazón que conoce las distancias" [the joy of the heart that knows distances] (ibid., 22).

Through a series of transculturating gestures, narrative authority in the novel is given to *el latinoamericano que vuelve a lo suyo*, a local Andean "us" returning after an absence in the city or on the coast. The authorization of this subject is a launching pad for a bold writing experiment in which arriving metropolitan discourses are folded into a transculturated Andean cosmos. Such processes of fusion, the tremendous pressures under which they occur, the passions they unleash, and the toll they exact in blood, are the subject matter of the novel.

In the letters of the neocolony, decolonizing requires that one pass not around but through the subject-producing discourses of the metropole. The great experimentalist of Brazilian modernism, Mário de Andrade, was explicit about this necessity. One of his most important creations, the comic travel novel *Macunaíma* (1928) was conceived as a parody of Karl Martius's classic *Voyage to Brazil 1817–1820*.[8] One of his goals, said de Andrade in his preface, was to "desrespeitar lendariamente a geografia e a fauna geográfica" [legendarily disrespect geography and the geographic fauna], to "deregionalize as much as possible [his] creation, and at the same time achieve a literary conception of Brazil as a single entity, an ethnic, national and geographic concert" (1988, 356). While Carpentier's decolonizing strategy was recuperative, and Arguedas seemed to strive for fusion, Esther Gabara in a brilliant study traces de Andrade's creation, in both prose and experimental photography, of "a practice of representation and self-representation founded in 'error'" (Gabara 2001, 41). De Andrade's decolonizing practice is to create an authentically Brazilian inauthenticity out of misappropriated metropolitan discourses of travel, geography, ethnography. The key to a Brazilian modernist aesthetic, de Andrade said, was the "superimposition of images." Gabara shows that this superimposition of images is the key dynamic of de Andrade's nonfiction travel book, *O turista aprendiz* (The apprentice tourist) (1929), a parodic work of internal travel and cultural apprenticeship. In this book de Andrade describes himself simultaneously as seer and seen; he uses double-exposed photographic images that, as Gabara observes, superimpose portraiture (an art form of home and the Self) with landscape (an art form of "away" and elsewhere). In a photo titled "Ridiculous Pose in Teffe" de Andrade depicts himself holding "the cane and hat of the European naturalist, the banana of the Afro and indigenous Brazilian, and the fan of the *dona* of a plantation" (Gabara 2001, 18). He performs a refusal of both colonial and neocolonial national imaginaries. At the same time, Gabara argues, he "marks the colonial trauma as the only nationally shared event" (ibid., 19). "South American pain," he says, "an irreconcilably human, immense and sacred pain," is at the heart of the enterprise, written "on [his own] face like the roads, streets, plazas of a city" (quoted in ibid., 26). It's an astonishing image, invoking the positivist vision of civilization engraved onto the face of the empty landscape, and underscoring its human cost.

The same sacred pain, and the same strategy of superimposition compose some of the most powerful poems of Mistral, in whose work travel and mobility also articulate the crisis of longing and belonging and the dilemma of the cultural referent in the neocolony. "La extranjera" (The Foreigner), one of the poems that most appealed to Mistral's first English translator, the African American poet Langston Hughes, uses a verbal equivalent of de Andrade's superimposed images of home and away. The poem is staged as the utterance of an unnamed voice who is describing the poetic I as a foreigner, an *arrivée*. It begins: "Habla con dejo de sus mares bárbaros / Con no sé qué algas y no sé qué arenas" ("País de la ausencia," 1938, 103, lines 1–2) [She speaks with the lilt of her barbarous seas / with who know what algae and who knows what sands] (Hughes trans., 1957).[9] Like de Andrade's ridiculous pose, the poem is thus a self-portrait refracted through the voice of an alien other who, however, sees itself as a self, encoded in images of South American otherness, which to a degree are also the poet's own: "En huerto nuestro que nos hizo extraño / ha puesto cactus y zarpadas hierbas" (103, lines 5–6) [In our gardens which she made strange to us / she has planted cactus and rough grasses]. The neocolonial reduction to nature constitutes the shared code between these two self/others. The condition of *extranjera* is permanent; it cannot be rectified by assimilation; her destination is a destiny. In eighty years, she will die among us, the poem says, "en una noche en la que más padezca / con sólo su destino por almohada" (l. 16) [one night when she suffers most / with only her destiny for a pillow]. Between the foreign (to them) stranger and the foreign (to her) hosts, the shared cultural capital is that which marks her as strange and them as not. At the same time, the foreigner is able to intervene in this normative reality, planting cactus and making their gardens strange to them, displaying their otherness to themselves.[10]

Published in sequence with "La extranjera," the beautiful poem "País de la ausencia" (Land of Absence) performs a complementary maneuver. Instead of a double exposure, it presents a blank photographic plate, a carefully elaborated picture of nothing. In this poem the stranger describes the place of belonging she has been able to construct for herself. Its building blocks are nonentities: absences, denials, and losses. This land of mine, she says,

> no echa Granada
> no cría jazmín
> y no tiene cielos
> ni mares de añil   (103, lines 9–12)

it bears no pomegranate
nor grows jasmine
and has no skies
nor indigo seas

"Yo no lo buscaba / ni lo descubrí" (lines 23–24) [I did not search for it / nor did I discover it]. It is a home born not out of discovery, conquest or acquisition, but out of the experience of loss sustained in "years of wandering": "Perdí cordilleras en donde dormí / . . . perdí huertos de oro. . . . islas de caña y añil" (lines 39–44) [I lost ranges of mountains / . . . orchards of gold . . . islands of indigo and sugar cane]. The foundational myths of América are denied or erased, along with the images of nature that are the vocabulary of neocolonialism. Nothing is put in their place; a semantic vacuum is proposed as a form of plenitude. In this ingenious way the poem breaks out of the rhetoric of destination and destiny. The land of absence cannot be a destination one can go to; it is a place that comes into being as one leaves other places and stories behind.

"South American pain"—does de Andrade's phrase denote an existential condition of the lettered subject of neocolonial modernity? Perhaps it does, if the ex-colonial literature of return is read against the vast phenomenon of departure and nonreturn, against the fact that for so many twentieth-century writers from the decolonizing world, living out their lives in their countries of origin is an existential if not a political impossibility. Carpentier, Asturias, Mistral, and virtually all the women writers of her generation lived abroad nearly all their adult lives, as did Cortázar, García Márquez, Vargas Llosa, and so many others of a later generation. (De Andrade and Arguedas are exceptions; Quiroga and Arguedas were suicides.) For many, particularly the women, awayness became a permanent condition, a way of conquering freedom and agency, and of living out an impossibility of belonging. When Mistral wrote the *Poema de Chile*, she had not lived in Chile for decades and never would again. Though her dilemma is often described in existential terms, it is easily linked to the politics of the neocolony. The neocolonial contract, which restricts development of all kinds in the neocolony, makes growth and flourishing into a struggle against the grain. The richest creative challenges seem to lie in seeking to entangle or, as in de Andrade's double-exposed photographs, superimpose the local/national and the metropolitan/universal, refracting them through each other or forcing them into excruciating, inventive fusion. Perhaps these modernist writers were trying to do what postcolonial critic Vijay Bahl (1997) thinks is an impossible trick: "to define themselves in opposition to the constructs of otherness thrust upon them by imperialist forces without allowing themselves to be subsumed by those categories" (1997, 12). In the neocolony the creative challenge is to produce, between "opposition" and "subsumed," a "land of presence."

NOTES

1 "New Romeo and Juliet," *Público* (Guadalajara), 2 April 1999, 1.
2 For example, with the exception of Fanon, anticolonial writers such as Amilcar Cabral and Kwame Nkrumah are not in the field of reference for postcolonial work, nor is the extensive South and Southeast Asian critique of Western science elaborated in the 1980s, nor the extensive elaboration African philosophy in the 1990s, whose aim is to decolonize philosophical thought.
3 De la Campa, as well as Chanady, in this volume, also examine literary texts in connection with Latin American (post)coloniality.
4 Unless otherwise indicated, English translations here and throughout are mine.
5 At one time I proposed this position be analyzed as that of the "*travelee*," the person or place traveled to (Pratt 1992).
6 Much of the essay "De lo real maravilloso americano" was written in the late 1940s and reflects the creative process that produced Carpentier's first novel of the *real maravilloso, El reino de este mundo (The Kingdom of This World)* (1948). But his attempts to grasp Cuba's transculturated reality predates this, for even by 1948 Carpentier had already published *Écue-Yamba-O*, a text he subtitled as an "afro-Cuban novel," and had collected afro-Cuban poetry.
7 Mistral did not complete the *Poema de Chile* during her lifetime.
8 For a detailed study of this aspect of the novel, see Lúcia de Sá 2004.
9 One is not surprised that the first translator of these poems of nonbelonging was the African American poet Langston Hughes (Mistral 1957, 83), who said he translated only those poems that he felt he understood. On the other hand, the documentation shows that Mistral was awarded the Nobel Prize for literature for her poetry about motherhood, rather than for these themes of travel and estrangement.
10 This is the space that the writer and critic Silviano Santiago calls "o entre-lugar" [the in-between]. For him, this is a place of power and privilege for the peripheral intellectual, who has the ability to reveal the metropole as it cannot reveal itself.

PART SIX

POSTCOLONIAL ETHNICITIES

The contributors in this section explore some of the key concepts of postcolonial critical theory such as miscegenation, hybridity, and transculturation, in an attempt to emphasize the role that race has played in the formation and consolidation of national projects, and as a continuous challenge to Europeanized projects of (neo)liberal and globalized modernity. Opening this section, Mario Roberto Morales deconstructs the connections between postcolonial theories, Occidentalism, and the Latin American field, establishing the historical and cultural differences that set this region apart from other postcolonial areas. Morales emphasizes the importance of *mestizaje* in the construction of intercultural and interethnic subjectivities, contrasting Latin American particularism with "the universal nature of Modernity." His article offers a strong critique of multiculturalism, neoliberalism, identity politics, subalternism, and, in general, of the production and recycling of discourses that often characterize intellectual exchanges. Since "the processes of modernity cannot be seen as alien to Latin America, but rather as an essential part of its self-construction, its self-creation, its origins and development as a mestizo continent," Morales advocates for a reflection on the ways Latin America can *appropriate* modernity in a productive and original manner.

The final two essays offer case studies related to the formation of collective subjectivities and the definition of cultural and political agency in two different regions of Latin America: Central America and the Andes. These pieces focus on countries that are characterized by the active mobilization of indigenous populations and that are traversed by ethnic, economic, and cultural problems deeply rooted in Latin America's coloniality.

Rather than analyzing the validity of postcolonial theories for Latin America, Catherine Walsh explores "the construction of new loci of enunciation that depart from the knowledge, experience, and understanding of those who are living in and thinking from colonial and postcolonial legacies." Her work focuses on the ways in which Ecuadorian indigenous movements have been contributing, in the last decades, to a process of resignification and restructuring of colonial-based concepts such as democracy, governance, and state. Walsh examines some of the conditions surrounding the formation and transformation of Indian and mestizo subjectivities, as well as the political actions of some specific organizations such as the Confederation of Indigenous Nationalities of Ecuador (CONAIE), which has embarked on the project of constructing a plurinational state in this country.

Finally, Arturo Arias concentrates his study on the case of Guatemala, from an ethnic and cultural perspective. In particular, he analyzes the Maya movement in the context of the challenges posed by globalization and reflects on the need to redefine local agendas. According to Arias, two salient aspects have contributed to the insertion of the Maya movement in the global scene: the militant revolutionary history of this movement and "the instrumentalization of [Rigoberta] Menchú as an iconic symbol of pluralist subalternity within the United States." Arguing against other positions on this matter, Arias analyzes the conflictive interrelations between Mayas and Ladinos, as well as the spaces in which these ethnic groups find confluence through mestizaje, transculturation, cultural hybridity, and the like. Arias's critical piece elaborates on issues of ethnicity, identity politics, political representation, and multiculturalism, arguing in favor of overcoming traditional dualisms as well as cultural and political stereotypes.

PERIPHERAL MODERNITY AND DIFFERENTIAL *MESTIZAJE* IN LATIN AMERICA: OUTSIDE SUBALTERNIST POSTCOLONIALISM

Mario Roberto Morales

K nowledge produced in Latin America often differs from and collides with the knowledge produced *about* it in the North American academy. The difference has to do with the divergent needs of the place and the subject of the enunciations and, therefore, with the objectives and the effect they produce in the receptors and actors of the ideological and political outcomes of that knowledge production. The debate that this divergence originates about the methodological criteria utilized to think Latin America has its immediate history and locus in the United States. But the Latin American voices that interpellate (*for* and *from* Latin America) the centralist criteria that theorizes it as periphery (including those that are solidarian and self-deconstructive) have earned, by their own right, a place as valid interlocutors that have become impossible for the hegemonic academe to ignore (see Volek 2002).

This essay, therefore, places its enunciation in the

framework of the theoretical currents that provide for the analysis of Latin America in the North American academy, where concepts like postmodernism, postcolonialism, and subalternism are applied as part of other methodologies, such as those used in Latin American (area) studies and those that were adopted during the postmodern and poststructuralist waves, among which we can count the ones conforming the fields of cultural studies. All this has produced interesting hybridizations such as that which is represented by what can be called Latin American Subaltern Cultural studies, a space of knowledge of extremely mobile and undetermined object of study and episteme.

Consequently, it is within the framework of theoretical approaches represented by Orientalism and postcolonialist subalternism (i.e., Said, Guha) and by *Occidentalismo* and *Posoccidentalismo* (Fernández Retamar, Coronil, and others) that this essay proposes to deconstruct the extrapolation of the postcolonial and subalternist categories for the study of Latin America, establishing the historical and cultural axis that differentiates this geocultural area from the ones whose study produced the aforementioned categories. This axis is originated by the concrete historical facts that determined the formation and development of the intricate differential and differentiated *mestizajes* that constituted the colonial and postcolonial history of Latin America, and which produced a pluralistic mestizo subject who is located in all social classes and who is ethnoculturally differentiated by his or her respective mestizaje. This intercultural subject lives and creates cultural identities that he or she exercises *from* his or her articulated differences when he or she identifies him or herself in the act of identifying his or her counterparts as criollo(a), Mestizo(a), *Indio(a)*, *Mulato(a)*, or as any other possible identification yet unnamed. In addressing this problem, I discuss concepts such as occidentalismo and posoccidentalismo (in their relation with the construction of world modernity) in order to intertwine them with the notion of *differential and differentiated interethnic and intercultural mestizajes*, through which I seek to establish theoretically the cultural specificity of Latin America and, with it, the need to theorize it with notions that can go beyond the mimicry that the use of the postcolonial-subalternist apparatus implies, thus evading the multiculturalist and politically correct ideologies of some of its representatives, which more suitably serve the careerist interests of North American academia than the democratization of Latin America. In so doing, this mimicry aligns itself with the agenda of neoliberal globalization that subalternizes the "rest" from the center of the West, turning the former into groups of homogenized, segmented consumers (often with their enthusiastic approval).

With relative independence regarding the location of who theorizes, the theoretical production *in*, *from*, and *for* Latin America thus collides with the one *about* it. This essay pretends to situate itself in the vortex of this collision. And I seek to situate the locus of my enunciation in a space of cultural mobility that goes *from* Latin America toward the world.

FROM ORIENTALISM TO SUBALTERNIST POSTCOLONIALISM

The so-called Postcolonial Theory, understood as a deconstructive method applied to colonial discourses and the nationalist postures derived from the former, articulates itself greatly from the concept of "Orientalism" as proposed by Edward Said at the end of the 1970s. A Western discourse that *produced* the notion of the Orient in Western mentalities, Orientalism thus made it possible to control the perception of Oriental culture with the act of transmitting its meanings in terms of the Western cultural code (Said 1994a [1978]). Discourse, control, knowledge, and power: this is the space of the deconstructive research that Said proposes. The author poses the urgency not only of rewriting the history of the West in terms of colonialism but also, and most important, of the rewriting of the history of the Westerly constructed Orient from the perspective of its formerly colonized subjects. But more than this, Said is interested in showing the places where this ad hoc "translation" into Western interests is perpetrated, and he finds those places in the lettered environments of society, thus turning his method into a form of analysis of texts and discourses, all of which had a great impact on the literature departments of North American universities where, at the time, the Marxist, structuralist, psychoanalytic, feminist, and poststructuralist theoretical approaches were being debated. The reason for this impact lies in the fact that Said gave all of these approaches a sort of diverse unity when he applied a deconstructive methodology to colonial discourse, thereby critiquing the Western/modern ideology underlying all of the previous anticolonialist projects (including that of Fanon), offering with it a political agenda for the professors of humanistic disciplines that at the time were going through the crisis of the leftist paradigm.[1]

Subaltern studies, for their part, are derived from Said's contribution, especially the original subalternist version represented by Ranajit Guha's proposal, dating back to the beginning of the 1980s, to read and rewrite the British colonial history of India "in reverse." Guha thereby criticized the posture of the colonized intellectuals and politicians of that country, as well as their nationalist and anticolonialist discourses, considering them penetrated by Western/modern ideology and, therefore, as constitutive of a space of misrepresentation of the popular subject in the history of India (Guha and Spivak 1988).[2]

In its failure to go beyond the colonial imaginary, anticolonialist representation (which included that of Gandhi and Nehru) ought to be substituted by another one that should be not-lettered, oral, popular, and subaltern (a term that Guha, Partha Chatterjee, Dipesh Chakrabarty, and later on Gayatri Spivak and Homi Bhabha took from Antonio Gramsci, who had applied it to any subject situated in a position of disadvantage in relation to any form of power).

Subaltern studies are, then, a form of postcolonial critical analysis, but one that wishes to distance itself from the structural-dependency relationship that postcolonial theory has with its Eurocentric matrix, given the fact that its deconstructionism totally depends on its deconstructed object, Western thought, without which postcolonialism cannot exist because it poses it as the sine qua non condition of its otherness when it defines the latter as a "creation" of the former. The dichotomic binarism that generates this vision of a colonized otherness as necessarily derived from the colonizing centrality concretizes itself as a method only at the price of, once again, depending on the power of the knowledge, the culture, and the science of the colonizer.

Because of this, subaltern studies imposes on itself the quest for something solid and positive in the realm of the colonized subalternity. Something that, in proposing itself as alien to Western knowledge and culture, must be necessarily marginal, uncontaminated, positive, and that must constitute an absolute otherness—not something non-Western, a simple affirmative negation of the West, but an affirmation in itself. Such otherness could only exist as a "strategic" intellectual construct that materialized itself theoretically in the notion of a "subaltern subject," which was assigned absolute marginality and a status totally uncontaminated by Western lettered culture.

The constructionist character that Said gave to the Western version of otherness implied a method with which to deconstruct that Western construction, a method that subalternists established as the patrimony of their subaltern subject, which was oral and popular but also postcolonial, and which they binarily opposed to the colonizing subject. Even though this binarism implied the essentialization of the subaltern subject—a danger that was denounced by Spivak in "Can the Subaltern Speak?" (1985)—the resource of strategism came to the theoretical rescue of the situation. In posing the binary essentialization of the subaltern as part of the anticolonial struggle, essentialism was justified as a mere temporal device with concrete political objectives, a characteristic that (in theory) would be surpassed when the emancipatory effort assumed the Marxist task that Fanon had already assigned to it, and on which Paulo Freire had insisted so much in his "liberating education" (*educación liberadora*): to free not only the oppressed from his chains, but also the oppressor from his power, so as to not just limit ourselves to flipping the coin of authoritarianism and thus lose the emancipatory nature of the struggle.

Some college professors in the United States, though, did not see this in entirely the same way. They were seduced by the deconstructionist insistence of Guha (which came from Foucault via Said) on the fact that humanistic disciplines traditionally played a subalternizing role toward colonized peoples through the local lettered classes that reproduced the values of liberalism and modernity to the detriment of subaltern voices. This notion unleashed innumerable critical works about the criollo and Mestizo writers of Latin America, who were lynched under the authority of those who judged them as "white," "modern," "Western," "machos," and "racist."[3] All this was perpetrated in the name of an essentialized subaltern subject that found its incarnation in Rigoberta Menchú, thus turning literary criticism into a witch-hunt and something of a tribunal to judge, from First World campuses, facts that were often entirely extraliterary.[4]

What had been a political act of national democratic transformation in the view of Third World intellectuals (that is, critical theory in the case of postcolonialism and subalternism applied to the Middle East and India) was, when appropriated by North American professors, made into a careerist dilemma regarding how to deal with the budgetary cuts that neoliberalism was perpetrating against the humanities. The result was a series of hybrid disciplines that, without having an official name, can be regarded in their totality as postcolonial subaltern Latin American studies. All of this led (in the case of excesses such as those of Beverley and Yúdice concerning testimonio theory) to the well-known cultural campus wars, among which the already prolonged, politically correct lynching of David Stoll for his well-known but almost unread book about the crucial inaccuracies that Rigoberta Menchú incurred in her testimonio is notorious. Stoll's work is field and archive research that, without proposing to do so, demolished the theorizations about Latin American subalternity and the voices of its "otherness" that were being constructed by the American academic (campus) Left.[5]

Between 1982 (when the first volume of *Subaltern Studies*, edited by Guha, appeared) and 1988 (the year of *Selected Subaltern Studies*, edited by Guha and Spivak with a foreword by Said), there was not much subalternist activity in the United States. But after the publication of this last volume, the transpolation of the Indian subalternism to an essentialized Latin American subaltern subject was exacerbated along with the academic leftist positioning of its representatives, especially some members of the Latin American Subaltern Studies Group, founded in 1993 (see Latin American Subaltern Studies Group 1994).

From then on, self-referentiality often became the axis of academic production and of the discussions on Latin Americanism, area studies and the uncertain future of the humanities (see Castro-Gómez 1998, 177–87). The need to subvert Western epistemological principles *within* the Western academic environment was justified for the original postcolonialist-subalternists by the argument that the very locus of reproduction of those principles was the best place from which to question and oppose them. What they did not anticipate was that the forms by which the North American educational system appropriated that questioning were to respond to what Jameson theorized as "the cultural logic of Late Capitalism," a logic that, in evading the perspective of the socioeconomic totality (Capital and the Market), evades the explanation of the material determinations of the different academic knowledges, including those of dissent and rebelliousness (Frank and Weiland 1997). It is in this direction that the criticism of postcolonial theory, realized by postcolonialists such as Aijaz Ahmad and Arif Dirlik (Mongia 1997, 276–94), has developed, and it is the aforementioned void that originates the uses that legions of university professors and graduate students make of that theory in the United States, essentializing and idealizing the notions of subalternity, otherness, and the people, among others.[6]

No doubt, the original sin of subaltern studies is the same as that of postcolonial theory: having originated and grown in the metropolitan academe and within the realm of the multiculturalism of the 1980s, which constituted the establishment's response to the civil rights movement of the 1960s and 1970s. This phenomenon originated the so-called new social movements, different from the "old ones" in that the latter wished to replace the capitalist system and the new ones sought only to be integrated into the space of the advantages of plain citizenship and the hegemony of national rights. Multiculturalism and its device for struggle, identity politics, functioned as domestic resources of integration without emancipatory possibilities. They lacked a utopian perspective because their activity was reduced to the struggle for the vindication of the cultural differences of minorities. They sought recognition of their legitimacy by the hegemonic subject, culture, identity, and state, all of which, in being thus interpellated, affirmed their hegemony, domination, and "superiority," thereby reinforcing their capacity to rule over the minorities that remained divided and isolated in their differential cultural compartments thanks to the politically correct and graciously given recognition and respect for their cultural difference. This difference became homogenized by the lifestyle that the minorities had struggled to integrate into, and it resolved itself in the disciplined consumerism, practiced by urban communities in the United States since the 1960s, of all sorts of "hip" and "cool" products (Thomas Frank 1997).

It is within this political and cultural framework that the academic efforts to found a "pure" marginality and otherness are developed in opposition to a powerful system that usually absorbs dissent and rebelliousness through consumerist offers that fit the affective and ideological needs of intellectualized and progressive groups (Frank and Weiland 1997). Ad hoc theoretical trends are thus created through the production and promotion of books and the marketing of university positions, specialized congresses, and "on edge" university gatherings.

In this sense, it is of primordial importance to understand the meaning of the critique of multiculturalism that Slavoj Žižek renders when he warns of the danger of remaining in a sort of celebrationism of differences and respect and consideration toward otherness from an alleged yet empty cultural universality that allows the person who celebrates, respects, and considers the "others" to decide that they are respectable, that they are eligible to be respected and, of course, studied. That is why, says Žižek, "multiculturalism is a form of denied, inverted, self-referential racism . . . that empties its position of all positive content (the multiculturalist is not directly racist, does not oppose to the Other the particular values of his own culture), but all the same he maintains this position as a privileged empty point of universality from which one can adequately appreciate (and also despise) the other particular cultures" (quoted in Castro-Gómez, Guardiola-Rivera, and Millán de Benevides 1999, 13; my translation).

To this denied racism inherent in the cultural logic of late capitalism (Castro-Gómez, Guardiola-Rivera, and Millán de Benevides 1999, 13), a denied and inverted classism is added. And it is applicable to the solidarism with the civil rights movement of the 1960s in the United States, that is (I add), the ideological matrix of the college professors who have appropriated postcolonialist subalternism as a political and ideological agenda that justifies their academic solidarism toward what they perceive as the Latin American postcolonial subalternity, which they also see incarnated in the figure of Rigoberta Menchú. This analysis can also be applied to all the Latin American new social movements whose existence depends, almost without exception, on funding through the international cooperation of the globalizing countries, thus making evident their dependency on the cultural logic that self-deceptively they try to contradict (Morales 2001, 2002).

The postcolonial subalternist binary oppositionalism, being a strictly First World academic device, reinforces the dominant cultural logic by contradicting its object of study in binary terms, thus posing it as totally and perennially determinant, and by commodifying its dissent and rebelliousness within the narrow confines of the campus. In the case of India and the Middle East, strategic binarism may have been the only way possible in which to move forward, given the recent and nonmestizo character of their colonization. But this is certainly not the case of Latin America, as I hope to demonstrate.

Consequent with what has been said, the discussion about the study of Latin America in the United States—which extends from area studies to a wide array of postmodern options combining cultural studies with innumerable appropriations of postcolonial subalternism—has transformed itself into a self-referential discussion about the positionality of the academic subject (North American, European, or Latin American). The principles of the postcolonial subalternist theoretical corpus (heir of the discourse-centered analysis of poststructuralism and postmodernism) and above all the nature of academic space (subject to the dominant cultural logic) oblige the enunciator to practice a strict self-referentiality as a constant, politically correct condition (often expiatory) of intellectual honesty. A typical dilemma of metropolitan intellectuals, this concern ends up distancing itself from the problems of its object of study.[7] These problems, on the other hand, constitute a different concern for Latin American intellectuals who are not immersed in the aforementioned dilemma, and whose theorizations collide with those of their First World colleagues. It is this dynamic that leads to questions such as that which has gathered us here: is it or is it not pertinent to apply the concept of postcoloniality to the historical, economic, social, political, and cultural problematics of Latin America? If it is, then we have to explain the reasons why we are postcolonial. And if it is not, we have to explain what it is that we are. The answer seems to revolve once again around the old problem of cultural identity, so many times (re)visited by Latin American intellectuals as a way of solving what they regard as their own particular and collective labyrinth.

THE UNIVERSAL NATURE OF MODERNITY AND THE EMERGENCE OF A PLURAL AND DIFFERENTIALLY MESTIZO CULTURE AND SUBJECT IN LATIN AMERICA

The key to answering the question just posed must be looked for in the process called modernity. For it is due to modernity that Latin America constitutes itself as a diverse, heterogeneous, and differentially mestizo cultural unity, and it is also due to this process that Latin America claims an ad hoc theoretical instrument to be thought not only in the epistemological terms of the modernity of which it forms a part but also in the terms that emerge from the marginalization that that modernity exerts toward it, terms which are the basis on which modernity bases its centrality, thus contributing to the production of the cultural specificity of its Latin American "otherness." Furthermore, the construction of Latin America responds not only to the interests and criteria of modern centrality but also to the self-perceptive notions resulting from the creative appropriations that Latin Americans have made of the science and the culture of modernity, "translating" them to their own cultural needs.

As we know, modernity has ceased to be thought of as a unidirectional process originating in Europe during the Renaissance and exerting a unilateral cultural influx on the European colonies of the New World (Habermas). It is now regarded as a world process resulting from the European expansionist needs and from the concomitant colonial order that Europe imposed on the regions it had "discovered," thus articulating a "universal" economic system whose balance depended basically on the exploitation of those colonies as a means of building the foundations of the industrial development of the regions that had constituted themselves as "central" in relation to the colonized "periphery" (Dussel, Wallerstein, and others). The colonies ultimately became markets for the central industrial products and also subjects of loans that were impossible to pay and which were supposedly going to finance an illusory development that was to be similar to that of the central countries. This process gave birth to the so-called sui generis modernity of Latin America, characterized by its chaotic hybridity.

This organic and holistic approach to modernity also functions as a basis for thinking the bipolar notions of center-periphery, Europe-America, hegemonic subject–subaltern subject, universal culture–national cultures, and so on, as ideological constructs resulting from the specular identitarian dynamics of the central power. This dynamic originates from the image that the dominant power constructs of itself when reflected in the mirror of "the other," to whom it conveniently assigns a lesser existential and cultural condition, with the approval, of course, of the others, an approval that emerges from the functional articulation of power that—as we all know— needs the contribution of those who endure it in order to be exercised efficiently. Those who suffer the exercise of power (the subaltern) relate to that power in multiple ways, negotiating their position in relation to it and affirming it as such. These forms of relation-negotiation can be of frontal and of oblique (or indirect) opposition, and also of submissive acceptance or passive resistance, among others.

The articulation and functioning of colonial power is, like modernity, organic and "universal." Modernity and the colonial order constitute an organic world-system-of-power in which the dominated or colonized or subaltern play an active role in maintaining the established order, thus giving origin to a colonial culture whose nature is diverse, plural, and differential, and also to colonial subjects who—in the case of Latin America— develop specific cultural emphases and identities characterized by a differential mestizaje which is not uniform nor unique and that obviously is not the same in Spaniards, Creoles (criollos), Indians, Mestizos, blacks, mulattoes, or any of the other ethnosocial and ethnocultural groups that are typical of the Latin American colonial era.

This organic approach to modernity assigns an active role to those who suffer its colonizing power, and therefore the study of the social, political, and cultural subject of the Latin American colonial period must be characterized with the specific terms by which colonization took place in Latin America; all this in turn points to the need to analyze the mestizo nature of Spain and Portugal in the fifteenth century in relation to the European countries that colonized Africa, the Middle East, and Asia, because the emergence of a diverse (in terms of power) colonial subject in the colonies varies from one reality to another. If in Africa and the Middle East a subaltern colonial subject that can be binarily opposed to the colonizer emerges, this is due to the fact that, in the colonizing adventure of the countries of the North of Europe, biological mestizaje was the exception and not the rule, whereas in the case of Spain and Portugal, it was the rule and not the exception. This was due above all to the well-known fact that these two countries were conformed by one of the most intense processes of mestizaje that Europe had experienced. This fact explains why a colonial subject who is neither unique nor uniform but rather plural and differentiated (in class and ethnicity) emerges in Latin America. This complicates the colonial landscape and forces us to think the colonial, postcolonial, and neocolonial realities of Latin America with notions that should go beyond the binary dichotomies, bipolar essentialisms (strategic or fundamentalist, it doesn't matter), and oppositional contradictions between hegemony and subalternity, elitist domination and popular resistance, hegemonic and counterhegemonic practices, and so on that animate all postcolonial and subalternist methodologies.

On the contrary, this complex reality demands that the analysis be located at the vortex of the articulation of the ethno- and sociocultural differences that make the conflictive intercultural dynamics of these subjects possible, and not in the extremes of those differences (as if they were not articulated and in intense mestizaje). The analysis of this reality requires that the point of view be fixed in the spaces where the intercultural and differentiated mestizajes occur and also in the infinite forms of identitarian negotiation that in frontal or oblique ways take place between the different mestizo subalternities and also the mestizo dominant powers. That is why I have proposed (2002) to study our intercultural realities by theorizing our plural and differentiated mestizaje, and not by mechanically applying multiculturalist criteria that artificially separate the groups through the magnification of their differences, thereby evading the fact that those differences are the product of mestizaje and that they have resulted from diverse articulations occasioned along the time and space first of colonial history and later of republican capitalist and "modern" historical development. The plural and differentiated colonial subject includes (from the bottom up) Indians, blacks, mulattoes, Mestizos, criollos, and Spaniards, all of whom differentiate themselves through the diverse nature of their mestizajes, that is, through the different forms by which the prevailing cultural differences are articulated in their cultural specificity and conditioned by their race, gender, and class.

According to this order of ideas, the question arises: what is the difference between "Latin American culture" and the culture of other formerly colonized countries in Africa, the Middle East, and Asia, if we take into consideration that the former is the result of an intense and conflictive process of biological and cultural mestizaje which does not erase the differences between the groups that form part of it, and that the latter denotes a category of mestizaje that is indeed exceptional and within which racial and cultural separateness was the rule of the colonizing processes? It would be false to respond that Latin America has a happy, harmonic, unified mestizo culture (even in its well-publicized heterogeneity). The problem here lies in characterizing the ethnocultural reality of Latin America in its intercultural dynamics, in order to extract from that characterization the adequate notions for its theorization, thus avoiding the application of concepts that emerged from the analysis of other realities that (even though colonized) are not identical to those of Latin America. Such is the case of concepts such as postcoloniality and postcolonialism.

How, then, can we define "Latin American culture" in light of the differential mestizaje that characterized all its colonial subjects, and given the fact that these subjects were not homogenous but, on the contrary, remained differentiated in matters of class and ethnicity, even though problematically articulated in their differentiation? Let us begin by characterizing those colonial subjects and the basic features of their differentiated mestizaje.

MESTIZO SPANIARDS, MESTIZO CRIOLLOS, AND MESTIZO INDIANS

The Spaniards who came to America were the result of a brutal mestizaje that included Celtics, Iberians, Visigoths, Carthaginians, Romans, Jews, and Arabs, among others. Therefore, mestizaje was nothing strange to them. Besides, the Spain of the Reconquista (their Spain) hosted the conflictive relationship between Christians, Muslims, and Jews. Of course, Christianity was the politically triumphant religion, and salvation through conversion became the ideological justification of political dominance, a fact that was decisive in the formation of the ethnoreligious identities of Spain, such as the Ladino ethno-identity, a term that emerged from the deformation of the word *Latino* (Latin) and that referred to Jews who had converted to the religion of the Latin world (Roman Catholicism) and who already spoke a language of Latin origin.[8]

It is interesting to note that in America, for instance in the Captaincy General of the Kingdom of Guatemala, converted Indios were called Indios Ladinos, thus originating a new ethnic identity that, in the end, became culturally hegemonic in that country during its republican era, because the name ceased to be applied just to acculturated Indios and was extended, from the seventeenth century on, to all those who decided not to self-identify as Indio, even if in fact they were physically and/or culturally Indian, and including the small mulatto and black population (Batres Jáuregui 1892).

But in addition to the capability of the Spanish power to boost the creation of new identities in relation to its European, Christian and mestizo identity, there were also forms of American cultural mestizaje experienced by the Spaniards, such as the one that we can deduce from the adventure of Álvar Núñez Cabeza de Vaca, narrated in his shocking book *Naufragios*. Even though Núñez returns to his civilization and culture after having assimilated himself (out of need) to the everyday life of several indigenous communities, it seems apparent that a number of Spaniards decided to mingle with the indigenous cultures for a variety of reasons. These processes need to be documented, but it is interesting to read a fictional version of this probable fact by the Guatemalan writer and winner of the Nobel Prize for literature Miguel Angel Asturias, in his novel *Maladrón*.

What is at stake in analyzing this problematic is the possibility of theorizing a cultural mestizaje that flows from the bottom up, which is what Recinos (2002, 28, 79, 80, and 353) calls a process of Americanization or Indianization of the European subject and culture, a mestizaje that flows from the subaltern toward the dominant groups, be it forced or voluntary in the individual who is subjected to the mestizaje, an individual who experiences a transculturation and produces an (other) subject who is culturally differentiated and who has a negotiated mestizo identity, modified in relation to his or her original identity.[9] If this was possible among colonial Spaniards who, furthermore, were discriminated against in Spain and in America because of their cultural mestizaje and their *Indiano* identity features, the same can be said of their descendants, the criollos or Indianos or American-born sons and grandsons of Spaniards.

It is a well-known fact that, from the end of the sixteenth century on, the criollos created what according to the criteria of the modern Eurocentric episteme is known as "Latin American culture," in reference to colonial and republican literature and arts. It was also the criollos who implemented the processes that led to independence from Spain and the popularization of liberal ideas and Enlightenment ideals in the educational systems, all the while enforcing fierce military dictatorships and semifeudal economic and social regimes. Ever since the contact of Latin America with the capitalist world market by way of the exportation of single products, the criollos delegate the exercise of political power in the hands of their mestizo military caudillos. And with the institutionalization of lay, mandatory, and free education, Latin American culture (literary and artistic) also became an exercise of lettered mestizo individuals. However, the Eurocentric and modern criollo cultural criteria became the cultural heritage of the mestizos who, in an illusory appropriation, also embraced the criollo ideals of "purity of blood" and, by way of a binary contradiction, made the Indians the counterpart of their "white" anxieties in the very same way in which the criollos use mestizos and Indians alike as a reference to validate their supremacist differentiation, characterizing them as inferior. This is the dynamic of ethnocultural differentiation and racist hierarchy that has animated our conflictive intercultural life since colonial times.

What is much less known is the fact that the criollos also experienced intense processes of cultural mestizaje from the bottom up. That is, they assimilated innumerable identitarian and cultural features from the Indians and from the Ladino Indians, all of which seems apparent in many of the forms of expression, as well as the rhythmic, phonetic, and semantic variations of the Spanish language that they speak throughout Latin America. Their mestizaje is also visible in customs, worldviews, mentalities, superstitions, diets, manners, religious notions, and the like. This leads us to think that the dominant culture, created by the criollos on the basis of the destruction of pre-Colombian cultures and the marginalization of their colonial residues, constitutes a differential mestizo culture, which means that it differentiates itself not only from Spanish culture but also from the autochthonous cultures, to the extent that the criollo mestizo subject emerges as an exceptional anomaly in relation to other colonizing experiences such as the British colonization of India and Arabia or the French colonization of Algiers, for example, neither of which gave birth to a colonial subject even remotely similar to the Latin American criollo. It is in this sense that the mestizo subject called criollo proposes itself as a basic key to establish, in History, the specificity of the hegemonic Latin American culture not only in relation to the culture of the metropolis but also in relation to the cultures of the other colonized regions with which it shares the condition of being part of the world project of modernity, and also in relation to the local subalternized cultures with which it establishes a mestizo interculturality within the context of a political and economic structure inherited from the colonial order.

Is it, then, pertinent, when studying the cultural differentiation of Latin America, to oppose the Indian culture as a binary otherness in relation to the criollo culture, if we know that historically they are permeated by one another? The question leads us to theorize the mestizaje of the Indians (which is much more documented that that of the criollos) and also to take into account that the study of the colonial institutions of domination has been carried out with binary assumptions that differentiate Spaniards from Indians and criollos from Indians, emphasizing the cultural imposition of the first over the second and thus ignoring the transcultural processes that take place inversely and are primordial to the study of the plural and differential colonial mestizaje as the axis of our identitarian interculturality (Recinos 2002, 28, 35). In this order of ideas, it is interesting to observe the colonial sequence of the biological mestizaje produced by the intense sexual relations between Spaniard-criollo males and Indian women, and afterward between Mestizo males and Spanish women, all of which originated large mestizo communities quite undifferentiated but with Eurocentric criollo mentalities. This is what Christopher Lutz indicates when he documents that, in the sixteenth-century Kingdom of Guatemala, the Mestizo girls and the legitimate male children were taken into the custody of their Spanish fathers.[10] This is a fact that, among others, makes the Latin American case different from those in which racial segregation was dominant and mestizaje was strictly prohibited.[11] On the contrary, the intensity of our biological mestizaje made physical differentiation difficult and even impossible, thus reinforcing ethnocultural differentiation.[12] This, in turn, ended the Indian character of the barrios of the city of Santiago de Guatemala by the eighteenth century, an epoch of clear criollo hegemony.[13]

The indigenous culture of Guatemala nowadays is thus the result of colonial mestizaje. What we would have to add to this statement is that the diversity of that mestizo result has consolidated itself throughout the centuries of colonial and republican experience as an ethnocultural differentiality. This is due precisely to the Eurocentric discrimination that the Indian mestizos have had to endure from the criollo and Ladino mestizos, and it is also due to the internalization of the dominant discriminating criteria by the dominated, subaltern, and discriminated subjects. All of this determines the wide variety of their responses to the social and moral reality of marginality and discrimination. These facts lead us to think our interculturality as interdiscriminatory, given the structure of colonial and republican power, and given the "modern" economic structure dominated by criollo elites, to which we must add, in descending order, indigenous bourgeois minorities and mestizo and indigenous middle classes whose prosperity is based on the work of the landless indigenous groups and of the poor that emigrate to the United States. It is worth noting in this context the existence—in the Guatemalan region of "Oriente," inhabited by a white and European-like population—of significant groups of poor Ladinos and even criollos that regularly have to endure famines that do not occur among the poorest Indian communities.

The Latin American colonial subject is, then, not a single but a plural subject. It is a differentiated subject because it is not culturally homogenous and because the nature of its heterogeneity varies in every specific group. It divides itself, in general terms, into mestizo criollos (Recinos 2002, 20), mestizo Indians, mestizo Ladinos (in the case of Guatemala), and Mestizos, according to the self-identification adopted by concrete subjects in a given situation. The theoretical challenge that this dynamic poses is that of thinking this multiple and differentiated mestizaje in its interactions, because those interactions originate the specific interculturality that animates our societies, where the articulation of differences and not their binary differentiation is the cultural rule. It is at this point that the question about the pertinence of the application of concepts such as postcoloniality and postcolonialism to the study of our intercultural dynamics must be posed, a question that is very much related to the one regarding the same pertinence in relation to notions coming from multiculturalism, identity politics, and subalternism. Does a reality of conflictive mestizo cultural articulation admit binary notions of analysis, bipolar oppositions, and "readings in reverse" à la Said, Guha, Spivak, and their North American would-be peers?

DIFFERENTIAL MESTIZAJE AND THE CRIOLLOS

The world-system that modernity has been since its beginnings determined that the knowledge it founded—Eurocentric, lettered, and white—to think itself and its counterparts (the othernesses that affirmed it as central) would be diffused in its colonies, thereby originating the innumerable ways in which (to use an expression proper to Latin American thought from Rodó to Fernández Retamar) the Prospero-Caliban dialectic (or syndrome) operates. In other words, the central knowledge—positive and affirmative—is exported to the colonies and incorporated into the dominated forms of knowledge, thus determining the way in which the colonized subalternity begins to think itself. However, this master-slave dialectic, in which the master gives name to the slave (as in the case of Robinson Crusoe and Friday), is different in the cases of colonization with no mestizaje and in those in which mestizaje constitutes the norm. That is, the Prospero-Caliban dialectic or syndrome functions differently in both historical experiences, basically because, in the case of mestizo colonization, intense biological mixing determines the emergence of several ethnocultural variants that push the individual subject closer to Prospero or to Caliban (it depends). The two extremes are blurred in favor of the enlarged gray area of the mestizajes, in which the innumerable variants, emphases, and possibilities of combination make the specific individual impossible to be named with any specificity, and only prone to being characterized as multiple and differentiated by the most general of features. In the case of the colonial experience with exceptional mestizaje or with no mestizaje at all, the culture of Prospero always constitutes a foreign imposition that never mingles in a radically transforming way with the dominated cultures.

These variations in transculturation, determined by the character and intensity of the mestizaje involved, originate diverse colonial subjects and, in the end, diverse nations and nationalities resulting from independentist and anticolonialist struggles, also diverse in and of themselves. In the case of Latin America, I think—along with Recinos—that the key to this difference resides in the mestizo criollo colonial subject and in its assumed role as founder of the nations, the nationalities, the identities, and the national cultures of the continent, with all the exclusions, injustices, and cruelties that this undeniable historical fact has implied.[14]

In effect, the criollos were the holders and multipliers of the ideologies, mentalities, and modern scientific knowledges that were exported to the colonies, and with these in hand they founded a notion of Latin and Spanish American cultural specificity, originality, and identity, in spite of the fact that these very names came from abroad (after all, modernity is a world cultural system). So, the criollo Latin Americanism—which can be traced through colonial literature from the moment it creates notions of fatherland (*patria*) and patriotic mentalities, as in the case of the Guatemalan criollo chronicler Francisco Antonio de Fuentes y Guzmán and the poet Rafael Landívar, through the national literatures in which literary tradition creates notions of Nation and nationalistic mentalities, as in the case of the criollo novel and essay of the nineteenth century—was an enlightened device that the criollos used to establish themselves as different from the Spaniards, although not so different as to be confused with the Indians and the Mestizos. This identitarian schizophrenia of the criollos, seen as a form of cultural mestizaje, constitutes the axes of the well-known Latin American Eurocentric ("white") patriotism, and also of its literature, painting, sculpture, and historiography, in which the material marginalization and the simultaneous (and simulated) ideological inclusion and instrumentalization of the subaltern sectors of society, situated at the margins of citizenship, are constant and generalized.

The question arises: does this ethnocultural marginalization and exclusion have a Eurocentric and racist character identical to the one operating between British colonizers and Indian (from India) subalternity, where a subject even remotely similar to the criollo never emerged? In other words, is it pertinent to oppose, in a binary way, an essentialized European and colonizing culture to another one, local and colonized, in identical terms in both cases or, on the contrary, is it necessary to introduce certain notions of relativity into the Latin American contradiction, taking into account that the hegemonic subject that creates and founds the Latin American nations is a culturally and ideologically mestizo, differentiated, and ambivalent subject, especially when it comes to its self-perception, which at the same time values and despises the Indian culture that has permeated him and her in his or her conduct, habits, and worldview?

The criollo is neither a colonizer nor a colonized, but at times he is both and tries to behave more as a colonizer than as a colonized. His mobile positionality determines a schizoid identitarian conduct that, when he is situated in the public sphere, makes him legitimize at all cost his European-ness vis-à-vis the majoritarian Indianness, while in the private sphere he exercises his mestizaje without restrictions (Recinos 2002). The differential mestizaje that is articulated mainly from the bottom up constitutes the axis of the identitarian criollo conflict, and from it originates his furious Euro-centism and the negation of his autochthonous component. These two fea-tures will be inherited by the Ladinos, who will assume them as an illusory "whiteness" of their own, and also by the Indians, who will assume them both by rejection and by mimicry. In any case, none of the cultural emphases in which the plural and differentiated mestizo colonial subject is diversified can exist without its counterparts. That is why the isolation of his differences and their elevation to binary oppositions constitute not only a theoretical inadequacy but also a falsification of reality and a historical distortion with serious political and ideological consequences worthy of being debated.

In responding to the previous questions, we have to take into account that the ambivalence in the self-perception of cultural identity is applicable to all colonial subjects, and not only to the criollos, according to the specificity of each and every one of them. Precisely because mestizaje was and is the rule and not the exception of our interculturality, Eurocentric modern values permeated the consciousness of all colonial groups and subjects, making identitarian dislocation a common feature. The Indians internalized criollo and Mestizo ideals as desirable because they perceived that those values somehow dignified their condition as colonial serfs, and at the same time they hated them for being unreachable, due to the discriminated cultural specificity of Indians. The hatred of the colonial Indians toward the Ladino Indians and that of the Indians of today toward the Ladinos constitute a clear example of the schizoid conflict underlying our differentiated intercultural and plural mestizajes, because it is a hatred, first toward those who negate their own communitarian culture (during colonial times), and afterward toward those who reject the ethnocultural Indian or indigenous specificity as well as its current identitarian constructionisms, as is the case of the "Maya" movement (Morales 2002, chap. 3). The basis of this hatred—which finds its active counterpart in the illusorily white Ladinos—resides in the colonial dialectic of desire-rejection toward the Eurocentric values that simultaneously offer themselves up as desirable (because they are hegemonic and powerful) and as repugnant (because they are hostile).

Given this mestizo, differential, conflictive, and schizoid axis that articulates the Latin American culture in all its diversity and heterogeneity, it is not pertinent to theoretically consider in the same way the problem of the British historiography of India and the criollo historiography of Latin America. The mestizo cultural component of the criollos complicates the problem and turns binarism (strategic or not) into a device that ends up being insufficient to explain the intercultural, interethnic, and interidentitarian Latin American dynamics. These demand that different categories be thought and, above all, democratized, given the fact that the colonial heritage continues to be the main obstacle to surmounting the purist mentalities of all the groups that originated from the colonial experience and who, precisely because of that experience, are still incapable of thinking and valuing their own (particular) mestizaje and of assuming it as the axis of their intercultural relationships with their counterparts who are also mestizo.

In this line of thought, is it pertinent to think of a Latin American postcoloniality and of a postcolonialist subalternist Latin Americanism?

PERTINENCE AND NONPERTINENCE OF SOME CONCEPTS

The Spaniards first, and then (most important) the criollos, but also some Mestizos and Indians, have created a theory about Latin America that, originating in the modern/European epistemologies, is developed *from/within* Latin American sociohistorical dynamics. We can say that this has been taking place since the letters of Columbus and the Spanish, Indian, and criollo chronicles, especially if we consider the fact that the subject that lets itself be portrayed in these narratives determines, with its mere presence and acts, a European content and a vision of what—through an appropriative action—we can call (even today) a mestizo "we." The latter has passed through contradictions such as those represented by the liberal-conservative, Americanist-Europeanist binarisms (as in Sarmiento-Martí, for instance), and also through explanatory efforts such as the refined modernist one of Rodó, up through the attempts at inclusive classist synthesis by Mestizos like Mariátegui and Ortíz, and the cultural synthesis of Fernández Retamar and Paz, among others.

Of course, the "we" that emerges from the European vision and that is developed thanks to the Eurocentric Americanist vision of the criollos is a homogenizing "we" that excludes and discriminates against the cultural differences and emphases that make up the Spanish and criollo mestizajes themselves. But the core of this discussion resides in the fact that the differential and articulated mestizaje that animates the Latin American inter-discrimination makes it impossible to introduce an oppositional binarism into the analysis of this problematic, and it forces us to theorize it in its complex dialectic. This view differentiates our analysis from the one developed by the nationalist and anticolonialist intelligentsia of India, which serves the Indian (from India) subalternists as the version about which they propose the "writing in reverse" of the history of their country. A similar matter animates Said's proposal regarding the Western construction of the Orient. And even though the construction of Latin America is a Western one, it is Western in a way that enables it to legitimize itself as original through the action of the differential, plural, intercultural, discriminating, and marginalizing mestizaje that was founded by the Spaniards, perfected by the criollos, and made functional by Indians, Mestizos, blacks, and mulattoes through the special articulation of power that has constituted us and that we are obliged to analyze with concepts and categories that emanate from the exact nature of that reality. The mechanical extrapolation of concepts originated from other realities and other cognitive needs not only do not work in our case, but they can turn out to be a set of neocolonizing devices, especially if—as in the case of postcolonialism and subalternism—they are strictly academic devices, originated in the campus and for the campus, but with influence in North American foreign policy, and also responsive to the dynamics of the First World academic and intellectual market, which has a decisive influence on our weak Latin American academic environment.

The criollos, then, are the founders and developers of what is known as "Latin American culture." They are also responsible for the interdiscriminatory criteria that rule our conflictive interculturality (the dialectics of criollo-Ladino, Indio-Ladino). Throughout our history there have been pro-colonial and anticolonial, conservative and liberal, dictatorial and democratic criollos. Thus ours is a historical problem related to the national integration of our mestizo differentiality and not to the rescue of some lost cultural originality; it is related to the democratization of the historical version of ourselves and not to the binary opposition of two versions of that history, which is the problem that, with all due pertinence, the intellectuals of the recently decolonized countries have to face.

Maybe, in terms of a temporal sequence, we could talk about a criollo-American colonial moment extending from the sixteenth century to the eighteenth, characterized by the processes of transculturation through which the criollos impose Western culture even as they are permeated by diverse forms of cultural mestizaje and as they adopt an ambivalent code that legitimizes them as Europeans and positions them as Americans. We could speak of an anticolonial moment that goes from the eighteenth century to the nineteenth, characterized by the independence struggles and the enlightened ideals adopted by the independentist forefathers, and also of a postcolonial moment that goes from the second third of the nineteenth century and that reaches its peak with the liberal revolutions and the republican linkage with the capitalist world market. And finally we could talk about a national moment that occupies the whole of the twentieth century, a moment in which Latin America seeks to modernize itself through a series of revolutions that begins with the Mexican Revolution (1910–20), continues with the Guatemalan Revolution (1944–54), the Cuban Revolution (1959), the Chilean Revolution (1970), the Sandinista Revolution (1979), and culminates with the electoral defeat of the Sandinistas, coinciding with the collapse of the socialist bloc in the second half of 1989. In all these revolutionary experiences the middle classes, composed of criollos and Mestizos, were the hegemonic protagonists over the popular Indian and peasant leaders. It so happened in Mexico with Carranza, Obregón, and Calles; in Guatemala with Arévalo and Arbenz; in Cuba with Fidel and Raúl Castro; in Chile with Allende; and in Nicaragua with the Ortega brothers.

Our postcoloniality has to do, then, with the intranational struggles that, inspired in the epistemological principles of modernity, the criollos and Mestizos led at the end of the eighteenth century. With the emergence of the criollo-liberal hegemony, the Mestizo and Indian groups also articulated their voices and actions around the modern episteme, although in its popular emancipative dimension, represented basically by the Indian rebellions during colonial and independentist times (vaguely inspired in enlightened ideas, as is the case of the revolt led by Atanasio Tzul and Lucas Aguilar in Guatemala), by authoritarian populism (Perón and his peers), and by Marxism in all its variants, among which we have to include the theology of liberation.

The myths of modernity also inspired the avant-gardist representations of what we have perceived as "ours" (Asturias, Carpentier, Mário de Andrade), all of which implied an attempt at widening the margins of the nation and of the criteria for the inclusion of Indians, Mestizos, blacks, and mulattoes as subjects of citizenship rights.[15] What is considered "ours" was constructed with European elements. Asturias, for example, constructs his "Mayan" reality-effect through surrealist "translations" of the imagery displayed in pre-Columbian texts.

Americanism, as synonymous with Latin Americanism, was, in consequence, a device of the lettered criollo (or white) minority that, involuntarily subjected to its own kind of mestizaje, founded a version of itself with which the subaltern groups conflictively identified, adding at the same time surviving elements of their destroyed cultures and others that emerged from the processes of transculturation. As we have seen, the complexity of this process, which originates multiple differentiated mestizajes, does not admit binary oppositions between cultures. Its mestizo dynamics demand that a different set of ideas be analyzed. So, in responding directly (once again) to the question that has gathered us in this theoretical space, the mechanical application of transplanted concepts and methods such as those pertaining to subalternist postcolonialism is not pertinent for the case of Latin America.

As we have said, our problem is not so much the search for and rescue of a cultural authenticity alternative to that of an oppositional colonizing subject who has written our history, which, for that very reason, ought to be rewritten "in reverse" as a condition for achieving the hegemony of that cultural authenticity. Our struggle has been and continues to be that of developing the capability of thinking ourselves, including in that reflection all the components and cultural emphases that constitute us, and above all characterizing our intercultural, interethnic, inter-identitarian dynamics in their relationality. As partial attempts at theorizing ourselves we can list proposals such as that of the Landivarian fatherland and the democratic nation of the independentist forefathers (Recinos 2002); that of the cruel miscegenation of Sarmiento; Martí's "Our América"; Mariátegui's refunctionalization of the pre-Columbian roots; Vasconcelos's "Cosmic Race"; Che Guevara's "New Man"; and others, such as Gutierrez's "Theology of Liberation" and Freire's "Pedagogy of the Oppressed."

In this sense, part of our challenge is, yes, to rewrite our history, but in a code that is intercultural, interclassist, interethnic (not binary, oppositional, or differentialist). The dominant Latin American subject is still located in the criollo elite. The culturally hegemonic subject is located within the Mestizo groups. And the subalternized subject dwells in the spaces of the communitarian indigenous peoples (especially in countries like Mexico, Guatemala, Ecuador, Bolivia, Peru, and Brazil). Our history should be rewritten in an intercultural way and not "in reverse" or inspired in the discourse of a constructed subaltern otherness, as in the case of the enshrinement of Rigoberta Menchú by North American university professors through a moralist solidarism toward all intolerant, ethnocentric essentialisms and through a violent censorship of the theoretical approaches and political proposals emerging from the criteria of transculturation and mestizaje.[16]

CODA

That we have been "Westernized"? Yes, although not in the same way as "Orientals" have been "Orientalized." The processes of modernity cannot be seen as alien to Latin America, but rather as an essential part of its self-construction, its self-creation, its origins and development as a mestizo continent. Our problem is not, therefore, the invention of an anti-Occidentalism, nor is it to critique Occidentalism as a negation of an essentialized alterity that would constitute "what we *really are*" (see Castro-Gómez in this volume). Our problem consists in defining our modernity and what we want it to be from now on, which implies explaining our intercultural dynamic and, with it, the character of our differential and plural mestizajes and our differences in constant and conflictive articulation, demanding the democratization of their practice. In fulfilling this task there is no space for notions such as those of postcoloniality, postcolonialism, or subalternism as they are used in North American academia to refer to a homogenized subaltern subject, manipulating the contributions of Said, Guha, and others, claiming it to be "universal" (sometimes by Eurocentric negation), and idealizing it (through the puritanical and behaviorist values that lie at the basis of the politically correct "leftist" morality of the campuses).

Our dilemma has an intra– and trans–Latin American character because, in spite of ourselves, we have been modern since the sixteenth century, when the mestizaje that constitutes us, creates us, constructs us, and imagines us began, to our advantage and disadvantage. The postcolonial dilemma of the Middle East, Asia, and Africa is not ours. The emergence and development of our colonial subject—plural, mestizo (criollo, Ladino, Indian) and differential (ethnicity, culture, gender)—marks our difference in relation to the rest of the colonized and subalternized world. Therefore, Latin American cultural criticism should be more interested in studying the interactions that exist between Capital (the Market) and the innumerable ways in which Latin Americans construct their cultures, their identities, their mirrors, and their originalities, than in celebrating, in an empty, cathartic self-gratifying, pater(mater)nalistic way, the magnified and idealized differences that, in the end, the dominant cultural logic either converts into tourist attractions and spectacles for the consumption of travelers addicted to "othernesses" and "cultural differences" (Morales 2002, chap. 4) or homogenizes in the sea of consumerism à la United Colors of Benneton. One way of exercising this criticism is by showing how the different knowledges of the dominant (Western) cultural logic that reproduces itself on North American campuses is articulated with the objects of study and "othernesses" that they manipulate in order to serve their epistemological principles and their charitable morality of respect toward the difference that they graciously dignify from the heights of their politically correct, behaviorist, and puritanical domination. These lines have sought to do just that.

NOTES

This chapter benefited from the editing of Juliet Lynd.

1 For a historical account of the original developments of postcolonial theory and postcolonialism, see Williams and Chrisman 1994. For a recent account of those developments, see Mongia 1997.

2 The Subaltern Studies series edited by Guha began in 1982 with the publication of the first volume by the Oxford University Press in Delhi, and it continued with the second volume in 1983, the third in 1984, the fourth in 1984, the fifth in 1987 and the sixth in 1989. A selection of essays from the six volumes was published in the United States in 1988 under the title *Selected Subaltern Studies*, coordinated by Guha and Spivak and with a foreword by Said. This was the volume that unleashed the wave of campus solidarity toward subalternism according to the ideological coordinates of North American academia at the moment: postcolonialism, multiculturalism, affirmative action, identity politics, political correctness, and cultural studies, all of which had inherited the principles of French structuralism applied to literary criticism (Roland Barthes) and those of Marxist literary criticism (Raymond Williams, Richard Hoggart). Afterward, the theoretical contributions of poststructuralist theoreticians such as Lacan, Foucault, and Derrida would be incorporated, along with those of feminist theory, psychoanalysis, and Marxism, all intermingled with postcolonial theory, subalternism, and Latin American (area) studies.

3 I will use the word *Mestizo* (with a capital M) to refer to a specific colonial ethnocultural subject, and the word *mestizo* (with a lowercase m) to refer to a general ethnocultural condition characterized by the mixture of cultural features in persons, symbolic objects, ideologies, mentalities, and environments.

4 Some excesses in this respect are notorious, such as those of the theory of *testimonio* proposed by John Beverley (1991), which limits this genre to the narrative of an eye-witness account that must be illiterate, oral, and belonging to a cultural otherness opposed in binary terms to the hegemonic culture. This prerequisite allegedly assures that the version given by this subject about his or her culture and experience is more adequate, in terms of the subaltern subject of representation, than the one given by "white" lettered intellectuals. Says Beverley: "There is a crucial difference in power terms between having someone like Rigoberta Menchú tell the story of her people (and win a Nobel Prize herself) and having it told, however well, by someone like the Nobel Prize–winning Guatemalan novelist Miguel Angel Asturias" (1993, 76). After David Stoll's findings, it is now known that what Beverley calls Menchú's "story of her people" is a narrative mediated by the "white," Marxist, Eurocentric left wing to

which Menchú belonged, and that Menchu's discourse is characterized by a cultural mestizaje influenced by the theology of liberation and the *indigenista* theories of the time, and not some oral, nonlettered, illiterate cultural otherness —a discourse that, in this way, excessively resembles that of Asturias, a fact proving quite inconvenient to the essentialist binarism that resulted from the North American appropriation of the original postcolonialism and subalternism. The contrast between the unlimited enthusiasm that Beverley used to feel for literature a few years before (Beverley and Zimmerman 1990) and this antiliterary posture is surprising. The following affirmations, whose authorship he shares with Marc Zimmerman, are a good example of this: "We argue that literature has been in Central America not only a means of politics but also a model for it. . . . While our thesis is that this poetry [revolutionary poetry] has been a materially decisive force in the Central American Revolutions, it is also important to stress that it is by no means their only significant or important ideological practice. There is, for example, the very rich heritage of Central American indigenous and mestizo oral culture" (ibid., 1990, xiii). Any Central American leftist militant and/or writer knows that, in itself, literary practice was never "materially decisive" in the revolutionary processes and that the writers who were killed owe their deaths to the fact they were militants and not to their writing. Writing could not be relevant, much less subversive, in an environment with more that 60 percent illiteracy. No doubt the paternalistic enthusiasm for an idealized "pueblo" can lead to the distortion of "the popular."

In the following statements made by George Yúdice we find another notorious example of these excesses: "The 'popular' was either essentialized in petit bourgeois recreations of peasant and indigenous speech and culture (e.g., Salarrué in El Salvador, Asturias in Guatemala), or pawned off as mass culture (Fuentes, Puig, Sarduy). . . . Like the Christian Base Communities, which are grassroots movements in which popular (i.e., exploited) sectors reread the gospels as the 'good news' of the coming of the Kingdom of God here on earth, the testimonial emphasizes a rereading of culture as lived history and a profession of faith in the struggles of the oppressed" (in Beverley 1993, 111). In the name of "the testimonial," this enthusiasm disqualifies the "petit-bourgeois essentialization" that the "White" writers perpetrate with "the popular." This logic would have led, in the end, to the negation of literature and culture as the elitist exercise that it has always been, in the name of "the people" and its interests. Something very similar happened during China's Cultural Revolution.

5   For an account of repressive academic actions that, from positions of power, several university professors perpetrated against Stoll and against those they considered as his "defenders," and for a definition of the terms of the pertinent debate that derives from Stoll's findings, see Morales 2001.

6   For an excellent archaeology of subalternist postcolonialism and its North American appropriations, see Castro-Gómez and Mendieta 1998; Castro-Gómez, Guardiola-Rivera, and Millán de Benavides 1999.

7   "One is sometimes inclined to believe that, in fact, postcolonialism as currently practiced has a great deal more to do with the reception of French 'theory' in

places like the United States, Britain, Canada and Australia than it does with the realities of cultural decolonization or the international division of labor" (Larsen 2002, 204–5).

8   Ladino is the name of a people and of a language spoken by Jewish communities that were expelled from Spain after the Reconquista. For an interesting study on the subject, see Isaac Jerusalmi, "El ladino, lengua del judaísmo y habla diaria" (in Alcalá 1995, 301–18).

9   "Es muy valiosa la observación que Roberto Fernández Retamar hace al indicar que el término occidentalizar abre una perspectiva diferente para analizar el proceso colonialista en América, y Walter Mignolo ha aportado también más luces al respecto. Sin embargo, a pesar de su valor, el concepto adolece de la consideración del proceso inverso, es decir, lo que constituye buena parte de nuestro trabajo, ni más ni menos que lo que nosotros llamamos la 'indianización' o la 'americanización' del imaginario occidental europeo. Lo que puede resumirse en que si el proceso de occidentalización de las Indias fue el impulso y esfuerzo primero de la conquista espiritual y cultural, a éste siguió el de 'americanización' o 'indianización' de la cultura de occidente. No olvidemos que la transculturación no es nunca un proceso en una sola dirección" (Recinos 2002, 79–80).

10   "Official views of mestizaje in the 1520s were exclusively defined by large numbers of unions between conquering Spaniards, overwhelmingly male and in the prime of their life, and Indian women. The resulting mestizo population, though numerous and unprovided for by the framers of the two republics, was largely accommodated by both the *república de los españoles* (republic of Spaniards) and the *república de los indios* (Indian republic). *Mestizas*, and legitimate children of both sexes, were generally absorbed by the Spanish sector; the illegitimate (especially boys), who represented the vast majority of early mestizo children, tended to assume the lowly status of their mothers; the rest, an insignificant minority, found doors to both republics closed" (Lutz 1994, 45).

11   "Santiago's post-1600 *cabildo* officials were largely indifferent to the rapid pace of mestizaje. Manifesting none of the racial hatred that prompted their counterparts in Manila . . . segregation had been implemented in Santiago de Guatemala and throughout Spanish America, not so much out of fear and hatred for any one group, but to protect Indians from the alleged harmful effects of contact with *castas*, blacks, and Spaniards. Once the racial purity of the all-Indian communities had been compromised, local Spanish officials lacked any reason, let alone the burning ones that for centuries motivated Spanish colonists in the Philippines to prosecute the Chinese, to continue a failed social policy on the Indians' behalf" (Lutz 1994, 47).

12   "Yet the inflow of Spaniards and ladinos (*castas* who, by 1700, after nearly two centuries of mestizaje, had become the dominant phenotype in Santiago de Guatemala; racially indistinguishable from each other, all could lay claim to some Spanish heritage, if only cultural) into the [Indian] barrios continued at such a rate that officials there were forced in 1682 to petition the Audiencia once again. . . . [L]*adino* came to describe all the *castas*. Precise racial categorization, at

best a speculative art in Spanish America, was made useless by widespread mestizaje among the *castas*. . . . Biological mestizaje was less direct yet more pervasive than its cultural counterpart. Whereas most acts of cultural mestizaje were voluntary, the thousands born into *castas* status . . . were the beneficiaries of circumstances beyond their control. Formal unions with free *castas* and Spaniards generally exemplified the offspring of Indian women from tributary status but provided no such benefits for the women themselves, who retained the status of their birth" (Lutz 1994, 50, 59, 61–62).

13 "The impact of mestizaje in both its forms so changed Santiago de Guatemala's peripheral communities that 'Indian barrio' fast became a contradiction in terms. When the Dominican friars sought permission in 1664 to build a new convent in Santa Cruz, a neighborhood then under their care, the barrio's population consisted of Indians, *mestizos* and mulattoes. A hundred years later, in the 1760s, Santa Cruz had practically lost its Indian identity. . . . By the time of Santiago de Guatemala's destruction by earthquakes in 1773, all of the capital's peripheral communities had been similarly transformed. Mestizaje, prompted and ever accelerated by ladino and poor-Spanish takeover, was the primary source of that transformation" (Lutz 1994, 62, 63).

14 "La existencia y naturaleza del criollo es uno de los elementos que radicalmente establecen diferencia entre los estudios sobre el colonialismo español y los que se realizan sobre las regiones del globo colonizadas por otras potencias europeas" (Recinos 2002, 18).

15 I further elaborate on this idea in my critical edition of Miguel Angel Asturias's *Cuentos y leyendas* (2000) and in the second chapter of *La articulación de las diferencias* (2002).

16 I analyze the repressive excesses of academic censorship and the boycott of the intellectual debate by an intolerant Menchuist religiosity in "El neomacartismo estalinista" (2000–2001), in the introduction to *Stoll-Menchú* (2001), and in the prologue to the second edition of *La articulación de las diferencias o el síndrome de Maximón* (2002).

Justamente hay que descolonizar, justamente lo que existe es la tara colonial, en nuestros países de la región andina existe desgraciadamente este problema estructural.

[Indeed it is necessary to decolonize, indeed what exists is a colonial tare, in our countries of the Andean region, there exists unfortunately this structural problem.]

—Luis Macas in an interview, August 2001

(POST)COLONIALITY IN ECUADOR: THE INDIGENOUS MOVEMENT'S PRACTICES AND POLITICS OF (RE)SIGNIFICATION AND DECOLONIZATION

Catherine E. Walsh

The applicability of postcolonial theory and discourse to the historical and social reality of Latin America is an issue of debate among academics both in metropolitan countries and Latin America.[1] However, the concern of this essay is not with how well postcolonial theory travels, nor is it with the geopolitical baggage that accompanies its epistemological formation in the metropolitan English-speaking world and the "universalization" implied in a possible movement south. My interest is rather with the construction of new loci of enunciation that depart from the knowledge, experience, and understanding of those who are living in and thinking from colonial and postcolonial legacies (Mignolo 1993), including the past and present relations of subordination and struggles of decolonization that such legacies structure, encourage, and define.

In Ecuador with the emergence in the 1990s of the indigenous movement as an important social and polit-

ical actor and its questioning of (post, neo) colonial power relations, institutional structures, modern nationhood, and the monocultural state, the tare
of colonialism and the task of decolonization have taken on new local,
national, and regional significances. The increasingly frequent use of these
terms in the discourse of indigenous leaders and in the political projects of
the indigenous organizations has not only helped evidence the present-day
colonial condition and its ties to the past but has also helped mark and
define a decolonizing politics aimed at social, cultural, political, as well as
epistemic transformations and the construction of an intercultural and democratic society. This essay analyzes how the politics and practices of the
Ecuadorian indigenous movement in recent years are contributing to a critical understanding of the dominance and subalternization advanced
through neocolonial relations and the manner in which these politics and
practices are enabling a resignification and restructuring of such colonial-
based concepts as democracy, governance, and state. Through a look at
discursive references to colonialism and decolonization and at indigenous
politics and practices that have enabled resignifications and restructurings
at both local and national levels (including the formation in January 2003 of
a military-indigenous alliance government), it affords a concrete example of
how (post)coloniality is lived and thought in Latin America. In this sense, it
gives reason for the specificity of time and place; the need to theorize *from*
Latin America and *from* the particularity of neocolonial relations within the
cultural fields of the Andes. Rather than an argument for boundary or en-
closure, this specificity should be seen as a means to visibilize what in
metropolitan-oriented postcolonial theory and writings is generally not seen
or considered, thus opening new spaces and dimensions for critical dialogue and debate both within and outside of Latin America, and not just
about but also *with* those subjects historically marked as subaltern others.

(RE)THINKING THE (POST)COLONIAL IN LATIN AMERICA

Most agree that there exists a postcolonial experience in Latin America. An
experience that, as Coronil (2002) points out, is characterized by renewed
and transnationalized forms of political and economic subjection as well as
by permanent internal exclusions: imperialism with its colonial, national,
and global modalities, and ongoing (neo)colonial relations, both of which
suggest a historical flow between past and present subordinations.[2]

Yet the obvious absence of Latin America in postcolonial studies' texts and
the added neglect of neocolonialism, imperialism, and internal colonialism

—central concerns in the Americas (Coronil 2000a, 2000b)—leave one to question in geopolitical terms the knowledge and subjectivity of postcolonial studies. What are the social inscriptions that mark and legitimize as such the postcolonial experiences that postcolonial studies take as its principal referents? Who are the subjects and objects of knowledge within the postcolonial gaze? And what are the connections among social inscriptions, the subjects and objects of knowledge, and geopolitical (and institutional) locations?

While postcolonial studies are based in the "historical fact" of European colonialism and the material effects of this experience (Ashcroft, Griffiths, and Tiffin 1995), that their primary focus is on French- and English-speaking "settler colonies" suggests a model, temporality, and experience of colonialism that is not universal. With much of the academic production in postcolonial studies involving intellectuals "in the diaspora," particularly in the United States, the issue of place takes on an added significance.

All of this points to the tensions that circumscribe the present debate, including what constitutes the localizations of the postcolonial and how the postcolonial is localized, why Latin America has remained (and whether it should continue to remain) on the margins, whether or not the particular experience of Latin America "fits" in the model of colonialism privileged by postcolonial theory, and if it is appropriate and necessary to consider a specifically (Latin) American postcolonial theoretical position (see, for example, Hulme 1996 and Klor de Alva 1995). An additional concern is the manner in which current postcolonial positions relate, or not, to the anti-colonialist narratives popular among U.S. programs of Third World studies in the 1960s and 1970s (see Castro-Gómez 1998).

While such tensions are certainly worthy of discussion, the intent here is not to deconstruct postcolonial theory nor to argue its applicability, or lack thereof, with regard to Latin America. Instead, it is to theorize *from* the lived experience of Latin American (post)coloniality, what Silvia Rivera Cusicanqui calls "the long-term colonial horizon" (1993, 99), and *from* ongoing struggles for decolonization—struggles that, in the Andean region in particular, are intimately linked to the dynamics of identity, power, and place, and to the nexus of power and knowledge that made and still make colonial situations possible.

In the Andes, a structuring feature of the colonial act was the formation and transformation of collective Indian and mestizo identities, "identities defined through their mutual opposition in the cultural-civilizatory plane, in terms of a basic polarity between native cultures and western culture that . . . continues to shape the modes of coexistence and the structures of *habitus* in force in our societies" (Rivera Cusicanqui 1993, 57; my translation).

The opposition and hierarchy constructed in the social identities of (white, criollo)-mestizo and *indio*, and the erasure of cultural, linguistic, and territorial difference implied in the latter were essential features of the establishment of a racialized *patrón* or norm of colonial power within the region, that which Quijano refers to as the "coloniality of power" (1999a, 99–109; and in this volume). Neither the use of ethnoracialized categories nor the coloniality of power itself ended with colonialism; in fact, both are reconstituted and restructured today within the discursive and cognitive constructions of the new official multiculturalism, all within the interests of global capitalism (see Walsh 2002a).

The resistance of indigenous peoples to the norms of colonial power and their agency within the political, cultural, and symbolic fields, particularly in recent years, are constitutive moments of the (post)colonial, of the inter-relatedness of identity, power, and place, and of projects of decolonization that involve the organization and strategic use of political subjectivities (e.g., Sanjinés 2002 and Walsh 2002b). Yet, interestingly enough, attention to agency (beyond the textual) has generally not been a defining feature of postcolonial theory. As a result, the lived subjectivities and actions of *the people* are frequently marginal to and within the postcolonial gaze.[3]

My rethinking of postcolonial places attention on these subaltern subjectivities, on what Ashcroft (1999) refers to as the creative, theoretical, and strategic production of colonized societies themselves, and on the ways people construct and contest the (post)colonial condition within local spaces but with globalized implications. As Ashcroft suggests, "If, rather than a new hegemonic field, we see the postcolonial as a way of talking about the political and discursive strategies of colonized societies, then we may more carefully view the various forms of anti-systemic operations within the global world system" (ibid., 14–15)

The postcolonial, in this sense, is a perspective, a lens for rereading the dynamic, experiential, and shifting nature of coloniality, its new fields and dispositions of power, its relations, practices, struggles, and resistances (Walsh 1998). A perspective that helps make visible anticolonial projects aimed at social, cultural, political, as well as epistemic transformations. Such a view coincides with Cooppan's call to consider "the post-colonial" not as a single, invading monolith, but rather as encompassing a wide range of critical practices and theoretical affiliations. As such, "Texts that fall within the category of 'the post-colonial' are not only those which fictionally thematize cultural contact and the absurdities, impurities, and syncretisms that it produces, but also those which represent . . . particular (and often particularist) anti-colonial, anti-imperial, and anti-capitalist energies, practices, politics, and polemics" (2000, 16). It is to these practices, politics, and polemics that we now turn.

THE POSTCOLONIAL STRATEGIES OF
THE INDIGENOUS MOVEMENT

"The indigenous presence and struggle in recent times has provoked a shaking up in the practice and conception of historic and cultural reality toward the recognition of Ecuadorian society as it truly is (that is, as a *mestizo* society). This represents a major step in the road to establish a process of dialogue among cultures that recognizes this reality as a structural problem" (Macas 2001, 29; my translation). The strengthening of the indigenous movement in the Confederation of Indigenous Nationalities of Ecuador (CONAIE) in 1986 and its public emergence, with the massive 1990 Inti Raymi uprising, as an important social and political actor began a process which has no parallel in the history of the country. From the outset, this process made explicit its intention to confront past and present colonial relations, both those considered as "internal" as well as those considered as more imperial in nature.

As a result and as part of what, in Ashcroft's words, might be referred to as "post-colonial strategies" (1999, 21), the movement has directed its discourse and actions on the political reality of (neo)colonialism as reflected in the existing models of state, democracy, and nation and on the need to rethink all three as part of a process of decolonization and transformation (Walsh 2002b).[4] The overall goal, as CONAIE's 1997 *Proyecto Político* (Political project) notes, is "to advocate for "the liberation of [indigenous] peoples, nationalities, and nations that live under colonial and neocolonial systems, as well as under false democracies" (14; my translation). In CONAIE's political projects throughout the 1990s, attention was to the construction of a "new democracy" that would be "anticolonialist, anticapitalist, anti-imperialist, and antisegregationist" in nature, one that would guarantee "the full and permanent participation of the [indigenous] peoples and nationalities in decision making and in the exercise of political power in the plurinational state" (CONAIE 1997, 11; my translation).[5]

RESIGNIFYING STATE AND NATION

The proposal for a plurinational state has, in fact, been a central component of the movement's postcolonial strategies for more than a decade. Arguing that the difference of Ecuador's indigenous peoples and nationalities is not just cultural but, more important, historical, political, and economic (similar to what Mignolo [2000d] refers to as the "colonial difference"), the proposal calls for a reordering of political, judicial, administrative, and economic structures, and for the right of indigenous peoples to determine their own processes of economic, social, cultural, scientific, and technological development: "The plurinational state is the organization of government that represents the joint political, economic, and social power of the peoples and nationalities. . . . [It] is formed when various peoples and nationalities unite under the same government, directed by a constitution. This is distinct from the present uninational state, which represents only dominant sectors" (CONAIE 1994, 52; my translation).

As such, the concept of a plurinational state not only places into question the neocolonial systems of governance that construct and assume a hegemonic homogeneity, but, more important, positions as key the agency of indigenous peoples in restructuring these systems and in determining, organizing, and administering their own development.[6] This agency attempts to undo the marginalization, subordination, and exclusion that defines the (neo)colonial legacy, to decolonize the "colonial tare" (Macas 2001).

Yet while the demand for a plurinational state has been a constant since 1990, including in the 1998 Constituent Assembly for constitutional reform, claims from dominant sectors that it would divide "the nation" and create ministates has prevented social adherence among non-indigenous sectors. The fact that white-mestizo society continues to define indigenous peoples as a homogeneous bloc, erasing sociohistorical differences and maintaining the racialized-colonial categories of power to which Quijano (1999a) refers, has limited an understanding of the concept of plurinationality and complicated its construction as a national state project. Moreover, it also has continued to use white—the "color of power"—as an instrument of subordination (Hoy cited by Ibarra 2002, 30).

In what might be referred to as a postcolonial strategic response to this problematic, CONAIE and the Council for the Development of Indigenous Nationalities and Peoples (CODENPE), a state institution under the control of the indigenous organizations, began an internal restructuring process in 1998 aimed, in part, at visibilizing and resignifying indigenous difference. This process has shifted the governance of both institutions from a structure based on regional and local organizational representation to one based on "ethnic-territorial" representation, that is to say, on the reconstitution of ancestral differences made evident in the categories of *nacionalidades y pueblos*, indigenous nationalities or nations, and peoples. The current identification of over thirty distinct nations and peoples, while CONAIE recognized only eleven in 1989, is illustrative of this process (see Walsh 2002b). Initially considered by the indigenous bases to be a construction of an elite group of indigenous intellectuals, these identity-based categories have begun to take hold in many communities, strengthening local identities, articulating past, present, and future temporalities, and pluralizing the indigenous difference. As a community-based *kichwa* intellectual recently noted, these processes and practices which include an increased use of indigenous-language names among the new generations, "form part of [the project of] decolonization."[7]

However, the project of decolonization and the strategies it constructs are not limited to the reconstitution of ancestral differences. The formation in January 2003 of a military-indigenous alliance government that includes two indigenous leaders as ministers—Luis Macas as minister of agriculture and Nina Pacari as minister of foreign relations—as well as a number of indigenous (and Afro-Ecuadorian) leaders in key government positions at the national and international levels, also has a decolonizing strategic significance. A recent newspaper editorial made reference to the indigenous presence in the government as "one of the histories . . . in its route to the conquest of autonomous power."[8] But more than an issue of power per se, Pachakutik, the pluriethnic political movement with which the indigenous officials in the government are associated, talks about this presence as another strategy or step toward a plurinational state, the transformation from within of the uni-national state structure.[9]

Yet as an article in the alternative media recently pointed out, the issue is not so much the inclusion of indigenous ministers per se, but rather the conduction of a political project and program, especially one focused on economics and an antineoliberal agenda. In this sense, the challenge for Pachakutik and the indigenous movement is the extent to which they can effectively put into practice the postcolonial strategic shift witnessed since 2001, from a social force based primarily on resistance to one based on a greater capacity for political action (Moreano 2003). Constructing democracy and local power from the colonial difference, "in the last years, we have been protagonists of an important change in favor of the country. We are renovating municipalities and provincial councils, we are constructing new paradigms of local administration, giving examples to the country of how to govern alongside the people, creating politics from below, opening up participation, building a true democracy very different from that managed by the owners *del dólar y el dolor* [of the dollar and the pain]" (Lluco 2001, 8; my translation).

Since its formation in the final months of 1995 and its entrance in the electoral process in 1996, a central (postcolonial) strategy of Pachakutik and the indigenous movement has been the building of local power, local democracy, and local alternative governments, "the building and taking of political power from the state toward the consolidation of a plurinational state and a true democracy" (Coordinación de Gobiernos Locales Alternativos 2002, 20; my translation). With the election in 1996 of ten mayors and seventy-five other local officials under the Pachakutik movement's banner (the majority indigenous) and in 2000 of twenty-seven mayors, 110 other local officials, and over 400 presidents and members of parochial councils, the structure and color of local power has begun a process of radical transformation. This has included a widening of popular participation, the creation of new public spaces for the dialogic problematization of collective local interests, and the resignifying in meaning and practice of "development." These changes have occurred within a framework of profound change, including the reduction and decentralization of the state apparatus and, above all, its mechanisms of symbolic, political, and cultural legitimization with respect to local citizenship (Franklin Ramírez 2000). Through the institutionalization of new forms of citizen participation and collective decision making, including popular parliaments, cantonal citizen assemblies, and participatory budgets, these local alternative governments are enabling the conformation of local social and political subjects and the construction of new conceptions and practices of local democracy. This conformation and construction has as its goal a new model and structure of social power "from below" that places in question the neocolonial framework of liberal representative democracy and its pretensions of a "universalized" citizenry.[10] As the indigenous mayor of Cotacachi, Auki Tituaña, has argued, it also questions "the forms of organization of the colonialist state, characterized as excessively exclusionary and corrupt, that which has served as an instrument of domination for landowners, bankers, and the managerial class who control the political, military, and economic power of the country and whose principal actors belong to the white-mestizo ethnicity which has permanently been in charge of marking racial, religious, and sociocultural differences" (Tituaña 2000, 110; my translation).

For the indigenous movement, then, the strategy has been to concentrate efforts locally, working up to the more difficult transformation of state and society, "the construction of a different society, in which systems of political representation imply processes of full and differentiated citizenship, and the construction of a state which accepts and respects the radical difference of ancestral peoples and nations, all within a context of political democracy,

social justice, and economic equality" (Instituto Científico de Culturas Indígenas 2001, 8; my translation).

RECOLONIZATION AND THE (RE)CONSTITUTION OF
COLONIAL MEDIUMS OF THOUGHT

"The issue is how we can decolonize the matter of the mind" (Lluco 2001, 9;
my translation). Peter Hulme maintains that "nothing in the word 'post
colonial' implies a divorce from colonialism, instead it implies a process of
liberation of the colonial mediums of thought" (1996, 6; my translation).
Such declarations coincide with the task currently confronting the indigenous movement in Ecuador and made evident in the words of Miguel Lluco,
an indigenous leader and the president of Pachakutik.

While the force and presence of the indigenous movement in the social,
political, and economic spheres of society have pushed transformations that
a decade or two ago seemed impossible to imagine, racism, polarities, and
colonial mediums of thought not only remain vigilant but, worse yet, appear
to be on the rise. This has become clearly evident, particularly with the
appointment of indigenous leaders in ministerial positions and the treatment of these appointments by the media.

For example, El comercio, a leading national newspaper, offered a series of
"humoristic" and "editorial" (i.e., not signed) opinions in its weekly page
"Infinite Justice," including various stereotyped views of Ministers Nina
Pacari and Luis Macas, and Pachakutik President Miguel Lluco. Phrases such
as "hopefully in the era of 'luciana' [referring to President Lucio Gutiérrez]
there will not be [indigenous] revenges" and "hopefully Lluco will not give
yucca, nor that Pacari will be a 'Mata Hari' and 'ortigar' the rear-end of her
slaves" appeared in the first several weeks after the positioning of the government, along with the use of nicknames like "Niña" (little girl) for Pacari
and "Patrón Luis" with reference to Luis Macas.[11] This latter use of patrón is
particularly revealing in that it references the idea that the ascendance to
power of indigenous leaders represents a kind of reversal of traditional
roles, that is to say, the inversion of those who have been treated as servants
now to positions from which they can order and control (Taller Intercultural
2003).

Similarly, an hour-long television interview in late January with Ministers Pacari and Macas and Congressman Salvador Quishpe on the program
Este Lunes worked to "further racialize and increase the indigenous–white-
mestizo divide." For example, by positioning the interviewees as "rational

Indians," ethnic minorities able to move within the (white-mestizo) government space of power, versus the "irrational" ones associated with the indigenous organizations and bases, and by suggesting that with the first, the latter might get into power, the show provoked fear and distrust as well as a stirring up of the sentiments that for centuries have defined colonial relations. It also played off the idea of different logics and rationalities, a particular concern for politics in the international sphere (Taller Intercultural 2003). These communicative acts, among many others in this and other media reports and portrayals, make evident the persistence (and reconstitution) of both racism and colonial mediums of thought, which have not permitted the society to overcome injustices or to construct a new social project grounded in difference and in the establishment of structural, institutional, and relational conditions focused on equality, dialogue, and interculturality—a concept, process, and project aimed at transforming these very structures, institutions, and relations, as well as the colonial mind.[12] As such, these acts function as counterstrategies to the indigenous movement's efforts toward decolonization.

The push and pull between de- and recolonization made evident here both marks and (re)presents the present nature and substance of postcoloniality in Ecuador, but also in the region (see recent struggles in Bolivia, for example). However, such struggles are not only "internal," that is to say, national, regional, or simply of the mind. Instead, as Coronil (2002) argues, they are characterized by renewed and transnationalized forms of political and economic subjection, the colonial, national, and global modalities of a somewhat differently clothed imperialism.

One clear example is Álca de Livre Comércio das Américas (ALCA), an issue of major debate in Latin America and one which in Ecuador has been referred to by indigenous leaders as a "project of recolonization." As Blanca Chancoso, a longtime indigenous leader and coordinator of the World Social Forum asserts, "The process of colonization to which our peoples have been subject has not yet ended. Now the colonizers have new mechanisms to pillage the riches of our lands, and to subject us to their interests. The Area of Free Commerce in the Americas is a project that prolongs this colonialism. . . . ALCA is not an agreement for an area of free commerce for everyone, nor is it a space of interrelation between governments and peoples. Rather it is a project that seeks to strengthen the opening of markets for North American and large transnational companies" (2002, 5; my translation).

In the meeting of indigenous peoples at the Continental Encounter "Another America is Possible" held in Ecuador in October 2002, leaders made clear the relation between colonialism and imperialism that ALCA represents, as well as the manner in which it reflects new forms and relations of postcolonial dependency.[13] The enunciation of such relations is important in that they reveal the imperialized and globalized nature of projects of recolonization in the region, their articulation with colonial mediums of thought, and the contribution both together make to the consolidation of hegemonic power relations and global capitalism.

THE PLACE OF ENUNCIATION

As this essay suggests, (post)coloniality in Latin America is a lived experience. More than a theoretical stance among university-based intellectuals, (post)coloniality marks a locus or place of enunciation that departs from lived experiences of domination and subalternization and from struggles of decolonization, a social, cultural, and political positioning that references the legacies of the past and their imbrications with the present within a project aimed at transformation.

Through the discourse, politics, and practices of the Ecuadorian indigenous movement in recent years, these lived experiences are signified, resignified, and reformed locally and nationally, but also in the international sphere. More than any other sector of society, it is the indigenous movement's reference to colonialism, neocolonialism, and re- and decolonization that, in Ecuador, gives meaning to these terms, a meaning constituted in a particular time and place and through the movement's own agency. The fact that academics in the country and region seldom take this into account or consider in their courses and writings how the indigenous movement constructs a localized significance for postcoloniality reveals the permanence of a dominant geopolitics of knowledge.

To speak of the "place of enunciation" does not mean to naturalize Latin America or Ecuador as sources of authentic or essentialized identities but rather to once again emphasize the dynamics of identity, power, and place—between the "creation of place and the creation of people" (Escobar 2000, 115)—that form an integral part, particularly in the Andean region, of ongoing struggles for decolonization (Rivera Cusicanqui 1993). In this sense, "place" is central not only because it helps make visible the "subaltern forms of thinking and local and regional modalities to configure the world" (Escobar 2000, 116) that Western theory (and metropolitan-oriented postcolonial theory and writings) tends to obfuscate, but also because it "locates" the postcolonial with regard to social inscriptions, to the organization and strategic use of political subjectivities, and to actions that have as their vision a new social power founded in a just, equitable, participatory, and truly plural democracy, state, and society.

NOTES

1 Luis Macas is an indigenous leader, a former president of the Confederation of Indigenous Nationalities of Ecuador, a former national congressman, and rector of the Universidad Intercultural de las Nacionalidades y Pueblos Indígenas. As of 15 January 2003, Macas held the post of minister of agriculture in the military-indigenous alliance government of Lucio Gutierrez. Macas left the government in 2003 and went back to CONAIE. He ran for president in 2006, but without success.

2 For Coronil, imperialism within the Latin American context is a category that is more inclusive than colonialism and that takes in a wide historic horizon including colonialism.

3 The exception is the field of subaltern studies, including the work of the now defunct Latin American Subaltern Studies Group. Yet as Coronil (2000a) argues, even within subaltern studies, the recognition of the subaltern as an agent of historical transformation is often muted. His critique of Spivak in this regard is useful.

4 For Ashcroft (1999, 21), postcolonial strategies focus on the political and historical reality of colonialism and are directed at transforming its discourses and institutions. These strategies are also evidenced in the movement's efforts to construct its own model of education as a response to the "generalized practice of neocolonial attitudes that tend to eliminate knowledge as an instrument of development and of solution to existing sociocultural and economic problems (Dirección Nacional de Educación Intercultural Bilingue del Ecuador 1994, 20).

5 In his essay in this volume Löwy proposes that the "militant style, the faith in the cause, and the predisposition toward sacrifice" present in CONAIE as well as in other social movements possibly spring from a religious source, a subject open to debate.

6 The concept and demand for a plurinational state is not limited to Ecuador but in fact has also formed an important part of indigenous demands in Bolivia, particularly in the 1980s.

7 Imbaya Cachiguango, Workshop on Identity and Interculturality, Peguche, Ecuador, 22 February 2003.

8 "El drama de Pachakutik," El comercio, 6 February 2003, 4; my translation.

9 Such process recalls what Žižek (1997) referred to as the "ethnization of the nation." However, there are important differences between Žižek's assertions and the processes mentioned here. For Žižek, this ethnization derives from and forms an essential part of the cultural logic of multinational capitalism. In contrast, the indigenous movement makes use of what Spivak (1993) calls a

strategic essentialism, a political agency (from below) that challenges and attempts to resignify and transform dominant concepts and structures: "a way to articulate what it has meant to be *culturally and epistemically* dehumanized by colonization and a way to reorganize 'national consciousness' in the struggles for decolonization" (Walsh 2002b, 67); or, as Mignolo suggests, "a way to critically think modernity from the colonial difference" (2000d, 8).

10   For a discussion of how the indigenous movement has contributed to a substantial modification in "the architecture of an essentialized, postcolonial and neo-colonial citizenship," see Guerrero 1997 (121).

11   *Ortigar* means "to beat with the stinging nettle," a common custom used in indigenous communities "to clean away" bad spirits and discipline acts against the community.

12   For a discussion of the concept of interculturality with regard to the indigenous movement, see Walsh 2002a.

13   This encounter, which brought together 10,000 people from forty-one countries, had as a central objective the exchange of strategies and of alternative proposals with reference to ALCA.

THE MAYA MOVEMENT:
POSTCOLONIALISM AND CULTURAL AGENCY

Arturo Arias

L et us begin with a clearly local issue. It could very well be a crime story. In reality, it is an event with clear political connotations. On 16 May 1998, at 7 p.m., two husky, armed men intimidated and threatened the life of Licenciado Ovidio Paz Bal, one of the attorneys for the Defensoría Maya (Maya Legal Defense Fund). This happened in the town of Sololá, in the "department" (province) of the same name. The victim had been traveling on a public bus coming from the capital, and when he got out of the van, he was followed by two strangers. The individuals told him: "Back off. If you don't let up we're going to put a bullet in your head, and that goes for Juan and Ricardo, too." The lawyer ran to a shop for help. When they saw this, the strangers left the scene. The names referred to by the thugs were those of Juan León, national coordinator of the Defensoría Maya, and Ricardo Sulugui Juracán, regional coordinator of Defensoría Maya for Sololá. Juan

León had worked for decades to promote and defend indigenous peoples' rights, not only within Guatemala but also in the international arena, including the United Nations. Ricardo Sulugui is a leader of the Maya Kaqchikel people who has worked tirelessly against both militarization and the eradication of civil self-defense patrols. When these events happened, he was one of the negotiators in Sololá for the establishment of a Maya university in the region, on the grounds previously occupied by Military Zone 14.

In a conventional political analysis, we could say that these acts of intimidation were framed within a general policy of threats and extrajudicial executions carried out by paramilitary bands in Guatemala, which intensified after the assassination of Bishop Juan Gerardi. On 26 April 1998, Monsignor Juan Gerardi, coordinator of the Guatemalan Archbishop's Human Rights Office (ODHAG), was bludgeoned to death. This happened just two days after the bishop had presented the "Recuperation of Historical Memory" (REHMI) report, which documented torture, kidnappings, massacres, and other crimes against humanity committed largely by the Guatemalan Army during the 1960–96 armed conflict.

Now let us turn to a different case. This one is decidedly less dramatic, but equally significant when addressing ethnic issues. The Maya writer Luis Enrique Sam Colop published a comment in his weekly column regarding the well-known director of the Guatemala City daily newspaper La hora, Oscar Clemente Marroquín: "But what I wish to call to your attention today is that columnist Oscar Clemente Marroquín, in his justified criticism of congressional president García Regás and in opposition to the immorality of other public officials, also adds: 'Although at bottom I must say that the fault lies not with the Indian but with those who side with him.' "[1]

Occurrences of this nature—from direct death threats to the unconscious racism that crops up in the thought processes of someone who is allegedly one of the most progressive journalists in the country—exemplify the obvious difficulty of fitting theories of cultural analysis engendered in urban, cosmopolitan academic circles, where concepts such as "globalization" or "postmodernism" have been common, to the concrete events that rule the daily realities of ethnic groups in distant localities that have been labeled "marginal" or "peripheral." Or is this really so?

This essay will explore the way in which concrete events not only challenge the authenticity of the ethnic subject on a constant basis but also challenge those theorists who attempt to place an ensemble of heterogeneous issues within the unifying context of globalization. From this discussion it will become clear that, within a globalized world, specificity still counts.

But I will also show the ways in which globalization affects the unfolding of the ethnic subject's identity when cultural power is reorganized within new parameters that push analyses in the direction of decentralized, multideter-mined sociopolitical relations.[2] Along the way, we shall see how different alternatives produce contradictory gazes in the space of alterity as well as in the mechanisms of production and distribution of meaning.

DISPUTING THE AUTHENTICITY OF "WHAT IS MAYAN" IN A GLOBAL WORLD

In a book published some years ago, José Joaquín Brünner defined the concept of globalization as an attempt to explain the encasing within a single capitalist system of markets and information networks extending "to the limits of the planet" (1998, 11).[3] He differentiated this economic process from postmodernism, which he saw as an attempt to "express the cultural style corresponding to this global reality" (ibid., 12). If indeed the current features of Maya culture must, by extension, fit within this decentered, port-able culture, the product of multiple fragmentations and convergences, it must be borne in mind that Maya culture is not simply a product or an off-shoot of globalization and postmodernism, though they brought renewed attention to a Maya subjectivity that had remained invisible for far too long. The Maya movement as such arose from the consequences of a brutal civil war in Central America. Mario Payeras sums up the situation: "Beyond their implications in other aspects, the social struggles of the 1970s were decisive in defining the ethnic problem, emphasizing Maya agency and testing in real life any unfounded beliefs and superficial theorizing on the subject. After what has happened, no one denies the depth of the conflict nor, in progres-sive sectors of society, the legitimacy of ethnic identity" (1997, 132).

In light of this particular political circumstance, the Maya movement's entrance on the global scene, generated mainly through the iconic role played by Rigoberta Menchú's book in the U.S. "culture wars" at the end of the 1980s, is a contradictory one because two of its salient aspects—a mili-tant revolutionary history, on the one hand, and the instrumentalization of Menchú as an iconic symbol of pluralist subalternity within the United States on the other—frequently contradict each other.

Yet this is not the whole story. Precisely because of deeply entrenched racism in their societies, Guatemala and all of Central America have tradi-tionally denied any representational space to Maya culture. For that reason, Mayas have had to use the high profile they acquired in the international arena to assert a representativity within the nation of which they technically form a part. In this process, however, they have established not only pan-Maya ties outside of the particular national space of Guatemala but also pan-ethnic ties on a continental scale, even, we could add, on a global level (the politicocultural movement of those self-described "first peoples" is a clear example of this last step).

It is as a result of these contradictions between the representativity of "the Maya" in both global and local scenarios that a national debate has emerged inside Guatemala regarding the Mayas' newly gained visibility. This is because the nation-state is still perceived by hegemonic Ladinos in a traditionally "modern" way: one ethnic group, one nation, one state. In this debate, "Ladino" forces have generated a negative critique of both Maya aspirations and Maya agency, purveying uneven and partial interpretations of the position they label "Mayista" that are at odds with what we now see in the global space.[4] Unlike traditional reactionary, anticommunist discourse on this very subject, neo-Ladinist positions argue that, politically, they are located within self-proclaimed "progressive sectors" of society.[5] Feeling threatened by Maya representativity, they attempt—with an adroit use of postmodern rhetoric—to save the Ladino world from the destructive forces unleashed by Mayanness. According to them, their critique targets only those essentialist and fundamentalist aspects of Mayista discourse, which they consider "anti-Ladino" (in this regard see Morales 2000, 2002). However, they claim to have no disagreements with regional autonomies or with the regularization of Maya languages presently taking place in the country. They assert that they respect Maya culture and identity, and even the "difference" existing between both ethnic groups, Ladinos and Mayas. But they also argue that democratization would be better served by celebrating those spaces where mutual differences find confluence (spaces of cultural mestizaje, hybridization, transculturation, etc.) than by "inventing" or magnifying the actual differences that do exist, as Morales explains: "It was also my intention to dismantle discourses by self-proclaimed 'Maya' intellectuals in order to situate the debate beyond essentialisms (strategic or otherwise), whether indigenous or Ladino, taking as a point of departure the constructed nature of ethnic and cultural identities and pointing to the possibilities of inter-ethnic negotiation" (Morales 2000, 448).

This concept in itself is not without merit or validity. To defend their arguments, however, these Ladino critics ignore many lessons garnered from the debates surrounding multiculturalism, claiming that concepts developed in the United States should not be mechanically transposed to other cultural spaces, given that those positions were formulated exclusively for the benefit of American minorities. This allows them to ignore or minimize the complexity of that other Guatemalan ethnicity—their own—even as they argue that current constructions of Maya identity in Guatemala are inauthentic because they are not wholly autonomous or identical to that of pre-conquest Mayas, but rather reflect the influence of modern technology and globalization. The revolution in communications, however, means that Mayas—like all other cultural groups in the world today—will have access to the knowledge, resources, and political strategies available everywhere, and it is to be expected that they should be able to use these tools for their own benefit and that they will be affected by this process. It is in the light of these essentialized constructions by Ladinos of "authentic" Maya culture that the conservative nature of Ladino postmodern critiques of Maya identity politics emerges.

A study by the Facultad Latinoamericana de Ciencias Sociales (FLACSO), edited by Alberto Esquit Choy and Victor Gálvez Borrel, sums up this position.

> From the ladino side the debate is led by columnists Mario Alberto Carrera and Mario Roberto Morales. Some of the points they have raised: The Mayas as a people have been extinct since the year 500 A.D. and that to talk of Mayans today is to resuscitate a people that have been dead for a thousand years; the present indigenous of Guatemala (principally the K'íche's) are descendants of the Toltecs who settled in Mexico; the majority of present day indigenous are in fact mestizos. . . . [I]dentity is a process of addition and not subtraction. . . . [I]n Guatemala we are all Guatemalans and to argue the contrary is to play into the interests of the powerful; in the context of ethnic and Mayan fundamentalism, ladinos could also feel discriminated against. (1997, 44)

In fact, the contradiction we find when it comes to Maya subjectivity is precisely the one that has divided cultural theorists between those who see a particular understanding of globalization as the negation of the ethnic subject, as a sort of worldwide Americanization of identities, in opposition to those who defend the authenticity of the so-called peripheral subject by arguing that specificity is more important than ever in a globalized world. In fact, neo-Ladinist positions do not recommend a return to those times when the Maya population was subjected to racism, oppression or exploitation. Rather, they articulate their positions as follows: "In the case of Guatemala it is worthwhile, rather, to propose an inter-ethnic negotiation based on the admission of cultural mestizaje that is diglossic, hybrid, and heterogeneous on both sides, in order to move in the direction of an ethnic-cultural democratization. That is to say, the free and egalitarian exercise of diverse cultural traditions that belong to the cultural ensemble known as Guatemala" (Morales 2000, 449).

However, the debate cannot be reduced to the fact that one Maya faction may favor certain "essentialist" elements to configure their own identity (which does happen) while Ladinos paternalistically point out to them that they are in error because essentialisms do not exist. Rather than the fabrication and articulation of one position or another via splendid theoretical pyramids, the real problem is the violence the Mayas still face and the asymmetrical relations of power that have existed between Ladinos and Mayas for more than 500 years. In light of this imbalance, and of the war unleashed by its exacerbation—followed in turn by a ferocious campaign of ethnocide on the part of the Guatemalan Army that killed nearly a quarter of a million indigenous people—Maya factions are justified in constituting their subjectivity at present in whatever fashion they wish, regardless of our possible disagreement with traces of essentialism that may creep into those constructs. To argue, as Morales does, that Mayas are presently an "atomized movement" seeking an "ethnocentric, anti-Ladino autonomy that emerged from the fact that both left- and right-wing contenders instrumentalized indigenous peoples in a war that those very same sectors never made their own despite massive incorporation into their ranks" (2000, 449) is not only politically dangerous in Guatemala (as both Morales and David Stoll have discovered) but it relies on gross generalities that deny Maya subjectivity all possibility of agency. Mayas are reduced to the racist stereotype of helpless subaltern victims, incapable not only of saying anything but also of doing anything. They are, in fact, reduced to hapless subjects who can go nowhere without the prior consent of Ladinos, who, as Westerners, have a legitimate handle on postmodernism. As Rigoberta Menchú aptly puts it, "For some I am still the Indian, the abusive woman, subversive woman, born in a humble cradle and lacking in knowledge. . . . There is so much envy because an indigenous woman has become a protagonist in small spaces of leadership in the country. . . . I must fear not only death but also the possibility of political harassment from sectors that will never be able to tolerate the prominence of an indigenous woman in politics. . . . New generations will have to be born, and the new generations will have a different mentality and a different way of coexisting in our country, so that indigenous and non-indigenous can be manifest in history and play a role benefiting our society" (1998, 177, 178).

Those who contravene Maya agency take the position that construction of identities within the "global village" is an impossibility (Brünner 1998, 179). They do recognize cultural hybridization, but deny the complex relationships that still exist between hegemonic and subaltern sectors at the symbolic level in an era when so-called peripheries have nearly the same access to symbolic goods as the center does.

As Esquit Choy and Gálvez Borrel have aptly noted, to analyze the contemporary Maya movement it is necessary to consider not only the qualitative changes that have taken place since the 1980s, placing them within the current paradigm of globalization, but also the diverse forms of cultural resistance that have appeared on the scene since the beginning of the colonial era (1997, 85), without either falling into Lyotardian games about the flux of history or seeing history itself as either irreversible or metadiscursive.

In this last context one understands how, for a broad sector of Mayas, the fuse lit with the revolutionary war was merely a mechanism, at times an excuse, for the communities to organize themselves, gain agency, and directly confront the racist state, as I have documented elsewhere.[6] As early as fifteen years ago, the top Maya leader in the Unidad Revolucionaria Nacional Guatemalteca (URNG), Pablo Ceto, was talking about participating in a "conspiracy within the conspiracy."[7] For him, the revolutionary struggle and Marxist ideology itself were nothing but vehicles, mere instruments to be employed in the defense of and struggle for Maya identity, independent of any other goals the revolutionary movement had in mind. As Demetrio Cojtí confirms today, Ceto's position on this has not changed. If anything, he has tried to reconcile, on the one hand, the URNG and its self-described "popular Maya" base, grouped more or less within the Coordinadora de los Pueblos Mayas de Guatemala (COPMAGUA), and, on the other, the supposedly "fundamentalist" positions defended by self-described "cultural Mayas."[8]

Given the conditions of structural racism on which the Guatemalan State rests, it is impossible for the nation to be truly democratized without first destroying the hegemony of Ladinos, allegedly the most Westernized sector within the country, although not necessarily the most globalized. As Haroldo Shetemul, then director of *Crónica*, noted in an editorial he wrote some years ago, the United Nations itself made a similar point in a document titled "Guatemala: Contrasts in Human Development."[9]

Those who object to this conclusion form a democratization-destruction binary opposition, even while they are accusing the Maya movement of creating a suprahistorical binary opposition, Maya-Ladino (Morales 2000, 449). The latter presupposes that those favoring the "destruction" of Ladino hegemony cannot possibly be in favor of "democratization." Nonetheless, even in the best of cases, this is a fallacy. As Marta Casaus Arzú points out,

> Due to the penetration and dispersion of racism throughout all spheres of civil society and the State in recent decades, it is necessary to seek new formulas for the interrelationship of both spheres. . . . This change can only come about with a reconsideration of the nature of the State and a reformulation of the nation. . . . It has become necessary to modify the constitution and current legislation, to substantially modify the educational system and the cultural values of the population. . . . In turn it would be necessary to try to modify the racist, exclusionary national imaginary for upcoming generations under other assumptions and by modifying schoolbooks, communications media, etc.
>
> But in our opinion the key lies in modifying the system of domination and in redefining the social space of the different actors on the basis of respect and recognition of Indigenous Peoples' identities and of their social and cultural rights, and also by respecting other social identities such as gender and class. (1998, 144)

In fact, since 1996, all Maya positions without exception have favored a democratization that includes the Ladino sector (see Cojtí Cuxil 1997). They also speak of sharing power in a multinational and plurilingual nation.[10] Or, rather, multiethnic and plurilingual, for those who would quibble about whether Maya groups are nations or not, a debate which is very far from being settled. The linguistic signifier may change, but the notion to which it refers remains the same, namely, a nation in which Ladinos and Mayas coexist, with a Maya government, with a legitimate exercise of power, and so on. Like it or not, this would mean the reconstitution of Ladino hegemony. We must remember that the word *hegemony* implies that one group exercises power while tolerating and respecting the legitimate spaces of other groups by negotiating agreements more or less democratically with them. In Guatemala, however, Ladinos construe their present subjectivity fundamentally on the basis of domination and not of hegemony. To their way of thinking, they have won the war, and therefore should continue to be the dominant group in the country. Nevertheless, within the framework of the 1996 peace accords, seriously undermined since the Portillo administration came to power in 2001, and making concessions to international policies of a globalized nature that reach Guatemala through institutions such as the United Nations or the Organization of American States, they are willing to tolerate and respect Mayas' subaltern spaces. But local spaces occupied by Mayas have become impregnated with a strong sense of their own subjectivity as a result of the globalized spaces in which they operate. For this reason, in their own conceptualization of a multinational and plurilingual nation, Mayas think that both ethnic groups—Mayas and Ladinos—should exercise an equal measure of power. This assertion alone would imply breaking, destroying, not only Ladino domination but also Ladino hegemony.

Neo-Ladinist critics duck this question by asserting that there is no such thing as a "Maya culture" that is diametrically opposed to a Ladino one, nor is there a Ladino culture essentially opposed to the Mayan. They go so far as to claim that recognizing a separate Maya culture would be no more than a form of paternalistic solidarity or a legitimization of inauthentic cultural formations that serve a strictly strategic purpose. This position suppresses the common knowledge held by all Guatemalans, Ladinos and Mayas alike, that Mayas are immediately and always recognized as an ethnic group, and that they are and have been the victims of exploitation, prejudice, violence, and neglect solely on the basis of that ethnicity. Therefore, at this point in the debate, the semantic question of whether the Mayas are "really" Mayas is spurious, given that the issue is not the abstract one of "identity," but the concrete one of social and political power. Garífunas aren't Garífunas, either, in this same logic, since their identity is a construct elaborated by African slaves who escaped from St. Vincent in the eighteenth century, nor are Miskitos anything more than a mingling of indigenous people with groups of African and English descent; pursuing this line even further, we could explain easily that "Americans" are not Anglo-Saxons, and Germans are not "Aryans." It would be a never-ending story because, as we all know, ethnic groups are de facto constructs deployed politically as positioning mechanisms to rearticulate power. Thus, since there is no metaphysical truth, or even an essentialized or metadiscursive one, any positionality, however artificial, can take on a sheen of an imaginary truth laden with symbolism when articulated within a social space where agency is exercised.

MAYAN TRANSFORMATIONS AND MIMICRIES IN THE UNFOLDING OF A NEW ETHNIC SUBJECT

The phenomenon of globalization can produce dubious identities, as it has with Mayas in places such as Chiapas, California, or even Florida. But the phenomenon is different in its traditional space, and as Brünner has pointed out, this is not due to any sort of "localized essence" (1998, 183). It proceeds, rather, from an intercultural conflict heightened by war. The space of a globalized postmodernity is now lived in Guatemala within the framework created by the peace accords, imposed in large measure by the United Nations, which aim to relaunch a viable, functional, and inclusive nation-state at a time when the parameters of most states have been surpassed by global dynamics.

Within the process of ethnic alliances that encompass even Mayas from Chiapas, of new mobility generated by the end of the war and the refugees' return, of the active intervention of a large number of nongovernmental agencies, all of them experts in development or in conflict resolution, and so on, Mayas have chosen ethnic affirmation because they lack political power within the traditional spaces in which they have lived. Even they do not consider themselves a homogeneous group, or anything of the sort, but rather recognize a plurality of cultural practices, strategies, and even political goals within the pan-Mayan movement. Indeed, Mayas themselves have recognized four tendencies existing within their ranks from the end of the nineties: those self-described as "cultural Mayas," whom their opponents have accused of fundamentalism or even anti-Ladino racism, represented especially by Kaqchikel intellectuals; "popular Mayas," organized in structures now monopolized by the URNG party; Mayas operating within regional grassroots political groups, represented mainly by the mayor of Quetzaltenango and the 2003 presidential candidate Rigoberto K'emé and his group, Xel-Huh, in alliance with other regional grassroots entities; and lastly, the "military Mayas" located on the Right of the political spectrum and linked to the power structure built by the army in the highlands.[11] The latter mainly groups the base of support developed by *comisionados militares*—army representatives within the community—during the war, of which "civil patrols" are the mainstay. The first three tendencies are coordinated informally, and not without contradictions, within the Consejo de Organizaciones Mayas de Guatemala (COMG) in order to negotiate accords that represent pan-Maya interests.[12] This body, however, is not strictly organic, nor does it necessarily guarantee agreements among the various groups. Basic conflicts tend to exist between cultural Mayas and popular Mayas due to the fact that the latter often prioritize the interests of the URNG party over ethnic interests. As a result cultural Mayas frequently form tactical alliances with regional grassroots political groups to oppose popular Mayas. Nevertheless, in the COMG an attempt has at least been made to negotiate the divergent positions and to create cohesive agreements that will benefit the Maya people as a whole. Military Mayas constitute the backbone of General Ríos Montt's support, although during the early part of 2003 their demands seemed to have eluded his grasp and that of the Portillo administration (Portillo represents Ríos Montt's Guatemalan Republican Front Party [FRG]).

Needless to say, the foregoing hardly implies that there are no problems within these political organizations. Machismo is still prevalent within Maya leadership, but it is masked with an added layer of secretivity to avoid showing a bad face to the public. There are also interethnic conflicts, such as the one still extant between the K'ichés and the Kaqchikels, the largest groups within the Guatemalan Maya family, who are still acting out a rivalry that originated before the Spanish conquest, as a result of both groups' attempt to hegemonize the ensemble of the Maya population. At present Kaqchikels monopolize the intellectual space, in large measure because that group is located at the edge of the Pan-American Highway, the conduit for all economic development associated with modernity in the twentieth century, while the K'ichés, outside of the city of Quetzaltenango, are located in more marginal areas with respect to the economic and cultural development of the country. From them, however, have emerged grassroots political leaders of great stature, among whom Rigoberta Menchú and Rigoberto K'emé are arguably the most famous.[13] As a consequence, K'ichés have had a greater presence in political groups, while Kaqchikels dominate the cultural, intellectual, and educational space. Other ethnic groups are at a substantial disadvantage compared to these two largest groups, although they negotiate tactical alliances with them according to their interests.

The overall problem continues to be one of marginality. However prevalent the globalizing rhetoric has become, Mayas do not find themselves in positions of power, but quite the contrary. A few examples will suffice. Even in international organizations such as the various structures linked to the United Nations that operate within the country, Mayas are not hired as part of the staff.[14] This employment policy, in perfect alignment with Ladino hegemony in the country, serves only to perpetuate the racist nature of the state with an international blessing. Similarly, the training program for former Maya combatants, implemented by the Organization of American States (OAS) within the framework of the peace accords, ended with much the same result. One of the people who worked on the project told Menchú that this program trained many former combatants who had no formal education in manual work: carpentry, driving vehicles, and so on.[15] But now that the program has ended and the OAS has left the country, no jobs exist for any of the trainees. The past government (Alvaro Arzú, 1996–2000) refused to hire them or even absorb a small number of the program's Maya personnel. They were very respectful when representatives of that international body consulted with them and listened to all their concerns, but when it came to the concrete act of hiring someone, they did not do it. In the meantime, the Arzú government also kept the few Maya cadres atomized, scattered in thousands of commissions of dubious utility, where the differences between the various sectors often flared up, to the glee of the government's Ladino functionaries. The Portillo administration only incorporated Mayas willing to align themselves with the FRG, and have mobilized former *patrulleros civiles* on their behalf.

Another example would be the following: the joint committees created by the peace accords, designed to create those very policies that would transform the Ladino composition of the state, finished their work during 1998. This meant that it was time to shape the bilingual education program, one of several key strategic instruments aimed at changing the very nature of the nation. According to the peace accords, the implementation of this initiative was to be carried out by a commission composed equally of Mayas and Ladinos. The government, however, proposed a commission with only two Maya members out of a total of eighteen. The government's rationale for the low number was the classic argument that there were not enough Maya cadres qualified to participate in such a high-level commission dealing with matters of critical importance for the future of the country. In this decision, however, the government not only nullified the principle of ethnic political representation but also refused to admit its responsibility for not producing more Maya professionals. After a great deal of negotiating, supporters of Maya inclusion managed to enlarge the commission to a total of twenty-two members, of whom seven were Mayas.[16] This is the commission charged with the creation of the first bilingual education program in the entire history of Guatemala.

The lack of Maya cadres is indeed a problem that limits whatever insertion indigenous groups can have within a national context. It affects, of course, Mayas' own interests and undermines any effort to advance more consistent ethnic policies throughout the length and breadth of the nation. Generally, the scarcity of qualified cadres implies that the majority of them lack strategic vision, viewing the political panorama only in terms of short-term goals, when not of actual self-interest. Many of them are poorly trained and will only mobilize around concrete political problems that concern ethnic matters specifically. This limitation was clearly evident in 1998, when, for the first time, a program to legislate the disastrous situation of the country's children was implemented. Mayas did not participate in these commissions, although they were invited, because many of them wrongly believed that the topic did not concern them. When the preliminary plan for the new law was issued at last, it turned out that it was eminently Ladino in its cultural characteristics. Only then, when it was practically a fait accompli, did Mayas fight to delay its implementation and add modifications appropriate to their own cultural norms.[17]

There were also, at times, Byzantine problems such as the debate between a linguistic group called Oxlajuuj Keej Maya "Ajtz'iib" (OKMA), which operated autonomously within the Centro de Investigaciones Regionales Meso-americanas (CIRMA), and the Academia Maya de la Lengua. For example, the former claimed that K'iché has a double vowel, while the academy insisted that this was not the case and attempted to impose its view based on the fact that it was legally recognized by the current constitution as the national body dealing with Mayan languages. The result of this singular dispute was that presently no texts in K'iché are being published at the institutional level, publicly or privately, at a time when they are more important than ever for training cadres and broadening civil and political rights.

The problems the few existing Maya organizations have to shoulder are numerous, and many of them should normally be the responsibility of other types of bodies or institutions. Here is another concrete example: according to Menchú, her foundation has had to take charge of groups of former combatants or members of the Comunidades Populares en Resistencia (CPR)—a support group for the former guerrillas—who out of ethical or moral compunction refused to surrender to United Nations organizations. Although they have renounced the use of arms, these individuals wandered unarmed all over Guatemalan territory for about three years, after the signing of the 1996 peace accords. "Just yesterday," said Menchú in August 1998, "we held a meeting because there are now 185 *compañeros* who have sought us out." Moreover, Menchú affirmed that, contrary to the beliefs of both supporters and critics of the Maya movement, there would be no increase in the number of Maya deputies in congress in the upcoming elections (2000), "because within all parties, Maya candidates appear as number twelve or thirteen on the list, or even further down, so the possibility of them being elected is minimal. None of the parties cares about placing them higher on the list" (personal communication, 1998). (The 2000 electoral results proved her right on this issue as well.) As a result, political hope for Mayas resides, not in placing candidates for national elections, but, rather, in increasing the local power of civic committees, and in their ability to win grassroots support at the town level. On this score, Menchú says that there are more Maya mayors now than ever and that both her own foundation and "cultural Mayas" have been working closely with them. "Not all of them have an ethnic consciousness, and not all are honest," she states, "but it is politically important that they get elected" (personal communication, 1998).

If we understand the modern state as a bureaucratic mechanism of control backed by force, it becomes clear not only that current internationalization processes have to a large extent surpassed the Guatemalan State, since it is in no position to tackle global problems, but also that should Mayas one day come to wield executive or legislative power within the nation, they would control the State, or rather part of it, but this would not make the country a "Maya nation" in which they would be able to "throw the Ladinos to the sea," the grotesque fear of diehard defenders of Ladinismo. No matter which group exercises political power at the national level, globalizing issues would weaken their effective control over "deterritorialized" factors such as the economy or communications, now beyond government control. This would "normalize" a Maya-run government, just as these factors have done with the Lula government in Brazil. Thus, in rearticulating their relationship to power and gaining access to symbolic domination, they would be forced to rebuild their own subjectivity, as has occurred with every formerly oppressed ethnic or political group that transforms its relationship to power, given that so-called essentialisms do not in fact exist outside of the symbolic spaces where identity is self-constructed.[18]

Maya racism, which of course also exists, is conceptually located within what has been called in the United States "reverse racism," analogous to the phenomenon of Afrocentrism. Whether one likes it or not, or else takes a critical stand against its most radical expressions, it must be recognized that it has arisen in reaction to a brutal oppression and discrimination, which makes it different from the racism of Ladinos for Mayas. But independent of whether we know the historical origins of this inequality, we must also understand that, in the present context of globalization, the nature of the state has changed in such a way that it is impossible for this type of domination, racism, or discrimination to develop again in the same way it did during the previous centuries, no matter who is playing the dominant role in the process.

PROBLEMS AND MORE PROBLEMS

The elements I have put forth in the previous sections might be seen as merely a discussion of nuances regarding local cultures within a broader framework of globalization of culture. What we are dealing with, however, is the elusive relation between specific cultures and globalizing tendencies. If for Europe the publishing sector is the basis for cultural politics and for the United States the entertainment industry plays an analogous role, it may be stated that the various expressions of ethnic cultures constitute this basis in a large part of what used to be called the Third World.[19] To say this is not to reduce the problem to an academic debate among experts in cultural studies. The painful consequences of the contradictions that arise within global culture implicate very specific, concrete events and lives, such as those of Ovidio Paz Bal, Juan León, and Ricardo Sulugui Juracán. Thus, from within this transformative subalternity arises a consistent discourse that is effectively constructing new relations of power/knowledge within a decentered intercultural festival of globality. These expressions do not generate homogenizing tendencies, but, rather, heterogeneous disjunctions, Lyotardian *differends*.

The real problem is not whether the present Maya leaders are capable of articulating concrete or coherent positions within this constant flux of the global and the local. It is, rather, that, because the discourses they do articulate and that circulate by means of global communications skip that hegemonic, Ladino national space that they are addressing, they seldom reach the very interlocutors with whom they want to engage in a dialogic relationship. As a result, whereas these enunciations contribute to the founding of new truths on a broader scale, they are not heard within the existing networks monopolized inside Guatemala by Ladinos. This brings about the paradox that, although Maya discourses do indeed contribute to the shaping of deterritorialized truths, they remain excluded from their own national communication and education systems. This is why the Ladino sector can qualify those discourses enunciated by the Maya movement as "imported ideas" from the outside, since they reach Ladino networks from abroad, and often through the writings in English of American scholars, even when they were originally enunciated inside the national space, and often by Maya cadres who transmitted those very forms of knowledge to American scholars who then published them as a product of their own academic research. However, an idea only acquires a ring of truth when adopted as a discourse of power within globalizing networks of communication and circulation of meaning. We already know that it is not enough to speak the truth. One must be "within the truth"—the dominant one—discursively speaking. Apart from Menchú, no Maya leader has managed to make this final step in the globalized world, and she herself has done so only partially inside the national space, and only after winning the Nobel Peace Prize.[20]

These Maya leaders—representatives of a certain fluctuating marginality within the larger global marginality that encompasses the whole of Guatemala—indeed articulate worthwhile discursive positions. The problem does not lie in the Mayas' skill at articulating weighty or meaningful discourses. It is rather that hegemonic Ladinos do not take those discourses seriously, precisely because they deconstruct the Ladino project of rearticulating their own postwar subjectivity as a triumph of the Americanizing Western model, and not as the recognition of a peripheral interculturality "of color." Horrified at the prospect of seeing themselves placed within such a space, some Ladinos refuse to hear of any Maya discourse, regardless of its merits.

It is all very well to acknowledge that authoritarian discourses can occur within subalternity, as well as within hegemonic groups. Subalterns are not and do not have to be saints. Their daily behavior is often exactly the opposite of such saintliness, given the miserable conditions of subalternity. But to arrive at some sort of workable, egalitarian society, or even one with a minimum of justice, asymmetrical power relations must be broken down. This can only be done by supporting the subaltern subject, not the dominant one, which in the Guatemalan case happens to be the one occupying the space of traditional Ladino political hegemony.[21] For the first time, however, thanks to the circulation of discourses through various communication and technological networks, one can actually see Maya and Ladino cultural differences colliding and also coexisting, like tectonic plates in the interior of this debilitated state named "Guatemala." This plurality, rather than diminishing, continues to intensify in the twenty-first century even though the armed conflict that seemingly represented its highest level of tension has ended. What has truly disappeared is a foundational discourse that could justify the existence of a Guatemalan State with a subaltern Maya population. Thus, the war may end, but at the symbolic level, ethnic differences are more polarized than ever. The representation of both groups in the mass media reflects the generally perceived difference in their singular identities, which are reinterpreted once more as they fuse with other globalizing tendencies.[22]

CONCLUSIONS

Brünner refers to the culture of globalization as a reorganization in time and space. As distance and time are compressed, global cultures have a nearly immediate local impact, thus shattering—among other things—many of those very differences that vertically inflected center-periphery relations during the modern era. In this new "architecture of networks" (Brünner 1998, 134), in this new nonlinear concept of temporality, the Maya ethnic problem previously located exclusively in a local space, marginalized from all modern truth, acquires a semblance of contemporaneity in the ensemble of interdependent links developed in those deterritorialized spaces we could label "postnational cultures," after García Canclini. It is in this context that, in another text, Mabel Moraña (1998b) speaks of the globalization of indigenous issues as well.[23]

With these developments, the traditional representational scheme of things—with its characteristically modern slant—comes tumbling down. I am referring here to the erroneous assumption that it is possible to have cultural models that hypothetically can be implemented solely within the United States but have no validity in alterity, in other spaces with allegedly different characteristics. In fact, just as there is now a hybrid, or heterogeneous, cultural identity on a global scale, there is also a hybridization of knowledge at the postnational (or deterritorialized) level, flowing in multiple directions, in such a fashion that local knowledges (Maya, in this particular case) become part of the global, and the theoretical/political discursivity that operates within globality is likewise appropriated by local forces—by means of the Internet, among other mechanisms of the digital age used by Mayas in their various organizations. Is it possible in this context to criticize contemporary Maya intellectuals for having recourse to theories allegedly formulated for different national spaces, in the process of subversively mimicking the academic discourse of the center to transgress ideologies that consolidate racist domination? Is it justified in the name of an imagined "national purity" to prolong the subordination/oppression of Mayas until the day they can produce a cultural theory as absolutely original and thoroughly national as are *frijolitos y tortillas* or marimba music? Certainly, such an attitude has no sound basis in a world ruled by the immediateness that is constantly modifying all power/knowledge relations. Globalization has in fact transformed, when not actually erased, center-periphery relations, despite the setbacks generated by 9/11, as well as the perception that formerly "peripheral" cultures had of themselves. Now, instead, these groups appropriate all those mechanisms that allow them to subvert the very notion of a cultural center or periphery.

The debate on this issue is far from over. My intention in this essay has been to outline a few of the conundrums emerging within it, with the intention of avoiding unidirectional binarisms in so-called center-periphery relations. Otherwise, we would indeed be guilty of fetishizing and essentializing subaltern cultures, as Frances Aparicio and Susana Chávez-Silverman have argued (1997, 14). Whether we like it or not, something as allegedly local as the K'iché-Kaqchikel conflict, the narrow-mindedness of certain strains of Ladino thought in Guatemala, or even the perils confronted by Maya lawyers receiving death threats on the outskirts of Sololá are presently being discussed, debated, and often even resolved in the global arena.

NOTES

Unless otherwise indicated, all English translations are my own.

1   Sam Colop, "Ucha'xik: Del racismo subyacente," *Prensa libre*, 12 August 1998, 13.
2   Here we follow closely García Canclini's analysis of "oblique powers "in *Culturas híbridas* (1992 [1989]).
3   For a further and broad discussion of globalization theory, modernity, and postcolonialism, see Mendieta's essay in this volume.
4   Ladino is the Mestizo subject, non-Maya, who aspires to a Western identity and wants to deny her or his own Maya origins or else underline her or his European ascendancy.
5   See Morales (2000, 2002). Morales's columns in Guatemala's *Siglo XXI* emphasized this topic throughout 1997 and 1998. Even though he has since been severely criticized for this position, as well as for siding with David Stoll in the Rigoberta Menchú controversy, he continues to express these opinions occasionally to date.
6   In reality, the war was more the unexpected outcome of the 4 February 1976 earthquake, which forced local communities to reorganize themselves, gain agency, and implement a whole gamut of mechanisms of self-management.
7   Pablo Ceto, personal communication, August 1983.
8   Demetrio Cojtí, personal communication, 18 August 1998.
9   Haroldo Shetemul, "La esquina del Director: La multietnicidad guatemalteca," *Crónica*, 9 July 1998, 3.
10 Concerning this matter, we can see, as just one example among many, an article published in *Guatemala Hoy* on 8 September: "All the proposals and political initiatives of Mayan organizations concerning the constitutional reforms presently being discussed in Congress, do not question relations among Guatemalans, but, rather, complement them," affirmed the Defensoría Maya, when it ratified its will to contribute to the advancement of the peace process. "In this historical moment," their spokesperson argued, "we have to avoid certain political sectors taking advantage of our proposals to create chaos by defending constitutional reforms that are not contemplated in the peace agreements," said the representative of Defensoría Maya. The organization "regretted that some political parties do not take seriously their proposals for constitutional reform, and that certain government sectors demand that the Maya people renounce their own aspirations, accusing them of putting the peace process at risk."
11 Haroldo Shetemul, personal communication, 13 August 1998. This information has been corroborated by Demetrio Cojtí (personal communication, 18 August 1998).
12 COMG was created on 20 June 1990 as a coordination effort for Maya institutions. It is integrated by fifteen member organizations, both nongovernmental as well as academic. COMG is also a part of the Coordinadora de Organiza-

ciones y Naciones Indígenas del Continente (CONIC). See Bastos and Camús 1996.

13 Besides, the K'ichés from the city of Quetzaltenango consider themselves the economic and cultural elite in Guatemala. As a result, they often distance themselves from other K'ichés residing elsewhere.

14 Demetrio Cojtí, who provided this information, is one of the few Mayas who has had an executive role in a nongovernmental organization, as director of UNICEF. Thus, his observations reflect his own experience. He is presently vice-minister of education, in charge of bilingual educational programs.

15 Rigoberta Menchú, personal communication, 13 August 1998.

16 There are other Mayas working in the commission, but they are there as government workers, and, thus, they represent the government, rather than representing Maya organizations.

17 In this regard, I want to quote a column that appeared in *Guatemala Hoy* on 1 September 1998: " 'The new Children and Youth Laws exclude the indigenous children in the country, but it is an instrument that pretends to regulate the situation of all children in the nation,' argued representative Manuela Alvarado of the New Guatemala Democratic Front (FDNG). Alvarado said that the FDNG's position has to do with the way Article 78–96 is written; it is basically a copy of similar laws in other countries, which all lack a Maya population. 'We know that the law will penalize those who violate children's rights, but its breadth should be greater, so that it truly protects peasant and indigenous children who work alongside their parents in situations that are unhealthy for their development,' added Alvarado. Demetrio Cojtí, Felisa Loarca, Juana Apen, Rolando López Godínez, Juan Batz, juridical advisor, of the Wukub Noj group; and Alfredo García Chuvac, representatives of the Uleu Foundation, Alfredo Tai Coyoy, congresswomen Rosalina Tuyuc and Manuela Alvarado, all form part of indigenous representatives that signed the document."

18 In this aspect, I also agree with both Morales and Carrera that there is no such thing as a "Maya culture" per se, that could be clearly differentiated from a Ladino one. This does not deny, however, that both groups have positioned themselves *politically* as binary opposites. We should not be fooled by the apparent contradiction generated by this uncanny situation. The same takes place in asymmetrical relations of power in which Ladinos have historically exercised both domination and hegemony, while Mayas have played a clearly subaltern role to them, with racism as the primary defining issue between both. Thus, politically, it is impossible to defend Ladino hegemony and not appear to be racist, even if one understands that there are no absolute and opposing ethnic differences between the two groups.

19 See "El 14o Encuentro de Editores termina con un homenaje a Pérez González," in *El país*, 18 July 1998, 24. Also see "19 Nations See U.S. as a Threat to Their Cultures," *New York Times*, 1 July 1998, B1.

20 This situation is analogous to that of Central American writers. Great literature has been produced in Central America, from the time of *Popol vuh* to the present, including outstanding names such as Landívar, Asturias, Cardoza y Aragón,

Monterroso, Ramírez, and the like. Nonetheless, this literature does not play a role in power/knowledge relations exercised from and by the metropolis, which tends to favor Southern Cone writers.

21   The position defended by Ladino intellectuals argues that to share hegemony, an interethnic negotiation has to take place. They understand this as a pact in which both sides negotiate under conditions of absolute quality. This is a fallacy to start with, as Mayas cannot have "conditions of absolute equality" in an asymmetrical relation of power tinged with racism. As a first step to break this asymmetry, Mayas are constructing their own subjectivity and gaining agency by employing many of the very symbolic elements that Ladinos disqualify, arguing that they are "ideological."

22   Whether it is publicly admitted or not, Ladino strategy has consisted in cornering Maya leaders by negating the importance of Maya subjectivity on the basis that their discursivity is essentialist, fundamentalist, anti-Ladino, and even guilty of reverse racism. This is done to stop the hegemonic reversal of ethnic relations. To achieve this, "Ladinoists" have attempted to categorize all Maya leaders as essentialist without nuances of any kind, so as to build a following among Ladino sectors that is, de facto, racist.

23   This same phenomenon could even explain the iconic role played by figures such as Rigoberta Menchú in cultural spaces very different from their own, without denying that part of its component might very well also be a mechanism of primitivist mythifying that escapes the confines of intercultural dialogue.

BIBLIOGRAPHY

Ábed Yabri, Mohamed. 2001a. Crítica de la razón árabe: Nueva visión sobre el legado filosófico andalusí. Barcelona: Icaria.

——. 2001b. El legado filosófico árabe: Alfarabi, Avicena, Avempace, Averroes, Abenjaldún: Lecturas contemporáneas. Madrid: Trotta.

Abu-Lughod, Janet L. 1989. Before European Hegemony: The World System A.D. 1250–1350. New York: Oxford University Press.

Abu-Lughod, Lila. 1986. Veiled Sentiments: Honor and Poetry in a Bedouin Society. Berkeley: University of California Press.

Aching, Gerard. 1997. The Politics of Spanish American Modernismo: By Exquisite Design. Cambridge: Cambridge University Press.

Achugar, Hugo. 1998. "Leones, cazadores e historiadores: A propósito de las políticas de la memoria y del conocimiento." In Santiago Castro-Gómez and Eduardo Mendieta, eds., Teorías sin disciplina: Latinoamericanismo, poscolonialidad and globalización en debate. Mexico City: Miguel Ángel Porrúa. 271–85.

——. 2000. "Sobre el 'balbuceo teórico' latinoamericano, a propósito de Roberto Fernández Retamar." In Elzbieta Sklodowska and Ben A. Heller, eds., Roberto Fernández Retamar y los estudios latinoamericanos. Serie "Críticas." Pittsburgh: Instituto Internacional de Literatura Iberoamericana. 89–115.

Acosta, Joseph de. 1979 [1590]. *Historia natural y moral de las Indias*. Ed. Edmundo O'Gorman. Mexico City: Fondo de Cultura Económica.

Acosta-Belén, Edna. 2001. "Reimagining Borders: A Hemispheric Approach to Latin American and U.S. Latino and Latina Studies." In Johnella A. Butler, ed., *Color-Line to Borderlands: The Matrix of American Ethnic Studies*. Seattle: University of Washington Press. 240–64.

Adam, Ian, and Helen Tiffin, eds. 1990. *Past the Last Post: Theorizing Postcolonialism and Postmodernism*. Calgary: University of Calgary Press.

Adorno, Rolena. 1986. *Guaman Poma: Writing and Resistance in Colonial Peru*. Austin: University of Texas Press.

——. 1988a. "Discourses on Colonialism: Bernal Díaz, Las Casas, and the Twentieth-Century Reader." *Modern Language Notes* 103: 239–58.

——. 1988b. "Nuevas perspectivas en los estudios coloniales literarios hispanoamericanos." *Revista de Crítica Literaria Latinoamericana* 28: 11–28.

——. 1993a. "The Genesis of the *Nueva corónica y buen gobierno*." *Colonial Latin American Review* 2, nos. 1–2: 53–92.

——. 1993b. "Reconsidering Colonial Discourse for Sixteenth- and Seventeenth-Century Spanish America." *Latin American Research Review* 28, no. 3: 135–45.

Adorno, Rolena, and Walter D. Mignolo, eds. 1989. "Colonial Discourse." Special issue, *Dispositio/n* 14, nos. 36–38.

Agamben, Giorgio. 1998 [1995]. *Homo Sacer: Sovereign Power and Bare Life*. Trans. Daniel Heller-Roazen. Stanford, Calif.: Stanford University Press.

——. 1999 [1994]. *The Man without Content*. Trans. Georgia Albert. Palo Alto, Calif.: Stanford University Press.

Agarwal, Bina. 1995. *A Field of One's Own: Gender and Land Rights in South Asia*. Cambridge: Cambridge University Press.

Agassiz, Louis, and Elizabeth Cabot Cary Agassiz. 1869 [1867]. *A Journey in Brazil*. Boston: Fields, Osgood.

Agney, John. 1998. *Geopolitics: Revisioning World Politics*. London: Routledge.

Aguilar, Alonso. 1968. *Pan-Americanism from Monroe to the Present: A View from the Other Side*. New York: Monthly Review Press.

Aguirre Beltrán, Gonzalo. 1972. *La población negra de México*. 2d ed. Mexico City: Fondo de Cultura Económica.

Ahmad, Aijaz. 1987. "Jameson's Rhetoric of Otherness and the 'National Allegory.'" *Social Text* 17 (fall): 3–25.

——. 1992a. *In Theory: Classes, Nations, Literatures*. London: Verso.

——. 1992b. "Three Worlds Theory: End of a Debate." In *Theory: Classes, Nations, Literatures*. London: Verso. 287–318.

——. 1995. "The Politics of Literary Postcoloniality." *Race and Class* 36, no. 3: 1–20.

Ahmed, Lelia. 1989. "Feminism and Cross-Cultural Inquiry: The Terms of Discourse in Islam." In Elizabeth Weed, ed., *Coming to Terms: Feminism, Theory, Politics*. London: Routledge, Chapman, Hall. 143–51.

Akiwowo, Akinsola. 1999. "Indigenous Sociologies: Extending the Scope of the Argument." *International Sociology* 14, no. 2: 115–38.

Alarcón, Norma. 1990. "The Theoretical Subject(s) of This Bridge Called My Back and Anglo-American Feminism." In Gloria Anzaldúa, ed., *Making Face, Making Soul: Haciendo caras*. San Francisco: Aunt Lute. 356–59.

——. 1994. "Conjugating Subjects: The Heteroglossia of Essence and Resistance." In Alfred Arteaga, ed., *An Other Tongue: Nation and Ethnicity in the Linguistic Borderlands*. Durham, N.C.: Duke University Press. 125–38.

Alavi, Hamza. 1972. "The State in Post-Colonial Societies." *New Left Review* 74: 59–81.

Alberro, Solange. 1992. *Del gachupín al criollo: O de cómo los españoles de México dejaron de serlo*. Mexico City: El Colegio de México.

——. 2000. "La emergencia de la conciencia criolla: El caso novohispano." In José Antonio Mazzotti, *Agencias criollas: La ambigüedad "colonial" en las letras hispanoamericanas*. Pittsburgh: Biblioteca de América. 37–54.

Alcalá, Ángel, ed. 1995. *Judíos. Sefarditas. Conversos. La expulsión de 1492 y sus consecuencias*. Valladolid: Ámbito Ediciones.

Alcoff, Linda. 1988. "Cultural Feminism versus Poststructuralism: The Identity Crisis in Feminist Theory." *Signs* 13: 405–36.

——. 1991. "The Problem of Speaking for Others." *Critical Inquiry* 20: 5–32.

Alcoff, Linda, and Eduardo Mendieta, eds. 2000. *Thinking from the Underside of History: Enrique Dussel's Philosophy of Liberation*. Lanham, Md.: Rowman and Littlefield.

Alexander, Jacqui, and Chandra Talpade Mohanty, eds. 1997. *Feminist Genealogies, Colonial Legacies and Democratic Futures*. New York: Routledge.

Allen, Theodore. 1994. *The Invention of the White Race*. 2 vols. London: Verso.

Almeida, F. J. Lacerda e. 1889. *Documentos para a História das Colónias Portuguezas: Diário da viagem de Moçambique para os rios de Senna*. Lisbon: Imprensa Nacional.

Almeida, Miguel Vale de. 2000. *Um mar da cor da terra: Raça, cultura e política da identidade*. Oeiras: Celta.

Al-Sa'dawi, Nawal. 1999. *Mujer en Punto Cero*. Madrid: Editorial Horas y Horas/Las Femineras.

Altuve-Febres Lores, Fernán. 1996. *Los reinos del Perú: Apuntes sobre la monarquía peruana*. Lima: Altuve-Febres y Dupuy.

Alvarez Curbelo, Silvia, Mary Frances Gallart, and Carmen I. Raffucci, eds. 1998. *Los Arcos de la Memoria: El '98 de los pueblos puertorriqueños*. San Juan: Postdata.

Alvarez Sonia, Elisabeth Friedman, et al. 2002. "Encountering Latin American and Caribbean Feminisms." *Signs* 28, no. 2: 539–79.

Alves, Claudete. 2002. "Que bom estar presente neste parto." *Cadernos negros: Poemas afro-brasileiros* 25: back cover.

Amin, Samir. 1989. *Eurocentrism*. Trans. Russell Moore. New York: Monthly Review Press.

——. 1992. *Empire of Chaos*. Trans. W. H. Locke Anderson. New York: Monthly Review Press.

Anaya, Rudolfo. 1976. *Heart of Aztlán*. Berkeley, Calif.: Editorial Justa.

Anaya, Rudolfo, and Francisco Lomelí, eds. 1989. *Aztlán: Essays on the Chicano Homeland*. Albuquerque, N.M.: El Norte Publications/University of New Mexico Press.

Anderson, Benedict. 1991. *Imagined Communities: Reflections on the Origin and Spread of Nationalism*. London: Verso.

Anderson, Perry. 1975. *Lineages of the Absolutist State*. London: New Left Books.

Andrade, Mário de. 1955–66. *Obras Completas*. São Paulo: Martins.

———. 1988. *Macunaíma*. Belo Horizonte, Brazil: Editora Itatiaia.

Antoine, Régis, ed. 1995. *A History of Literature in the Caribbean: Hispanic and Francophone Regions*. Philadelphia: John Benjamins.

Anzaldúa, Gloria. 1987. *Borderlands: The New Mestiza—La frontera*. San Francisco: Spiters-Aunt Lute.

———. 1990. "How to Tame a Wild Tongue?" In Russel Ferguson, Martha Grever, Trinh Minh-ha, Cornell West, eds., *Out There: Marginalization and Contemporary Cultures*. Cambridge, Mass.: MIT Press. 205–14.

———. 2000. *Interviews/Entrevistas*. Ed. AnaLouise Keating. New York: Routledge.

Anzaldúa, Gloria, and AnaLouise Keating, eds. 2002. *This Bridge We Call Home: Radical Visions for Social Transformation*. New York: Routledge.

Aparicio, Frances R., and Susana Chávez-Silverman, eds. 1997. *Tropicalizations: Transcultural Representations of Latinidad*. Hanover, N.H.: Dartmouth University Press.

Apel, Karl-Otto. 1996. " 'Discourse Ethics' before the Challenge of 'Liberation Philosophy.' " *Philosophy and Social Criticism* 22, no. 2: 1–25.

Apollon, Willy. 1999. "Vodou: The Crisis of Possession." *Jouvert* 3, nos. 1–2. Online. http://social.chass.ncsu.edu/jouvert/v3i12/apollo.htm.

Appadurai, Arjun. 1996. *Modernity at Large: Cultural Dimensions of Globalization*. Minneapolis: University of Minnesota Press.

Appelbaum, Nancy, Anne Macpherson, and Karin Rosemblatt, eds. 2003. *Race and Nation in Modern Latin America*. Chapel Hill: University of North Carolina Press.

Appiah, Kwame Anthony. 1991. "Is the Post- in Postmodernism the Post- in Postcolonial?" *Critical Inquiry* 17: 336–57.

———. 1992. *In My Father's House: Africa in the Philosophy of Culture*. New York: Oxford University Press.

Arac, Jonathan, ed. 1986. *Postmodernism and Politics*. Minneapolis: University of Minnesota Press.

Arac, Jonathan, and Christopher Norris. 1987. *Derrida*. Cambridge, Mass.: Harvard University Press.

Arac, Jonathan, and Harriet Ritro, eds. 1991. *Macropolitics of Nineteenth-Century Literature: Nationalism, Exoticism, Imperialism*. Philadelphia: University of Pennsylvania Press.

Arce, Alberto, and Norman Long. 2000. *Anthropology, Development, and Modernities: Exploring Discourses, Counter-Tendencies, and Violence*. London; New York: Routledge.

Arce, Bayardo. 1980. "El difícil terreno de la lucha: El ideológico." *Nicaráuac* 1: 155–56.

Arciniegas, Germán. 1975. *America in Europe: A History of the New World in Reverse*. New York: Harcourt Brace.

Ardao, Arturo. 1980. *Génesis de la Idea y el nombre de América Latina*. Caracas: Centro de Estudios Latinoamericanos Rómulo Gallegos.

———. 1993. *América Latina y la latinidad*. Mexico City: Universidad Nacional Autónoma de México.

Ardiles, Osvaldo. 1975. *Cultura popular y filosofía de la liberación: Una perspectiva latinoamericana*. Buenos Aires: F. G. Cambeiro.

Arenas, Reinaldo. 1982 [1966]. *El mundo alucinante*. Caracas: Monte Avila.

Arguedas, José María. 1975. *Formación de una cultura nacional indoamericana*. Mexico City: Siglo XXI.

——. 1980. *Yawar Fiesta*. Lima: Editorial Horizonte.

——. 1985. *Yawar Fiesta*. Trans. Frances Horning Barraclough. Austin: University of Texas Press.

——. 1986. *Los ríos profundos*. Caracas: Biblioteca Ayacucho.

——. 1990. *El zorro de arriba y el zorro de abajo*. Nanterre, France: ALLCA XXe.

——. 1992. "No soy un aculturado." In *El zorro de arriba y el zorro de abajo*. Mexico City: Colección Archivos. 256–58.

Arias, Arturo. 1997a. "Forum on Anthropology in Public: Consciousness, Violence, and the Politics of Memory in Guatemala: Comments to Charles R. Hale." *Current Anthropology* 38, no. 5.

——. 1997b. "La psique interior de los guatemaltecos, las cuestiones del biculturalismo." *Mesoamerica* 34: 633–36.

——. 1998. "Latin America and Globalization: Response to Jeremy Adelman's Paper." *LASA Forum* 29, no. 1.

Aricó, José. 1980. *Marx y América Latina*. Lima: Centro de Estudios para el Desarrollo y la Participación.

Armas Wilson, Diana de. 2000. *Cervantes, the Novel and the New World*. Oxford: Oxford University Press.

Arnold, A. James, ed. 1997. *Cross-Cultural Studies*. Vol. 3 of *A History of Literature in the Caribbean*. Amsterdam: John Benjamins.

Arriarán, Samuel. 1997. *Filosofía de la posmodernidad: Crítica a la modernidad desde América Latina*. Mexico City: Facultad de Filosofía y Letras, Dirección General de Asuntos del Personal Académico, Universidad Nacional Autónma de México.

Arrighi, Giovanni. 1994. *The Long Twentieth Century: Money, Power, and the Origins of Our Times*. London: Verso.

Arrighi, Giovanni, Terence Hopkins, and Immanuel Wallerstein. 1989. *Antisystemic Movements*. New York: Verso.

Arrighi, Giovanni, and Beverly J. Silver. 1999. *Chaos and Governance in the Modern World-System*. Minneapolis: University of Minnesota Press.

Arthur, Charles, and Michael Dash, eds. 1999. *A Haití Anthology: Libète*. Princeton, N.J.: Markus Wiener Publishers.

Artía Rodríguez, Patricia. 2001. "Desatar las Voces, Construir las Utopías: La Coordinadora Nacional de Mujeres Indígenas en Oaxaca." Master's thesis, Centro de Investigaciones y Estudios Superiores en Antropología Socia, Mexico.

Ashcroft, Bill. 1998. "Modernity's First Born: Latin America and Post-colonial Transformation." *Ariel* 29, no. 2 (April): 7–29.

——. 1999. "Modernity's First Born: Latin America and Post-colonial Transformation." In Alfonso de Toro and Fernando de Toro, eds., *El debate de la postcolonialidad en Latinoamérica: Una postmodernidad periférica o cambio de paradigma en el pensamiento latinoamericano*. Madrid: Iberoamericana. 13–30.

——. 2001. *On Post-Colonial Futures: Transformations of Colonial Culture*. London: Continuum.

Ashcroft, Bill, Gareth Griffiths, and Helen Tiffin, eds. 1989. *The Empire Writes Back: Theory and Practice in Post-colonial Literatures.* London: Routledge.

———. 1995. *The Post-colonial Studies Reader.* London: Routledge.

———, eds. 1998. *Key Concepts in Post-colonial Studies.* London: Routledge.

Assad, Talal, ed. 1973. *Anthropology and the Colonial Encounter.* New York: Humanities Press.

Asturias, Miguel Angel. 1967. "Hearing the Scream: A Rare Interview with the Surprise Nobel Prize Winner, Miguel Angel Asturias." *Atlas* 14, no. 6: 57–58.

Avelar, Idelber. 1999. *The Untimely Present: Postdictatorial Latin American Fiction and the Task of Mourning.* Durham, N.C.: Duke University Press.

Aveni, Anthony, and G. Brotherston. 1983. *Calendars in Mesoamerica and Peru.* Oxford: Bar Publications.

Azevedo, Célia Maria M. de. 1987. *Onda negra, medo bronco.* São Paulo: Paz e Terra.

Azevedo, Elciene. 1999. *Orfeu de carapinha: A trajetória de Luiz Gama na imperial cidade de São Paulo.* Campinas, Brazil: Editora da Unicamp, Cecult.

Azevedo, Marcello, SJ. 1986. *Communidades Eclesiais de Base e Inculturação da Fé.* São Paulo: Loyola.

Bacon, Francis. 1875 [1620]. *Novum organum.* Vol. 4 of *Complete Works.* Ed. I. Spedding, R. Ellis, and D. D. Heath. London: Lawrence Chapman.

Baer, Werner. 1962. "The Economics of Prebisch and ECLA." *Economic Development and Cultural Change* 10: 169–82.

Baganha, Maria Ioannis. 1990. *Portuguese Emigration to the United States, 1820–1930.* New York: Garland Publishing.

———. 1991. Review of David Higgs, ed., *Portuguese Migration in Global Perspective. Análise Social* 26, no. 111: 443–49.

Bagú, Sergio. 1949. *Economía de la sociedad colonial: Ensayo de historia comparada de América Latina.* Buenos Aires: El Ateneo.

———. 1952. *Estructura social de la colonia: Ensayo de historia comparada de América Latina.* Buenos Aires: El Ateneo.

Bahl, Vinay. 1997. "Cultural Imperialism and Women's Movements: Thinking Globally." *Gender and History* 9, no. 1: 1–14.

Bakhtin, Mikhail. 1981 [1935]. "Discourse in the Novel." In *The Dialogic Imagination: Four Essays.* Trans. Caryl Emerson and Michael Holquist. Austin: University of Texas Press. 259–422.

Balandier, George. 1951. "La situation coloniale: Approache théorique." *Cahiers internationaux de sociologie* 11, no. 51: 44–79.

Balbuena, Bernardo de. 1604. *Grandeza mexicana.* Mexico City: Melchior Ocharte.

Balfour, Sebastian. 1998. *The End of the Spanish Empire, 1898–1923.* London: Clarendon Press.

Balibar, Étienne. 2002. "World Borders, Political Borders." Trans. Emily Apter. *PMLA* 117, no. 1: 71–78.

Balibar, Étienne, and Immanuel Wallerstein. 1991 [1988]. *Race, Nation, Class: Ambiguous Identities.* London: Verso.

Bambirra, Vania. 1978. *Teoría de la dependencia: Una anticrítica.* Mexico City: Serie Popular Era.

Barker, Francis, and Peter Hulme. 1985. "Nymphs and Reapers Heavily Vanish: The Discursive Con-texts of The Tempest." Drakakis 1985: 191–205.

Barker, Francis, Peter Hulme, and Margaret Iversen, eds. 1994. Colonial Discourse, Postcolonial Theory. Manchester, U.K.: Manchester University Press.

Barnes, Sandra T. 1989. "Introduction: The Many Faces of Ogun." In Sandra T. Barnes, ed., Africa's Ogun: Old World and New. Bloomington: Indiana University Press. 1–26.

Barnes, Sandra T., and Paula Girshick Ben-Amos. 1989. "Ogun, the Empire Builder." In Sandra T. Barnes, ed., Africa's Ogun: Old World and New. Bloomington: Indiana University Press. 39–64.

Barnet, Miguel. 1966. Biografía de un cimarrón. Havana: Academia de Ciencias de Cuba.

——. 1973 [1966]. Esteban Montejo: Autobiography of a Runaway Slave. New York: Random House.

Barradas, Ana. 1992. Ministros da noite: Livro negro da expansão portuguesa. Lisbon: Antígona.

Barreca, Regina. 1993. "Writing as Voodoo: Sorcery, Hysteria and Art." In Death and Representation. Baltimore: Johns Hopkins University Press. 174–91.

Barthes, Roland. 1972a. Critical Essays. Trans. Richard Howard. Evanston, Ill.: Northwestern University Press.

——. 1972b. Mythologies. Trans. Annette Lavers. New York: Hill and Wang.

——. 1977. Rarities, Image, Music, Text. Trans. Stephen Heath. New York: Hill and Wang.

Bartra, Roger. 1992. El Salvaje en el Espejo. Mexico City: Ediciones Era.

Bastos, Santiago, and Manuela Camús. 1996. Quebrando el silencio: Organizaciones del pueblo maya y sus demandas 1986–1992. Guatemala: Facultad Latinoamericana de Ciencias Sociales.

Batres Jáuregui, Antonio. 1892. Vicios del lenguaje y provincialismos de Guatemala. Guatemala: Encuadernación y Tipografía Nacional.

Baudrillard, Jean. 1981. For a Critique of the Political Economy of the Sign. Trans. Charles Levin. New York: Telos.

Bauman, Zygmunt. 1991. "How the Defeated Answer Back." New York Times Literary Supplement, 11 January 1991, 7.

Bazin, Jean. 1990. "A chacun son Bambara." In J.-L. Amselle and E. M'Bokolo, eds., Au coeur de l'éthnie: Ethnie, tribalisme et Etat en Afrique. Paris: La Découverte. 87–127.

Beaud, Michel. 1983. A History of Capitalism, 1500–1980. Trans. Tom Dickman and Anny Lefebvre. New York: Monthly Review Press.

Beck, U. 1992. Risk Society: Toward a New Modernity. London: Sage.

Behar, Ruth, and Deborah Gordon, eds. 1995. Women Writing Culture. Berkeley: University of California Press.

Behn, Aphra. 1688. Oroonoko, or, the Royal Slave: A True History. London: Printed for William Canning.

Belausteguigoitia, Marisa. 1998. "Visualizing Places: 'She Looks, therefore . . . Who Is?'" Development 41, no. 2: 44–52.

——. 2002. "The Color of the Earth: Indigenous Women 'Before the Law.'" Development 45, no. 1: 47–53.

Benítez Rojo, Antonio. 1972 [1967]. "La tierra y el cielo." In *El escudo de hojas secas*. Buenos Aires: Centro Editor de America Latina.

——. 1998. "Heaven and Earth." *A View from the Mangrove*. Trans. James Maraniss. Amherst: University of Massachusetts Press. 190–205.

Benjamin, Walter. 1998. *The Origin of German Tragic Drama*. London: Verso.

Berdan, Frances F., and Patricia Rieff Anawalt. 1992. *Codex Mendoza*. 4 vols. Berkeley: University of California Press.

Bergad, Laird. 1988. "¿Dos alas de un mismo pájaro? Notas sobre la historia socio-economica comparativa de Cuba y Puerto Rico." *Historia y Sociedad* 1, no. 1: 144–53.

Berger, John. 2002. "Prólogo: Un Esfuerzo por Comprender." In Arundhaty Roy, *El álgebra de la justicia Infinita*. Barcelona: Anagrama. 11–19.

Berlin, Henrich, ed. 1948. *Anales de Tlatelolco: Unos anales históricos de la nación mexicana* and *Códice de Tlatelolco*. Annotated version in Spanish by Heinrich Berlin with a summary of the *Anales* and an interpretation of the *Codex of Tlatelolco* by Robert H. Barlow. Mexico City: Robredo.

Berman, Bruce, and John Lonsdale. 1992. *Unhappy Valley: Conflict in Kenya and Africa: Book One: State and Class*. London: James Currey.

Bernal, Martin. 1987. *Black Athena: The Afroasiatic Roots of Classical Civilization*. Vol. 1 of *The Fabrication of Ancient Greece, 1785–1985*. New Brunswick, N.J.: Rutgers University Press.

Bernasconi, Robert. 1997. "African Philosophy's Challenge to Continental Philosophy." In Emmanuel Chukwudi Eze, ed., *Postcolonial African Philosophy: A Critical Reader*. London: Blackwell. 183–96.

Bethencourt, Francisco. 1991. "A sociogénese do sentimento nacional." In *A Memória da Nação*. Lisbon: Sá da Costa. 473–503.

Beverley, John. 1991. " 'Through All Things Modern': Second Thoughts on Testimonio." *boundary 2* 18, no. 2: 1–21.

——. 1993. *Against Literature*. Minneapolis: University of Minnesota Press.

——. 1999. *Subalternity and Representation: Arguments in Cultural Theory*. Durham, N.C.: Duke University Press.

——. 2000. "The Dilemma of Subaltern Studies at Duke." *Nepantla* 1, no. 1: 33–44.

——. 2002. "La persistencia del subalterno." *Nomadas*, no. 17 (October): 48–57. Bogotá: Universidad Central.

Beverley, John, and Hugo Achugar, ed. 1991. *La voz del otro: Revista de crítica literaria latinoamericana no. 36*. Lima: Latinoamericana Editores.

Beverley, John, Michael Aronna, and José Oviedo, eds. 1995. *The Postmodernism Debate in Latin America*. Durham, N.C.: Duke University Press.

Beverley, John, and Marc Zimmerman. 1990. *Literature and Politics in the Central American Revolutions*. Austin: University of Texas Press.

Bhabha, Homi. 1984. "Of Mimicry and Man: The Ambivalence of Colonial Discourse." *October* 28: 125–33.

——. 1985a. "Signs Taken for Wonders: Questions of Ambivalence and Authority under a Tree outside Delhi, May 1817." *Critical Inquiry* 12, no. 1 (autumn): 144–65.

——. 1985b. "Sly Civility." *October* 34: 71–80.

——. 1986. "Signs Taken for Wonders: Questions of Ambivalence and Authority under a tree outside Delhi, May 1817." In Henry Louis Gates Jr., ed., *"Race," Writing and Difference*. Chicago: University of Chicago Press. 163–84.

——. 1990a. "DissemiNation: Time, Narrative, and the Margins of the Modern Nation." In Homi K. Bhabha, ed., *Nation and Narration*. London: Routledge. 291–322.

——. 1990b. "The Third Space." In Jonathan Rutherford, ed., *Identity: Community, Culture, Difference*. London: Lawrence and Wishart. 207–21.

——. 1992a. "Postcolonial Authority and Postmodern Guilt." In Lawrence Grossberg, Cary Nelson, and Paul A Treichler, eds., *Cultural Studies*. New York: Routledge. 56–68.

——. 1992b. "Postcolonial Criticism." In Stephen J. Greenblatt and Giles Gunn, eds., *Redrawing the Boundaries: The Transformation of English and American Literary Studies*. New York: Modern Language Association of America. 437–65.

——. 1994a. *The Location of Culture*. London: Routledge.

——. 1994b. "Of Mimicry and Man: The Ambivalence of Colonial Discourse." In *The Location of Culture*. London: Routledge. 85–92.

——. 1997. "The Global Bazaar and the English Gentlemen's Club." In *Cânones e Contextos*. Rio de Janeiro: ABRALIC.

Bhavani, Kum-Kum, John Foran, and Priya Kurian, eds. 2003. *Feminist Futures: Re-Imagining Women, Culture and Development*. London: Zed Books.

Bierhorst, John. 1992. *History and Mythology of the Aztecs: The Codex Chimalpopoca*. Tucson: University of Arizona Press.

Bilbao, Francisco. 1864. *El evangelio americano*. Buenos Aires: Sociedad tipográfica bonaerense.

Blackburn, Robin. 1988. *The Overthrow of Colonial Slavery, 1776–1848*. London, Verso.

Blaut, J. M. 1993. *The Colonial Model of the World: Geographical Diffusionism and Eurocentric History*. New York: Guilford.

Bloom, Harold. 1973. *The Anxiety of Influence*. Oxford: Oxford University Press.

——, ed. 1992. *Caliban (Major Literary Characters)*. New York: Chelsea House.

——. 1994. *The Western Canon: The Books and School of the Ages*. New York: Harcourt Brace.

Boddy, Janice. 1994. "Spirit Possession Revisited: Beyond Instrumentality." *Annual Review of Anthropology* 23: 407–34.

Bodenheimer, Susanne. 1971. "Dependency and Imperialism: The Roots of Latin American Underdevelopment." In K. T. Fann and Donald C. Hodges, eds., *Readings in U.S. Imperialism*. Boston: Porter Sargent. 155–82.

Boëtsch, Gilles, and Eric Savarese. 1999. "Le corps de l'africaine: érotisation et inversion." *Cahiers d'Études Africaines* 39, no. 153: 123–44.

Boff, Leonardo. 1978. *Église en genèse: Les communautés de base*. Paris: Desclée.

——. 2002. *El Cuidado Esencial*. Madrid: Editorial Trotta.

Bolaños, Alvaro Felix, and Gustavo Verdesio, eds. 2002. *Colonialism Past and Present: Reading and Writing and Colonial Latin America Today*. Albany: State University of New York Press.

Bonfil Batalla, Guillermo, ed. 1981. *Utopía y revolución: El pensamientos político contemporáneo de los indios en América Latina*. Mexico City: Ediciones Nueva Imagen.

——. 1987. *México Profundo*. Mexico City: SEP-CIESAD.

Bonilla, Frank, Edwin Meléndez, Rebecca Morales, and María de los Angeles Torres, eds. 2001. *Borderless Borders: U.S. Latinos, Latin Americans, and the Paradox of Independence*. Philadelphia: Temple University Press.

Boone, Elizabeth. 2000. *Stories in Red and Black: Pictorial Histories of the Aztecs and Mixtecs*. Austin: University of Texas Press.

Borah, Woodrow, and Sherburne F. Cook. 1963. *The Aboriginal Population of Central Mexico on the Eve of the Spanish Conquest*. Ibero-Americana. Berkeley: University of California Press.

Borunda, Ignacio. 1898. *Clave de los jeroglíficos americanos*. Rome: Vatican.

Bosi, Ecléa. 1972. *Cultura de massa e cultura popular: Leituras de operárias*. Petrópolis, Brazil: Vozes.

Boturini, Lorenzo. 1746. *Idea de una nueva historia general de la América Septentrional: Fundad sobre material copioso de figuras, symbolos, carateres, y geroglifiocs, cantares, y manuscritos de autores indios, ultimamente descubiertos*. Madrid: En la imprenta de Juan de Zuñiga.

Bourdieu, Pierre. 1993 [1968]. "Outline of a Sociological Theory of Art Perception." In *The Field of Cultural Production*. New York: Columbia University Press. 215–37.

———. 2001 [1998]. *Masculine Domination*. Trans. Richard Nice. Stanford, Calif.: Stanford University Press.

Bourdieu, Pierre, and Loïc Wacquant. 1999. "The New Global Vulgate." *Baffler* 12: 69–78.

Bousquié, Paul. 1994. *Le corps, cet inconnu*. Paris: L'Harmattan.

Bouysse-Cassagne, Thérèse, and Olivia Harris. 1987. "Pacha: En torno al pensamiento Aymara." In Thérèse Bouysse-Cassagne, Olivia Harris, and V. Cereceda, eds., *Tres reflexiones sobre el pensamiento Andino*. La Paz: Hisbol. 11–60.

Boxer, Charles R. 1963. *Race Relations in the Portuguese Colonial Empire, 1415–1825*. Oxford: Clarendon Press.

Boyarin, Jonathan, ed. 1993. *Ethnography of Reading*. Berkeley: University of California Press.

Brading, David. 1991. *Orbe indiano: De la monarquía católica a la república criolla, 1492–1867*. Mexico City: Fondo de Cultura Económica.

Braidotti, Rosi. 1994. *Nomadic Subjects: Embodiment and Sexual Difference in Contemporary Feminist Theory*. New York: Columbia University Press.

Brathwaite, Edward Kamau. 1983. *Third World Poems*. Essex: Longman.

———. 1984. *History of the Voice: The Development of National Language in Anglophone Caribbean Poetry*. London: New Beacon.

———. 1992. "Reading of His Poetry." Paper presented at the Inventions of Africa: Africa in the Literature of the Continent and the Diaspora workshop, Center for Afroamerican and African Studies, University of Michigan, Ann Arbor, 17 April.

Braudel, Fernand. 1992 [1979]. *The Perspective of the World*. Vol. 3 of *Civilization and Capitalism, 15th–18th Century*. Trans. Sian Reynolds. Berkeley: University of California Press.

———. 1995 [1949]. *The Mediterranean and the Mediterranean World in the Age of Philip II*. Trans. by Sian Reynolds. 2 vols. Berkeley: University of California Press.

Bravo, José Antonio. 1978. *Lo real maravilloso en la narrativa latinoamericana actual: Cien años de soledad: El reino de este mundo: Pedro Páramo*. Lima: Editoriales Unidas.

Brendbekken, Marit. 2002. "Beyond Vodou and Anthroposophy in the Dominican-Haitian Borderlands." *Social Analysis* 46, no. 3: 31–45.

Bricker, Victoria R., ed. 1986. *Supplement to the Handbook of Middle American Indians*. Vol. 4, ed. Ronald Spores. Austin: University of Texas Press.

Briones, Claudia. 1990. "Disputas y consentimientos en la identidad étnica de los mapuche argentinos." Paper presented at the 3d Congreso Argentino de Antropología Social, Rosario, July 1990.

——. 1991. "The Race for Authenticity: A Contest without Winners." Unpublished manuscript.

British Library of Information. 193[9]. *What Is British Imperialism?* New York: British Library of Information.

Broda, Johanna, and Félix Baez Jorge. 2001. *Cosmovisión, ritual e identidad de los pueblos indígnas de México*. Mexico City: Fondo de Cultura Económica.

Bronner, Fred. 1986. "Urban Society in Colonial Spanish America: Research Trends." *Latin American Research Review* 21: 7–72.

Bronseval, Frère Claude. 1970. *Peregrinatio Hispanica 1531–1533*. Paris: Presses Universitaires de France et Fondation Calouste Gulbenkian.

Brotherston, Gordon. 1992. *Book of the Fourth World: Reading the Native Americas through Their Literature*. Cambridge: Cambridge University Press.

——. 1995. *Painted Books from Mexico*. London: British Museum Press.

Brown, Paul. 1985. " 'This Thing of Darkness I Acknowledge Mine': *The Tempest* and the Discourse of Colonialism." In Jonathan Dollimore and Alan Sinfield, eds., *Political Shakespeare: New Essays in Cultural Materialism*. Ithaca, N.Y.: Cornell University Press. 48–71.

Bruce-Novoa, Juan. 1994. "Dialogical Strategies, Monological Goals: Chicano Literature." In Alfred Arteaga, ed., *An Other Tongue*. Durham, N.C.: Duke University Press. 225–45.

Brünner, José Joaquín. 1998. *Globalización cultural y posmodernidad*. Chile: Fondo de Cultura Económica.

Buell, Lawrence. 2000. "Postcolonial Anxiety in Classic U.S. Literature." In Amritjit Singh and Peter Schmidt, eds., *Postcolonial Theory and the United States: Race, Ethnicity, and Literature*. Jackson: University Press of Mississippi. 196–219.

Bueno, Raúl. 1996. "Sobre la heterogeneidad literaria y cultural de América Latina." In José Antonio Mazzotti and Juan Zevallos-Aguilar, eds., *Asedios a la heterogeneidad cultural: Libro de homenaje a Antonio Cornejo Polar*. Philadelphia: Asociación Internacional de Peruanistas. 16–32.

Bukharin, Nicolai. 1929. *Imperialism and World Economy*. New York: International Publishers.

Burga, Manuel. 1988. *Nacimiento de una utopía: Muerte y resurrección de los Incas*. Lima: Instituto de Apoyo Agrario.

Burns, E. Bradford. 1993. *A History of Brazil*. 3d ed. New York: Columbia University Press.

Bustos, Guillermo. 2002. Enfoque subalterno e historia latinoamericana: Nación y escritura de la historia en el debate Mallon-Beverley. Unpublished manuscript.

Butler, Judith. 1990. *Gender Trouble*. London: Routledge.

———. 1997. *The Psychic Life of Power: Theories in Subjection*. Stanford, Calif.: Stanford University Press.

———. 2001. *El Género en Disputa: El feminismo y la subversión de la identidad*. Mexico City: Paidos/PUEG, Universidad Nacional Autónoma de México.

Byron, George Gordon, Lord. 1966. *The Poetical Works*. London: Oxford University Press.

Cabral, Amílcar. 1974. *Guiné-Bissau: Nação africana forjada na luta*. Lisbon: Publicações Nova Aurora.

———. 1981. *Cultura y liberación nacional*. Mexico City: Escuela Nacional de Antropología e Historia, Instituto Nacional de Antropología e Historia.

Cadava, Eduardo. 1998. *Words of Light: Theses on the Photography of History*. Princeton: Princeton University Press.

Cadena, Marisol de la. 2000. *Indigenous Mestizos: The Politics of Race and Culture in Cuzco, Peru, 1919–1991*. Durham, N.C.: Duke University Press.

Calancha, Antonio de la. 1638. *Chronica Moralizada del Orden de San Agustín en el Perú con sucesos exemplares vistos en esta Monarchia*. Barcelona: Por Pedro de Lacavalleria.

Calinescu, Matei. 1987. *Five Faces of Modernity: Modernism, Avant-Garde, Decadence, Kitsch, Postmodernism*. Durham, N.C.: Duke University Press.

Candido, Antonio. 1959. *Formação da Literatura Brasileira*. São Paulo: Martins.

———. 1967 [1950]. "Literatura e cultura de 1900 a 1945." In *Literatura e sociedade*. São Paulo: Nacional. 129–60.

———. 1973. "Literatura e Subdesenvolvimiento." *Argumento* 1: 140–62.

———. 1991. "Uma Visão Latino-americana." Lecture delivered at the conference Literatura e História em América Latina, Center for Latin American Studies "Angel Rama," São Paulo, 2 August.

———. 1995 [1970]. "Literature and Underdevelopment." In *Antonio Candido: On Literature and Society*. Ed. and trans. Howard Becker. Princeton: Princeton University Press. 119–41.

Cañizares Esguerra, Jorge. 1999. "New World, New Stars: Patriotic Astrology and the Invention of Indian and Creole Bodies in Colonial Spanish America, 1600–1650." *American Historical Review* 104, no. 1: 33–68.

Cardenal, Ernesto. 1980. "Cultura revolutionaria, popular, nacional, anti-imperialista." *Nicaráuac* 1: 163–88.

Cárdenas, Juan de. 1945 [1591]. *Problemas y secretos maravillosos de las Indias*. Facsimile ed. Madrid: Ediciones Cultura Hispánica.

Cardoso, Fernando Henrique. 1962. *Capitalismo e Ecravidão*. São Paulo: DIFEL.

———. 1964. *Empresário industrial y desenvolvimento econômico no Brazil*. São Paulo: Difusao Européia do Livro.

———. 1973. "Notas sobre el estado actual de los estudios de la dependencia." In Sergio Bagú, ed., *Problemas del subdesarrollo latinoamericano*. Mexico City: Editorial Nuestro Tiempo. 100–110.

———. 1976. "Les Etat-Unis et la théorie de la Dépendance." *Revue Tiers Monde* 17, no. 68: 805–25.

———. 1977. "The Consumption of Dependency Theory in the United States." *Latin American Research Review* 12: 7–24.

———. 1985. *Estado y sociedad en América Latina.* Buenos Aires: Ediciones Nueva Visión.

Cardoso, Fernando Henrique, and Enzo Faletto. 1969. *Dependencia y Desarrollo en América Latina.* Mexico City: Fondo de Cultura Económica.

Carochi, Horacio, S. J. 2001 [1645]. *Grammar of the Mexican Language with an Explanation of the Adverbs.* English-Spanish edition. Trans. and ed. with commentary by James Lockhart. Stanford, Calif.: Stanford University Press.

Carpentier, Alejo. 1964. "De lo real maravillosamente americano" [*sic*]. *Tientos y diferencias.* Mexico City: Universidad Nacional Autónoma de México. 115–35.

———. 1964. "Problemática de la actual novela latinoamericana." *Tientos y diferencias.* Mexico City: Universidad Nacional Autónoma de México. 5–46.

———. 1967 [1949]. *El reino de este mundo.* Mexico City: Compañía General de Ediciones.

———. 1968 [1933]. *Écue-Yamba-O! Novela afrocubana.* Buenos Aires: Editora Xanandú.

———. 1987. *Tientos, diferencias y otros ensayos.* Esplugues de Llobregat, Barcelona: Plaza and Janés.

Carrier, James G., ed. 1995. *Occidentalism: Images of the West.* Oxford: Oxford University Press.

Casaus Arzú, Marta. 1995. *Guatemala: Linaje y racismo.* San José: Facultad Latinoamericana de Ciencias Sociales.

———. 1998. *La metamorfosis del racismo en Guatemala.* Guatemala: Cholsamaj.

Cassano, Franco. 1995. *Il pensiero meridiano.* Bari: Sagittari Laterza.

Castanheira, Zulmira. 1996. "Robert Southey, o primeiro lusófilo ingles." *Revista de Estudos Anglo-Ingleses* 5.

Castells, Manuel. 1996. *The Rise of the Network Society.* Cambridge: Blackwell.

Castro-Gómez, Santiago. 1996. *Crítica de la razón latinoamericana.* Barcelona: Puvill Libros.

———. 1998. "Latinoamericanismo, modernidad, globalización: Prolegómenos a una crítica poscolonial de la razón." In Santiago Castro-Gómez and Eduardo Mendieta, eds., *Teorías sin disciplina: Latinoamericanismo, poscolonialidad y globalización en debate.* Mexico City: Miguel Ángel Porrúa. 169–205.

———. 1999. "Epistemologías coloniales, saberes latinoamericanos: El proyecto teórico de los estudios subalternos." In Alfonso de Toro and Fernando de Toro, eds., *El debate de la postcolonialidad en Latinoamérica: Una postmodernidad periférica o cambio de paradigma en el pensamiento latinoamericano.* Madrid: Iberoamericana. 79–100.

———. 2000a. "Ciencias sociales, violencia epistémica y el problema de la "invención del otro." In Edgardo Lander, ed., *La colonialidad del saber: Eurocentrismo and ciencias sociales: Perspectivas latinoamericanas.* Buenos Aires: Consejo Latinoamericano de Ciencias Sociales/UNESCO. 145–61.

———, ed. 2000b. *La reestructuración de las ciencias sociales en América Latina.* Bogotá: Pensar, Instituto de Estudios Sociales y Culturales, Pontificia Universidad Javeriana.

Castro-Gómez, Santiago, Oscar Guardiola-Rivera, and Carmen Millán de Benavides, eds. 1999. *Pensar (en) los intersticios: Teoría and práctica de la crítica poscolonial.* Bogotá: Centro Editorial Javierano.

Castro-Gómez, Santiago, and Eduardo Mendieta, eds. 1998. *Teorías sin disciplina:*

Latinoamericanismo, poscolonialidad y globalización en debate. Mexico City: Miguel Ángel Porrúa.

Castro-Klaren, Sara. 1995. "Writing Sub-Alterity: Guamán Poma and Garcilaso, Inca." In Fernando de Toro and Alfonso de Toro, eds., *Borders and Margins: Postcolonialism and Post-modernism*. Madrid: Iberoamericana. 45–60.

——. 1999. "Mimicry Revisited: Latin America, Post-colonial Theory and the Location of Knowledge." In Alfonso del Toro and Fernando del Toro, eds., *El debate de la poscoloneidad en América Latina: Una postmodernidad periférica o cambio de paradigma en el pensamiento latinoamericano*. Madrid: Iberoamericana. 137–64.

——. 2001. "Historiography on the Ground: The Toledo Circle and Guamán Poma." In Ileana Rodríguez, ed., *The Latin American Subaltern Studies Reader*. Durham, N.C.: Duke University Press. 143–71.

——. 2002. "Writing with His Thumb in the Air." In Alvaro Felix Bolaños and Gustavo Verdesio, eds., *Colonialism Past and Present: Reading and Writing and Colonial Latin America Today*. Albany: State University of New York Press. 261–87.

——. 2003. "The Nation in Ruins: Archeology and the Rise of the Nation." In Sara Castro-Klaren and John Chasteen, eds., *Beyond Imagined Communities*. Washington: Woodrow Wilson Center Press; Baltimore: Johns Hopkins University Press. 161–96.

Celso, Afonso. 1943. *Porque me ufano do meu país*. 12th ed. Rio de Janeiro: F. Briquiet.

Cervantes de Salazar, Francisco. 1972. *México en 1554 y Túmulo imperial*. Mexico City: Porrúa.

Césaire, Aimé. 1972. *Discourse on Colonialism*. Trans. Joan Pinkham. New York: Monthly Review Press.

——. 1983. *Cahier d'un retour au pays natal*. Paris: Présence Africaine.

——. 1989. *Discours sur le colonialisme*. Paris: Présence Africaine.

Chabal, Patrick. 1997. "Apocalypse Now? A Post-colonial Journey into Africa." Inaugural lecture presented at King's College, London, 12 March 1997.

Chakrabarty, Dipesh. 1992. "Provincializing Europe: Postcoloniality and the Critique of History." *Cultural Studies* 6, no. 3: 337–57.

——. 1997. "The Time of History and Time of Gods." In Lisa Lowe and David Lloyd, eds., *The Politics of Culture in the Shadow of Capital*. Durham, N.C.: Duke University Press. 35–60.

——. 2000. *Provincializing Europe: Postcolonial Thought and Historical Difference*. Princeton: Princeton University Press.

Chalhoub, Sidney. 1990. *Visões da liberdade: Uma história das últimas décadas da escravidão na Corte*. São Paulo: Companhia das Letras.

Chambers, Iain. 1994. *Migrancy, Culture, Identity*. London: Routledge.

Chanady, Amaryll. 1990. "Latin American Discourses of Identity and the Appropriation of the Amerindian Other." *Sociocriticism* 6, nos. 1–2: 33–48.

Chancoso, Blanca. 2002. "Las intensiones del ALCA: Un proyecto de recolonización." *Boletín ICCI ARY-RIMAY* 44: 5–18.

Chandra, Bipan. 1981. "Karl Marx: His Theories of Asian Societies and Colonial Rule." In *Review* V, no. 1: 13–91.

Chang-Rodríguez, Raquel. 1988. *La apropiación del signo: Tres cronistas indígenas del Perú*. Tempe, Ariz.: Center for Latin American Studies, Arizona State University.

———. 1991. *El discurso disidente: Ensayos de literatura colonial peruana*. Lima: Fondo Editorial de la Pontificia Universidad Católica del Perú.

Chartier, Roger. 1988. *Cultural History*. Trans. Lydia G. Cochrane. Ithaca, N.Y.: Cornell University Press.

Chatterjee, Partha. 1986. *Nationalist Thought and the Colonial World: A Derivative Discourse?* London: Zed Books for the United Nations University.

———. 1993. *The Nation and Its Fragments: Colonial and Postcolonial Histories*. Princeton: Princeton University Press.

———. 1997. *A Possible India: Essays in Political Criticism*. Delhi: Oxford University Press.

Chaturvedi, Vinayak, ed. 2000. *Mapping Subaltern Studies and the Postcolonial*. London: Verso.

Chaves, Castelo Branco. 1983. *O Portugal de D. João V visto por três forasteiros*. Lisbon: Biblioteca Nacional.

Chiampi, Irlemar. 1980. "Carpentier y el surrealismo." *Revista Língua e Literatura* 9: 155–74.

Chiaramonte, José Carlos. 1971. *Nacionalismo y liberalismo económicos en Argentina, 1860–1880*. Buenos Aires: Ediciones Solar.

Chimalpahin Quauhtlehuanitzin, Domingo de San Antón Muñón. 1997 [ca. 1620]. *Codex Chimalpahin: Society and Politics in Mexico: Tenochtitlan, Tlatelolco, Texcoco, Culhuacan, and Other Nahua Altepetl in Central Mexico*. Ed. and trans. Arthur J. O. Anderson and Susan Schroeder. 2 vols. Norman: University of Oklahoma Press.

———. 1998. *Las ocho relaciones y el memorial de Colhuacan: Relaciones séptima y octava*. Ed. and trans. Rafael Tena. Mexico City: Consejo Nacional para la Cultura y las Artes.

Chinweizu. 1975. *The West and the Rest of Us: White Predators, Black Slavers, and the African Elite*. New York: Vintage.

Chomsky, Aviva. 2000. "Barbados or Canada? Race, Immigration and Nation in Early Twentieth-Century Cuba." *Hispanic American Historical Review* 80, no. 3: 415–62.

Chomsky, Noam, et al. 1997. *The Cold War and the University: Toward an Intellectual History of the Postwar Years*. New York: New Press.

Cláudio, Afonso. 1979. *Insurreição do Queimado*. Vitória, Brazil: Editora da Fundação Ceciliano Abel de Almeida.

Cliff, Michelle. 1985. *The Land of Look Behind*. Ithaca, N.Y.: Firebrand.

Clifford, James. 1988. *The Predicament of Culture*. Cambridge, Mass.: Harvard University Press.

———. 1992. "Borders and Diasporas in Late-Twentieth-Century Culture." Lecture presented at the East-West Center, Honolulu, 18 September 1992.

Clifford, James, and George E. Marcus. 1986. *Writing Culture: The Poetics and Politics of Ethnography*. Berkeley: University of California Press.

Cline, S. L. 1986. *Colonial Culhuacan, 1580–1600: A Social History of an Aztec Town*. Albuquerque: University of New Mexico Press.

Closs, Michael, ed. 1986. *Native American Mathematics*. Austin: University of Texas Press.

Codex Madrid. 2002. Mexico city: Libros mas cultura.

Codex Mexicanus. Bibliothèque Nationale de Paris Nos. 23–24. 1952. Edited by Ernst Mengin. Paris: Société des Américanistes.

Codex Vaticanus 3738 ("Codex Vaticanus A," "Codex Ríos"). 1979. Biblioteca Apostolica Vaticana Facsimile ed. Graz, Austria: Akademische Druck.

Cohen, Hermann. 1914. *Logik der Reinen Erkenntnis*. Berlin: Bruno Cassirer.

Cojtí Cuxil, Demetrio. 1991. *Configuración del Pensamiento Político del Pueblo Maya*. Quezaltenango: Asociación de Escritores Mayas de Guatemala.

———. 1997. *Ri Maya Moloj pa Iximuleu: El movimiento maya (en Guatemala)*. Guatemala: IWGIA/Cholsamaj.

Colás, Santiago. 1995. "Of Creole Symptoms, Cuban Fantasies, and Other Latin American Postcolonial Ideologies." *Publications of the Modern Language Association of America* 110, no. 3: 382–96.

Collier, George, and Elizabeth Lowery Quaratiello. 1994. *Basta! Land and the Zapatista Rebellion in Chiapas*. Oakland, Calif.: Food First Book.

Comaroff, John, and Jean Comaroff. 1991. *Of Revelation and Revolution: Christianity and Colonialism in South Africa*. Chicago: University of Chicago Press.

Confederation of Indigenous Nationalities of Ecuador. 1994. *Proyecto Político*. Quito: Confederation of Indigenous Nationalities of Ecuador.

———. 1997. *Proyecto Político*. Quito: Confederation of Indigenous Nationalities of Ecuador.

cooke, miriam. 2000. "Multiple Critique: Islamic Feminist Rhetorical Strategies." *Nepantla* 1, no. 1: 91–110.

Cooper, Frederick. 1989. "From Free Labor to Family Allowances: Labor and African Society in Colonial Discourse." *American Ethnologist* 16, no. 4: 745–65.

Cooper, Frederick, and Ann Laura Stoler, eds. 1997. *Tensions of Empire: Colonial Cultures in a Bourgeois World*. Berkeley: University of California Press.

Cooppan, Vilashini. 2000. "W(h)ither Post-colonial Studies? Towards the Transnational Study of Race and Nation." In Laura Chrisman and Benita Parry, eds., *Postcolonial Theory and Criticism*. Cambridge: D. S. Brewer. 1–36.

Coordinación de Gobiernos Locales Alternativos. 2002. "Logros, avances y retos." *Gobiernos Locales Alternativos* 1: 20–24.

Cornejo Polar, Antonio. 1994a. *Escribir en el aire: Ensayo sobre la heterogeneidad sociocultural de las literaturas andinas*. Lima: Editorial Horizonte.

———. 1994b. "Mestizaje, transculturación, heterogeneidad." *Revista de Crítica Literaria* 20, no. 40: 368–71.

———. 1998. "Mestizaje e hibridez: Los riesgos de las metáforas: Apuntes." *Revista de Crítica Literaria Latinoamericana* 24, no. 47: 7–11.

Coronil, Fernando. 1992. "Can Postcoloniality Be Decolonized? Imperial Banality and Postcolonial Power." *Public Culture* 5, no. 1: 89–108.

———. 1994. "Listening to the Subaltern: The Poetics of Neocolonial States." *Poetics Today* 15, no. 4: 645–58.

———. 1995. "Introduction: Transculturation and the Politics of Theory: Countering the Center, Cuban Counterpoint." In Fernando Ortiz, *Cuban Counterpoint: Tobacco and Sugar*. Trans. Harriet de Onís. Durham, N.C.: Duke University Press. ix–lvi.

———. 1996. "Beyond Occidentalism: Toward Nonimperial Geohistorical Categories." *Cultural Anthropology* 11, no. 1 (February): 51–87.

———. 1997. *The Magical State: Nature, Money and Modernity in Venezuela*. Chicago: University of Chicago Press.

——. 1999. "Más allá del occidentalismo: Hacia categorías geohistóricas no imperiales." *Casa de las Américas* 21, no. 214: 21–49.

——. 2000a. "Listening to the Subaltern: Postcolonial Studies and the Neocolonial Poetics of Subaltern States." In Laura Chrisman and Benita Parry, eds., *Postcolonial Theory and Criticism*. Cambridge: D. S. Brewer. 37–56.

——. 2000b. "Naturaleza del pocolonialismo: Del eurocentrismo al globocentrismo." In Edgardo Lander, ed., *El colonialidad del saber: Eurocentrismo y ciencias sociales: Perspectivas latinoamericanas*. Buenos Aires: Consejo Latinoamericano de Ciencias Sociales. 87–111.

——. 2000c. "Towards a Critique of Globalcentrism: Speculations on Capitalism's Nature." *Public Culture* 12, no. 2: 351–74.

——. 2002. "Globalización liberal o imperialismo global? El presente y sus diferencias." Paper presented at the Rethinking Imperialism conference, Universidad Torcuato Di Tella, Italy.

——. 2003. "Globalización liberal o Imperialismo Global: Cinco piezas para armar el rompecabezas del presente." *Temas* 33–34, no. 14: 27.

Cortázar, Julio. 1984. *Nicaragua, tan violentamente dulce*. Barcelona: Muchnik Editores.

Costa, Emilia Viotti da. 1998. *Coroas de glória, lágrimas de sangue*. São Paulo: Companhia das Letras.

Coulthard, G. R. 1962. *Race and Colour in Caribbean Literature*. London: Oxford University Press.

Covarrubias Horozco, Sebastian de. 1611. *Tesoro de la lengva castellana, o española*. Madrid: Por L. Sánchez, impressor del rey n.s.

Cox, Harvey. 1984. *Religion in the Secular City: Toward a Post-Modern Theology*. New York: Simon and Schuster.

Craton, Michael. 1982. *Testing the Chains*. Ithaca, N.Y.: Cornell University Press.

Culler, Jonathan. 1982. *On Deconstruction*. Ithaca, N.Y.: Cornell University Press.

Dario, Ruben. 1998. "El Triunfo de Caliban (1898)." Ed. and notes by Carlos Jáuregui. *Revista Iberoamericana* 64, nos. 184–85: 451–56.

David, Alexandra. 1989. "The Quest for Public Order." Paper presented at the meeting of the Southwestern Historical Association, Fort Worth, Texas. 28–31 March.

Davis, Wade. 1988. *Passage of Darkness: The Ethnobiology of the Haitian Zombi*. Chapel Hill: University of North Carolina Press.

Dayan, Joan. 1993a. "France Reads Haiti: An Interview with Rene Depestre." *Yale French Studies* 83: 136–53.

——. 1993b. "France Reads Haiti: Rene Depestre's *Hadriana dans tous mes rêaves*." *Yale French Studies* 83: 154–75.

——. 1995. *Haiti, History, and the Gods*. Berkeley: University of California Press.

——. 2001. "Legal Slaves and Civil Bodies." *Nepantla* 2, no. 1: 3–39.

Dean, Carolyn, and Dana Leibsohn. 2003. "Hybridity and Its Discontents: Considering Visual Culture in Colonial Spanish America." *Colonial Latin American Review* 12, no. 1 (June): 5–36.

de Certeau, Michel. 1986 [1981]. *Heterologies: Discourse on the Other*. Trans. Brian Massumi. Minneapolis: University of Minnesota Press.

——. 1988. *The Writing of History.* Trans. Tom Conley. New York: Columbia University Press.

de Grandis, Rita. 2000. "Pursuing Hybridity: From the Linguistic to the Symbolic." In Rita de Grandis and Zila Bernd, eds., *Unforeseeable Americas: Questioning Cultural Hybridity in the Americas.* Amsterdam: Rodopi. 208–25.

de la Campa, Román. 1996. "Latinoamérica y sus nuevos cartógrafos: Discurso poscolonial, diásporas intelectuales y miradas fronterizas." *Revista Iberoamericana* 176–77: 697–719.

——. 1999. *Latin Americanism.* Minneapolis: University of Minnesota Press.

——. 2001. "Latin, Latino, American: Split States and Global Imaginaries." *Comparative Literature* 53, no. 4: 373–88.

——. 2003a. "Deconstruction, Cultural Studies and Global Capitalism: Implications for Latin America." In *Critical Latin American and Latino Studies.* Minneapolis: University of Minnesota Press. 154–71.

——. 2003b. "On New American Subjects and Intellectual Models." *Nepantla* 4, no. 2: 235–45.

Deleuze, Gilles. 1983. *Nietzsche and Philosophy.* New York: Columbia University Press.

——. 1991. *Foucault.* Mexico City: Paidos.

Deleuze, Gilles, and Félix Guattari. 1972. *Capitalisme et schizophrénie: L'Anti-Oedipe.* Paris: Minuit.

——. 1986. *Kafka: Toward a Minor Literature.* Minneapolis: University of Minnesota Press.

Delgado Pop, Adela. 2000. "¿Qué es ser mujer indígena a las puertas del nuevo milenio?" In Morna MacLeod and M. Luisa Cabrera, eds., *Identidad: Rostros sin márcara (Reflexiones sobre cosmovisión, género y etnicidad).* Guatemala City: OXFAM. 15–25.

Deloria, Vine, Jr. 1994 [1972]. *God Is Red: A Native View of Religion.* Colorado: Fulcrum.

de Man, Paul. 1983. *Blindness and Insight: Essays in the Rhetoric of Contemporary Criticism.* Minneapolis: University of Minnesota Press.

Deren, Maya. 1970. *Divine Horsemen: The Living Gods of Haiti.* Kingston, N.Y.: McPherson.

Derrida, Jacques. 1964. "Violence et Métaphysique, essai sur la penseé d' Emmanuel Levinas." *Revue de Métaphysique et Morale* 69, nos. 3 and 4: 322–54, 425–43.

——. 1967a. *De la Grammatologie.* Paris: Minuit.

——. 1967b. *L'Ecriture et la Différence.* Paris: Seuil.

——. 1976. *Of Grammatology.* Trans. Gayatri Spivak. Baltimore, Md.: Johns Hopkins University Press.

——. 1977. *Limited, Inc.* Baltimore, Md.: Johns Hopkins University Press.

——. 1978. *Writing and Difference.* Trans. Alan Bass. Chicago: University of Chicago Press.

——. 1980. "The Law of Genre." *Glyph: Textual Studies* 7: 202–32.

——. 1982. *Margins of Philosophy.* Chicago: University of Chicago Press.

——. 1985. "Racism's Last Word." *"Race," Writing and Difference.* Henry Louis Gates Jr., ed. Chicago: University of Chicago Press. 329–38.

——. 1994. *Specters of Marx.* London: Routledge.

——. 1995. *El Lenguaje y las instituciones filosoficas.* Barceolona: Ediciones Paidos.

——. 1998. *Monolingualism of the Other, or, The Prosthesis of Origin.* Trans. Patrick Mensah. Stanford, Calif.: Stanford University Press.

Descartes, René. 1963–67. *Oeuvres philosophiques.* Paris: Editions Alquie.

Deslauriers, Pierre. 2001. "African Magico-Medicine at Home and Abroad: Haitian Religious Traditions in a Neocolonial Setting: The Fiction of Dany Laferriere and Russel Banks." In Jamie S. Scott and Paul Simpson Housley, eds., *Mapping the Sacred: Religion, Geography and Postcolonial Literatures.* Amsterdam: Rodopi. 337–53.

Desmangles, Leslie. 1992. *The Faces of the Gods: Vodou and Roman Catholicism in Haiti.* Chapel Hill: University of North Carolina Press.

Dias, Jorge. 1961. *Os elementos fundamentais da cultura portuguesa.* Lisbon: Junta de Investigação do Ultramar.

Díaz, Alberto Pedro. 1966. "Guanamaca, una comunidad haitiana." *Etnología y folklore* 1 (January–June): 25–39.

Díaz-Quinoñes, Arcadio. 1993. *La Memoria Rota.* Rio Piedras: Ediciones Huracán.

——. 1998. "1898: Hispanismo y Guerra." In Walter L. Bernecker, ed., *1898: Su significado para Centroamerica y el Caribe.* Frankfurt and Madrid: Iberoamericana. 17–35.

——. 2000. *El Arte de Bregar: Ensayos.* San Juan: Ediciones Callejon.

Dietz, James. 1986. *Economic History of Puerto Rico.* Princeton: Princeton University Press.

Dirección Nacional de Educación Intercultural Bilingue del Ecuador. 1994. "Modelo de educación intercultural bilingüe." *Pueblos indígenas y educación* 29–30: 4–142.

Dirlik, Arif. 1994. "The Postcolonial Aura: Third World Criticism in the Age of Global Capitalism." *Critical Inquiry* 20 (winter): 328–56.

Dollimore, Jonathan, and Alan Sinfield, eds. 1985. *Political Shakespeare: New Essays in Cultural Materialism.* Ithaca, N.Y.: Cornell University Press.

Donaldson, Laura E., and Kwok Pui-lan, eds. 2002. *Postcolonialism, Feminism and, Religious Discourse.* New York: Routledge.

Douglas, Kelly Brown. 1993. *The Black Christ.* Maryknoll, N.Y.: Orbis Books.

Drakakis, John, ed. 1988. *Alternative Shakespeares.* London: Routledge.

Dreyfus, Herbert, and Paul Rabinow. 1983. *Michel Foucault: Beyond Structuralism and Hermeneutics.* Chicago: University of Chicago Press.

Duarte, Angela Ixkic. Forthcoming. "Alma López: La doble mirada del género y la etnicidad." Estudios Latinoamericanos, Facultad de Ciencias Políticas, Universidad Nacional Autónoma de México.

Dube, Saurabh, ed. 1999. *Pasados poscoloniales.* Mexico City: El Colegio de Mexico.

Dubois, Claude-Gilbert. 1979. *Le manierisme.* Paris: Presses Universitaires de France.

Duque, Felix, and German Gutierrez, eds. 2001. *Itinerarios de la Razón Crítica: Homenaje a Franz Hinkelammert en sus 70 años.* San José: Editorial Departamento Ecuménico de Investigaciones.

Durán, Diego de. 1984 [ca. 1581]. *Historia de la Nueva España e islas de Tierra Firme.* Ed. María Garibay K. 2 vols. Mexico City: Porrúa.

Durán Casas, Vincente S. J. 1991. "¿De qué ética hablamos? Etica ciudadana como ética del consenso." In *Colombia: Una casa para todos.* Bogotá: Ediciones Antropas. 69–86.

Durand, José. 1976. El Inca Garcilaso, clasico de América. Mexico City: Sep Setentas.

Durkheim, Émile. 1947. The Elementary Forms of the Religious Life: A Study in Religious Sociology. Trans. Joseph Ward Swain. Glencoe, Ill.: Free Press.

Dussel, Enrique. 1965. "Iberoamérica en la Historia Universal." Revista de Occidente 25: 85–95.

———. 1967. Hipótesis para una historia de la iglesia en América Latina. Barcelona: Editorial Estela.

———. 1969. El humanismo semita: Estructuras intencionales radicales del pueblo de Israel y otros semitas. Buenos Aires: Editorial Universitaria de Buenos Aires.

———. 1969–71. El episcopado hispanoamericano: Institución misionera en defensa del indio, 1504–1620. Cuernavaca, Mexico: Centro Intercultural de Documentación.

———. 1972. Historia de la Iglesia en América Latina: Coloniaje y Liberación 1492–1972. Barcelona: Editorial Nova Terra.

———. 1973. Para una ética de la liberación latinoamericana. Buenos Aires: Siglo Veintiuno Argentina Editores.

———. 1974a [1969]. Para una de-strucción de la historia de la Etica. Mendoza, Argentina: Ser y Tiempo.

———. 1974b. El dualismo en la antropología de la Cristianidad: Desde el origen del cristianismo hasta antes de la conquista de América. Buenos Aires: Editorial Guadalupe.

———. 1975a. El humanismo helénico. Buenos Aires: Editorial Universitaria de Buenos Aires.

———. 1975b. Liberación Latinoamericana y Emmanuel Levinas. Buenos Aires: Editorial Bonum.

———. 1976. History and the Theology of Liberation: A Latin American perspective. New York: Orbis Books.

———. 1977a. Filosofía de la liberación. Mexico City: Editorial Edicol.

———. 1977b. Caminos de liberación latinoamericana I: Interpretación histórico-teológica de nuestro continente latinoamericano. Buenos Aires: Latinoamérica Libros.

———. 1978. Desintegración de la cristiandad colonial y liberación: Perspectiva latinoamericana. Salamanca, Spain: Ediciones Sígueme.

———. 1980. La pedagógica latinoamericana. Bogotá: Editorial Nueva América.

———. 1981. Historia general de la Iglesia en América Latina. Vol 1. Salamanca, Spain: Ediciones Sígueme.

———. 1983 [1975]. Introducción a la Filosofía de la Liberación. 2d ed. Bogotá: Editorial Nueva América.

———. 1985a. Caminhos de libertação latino-americana. Vol. 1 of Interpretação histórico-teológica. São Paulo: Paulinas.

———. 1985b. La Producción téorica de Marx. Mexico City: Siglo XXI.

———. 1988. Hacia un Marx desconocido: Un comentario de los manuscritos del 61–63. Ixtapalpa, Mexico: Universidad Autónoma Metropolitana.

———. 1990a. "Marx's Economic Manuscripts of 1861–63 and the 'Concept' of Dependency." Latin American Perspectives 17, no. 1: 62–101.

———. 1990b. El último Marx (1863–1882) y la liberación latinoamericana. Iztapalapa, Mexico: Siglo Veintiuno Editores.

———. 1992. 1492: El encubrimiento del otro: El origen del mito de lamodernidad: Conferencias de Frankfurt 1992. Bogotá: Ediciones Antropos.

———. 1993. *Von der Erfindung Amerikas zur Entdeckung des Anderen: Ein Projekt der Transmoderne.* Düsseldorf: Patmos Verlag.

———, ed. 1994a. *Debate en torno a la ética del discurso de Apel: Diálogo filosófico Norte-Sur desde América Latina.* Iztapalapa, Mexico: Siglo Veintiuno Editores.

———. 1994b [1987]. *Historia de la Filosofía Latinoamericana y Filosofía de la Liberación.* Bogotá: Editorial Nueva América.

———. 1994c. "Una década argentina (1966–1976) y el origen de la Filosofía de la Liberación." In *Historia de la filosofía y filosofía de la liberación.* Bogotá: Editorial Nueva América. 55–96.

———. 1995a. "Eurocentrism and Modernity (Introduction to the Frankfurt Lectures)." In John Beverley, Michael Aronna, and José Oviedo, eds., *The Postmodernism Debate in Latin America.* Durham, N.C.: Duke University Press. 65–76.

———. 1995b. *Introducción a la filosofía de la liberación.* Bogotá: Editorial Nueva América.

———. 1995c. *The Invention of the Americas: Eclipse of the "Other" and the Myth of Modernity.* Trans. Michael Barber. New York: Continuum.

———. 1996a [1977]. *Filosofía de la liberación.* Bogotá: Editorial Nueva América.

———. 1996b. *The Underside of Modernity: Apel, Ricoeur, Rorty, Taylor and the Philosophy of Liberation.* Trans. and ed. Eduardo Mendieta. New Jersey: Humanities Press.

———. 1997. *Oito ensaios sobre cultura latino-americana e libertação.* São Paulo: Paulinas.

———. 1998a. "Beyond Eurocentrism: The World-System and the Limits of Modernity." Trans. Eduardo Mendieta. In Fredric Jameson and Masao Miyoshi, eds., *The Cultures of Globalization.* Durham, N.C.: Duke University Press. 3–31.

———. 1998b. "En busqueda del sentido (Origen y desarrollo de una Filosofia de la Liberación)." *Anthropos* 180: 14–19.

———. 1998c. *Etica de la liberación en la edad de la globalización y de la exclusión.* Madrid: Editorial Trotta.

———. 1999a. "Más allá del eurocentrismo: El sistema mundo y los límtes de la modernidad." In Santiago Castro-Gómez, Oscar Guardiola-Rivera, and Carmen Millán de Benavides, eds., *Pensar (en) los intersticios: Teoría y práctica de la crítica poscolonial.* Bogotá: Centro Editorial Javierano. 147–62.

———. 1999b. *Posmodernidad y transmodernidad: Diálogos con la filosofía de Gianni Vattimo.* Mexico City: Universidad Iberoamericana Plantel Golfo Centro.

———. 2000a. "Europa, modernidad y eurocentrismo." In Edgardo Lander, ed., *La colonialidad del saber: Eurocentrismo y ciencias sociales: Perspectivas latinoamericanas.* Buenos Aires: Consejo Latinoamericano de Ciencias Sociales/UNESCO. 41–54.

———. 2000b. "Europe, Modernity, and Eurocentrism." *Nepantla* 1, no. 3: 465–78.

———. 2001a. "Eurocentrismo y modernidad: Introducción a las lecturas de Frankfurt." In Walter Mignolo, ed., *Capitalismo y geopolítica del conocimiento: El eurocentrismo y la filosofía de la liberación en el debate intelectual contemporáneo.* Buenos Aires: Ediciones del Signo/Duke University. 57–70.

———. 2001b. *Hacia una Filosofía Política Crítica.* Bilbao, Spain: Editorial Desclée de Drouwer.

———. 2001c. *Towards an Unknown Marx: A Commentary on the Manuscripts of 1861–1863.* London: Routledge.

———. 2002. "World System and 'Trans'-Modernity." *Nepantla* 3, no. 2: 221–44.

Duviols, Pierre. 1983. "Guamán Poma, historiador del Perú antiguo: Una nueva pista." *Revista Andina* 1: 103–15.

Eakin, Marshall C. 1998. *Brazil: The Once and Future Country*. New York: St. Martin's Press.

Edmonson, Munro S. 1971. *The Book of Counsel: The Popol vuh of the Quiché Maya of Guatemala*. New Orleans: Tulane University Middle American Research Institute.

——. 1988. *The Book of the Year*. Salt Lake City: University of Utah Press.

Elliot, J. H. 1963. *Imperial Spain, 1469–1716*. New York: New American Library.

Eltit, Damiela. 1989. *El padre mío*. Santiago, Chile: Francisco Zegers.

Emery, Amy Fass. 1996. *The Anthropological Imagination in Latin American Literature*. Columbia: University of Missouri Press.

Englund, Harri, and James Leach. 2000. "Ethnography and the Meta-Narratives of Modernity." *Current Anthropology* 41, no. 2: 225–48.

Ennes, António. 1946 [1873]. *Moçambique: Relatório apresentado ao governo*. Lisbon: Imprensa Nacional.

Eribon, Didier. 1989. *Michel Foucault: 1926–1984*. Paris: Flammarion.

Escobar, Arturo. 1995. *Encountering Development: The Making and Unmaking of the Third World*. Princeton: Princeton University Press.

——. 2000. "El lugar de la naturaleza y la naturaleza del lugar ¿Globalización o postdesarrollo?" In Edgardo Lander, ed., *La colonialidad del saber: Eurocentrismo y ciencias sociales: Perspectivas latinoamericanas*. Buenos Aires: Consejo Latinoamericano de Ciencias Sociales. 113–44.

Esquit Choy, Alberto, and Victor Gálvez Borrel. 1997. *The Mayan Movement Today: Issues of Indigenous Culture and Development in Guatemala*. Guatemala: Facultad Latinoamericana de Ciencias Sociales.

Esteva, Gustavo, and Madhu Suri Prakash. 1998. *Grassroots Post-modernism: Remaking the Soil of Cultures*. Zed Press, London.

Etienne Balibar. 1997. *La crainte des masses: Politique et philosophie avant et après Marx*. Paris: Galilée.

Everdell, William R. 1997. *The First Moderns*. Chicago: University of Chicago Press.

Eze, Chukwudi Emmanuel. 1997. "The Color of Reason: The Idea of 'Race' in Kant's Anthropology." In Chukwudi Emmanuel Eze, ed., *Postcolonial African Philosophy*. New York: Blackwell. 103–40.

Fabian, Johannes. 1983. *Time and the Other*. New York: Columbia University Press.

——. 1993. "Keep Listening: Ethnography and Reading." In Jonathan Boyarin, ed., *Ethnography of Reading*. Berkeley: University of California Press. 80–98.

Falla, Ricardo. 1999. *Lo peruano en la obra de Pedro de Peralta y Barnuevo: El caso de la Lima fundada*. Lima: Universidad Nacional Mayor de San Marcos.

Fals-Borda, Orlando. 1971. *Ciencia propia y colonialismo intelectual: Los nuevos rumbos*. Bogotá: C. Valencia Editores.

Fanon, Frantz. 1961. *Les damnés de la terre*. Paris: Maspero.

——. 1967 [1952]. *Black Skins, White Masks*. Trans. Charles Lam Markmann. New York: Grove Press.

——. 1991. *The Wretched of the Earth*. Trans. Constance Farrington. New York: Grove Press.

Federici, Silvia, ed. 1995. *Enduring Western Civilization: The Construction of the Concept of Western Civilization and Its "Others."* New York: Praeger.

Feld, Steven. 1995. "From Schizophonia to Schismogenesis: The Discourses and Practices of World Music and World Beat." In George Marcus and Fred Myers, eds., *The Traffic in Culture.* Los Angeles: University of California Press. 96–126.

Feliciano, J. F., and V. H. Nicolau, eds. 1998. *Memórias de Sofala por João Julião da Silva, Herculano da Silva e Guilherme Ezequiel da Silva.* Lisbon: Comissão Nacional para os Descobrimentos Portugueses.

Fernández de Córdoba, Francisco. 1976 [1620]. "Prólogo al lector" (fechado el 8-9-1620). In Alonso Ramos Gavilán, *Historia de Nuestra Señora de Copacabana.* 2d ed. La Paz: Academia Boliviana de la Historia. 7–9.

Fernández Olmos, Margarite, and Lizabeth Paravisini-Gebert, eds. *Sacred Possessions: Voudou, Santería, Obeah, and the Caribbean.* New Brunswick, N.J.: Rutgers University Press, 1997.

Fernández Retamar, Roberto. 1973. *Calibán.* Montevideo: Aquí Testimonio.

——. 1976. "Nuestra América y Occidente." *Casa de las Américas* 16, no. 98: 36–57.

——. 1989a [1971]. "Caliban: Notes towards a Discussion of Culture in Our America." In *Caliban and Other Essays.* Trans. Edward Baker. Foreword by Fredric Jameson. Minneapolis: University of Minnesota Press. 3–45.

——. 1989b. *Caliban and Other Essays.* Trans. by Edward Baker. Foreword by Fredric Jameson. Minneapolis: University of Minnesota Press.

——. 1989c [1986]. "Caliban Revisited." In *Caliban and Other Essays.* Trans. by Edward Baker. Foreword by Fredric Jameson. Minneapolis: University of Minnesota Press. 46–55.

——. 1993a. "Adiós a Calibán." *Casa de las Américas* 33, no. 191: 116–22.

——. 1993b. "Calibán, quinientos años más tarde." *Nuevo Texto Crítico* 11: 223–44.

——. 1996. "Pensamiento de Nuestra América: autorreflexiones y propuestas." *Casa de las Américas* 37, no. 204: 41–56.

——. 2000. *Todo Calibán.* Havana: Letras cubanas.

Ferrer, Ada. 1999. *Insurgent Cuba: Race, Nation, and Revolution, 1868–1898.* Chapel Hill: University of North Carolina Press.

Ferro, Marc. 1996. *História das colonizações.* Lisbon: Estampa.

Fick, Carolyn. 1990. *The Making of Haiti.* Knoxville: University of Tennessee Press.

Fiddian, Robin, ed. 1988. *Postcolonial Perspectives on the Cultures of Latin America and Lusophone Africa.* Liverpool: Liverpool University Press.

Flores, Juan. 1992. *Divided Borders: Essays on Puerto Rican Identity.* Texas: Arte Público Press.

Flores Galindo, Alberto. 1987. *Buscando un Inca: Identidad y utopía en los andes.* Lima: Instituto de Apoyo Agrario.

Flórez, Juliana. 2003. "Notas sobre teoría feminista y modernidad/colonialidad." Unpublished manuscript.

Follari, Roberto. 1991. *Modernidad y postmodernidad: Una óptica desde América Latina.* Buenos Aires: Rei.

Fontanella de Weinberg, María Beatriz. 1993. *El español de América.* 2d ed. Madrid: Editorial MAPFRE.

Fortuna, Carlos. 1993. *O Fio da meada: O algodão de Moçambique, Portugal e a economia-mundo (1860–1960)*. Porto: Afrontamento.

Foucault, Michel. 1966. *Les Mots et les Choses*. Paris: Gallimard.

——. 1969. *L'Archeologie du savoir*. Paris: Gallimard.

——. 1970. *The Order of Things*. New York: Random House.

——. 1971. *The Archaeology of Knowledge*. Trans. A. M. Sheridan Smith. New York: Pantheon.

——. 1972. *Histoire de la folie 'a l'age Classique*. Paris: Gallimard.

——. 1975. *Surveiller et Punir*. Paris: Gallimard.

——. 1976. *La Volonté de Savoir*. Paris: Gallimard.

——. 1978 [1976]. *The History of Sexuality*. Trans. Robert Hurley. New York: Pantheon.

——. 1979. *Discipline and Punish: The Birth of the Prison*. Trans. A. Sheridan. New York: Vintage.

——. 1980. *Power/Knowledge*. Trans. Colin Gordon et al. New York: Pantheon.

——. 1982. *I, Pierre Rivière, Having Slaughtered My Mother, My Sister, and My Brother: A Case of Parricide in the 19th Century*. Lincoln: University of Nebraska Press.

——. 1984. *Le souci de soi*. Paris: Gallimard.

——. 1986. *El uso de los placeres*. Mexico City: Siglo XXI.

——. 1991a. *Enfermedad mental y personalidad*. Barcelona: Paidós.

——. 1991b. "Governmentality." In Graham Burchell, Colin Gordon, and Peter Miller, eds., *The Foucault Effect: Studies in Governmentality*. Chicago: University of Chicago Press. 87–104.

——. 2003 [1976]. *"Society Must Be Defended": Lectures at the College de France, 1975–1976*. Trans. David Macey. New York: Picador.

Fox, Richard, ed. 1991. *Recapturing Anthropology*. Santa Fe, N.M.: School of American Research.

Frank, Andre Gunder. 1969a [1967]. *Capitalism and Underdevelopment in Latin America*. Rev. and enlarged ed. New York: Monthly Review Press.

——. 1969b. *Latin America: Underdevelopment or Revolution*. New York: Monthly Review Press.

——. 1970. *Capitalismo y subdesarrollo en América Latina*. Mexico City: Siglo XXI.

——. 1988. *ReOrient: Global Economy in the Asian Age*. Berkeley: University of California Press.

Frank, Thomas. 1997. *The Conquest of Cool: Business Culture, Counterculture, and the Rise of Hip Consumerism*. Chicago: University of Chicago Press.

Frank, Thomas, and Matt Weiland, eds. 1997. *Commodify Your Dissent*. New York: W. W. Norton.

Frank, Waldo David. 1919. *Our America*. New York: Boni and Liveright.

Frente Sandinista de Liberación Nacional, Dirección Nacional. 1981. *Habla la dirección de la vanguardia*. Managua, Nicaragua: Departamento de Propaganda y Educación Política del FSLN.

Freud, Sigmund. 1953–74. *The Standard Edition of the Psychological Works of Sigmund Freud*. Trans. from the German under the general editorship of James Strachey, in collaboration with Anna Freud, assisted by Alix Strachey and Alan Tyson. 24 vols. London: Hogarth Press and the Institute of Psycho-Analysis.

Freyermuth, Graciela, and Mariana Fernández. 1995. "Migration, Organization and Identity: The Case of a Women's Group from San Cristóbal las Casas." *Signs* 20, no. 4: 970–95.

Freyre, Gilberto. 1947. *Interpretação do Brasil: Aspectos da formação social brasileira com o processo de amalgamento de raças e culturas*. Rio de Janeiro: Livraria José Olympio.

———. 1966 [1946]. *The Masters and the Slaves: A Study in the Development of Brazilian Civilization*. Trans. Samuel Putnam. New York: Knopf.

———. 1992 [1933]. *Casa-grande e senzala*. Rio de Janeiro: Editora Record.

———. n.d. *O mundo que o português criou*. Lisbon: Livros do Brasil.

Fukuyama, Francis. 1989. "The End of History." *National Interest* 16: 3–18.

Furtado, Celso. 1971. *La economía latinoamericana: Formación histórica y problemas contemporáneos*. Mexico City: Siglo XXI.

Furtado, Filipe. 1997. "Portugal em histórias da Inglaterra." *Revista de Estudos Anglo-Portugueses* 6: 71–81.

Gabara, Esther. 2001. "The Ethos of Modernism: Photography and Literature in Brazil and Mexico, 1920–1940." Ph.D. diss., Stanford University.

Galarza, Joaquín. 1966. "Glyphes et attributs chrétiens dans les manuscrits pictographiques mexicains du xvie siècle: Le Codex Mexicanus 23–24." *Journal de la Société des Américanistes* 55: 7–42.

Galeano, Eduardo. 1973 [1971]. *Open Veins of Latin America*. Trans. Cedric Belfrage. New York: Monthly Review Press.

Galván, Sergia. 1995. "El mundo étnico-racial dentro del feminismo latinoamericano." Special issue, *Fempress*, no. 19: 33–36.

Gandhi, Leela. 1998. *Postcolonial Theory: A Critical Introduction*. New York: Columbia University Press.

Gaonkar, Dilip P., ed. 2001. *Alternative Modernities*. Durham, N.C.: Duke University Press.

García Canclini, Néstor. 1989. *Culturas híbridas: Estrategias para entrar y salir de la Modernidad*. Mexico City: Grijalbo.

———. 1992 [1989]. *Culturas híbridas: Estrategias para entrar y salir de la modernidad*. Buenos Aires: Sudamericana.

———. 2003. *Latinoamericanos buscando lugar en este siglo*. Buenos Aires: Paidos.

García Márquez, Gabriel. 1979. "Fantasía y creación artística en America Latina y el Caribe." *Texto crítico* 14: 3–8.

García Mora, Carlos, ed. 1987–88. *La antropología en México*. 12 vols. Mexico City: Instituto Nacional de Antropología e Historia.

Garza Caligaris, Anna María, and Sonia Toledo. Forthcoming. "Campesinos, indígenas and mujeres en Chiapas: Movimientos sociales en las décadas de los setenta y ochenta." In Maya Lorena Pérez, ed., *Chiapas desde las Mujeres*. Mexico City: Instituto Nacional de Antropología e Historia.

Geertz, Clifford. 1973. *The Interpretation of Cultures*. New York: Basic Books.

Geggus, David, ed. 2001. *The Impact of the Haitian Revolution in the Atlantic World*. Columbia: University of South Carolina Press.

Genovese, Eugene. 1979. *From Rebellion to Revolution*. New York: Vintage.

Gera, Lucio, Enrique Dussel, and Julio Arch. 1969. *Contexto de la Iglesia argentina:*

Informe sobre diversos aspectos de la situación argentina. Buenos Aires: Facultad de Teología de la Pontificia Universidad Católica Argentina.

Gibson, Charles. 1952. *Tlaxcala in the Sixteenth Century.* New Haven, Conn.: Yale University Press.

——. 1964. *The Aztecs under Spanish rule.* Stanford, Calif.: Stanford University Press.

Gibson-Graham, J. K. 1996. *The End of Capitalism (As We Knew It).* Oxford: Blackwell.

——. 2003. "Politics of Empire, Politics of Place." Unpublished manuscript.

Giddens, Anthony. 1990. *The Consequences of Modernity.* Stanford, Calif.: Stanford University Press.

Gilbert, Alan. 1997. *La Ciudad Latinoamericana.* Mexico City: Siglo XXI.

Gilroy, Paul. 1993. *The Black Atlantic: Modernity and Double Consciousness.* Cambridge: Cambridge University Press.

——. 2000. *Against Race: Imagining Political Culture beyond the Color Line.* Cambridge, Mass.: Harvard University Press.

Gobineau, Arthur de. 1853–57. *Essais sur l'inégalité des races humaines.* Paris: P. Belfond.

Godleskwa, Anne, and Neil Smith, eds. 1994. *Geography and Empire.* Cambridge: Blackwell.

Goldberg, Jonathan. 1982. "The Politics of Renaissance Literature: A Review Essay" *English Literary History* 49: 514–42.

——. 1983. *James I and the Politics of Literature: Johnson, Shakespeare, Donne, and Their Contemporaries.* Baltimore, Md.: Johns Hopkins University Press.

Goldberg, Theo, and Ato Quayson, eds. 2002. *Relocating Postcolonialism.* Oxford: Blackwell.

Gomes, Flávio. 1995. *Histórias de quilombolas.* Rio de Janeiro: Arquivo Nacional.

Gómez-Peña, Guillermo. 1988. "Documented/Undocumented." In R. Simonson and S. Walker, eds., *Multicultural Literacy.* Saint Paul, Minn.: Graywolf. 127–34.

——. 1996. *The New World Border.* San Francisco: City Lights.

González, Rodolfo (Corky). 2001. "Yo soy Joaquín/I am Joaquín: An Epic Poem." In *A Message to Aztlán.* Houston: Arte Público Press. 2–31.

González Casanova, Pablo. 1965a. *La democracia en México.* Mexico City: Ediciones Era.

——. 1965b. "Internal Colonialism and National Development." *Studies in Comparative International Development* 1, no. 4: 27–37.

——. 1970. "El Colonialismo Interno." In *Sociología de la explotación.* Mexico City: Siglo XXI. 221–50.

González Echevarría, Roberto. 1974. "Isla a su vuelo fugitiva: Carpentier y el realismo mágico." *Revista Iberoamericana* 40, no. 86 (January–March): 9–64.

——. 1985. Prologue to Antonio Benítez Rojo, *Estatuas sepultadas y otros relatos.* Hanover: Ediciones del Norte. vii–xxi.

——. 1990a. *Alejo Carpentier: The Pilgrim at Home.* Austin: University of Texas Press.

——. 1990b. *Myth and Archive: A Theory of Latin American Narrative.* Cambridge: Cambridge University Press.

González Stephan, Beatriz, ed. 1996. *Cultura y tercer mundo.* 2 vols. Caracas: Nueva Sociedad.

——. 2003. "On Citizenship: The Grammatology of the Body Politic." In Eduardo Mendieta, ed., *Latin American Philosophy: Currents, Issues, Debates.* Bloomington: Indiana University Press. 188–206.

González Vales, Luis E., ed. 1997. *1898: Enfoques y Perspectivas*. San Juan: Academia Puertorriquena de la Historia.

Goodman, Nelson. 1978. *Ways of Worldmaking*. Indianapolis: Hackett.

Goody, Jack. 1977. *The Domestication of the Savage Mind*. Cambridge: Cambridge University Press.

Gordon, Lewis R. 1995. *Fanon and the Crisis of European Man: An Essay on Philosophy and the Human Sciences*. New York: Routledge.

Gramsci, Antonio. 1975. *Quaderni del Carcere*. Vol. 1. Milan: Einaudi.

Greenblatt, Stephen. 1980. *Renaissance Self-Fashioning: From More to Shakespeare*. Chicago: University of Chicago Press.

———. 1982. *Power and the Power of Forms in the Renaissance*. Norman: University of Oklahoma Press.

———. 1988. "Martial Law in the Land of Cockaigne." In *Shakespearean Negotiations*. Berkeley: University of California Press. 129–98.

———. 1990a. "Culture." In Frank Lentricchia and Thomas McLaughlin, eds., *Critical Terms for Literary Study*. Chicago: University of Chicago Press. 225–32.

———. 1990b [1976]. "Learning to Curse: Aspects of Linguistic Colonialism in the Sixteenth Century." In *Learning to Curse: Essays in Early Modern Culture*. New York: Routledge. 16–39.

——— 1991. *Marvelous Possessions: The Wonder of the New World*. Chicago: University of Chicaco Press.

Greenblatt, Stephen J., and Giles Gunn, eds. 1992. *Redrawing the Boundaries: The Transformation of English and American Literary Studies*. New York: Modern Language Association of America.

Griffiths, Trevor. 1983. "This Island's Mine: Caliban and Colonialism." *Yearbook of English Studies* 13: 159–80.

Grijalva, Juan de. 1985 [1624]. *Crónica de la Orden de N. P. S. Agustín en las provincias de la Nueva España*. Mexico City: Porrúa.

Grinberg, Keila. 1994. *Liberata, a lei da ambigüidade*. Rio de Janeiro: Relume Dumará.

Grosfoguel, Ramón. 1997. "A TimeSpace Perspective on Development: Recasting Latin American Debates." *Review* 20, nos. 3–4: 465–540.

———. 2000. "Developmentalism, Modernity and Dependency Theory in Latin America." *Nepantla* 1, no. 2: 347–74.

———, ed. 2002. "Eurocentrism, Border Thinking and Coloniality of Power in the Modern/Colonial World-System." Dossier published by *Review* 20, no. 5: 3.

Grossberg, Lawrence. 1996. "The Space of Culture, the Power of Space." In Iain Chambers and Lidia Curti, eds., *The Post-colonial Question*. London: Routledge. 169–88.

Grupo de Estudios Subalternos Latinoamericanos. 1998. "Declaración de fundación del Grupo de Estudios Subalternos Latinoamericanos." In Santiago Castro-Gómez and Eduardo Mendieta, eds., *Teorías sin disciplina: Latinoamericanismo, poscolonialidad y globalización en debate*. Mexico City: Miguel Ángel Porrúa. 84–100.

Gruzinski, Serge. 1988. *La colonisation de l'imaginaire: Sociétés indigènes et occidentalisation dans le Mexique espagnol, XVI–XVIII*. Paris: Gallimard.

———. 1993. *The Conquest of Mexico: The Incorporation of Indian Societies into the Western World, 16th–18th Centuries*. Trans. Eileen Corrigan. Cambridge: Polity.

——. 2001. *La Pensée metisse*. Paris: Fayard.

——. 2002 [1999]. *The Mestizo Mind*. Trans. Deke Dusinberre. London: Routledge.

Guardino, Peter F. 1996. *Peasants, Politics, and the Formation of Mexico's National State: Guerrero, 1800–1857*. Stanford, Calif.: Stanford University Press.

Guerrero, Andrés. 1997. "Ciudadanía, frontera étnica y compulsión binaria." *Iconos* 4: 106–18.

Gugelberger, Georg M., ed. 1996. *The Real Thing: Testimonial Discourse and Latin America*. Durham, N.C.: Duke University Press.

Guha, Ranajit. 1981. *A Rule of Property for Bengal*. Delhi: Orient Longman.

——, ed. 1982–89. *Subaltern Studies: Writings on South Asian History and Society*. 6 vols. Delhi: Oxford University Press.

——. 1983. *Elementary Aspects of Peasant Insurgency in Colonial India*. Delhi: Oxford.

——. 1988a. *An Indian Historiography of India: A Nineteenth-century Agenda and Its Implications*. Calcutta: K. P. Bagchi, Centre for Studies in Social Sciences.

——. 1988b. "On Some Aspects of the Historiography of Colonial India." In Ranajit Guha and Gayatri Chakravorty Spivak, eds., *Selected Subaltern Studies*. Delhi: Oxford University Press. 37–44.

——. 1989. "Dominance without Hegemony and Its Historiography." In Ranajit Guha, ed., *Subaltern Studies: Writings on South Asian History and Society*. Delhi: Oxford University Press. 6:210–309.

——. 1997a. *Dominance without Hegemony: History and Power in Colonial India*. Cambridge, Mass.: Harvard University Press.

——. 1997b. "An Indian Historiography of India: Hegemonic Implications of a Nineteenth-Century Agenda." In *Dominance without Hegemony: History and Power in Colonial India*. Cambridge, Mass.: Harvard University Press. 152–212.

——, ed. 1997c. *A Subaltern Studies Reader, 1986–1995*. Minneapolis: University of Minnesota Press.

——. 2002. *History at the Limit of World-History*. New York: Columbia University Press.

Guha, Ranajit, and Gayatri Chakravorti Spivak, eds. 1988. *Selected Subaltern Studies*. New York: Oxford University Press.

Guillén, Nicolás. 1972. *Man-making Words: Selected Poems*. Trans. Roberto Márquez and David Arthur McMurray. Amherst: University of Massachusetts Press.

Guimerá, Agustín., ed. 1996. *El reformismo borbónico*. Madrid: Alianza Editorial.

Gupta, Akhil. 1998. *Postcolonial Developments: Agriculture in the Making of Modern India*. Durham, N.C.: Duke University Press

Gutiérrez, Gustavo. 1971. *Teologia de la liberación: Perspectivas*. Lima: CEP.

——. 1986. *La force historique des pauvres*. Paris: Cerf.

Habermas, Jürgen. 1973. *Legitimation Crisis*. Boston: Beacon.

——. 1984–87. *The Theory of Communicative Action*. 2 vols. Trans. Thomas McCarthy. Boston: Beacon.

——. 1987. *The Philosophical Discourse of Modernity: Twelve Lectures*. Trans. Frederick Lawrence. Cambridge, Mass.: MIT Press.

——. 1996. *Between Facts and Norms: Contributions to a Discourse Theory of Law and Democracy*. Trans. William Rehg. 2 vols. Cambridge, Mass.: MIT Press.

——. 1998. *The Inclusion of the Other: Studies in Political Theory*. Ed. Ciaran Cronin and Pablo De Greiff. Cambridge, Mass.: MIT Press.

Hall, Stuart. 1996a [1989]. "New Ethnicities." In David Morley et al., eds., *Stuart Hall: Critical Dialogues in Cultural Studies*. London: Routledge. 441–49.

———. 1996b. *Race: The Floating Signifier*. Dir. Sut Jhally. Northampton: Media Education Foundation.

———. 1996c. "When Was 'the Post-colonial'? Thinking at the Limit." In Ian Chambers and Lidia Curti, eds., *The Post-colonial Question: Common Skies, Divided Horizons*. New York: Routledge. 242–59.

Hallward, Peter. 2001. *Absolutely Postcolonial*. Manchester, U.K.: Manchester University Press.

Halperin, David. 1995. *Saint Foucault: Toward a Gay Hagiography*. New York: Oxford University Press.

Halperin Donghi, Tulio. 1993. *The Contemporary History of Latin America*. Trans. John Charles Chasteen. Durham, N.C.: Duke University Press.

Hanchard, Michael. 1994. *Orpheus and Power: The Movimento Negro of Rio de Janeiro and São Paulo, Brazil, 1945–1988*. Princeton: Princeton University Press.

Handley, George B. 2000. *Postslavery Literatures in the Americas: Family Portraits in Black and White*. Charlottesville: University Press of Virginia.

Haraway, Donna. 1990. "A Manifesto for Cyborgs: Science, Technology and Socialist Feminism in the 1980s." In L. Nicholson, ed., *Feminism/Posmodernism*. New York: Routledge. 190–234.

———. 1991. "Situated Knowledges: The Science Question in Feminism and the Privilege of Partial Perspective." In *Simians, Cyborgs, and Women: The Reinvention of Nature*. New York: Routledge. 183–201.

Harcourt, Wendy, and Arturo Escobar. 2002. "Lead Article: Women and the Politics of Place." *Development* 45, no. 2: 7–14.

Hardt, Michael, and Antonio Negri. 2000. *Empire*. Cambridge, Mass.: Harvard University Press.

Haring, Clarence W. 1947. *The Spanish Empire in America*. New York: Harcourt, Brace, and World.

Harney, R. T. 1990. " 'Portygees and Other Caucasians': Portugueses Migrants and the Racialism of the English-Speaking World." In D. Higgs, ed., *Portuguese Migration in Global Perspective*. Toronto: Multicultural History Society of Ontario. 113–35.

Harrison, Faye. 1991. *Decolonizing Anthropology*. Washington: American Anthropology Association Monograph.

Hart, William D. 2000. *Edward Said and the Religious Effects of Culture*. Cambridge: Cambridge University Press.

Harvey, David. 1989. *The Condition of Postmodernity*. Oxford: Blackwell.

———. 2000. "The Geography of the Manifesto." In *Spaces of Hope*. Berkeley: University of California Press. 21–40.

Harvey, Herbert R., and Barbara Williams. 1986. "Decipherment of Some Implications of Aztec Numerical Glyphs." In Michael Closs, ed., *Native American Mathematics*. Austin: University of Texas Press. 237–60.

Harvey, Neil. 1998. *The Chiapas Rebellion: The Struggle for Land and Democracy*. Durham, N.C.: Duke University Press.

Hatem, Mervat. 1998. "Aísha Taymur's Tears and the Critique of Modernist and Feminist Discourses on Nineteenth Century Egypt." In Lila Abu-Lughod, ed.,

Remaking Women: Feminism and Modernity in the Middle East. Princeton: Princeton University Press. 19–43.

Haskett, Robert. 1991. *Indigenous Rulers: An Ethnohistory of Town Government in Colonial Cuernavaca.* Albuquerque: University of New Mexico Press.

Hayden, Tom. 2001. *The Zapatista Reader.* New York: Thunder's Mouth Press/Nation Books.

Hedley, Jane. 1996. "Nepantilist Poetics: Narrative and Cultural Identity in the Mixed Language Writings of Irena Klepfisz and Gloria Anzaldúa." *Narrative* 4, no. 1: 36–54.

Hegel, Georg Wilhelm Friedrich. 1956 [1835]. *The Philosophy of History.* Trans. J. Sibree. New York: Dover.

——. 1970. *Vorlesungen über die Philosophie der Geschichte.* Ed. Eva Moldenhauer and Karl Markus Michel. Frankfurt am Main: Suhrkamp.

——. 1997. "Geographical Basis of World History." In Emmanuel Chukwudi Eze, ed., *Race and the Enlightenment: A Reader.* Oxford: Blackwell. 109–53.

Heidegger, Martin. 1966. *Einführung in die Metaphysik.* Tübingen, Germany: Max Niemeyer.

——. 1977. "The Age of the World Picture." In *The Question Concerning Technology.* New York: Harper and Row. 115–54.

——. 1981 [1944]. *Saggi sulla poesia di Hölderlin* [Heimkunft/An die Verwandten]. Milan: Adelphi. 10–31.

Helg, Aline. 1995. *Our Rightful Share: The Afro-Cuban Struggle for Equality, 1886–1912.* Chapel Hill: University of North Carolina Press.

Henrique Dias Tavares, Luís. 1975. *História da sedição intentada na Bahia em 1798 ("a conspiração dos alfaiates").* São Paulo: Livraria Pioneira Editora.

Herlinghaus, Hermann, and Monika Walter. 1994. *Posmodernidad en la periferia: Enfoques latinoamericanos de la nueva teoría cultural.* Berlin: Langer Verlag.

Hernández Castillo, Rosalva Aída. 2001a. "Entre el etnocentrismo feminista y el esencialismo étnico: Las mujeres indígenas y sus demandas de género." *Debate Feminista* 12, no. 24 (October): 206–30.

——. 2001b. *La Otra Frontera: Identidades Múltiples en el Chiapas Poscolonial.* Mexico City: Porrúa/CIESAS.

——. 2002. "Indigenous Law and Identity Politics in México: Indigenous Men's and Women's Perspective for a Multicultural Nation." *Political and Legal Anthropology Review* 25, no. 1: 90–110.

——. 2004. "Feminismos y posmodernismos: Diálogos, coincidencias y resistencias." *Desacatos Journal of Anthropological Research.* 107–21.

Hernández Castillo, Rosalva Aída, and Héctor Ortíz Elizondo. 1996. "Constitutional Amendments and New Imaginings of the Nation: Legal Anthropology and Gendered Perspectives on Multicultural Mexico." *Political and Legal Anthropology Review* 19, no. 1: 59–69.

Herrera Flores, Joaquin, ed. 2000. *El vuelo de anteo: derechos humanos y crítica de la razón liberal.* Bilbao, Spain: Editorial Desclée de Brouwer.

Hervieu-Léger, Danièle, and Francoise Champion. 1986. *Vers un nouveau christianisme? Introduction à la sociologie du christianisme occidental.* Paris: Cerf.

Herzfeld, Michael. 1987. *Anthropology through the Looking Glass: Critical Ethnography in the Margins of Europe*. Cambridge: Cambridge University Press.

Heusch, Luc de. 1989. "Kongo in Haiti: A New Approach to Religious Syncretism." *Man* 24, no. 2 (June): 290–303.

Hilferding, Rudolf. 1981. *Finance Capital*. Trans. Morris Watnick and Sam Gordon. London: Routledge and Kegan Paul.

Hinkelammert, Franz, ed. 1999. *El huracán de la globalización*. San José: Departamento Ecuménico de Investigaciones.

——. 2000a. "La inversión de los derechos humanos: El caso de John Locke." In Joaquin Herrera Flores, ed., *El vuelo de anteo: derechos humanos y crítica de la razón liberal*. Bilbao, Spain: Editorial Desclée de Brouwer. 79–114.

——. 2000b. "El proceso actual de globalización y los derechos humanos." In Joaquin Herrera Flores, ed., *El vuelo de anteo: derechos humanos y crítica de la razón liberal*. Bilbao, Spain: Editorial Desclée de Brouwer. 117–28.

Hobsbawm, Eric J. 1962. *The Age of Revolution, 1789–1848*. New York: Mentor.

——. 1987. *The Age of Empire, 1875–1914*. London: Widenfeld and Nicholson.

Hobson, J. A. 1938. *Imperialism: A Study*. London: Allen and Unwin.

Hofman, S. 1997. "Transculturation and Creolization: Concepts of Caribbean Cultural Theory." In Richard A. Young, ed., *Latin American Postmodernisms*. Amsterdam: Rodopi. 73–86.

Hopkins, Terence K. 1990. "Notes on the Concept of Hegemony." *Review* 13, no. 3: 409–11.

Hopkins, Terence K., and Immanuel Wallerstein. 1982. *World-Systems Analysis: Theory and Methodology*. Vol. 1. Beverly Hills, Calif.: Sage.

——. 1996. *The Age of Transition*. London: Zed Press.

Horswell, Michael J. Forthcoming. *Chuquichinchay, Ipas, and Sodomitas: Queer Tropes of Sexuality in Colonial Andean Literature*.

Hoselitz, Bert F. 1960. *Sociological Factors in Economic Development*. Glencoe, U.K.: Free Press.

Hountondji, Paulin J. 1977. *Sur la philosophie africaine: Critique de l'ethnophilosophie*. Paris: F. Maspero.

——. 1992. "Recapturing." In Valentine Mudimbe, ed., *The Surreptitious Speech: Présence Africaine and the Politics of Otherness, 1947–1987*. Chicago: University of Chicago Press. 238–48.

Hulme, Peter. 1986. *Colonial Encounters: Europe and the Native Caribbean, 1492–1797*. London: Methuen.

——. 1992. "Towards a Cultural History of America." *New West Indian Guide* 66, nos. 1–2: 77–81.

——. 1996. "La teoría poscolonial y la representación de la cultura en las Américas." *Casa de las Américas* 202 (January–March): 3–8.

Hulme, Peter, and Francis Barker, eds. 1994. *Postcolonial Theory and Colonial Discourse*. Manchester, U.K.: Manchester University Press.

Humboldt, Alexander von. 1805–35. *Voyage aux régions équinoctiales du Nouveau Continent, fait dans les années 1799–1804*. Paris: Imprimerie Impériale.

Huntington, Samuel P. 1996. *The Clash of Civilizations and the Remaking of World Order.* New York: Simon and Schuster.

Hurbon, Laënec. 1992. "Vodou: A Faith for Individual, Family, and Community from *Dieu dans le vaudou haïtien.*" *Callaloo* 15, no. 3: 787–96.

——. 1995. *Voodoo: Search for the Spirit.* Discoveries Series. New York: Harry N. Abrams.

Hurston, Zora Neale. 1990. *Tell My Horse: Voodoo and Life in Haiti and Jamaica.* New York: Harper Collins.

Hurtado, Aída. 2000. "Sitios y Lenguas: Chicanas Theoriza Feminism." In Uma Narayan and Sandra Harding, eds., *Decentering the Center: Philosophy for a Multi-cultural, Postcolonial, and Feminist World.* Bloomington: Indiana University Press. 128–56.

Hussein, Nasser. 1990. "Hyphenated Identity: Nationality, Discourse, History, and the Anxiety of Criticism in Salma Rushdie's *Shame.*" *Qui Parle?* (summer): 8–11.

Husserl, Edmund. 1965. "Philosophy and the Crisis of European Man." In *Phenomenology and the Crisis of Philosophy.* New York: Harper and Row. 149–92.

——. 1982. *Ideas Pertaining to a Pure Phenomenology and to a Phenomenological Philosophy: First Book.* Trans. F. Kersten. Dordrecht, The Netherlands: Kluwer Academic Publishers.

Huyssen, Andreas. 2002. *Valores: Arte, Mercado, Politica.* Ed. Reinaldo Marques and Lucia Helena Vilela. Belo Horizonte, Brazil: Universidade Federal de Minas Gerais.

Huyssen, Andreas, and David Bathrick. 1989. *Modernity and the Text: Revisions of German Modernism.* New York: Columbia University Press.

Hymes, Dell. 1974. *Reinventing Anthropology.* New York: Vintage.

Ianni, Octavio. 1998. *La Sociedad Global.* Mexico City: Siglo XXI.

——. 2000. *Enigmas de la modernidad-mundo.* Mexico City: Siglo XXI.

Ibarra, Hernán. 2002. "El triunfo del coronel Gutiérrez y la alianza indígena militar." *Ecuador Debate* 57: 21–34.

Ileto Reynaldo. 1979. *Pasyon and Revolution: Popular Movements in the Philippines, 1840–1910.* Quezon City: Ateneo de Manila University Press.

Imaz, Eugenio. 1964. *Nosotros mañana.* Buenos Aires: Editorial Sudamericana.

Instituto Científico de Culturas Indígenas. 2001. "The Indigenous Uprising, Institutionality and Status." *Boletín ICCI-RIMAI* 23: 2–8.

Ippolito, Emilia. 2000. *Caribbean Women Writers: Identity and Gender.* Suffolk: Camden House.

Isaacman, A. 1976. *A tradição da resistência em Moçambique: O vale do Zambeze, 1850–1921.* Porto: Afrontamento.

Jacobson, Mathew Frye. 1998. *Whiteness of a Different Color.* Cambridge, Mass.: Harvard University Press.

James, C. L. R. 1963. *The Black Jacobins Toussaint L'Ouverture and the San Domingo Revolution.* 2d ed. New York: Vintage Books.

James, Conrad, and John Perivolaris, eds. 2000. *The Cultures of the Hispanic Caribbean.* Gainsville: University Press of Florida.

James Figarola, Joel, José Millet, and Alexis Alarcón. 1992. *El Vodú en Cuba.* Santo Domingo: Santiago de Cuba, Casa del Caribe.

Jameson, Fredric. 1985. "El posmodernismo o la lógica cultural del capitalismo tardío." *Casa de las Américas,* 26 nos. 155–56: 141–74.

——. 1986. "Third World Literature in the Era of Multinational Capitalism." *Social Text*, no. 15: 65–88.

——. 1990. "Modernism and Imperialism." In Seamus Deane, ed., *Nationalism, Colonialism, and Literature*. Minneapolis: University of Minnesota Press. 43–68.

——. 1991. *Postmodernism, or, The Cultural Logic of Late Capitalism*. Durham, N.C.: Duke University Press, 1991.

——. 1998. "Notes on Globalization as a Philosophical Issue." In Fredric Jameson and Masao Miyoshi, eds., *The Cultures of Globalization*. Durham, N.C.: Duke University Press. 54–80.

Jaramillo Edwards, Isabel. 1997–98. "Alfred Thayer Mahan y el paisaje de fin de siglo." *Temas*, nos. 12–13: 152–61.

Jáuregui, Carlos. 2005. *Canibalia*. Havana: Casa de las Américas.

Jáuregui, Carlos, and Juan P. Dabove, eds. 2003. *Heterotropías: Narrativas de identidad y alteridad latinoamericana*. Pittsburgh: Instituto Internacional de Literatura Iberoamericana.

Jayawardena, Kumari. 1996. *Feminism and Nationalism in the Third World*. London: Zed Books.

John, Mary E. 1996. *Discrepant Dislocations: Feminism, Theory and Poscolonial History*. Berkeley: University of California Press.

Jomard, Francois, ed. 1809–28. *Description de l'Egypte: Ou, Recueil des observations et des recherches qui ont été faites en Egypte pendant l'expédition de l'armee française*. 23 vols. Paris: Impr. Impériale.

Joseph, Gilbert Michael, Catherine LeGrand, and Ricardo Donato Salvatore. 1998. *Close Encounters of Empire: Writing the Cultural History of U.S.-Latin American Relations*. Durham, N.C.: Duke University Press.

Jrade, Cathy L. 1991. *Modernismo Modernity and the Development of Spanish American Literature*. Austin: University of Texas Press.

Julien, Catherine. 2000. *Reading Inca History*. Iowa City: University of Iowa Press.

Júnior, José F. 1955. *Narração do distrito de Tete, contada por José Fernandes Júnior "O Chiphazi."* Maputo, Mozambique: Arquivo Histórico de Moçambique (mimeograph).

Júnior, Rodrigues. 1955. *O Negro de Moçambique (estudo)*. Lourenço Marques, Mozambique: África Editora.

Junod, Henry. 1946. *Usos e costumes dos Bantos: A vida de uma tribo sul-africana*. 2 vols. Lourenço Marques, Mozambique: Imprensa Nacional.

——. 1996 [1917]. *Usos e costumes dos Bantu*. 2 vols. Maputo, Mozambique: Arquivo Histórico de Moçambique.

Kaarsholm, Preben. 1989. "The Past as Battlefield in Rhodesia and Zimbabwe: The Struggle of Competing Nationalisms over History from Colonization to Independence." *Culture and History* 6: 85–106.

Kahn, Joel. 2001. "Anthropology and Modernity." *Current Anthropology* 42, no. 5: 651–80.

Kale, Madhavi. 1998. *Fragments of Empire: Capital, Slavery, and Indian Indentured Labor Migration in the British Caribbean*. Philadelphia: University of Pennsylvania Press.

Kaminsky, Amy. 1993. *Reading the Body-Politics: Feminist Criticism and Latin American Women Writers*. Minneapolis: University of Minnesota Press.

Kant, Immanuel. 1990. *Foundations of the Metaphysics of Morals, and What Is Enlightenment?* 2d ed. New York: Macmillan.

Kaplan, Amy, and Donald E. Pease, eds. 1993. *Cultures of United States Imperialism.* Durham, N.C.: Duke University Press.

Karasch, Mary. 1987. *Slave Life in Rio de Janeiro, 1808–1850.* Princeton: Princeton University Press.

Kaufman, Peter Iver. 1990. *Redeeming Politics: Studies in Church and State.* Princeton: Princeton University Press.

Kautsky, Karl. 1988. *The Agrarian Question.* Trans. Peter Burgess/London: Zwan Publications.

Kearney, Richard. 1991. *Poetics of Imagining: From Husserl to Lyotard.* London: Routledge.

Keene, Benjamin. 1985. "Main Currents in United States Writings on Colonial Spanish America, 1884–1984." *Hispanic American Historical Review* 65, no. 4: 657–82.

Keller, Evelvn Fox. 1985. *Reflections on Gender and Science.* New Haven, Conn.: Yale University Press.

Khadiagala, Lynn. 2001. "The Failure of Popular Justice in Uganda: Local Councils and Women's Property Rights." *Development and Change* 32, no. 1: 55–76.

Kicza, John E. 1988. "The Social and Ethnic Historiography of Colonial Latin America: The Last Twenty Years." *William and Mary Quarterly,* 3d series, 45, no. 3: 453–88.

Kincaid, Jamaica. 1988. *A Small Place.* New York: Farrar, Straus, Giroux.

King, Richard. 1999. *Orientalism and Religion: Postcolonial Theory, India, and "The Mystic East."* London: Routledge.

Kinsbruner, Jay. 1994. *Independence in Spanish America: Civil Wars, Revolutions, and Underdevelopment.* Albuquerque: University of New Mexico Press.

Kirk-Duggan, Cheryl A. 1997. *Exorcizing Evil: A Womanist Perspective on the Spirituals.* Maryknoll, N.Y.: Orbis Books.

Kirpal, Viney. 1988. "What Is the Modern Third World Novel?" *Commonwealth Literature* 23, no. 1: 144–56.

Klarén, Peter Flindell. 2000. *Peru: Society and Nationhood in the Andes.* Oxford: Oxford University Press.

Klor de Alva, J. Jorge. 1982. "Spiritual Conflict and Accommodation in New Spain: Toward a Typology of Aztec Responses to Christianity." In G. A. Collier et al., eds., *The Inca and Aztec States, 1400–1800: Anthropology and History.* New York: Academic Press. 345–66.

———. 1989. "Aztlán, Borinquen, and Hispanic Nationalism in the U.S." In R. Anaya and F. Lomelf, eds., *Aztlán: Essays on the Chicano Homeland.* Albuquerque: El Norte Publications/New Mexico University Press. 135–63.

———. 1991. "Religious Rationalization and the Conversion of the Nahuas: Some Reflections on Social Organization and Colonial Epistemology." In D. Carrasco, ed., *To Change Place: Aztec Ceremonial Landscapes.* Boulder: University of Colorado Press. 233–45.

———. 1992a. "Colonialism and Postcolonialism as (Latin) American Mirages." *Colonial Latin American Review* 1, nos. 1–2: 3–23.

———. 1992b. "La invención de los orígenes y la identidad latina en los Estados Unidos (1969–81)." In J. Jorge Klor de Alva et al., eds., *Encuentros interétnicos: De palabra y obra en el Nuevo Mundo*. Madrid: Siglo XXI. 467–88.

———. 1992c. "Nahua Studies, the Allure of the 'Aztecs,' and Miguel León-Portilla." In Miguel León-Portilla, *The Aztec Image of Self and Society: Introduction to Nahua Culture*. Ed. and with an introduction by J. Jorge Klor de Alva. Salt Lake City: University of Utah Press. vi–xxiv.

———. 1995. "The Postcolonization of the (Latin) American Experience: A Reconsideration of 'Colonialism,' 'Postcolonialism,' and 'Mestizaje.'" In Gyan Prakash, ed., *After Colonialism: Imperial Histories and Postcolonial Displacements*. Princeton: Princeton University Press. 241–75.

Kocher, Paul. 1962. *Christopher Marlowe: A Study of His Thought*. New York: Russell and Russell.

Kokotovic, Misha. 2000. "Hibridez y desigualdad: García Canclini ante el neoliberalismo." *Revista de Crítica Literaria Latinoamericana* 36, no. 52: 289–300.

Konetzke, Richard. 1950. "La condición legal de los criollos y las causas de la Independencia." *Estudios americanos* 2, no. 5 (January): 31–54.

———. 1953. *Colección de documentos para la historia de la formación social de Hispanoamérica, 1493–1810*. 3 vols. Madrid: Consejo Superior de Investigaciones Científicas.

Kortenaar, Neil ten. 1996. "The Trick of Divining a Postcolonial Canadian Identity: Margaret Laurence between Race and Nation." *Canadian Literature* 149 (summer): 11–33.

Koso-Thomas, Olayinka. 1987. *The Circumcision of Women: A Strategy for Eradication*. London: Zed Books.

Kossok, Manfred. 1968. *Historia de la Santa Alianza y la emancipación de América Latina*. Buenos Aires: Ediciones Sílaba.

Kossok, Manfred, and Walter Markov. 1961. "Las Indias no eran Colonias? Hintergründe einer Kolonialapologetik." In *Lateinamerika zwischen Emanzipation und Imperialismus (1810–1960)*. Berlin: Akademie Verlag. 1–34.

Kramer, Fritz W. 1989. "The Otherness of the European." *Culture and History* 6: 107–23.

Kraniauskas, John. 2000. "Hybridity in a Transnational Frame: Latin-Americanist and Postcolonial Perspectives on Cultural Studies." *Nepantla* 1, no. 1: 111–38.

Kristeva, Julia. 1988. *Étrangers a nous-mêmes*. Paris: Fayard.

Kubayanda, Josephat. 1992. "On Colonial/Imperial Discourse and Contemporary Critical Theory." Lecture presented in College Park, Maryland.

Kubler, George, and Charles Gibson. 1951. *The Tovar Calendar: Reproduced with a Commentary and Handlist of Sources on the Mexican 365-day Year*. Vol. 11 of *Memoirs of the Connecticut Academy of Arts and Sciences*. New Haven, Conn.: Yale University Press.

Kurz, Robert. 1991. *Der Kollaps der Modernisierung: Von Zusammenbruch des Kasernsozialismus zur Krise der Weltökonomie*. Frankfurt am Main: Eichborn Verlag.

———. 1993. *O retorno do Potemkin: Capitalismo de fachada e conflicto distributivo na Alemanha*. Trans. Wolfgang Leo Maar. Sao Paulo: Paz e Terra.

Kuznesof, Elizabeth Anne. 1988. "Household, Family, and Community Studies, 1976–1986." *Latin American Population History Bulletin*, no. 14: 9–22.

——. 1995. "Ethnic and Gender Influences on 'Spanish' Creole Society in Colonial Spanish America." *Colonial Latin American Review* 4, no. 1: 153–76.

Lacan, Jacques. 1977a. *Ecrits: A Selection.* London: Tavistock.

——. 1977b. *The Four Fundamental Concepts of Psychoanalysis.* London: Hogarth Press.

Laclau, Ernesto. 1977. *Politics and Ideology in Marxist Theory.* London: New Left Books.

——. 1985. *Hegemony and Socialist Strategy: Towards a Radical Democratic Politics.* London: Verso.

——. 1990. *New Reflections on the Revolution of Our Time.* London: Verso.

——. 1995. "Universalism, Particularism, and the Question of Identity." In John Rajchman, ed., *The Identity Question.* New York: Routledge. 93–108.

——. 1996. *Emancipation(s).* London: Verso.

——, ed. 1994. *Making of Political Identities.* London: Verso.

Lafaye, Jacques. 1976 [1974]. *Quetzalcoatl and Guadalupe: The Formation of Mexican National Consciousness, 1531–1813.* Trans. Benjamin Keen. Chicago: University of Chicago Press.

LaFeber, Walter. 1963. *The New Empire: An Interpretation of American Expansion 1860–1898.* Ithaca, N.Y.: Cornell University Press.

Laite, Glacyra. 1989. *Pernambuco 1824: A Confederação do Equador.* Recife, Brazil: Massangana.

Lambert, Richard D. 1990. "Blurring Disciplinary Boundaries: Area Studies in the United States." *American Behavioral Scientist* 33, no. 6: 712–32.

Lander, Edgardo. 1997a. Colonialidad, modernidad, postmodernidad." *Estudios latinoamericanos* 4, no. 8: 31–46.

——. 1997b. *La democracia en las ciencias sociales contemporáneas.* Serie Bibliográfica FOBAL-CS no. 2. Caracas: Facultad de Ciencias Económicas y Sociales, Universidad Central de Venezuela, and Instituto Autónomo Biblioteca Nacional.

——. 1998. "Eurocentrismo y colonialismo en el pensamiento latinoamericano." In Roberto Briceño-Leon and Heinz R. Sonntag, eds., *Pueblo, epoca y desarrollo: La sociología de América Latina.* Caracas: Nueva Sociedad. 87–96.

——. 2000a. "Ciencias sociales: Saberes coloniales eurocéntricos." In Edgardo Lander, ed., *La colonialidad del saber: Eurocentrismo y ciencias sociales: Perspectivas latinoamericanas.* Buenos Aires: Consejo Latinoamericano de Ciencias Sociales/UNESCO. 11–40.

——, ed. 2000b. *La colonialidad del saber: Eurocentrismo y ciencias sociales: Perspectivas latinoamericanas.* Buenos Aires: Consejo Latinoamericano de Ciencias Sociales/UNESCO.

——. 2001. "Eurocentrism and Colonialism in Latin American Social Thought." *Nepantla* 1, no. 3: 519–32.

——. 2002. "Los derechos de propiedad intelectual en la geopolítica del saber de la sociedad global." In Catherine Walsh, Freya Schiwy, and Santiago Castro-Gómez, eds., *Interdisciplinar las ciencias sociales.* Quito: Universidad Andina/Abya Yala. 73–102.

Lao-Montes, Agustin. 2001. "Latin American Areas Studies and Latino Ethnic Studies: From Civilizing Mission to the Barbarian's Revenge." *APA Newsletter on Hispani/Latino Issues in Philosophy,* no. 2 (spring): 112–22.

Lao-Montes, Agustin, and Arlene Dávila, eds. 2001. *Mambo Montage: The Latinization of New York*. New York: Columbia University Press.

Laroche, Maximilien. 1978. "Violence et langage dans les littératures d'Haiti et des Antilles françaises." *Présence Francophone: Revue Littéraire Sherbrooke*, no. 16: 111–21.

Larsen, Neil. 1990. *Modernism and Hegemony: A Materialist Critique of Aesthetic Agencies*. Minneapolis: University of Minnesota Press.

———. 2001. *Determinations: Essays on Theory, Narrative and Nation in the Americas*. London: Verso.

———. 2002. "Marxism, Postcolonialism, and *The Eighteen Brumaire*." In Crystal Bartolovich and Neil Lazarus, eds., *Marxism, Modernity and Postcolonial Studies*. Cambridge: Cambridge University Press. 204–20.

Larson, Brooke. 1988. *Colonialism and Agrarian Transformation in Bolivia: Cochabamba, 1550–1900*. Princeton: Princeton University Press.

Latasa Vassallo, Pilar. 1999. "¿Criollismo peruano versus administración española? Posición criollista del virrey Montesclaros (1607–1615)." In *Actas del Primer Congreso Internacional de Peruanistas en el Extranjero*, http://www.fas.harvard.edu/icop/pilar latasa.html.

Latin American Subaltern Studies Group. 1994. "Founding Statement." *Dispositio/n* 19, no. 46: 9–11.

Latouche, Serge. 1996. *The Westernization of the World*. Cambridge: Polity.

Latour, Bruno. 1993. *We Have Never Been Modern*. New York: Harvester Wheatsheaf.

Lavallé, Bernard. 1978. "Del 'espíritu colonial' a la reivindicación criolla o los albores del criollismo peruano." *Histórica* 2, no. 1: 39–61.

———. 1984. "La rebelión de las alcabalas (Quito, julio de 1592–abril de 1593): Ensayo de interpretación." *Revista de Indias* 44, no. 173: 141–201.

———. 1992. *Quito et la crise de l'Alcabala (1580–1600)*. Paris: Editions du Centre National de la Recherche Scientifique.

———. 1993. *Las promesas ambiguas: Ensayos sobre el criollismo colonial en los Andes*. Lima: Fondo Editorial de la Pontificia Universidad Católica del Perú.

———. 2000. "El criollismo y los pactos fundamentales del imperio americano de los Habsburgos." In José Antonio Mazzotti, ed., *Agencias criollas: La ambigüedad "colonial" de las letras hispanoamericanas*. Pittsburgh: Instituto Internacional de Literatura Iberoamericana. 37–54.

Lazarus, Neil. 1999. *Nationalism and Cultural Practice in the Postcolonial World*. Cambridge: Cambridge University Press.

Leff, Enrique. 2000. *Saber Ambiental*. Mexico: Siglo XXI.

———. 2003. "La Ecología Política en América Latina: Un Campo en Construcción (Borrador para discusión)." Consejo Latinoamericano de Ciencias Sociales Grupo de Trabajo en Ecología Política. Unpublished manuscript.

Lenin, V. I. 1970. *Selected Works*. 3 vols. Moscow: Progress Publishers.

Leon, António Garcia de. 1993. "Contrapunto entre lo Barroco y lo Popular en el Veracruz Colonial." Paper presented at the Colóquio Internacional Modernidad Europea, Mestizaje Cultural y Ethos Barroco, Universidad Nacional Autonoma de México, 17–20 May.

León-Portilla, Miguel. 1963. *Aztec Thought and Culture.* Norman: University of Oklahoma Press.

——. 1974. "Testimonios nahuas sobre la conquista espiritual." *Estudios de cultura nahuatl* 11: 11–36.

Levene, Ricardo. 1951. *Las Indias no eran colonias.* Buenos Aires: Espasa-Calpe.

Levillier, Roberto. 1935. *Don Francisco de Toledo: Supremo organizador del Perú.* 3 vols. Buenos Aires: Publicaciones del Congreso Argentino.

Levinas, Emmanuel. 1971. *Totalité et infini.* The Hague: Nijhoff.

——. 1998. *La huella del otro.* Mexico City: Taurus.

Lezama, José Luis. 1993. *Teoría social, espacio y ciudad.* Mexico City: Colegio de Mexico.

Lienhard, Martin. 1989. *La voz y su huella: Literatura y conflicto étnico-social en América Latina, 1492–1989.* La Habana: Casa de las Américas.

——. 1990. *La voz y su huella: Escritura y conflicto étnico-social en América Latina (1492–1988).* Havana: Casa de las Américas.

——. 1992. "La interrelación creativa del quechua y del español en la literatura peruana de lengua española." In Luis Millones and Hiroyasu Tomoeda, eds., *500 años de mestizaje en los Andes.* Osaka: Museo Nacional de Etnología. 27–49.

Lima, Manuel de Oliveira. 1984 [1896]. *Aspectos da literatura colonial brasileira.* Rio de Janeiro: F. Alves.

Limón, Graciela. 1993. "Haitian Gods, African Roots: Identity and Freedom in Alejo Carpentier's *The Kingdom of This World.*" *Caribbean Studies* 9, no. 3: 195–201.

Lisboa, Karen Macknow. 1995. "A Nova Atlântida ou o gabinete naturalista dos Doutores Spix e Martius: Natureza e civilização na Viagem pelo Brasil (1817–1820)." Master's thesis, Universidade de São Paulo.

Liss, Peggy K. 1986 [1975]. *Orígenes de la nacionalidad mexicana, 1521–1556: La formación de una nueva sociedad.* Trans. Agustín Bárcena. Mexico City: Fondo de Cultura Económica.

Llach, Juan José. 1974. *Dependencia cultural y creación de cultura en América Latina.* Buenos Aires: Editorial Bonum.

Llopis, Rogelio. 1970. "El escudo de hojas secas." *Casa de las Américas* 62 (September–October): 199–201.

Lluco, Miguel. 2001. "Presentación del taller." In *Taller Intercultural de Mujeres Líderes en Poderes Locales: Construyendo el poder local desde la diferencia.* Quito: Instituto Científico de Culturas Indígenas. 7–10.

Lobato, Alexandre. 1952. *Sobre cultura moçambicana.* Lisbon: Gradiva.

Lockhart, James. 1972. "The Social History of Colonial Latin America: Evolution and Potential." *Latin American Research Review* 7: 5–45.

——. 1985. "Some Nahua Concepts in Postconquest Guise." *History of European Ideas* 6, no. 4: 465–82.

——. 1991. *Nahuas and Spaniards: Postconquest Central Mexican History and Philology.* UCLA Latin American Studies vol. 76, Nahuatl Studies Series no. 3. Stanford, Calif.: Stanford University Press.

——. 1992. *The Nahuas after the Conquest: A Social and Cultural History of the Indians of Central Mexico, Sixteenth through Eighteenth Centuries.* Stanford, Calif.: Stanford University Press.

——, ed. 1993. *We People Here: Nahuatl Accounts of the Conquest of Mexico*. Trans. James Lockhart. Berkeley: University of California Press.

Lohmann Villena, Guillermo. 1974. *Los ministros de la Audiencia de Lima en el reinado de los Borbones (1700–1821)*. Seville: Consejo Superior de Investigaciones Científicas.

Lonsdale, John. 1989. "African Pasts in Africa's Future." *Revue Canadienne des Etudes Africaines* 23: 126–46.

Loomba, Ania. 1998. *Colonialism/Postcolonialism*. The New Critical Idiom Series. London: Routledge.

Lope Blanch, Juan M. 1968. *El español de América*. Madrid: Ediciones Alcalá.

López, Silvia. 2000. " 'Hybrid Cultures': Modern Experience and 'Institution Kunst.' In Rita de Grandis and Zila Bernd, eds., *Unforeseeable Americas: Questioning Cultural Hybridity in the Americas*. Amsterdam: Rodopi. 254–70.

López-Baralt, Mercedes. 1988. *Ícono y conquista: Guaman Poma de Ayala*. Madrid: Hiperión.

López de Gómara, Francisco. 1979 [1552]. *Historia general de las Indias*. Caracas: Biblioteca Ayacucho.

López Martínez, Héctor. 1971. *Rebeliones de mestizos y otros temas quinientistas*. Lima: Imprenta Gráfica Villanueva.

Love, Joseph. 1980. "Raúl Prebisch and the Origin of the Doctrine of Unequal Exchange." *Latin American Research Review* 15, no. 3: 45–72.

Lowenhaupt Tsing, Anna. 1993. *In the Realm of the Diamond Queen: Marginality in an Out-of-the-Way Place*. Princeton: Princeton University Press.

Lugo-Ortiz, Agnes. 1999. *Identidades imaginadas: Biografía y nacionalidad el el horizonte de la Guerra (Cuba 1860–1898)*. Río Piedras: Editorial Universidad de Puerto Rico.

Luhmann, Niklas. 1995. *Social Systems*. Stanford, Calif.: Stanford University Press.

Lutz, Christopher. 1994. *Santiago de Guatemala 1541–1773: City, Caste and the Colonial Experience*. Norman: University of Oklahoma Press.

Luxemburg, Rosa. 1976. *The Accumulation of Capital*. Trans. Rudolf Wichmann. New York: Monthly Review Press.

Lynch, John. 1973. *The Spanish American Revolutions, 1808–1826*. New York: Norton.

——. 1996. "El reformismo borbónico e Hispanoamérica." In Agustín Guimerá, ed., *El reformismo borbónico*. Madrid: Alianza Editorial. 37–59.

Lyotard, Jean François. 1984. *The Postmodern Condition: A Report on Knowledge*. Minneapolis: University of Minnesota Press.

——. 1992. *The Postmodern Explained to Children: Correspondence 1982–1985*. Trans. and ed. Julian Pefanis and Morgan Thomas. Sydney: Power Publications.

Maalouf, Amin. 1998. *Les identités meurtrières*. Paris: Grasset.

Mabille, Pierre. 1940. *Le miroir du merveilleux*. Paris: Minuit.

Macas, Luis. 2001. "Diálogo de culturas: Hacia el reconocimiento del otro." *Revista Yachaikuna* 2: 26–33.

Macaulay, Rose. 1946. *They Went to Portugal*. Oxford: Alden Press.

——. 1990. *They Went to Portugal Too*. Manchester, U.K.: Carcanet.

Machado, Maria Helena. 1994. *O plano e o pânico*. Rio de Janeiro: EDFRJ / EDUSP.

MacNeill, J., P. Winsemius, and T. Yakushiji. 1991. *Beyond Interdependence: The Meshing*

of the World's Economy and the Earth's Ecology. A Trilateral Commission Book. Foreword by David Rockefeller. New York: Oxford University Press.

Maffie, James. 2001. "Truth from the Perspective of Comparative World Philosophy."
Social Epistemology 15: 263–73.

Mahan, Alfred Thayer. 1975. *Letters and Papers of Alfred Thayer Mahan.* Annapolis, Md.:
Naval Institute Press.

Mahmood, Saba. 2001. "Feminist Theory, Embodiment, and the Docile Agent: Some
Reflections on the Egyptian Islamic Revival." *Cultural Anthropology* 16: 203–31.

——. 2003. *Pious Transgressions: Embodied Disciplines of the Islamic Revival.* Princeton:
Princeton University Press.

Majid, Anouar. 2000. *Unveiling Traditions: Postcolonial Islam in a Polycentric World.* Durham, N.C.: Duke University Press.

——. 2001. "Provincial Acts: The Limits of Postcolonial Theory." Paper presented at
the international congress "Postcolonial/Political Correctnesses," Casablanca,
12–14 April.

Maldonado-Torres, Nelson. 2002. "Post-imperial Reflections on Crisis, Knowledge,
and Utopia: Transgresstopic Critical Hermeneutics and the 'Death of European
Man.'" *Review* 25, no. 3: 277–315.

——. 2003. "Imperio y colonialidad del ser." Paper presented at the 24th International Congress, Latin American Studies Association, Dallas, 27–29 March.

Maliandi, Ricardo. 1993. *Dejar la posmodernidad: La ética frente al irracionalismo actual.*
Buenos Aires: Editorial Almagesto.

Mallon, Florencia E. 1994. "The Promise and Dilemma of Subaltern Studies: Perspectives from Latin American History." *American Historical Review* 99, no. 5: 1491–515.

——. 1995. *Peasant and Nation: The Making of Postcolonial Mexico and Peru.* Berkeley:
University of California Press.

——. 2001. "Promesa y dilema de los estudios subalternos: Perspectivas a partir de la
historia latinoamericana." In Ileana Rodríguez, ed., *Convergencia de tiempos.* Amsterdam: Rodopi. 117–54.

Mama, Amina. 1995. "Sheroes and Villains: Conceptualizing Colonial and Contemporary Violence against Women in Africa." In Jacqui Alexander and Chandra Talpade Mohanty, eds., *Feminist Genealogies, Colonial Legacies and Democratic Futures.* New
York: Routledge. 46–63.

Manghezi, Nadja. 1999. "Eduardo Mondlane nos Estados Unidos da América (1951–
1961)." *Estudos Moçambicanos* 17: 7–34.

Mani, Lata. 1987. "Contentious Traditions: The Debate on Sati in Colonial India."
Cultural Critique 7: 119–56.

——. 1998. *Contentious Traditions: The Debate on Sati in Colonial India.* Berkeley: University
of California Press.

Mao Tse-tung. 1967. "On New Democracy." In *Select Works of Mao Tse-tung,* vol. 2.
Peking: Foreign Languages Press. 339–84.

—— [Mao Zedong]. 1980. *Talks at the Ya'nan Conference on Literature and Art.* Trans.
Bonnie S. McDougall. Ann Arbor: Center for Chinese Studies, University of Michigan Press.

Maravall, José Antonio. 1975. *La cultura del barroco: Análisis de una estructura histórica.*
Barcelona: Ariel.

——. 1990. *La cultura del barroco: Análisis de una estructura histórica*. Barcelona: Ariel.

Marcos, Sylvia. 1999a. "La Otra Mujer: Una propuesta de reflexión para el 8 Congreso Feminista Latinoamericano y del Caribe." *Cuadernos Feministas* 2, no. 9.

——. 1999b. "Twenty-five Years of Mexican Feminisms." *Women's Studies International Forum* 22, no. 4: 431–33.

Marcus, George E., and Michael Fischer. 1986. *Anthropology as Cultural Critique*. Chicago: University of Chicago Press.

Marcuse, Herbert. 1964. *One-dimensional Man*. Boston: Beacon Press.

Mariátegui, José Carlos. 1928a. "Aniversario y balance." *Amauta*, no. 17 (September).

——. 1928b. *Siete ensayos de interpretación de la realidad peruana*. Lima: Biblioteca Amauta.

——. 1929. "Punto de vista antimperialista." In *Obras completas*. Vol. 11. Lima: Biblioteca Amauta.

——. 1971 [1928]. *Seven Interpretative Essays on Peruvian Reality*. Trans. Marjory Urquidi. Austin: University of Texas Press.

Mark, Jonathan. 1994. *Human Biodiversity, Genes, Race, and History*. New York: Aldyne de Gruyter.

Marshall, J. P., ed. 1996. *The Cambridge Illustrated History of the British Empire*. Cambridge: Cambridge University Press.

Martí, José. 1963–65. *Obras completas*. Havana: Editorial Nacional.

——. 1975. *Inside the Monster: Writings on the United States and American Imperialism*. Ed., intro., and notes by Philip S. Foner. New York: Monthly Review Press.

——. 1977. *Our America: Writings on Latin America and the Struggle for Cuban Independence*. Ed., intro., and notes by Philip S. Foner. New York: Monthly Review Press.

——. 1999. "Our America." In *José Martí Reader: Writings on the Americas*. Ed. D. Schnookal and M. Muñiz. Melbourne: Ocean Press. 111–20.

Martín-Barbero, Jesús. 1993 [1987]. *Communication, Culture and Hegemony: From the Media to Mediations*. Trans. Elizabeth Fox and Robert White. London: Sage.

Martínez-San Miguel, Yolanda. 1999. *Saberes americanos: Subalternidad y epistemología en los escritos de Sor Juana*. Pittsburgh: Instituto Internacional de Literatura Iberoamericana.

Martins, J. P. Oliveira. 1904. *O Brasil e as colónias portuguesas*. Lisbon: Parceria António Mário Pereira.

Mártir de Anglería, Pedro. 1944 [1530]. *Décadas del Nuevo Mundo*. Trans. Joaquín Torres Asensio. Buenos Aires: Editorial Bajel.

——. 1966. *Opera: Legatio Babylonica* [1516], *de Orbe Novo Decades Octo* [1530], *Opus Epistolarium*. Facsimile ed. Graz, Austria: Akademische Druck.

Marx, Karl. 1930. *The Communist Manifesto*. London: New York International.

——. 1974. *The First International and After*. Vol. 3 of *Political Writings*. Harmondsworth, U.K.: Penguin.

——. 2001. *Simón Bolívar*. Madrid: Ediciones Sequitur.

Mason, Peter. 1989. "Portrayal and Betrayal: The Colonial Gaze in Seventeenth Century Brazil." *Culture and History* 6: 37–62.

——. 1990. *Deconstructing America: Representations of the Other*. London: Routledge.

Matibag, Eugenio. 1996. *Afro-Cuban Religious Experience: Cultural Reflections in Narrative*. Gainesville: University Press of Florida.

Matos, Félix V. 2000. "Their Islands and Our People: U.S. Writing about Puerto Rico 1898–1920." *Centro: Centro de estudios puertorriqueños* 11, no. 1: 33–50.

Matos Moctezuma, Eduardo, and Felipe Solís. 2002. Introduction to *Aztecs*. London: Royal Academy.

Mattoso, José. 1998. *A identidade nacional*. Lisbon: Gradiva.

Mazrui, Ali A., and Michael Tidy. 1984. *Nationalism and New States in Africa*. London: Heinemann.

Mazzotti, José Antonio. 1996. "La heterogeneidad colonial peruana y la construcción del discurso criollo en el siglo 17." In José Antonio Mazzotti and U. Juan Zevallos-Aguilar, eds., *Asedios a la heterogeneidad cultural: Libro de homenaje a Antonio Cornejo Polar*. Philadelphia: Asociación Internacional de Peruanistas. 173–96.

———. 1998. "Indigenismos de ayer: Prototipos perdurables del discurso criollo." In Mabel Moraña, ed., *Indigenismo hacia el fin de milenio: Homenaje a Antonio Cornejo Polar*. Pittsburgh: Instituto Internacional de Literatura Iberoamericana. 77–102.

———. 2000. *Agencias criollas: La ambigüedad "colonial" en las letras hispanoamericanas*. Pittsburgh: Biblioteca de América.

———. 2002. "Heterogeneidad cultural y estudios coloniales: La prefiguración y la práctica de una ruptura epistémica." In Friedhelm Schmidt, ed., *Antonio Cornejo Polar y los estudios latinoamericanos*. Pittsburgh: Instituto Internacional de Literatura Iberoamericana. 37–54.

Mazzotti, José Antonio, and U. Juan Zevallos-Aguilar, eds. 1996. *Asedios a la heterogeneidad cultural: Libro de homenaje a Antonio Cornejo Polar*. Philadelphia: Asociación Internacional de Peruanistas.

Mbembe, Achille. 2000. *De la postcolonie: Essai sur l'imagination politique dans l'Afrique contemporaine*. Paris: Khartala.

McClintock, Anne. 1994. "The Angel of Progress: Pitfalls of the Term Postcolonial." In Patrick Williams and Laura Chrisman, eds., *Colonial Discourse and Postcolonial Theory: A Reader*. New York: Columbia University Press. 291–304.

———. 1995. *Imperial Leather: Race, Gender and Sexuality in the Colonial Conquest*. New York: Routledge.

McLeod, John. 2000. *Beginning Postcolonialism*. Manchester, U.K.: Manchester University Press.

McLeod, Marc. 1998. "Undesirable Aliens: Race, Ethnicity, and Nationalism in the Comparison of Haitian and British West Indian Immigrant Workers in Cuba, 1912–1939." *Social History* 31, no. 3: 599–623.

Medina, Javier. 1992. *Repensar Bolivia: Cicatrices de un viaje hacia sí mismo*. La Paz: Hisbol.

Meléndez, Juan. 1681. *Teſoros Verdaderos de las Yndias en la Hiſtoria de la Gran Prouincia de San Iuan Bautiſta de el Perú de el Orden de Predicadores*. Rome: Por Nicolas Angel Tinaſſio.

Memmi, Albert. 1965. *The Colonizer and the Colonized*. New York: Orion Press.

———. 1967 [1957]. *The Colonizer and the Colonized*. Boston: Beacon.

———. 1979. *Portrait du colonisé précédé du portrait du colonisateur*. Paris: Payot.

Menchú, Rigoberta. 1984. *I, Rigoberta Menchú: An Indian Woman in Guatemala*. Ed. Elisabeth Burgos Debray. Trans. Ann Wright. London: Verso.

———, in collaboration with Dante Liano and Gianni Minà. 1998. *Rigoberta: La nieta de los mayas*. Madrid: El País/Aguilar.

Mendieta, Eduardo. 1998. "Modernidad, posmodernidad y poscolonialidad: Una búsqueda esperanzadora en el tiempo." In Santiago Castro-Gómez and Eduardo Mendieta, eds., *Teorías sin disciplina: Latinoamericanismo, poscolonialidad y globalización en debate*. Mexico City: Miguel Ángel Porrúa. 147–68.

———. 2001a. "Chronotopology: Critique of Spatio-Temporal Regimes." In Jeffrey Paris and William Wilkerson, eds., *New Critical Theory: Essays on Liberation*. Lanham, Md.: Rowman and Littlefield. 175–97.

———. 2001b. "The City and the Philosopher: On the Urbanism of Phenomenology." *Philosophy and Geography* 4, no. 2: 203–18.

———, ed. 2002. *Latin American Philosophy: Currents, Issues, Debates*. Bloomington: Indiana University Press.

———. 2003. "What Can Latinas/os Learn from Cornel West? The Latino Postcolonial Intellectual in the Age of the Exhaustion of Public Spheres." *Nepantla* 4, no. 2: 305–25.

———. 2004. "The Emperor's Map: Latin American Critiques of Globalism." In Manfred Steger, ed., *Rethinking Globalism*. Lanham, Md.: Rowman and Littlefield. 231–42.

Mengin, Ernst. 1945. *Unos annales históricos de la Nación Mexicana: Manuscrit mexicain no. 22; liber in lingua Nahuatl manuscriptus paucisque picturis linearibus ornatus ut est conservatus in Bibliotheca Nationis Gallicae Parisiensi sub numero 22, archetypum. Manuscrit mexicain no. 22bis; ejusdem operis exemplum aetate posterius nonnullisque picturis linearibus ornatum, ut est conservatum in Bibliotheca Nationis Gallicae Parisiensi sub numero 22bis*. Paris: Bibliothèque nationale.

———. 1952. "Commentaire du Codex Mexicanus." *Journal de la Société des Americanistes* 41: 387–498.

Mernissi, Fatima. 1993. *El Poder olvidado: Las mujeres ante un Islam en cambio*. Barcelona: Icaria-Antrazyt.

Merrim, Stephanie, ed. 1991. *Feminist Perspectives on Sor Juana Inés de la Cruz*. Detroit: Wayne State University.

———. 1999. *Early Modern Women's Writing and Sor Juana Inés de la Cruz*. Nashville: Vanderbilt University Press.

Métraux, Alfred. 1972. *Voodoo in Haiti*. New York: Schocken.

Migerel, Helene. 1987. *La Migration des Zombis: Survivances de la magie antillaise en France*. Paris: Editions Caribeennes.

Mignolo, Walter D. 1989a. "Afterword: From Colonial Discourse to Colonial Semiosis." In Roleno Adorno and Walter Mignolo, eds., "Colonial Discourse," special issue, *Dispositio/n* 14, nos. 36–38: 333–37.

———. 1989b. "Colonial Situations, Geographical Discourses, and Territorial Representations: Toward a Diatopical Understanding of Colonial Semiosis." In Roleno Adorno and Walter Mignolo, eds., "Colonial Discourse," special issue, *Dispositio/n* 14, nos. 36–38: 93–140.

———. 1989c. "Literacy and Colonization: The New World Experience." In R. Jara and N. Spadaccini, eds., "Re-writing the New World," special issue, *Hispanic Issue* 4: 55–96.

———. 1992a. "On the Colonization of Amerindian Languages and Memories of Writing and the Discontinuity of the Classical Tradition." *Society and History* 34, no. 2: 301–30.

——. 1992b. "La semiosis colonial: La dialéctica entre representaciones fracturadas y hermenéuticas pluritópicas." In Beatriz González Stephan and Lúcia Helena Costigan, eds., *Crítica y descolonización: El sujeto colonial en la cultura latinoamericana.* Caracas: Universidad Central de Venezuela. 27–47.

——. 1993. "Colonial and Postcolonial Discourse: Cultural Critique or Academic Colonialism?" *Latin American Research Review* 28: 120–34.

——. 1994a. "Are Subaltern Studies Postmodern or Postcolonial? The Politics and Sensibilities of Geo-Cultural Locations." In José Rabasa, Javier Sanjínes C., and Robert Carr, eds., "Subaltern Studies in the Americas," special issue, *Dispositio/n* 46 (1996): 45–71.

——. 1994b. Foreword to José Rabasa, Javier Sanjínes C., and Robert Carr, eds., "Subaltern Studies in the Americas," special issue, *Dispositio/n* 46 (1996): iii–iv.

——. 1995. *The Darker Side of the Renaissance: Literacy, Territoriality, and Colonization.* Ann Arbor: University of Michigan Press.

——. 1996a. "Herencias coloniales y teorías postcoloniales." In Beatriz González Stephan, ed., *Cultura y Tercer Mundo.* Caracas: Nueva Sociedad. 99–136.

——. 1996b. "Posoccidentalismo: Las epistemologías fronterizas y el dilema de los estudios (latinoamericanos) de área." *Revista Iberoamericana* 62, nos. 176–77: 676–96.

——. 1997. "La razón postcolonial: Herencias coloniales y teorías postcoloniales." In Alfonso de Toro, ed., *Postmodernidad y postcolonialidad: Breves reflexiones sobre Latinoamérica.* Madrid: Iberoamericana. 51–70.

——. 1998a. "Globalization, Civilization Processes, and the Relocation of Languages and Cultures." In Fredric Jameson and Masao Miyoshi, eds., *The Cultures of Globalization.* Durham, N.C.: Duke University Press. 32–53.

——. 1998b. "Posoccidentalismo: El argumento desde América Latina." In Santiago Castro-Gómez and Eduardo Mendieta, eds., *Teorías sin disciplina: Latinoamericanismo, poscolonialidad y globalización en debate.* Mexico City: Miguel Ángel Porrúa. 31–58.

——. 2000a. "La colonialidad a lo largo y a lo ancho: El hemisferio occidental en el horizonte colonial de la modernidad." In Edgardo Lander, ed., *La colonialidad del saber: Eurocentrismo, y ciencias sociales, perspectivas latinoamericanas.* Buenos Aires: Consejo Latinoamericano de Ciencias Sociales. 55–86.

——. 2000b. "Coloniality at Large: Time and the Colonial Difference." In Cándido Mendes, coord., and Enrique Rodríguez Larreta, ed., *Time in the Making and Possible Futures.* Rio de Janeiro: UNESCO/Instituto de Pluralismo Cultural. 237–72.

——. 2000c. "From Cross-genealogies and Subaltern Knowledges to Nepantla." *Nepantla* 1, no. 1: 1–8.

——. 2000d. *Local Histories/Global Designs: Coloniality, Subaltern Knowledges, and Border Thinking.* Princeton: Princeton University Press.

——. 2000e. "Rethinking the Colonial Model." In L. Hutcheon and M. Valdes, eds., *Rethinking Literary History.* Oxford: Oxford University Press. 78–142.

——, ed. 2001a. *Capitalismo y geopolítica del conocimiento: El eurocentrismo y la filosofía de la liberación en el debate intelectual contemporáneo.* Buenos Aires: Ediciones del Signo/Duke University.

——. 2001b. "Latin American Social Thought and Latino/as American Studies." *Newsletter on Hispanic/Latino Issues in Philosophy* (American Philosophical Association) 1, no. 2 (spring 2001): 105–12.

——. 2001c. "Local Histories and Global Designs: An Interview with Walter Mignolo." *Discourse* 22, no. 3: 7–33.

Mignolo, Walter, and Freya Schiwy. 2002. "Translation/Transculturation and the Colonial Difference." In Elisabeth Mudimbe-Boyi, ed., *Beyond Dichotomies*. Albany: State University of New York Press. 251–86.

Miller, Ivor L. 2000. "Religious Symbolism in Cuban Political Performance." *Drama Review* 44, no. 2: 30–55.

Millones, Luis. 1995. *Perú colonial: De Pizarro a Túpac Amaru 2*. Lima: Corporatión Financiera de Desarollo.

Minh-ha, Trinh T. 1989. *Woman, Native, Other: Writing Postcoloniality and Feminism*. Bloomington: Indiana University Press.

Mira-Caballos, Esteban. 1997. *El indio antillano: Repartimiento, encomienda y esclavitud (1492–1542)*. Seville: Muñoz Moya Editor.

Miranda, A. P. 1954. "Memória sobre a costa de Africa e da Monarquia Africana (c. 1766)." In L. F. C. Dias, ed., *Fontes para a história, geografia e comércio de Moçambique (século 18)*. Lisbon: Agência Geral do Ultramar. 47–121.

Mires, Fernando. 1990. *El Discurso de la Naturaleza: Ecologia y Politica en América Latina*. San José: DEI.

Mistral, Gabriela. 1938. *Tala*. Buenos Aires: Sur.

——. 1957. *Selected Poems of Gabriela Mistral*. Trans. Langston Hughes. Bloomington: Indiana University Press.

——. 1966. *Poesías completas*. Madrid: Aguilar.

Mitchell, Timothy. 1988. *Colonizing Egypt: Orientalism Reconsidered*. Cambridge: Cambridge University Press.

Mohanty, Chandra. 1991 [1986]. "Under Western Eyes: Feminist Scholarship and Colonial Discourses." In Chandra Mohanty, Ann Russo, and Lourdes Torres, eds., *Third World Women and the Politics of Feminism*. Bloomington: Indiana University Press. 51–81.

——. 2002. "'Under Western Eyes' Revisited: Feminist Solidarity through Anti-capitalist Struggles." *Signs* 28, no. 2: 499–535.

Molina, Alonso de. 1970. *Vocabulario en lengua castellana y mexicana y mexicana y castellana*. Mexico City: Porrúa.

Monclaro, Padre. 1899. "Relaçaõ da Viagem q Fizeraõ os Padres da Companhia de Jesus com Francisco Barreto na conquista de Monomotapa no Anno de 1569." In G. M. Theal, ed., *Records of South-Eastern Africa*. Vol. 3. Cape Town: Struik. 157–201.

Mondlane, Eduardo C. 1969. *The Struggle for Mozambique*. Harmondsworth, U.K.: Penguin.

Mongia, Padmini, ed. 1997. *Contemporary Postcolonial Theory*. London: Arnold.

Monjarás Ruiz, Jesús. 1987. *Mitos cosmogónicos del México indígena*. Mexico: Instituto Nacional de Antropología e Historia.

Montaigne, Michel. 1893. *The Essays Done into English by John Florio, anno 1603*. London: D. Nutt.

———. 1965. *Complete Essays*. Stanford, Calif.: Stanford University Press.

Montaldo, Graciela. 1977. "Strategies at the End of the Century: A Review Essay." *Organization* 44 (November): 628–34.

Montalvo, Juan. 2000. *El espectador*. Ambato, Ecuador: Editorial Pio XII.

Montejo, Víctor. 1997. "Pan-Mayanismo: La pluriformidad de la cultura maya y el proceso de autorrepresentación de los mayas." *Mesoamérica* 18, no. 33: 93–123.

Montrose, Louis A. 1980a. "The Purpose of Playing: Reflections on a Shakespearean Anthropology." *Helios* 7: 51–74.

———. 1980b. "Renaissance Literary Studies and the Subject of History." *English Literary Renaissance* 10: 153–82.

Moore, Rachel. 1992. "Marketing Alterity." *Visual Anthropology Review* 8: 16–26.

Moore-Gilbert, Bart. 1997. *Postcolonial Theory: Contexts, Practices, Politics*. London: Verso.

Mora, Pat. 1992. *Nepantla: Essays from the Land in the Middle*. Albuquerque: University of New Mexico Press.

Moraga, Cherríe, and Gloria Anzaldúa, eds. 1981. *This Bridge Called My Back: Writings by Radical Women of Color*. Watertown, Mass.: Persephone Press.

Morales, Mario Roberto, ed. 2000. *Miguel Angel Asturias: Cuentos y leyendas*. Critical ed. Paris: Colección Archivos.

———. 2000–2001. "El neomacartismo estalinista (o la cacería de brujas en la academia 'posmo')." *Encuentro de la cultura cubana* 19 (winter): 47–58.

———, ed. 2001. *Stoll-Menchú: La invención de la memoria*. Guatemala City: Consucultura.

———. 2002. *La articulación de las diferencias o el síndrome de Maximón*. 2d ed. Guatemala: Consucultura-Editorial Palo de Hormigo.

Moraña, Mabel. 1998a. "El boom del subalterno." *Cuadernos Americanos* 67, no. 1: 216–22.

———, ed. 1998b. *Indigenismo hacia el fin del milenio: Homenaje a Antonio Cornejo Polar*. Pittsburgh: Instituto Internacional de Literatura Iberoamericana.

———, ed. 1998c. *Viaje al silencio: Exploraciones del discurso barroco*. Mexico City: Universidad Nacional Autónoma de México.

———. 2000. "El 'tumulto de indios' de 1692 en los pliegues de la fiesta barroca." In José Antonio Mazzotti, ed., *Agencias criollas: La ambigüedad "colonial" en las letras hispanoamericanas*. Pittsburgh: Biblioteca de América. 161–75.

Moreano, Alejandro. 2003. "Del agua y del aceite y del aceite de ricino." *Tintají* 18 (February): 2.

Moreiras, Alberto. 1994. "Pastiche, Identity and Allegory of Allegory." In Amaryll Chanady, ed. *Latin American Identity and the Constructions of Difference*. Minneapolis: University of Minnesota Press. 118–40.

———. 1995. "Restitution and Appropiation in Latinoamericanism." *Interdisciplinary Literary Studies* 1: 1–43.

———. 1997. "The End of Magical Realism: José María Arguedas's Passionate Signifier (El zorro de arriba y el zorro de abajo)." *Narrative Technique* 27, no. 1: 84–111.

———. 1998. "Fragmentos globales: Latinoamericanismo de segundo orden." In Santiago Castro-Gómez and Eduardo Mendieta, eds., *Teorías sin disciplina: Latinoamericanismo, poscolonialidad and globalización en debate*. Mexico City: Miguel Ángel Porrúa. 59–83.

———. 2001. *The Exhaustion of Difference: The Politics of Latin American Cultural Studies*. Durham, N.C.: Duke University Press.

Mörner, Magnus. 1967. *Race Mixture in the History of Latin America*. Boston: Little, Brown.

———. 1970. *La corona española y los foráneos en los pueblos de indios en América*. Stockholm: Latinamerikanska-institutet, Almqvist, and Wiksell.

Morris, Wesley. 1972. *Toward a New Historicism*. Princeton: Princeton University Press.

Mowitt, John. 1988. "Foreword: The Resistance in Theory." In *Discerning the Subject*. Minneapolis: University of Minnesota Press. ix–xxiii.

———. 1992. *Text: The Genealogy of an Antidisciplinary Object*. Durham, N.C.: Duke University Press.

Mudimbe, Valentine. 1988. *The Invention of Africa: Gnosis, Philosophy, and the Order of Knowledge*. Bloomington: Indiana University Press.

Mudimbe-Boyi, Elisabeth. 2002. *Beyond Dichotomies*. New York: State University of New York Press. 251–86.

Mueller-Vollmer, Kurt. 1985. *Hermeneutics Reader*. New York: Continuum.

Mukherjee, Arun. 1990. "Whose Post-Colonialism and Whose Postmodernism?" *World Literature Written in English* 30, no. 2: 1–9.

Mullaney, Steven. 1983. "Strange Things, Gross Terms, Curious Customs: The Rehearsal of Cultures in the Late Renaissance." *Representations* 1: 40–67.

Myrdall, Gunnar. 1944. *American Dilemma*. New York: Harper and Brothers.

Nagy-Zekmi, Silvia. 2001. "Angel Rama y su ensayística transcultural(izadora) como autobiografía en clave crítica." *Revista Chilena de Literatura* 58: 123–31.

Najenson, José Luis. 1979. *Cultura nacional y cultura subalterna*. Toluca, Mexico: Universidad Autónoma del Estado de México.

Nandy, Ashis. 1983. *The Intimate Enemy: Loss and Recovery of Self Under Colonialism*. Delhi: Oxford University Press.

———. 1999. *Traditions, Tyranny and Utopia: Essays in the Politics of Awareness*. Delhi: Oxford University Press.

Naranjo Orovio, Consuelo, Miguel Angel Puig-Samper, and Luis Miguel García Mora. 1996. *La nación soñada: Cuba, Puerto Rico y Filipinas ante el 98: Actas del congreso internacional celebrado en Aranjuez del 24 al 28 de abril de 1995*. Madrid: Doce Calles.

Narayan, Uma. 2000. "Essence of Culture and a Sense of History: A Feminist Critique to Cultural Essentialism." In Uma Narayan and Sandra Harding, eds., *Decentering the Center: Philosophy for a Multicultural, Postcolonial, and Feminist World*. Bloomington: Indiana University Press. 80–101.

Navarro, Mireya. 2002. "Promoting Hispanic TV, Language, and Culture." *New York Times*, 30 December, C7.

Newson, Linda A. 1985. "Indian Population Patterns in Colonial Spanish America." *Latin American Research Review* 20: 41–74.

Ngugi wa Thiong'o. 1973. *Homecoming: Essays on African and Caribbean Literature, Culture, and Politics*. New York: Lawrence Hill.

———. 1986. *Decolonizing the Mind: The Politics of Language in African Literature*. London: Heinemann.

———. 1992. "Resistance in the Literature of the African Diaspora: Post-emancipation and Post-colonial Discourses." Lecture delivered at the conference, "Inventions of Africa: Africa in the Literatures of the Continent and the Diaspora," Center for Afroamerican and African Studies, University of Michigan, Ann Arbor, 17 April.

Nicholson, Linda, ed. 1990. *Feminism/Postmodernism*. New York: Routledge.

Nietzsche, Friedrich. 1954. *The Portable Nietzsche*. Trans. Walter Kaufmann. New York: Viking Press.

——. 1968. *Basic Writings of Nietzsche*. New York: Modern Library.

——. 1968. *The Will to Power*. Trans. Walter Kaufmann and R. J. Hollingdale. New York: Random House.

Nixon, Rob. 1987. "Caribbean and African Appropriations of *The Tempest*." *Critical Inquiry* 13: 557–78.

Nkrumah, Kwame. 1961. *I Speak of Freedom. A Statement of African Ideology*. London: Heinemann.

——. 1965. *Neo-Colonialism. The Last Stage of Imperialism*. London: Thomas Nelson.

Nowotny, Karl Anton. 1961. *Tlacuilolli: Die mexikanischen Bilderhandschriften, Stil und Inhalt*. Berlin: Gebr. Mann.

Nunberg, Geoffrey. 2002. "Keeping Ahead of the Joneses." *New York Times*, 24 November, national ed., sec. 4, 4.

Nyerere, Julius K. 1966. *Freedom and Unity*. Dar es Salaam: Oxford University Press.

O'Gorman, Edmundo. 1952. *La idea del descubrimiento de América: Historia de esa interpretación y crítica de sus fundamentos*. Mexico City: Universidad Nacional Autónoma de México.

——. 1991 [1958]. *La invención de América: Investigación acerca de la estructura histórica del Nuevo Mundo y del sentido de su devenir*. Mexico City: Fondo de Cultura Económica.

——. 1961. *The Invention of America: An Inquiry into the Historical Nature of the New World and the Meaning of Its History*. Bloomington: Indiana University Press.

O'Hanlon, Rosalind. 1986. "Recovering the Subject: Subaltern Studies and Histories of Resistance in Colonial South Asia." *Modern Asian Studies* 22: 189–224.

Oldenburg, Veena Talwar. 1994. "The Continuing Invention of the Sati Tradition." In John Stratton Hawley, ed., *Sati: The Blessing and the Curse the Burning of Wives in India*. New York: Oxford University Press. 120–67.

Oré, Luis Jerónimo de Oré. 1598. *Símbolo Católico Indiano*. Lima: Por Antonio Ricardo.

Orgen, Stephen. 1975. *The Illusion of Power: Political Theatre in the English Renaissance*. Berkeley: University of California Press.

Orozco Abad, Iván. 1991. "Etica y proceso de paz." In *Colombia: Una casa para todos*. Bogotá: Ediciones Antropas. 353–74.

Ortega, Julio. 1973a. "Cuentos de Antonio Benítez Rojo." In *Relato de la utopía*. Barcelona: La Gaya Ciencia. 173–90.

——. 1973b. "Los cuentos de Antonio Benítez Rojo." In Enrique Pupo Walker, ed., *El cuento hispanoamericano ante la crítica*. Madrid: Castalia. 264–78.

Ortiz, Fernando. 1978. *Contrapunteo cubano del tabaco y el azúcar*. Caracas: Biblioteca Ayacucho.

Osterhammel, Jürgen. 1997. *Colonialism: A Theoretical Overview*. Trans. Shelley L. Frisch. Princeton, N.J.: Markus Wiener.

Ots Capdequí, J. M. 1993. El Estado español en Indias. Mexico City: Fondo de Cultura Económica.

Outlaw, Lucius. 1987. "African 'Philosophy': Deconstructive and Reconstructive Challenges." In Floistad Guttorm, ed., African Philosophy, vol. 5 of Contemporary Philosophy: A New Survey. Dordrecht: Martinus Nijhoff. 9–44.

Owen, Roger, and Bob Sutcliffe, eds. 1975 [1972]. Studies in the Theory of Imperialism. London: Longman.

Owen, W. F. W. 1964. "Letter from Captain W. F. W. Owen to J. W. Crocker, 9 October, 1823." In G. M. Theal, ed., Records of South-East Africa. Vol. 9. Cape Town: Struik. 32–35.

Pabón Ortega, Carlos E. 1996. "El 98 en el imaginario nacional: Seva o la 'nación soñada.'" In Consuelo Naranjo Orovio, Miguel Angel Puig-Samper, and Luis Miguel García Mora, La nación soñada: Cuba, Puerto Rico y Filipinas ante el 98: Actas del congreso internacional celebrado en Aranjuez del 24 al 28 de abril de 1995. Madrid: Doce Calles. 547–58.

Pacheco, Joaquín, Francisco Cárdenas, and Luis Torres, eds. 1864–89. Colección de documentos inéditos relativos al descubrimiento, conquista y organización de las antiguas posesiones españolas de América y Oceanía, sacados de los archivos del reino, y muy especialmente del de Indias. 42 vols. Madrid: Competentemente autorizada.

Packard, Randall. 1989. "The Healthy Reserve and the 'Dressed Native': Discourses on Black Health and the Language of Legitimation in South Africa." American Ethnologist 16, no. 4: 686–703.

Pagden, Anthony. 1987. "Identity formation in Spanish America." In Nicholas Canny and Anthony Pagden, eds., Colonial Identity in the Atlantic World, 1500–1800. Princeton: Princeton University Press. 51–93.

———. 1990. Spanish Imperialism and the Political Imagination: Studies in European and Spanish-American Social and Political Thought 1513–1830. New Haven, Conn.: Yale University Press.

———. 1995. Lords of All the World: Ideologies of Empire in Spain, Britain, and France c. 1500–1800. New Haven, Conn.: Yale University Press.

Palmié, Stephan. 2002. Wizards and Scientists: Explorations in Afro-Cuban Modernity and Tradition. Durham, N.C.: Duke University Press.

Panikkar, Raimundo. 1988. "What Is Comparative Philosophy Comparing?" In Gerald James Larson and Eliot Deutsch, eds., Interpreting Across Boundaries: New Essays in Comparative Philosophy. Princeton: Princeton University Press. 116–37.

———. 1993. The Cosmotheandric Experience: Emerging Religious Consciousness. Maryknoll, N.Y.: Orbis Books.

Paravisini-Gebert, Lisabeth. 1997. "Writers Playin' Mas': Carnival and the Grotesque in the Contemporary Caribean Novel." In James Arnold, ed., A History of Literature in the Caribbean, vol. 3. Amsterdam: John Benjamins Publishing. 215–36.

Parisot, Jean-Paul, and Françoise Suagher. 1996. Calendriers et chronologie. Paris: Masson.

Parry, Benita. 1987. "Problems in Current Theories of Colonial Discourse." Oxford Literary Review 9: 27–57.

Pastor, Beatriz. 1988. Discursos narrativos de la conquista: Mitificación y emergencia. 2d ed. Hanover, N.H.: Ediciones del Norte.

Patterson, Thomas C. 1997. *Inventing Western Civilization*. New York: Monthly Review Press.

Payeras, Mario. 1997. *Los pueblos indígenas y la revolución guatemalteca: Ensayos étnicos 1982–1992*. Guatemala City: Magna Terra.

Paz, Octavio. 1997 [1950]. *El laberinto de la soledad*. New York: Penguin.

Pearce, Roy Harvey. 1969. *Historicism Once More*. Princeton: Princeton University Press.

Peralta Barnuevo, Pedro de. 1863 [1732]. *Lima fundada, o, Conquista del Peru: Poema heroico en que se decanta toda la historia del descubrimiento, y sujecion de sus provincias por Don Francisco Pizarro, Marques de los Atabillos*. Lima: Imprenta de Sobrino y Bados.

Pérez, Alberto Julián. 1999. "El poscolonialismo y la inmadurez de los pensadores hispanoamericanos." In Alfonso de Toro and Fernando de Toro, eds., *El debate de la postcolonialidad en Latinoamérica: Una postmodernidad periférica o cambio de paradigma en el pensamiento latinoamericano*. Madrid: Iberoamericana. 199–213.

Pérez, Louis A. 1998. *The War of 1898: The United States and Cuba in History and Historiography*. Chapel Hill: University of North Carolina Press.

Pérez de Mendiola, Marina, ed. 1996. *Bridging the Atlantic: Toward a Reassessment of Iberian and Latin American Cultural Ties*. Albany: State University of New York Press.

Pérez-Luño, Antonio Enrique. 1992. *La polémica sobre el Nuevo Mundo: Los clásicos españoles en la Filosofía del Derecho*. Madrid: Editorial Trotta.

Peyser, Thomas. 1998. *Utopia and Cosmopolis: Globalization in the Era of American Literary Realism*. Durham, N.C.: Duke University Press.

Phelan, John Leddy. 1960. "Neo-Aztecism in the Eighteenth Century and the Genesis of Mexican Nationalism." In Stanley Diamond, ed., *Culture in History: Essays in Honor of Paul Radin*. New York: Columbia University Press.

———. 1979. *El Origen de la idea de America*. Mexico City: Universidad Nacional Autónoma de México.

Pico, Fernando. 1998. *1898: La Guerra después de la Guerra*. Río Piedras, Puerto Rico: Ediciones Huracán.

Piglia, Ricardo. 1992. *La ciudad ausente*. Buenos Aires: SudAmericana.

Pinaud, João Luiz, et al. 1987. *Insurreição negra e justiça*. Rio de Janeiro: Expressão e Cultura/OAB.

Pires, Maria Laura Bettencourt. 1981. *Portugal visto pelos Ingleses*. Lisbon: Centro de Estudos Comparados de Línguas e Literaturas Modernas da Universidade Nova de Lisbon.

Pletsch, Carl E. 1981. "The Three Worlds, or, the Division of Social Scientific Labor, circa 1950–1975." *Comparative Study of Society and History* 23, no. 4: 565–90.

Pomeranz, Kenneth. 2000. *The Great Divergence: China, Europe and the Making of the Modern World Economy*. Princeton: Princeton University Press.

Poot-Herrera, Sara. 1995. "Los criollos: Nota sobre su identidad y su cultura." *Colonial Latin American Review* 4, no. 1: 177–84.

Pop Bol Amanda. 2000. "Racismo y machismo: Deshilando la opresión." In Morna MacLeod and M. Luisa Cabrera, eds., *Identidad: Rostros sin márcara (reflexiones sobre cosmovisión, género y etnicidad)* Guatemala City: OXFAM. 111–41.

Portugal, Ana María. 1989. *Mujeres e iglesia: Sexualidad and aborto en América Latina Católicas por el derecho a decidir*. Washington: Catholics for a Free Choice/Distribuciones Fontamara.

Portugal, Joaquim José da Costa. 1954. "Notícias das Ilhas de Cabo Delgado." In L. F. C. Dias, ed., *Fontes para a história, geografia e comércio de Moçambique (século 18)*. Lisbon: Agência Geral do Ultramar. 275–310.

Potasch, Robert A. 1959. *El Banco de Avío de México, 1821–1846*. Mexico City: Fondo de Cultura Económica.

Poulantzas, Nicos. 1979. *State, Power, Socialism*. London: New Left Books.

Prado Tello, Elías, and Alfredo Prado Prado, eds. 1991. *Phelipe Guaman Poma de Ayala: Y no ay [sic] rremedio. . . .* Lima: Centro de Investigación y Promoción Amazónica.

Praeger, Michele. 1996. "René Depestre: Théorie et fiction du zombie." *Etudes francophones* 11, no. 1: 83–94.

Prakash, Gyan. 1995. *After Colonialism: Imperial Histories and Postcolonial Displacements*. Princeton: Princeton University Press.

———. 1997. "Los estudios de la subalternidad como crítica post-colonial." In Silvia Rivera Cusicanqui and Rossana Barragán, eds., *Debates post-coloniales: Una introducción a los estudios de la subalternidad*. La Paz: Historias-Sephis-Aruwiyiri. 293–314.

Pratt, Mary Louise. 1992. *Imperial Eyes: Travel Writing and Transculturation*. London: Routledge.

Prebisch, Raúl. 1959. "Commercial Policy in the Underdeveloped Countries." *American Economic Review, Papers and Proceedings* 49: 251–73.

———. 1960. *The Economic Development in Latin America and Its Principal Problems*. New York: Economic Commission for Latin America, United Nations.

Prem, Hanns. 1978. "Comentario a las partes calendáricas del Codex Mexicanus." *Estudios de cultura nahuatl* 13: 267–88.

Prieto, René. 1990. "Antonio Benítez Rojo." In Julio A. Martínez, ed., *Dictionary of Twentieth Century Cuban Literature*. New York: Greenwood Press. 65–71.

Quayson, Ato. 2000. *Postcolonialism: Theory, Practice or Process?* Cambridge: Polity.

Queiroz, Suely R. Reis de. 1977. *Escravidão negra em São Paulo*. Rio de Janeiro: José Olympio.

Querino, Manuel. 1954. *O africano como colonisador*. Salvador, Brazil: Livraria Progresso Editora.

———. 1978. *The African Contribution to Brazilian Civilization*. Trans. with intro. by E. Bradford Burns. Tempe: Arizona State University.

Quijano, Aníbal. 1966. *Notas sobre el concepto de marginalidad social*. Lima: Comisión Económica para América Latina.

———. 1967. "Urbanización, cambio social y dependencia." In Fernando Henrique Cardoso and Francisco Weffort, eds., *América Latina: Ensayos de interpretación sociológica*. Santiago: Editorial Universitaria.

———. 1972. *Qué es y qué no es socialismo*. Lima: Ediciones Sociedad y Política.

———. 1977. *Imperialismo y marginalidad en América Latina*. Lima: Mosca Azul.

———. 1981a. *Introducción a Mariátegui*. Mexico City: Siglo XXI.

———. 1981b. "Poder y democracia en el socialismo." *Sociedad y Política* 12.

———. 1988a. *Modernidad, identidad y utopía en América Latina*. Lima: Sociedad y Política Ediciones.

———. 1988b. "La nueva heterogeneidad estructural de América Latina." In Heinz Sonntag, ed., *Nuevo temas, nuevos contenidos*. Caracas: UNESCO/Nueva Sociedad. 29–51.

——. 1992a. "Colonialidad y Modernidad/Racionalidad." In Robin Blackburn and Heraclio Bonilla, eds., *Los Conquistados: 1492 y la población indígena de las Américas.* Bogotá, Colombia: Tercer Mundo Editores. 437–47.

——. 1992b. "Colonialidad y modernidad/racionalidad." *Perú indígena* 13, no. 29. 11–20.

——. 1992c. "Réflexions sur l'interdisciplinarité, le développement et les relations interculturelles." In Eduardo Portella, ed., *Entre savoirs: L'interdisciplinarité en acte: Enjeux, obstacles, perspectives.* Toulouse: Erès.

——. 1993a. "América Latina en la economía mundial." *Problemas del desarollo* 24: 5–18.

——. 1993b. " 'Raza,' 'etnia,' 'nación,' cuestiones abiertas en América Latina." In Roland Forgues, ed., *Encuentro internacional José Carlos Mariátegui y Europa: El otro aspecto del descubrimiento.* Lima: Editorial Amauta. 167–88.

——. 1994. "Colonialité du pouvoir, démocratie et citoyenneté en Amérique Latine." In *Amérique Latine: Démocratie et exclusion.* Paris: L'Harmattan. http://multitudes .samizdat.net/.

——. 1995. "Modernity, Identity and Utopia in Latin America." In John Beverley, Michael Aronna, and José Oviedo, eds., *The Postmodernism Debate in Latin America.* Durham, N.C.: Duke University Press. 201–16.

——. 1997. "Colonialidad de poder, cultura y conocimiento en América Latina." *Anuario Mariateguiano* 9, no. 9: 113–22.

——. 1998a. "The Colonial Nature of Power in Latin America." In Roberto Briceño-León, Heinz Rudolf Sonntag, and María Luz Morán, eds., *Sociology in Latin America: Proceedings of the ISA Regional Conference for Latin America, Colonia Tovar, Venezuela, July 7–8, 1997.* Montreal: Service de l'information et des relations publiques de l'UQAM, Service de graphisme. 27–38.

——. 1998b. "Estado-nación, ciudadanía y democracia: Cuestiones abiertas." In Helena Gonzales and Heidulf Schmidt, eds., *Democracia para una nueva sociedad.* Caracas: Nueva Sociedad. 139–57.

——. 1999a. "Colonialidad del poder, cultura y conocimiento en América Latina." In Santiago Castro-Gómez, Oscar Guardiola-Rivera, and Carmen Millán de Benavides, eds., *Pensar (en) los intersticios: Teoría and práctica de la crítica poscolonial.* Bogotá: Centro Editorial Javeriano. 99–109.

——1999b. "Coloniality and Modernity/Rationality." In Goran Therborn, ed., *Globalizations and Modernities.* Stockholm: Forksningsradnamnden.

——. 1999c. "Coloniality of Power and Its Institutions." Paper presented at conference, "World Historical Sites of Colonial Disciplinary Practices: The Nation State, the Bourgeois Family, and the Enterprise," Binghamton University, Binghamton, New York, 22–24 April.

——. 1999d. "¡Qué tal raza!" In Edith Benado Calderón, ed., *Familia y cambio social.* Lima: CECOSAM. 186–203.

——. 2000a. "Colonialidad del poder, eurocentrismo y América Latina." In Edgardo Lander, ed., *La colonialidad del saber: Eurocentrismo y ciencias sociales: Perspectivas Latinoamericanas.* Buenos Aires: Consejo Latinoamericano de Ciencias Sociales. 201–46.

——. 2000b. "Coloniality of Power, Eurocentrism, and Latin America." *Nepantla* 1, no. 3: 533–80.

——. 2000c. "El fantasma del desarrollo en América Latina." *Revista venezolana de ciencias sociales* 6, no. 2: 73–90.

——. 2000d. "Modernidad y democracia: Intereses y conflictos." *Anuario Mariateguiano* 12.

——. 2001. "Globalización, colonialidad y democracia." In Instituto de Altos Estudios Diplomáticos "Pedro Gual," ed., *Tendencias básicas de nuestra época: Globalización y democracia*. Caracas: Instituto de Altos Estudios Diplomáticos "Pedro Gual." 25–61.

Quijano, Aníbal, and Immanuel Wallerstein. 1992. "Americanity as a Concept, or the Americas in the Imaginary of the Modern World-System." *International Journal of Social Science* 134: 549–59.

Quine, Willard Van Orman. 1960. *Word and Object*. Cambridge: MIT University Press.

Quiñones-Keber, Eloise, ed. 1995. *Codex Telleriano-Remensis: Ritual, Divination, and History in a Pictorial Aztec Manuscript*. Austin: University of Texas Press.

Quiroga, Horacio. 1990. *Los desterrados y otros textos*. Ed. Jorge Lafforgue. Madrid: Clásicos Castalia.

Rabasa, José. 1993. *Inventing America: Spanish Historiography and the Formation of Eurocentrism*. Norman: University of Oklahoma Press.

——. 1996. "Pre-Colombian Pasts and Indian Presents in Mexican History." In José Rabasa, Javier Sanjinés C., and Robert Carr, eds., "Subaltern Studies in the Americas," special issue, *Dispositio/n* 19, no. 46: 245–70.

——. 1997. "On Zapatismo: Reflections of the Folkloric and the Impossible in a Subaltern Insurrection." In Lisa Lowe and David Lloyd, eds., *The Politics of Culture in the Shadow of Capital*. Durham, N.C.: Duke University Press. 399–432.

——. 1998. "Franciscans and Dominicans under the Gaze of a Tlacuilo: Plural-World Dwelling in an Indian Pictorial Codex." Morrison Library Inaugural Lecture Series 14. Manuscript, Doe Library, University of California, Berkeley.

——. 2000. *Writing Violence on the Northern Frontier: The Historiography of Sixteenth-Century New Mexico and Florida and the Legacy of Conquest*. Durham, N.C.: Duke University Press

——. 2006. "Elsewheres: Radical Relativism and the Frontiers of Empire." *Qui Parle* 16, no. 1: 71–94.

Rabasa, José, and Javier Sanjinés. 1994. "Introduction: The Politics of Subaltern Studies." In José Rabasa, Javier Sanjinés C., and Robert Carr, eds., "Subaltern Studies in the Americas," special issue, *Dispositio/n* 19, no. 46: v–xi.

Rabasa, José, Javier Sanjínes C., and Robert Carr. 1994. "Subaltern Studies in the Americas." Special issue, *Dispositio/n* 19, no. 46.

Radaelli, Sigfrido. 1957. *La institución virreinal en las Indias: Antecedentes históricos*. Buenos Aires: Editorial Perrot.

Rafael, Vicente. 1988. *Contracting Colonialism: Translation and Christian Conversion in Tagalog Society under Early Spanish Rule*. Ithaca, N.Y.: Cornell University Press.

——. 1994. "The Cultures of Area Studies in the United States." *Social Text* 33: 91–111.

Raichman, John. 1985. *Michel Foucault: Beyond Structuralism and Hermeneutics*. New York: Columbia University Press.

Rama, Angel. 1982. *Transculturación narrativa en América Latina*. Mexico City: Siglo XXI.

——. 1984. *La ciudad letrada*. Hanover, N.H.: Ediciones del Norte.

Ramírez, Franklin. 2000. *Participación, desarrollo y actores locales: Innovación política y gestión para el desarrollo en dos cantones indígenas del Ecuador.* Quito: Ciudad.

Ramírez, Sergio. 1988. "La revolución: El hecho cultural más grande de nuestra historia." *Ventana (Barricada)* (30 January 1982): 8.

Ramos, Alcida. 1982. "Indian Voices: Contact Experienced and Expressed." In Jonathan Hill, ed., *Rethinking History and Myth: Indigenous Perspectives on the Past.* Urbana: University of Illinois Press. 214–34.

——. 1990. "Indigenismo de Resultados." *Revista Tempo Brasileiro* 100: 133–50.

——. 1994. "The Hyperreal Indian." *Critique of Anthropology* 14, no. 2: 153–71.

Ramos, Julio. 1989. *Desencuentros de la modernidad en América Latina: Literatura y pólitica en el Siglo XIX.* Mexico City: Fondo de Cultura Económica.

Ranger, Terence. 1988. "The Invention of Tradition in Colonial Africa." In E. Hobsbawm and Terence Ranger, eds. *The Invention of Tradition.* Cambridge: Cambridge University Press. 211–62.

Readings, Bill. 1996. *The University in Ruins.* Cambridge: Harvard University Press.

Reardon, Bernard M. G. 1977. *Hegel's Philosophy of Religion.* New York: Barnes and Noble.

Recinos, Ivonne N. 2002. "Narrar la patria y prefigurar una nación excluyente en el Reino de Guatemala: 1680–1824." Ph.D. diss., University of Pittsburgh.

Recopilación de leyes de los reynos de las Indias: Mandadas imprimir, y publicar por la Magestad catolica del rey don Carlos II, nuestro señor: Va dividida en qvatro tomos, con el indice general, y al principio de cada tomo el indice especial de los titulos, que contiene. 1681. 4 vols. Madrid: I. de Paredes.

Reimers, David M. 1985. *Still the Golden Door: The Third World Comes to America.* New York: Columbia University Press.

Reis, Roberto. 1991. "Hei de Convencer: Autoritarismo no Discurso Colonial Brasileiro." Paper read at the meeting of the Latin American Studies Association, 4–6 April.

Renan, Ernest. 1990 [1882]. "What Is a Nation?" In Homi K. Bhabha, ed., *Nation and Narration.* London: Routledge. 8–22.

Rex, John, and David Mason, eds. 1986. *Theories of Race and Ethnic Relations.* Cambridge: Cambridge University Press.

Ribeiro, Darcy. 1974. *Fronteras indígenas de la civilización.* Mexico City: Siglo XXI.

——. 1995. *O povo brasileiro: A formação e o sentido do Brasil.* 2d ed. São Paulo: Editora Schwarcz.

Ricard, Robert. 1933. *La "Conquête spirituelle" de Méxique.* Paris: Université de Paris.

Richard, Nelly. 1989. *La estratificación de los márgenes.* Santiago: Francisco Zegers.

——. 1993. "The Latin American Problematic of Theoretical-Cultural Transference: Postmodern Appropriations and Counterappropriations." *South Atlantic Quarterly* 92, no. 3: 453–60.

——. 1994a. "Bordes, diseminación, postmodernismo: Una metáfora latinoamericana de fin de siglo." In Josefina Ludmer, ed., *Las culturas de fin de siglo en América Latina.* Buenos Aires: Beatriz Viterbo. 240–53.

——. 1994b. *La insubordinación de los signos: Cambio político, transformaciones culturales y poéticas de la crisis.* Santiago: Cuarto Propio.

———. 1996. "Signos culturales y mediaciones académicas." In Beatriz González Stephan, ed., *Cultura y tercer mundo*. Caracas: Editorial Nueva Sociedad. 1–22.

———. 1998a. "Intersectando Latinoamérica con el latinoamericanismo: Discurso académico y crítica cultural." In Santiago Castro-Gómez and Eduardo Mendieta, eds., *Teorías sin disciplina: Latinoamericanismo, poscolonialidad and globalización en debate*. Mexico City: Miguel Ángel Porrúa. 245–70.

———. 1998b. *Residuos y metáforas: Ensayos de crítica cultural sobre el Chile de la transición*. Santiago: Cuarto Propio.

Ricoeur, Paul. 1964. *Histoire et verité*. Paris: Seuil.

Rivarola, Luis. 1990. *La formación lingüística de Hispanoamérica*. Lima: Fondo Editorial de la Pontificia Universidad Católica del Perú.

Rivera Cusicanqui, Silvia. 1993. "La raíz: Colonizadores y colonizados." In Xavier Albó and Raúl Barrios, eds., *Violencias encubiertas en Bolivia*. La Paz: CIPCA. 27–139.

Rivera Cusicanqui, Silvia, and Rossana Barragán, eds. 1997. *Debates post-coloniales: Una introducción a los estudios de la subalternidad*. La Paz: Historias-Sephis-Aruwiyiri.

Rodó, José Enrique. 1967. *Ariel*. Ed., intro., and notes by Gordon Brotherston. Cambridge: Cambridge University Press.

———. 1988. *Ariel*. Austin: University of Texas Press.

Rodríguez, Ileana. 1998. "Hegemonía y dominio: Subalternidad un significado flotante." In Santiago Castro-Gómez and Eduardo Mendieta, eds., *Teorías sin disciplina: Latinoamericanismo, poscolonialidad y globalización en debate*. Mexico City: Miguel Ángel Porrúa. 101–19.

———, ed. 2001a. *Convergencia de Tiempos*. Amsterdam: Rodopi.

———, ed. 2001b. *The Latin American Subaltern Studies Reader*. Durham, N.C.: Duke University Press.

Rodríguez, Richard. 1988. *Hunger of Memory*. New York: Bantam.

Rodríguez Monegal, Emir. 1972. "Lo real y lo maravilloso en El reino de este mundo." In Klaus Müller-Bergh, ed., *Asedios a Alejo Carpentier*. Santiago de Chile: Editorial Universitaria. 101–33.

Rojas, Cristina. 2001. *Civilization and Violence: Regimes of Representation in Nineteenth Century Colombia*. Minneapolis: University of Minnesota Press.

Rojinski, David. 1998. "The Writing of Eurocentrism in Pre-Modern Castile and Colonial Spanish America." Ph.D. diss., University of Michigan.

Rojo, Grínor. 1997. "Crítica del canon, estudios culturales, estudios postcoloniales y estudios latinoamericanos: Una convivencia difícil." *Kipus* 6: 5–17.

Romano, Carlin. 2004. "The Unexamined Life May Be Your Own." *Chronicle of Higher Education*, 9 April, B13.

Romero, Emilio. 1927. "El Cuzco catolico." *Amauta*, no. 10 (December): 54.

Romero, José Luis. 2001. *Latinoamérica: Las ciudades y las ideas*. Mexico City: Siglo XXI.

Rorty, Richard. 1979. *Philosophy and the Mirror of Nature*. Princeton: Princeton University Press.

Rosaldo, Renato. 1988. "Ideology, Place, and People without Culture." *Cultural Anthropology* 3, no. 1: 77–87.

———. 1991. *Cultura y verdad: Nueva propuesta de análisis social*. Mexico City: Grijalbo/CNCA.

Rosario, Rubén del. 1970. El español de América. Sharon, Conn.: Troutman Press.

Rosenblat, Ángel. 1954. La población indígena y el mestizaje en América. 2 vols. Buenos Aires: Nova.

Ross, Kathleen. 2000. "Chisme, exceso y agencia criolla: Tratado del descubrimiento de las Indias y su conquista (1589) de Juan Suárez de Peralta." In José Antonio Mazzotti, ed., Agencias criollas: La ambigüedad "colonial" en las letras hispanoamericanas. Pittsburgh: Instituto Internacional de Literatura Iberoamericana. 131–42.

———. 1993. The Baroque Narrative of Carlos de Sigüenza y Góngora: A New World Paradise. Cambridge: Cambridge University Press.

Rostow, Walt W. 1960. The Stages of Economic Growth: A Non-Communist Manifesto. Cambridge: Cambridge University Press.

Rotenstreich, Nathan. 1984. Jews and German Philosophy: The Polemics of Emancipation. New York: Schocken Books.

Roth, Richard. 1989. "The Colonial Experience and Its Postmodern Fate." Salmagundi 85: 248–65.

Rowe, William, and Vivian Schelling. 1991. Memory and Modernity: Popular Culture in Latin America. London: Verso.

Rushdie, Salman. 1989. The Satanic Verses. New York: Viking.

———. 1992. Imaginary Homelands: Essays and Criticism, 1981–1991. New York: Penguin.

Rus Jan, Shannan Mattiace, and R. Aída Hernández Castillo. 2003. Mayan Lives, Mayan Utopias: The Indigenous Peoples of Chiapas and the Zapatista Rebellion. San Francisco: Latin American Perspectives in the Classroom/Rowman and Littlefield.

Russell-Wood, A. J. R. 1985. "United States Scholarly Contributions to the Historiography of Colonial Brazil." Hispanic American Historical Review 65, no. 4: 683–723.

Sá, Lúcia de. 2004. Rain Forest Literatures: Amazonian Texts and Latin American Culture. Minneapolis: University of Minnesota Press.

Saénz, Mario. 1999. The Identity of Liberation in Latin American Thought: Latin American Historicism and the Philosophy of Leopoldo Zea. Lanham, Md.: Lexington Books.

Sahagún, Bernardino de. 1829–30 [ca. 1575–80]. Historia general de las cosas de la Nueva España. Mexico City: A. Valdés.

———. 1946 [ca. 1575–80]. Historia general de las cosas de la Nueva España. Ed. Miguel Acosta Saignes. 3 vols. Mexico City: Editorial Nueva España. (Based on 1829–30 edition.)

———. 1950–82 [ca. 1579]. Florentine Codex: General History of the Things of New Spain. Trans. and ed. Arthur J. O. Anderson and Charles Dibble. 13 parts. Santa Fe, N.M.: School of American Research and University of Utah.

———. 1989 [1585]. Conquest of New Spain: 1585 Revision. Trans. Howard Cline. Ed. S. L. Cline. Salt Lake City: University of Utah Press.

———. 1993 [ca. 1558–60]. Primeros Memoriales. Facsimile edition. Photographs by Ferdinand Anders. Norman: University of Oklahoma Press.

———. 1997 [ca. 1547]. Primeros Memoriales. Paleography of Nhautl text and translation to English by Thelma D. Sullivan. Norman: University of Oklahoma Press.

Said, Edward. 1980. The Question of Palestine. New York: Vintage.

———. 1983. The World, the Text, and the Critic. Cambridge, Mass.: Harvard University Press.

———. 1989. "Representing the Colonized: Anthropology's Interlocutors." *Critical Inquiry* 15: 205–25.

———. 1990a [1973]. *Orientalismo.* Madrid: Libertarias/Prodhufi.

———. 1990b. "Reflection on Exile." In Russel Ferguson, Martha Grever, Trinh Minh-ha, Cornell West, eds., *Out There: Marginalization and Contemporary Cultures.* Cambridge, Mass.: MIT University Press. 357–63.

———. 1993. *Culture and Imperialism.* New York: Knopf.

———. 1994a [1978]. *Orientalism.* New York: Vintage.

———. 1994b. *Representations of the Intellectual.* New York: Random House.

———. 2000. *La paradoja de la identidad.* Barcelona: Ediciones Bellaterra.

———. 2002. "A Conversation with Neeldari Bhattacharya, Suvir Kaul and Ania Loomba." In Theo Goldberg and Ato Quayson, eds., *Relocating Postcolonialism.* Oxford: Blackwell. 1–14.

Sakai, Naoki. 1997. *Translation and Subjectivity: On "Japan" and Cultural Nationalism.* Minneapolis: University of Minnesota Press.

Salazar Bondy, Augusto. 1969. *Existe una filosofía de nuestra América?* Mexico City: Siglo XXI.

Saldívar, José David. 1997. *Border Matters: Remapping American Cultural Studies.* Berkeley: University of California Press.

Salgado, César. 1998. "El entierro de González: Con(tra)figuraciones del 98 en la narrativa ochentista puertorriqueña." *Revista Iberoamericana* 184–85: 441–50.

Salih, Tayeb. 1969. *Season of Migration from the North.* Trans. Denys Johnson-Davies. London: Heinemann.

Salinas y Córdova, Fray Buenaventura de. 1951 [1630]. *Memorial de las historias del Nuevo Mundo Piru.* Lima: Geronimo de Contreras.

Salvador Lara, Jorge. 1991. "Influencias hispánicas: Perspectivas sobre los 500 años." Paper presented at the Symposium of the Americas, Smithsonian Institution, Washington, 4–7 September.

Salvatore, Ricardo 1991. "Yankee Merchant's Narratives: Visions of Social Order in Latin America and the U.S., 1800–1870." Paper read at the meeting of the Latin American Studies Association, Crystal City, Virginia, 4–6 April 1991.

Samaniego Salazar, Filoteo. 1991. "Identidad cultural iberoamericana: Unidad y diversidad." Paper presented at the Symposium of the Americas, Smithsonian Institution, Washington, 4–7 September.

Sánchez, Napoleón N. 1976. "Lo real maravilloso americano o la americanización del surrealismo." *Cuadernos Americanos* 219, no. 4 (July–August): 69–95.

Sánchez-Albornoz, Nicolás. 1974. *The Population of Latin America: A History.* Trans. W. A. R. Richardson. Berkeley: University of California Press.

Sánchez Nestor, Martha. 2001. "Ya las mujeres quieren todo." *Cuadernos Feministas* 3, no. 15.

Sandoval, Chela. 2000. *Methodology of the Oppressed.* Minneapolis: University of Minnesota Press.

———. 2002. "Foreword: AfterBridge: Technologies of Crossing." In Gloria Anzaldúa and AnaLouise Keating, eds., *This Bridge We Call Home: Radical Visions for Social Transformation.* New York: Routledge. 21–26.

Sandstrom, Alan, and P. Effrein. 1986. *Traditional Papermaking and Paper Cult Figures of Mexico*. Norman: University of Oklahoma Press.

Sangari, Kumku. 1990. "The Politics of the Possible." In Abdul JanMohamed and David Lloyd, ed., *The Nature and Context of Minority Discourse*. New York: Oxford University Press. 216–45.

Sanjinés, Javier. 2002. "Mestizaje Upside Down: Subaltern Knowledges and the Known." *Nepantla* 3, no. 1: 39–60.

San Juan, Epifanio. 1998. *Beyond Postcolonial Theory*. New York: St. Martins.

Sant' Anna, José Firmino. 1911. *Missão da doença do sonno: Trabalhos de outubro a novembro de 1911 (N'hantsua, Tete)*. Mimeograph. Maputo, Mozambique: Arquivo Histórico de Moçambique, Secção dos Serviços de Saúde.

Santiago, Silviano. 1978. "O Entre-Lugar do Discurso Latino-americano." In *Uma literatura nos trópicos*. São Paulo: Editora Perspectiva. 9–26.

Santiago-Valles, Kelvin. 1994. *Subject People, Colonial Discourses: Economic Transformation and Social Disorder in Puerto Rico 1898–1947*. Albany: State University of New York Press.

——. 1999. " 'Higher Womanhood' among the 'Lower Races': Julia McNair Henry in Puerto Rico and the Burdens of 1898." *Radical History Review* 73: 47–73.

Santos, Boaventura de Sousa. 1994. *Pela mão de Alice: O social e o político na pós-modernidade*. Porto: Afrontamento.

——. 1995. *Toward a New Common Sense: Law, Science and Politics in the Paradigmatic Transition*. New York: Routledge.

——. 1998. *De la mano de Alicia: Lo social y lo político en la postmodernidad*. Trans. from Portuguese to Spanish by Consuelo Bernal and Mauricio G. Villegas. Bogotá: Ediciones Uniandes.

——. 1999. "On Oppositional Postmodernism." In R. Munck and D. O'Hearn, eds., *Critical Development Theory*. London: Zed Books. 29–43.

——. 2000. *A crítica da razão indolente: Contra o desperdício da experiência*. Porto: Afrontamento.

——. 2001. "Os processos da globalização." In Boaventura de Sousa Santos, ed. *Globalização: Fatalidade ou utopia?* Porto: Afrontamento. 31–106.

——. 2002. "Between Prospero and Caliban: Colonialism, Postcolonialism, and Inter-identity." *Luso-Brazilian Review* 39, no. 2: 9–43.

——. 2003. "The World Social Forum: Toward a Counter-Hegemonic Globalization." Paper presented at the 24th International Congress, Latin American Studies Association (LASA), Dallas, 27–29 March.

——, ed. 1993. *Portugal: Um retrato singular*. Porto: Afrontamento.

Santos, Frei João dos. 1999 [1609]. *Etiópia Oriental e Vária história de cousas notáveis do Oriente*. Lisbon: Comissão Nacional para as Comemorações dos Descobrimentos Portugueses.

Santos, Ronaldo Marcos dos. 1980. *Resistência e superação do escravismo na Província de São Paulo (1885–1888)*. São Paulo: Instituto de Pesquisas Econômicas.

Santos, Theotonio dos. 1970. "La crisis de la teoría del desarrollo y las relaciones de dependencia en América Latina." In Helio Jaguaribe, ed., *La dependencia política-económica de América Latina*. Mexico City: Siglo XXI.

———. 2002. *La teoría de la dependencia: Balances y perspectivas*. Mexico City: Plaza and Janés.

Santos Junior, J. R., and F. Barros. 1950. "Notas etnográficas de Moçambique." In *13th Congresso Luso-Espanhol para o Progresso das Ciências*. Vol. 5. Lisbon. 609–23.

Sarkar, Sumit. 1997. *Writing Social History*. Delhi: Oxford University Press.

Sarmiento, Domingo Faustino. 1868. *Life in the Argentine Republic in the Days of the Tyrants, or, Civilization and Barbarism*. New York: Hafner Library Classics.

———. 1970 [1845]. *Facundo: Civilización y barbarie*. Buenos Aires: Espasa-Calpe.

Scannone, J. C. 1975. "Théologie et politique." In Enrique Dussel, Gustavo Gutiérrez, and J. L. Secundo, eds., *Les Luttes de libération bousculent la théologie*. Paris: Cerf. 144–48.

Scarano, Francisco. 1998. "Intervention of Possession? Puerto Rico, 1898, and the American Colonial Periphery." Paper presented at the Conference on the 1898 War, Lehman College, City University of New York, October.

Schmidt, Friedhelm. 1996. "Literaturas heterogéneas o literatura de la transculturación?" In José Antonio Mazzotti and Juan Cevallos-Aguilar, eds., *Asedios a la heterogeneidad cultural: Libro de homenaje a Antonio Cornejo Polar*. Philadelphia: Asociación Internacional de Peruanistas. 33–40.

Schwartz, Stuart. 1995. "Colonial Identities and *Sociedad de Castas*." *Colonial Latin American Review* 4, no. 1: 185–201.

Schwarz, Henry. 2000. "Mission Impossible: Introducing Postcolonial Studies in the U.S. Academy." In Henry Schwarz and Sangeeta Ray, eds., *A Companion to Postcolonial Studies*. Oxford: Blackwell. 1–20.

Schwarz, Henry, and Sangeeta Ray. 2000. *A Companion to Postcolonial Studies*. Oxford: Blackwell.

Schwarz, Roberto. 1986. "Nacional por Subtração." In *Que horas são?* São Paulo: Companhia das Letras. 29–48.

———. 1992. *Misplaced Ideas: Essays on Brazilian Culture*. London: Verso.

Scott, David. 1999. *Refashioning Futures: Criticism after Postcoloniality*. Princeton: Princeton University Press.

Scott, James C. 1985. *Weapons of the Weak*. New Haven, Conn.: Yale University Press.

———. 1990. *Domination and the Arts of Resistance: Hidden Transcripts*. New Haven, Conn.: Yale University Press.

Seed, Patricia. 1991. "Colonial and Postcolonial Discourse." *Latin American Research Review* 26, no. 3: 181–200.

———. 1993. "Taking Possession and Reading Texts: Establishing the Authority of Overseas Empire." In Jerry M. Williams and Robert E. Lewis, eds., *Early Images of the Americas*. Tucson: University of Arizona Press. 111–47.

Séguy, Jean. 1999. *Conflit et utopie, ou réformer l'Eglise*. Paris: Cerf.

Seidman, Steven, and Wagner David G., eds. 1992. *Postmodernism and Social Theory*. New York: Blackwell.

Sekyi-Otu, Ato. 1996. *Fanon's Dialectic of Experience*. Cambridge, Mass.: Harvard University Press.

Senghor, Leopold S. 1964. *Liberté 1: Négritude et Humanisme*. Paris: Seuil.

———. 1977. *Anthologie de la nouvelle poesie nègre et malgache de langue francaise (precedée de Orphée noir par Jean-Paul Sartre)*. Paris: Presses Universitaires de France.

Sepúlveda, Juan Ginés de. 1975 [1547]. *Democrates alter: Tratado sobre las causas justas de la guerra contra los indios.* Latin/Spanish ed. Trans. Marcelino Menéndez Pelayo. Mexico City: Fondo de Cultura Económica.

Shapiro, Michael J. 1981. *Language and Political Understanding: The Politics of Discursive Practices.* New Haven, Conn.: Yale University Press.

——. 1988. *The Politics of Representation: Writing Practices in Biography, Photography, and Policy Analysis.* Madison: University of Wisconsin Press.

Shapiro, Michael J., and Der Derian, James, eds. 1989. *International/Intertextual Relations: Postmodern Readings of World Politics.* Lexington, Mass.: Lexington Books.

Shaw, Donald. 1997. *La Generación del 98.* Madrid: Cátedra.

Sherman, Steven. 1999. "Hegemonic Transitions and the Dynamics of Cultural Change." *Review* 22, no. 1: 87–117.

Shiva, Vandana. 1995. *Abrazar la vida: Mujer, ecología y supervivencia.* Madrid: Horas y Horas.

Shohat, Ella. 1993. "Notes on the Postcolonial." *Social Text* 3, no. 2: 99–113.

——, ed. 1998. *Talking Visions: Multicultural Feminism in a Transnational Age.* Cambridge: MIT University Press.

Shohat, Ella, and Stam, Robert. 1994. *Unthinking Eurocentrism: Multiculturalism and the Media.* New York: Routledge.

Showalter, Elaine. 2003. "What Teaching Literature Should Really Mean." *Chronicle of Higher Education,* 17 January, B79.

Shutte, Ofelia. 2000. "Cultural Alterity: Cross-cultural Communication and Feminist Theory in North-South Context." In Uma Narayan and Sandra Harding, eds., *Decentering the Center: Philosophy for a Multicultural, Postcolonial, and Feminist World.* Bloomington: Indiana University Press. 47–67.

Sigüenza y Góngora, Carlos de. 1986 [1680]. *Teatro de virtudes políticas, que constituyen á un príncipe advertidas en los monarcas antiguos del Mexicano imperio: Alboroto y motín de los indios de México.* Mexico City: Universidad Nacional Autónoma de México, Coordinación de Humanidades/Miguel Ángel Porrúa.

——. 1995. *Paraíso occidental.* Mexico City: Consejo Nacional para la Cultura y las Artes.

Silko, Leslie Marmon. 1977. *Ceremony.* New York: Viking.

——. 1991. *Almanac of the Dead.* New York: Simon and Schuster.

Silva, A. L. 1679. *Carta de António Lobo da Silva para o vice rei [da India], escrita no Zimbaboé em 15 de Dezembro de 1679.* Lisbon: Arquivo Histórico Ultramarino, Caixa 3 (Documento 77).

Simeon, Remi. 1988. *Diccionario de Lengua Nahuatl o Mexicano.* Mexico City: Siglo XXI.

Sivaramakrishnan, K., and Arjun Agarwal. 2003. *Regional Modernities: The Cultural Politics of Development in India.* New Delhi: Oxford University Press.

Sklodowska, Elzbieta, and Ben A. Heller, eds. 2000. *Roberto Fernández Retamar y los estudios latinoamericanos.* Serie "Críticas." Pittsburgh: Instituto International de Literatura Iberoamericana.

Slater, David. 1994. "Exploring Other Zones of the Postmodern." In Ali Rattansi and Sallie Westwood, eds., *Racism, Modernity, and Identity: On the Western Front.* Cambridge: Polity. 87–125.

Slemon, Stephen. 1990. "Unsettling the Empire: Resistance Theory for the Second World." *World Literature Written in English* 30, no. 2 (fall): 30–41.

——. 1995a. "The Scramble for Post-Colonialism." In Bill Ashcroft, Gareth Griffiths, and Helen Tiffin, eds., *The Post-colonial Studies Reader*. London: Routledge. 6–45.

——. 1995b. "Unsettling the Empire: Resistance Theory for the Second World." In Bill Ashcroft, Gareth Griffiths, and Helen Tiffin, eds., *The Post-colonial Studies Reader*. London: Routledge. 104–13.

Slenes, Robert. 1991–92. " 'Malungu'Ngoma Vem.' " *Revista Universidade de São Paulo* 12: 48–49.

Smith, Paul. 1988. *Discerning the Subject*. Minneapolis: University of Minnesota Press.

Smith, Simon C. 1998. *British Imperialism 1750–1970*. Cambridge: Cambridge University Press.

Smith, Angel, and Emma Dávila-Cox, eds. 1999. *The Crisis of 1898: Colonial Redistribution and Nationalist Mobilization*. London: Macmillan.

Solomon, J. Fisher. 1988. *Discourse and Reference in the Nuclear Age*. Norman: University of Oklahoma Press.

Solórzano Pereira, Juan de. 1648. *Política indiana / sacada en lengua castellana de / los dos tomos de derecho, i govierno municipal / de las Indias Occidentales que mas copiosamente escribio en la latina*. Translation of *De Indiarum jure* [1629]. Madrid: Por Diego Díaz de la Carrera.

Sommer, Doris. 1991. *Foundational Fictions: The National Romances of Latin America*. Berkeley: University of California Press.

——. 1998. "José Martí, Author of Walt Whitman." In Jeffrey Belnap and Raul Fernandez, eds., *José Martí's "Our America": From National to Hemispheric Cultural Studies*. Durham, N.C.: Duke University Press. 77–90.

Sommer, Doris, and Esteban Torres. 1992. "Dominican Republic." In David William Foster, ed., *Handbook of Latin American Literature*. 2d ed. New York: Garland. 271–86.

Spalding, Karen. 1974. *De indio a campesino: Cambios en la estructura social del Perú colonial*. Lima: Instituto de Estudios Peruanos.

——. 1984. *Huarochirí: An Andean Society under Inca and Spanish Rule*. Stanford, Calif.: Stanford University Press.

Spengemann, William. 1984. "The Earliest American Novel: Aphra Behn's *Oroonoko*." *Nineteenth-Century Fiction* 38: 384–414.

Spiller Pena, Eduardo. 1989. "Liberdades em arbítrio." *Padê* 1: 45–57.

Spitta, Sylvia. 1995. *Between Two Waters: Narratives of Transculturation in Latin America*. Houston: Rice University Press.

Spivak, Gayatri Chakravorty. 1985. "Three Women's Texts and a Critique of Imperialism." *Critical Inquiry* 12: 243–61.

——. 1987. "Subaltern Studies: Deconstructing Historiography and Value." In *In Other Worlds: Essays in Cultural Politics*. New York: Methuen. 197–221.

——. 1988a [1985]. "Can the Subaltern Speak?" In Lawrence Grossberg and Cary Nelson, eds., *Marxism and the Interpretation of Culture*. Champagne: University of Illinois Press. 271–313.

——. 1988b. *In Other Worlds: Essays in Cultural Politics*. New York: Routledge.

———. 1990. *The Post-colonial Critic: Interviews, Strategies, Dialogues*. Ed. Sarah Harasym. London: Routledge.

———. 1993. *Outside in the Teaching Machine*. New York: Routledge.

———. 1994 [1985]. "Can the Subaltern Speak?" In Patrick Williams and Laura Chrisman, eds., *Colonial Discourse and Post-colonial Theory: A Reader*. New York: Columbia University Press. 66–111.

———. 1996. "How to Teach a 'Culturally Different' Book." In *The Spivak Reader: Selected Works of Gayatri Chakravorty Spivak*. Ed. Donna Landry and Gerald MacLean. New York: Routledge. 237–66.

———. 1999. *A Critique of Postcolonial Reason: Toward a History of the Vanishing Present*. Cambridge, Mass.: Harvard University Press.

———. 2000. "The New Subaltern: A Silent Interview." In Vinayak Chaturvedi, ed., *Mapping Subaltern Studies and the Postcolonial*. London: Verso. 324–40.

Spivak, Gayatri Chakravorty, and Chandra Talpade Mohanty. 1984. "Under Western Eyes: Feminist Scholarship and Colonial Discourses." *Boundary 2*, no. 12: 3–13.

Starn, Orin. 1991. "Missing the Revolution: Anthropologists and the War in Peru." *Cultural Anthropology* 6: 63–91.

Stavenhagen, Rodolfo. 1965. "Classes, Colonialism, and Acculturation." *Studies in Comparative International Development* 1, no. 7: 53–77.

———. 1969. *Las clases sociales en las sociedades agrarias*. Mexico City: Siglo XXI.

Stein, Stanley J., and Barbara H. Stein. 1970. *The Colonial Heritage of Latin America: Essays on Economic Dependence in Perspective*. New York: Oxford University Press.

Stephanson, Anders. 1995. *Manifest Destiny: American Expansionism and the Empire of Right*. New York: Hill and Wang.

Stern, Steve J. 1982. *Peru's Indian Peoples and the Challenge of Spanish Conquest*. Madison: University of Wisconsin Press.

———. 1992. "Paradigms of Conquest: History, Historiography, Politics." *Latin American Studies* 24, Quincentennial Supplement: 1–34.

Stocking, George W., Jr. 1968. *Race, Culture, Evolution: Essays in the History of Anthropology*. New York: Free Press.

———. 1987. *Victorian Anthropology*. New York: Free Press.

———, ed. 1991. *Colonial Situations: Essays on the Contextualization of Ethnographic Knowledge*. History of Anthropology Series, vol. 7. Madison: University of Wisconsin Press.

Stoetzer, O. Carlos. 1979. *The Scholastic Roots of the Spanish American Revolution*. New York: Fordham University Press.

Stoler, Ann Laura. 1995. *Race and the Education of Desire*. Durham, N.C.: Duke University Press.

Stoll, David. 1999. *Rigoberta Menchú and the Story of All Poor Guatemalans*. Boulder, Colo.: Westview Press.

Stoner, K. Lynn. 1987. "Directions in Latin American Women's History, 1977-1984." *Latin American Research Review* 22: 101–34.

Suárez, Margarita. 2001. *Desafíos transatlánticos: Mercaderes, banqueros y el estado en el Perú virreinal, 1600–1700*. Lima: Fondo de Cultura Económica.

Suárez de Figueroa, Cristóbal. 1914 [1617]. *El passagero*. Madrid: Sociedad de Bibliófilos Españoles.

Sullivan, Paul R. 1989. *Unfinished Conversations: Mayas and Foreigners between Two Wars.* New York: Knopf.

Taller Intercultural. 2003. "Análisis del Programa 'Este Lunes.'" Document prepared for the Ministry of External Relations. Quito: Universidad Andina Simón Bolívar.

Tamayo Herrera, José. 1980. *Historia del Indigenismo Cuzqueño.* Vols. 16–20. Lima: Instituto Nacional de Cultura.

Taussig, Michael. 1984. "History as Sorcery." *Representations* 7 (summer): 87–109.

———. 1987. *Shamanism, Colonialism, and the Wild Man: A Study in Terror and Healing.* Chicago: University of Chicago Press.

———. 1993. *Mimesis and Alterity: A Particular History of the Senses.* New York: Routledge.

Tavares, Ildásio. 1996. *Nossos colonizadores africanos: Presença e tradição negra na Bahia.* Salvador, Brazil: Editora da Universidade Federal da Bahia.

———. 1999. *IX sonetos da Inconfidência.* São Paulo: Editora Giordano.

Taylor, Charles. 2002. "Modern Social Imaginaries." *Public Culture* 14, no. 1: 91–124.

Taylor, Patrick. 1989. *The Narrative of Liberation: Perspectives on Afro-Caribbean Literature, Popular Culture and Politics.* Ithaca, N.Y.: Cornell University Press.

———. 1992. "Anthropology and Theology in Pursuit of Justice." *Callaloo* 15, no. 3 (summer): 811–23.

Taylor, Peter. 1999. *Modernities: A Geohistorical Interpretation.* Minneapolis: University of Minnesota Press.

Taylor, William. 1991. "Mexico as Orient: Introduction to a History of American and British Representations since 1821." Paper presented at the Latin American Studies Association, Crystal City, Virginia, 4–6 April.

Tedlock, Dennis. 1985. *The Popol Vuh.* New York: Simon and Schuster.

Tempels, Placide. 1949. *La philosophie bantoue.* Paris: Éditions africaines.

Thomas, Nicholas. 1994. *Colonialism's Culture: Anthropology, Travel, and Government.* Princeton: Princeton University Press.

Thompson, Lanny. 2000. "Las guerras (anti)imperialistas de 1895–1902." *Revista de Ciencias Sociales Nueva Epoca* 9: 166–80.

Thurner, Mark. 1997. *From Two Republics to One Divided: Contradictions of Postcolonial Nationmaking in Andean Peru.* Durham, N.C.: Duke University Press.

Tibesar, O. F. M., Antonino. 1991 [1953]. *Comienzos de los franciscanos en el Perú.* Iquitos, Peru: Centro de Estudios Teológicos de la Amazonía.

Tiffin, Helen. 1995 [1987]. "Post-colonial Literatures and Counter-discourse." In Bill Ashcroft, Gareth Griffiths, and Helen Tiffin, eds., *The Post-colonial Studies Reader.* London: Routledge. 95–98.

Tilly, Charles. 1990. *Coercion, Capital, and European States, A.D. 990–1992.* Cambridge: Blackwell.

Tituaña, Auki. 2000. "Autonomía y poder local: el caso de Cotacachi, Ecuador." In Fernando García, ed., *Las sociedades interculturales: Un desafío para el Siglo XXI.* Quito: Facultad Latinoamericana de Ciencias Sociales/IBIS. 107–18.

Tocqueville, Alexis de. 1835. *Democracy in America.* New York: Vintage Classics.

Todorov, Tzvetan. 1989 [1982]. *La conquista de América: El problema del Otro.* Mexico City: Siglo XXI.

Tomkinson, J. 1964. "Report of Captain J. Tomkinson to Vice-Admiral Albermarble

Bertie (1809)." In G. M. Theal, ed., *Records of South-East Africa*, vol. 9. Cape Town: Struick. 1–6.

Toro, Alfonso de. 1999. "La postcolonialidad en Latinoamérica en la era de la globalización: Cambio de paradigma en el pensamiento teórico-cultural latinoamericano?" In Alfonso de Toro and Fernando de Toro, eds., *El debate de la postcolonialidad en Latinoamérica: Una postmodernidad periférica o cambio de paradigma en el pensamiento latinoamericano*. Madrid: Iberoamericana. 31–77.

Toro, Alfonso de, and Fernando de Toro, eds. 1999. *El debate de la postcolonialidad en Latinoamérica: Una postmodernidad periférica o cambio de paradigma en el pensamiento latinoamericano*. Madrid: Iberoamericana.

Toro, Fernando de. 1995. "From Where to Speak? Post-modern/Post-colonial Positionalities." In Fernando de Toro and Alfonso de Toro, eds., *Borders and Margins: Post-colonialism and Post-modernism*. Madrid: Iberoamericana. 131–48.

——. 1999. "The Postcolonial Question: Alterity, Identity and the Other(s)." In Alfonso de Toro and Fernando de Toro, eds., *El debate de la postcolonialidad en Latinoamérica: Una postmodernidad periférica o cambio de paradigma en el pensamiento latinoamericano*. Madrid: Iberoamericana.

Torquemada, Juan de. 1975 [1615]. *Monarquía indiana: De los veinte y un libros rituales y monarquía indiana, con el origen y guerras de los indios occidentales, de sus poblazones, descubrimiento, conquista, conversión y otras cosas maravillosas de la mesma tierra*. Ed. under the supervision of Miguel León Portilla. 7 vols. Mexico City: Universidad Nacional Autónoma de Mexico, Instituto de Investigaciones Históricas.

Torres Tovar, Carlos Alberto, Fernando Viviescas Monsalve, and Edmundo Pérez Hernández, eds. 2000. *La ciudad: Hábitat de diversidad y complejidad*. Bogotá: Universidad Nacional de Colombia.

Toussaint, Manuel, et al. 1990. *Planos de la Ciudad de Mexico Siglos 16 y 17*. Mexico City: Universidad Nacional Autónoma de México.

Trigo, Abril. 2000. "Migrancia, memoria, modernidá." In Mabel Moraña, ed., *Nuevas perspectivas desde/sobre América Latina*. Santiago: Cuarto Propio. 273–91.

Trigo, Benigno. 2000. *Subjects of Crisis: Race and Gender as Disease in Latin America*. Hanover, N.H.: University Press of New England.

——, ed. 2001. *Foucault and Latin America: Appropriations and Deployments of Discoursive Analysis*. New York: Routledge.

Tripp, Aili Mari. 2002. "The Politics of Women's Rights and Cultural Diversity in Uganda." In Maxine Molyneux and Shahra Razavi, eds., *Gender, Justice, Development and Rights*. Oxford: Oxford University Press. 384–413.

Trouillot, Michel-Rolph. 1990. "The Odd and the Ordinary: Haiti, the Caribbean and the World." *Cimarron* (winter): 3–13.

——. 1992. "The Caribbean Region: An Open Frontier in Anthropological Theory." *Annual Review of Anthropology* 21: 19–42.

——. 1995. *Silencing the Past: Power and the Production of History*. Boston: Beacon.

Tuathail, Gearoid O. 1996. *Critical Geopolitics: The Politics of Writing Global Space*. Minneapolis: University of Minnesota Press.

Turner, Terry. 1991. "Representing, Resisting, Rethinking: Historical Transformations of Kayapo Culture and Anthropological Consciousness." In George W.

Stocking Jr., ed., *Colonial Situations: Essays on the Contextualization of Ethnographic Knowledge*. History of Anthropology Series, vol. 7. Madison: University of Wisconsin Press. 285–313.

Turtis, Richard Lee. 2002. "A World Destroyed, a Nation Imposed: The 1937 Haitian Massacre in the Dominican Republic." *Hispanic American Historical Review* 82, no. 3: 589–635.

Ubaldo Ribeiro, João. 1984. *Viva o povo brasileiro*. 14th ed. Rio de Janeiro: Nova Fronteira.

——. 1989. *An Invincible Memory*. New York: Harper and Row.

Ulrich, Ruy Ennes. 1909. *Política colonial, lições feitas ao curso do 4° ano jurídico no ano de 1908/1909*. Coimbra: Imprensa da Universidade.

United Nations Centre for Human Settlements (Habitat). 2001. *Cities in a Globalizing World: Global Report on Human Settlements 2001*. London: Earthscan Publications.

Unsworth, Barry. 1992. *Sacred Hunger*. London: Hamish Hamilton.

Urton, Gary. 2003. *Signs of the Inka Khipu*. Austin: University of Texas Press.

Valdes, Rodrigo de. 1687. *Poema heroyco hispano-latino panegyrico de la fundacion, y grandeza de la muy noble, y leal ciudad de Lima*. Madrid: Imprenta de Antonio Roman.

Valdez, Luis. 1992. *Zoot Suit and Other Plays*. Houston: Arte Público.

Vallejo, César. 1996. *Obra Poética*. Nanterre, France: ALLCA XXe.

Vallier, Ivan. 1972. "Radical Priests and Révolution." In Douglas A. Chalmers, ed., *Changing Latin America: New Interpretations of Its Politics and Society*. New York: New York Academy of Political Sciences. 17–23.

Vanden, H. E. 1986. *National Marxism in Latin America: José Carlos Mariátegui, Thought and Politics*. Boulder, Colo.: Lynne Rienner.

Van Nief, Robert. 1990. "Colonialism Revisited: Recent Historiography." *World History* 1: 109–24.

Van Young, Eric. 1983. "Mexican Rural History since Chevalier: The Historiography of the Colonial Hacienda." *Latin American Research Review* 18: 5–61.

——. 1985. "Recent Anglophone Scholarship on Mexico and Central America in the Age of Revolution (1750–1850)." *Hispanic American Historical Review* 65, no. 4: 725–43.

——. 1993. "The Cuautla Lazarus: Double Subjectives in Reading Texts on Popular Collective Action." *Colonial Latin American Review* 2, nos. 1–2: 3–26.

Vargas-Valente, Virginia. 1993. *Los intereses de las Mujeres y los Procesos de Emancipación en América Latina*. Mexico City: Programa Universitario de Estudios de Género/Universidad Nacional Autónoma de México.

——. 2002. "Los feminismos latinoamericanos en su tránsito al nuevo milenio (Una lectura político personal)." In Daniel Mato, ed., *Estudios y otras prácticas intelectuales Latinoamericanas en cultura y poder*. Caracas Consejo Latinoamericano de Ciencias Sociales and CEAP, FACES, Universidad Central de Venezuela. 307–16.

Vasconcelos, José de. 1979 [1925]. *The Cosmic Race/La raza cósmica*. Baltimore: Johns Hopkins University Press.

Vattimo, Gianni. 1963. *Essere, storia e linguaggio in Heidegger*. Turin: Edizioni di "Filosofia."

——. 1968. *Schleiermacher filosofo dell'interpretazione*. Milan: Mursia.

——. 1985. *La fine della modernitá: Nichilismo ed ermeneutica nella cultura post-moderna.* Milan: Garzanti.

——. 1988. *Le aventure della differenza.* Milan: Garzanti.

——. 1989a. *Essere, storia e linguaggio in Heidegger.* Genoa: Marietti.

——. 1989b. *El sujeto y la máscara.* Barcelona: Península.

——. 1991. *The End of Modernity.* Baltimore: Johns Hopkins University Press.

——. 1998a. *Credere di credere: E possibile essere cristiani nonostante la Chiesa?* Milan: Garzanti.

——. 1998b. "The Trace of the Trace." In Jacques Derrida and Gianni Vattimo, eds., *Religion.* Stanford, Calif.: Stanford University Press. 79–94.

——. 1999. *Belief.* Trans. Luca D'Isanto and David Webb. Stanford, Calif.: Stanford University Press.

Vega, Inca Garcilaso de la. 1605. *La Florida del Ynca: Hiſtoria del Adelantado Hernando de Soto, Gobernador y Capitan General del Reino de la Florida, y de Otros Heroicos Caballeros Eſpañoles e Yndios, escrita por el Ynca Garcilaſſo de la Vega, Capitan de Su Magestad, Natural de la Gran Ciudad del Cozco, Cabeça de los Reinos y Provinçias del Peru.* Lisbon: Imprenta de Pedro Crasbeeck.

——. 1996. *Comentarios reales.* Caracas: Ayacucho.

Venn, Couze. 2000. *Occidentalism: Modernity and Subjectivity.* London: Sage.

Verdesio, Gustavo. 1997. "Andanzas y vaivenes teóricos y epistemológicos en un mundo comunicado." Paper presented at the Proyecto Diáspora de Investigación y Edición meeting, Montevideo, Uruguay, 15, 16, and 17 August.

Verson Vadillo, Lidia A. 1999. "Las religiones africanas como lenguajes culturales en la narrativa cubana contemporánea." Ph.D. diss., University of Pennsylvania.

Vianna, Luiz Werneck. 1997. *A revolução passiva: Iberismo e Americanismo no Brasil.* Rio de Janeiro: Editora Revan.

Vidal, Hernán. 1993. "The Concept of Colonial and Postcolonial Discourse: A Perspective from Literary Criticism." *Latin American Research Review* 28, no. 3: 113–19.

Vidales, Raúl. 1983. "Filosofia y política de las étnias en la última década." In *Ponencias do 2d Congreso de Filosofia Latinoamericana.* Bogotá: Universidad de Santo Tomás/Centro de Enseñanza Desescolarizada. 385–401.

Vila, Carlos M. 1992. *Estado, clase y etnicidad: La costa atlántica de Nicaragua.* Mexico City: Fondo de Cultura Económica.

Villanueva, Tino. 1984. *Shaking off the Dark.* Tempe, Ariz.: Bilingual Review Press.

Villarreal, José Antonio. 1959. *Pocho.* New York: Doubleday.

Villegas, Abelardo. 1986. "Panorama de los procesos de cambio: Revolución, reformismo, y lucha de clases." In Leopoldo Zea, ed., *América Latina en sus ideas.* Mexico City: UNESCO/Siglo XXI. 85–117.

Viola, H., and C. Margolis. 1991. *Seeds of Change: Five Hundred Years since Columbus.* Washington: Smithsonian Institute.

Virilio, Paul. 2000. *Politics of the Very Worst.* New York: Semiotext(e).

Viswanathan, Gauri. 1998. *Outside the Fold: Conversion, Modernity, and Belief.* Princeton: Princeton University Press.

Voekel, Pamela. 1991. "Forging the Public: Bourbon Social Engineering in Late Colonial Mexico." Master's thesis, University of Texas, Austin.

Vogeley, Nancy. 1989. "Colonial Discourse in a Postcolonial Context: Nineteenth Century Mexico." Paper presented at the meeting of the Latin American Studies Association, Miami, 4–6 December.

Vogt, Evon Z. 1964. "The Genetic Model and Maya Cultural Development." In Evon Z. Vogt and A. Ruz Lhuillier, eds., *Desarrollo cultural de los Mayas*. Mexico City: Universidad Nacional Autónoma de México. 9–48.

——. 1995. "On the Application of the Phylogenetic Model to the Mayas." In R. J. DeMallie and Alfonso Ortiz, eds., *North American Indian Anthropology*. Norman: University of Oklahoma Press. 377–414.

Volek, Emil, ed. 2002. *Latin America Writes Back: Postmodernity in the Periphery*. New York: Routledge.

Vollmer, Günter. 1981. *Geschichte der Azteken: Der Codex Aubin und verwandte Dokumente*. Berlin: Mann.

Volpato, Luiza R. C. 1993. *Cativos do Sertão*. São Paulo: Marco Zero/Universidade Federal do Mato Grosso.

Vuola, Elina. 1997. *Limits of Liberation: Praxis as Method of Latin American Liberation Theology and Feminist Theology*. Helsinki: Suomalainen Tiedeakatemia.

——. 2000. "Thinking Otherwise: Dussel, Liberation Theology, and Feminism." In Linda Alcoff and Eduardo Mendieta, eds., *Thinking from the Underside of History: Enrique Dussel's Philosophy of Liberation*. Lanham, Md.: Rowman and Littlefield. 149–80.

——. 2002. "Remaking Universals? Transnational Feminism(s) Challenging Fundamentalist Ecumenism." *Theory, Culture, and Society* 19, nos. 1–2: 175–95.

——. 2003. "Option for the Poor and the Exclusion of Women: The Challenge of Postmodernism and Feminism to Liberation Theology." In Joerg Rieger, ed., *Opting for the Margins: Theological and Other Challenges in Postmodern and Postcolonial Worlds*. Oxford: Oxford University Press. 105–26.

Wade, Peter. 1997. *Race and Ethnicity in Latin America*. London: Pluto Press.

Wade-Gayles, Gloria, ed. 1995. *My Soul Is a Witness: African-American Women's Spirituality*. Boston: Beacon.

Wald, Alan. 1992. "The Subaltern Speaks: The Colonial Subject in U.S. Radical Fiction." *Monthly Review* 43, no. 11: 17–28.

Wallerstein, Immanuel. 1974–89. *The Modern World-System*. 3 vols. San Diego: Academic Press.

——. 1983. *Historical Capitalism and Capitalist Civilization*. London: Verso.

——. 1987. "World-Systems Analysis." In A. Giddens and J. H. Turner, eds., *Social Theory Today*. Cambridge: Polity. 309–24.

——. 1991. *Unthinking Social Science: The Limits of Nineteenth-Century Paradigms*. Cambridge: Polity.

——. 1992a. "The Collapse of Liberalism." In Ralph Miliband and Leo Panitch, eds., *The Socialist Register 1991*. London: Merlin. 96–110.

——. 1992b. "The Concept of National Development, 1917–1989: Elegy and Requiem." *American Behavioral Scientist* 35: 517–29.

——. 1994. *Geopolitics and Geoculture: Essays on the Changing World-System*. Cambridge: Cambridge University Press.

——. 1995. *After Liberalism*. New York: New Press.

——, ed. 1996a. *Abrir las ciencias sociales: Informe de la Comisión Gulbenkian para la estructuración de las ciencias sociales*. Mexico City: Siglo XXI.

——. 1996b. "La restructuración capitalista y el sistema mundo." In Raquel Sosa, ed., *América Latina y el Caribe: Perspectivas de Reconstrucción*. Mexico City: ALAS/Universidad Nacional Autónoma de México. 69–85.

——. 1997a. "Eurocentrism and Its Avatars: The Dilemmas of Social Science." *New Left Review*, no. 226: 93–159.

——. 1997b. "The Unintended Consequences of Cold War Area Studies." In D. Montgomery, ed., *The Cold War and the University: Toward an Intellectual History of the Postwar Years*. New York: New Press. 195–232.

——. 1999. *The End of the World as We Know It: Social Science for the Twenty-First Century*. Minneapolis: University of Minnesota Press.

——. 2000. "Globalization, or the Age of Transition? A Long-term View of the Trajectory of the World System." *International Sociology* 15, no. 2: 249–65.

Wallerstein, Immanuel, et al. 1996. *Open the Social Sciences: Report of the Gulbenkian Commission on the Restructuring of the Social Sciences*. Stanford, Calif.: Stanford University Press.

Walsh, Catherine E. 1998. "'Staging Encounters': The Educational Decline of U.S. Puerto Ricans in (Post)-Colonial Perspective." *Harvard Educational Review* 68, no. 2: 218–43.

——. 2001. "Geopolíticas del conocimiento." Dossier published by *Comentario Internacional*. Quito: Universidad Andina Simón Bolívar.

——. 2002a. "(De)construir la interculturalidad: Consideraciones críticas desde la política, la colonialidad y los movimientos indígenas y negros en el Ecuador." In Norma Fuller, ed., *Interculturalidad y política: Desafíos y posibilidades*. Lima: Red para el desarrollo de las ciencias sociales en el Perú. 115–42.

——. 2002b. "The (Re)articulation of Political Subjectivities and Colonial Difference in Ecuador: Reflections on Capitalism and the Geopolitics of Knowledge." *Nepantla* 3, no. 1: 61–97.

——. 2003. "Ecuador 2003: Promises and Challenges." Paper presented at the University of North Carolina–Duke Latin American Studies "Burning Issues" Series conference, 25 April.

Walsh, Catherine E., Freya Schiwy, and Santiago Castro-Gómez, eds. 2002. *Indisciplinar las ciencias sociales: Geopolíticas del conocimiento y colonialidad del poder: Perspectivas desde lo andino*. Quito: Editorial Abya Yala.

Warman, Arturo. 1969. "Cultura popular y cultura nacional." In Leopoldo Zea, ed., *Características de la cultura nacional*. Mexico City: Universidad Nacional Autónoma de México, Instituto de Investigaciones Sociales.

Warner, Marina. 1992. *Indigo, or, Mapping the Waters*. London: Chatto and Windus.

Wauchope, Robert, ed. 1972–75. *Handbook of Middle American Indians*. Vols. 12–15. Austin: University of Texas Press.

Weber, Max. 1986. "Parenthèse théorique: Le refus religieux du monde, ses orientations et ses degrés." *Archives de Sciences Sociales des Religions* 61, no. 1: 11–12.

——. 1922. *Wirtschaft und Gesellschaft*. Tübingen, Germany: J. C. B. Mohr (P. Siebeck).

Weber, Max, et al. 1923. *Wirtschaftsgeschichte: Abriss der universalen Sozial- und Wirtschafts-Geschichte: Aus den nachgelassenen Vorlesungen*, hrsg. von S. Hellmann und M. Palyi. Munich: Duncker und Humblot.

Welsch, Wolfgang. 1993. *Unsere postmoderne Moderne.* Berlin: Akademie Verlag.

West, Cornel. 1989. *The American Evasion of Philosophy: A Genealogy of Pragmatism.* Madison: University of Wisconsin Press.

———. 1993. *Race Matters.* Boston: Beacon.

Wheeler, Douglas L. 1998. *The Empire Time Forgot: Writing a History of the Portuguese Overseas Empire, 1808–1975.* Porto: Universidade Fernando Pessoa.

Whitaker, Arthur, P. 1954. *The Western Hemisphere Idea: Its Rise and Decline.* Ithaca, N.Y.: Cornell University Press.

White, Hayden. 1978. *Tropics of Discourse: Essays in Cultural Criticism.* Baltimore, Md.: Johns Hopkins University Press.

Williams, Jerry. 1996. *Peralta Barnuevo and the Discourse of Loyalty: A Critical Edition of Four Selected Texts.* Tempe, Ariz.: Arizona State University Center for Latin American Studies Press.

———. 2001. *Peralta Barnuevo and the Art of Propaganda: Politics, Poetry, and Religion in Eighteenth-century Lima.* Newark, N.J.: Juan de la Cuesta.

Williams, Patrick, and Laura Chrisman, eds. 1994. *Colonial Discourse and Post-colonial Theory: A Reader.* New York: Columbia University Press.

Willis Paau, Lucía. 2000 "Reflexiones desde mi experiencia de Mujer." In Morna MacLeod and M. Luisa Cabrera, eds., *Identidad: Rostros sin márcara (reflexiones sobre cosmovisión, género y etnicidad).* Guatemala City: OXFAM. 73–95.

Wolf, Eric. R. 1959. *Sons of the Shaking Earth.* Chicago: University of Chicago Press.

———. 1982. *Europe and the People without History.* Berkeley: University of California Press.

———. 1987. "The Historiography of Modern Central America since 1960." *Hispanic American Historical Review* 67: 461–96.

Wolpe, Harold, ed. 1980. *The Articulation of Modes of Production.* London: Routledge and Kegan Paul.

Wright, Elizabeth, and Edmond Wright, eds. 1999. *The Žižek Reader.* London: Blackwell.

Wyrick, Deborah. 1999. "Divine Transpositions: Recent Scholarship on Vodou and Santería Religious Art." *Jouvert* 3, nos. 1–2. Online. http://social.chass.ncsu.edu/jouvert/v3i12/vodou.htm.

Xavier, Ignacio Caetano. 1954. "Relação do estado presente de Moçambique, Sena, Sofala, Inhambane e de todo o continente da Africa Oriental." In L. F. C. Dias, ed., *Fontes para a história, geografia e comércio de Moçambique (século 18).* Lisbon: Agência Geral do Ultramar. 171–217.

Young, Marilyn B. 1991. *The Vietnam Wars 1945–1990.* New York: Harper Collins.

Young, Robert. 1990. *White Mythologies: Writing History and the West.* London: Routledge.

———. 1995. *Colonial Desire: Hybridity in Theory, Culture, and Race.* London: Routledge.

———. 2001. *Postcolonialism: An Historical Introduction.* Cambridge: Blackwell.

Yovel, Yirmiahu. 1998. *Dark Riddle: Hegel, Nietzsche, and the Jews.* University Park: Pennsylvania State University Press.

Yúdice, George. 1993. "Postmodernism in the Periphery." *South Atlantic Quarterly* 92, no. 3: 543–56.

——. 1996. "Puede hablarse de la postmodernidad en América Latina?" *Revista de Crítica Literaria Latinoamericana* 15, no. 29: 105–28.

——. 2001. "From Hybridity to Policy: For a Purposeful Cultural Studies." Translator's intro. to Néstor García Canclini, *Consumers and Citizens*. Minneapolis: University of Minnesota Press. ix–xxxvii.

Zamora, Margarita. 1988. *Language, Authority and Indigenous History in the "Comentarios reales de los incas."* Cambridge: Cambridge University Press.

Zea, Leopoldo. 1957. *America en la Historia*. Mexico City: Fondo de Cultura Económica, Universidad Nacional Autónoma de México, Centro de Estudios Filosóficos.

——, ed. 1986. *América Latina en sus ideas*. Mexico City: UNESCO/Siglo XXI.

——. 1988. *Discurso desde la marginación y la barbarie*. Barcelona: Anthropos.

Zermeño Padilla, Guillermo. 1999. "Condición de subalternidad, condición postmoderna y saber histórico. ¿Hacia una nueva forma de escritura de la historia?" In *Historia and Grafía*, no. 12. Mexico City: Universidad Iberoamericana. 11–47.

Zielina, María Carmen, ed. 1992. *La africanía en el cuento cubano y puertorriqueño*. Miami: Ediciones Universal.

Zimmerman, Marc. 2000. "Calibán y la literature de nuestra América, muchos años después." In Elzbieta Sklodowska and Ben A. Heller, eds., *Roberto Fernández Retamar y los estudios latinoamericanos*. Serie "Críticas." Pittsburgh: Instituto International de Literatura Iberoamericana. 327–51.

Žižek, Slavoj. 1989. *The Sublime Object of Ideology*. London: Verso.

——. 1991. "The Missing Link of Fantasy." *Analysis* 3: 36–49.

——. 1994. *The Metastases of Enjoyment*. London: Verso.

——. 1997. "Multiculturalism: Or, the Cultural Logic of Multinational Capitalism." *New Left Review* 225: 29–49.

——. 1998. "A Leftist Plea for 'Eurocentrism.'" *Critical Inquiry* 24: 989–1007.

——. 1999. *The Ticklish Subject: The Absent Centre of Political Ontology*. London: Verso.

——. 2000. *The Fragile Absolute, or, Why Is the Christian Legacy Worth Fighting For?* London: Verso.

Zumárraga, Juan de, ed. 1546. *Doctrina cristiana: Mas cierta y verdadera para gente sin erudicion y letras: En que se contiene el catecismo o informacion pa indios con todo lo principal y necessario que el cristiano debe saber y obrar. Impressa en Mexico por mandado del reverendisimo señor don fray Juan de Çumarraga: Primer Obispo de Mexico*. Mexico City: Juan Pablos.

CONTRIBUTORS

ARTURO ARIAS is the director of Latin American Studies at the University of Redlands. He served as the president of the Latin American Studies Association for 2001–2003. His publications include *Ideologías, literatura y sociedad durante la revolución guatemalteca 1944–1954* (1979) and the novels *Después de las bombas* (1979), *Itzam Na* (1981), *Jaguar en llamas* (1989), *Caminos de Paxil* (1990), and *Cascabel* (1998). He also co-wrote the screenplay for the film *El Norte* (1984) and published a critical edition of Miguel Angel Asturias's *Mulata* (2001).

GORDON BROTHERSTON is a professor and the chair of the Department of Spanish and Portuguese at Stanford University. He has written extensively on the cumulative history of the American continent, the Mexican Codices and the intellectual interface between the Old and New Worlds, and poetry and narrative in Latin America. His publications include *The Emergence of the Latin American Novel* (1977), *Book of the Fourth World: Reading the Native Americas through Their Literature* (1992), *Footprints through Time: Mexican Pictorial Manuscripts* (1995), and *La América indígena en su literatura* (1997).

SANTIAGO CASTRO-GÓMEZ is a professor at the Universidad Javeriana, Bogotá, Colombia, and a full-time researcher at the Instituto de Estudios Sociales y Culturales PENSAR. He was visiting professor at Duke University, the University of Pittsburgh, and Universidad Andina Simón Bolívar, Quito. His publications include *Crítica de la razón latinoamericana* (1996), *Teorías sin disciplina* (1998), *Pensar (en) los intersticios* (coedited, 1999), *Indisciplinar las ciencias sociales* (2002), and two edited volumes *La reestructuración de las ciencias sociales en América Latina* (2000) and *Pensar en el siglo 19: Cultura, biopolítica y modernidad en Colombia* (2004).

SARA CASTRO-KLAREN is a professor in the Department of Spanish and Portuguese at Johns Hopkins University. She has published many articles about José María Arguedas, Euclides da Cunha, Rosario Ferré, and Diamela Eltit, among others. Her publications include *Escritura, transgresión y sujeto en la literatura latinoamericana* (1989) and *Understanding Mario Vargas Llosa* (1990). She has also recently published articles on Guaman Poma, el Inca Gracilaso de la Vega, and postcolonial theory.

AMARYLL CHANADY is a professor of comparative literature and the departmental chair at the Université de Montréal, Canada. She has published primarily on marginalization, the constitution of national identity, the question of the other, multiculturalism, postcolonialism, and Latin American literature and culture. Her articles have appeared in numerous international journals, as well as in various collected volumes. Her books include *Entre inclusion et exclusion: La symbolisation de l'autre dans les Amériques* (1999) and the edited volume *Latin American Identity and Constructions of Difference* (1994).

FERNANDO CORONIL is an associate professor in the Department of History at the University of Michigan, Ann Arbor, and director of the Latin American and Caribbean Studies Program. He has published articles on historical anthropology, state formation, capitalism, popular culture, and gender in Latin America. His publications include *Magical State: Nature, Money and Modernity in Venezuela* (1997).

ROMÁN DE LA CAMPA is a professor and the chair of the Department of Spanish and Portuguese at State University of New York, Stony Brook. His publications include books and essays on Latin American literature and culture, latinos in the United States, and essays on Cultural Theory. His publications include *América Latina y sus comunidades discursivas: Literatura y cultura en la era global* (1998), and *Latin Americanism* (1999). He also coedited, with Ann Kaplan and Michael Sprinker, *Late Imperial Culture* (1995).

ENRIQUE DUSSEL is a professor of ethics in the Department of Philosophy at Universidad Autónoma Metropolitana, Iztapalapa and Mexico City. His publications include more than thirty books, among them *Filosofía ética latinoamericana* (1977), *Ethics and Community* (1988), *Church in Latin America: 1492–1992* (1992), *Debate en torno a la épica del discurso de Apel: Diálogo filosófico norte-sur desde América Latina* (1994), *1492: El encubrimiento del otro: hacia el origen del mito de la modernidad* (1994), *Ética de la liberación en la edad de la globalización y la exclusión* (1998), *Towards an Unknown Marx: A Commentary on the Manuscripts of 1861–63* (2001).

RAMÓN GROSFOGUEL is an associate professor in the Department of Ethnic Studies at the University of California, Berkeley, and a senior research associate of the Maison des Science de l'Homme in Paris. He has published many articles on and edited many journals and volumes that explore Caribbean migration to Western Europe and the United States, world-system analysis, and postcoloniality. He is the author of *Colonial Subjects: Puerto Ricans in a Global Perspective* (2003).

RUSSELL G. HAMILTON is a professor emeritus of Spanish and Portuguese at Vanderbilt University. He specializes in Lusophone African and Brazilian literature and culture. He is the author of two books—*Voices from an Empire: A History of Afro-Portuguese Literature* (1975) and *Literatura Africana, Literatura Necessária* (1984)—as well as several essays that appeared in collected volumes and numerous articles and essays published in disciplinary journals.

PETER HULME is a professor of literature at the University of Essex. His publications include *Colonial Encounters: Europe and the Native Caribbean, 1492–1797* (1992), *Elegy for a Dying Race: The Caribs and Their Visitors* (1993), and *Remnants of Conquest: The Island Caribs and their Visitors, 1877–1998* (2000). He coedited, with Neil Whitehead, *Wild Majesty: Encounters with Caribs from Columbus to the Present Days: An Anthology* (1992); with William H. Sherman, *"The Tempest" and Its Travels* (2000); and, with Tim Youngs, *The Cambridge Companion to Travel Writing* (2002).

CARLOS A. JÁUREGUI is an associate professor of Spanish and anthropology and the director of graduate studies at Vanderbilt University. His book *Canibalia* (2005, 2007) won the "Premio Casa de las Américas." His other publications include *Querella de los indios en las "Cortes de la Muerte" (1557) de Michael de Carvajal* (2002) and, with coeditor Juan P. Dabove, *Heterotropías: Narrativas de identidad y alteridad latino-americana* (2003).

MICHAEL LÖWY has been the research director in sociology at the National Center for Scientific Research, Paris, since 1978 and Lecturer at the École des Hautes Études en Sciences Sociales, Paris, since 1981. Some of his publications include *Georg Lukács: From Romanticism to Bolshevism* (1981), *Redemption and Utopia: Libertarian Judaism in Central Europe* (1992), *On Changing the World: Essays in Political Philosophy, from Karl Marx to Walter Benjamin* (1993), *The War of Gods: Religion and Politics in Latin America* (1996), and, with Robert Sayre, *Romanticism against the Tide of Modernity* (2001).

NELSON MALDONADO-TORRES is the co-chair of the Religion in Latin America and the Caribbean Group of the American Academy of Religion. He is also a professor in the Department of Ethnic Studies at the University of California, Berkeley. He teaches theory and philosophy of religion, critical theory, religion and society, and liberation thought, and was 2003–2004 Andrew W. Mellon Assistant Professor of Religion at Duke University. He was also a founding member of the Caribbean Philosophical Association and participates in the Society of Phenomenology and Existential Philosophy. His publications include articles on Emmanuel Lévinas and Frantz Fanon, among many others.

JOSÉ ANTONIO MAZZOTTI is an associate professor at Tufts University. His publications include *Coros Mestizos del Inca Garcilaso* (1996) and *Poética del flujo: Migración y violencia verbales en el Perú de los 80* (2002). He has also edited many books on colonial literature. He coedited, with U. Juan Zevallos Aguilar, *Asedios a la heterogeneidad cultural: Libro de homenaje a Antonio Cornejo Polar* (1996) and *Edición y anotación de textos andinos* (2000). Another area of study is Latin American poetry.

EDUARDO MENDIETA is an assistant professor in the Philosophy Department at State University of New York, Stony Brook. His edited works include *Towards a Trascendental Semiotics: Selected Essays of Karl-Otto Apel*, vols. 1 and 2 (1994); with David Batstone, *The Good Citizen* (1999); and, with Linda Martin Alcoff, *Thinking from the Underside of History: Enrique Dussel's Philosophy* (2000). He is the author of *From Hermeneutics to Semiotics: Karl-Otto Apel's Transformation of Trascendental Philosophy* (forthcoming).

WALTER D. MIGNOLO is William H. Wannamaker Distinguished Professor and the director of the Center for Global Studies and the Humanities at Duke University. Among his recent publications are *The Darker Side of the Renaissance: Literacy, Territoriality, and Colonization* (1995) and *Local Histories/Global Designs: Coloniality, Subaltern Knowledges, and Border Thinking* (2000). He has also edited *Capitalismo y geopolítica del conocimiento: La filosofía de la liberación en el debate intelectual contemporáneo* (2001).

MARIO ROBERTO MORALES currently teaches Latin American literature in the Graduate International Program in the Department of Modern Languages at the University of Northern Iowa. He has published two books of literary criticism: *La ideología y la lírica de la lucha armada* (1994) and *La articulación de las diferencias o el síndrome de Maximón* (1999, 2002). He is also the editor of the critical edition of Miguel Angel Asturias's *Cuentos y leyendas* (2000) and of *Stoll-Menchú: La invención de la memoria* (2001). He has also published five novels, one of them in English: *Face of the Earth, Heart of the Sky* (2000). He is also a columnist for the Spanish daily *La Insignia* and for the Mexican website México.com.

MABEL MORAÑA is William H. Gass Professor of Romance Languages and International and Area Studies at Washington University, St. Louis, where she directs the Latin American Studies Program. She is also the director of publications of the Instituto Internacional de Literatura Iberoamericana, which publishes *Revista Iberoamericana* and five series of books on Latin American literary and cultural criticism. She has written extensively on colonial and contemporary topics and has edited numerous volumes on Latin American Cultural Studies. Her publications include *Viaje al silencio: Exploraciones del discurso barroco* (1998; the French translation: *Le discours baroque dans l'Amérique espagnole coloniale: Voyage vers le silence* [2005]), *Crítica impura* (2004), and the edited volume *Ideologies of Hispanism* (2004).

MARY LOUISE PRATT is Silver Professor of Spanish and Portuguese and affiliated faculty at the Hemispheric Institute for Performance and Politics at New York University. She has recently written on Nellie Campobello, Rigoberta Menchú, and the transnational pilgrimage of the Virgen de Zapopan. Her publications include *Imperial*

Eyes: Travel Writing and Transculturation (1992) and, with coeditor Kathleen Newman, *Critical Passions: Collected Essays of Jean Franco* (1999).

ANÍBAL QUIJANO is the director of the Centro de Investigaciones Sociales and of the review *Anuario Mariáteguiano* in Lima, Perú, and is currently teaching in the Department of Sociology at Binghamton University. He has been a visiting scholar at many universities in Latin America, the United States, and Europe. Power, knowledge, and social change are his main topics of research. He has published fourteen books—among them *Modernidad, identidad y utopia* (1988), *El fujimorismo y el Perú* (1995), and *La economía popular en América Latina* (1999)—as well as many articles in academic journals.

JOSÉ RABASA is a professor of Latin American literature and culture at the University of California, Berkeley. His publications include *Inventing America: Spanish Historiography and the Formation of Eurocentrism* (1993) and *Writing Violence on the Northern Frontier: The Historiography of Sixteenth-Century New Mexico and Florida* (2000).

ELZBIETA SKLODOWSKA is a professor of Spanish American literature and Randolph Family Professor in Arts and Sciences at Washington University in Saint Louis. She is currently Chair of the Department of Romance Languages and general editor for Spanish American Literature of *Revista de Estudios Hispánicos*. She has written several books and numerous articles on Spanish American *testimonio*, parody, and various aspects of Spanish American contemporary narrative. Her publications include *Parodia en la nueva novela hispanoamericana 1960–1985* (1991) and *Todo ojos, todo oídos: Control e insubordinación en la novela hispanoamericana 1895–1935* (1997).

CATHERINE E. WALSH is a professor and the director of the Latin American Cultural Studies doctoral program at the Universidad Andina Simón Bolívar in Quito, Ecuador, where she also coordinates the Fondo Documental Afro-Andino. Her recent publications include *Estudios culturales latinoamericanos: Retos desde y sobre la región andina* (2003) and, with coeditors Freya Schiwy and Santiago Castro-Goméz, *Indisciplinar las ciencias socials: Geopolíticas del conocimiento y colonialidad del poder: Perspectivas desde lo andino* (2002).

INDEX

GROSFOGUEL, RAMÓN. "Developmentalism, Modernity, and Dependency Theory in Latin America." *Nepantla* 1, no. 2 (2000): 347–74.

HULME, PETER. "Postcolonial Theory and the Representation of Culture in the Americas." *Ojo de buey* 2, no. 3 (1994): 14–25.

QUIJANO, ANÍBAL. "Coloniality, Eurocentrism, and Social Classification." *Nepantla* 1, no. 3 (2000): 533–80.

MIGNOLO, WALTER. "The Geopolitics of Knowledge and the Colonial Difference." *South Atlantic Quarterly* 101, no. 1 (winter 2002): 57–96.

ENRIQUE DUSSEL is a professor of ethics in the Department of Philosophy at Universidad Autónoma Metropolitana (UNAM), Iztapalapa, and at UNAM, Mexico City.

CARLOS A. JÁUREGUI is an associate professor of Spanish and anthropology and the director of graduate studies at Vanderbilt University.

MABEL MORAÑA is William H. Gass Professor of Romance Languages and International and Area Studies at Washington University, St. Louis, where she directs the Latin American Studies Program.

Library of Congress Cataloging-in-Publication Data

Coloniality at large : Latin America and the postcolonial debate / edited by Mabel Moraña, Enrique Dussel, and Carlos Jáuregui.
p. cm. — (Latin America otherwise : languages, empires, nations)
Includes bibliographical references and index.
ISBN-13: 978-0-8223-4147-5 (cloth : alk. paper)
ISBN-13: 978-0-8223-4169-7 (pbk. : alk. paper)
1. Latin America—Civilization.
2. Spain—Colonies—America—History.
3. Imperialism—Historiography.
I. Moraña, Mabel.
II. Dussel, Enrique D.
III. Jáuregui, Carlos A.
F1408.3.C5954 2008
980—dc22   2008003009